classic and elegant flair!

Contemporary metal design
A combination of 2 exciting looks—ribbed serving rings and smooth ball feet.

Easy to set up and take apart
Legs and plates insert in minutes for easy presentation, cleanup and storage.

Party Cakes

Shower Cakes

Appetizers

Desserts

Birthday Cakes

The Party Starts Here!

Dear Friend,

Planning a party is more fun when you start with an exciting theme. There is no better place than the Wilton Yearbook to find the perfect theme designs to please your guests. In the Yearbook, you will discover the cake and treat ideas you need to create an unforgettable theme party, along with products that make decorating a pleasure.

With this 2007 edition, creating a theme is easier than ever. In our Theme Parties special section, you will discover some of the most exciting celebration scenes we've ever presented. The fun starts with our cover cake, which also kicks off the special section. We're showing stars all around, from the smiling star cupcakes which top the rainbow fondant cakes to the sparkling cookie pop faces and pizza stars that surround it. What a great way to add fun to a traditional shape, and help your entire menu work together.

Theme party thrills continue with an amazing roller coaster cake. We've linked three tiers with a gum paste track which dips and turns like a real ride. Our new Cakes 'N More™ 3-Tier Party Stand is the key—its stairstep design is ideal for building a cake where separated tiers can connect in spectacular new ways. Don't miss our other theme designs featuring this stand, including wonderful water slide and wedding castle cakes that will captivate everyone.

Elsewhere, you'll find fantastic holiday fun, with a sunbathing Santa, a spooky Halloween cookie graveyard and a fishing Valentine bear among the highlights. And this year, Mardi Gras is added to the calendar, with a cupcake display featuring colorful beads and masks. And, as always, there are wonderful birthday and special event cakes to inspire your decorating best, including an adorable fondant nursery, complete with baby toys and furniture.

If you enjoy the many themed presentations in this Yearbook, you will love our new decorating show on Public Television, BAKE DECORATE CELEBRATE!™ In each episode, you will see how to make celebrations more fun, with exciting cakes and treats decorated before your eyes. Like the Yearbook, BAKE DECORATE CELEBRATE! and www.bakedecoratecelebrate.com make it easy for everyone to serve something spectacular. Look for it in your area soon or check out the website.

It's time to start planning your next party. I hope this 2007 Yearbook will be the beginning of many wonderful celebrations with your friends and family.

Vince Naccarato

Vince Naccarato
Chairman and CEO
Wilton Industries, Inc.

Cake Decorating!

2007 WILTON YEARBOOK

NASCAR® is a registered trademark of The National Association for Stock Car Auto Racing, Inc.

It's no time to be shy! Make some noise with our featured fondant cake that's dripping with embossed garlands and topped with Technicolor skyrockets. Then, hold on to your hats—get ready for wall-to-wall party hats, on a petal cake, cereal treats and lollipops. Find castles and carousels for girls and a multi-tiered city skyline for boys. Plus great theme ideas for adults like neon-colored daisies and tropical treats.

Let the kids have their friends over for the day! Imagine how a visit from the stars of Disney/Pixar Cars, Superman or Strawberry Shortcake will rock their world. Meanwhile, you can catch up with your heroes—the champions of NASCAR. Whoever you choose, you'll find great treat ideas, plus a complete product selection to make a theme party worthy of a star.

There's something to look forward to in every season, starting with the cookie graveyard centerpiece for your Halloween party. Keep the holiday fun going with a great sunbathing Santa cake. For your Valentine, there's a an adorable bear, fishing for the perfect catch. Also, look for our new Mardi Gras celebration ideas.

CREATIVE DIRECTOR
Daniel Masini

ART DIRECTOR/CAKE DESIGNER
Steve Rocco

DECORATING ROOM SUPERVISOR
Mary Gavenda

SENIOR CAKE DECORATOR
Susan Matusiak

CAKE DECORATORS
Jenny Jurewicz • Diane Knowlton
Julie Kurnat • Mark Malak
Tracey Wurzinger • Judy Wysocki

EDITOR/WRITER
Jeff Shankman

WRITERS
Mary Enochs
Marita Seiler
Jessica Radzak

COPY EDITOR
Jane Mikis

PRODUCTION MANAGER
Challis Yeager

ASSOCIATE PRODUCTION MANAGER
Mary Stahulak

GRAPHIC DESIGN/PRODUCTION
Deborah Casciato
RNB Graphics
Courtney Kieras

PHOTOGRAPHY
Peter Rossi—PDR Productions
Pirrello Digital Imaging

PHOTO STYLIST
Carey Thornton

CREATIVE SERVICES ASSISTANT
Sharon Gaeta

PRODUCT DEVELOPMENT/PUBLICATIONS
Sandie Della Bella
Tina Celeste

For photography purposes, many cakes in this book were decorated (by right- and left-handed decorators) with royal icing. Printed in U.S.A.

IN U.S.A.
Wilton Industries, Inc.
2240 West 75th Street
Woodridge, IL 60517
www.wilton.com

Retail Customer Orders:
Phone: 800-794-5866 • Fax: 888-824-9520
Online: www.wilton.com

Class Locations:
Phone: 800-942-8881
Online: www.wilton.com/classes/classlocator.cfm

IN CANADA
Wilton Industries, Canada, Ltd.
98 Carrier Drive
Etobicoke, Ontario M9W5R1 Canada
Retail Customer Orders: Phone: 416-679-0798

Class Locations:
Phone: 416-679-0790, ext. 200
E-mail: classprograms@wilton.ca

¡SE HABLA ESPAÑOL!
Para mas informacion, marque 800-436-5778

Birthday Blast!

Even if it's not a surprise party, your cake can knock everyone for a loop! Thrill guests with high-volume color, as seen here on our 3-story rainbow cake, boasting bright swirled fondant garlands and candles. Or pass out the party hats—and desserts shaped to match—for a theme look featuring a cake topped with ice cream cone caps and served with gelatin lollipops and cookie treats. For kids, check out our girls castle and carousel cakes and the boys city scene with a color flow cookie skyline built on a tiered cake.

Instructions for projects shown on these two pages are on page 8.

Make Some Noise!

Pan: 8 x 2 in. Round, p. 148

Colors:* Lemon Yellow, Rose, Leaf Green, Violet, Royal Blue, p. 135

Fondant: White Ready-To-Use Rolled Fondant (192 oz.), Brush Set, p. 128; Easy-Glide Fondant Smoother, p. 129; Star Cut-Outs™, p. 130; Rolling Pin, Roll & Cut Mat, Spiral Pattern Roller, p. 131

Recipe: Buttercream Icing, p. 114

Also: Plastic Dowel Rods (2 pks.), p. 224; 8 in. Cake Circles (3), 12 in. Silver Cake Base, p. 225; Piping Gel, p. 134; Yellow Cake Sparkles™, p. 136; Circle Metal Cookie Cutter, p. 158; paring knife, black shoestring licorice, cornstarch, cellophane tape

In advance: Make fondant star flames and candles (p. 120). **Also:** Prepare cake base. Brush with piping gel and cover with light blue fondant (p. 113).

Prepare three 2-layer 8 in. cakes for stacked construction (p. 112). Prepare cakes for rolled fondant (p. 113). Cover cakes with light yellow, rose and green fondant; smooth with Fondant Smoother and position on base board. For icing between cakes, roll a ¾ in. diameter white fondant rope; indent with fingers to create irregular shapes. Attach ropes with damp brush. For swags, roll out light rose, blue and violet fondant ¼ in. thick. Imprint design with Spiral Roller. Cut crescent shapes using circle cookie cutter; first cut circles, then move up cutter 1 in. and cut again to make a 3 in. long crescent. Attach to cake with damp brush, halfway down side. Roll ½ in. balls of light violet, green and blue; attach at swag points with damp brush. Insert candles in cake top. Serves 60.

*Combine Leaf Green with Lemon Yellow for green shown. Combine Violet with Rose for violet shown.

Candy-Coated Cakes

Pans: 12 x 18 in. Jelly Roll, Jumbo Muffin, p. 149

Candy: White Candy Melts®† p. 162; Primary, Garden Candy Color Sets, Decorator Brush Set, p. 163; Party/Birthday Lollipop Mold, p. 164

Recipe: Buttercream Icing, p. 114

Also: Parchment Triangles, p. 138; Circle Metal Cookie Cutter, p. 158; White Jumbo Baking Cups, p. 184; serrated knife

In advance: Make birthday cake candies and candy shells. Tint portions of melted white candy pink, violet, yellow, green and blue. Mold birthday cake candies without sticks using painting method (p. 123); refrigerate until firm. Make candy shells in baking cups (p. 123) using jumbo muffin cups and 3 tablespoons melted white candy for each; refrigerate until firm. Leave shells in baking cups.

Bake and cool 1-layer cake. Cut cake into rounds using circle cutter. Tort cakes with knife; fill with icing. Place cakes in shells; seal bottom with a thin layer of melted candy. Refrigerate until firm; carefully remove baking cups. Position cakes bottom side up. Using melted candy in cut parchment bags, pipe garlands 7 pleats wide. Pipe candy dots at garland points. Attach birthday cake candy to each with dots of melted candy. Each serves 1.

Pop These Balloons!

Candy: White Candy Melts®† p. 162; Garden, Primary Candy Color Sets, Decorator Brush Set, p. 163 Party/Birthday Lollipop Mold, p. 164; 4 in. Lollipop Sticks, p. 165;

Also: Parchment Triangles, p. 138; curling ribbon in pink, blue, green, yellow; white card stock paper, hole punch, scissors, black marker

Tint portions of melted white candy pink, blue, yellow and green (combine green and yellow candy colors for green shown). Mold candies using painting method (p. 123). After filling top layer, add lollipop sticks and refrigerate until set; unmold. Cut 2 x ¾ in. card stock nametags; print names with marker. Punch hole in upper right hand corner. Thread a 10 in. length of ribbon through hole and tie to lollipop stick; curl ribbon. Each serves 1.

◀ Plenty of Fun to Go Around!

Pan: Petal Set (12 x 2 in. used), p. 148

Tip: 2A, p. 140

Colors:* Royal Blue, Lemon Yellow, Golden Yellow, Leaf Green, Violet, Rose, p. 135

Fondant: White Ready-To-Use Rolled Fondant (55 oz.), Natural Colors Fondant Multi Pack, Brush Set, p. 128; Cutter/Embosser, p. 129; Rolling Pin, Roll & Cut Mat, p. 131

Recipe: Buttercream Icing, p. 114

Also: 2007 Pattern Book (Shirt), p. 126; 101 Cookie Cutters Set, p. 160; Gum-Tex™, p. 131; Piping Gel, p. 134; Fine Tip Primary Colors FoodWriter™ Edible Color Markers, p. 128; Cake Circles, Fanci-Foil Wrap, p. 225; sugar cones, confectioner's sugar, waxed paper, embroidery scissors

In advance: Tint 8 oz. white fondant each in rose, yellow, blue, green and violet. Add ½ teaspoon Gum-Tex to each color. Tint 3 oz. of each color a darker shade for trims. Make party hats (p. 120).

Ice 2-layer cake smooth. Roll out reserved light colored fondant ⅛ in. thick; using pattern, cut 8 shirts in various colors. Position one shirt on side of each petal, trimming as needed. For faces, roll out light and dark brown fondant from Multi Pack ⅛ in. thick; cut 4 faces in each shade using largest round cookie cutter. Position above shirts; trim as needed.

Draw eyes, hair and mouth with FoodWriters. Roll a small ball of fondant for nose; attach with damp brush. Position hats on cake. Serves 38.

*Combine Lemon Yellow with Golden Yellow for yellow shown. Combine Leaf Green with Lemon Yellow for green shown. Combine Violet with Rose for violet shown.

▶ Hat Hysteria!

Pan: Party Hat, p. 153
Colors:* Leaf Green, Lemon Yellow, Rose, p. 135
Candy: White Candy Melts®†, p.162; Primary and Garden Candy Color Sets, p. 163; Truffles Mold, p. 165
Recipe: Buttercream Icing, p. 114
Also: 2007 Pattern Book (Spirals), p. 126; 101 Cookie Cutters Set, p. 160; Non-Stick Cookie Sheet, p. 161; Parchment Triangles, p. 138; Cake Board, Fanci-Foil Wrap, p. 225; waxed paper

In advance: Tint portions of melted white candy blue, violet, yellow, pink and green (match shade on cake) using candy colors. Make 12 blue truffles, ¼ in. deep; refrigerate until firm. Add a little more blue color for darker shade; pipe swirl on top using melted candy in cut parchment bag. **Also:** Make candy plaques for pompom. Position smallest and largest circle cookie cutters on non-stick cookie sheet; fill ¼ in. deep with yellow and pink candy; refrigerate until firm. For spirals, position pattern on board and cover with waxed paper. Thicken violet candy with a few drops of water and pipe 8 spirals; refrigerate until firm. Reserve remaining violet candy. **And:** On waxed paper, pipe approximately 21 polka dots, ½ in. diameter, using melted green candy in cut parchment bag; refrigerate until firm.

Bake and cool cake. Trim pompom, using the medium round cutter as a guide. Ice cake smooth. Using reserved violet candy, pipe a curved outline on brim. Position truffles and polka dots on cake, securing with dots of icing if necessary. Attach pink candy plaque and violet spirals to yellow plaque with dots of melted candy. Attach plaque to cake with dots of icing. Serves 12.

*Combine Leaf Green with Lemon Yellow for green shown.

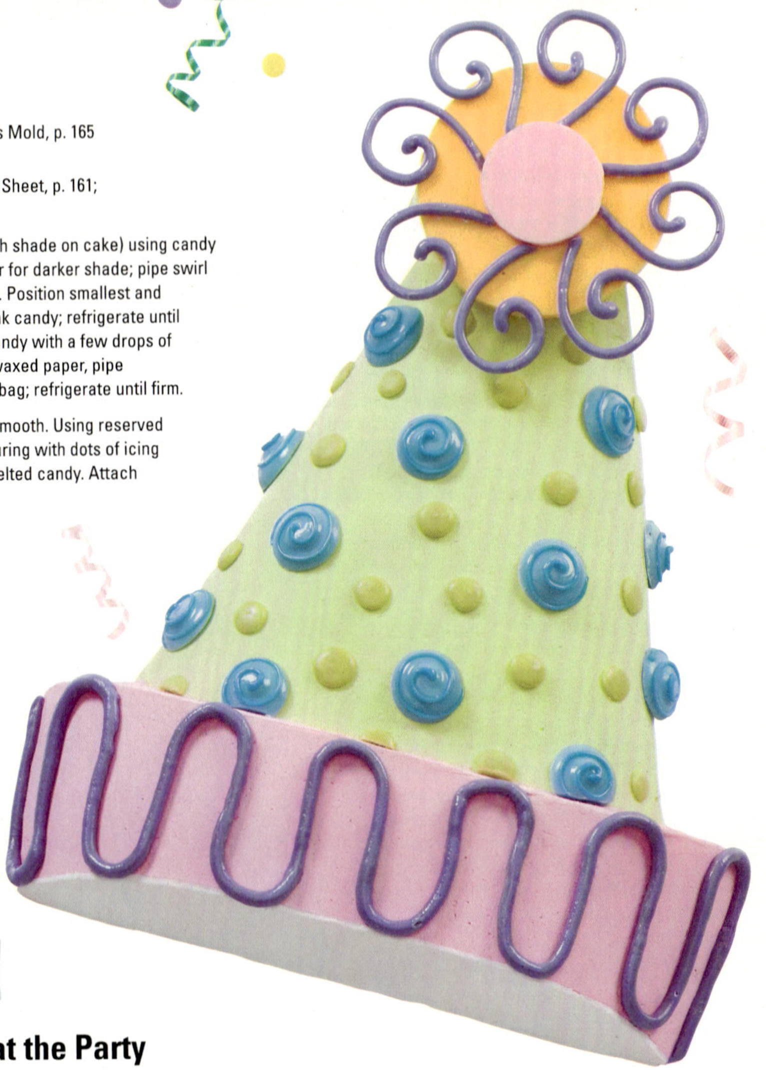

▲ Crispy Caps

Pan: 8 x 2 in. Round (2), p. 148
Candy: Stars Candy Mold, p. 164; White Candy Melts®† (3 pks.), p. 162; Primary, Garden Candy Color Sets, p. 163
Recipes: Candy Clay, p. 115; favorite crisped rice cereal treats
Also: Round Cut-Outs™, p. 130; Rolling Pin, Roll & Cut Mat, p. 131; Cookie Sheet, Cooling Grid, p. 161; Cake Dividing Set, p. 133; Parchment Triangles, p. 138; corn syrup, vegetable oil pan spray, plastic wrap, paring knife

In advance: Prepare candy clay using 1 package of Candy Melts. Divide in 5ths and tint pink, blue, violet, green and yellow using candy colors. Wrap each color in plastic wrap and let set overnight at room temperature.

Prepare cereal treats recipe and press into two pans prepared with pan spray; unmold. Divide treats into 8ths using cake divider; cut 8 wedges from each round. Melt remaining packages of candy; tint portions to match candy clay colors. Cover treats with melted candy (p. 124); let set. Roll out candy clay ⅛ in. thick. Cut dots using smallest Cut-Out; cut ½ in. wide strips for hat brims and stripes. For brims, gently gather strips to form loops. Mold stars using remaining candy clay. Attach all decorations to treats using melted candy. Each serves 1.

†Brand confectionery coating.

▼ Chilling at the Party

Candy: Party/Birthday Large Lollipop Mold, p. 164; 6 in. Lollipop Sticks, p. 165
Tip: 4, p. 140
Colors:* Royal Blue, Leaf Green, Lemon Yellow, p. 135
Recipe: Wilton Gelatin Treats, p. 114
Also: Vanilla Whipped Icing Mix, p. 134; Disposable Decorating Bags, p. 138; Rainbow Jimmies Sprinkles Decorations, p. 136; strawberry, lemon, lime, blueberry gelatin mix (3 oz. pk. each), vegetable shortening, vegetable oil pan spray

Lightly spray mold cavities with vegetable oil pan spray. Apply a small amount of shortening in indented stick areas of mold to create a barrier which will prevent gelatin from seeping out. Position stick up to top edge of mold; smooth additional shortening over stick above indented area. Prepare gelatin treat mixtures and fill mold. (gelatin treats mixture makes 4-5 treats). Refrigerate until firm and unmold. Using tinted or white whipped icing, pipe tip 4 outlines and balls. Fill in tops of cupcake shapes; sprinkle with jimmies. Each serves 1.

*Combine Leaf Green with Lemon Yellow for green shown.

A Swinging Party!

Pans: 8, 12 x 2 in. Round, p. 148

Tips: 2, 4, 8, p. 140

Colors: Lemon Yellow, Golden Yellow, Violet, Rose, Royal Blue, Black, Brown, Leaf Green, p. 135

Fondant: White Ready-To-Use Rolled Fondant (48 oz.), Brush Set, p. 128; Cutter/Embosser, p. 129; Square, Alphabet/Number Cut-Outs™, p. 130; Rolling Pin, Roll & Cut Mat, p. 131

Recipes: Buttercream, Royal Icings, p. 114; Thinned Fondant Adhesive, p. 115

Also: 2007 Pattern Book (Body, Paws, Muzzle, Hat, Romper, Swing Seat Harness, Yellow Cake, Icing, Assembled Bear), p. 126; 14 in. plate (from Tall Tier Cake Stand), 7¾ in. Columns (2 needed), Bottom Column Bolt, Glue-On Plate Legs (6 needed), Cake Corer Tube, p. 222; Plastic and Wooden Dowel Rods, p. 224; 6 in. Cookie Treat Sticks, p. 161; Cake Dividing Set, p. 133; Gum-Tex™, p. 131; Meringue Powder, p. 134; Assorted Celebration Candles, p. 187; hot glue gun, scissors, craft knife, ruler, heavy-duty glue for plastics, ¾ in. wide white satin ribbon (1 yd.), cellophane tape, curling ribbon in yellow, violet, white, rose, blue (2 yds. each)

In advance: Make fondant bear, romper, hat and swing seat harness. Tint 8 oz. portions of fondant violet, blue, rose, green and yellow; a 2 in. ball of brown; reserve a 1 in. white ball. Add 1 teaspoon Gum-Tex to brown fondant. Roll out fondant ⅛ in. thick; trace patterns and cut with knife. Cut brown bear, muzzle and paws; attach muzzle to face with damp brush. Cut green romper and attach to body with damp brush. Cut blue swing seat harness; position and wrap around to back, attaching with damp brush. Cut two 8 in. pieces of white ribbon; with thinned fondant adhesive, attach a piece of ribbon to each hand area on body, leaving 1½ in. extending inside harness. Attach paws to body with damp brush; press in place. Cut and attach violet hat. For hatband fringe cut a ¼ x 2½ in. strip of white fondant; cut slits in one end with scissors and attach with damp brush. Repeat same process for yellow pompom, rolling fringed strip into a ball before attaching. In royal icing, pipe in tip 2 mouth, bead tongue and outline eyes. Tint a ½ in. ball of brown fondant black; roll a ⅜ in. oval for nose and tiny balls for pads on foot; flatten and attach with damp brush. **Also:** Make swing (p. 119). Attach glue-on legs to plate with heavy-duty glue; set aside.

In buttercream, ice smooth 2-layer 12 in. cake (bake two 1½ in. layers to make 3 in. high cake) and 8 in. cake (4 in. high). Prepare for stacked and center column construction (p. 112). Divide 8 in. cake into 8ths. Roll out violet fondant ⅛ in. thick; cut strips ¼ in. x 5 in. Twist strips and attach at division points in garland formation 1½ in. deep with dots of icing. Roll ¾ in. balls of yellow, rose and blue fondant; attach at garland points in groups of 3. Position 8 in. cake on top of 12 in. cake; pipe tip 8 bead bottom border. To decorate 12 in. cake, roll out all fondant colors ⅛ in. thick. Cut yellow cake and rose icing using patterns; cut various color gifts using largest and medium square Cut-Outs. Attach gifts and yellow cake to sides with dots of icing; attach icing with damp brush. For yellow cake, cut three 1¼ x ½ in. blue crescents for garland; attach with damp brush. Roll and attach four ¼ in. balls at garland points; roll and attach ½ in. balls at bottom. For gift ribbons, cut ¼ in. wide strips; attach with water. For bows, roll ¼ in. ball knot and two ¾ in. log loops; flatten logs and attach all to top of gifts with icing. Cut name using alphabet Cut-Outs; attach with icing. With knife, cut various size confetti pieces in assorted colors; attach to 8 in. cake sides and top. Assemble columns and insert center pole at top column opening. Hang bear on swing from top. Cut curling ribbon into 1-yard lengths, tie to swing and curl. Insert candle. Serves 60.

Bear's on the Ball

Pans: 10 in. Round, p. 148; Standard Muffin, p. 149; Sports Ball Set, p. 155; Cookie Sheet, p. 161

Tips: 1M (2110), 2, 3, 16, 18, p. 140-141

Colors: Leaf Green, Lemon Yellow, Royal Blue, Brown, Black, p. 135

Recipes: Buttercream, Royal Icings, Roll-Out Cookie, p. 114

Also: 2007 Pattern Book (Bear, Balloon), p. 126; 16 in. Tall Tier Plate, 6½ and 7¾ in. Columns (1 each), Glue-On Plate Legs (6), Cake Corer Tube, p. 222; 6 in. Lollipop Sticks, p. 165; Pastel Baking Cups, p. 184; Icing Sculptor™, p. 133; Nesting Star Cutter Set, p. 160; Meringue Powder, p. 134; Dowel Rods, p. 224; Cake Circles, Fanci-Foil Wrap, p. 225; Smiley Flames Chunky Candles (3 pks.), p. 180; Flowerful Medley 6-Mix Sprinkles Assortment, p. 136; Rolling Pin, p. 131; marshmallows, cardstock with matching curling ribbon, non-toxic markers, toothpick, heavy-duty glue for plastics, paring knife, scissors

In advance: Roll out dough and trace bear pattern using toothpick. Cut cookie using knife; bake and cool. Decorate bear using royal icing. Ice inside ears, hat, nose, eyes and mouth smooth. Outline mouth with tip 3. Cover body and muzzle with tip 16 stars. Position lollipop sticks on hands and overpipe with tip 16 stars. Pipe tip 2 age on hat; add tip 2 pull-out fringe pompom and hat band. Let dry.

Prepare Tall Tier Stand. Glue legs to 16 in. separator plate; assemble stand with 6½ in. and 7¾ in. columns. Prepare 6 in. and 16 in. cake circles and 10 in. round cake (two 1½ in. layers for 3 in. high cake) and ball cake (use firm-textured batter such as pound cake) for Stacked and Tall Tier Construction (p. 112). Position round cake on 16 in. foil-wrapped cake circle and position over columns and onto plate.

Using buttercream icing, ice round cake top smooth; ice sides ½ in. thick, and immediately comb with Icing Sculptor fitted with white W-shaped blades. Ice 6 in. cake circle smooth and position on round cake. Position ball cake over columns and onto 6 in. circle. Lightly ice ball cake and imprint stars using smallest star cutter. Cover cake with tip 16 stars. Attach bear cookie to column with royal icing. For each leg, slightly trim marshmallow vertically to lay flat on board. Cut 2 lollipop sticks in half. Insert into marshmallows and insert in cake, cut side down. Fill in space between cookie and marshmallow with buttercream. For feet, cut 1 marshmallow vertically in half; attach 1 half to each leg, cut side out. For foot pads, ice cut side of marshmallow smooth. Cover remainder of foot and leg with tip 16 stars. Trace balloon pattern on cardstock; cut balloons. Write messages with markers. Tape balloons to sticks; tie on curling ribbon.

Pipe tip 18 shell borders on 10 in. round cake; edge 6 in. board with tip 16 shells. Cover cupcakes with tip 1M swirls; sprinkle with confetti from Flowerful Medley assortment. Insert candles. Position cupcakes around cake. Cakes serve 38; each cupcake serves 1.

One Grrreat Pan, Many Wild Designs!

With our versatile new Friendly Lion Pan (p. 178), it's easy to make kids a fun birthday cake featuring any creature in the jungle. They'll be all smiles—like the happy animals shown here!

▼ Elephant's Birthday Blowout!

Pan: Friendly Lion, p. 178
Tips: 3, 4, 12, 16, 21, p. 140-141
Colors: Red-Red, Lemon Yellow, Royal Blue, Rose, Black, p. 135
Recipes: Buttercream, Royal Icings, Roll-Out Cookie, p. 114
Also: 2007 Pattern Book (Elephant Ear, Trunk, Mini Birthday Cake), p. 126; Cookie Sheet, Cooling Grid, p. 161; Meringue Powder, p. 134; Numeral Candle, p. 186; Rainbow Jimmies Sprinkle Decorations, p. 136; 13 x 19 in. Cake Boards, Fanci-Foil Wrap, p. 225; Disposable Decorating Bags, p. 138; Flower Spikes, p. 224; Rolling Pin, p. 131; 22-gauge florist wire (three 8 in. lengths), waxed paper, marshmallows, cornstarch, paring knife, toothpick

In advance: Make water drops using royal icing. Pipe approximately 20 tip 3 beads on waxed paper-covered board; let dry. Attach beads to 8 in. lengths of florist wire using dots of royal icing; let dry. Roll out cookie dough; using patterns and toothpick, trace 2 ears (reverse 1 pattern), 1 trunk and 4 birthday cakes. Cut cookies using knife; bake and cool.

For mini birthday cake, stack cookies together, layering each with buttercream. Ice top and sides smooth. Pipe iced top with tip 12; immediately sprinkle with jimmies. Add tip 12 ball bottom border; edge border with tip 4 outline scallops. Mark 1 in. divisions at center; pipe tip 4 zigzag garland between division marks. Add tip 4 dot at garland points.

On lion cake, trim off lower mane area from ear to ear. Ice cookie ears, cake sides and background areas smooth. Outline body, eyes, mouth and ears with tip 3. Pipe in tip 3 eyes and mouth (smooth with finger dipped in cornstarch). Cover head, body, ears and trunk cookie with tip 16 stars. Pipe tip 3 strings at end of tail and for eyebrows. Pipe tip 21 shell bottom border. Position ears and trunk, support ears with marshmallows. Fill in any gaps between ears and cake with tip 16 stars. Insert flower spike into cake at end of trunk. Fill spike with icing, insert water drop wires and cover spike with tip 16 stars. Pipe tip 3 message. Position mini cake. Position candle at top of mini cake, supporting with a marshmallow half. Add tip 4 pull-out flame. Cake serves 12, cookies serve 4.

▲ Consider Him Tamed

Pan: Friendly Lion, p. 178
Tips: 3, 5, 16, 233, p. 140-141
Colors:* Leaf Green, Lemon Yellow, Brown, Kelly Green, Red-Red, Orange, p. 135
Fondant: White Ready-To-Use Rolled Fondant (24 oz.), p. 128; Rolling Pin, Roll & Cut Mat, p. 131; Cutter/Embosser, p. 129
Recipe: Buttercream Icing, p. 114
Also: Cake Board, Fanci-Foil Wrap, p. 225; Gum-Tex™, p. 131; cornstarch, ruler

One day in advance: Make fondant loops. Tint 12 oz. fondant red, 12 oz. orange; mix each color with 1 teaspoon Gum-Tex. Roll out fondant ⅛ in. thick. Using straight-edge wheel of Cutter/Embosser, cut fifty 3½ x 3/16 in. strips in each color. Fold in half to form loops, pinch ends to secure; let dry overnight on cornstarch-dusted boards.

Ice cake sides and background areas smooth. Outline and pipe in area under mane and tail with tip 5 (smooth with finger dipped in cornstarch). Outline body, tail, face and facial features with tip 3. Pipe in eyes and nose with tip 3; overpipe nose for dimension. Cover body, face and tail with tip 16 stars. Attach fondant loops on tail and mane with dots of icing. Pipe tip 16 swirl on ears; add tip 3 dot whiskers and string eyebrows. Pipe tip 233 pull-out grass bottom border. Serves 12.

*Combine Leaf Green with Lemon Yellow for light green shown.

▲ Call of the Wild

Pan: Standard Muffin, p. 148
Tips: 3, 21, p. 140-141
Colors:* Violet, Rose, Golden Yellow, Kelly Green, Royal Blue, Orange, p. 135
Recipe: Buttercream Icing, p. 114
Also: Jungle Pals Baking Cups, Jungle Pals Fun Pix®, p. 178

Ice cupcakes smooth. For zebra cupcake, pipe tip 3 lines from center to edge. Pipe tip 3 outline circle for lion cupcake and tip 3 dots for tiger cupcake. Pipe tip 21 rosette center for all. Insert picks in rosette. Each serves 1.

*Combine Violet with Rose for light and dark violet shown.

▼ Safari on a Stick!

Candy: White Candy Melts®†, p. 162; Garden, Primary Candy Color Sets, p. 163
Cookie: Round Cookie Treat Pan, Cookie Sheet, 8 in. Cookie Treat Sticks, p. 161
Also: Jungle Pals Icing Decorations, p. 178; Parchment Triangles, p. 138 ; waxed paper, curling ribbon, markers, card stock paper, paper punch

Using candy colors, tint portions of melted white candy yellow, green/yellow combination, blue, pink, violet/pink combination and orange. Using pan, insert sticks and mold lollipops in blue, green/yellow and yellow; refrigerate until firm. For candy plaques, draw 2 in. circles on waxed paper; position on cookie sheet. Using melted orange, yellow and blue candy in cut parchment bag, fill in circles; tap cookie sheet gently to smooth, refrigerate until firm. Place green, violet and pink candy in small bowls; add 1-2 drops of water to thicken. Using cut parchment bag, pipe stripes, dots or zigzags. Use melted candy to attach plaques to lollipops and icing decorations to plaques. Make name tags using card stock and markers; punch hole in tag and tie to lollipop sticks with curling ribbon. Each serves 1.

†Brand confectionery coating.

◀ Impish Chimp

Pan: Friendly Lion, p. 178
Tips: 1, 4, 6, 13, 16, 19, p. 140-141
Colors:* Red-Red, Christmas Red, Leaf Green, Lemon Yellow, Brown, Royal Blue, Rose, Black, p. 135
Recipes: Buttercream Icing, Roll-Out Cookie, p. 114
Also: 2007 Pattern Book (Left Arm, Right Arm, Tail, Hat, Ear), p. 126; Cookie Sheet, Cooling Grid, p. 161; Rainbow Nonpareils Sprinkle Decorations, p. 136; Rolling Pin, p. 131; Cake Board, Fanci-Foil Wrap, p. 225; paring knife, balloons, curling ribbon in red, yellow and blue (18 in. each), cornstarch, toothpick

In advance: Make cookie arms, tail, hat and 2 ears. Roll out dough, trace patterns with toothpick; cut cookies with paring knife. Bake and cool.

Trim off tail, ears, lower mane area from ear to ear and toes of middle paw from cake. Ice sides and background areas smooth. Attach cookies, except long arm, to cake with dots of icing. Ice mouth, ears and hat smooth. Outline body, arms, hands, tail and ears with tip 4. Pipe tip 1 outline teeth. Pipe tip 4 outline eyes and fill in nose (smooth nose with finger dipped in cornstarch). Cover remainder of chimp with tip 16 stars; overpipe face for dimension. Attach long arm; outline with tip 4, fill in with tip 16 stars. Overpipe fingers with tip 13 stars for dimension. Add tip 13 pull-out fringe on hat; pipe tip 6 age (smooth with finger dipped in cornstarch). Pipe tip 19 shell bottom border; sprinkle with rainbow nonpareils. Tie curling ribbon to balloons and attach under hands with dots of icing. Cake serves 12; each cookie serves 1.

*Combine Brown with Red-Red for dark and light brown shown. Combine Leaf Green with Lemon Yellow for green shown. Combine Red-Red with Christmas Red for red shown.

◀ Take a Whirl, Girl!

Pans: 8, 12 x 2 in. Round, p. 148

Tips: 3, 349, p. 140-141

Colors:* Rose, Violet, Lemon Yellow, Golden Yellow, Leaf Green, p. 135

Fondant: White Ready-To-Use Rolled Fondant (48 oz.), p. 128; Flower Cut-Outs™, p. 130; Fondant Shaping Foam, p. 129; Rolling Pin, Roll & Cut Mat, p. 131; Brush Set, p. 128

Recipes: Buttercream, Royal Icings, p. 114

Also: 2007 Pattern Book (Carousel Awning Sections), p. 126; Animal Pals 50 Pc. Cutter Set, p. 160; Confectionery Tool Set, p. 129; Plastic Dowel Rods, p. 224; 10 in. Plate, 9 in. Crystal Twist Legs from Crystal Clear Cake Divider Set, p. 220; 14 in. Round Silver Cake Base, p. 225; Cake Dividing Set, p. 133; White Candy Melts®†, p. 162; Gum-Tex™, p. 131; Meringue Powder, p. 134; 8 in. Cake Circles, Cake Board, p. 225; 18-gauge florist wire (three 8 in. lengths), green florist tape, cornstarch, ruler, paring knife

At least 48 hours in advance: Make fondant flowers. Tint 8 oz. portions of fondant light pink and lavender. Tint a 2 in. ball yellow. Combine each tinted fondant with ¾ teaspoon Gum-Tex. Roll out ⅛ in. thick. Using small Cut-Out, cut 40 flowers each in pink, yellow and lavender. Cup centers on foam using small ball tool and let dry on cornstarch-dusted board. Using medium Cut-Out, make 12 pink flowers; using large Cut-Out make 1 pink flower. Do not cup medium and large flowers. Let dry. Tape florist wires together, wrapping 4 in. at bottom end. Shape wire on each side into spiral leaves. Attach large flower at end of center wire with melted candy; let dry. **Also:** Make fondant horses and awning sections. Combine 8 oz. white fondant with ¾ teaspoon Gum-Tex. Roll out white and remaining lavender fondant ⅛ in. thick. Using pattern, cut 5 each lavender and white awning sections. Using horse cutter from set, cut 4 white horses. Let all dry on cornstarch-dusted board. **And:** Decorate flowers and horses using royal icing and tip 3. Pipe dot centers on small flowers. Add bead petals and dot centers on large and medium flowers. On horses, pipe dot eyes and nose; outline saddle and harness. Outline and pipe in saddle and hooves. Pipe pull-out string mane and tail. Let dry.

Prepare 2-layer 8 in. cake (bake two 1½ in. high layers to make a 3 in. high cake) and 2-layer 12 in. cake for Push-In Pillar Construction (p. 112). Ice smooth in buttercream. Divide 12 in. cake into 12ths. Pipe tip 3 drop strings 1½ in. deep from division points. Attach 3 small flowers to each drop string and 1 medium pink flower at each division point. Add tip 349 leaves. Pipe tip 3 dots between flowers. Roll out remaining rose fondant ⅛ in. thick. Cut ¾ in. strips, long enough to wrap around 12 in. cake; position at base of cake. Attach flowers around strip with dots of icing; add tip 349 leaves. Trim top of strip with tip 3 dots, 1½ in. apart. Place 8 in. cake on separator plate; divide into 10ths. Pipe tip 3 drop strings 1½ in. deep. Attach a flower at each division point and at lowest point of drop strings. Add tip 349 leaves. Pipe tip 3 dots between flowers. Cut and attach a ½ in. wide pink fondant strip at base as above. Pipe tip 3 bead bottom border; trim top of strip with tip 3 dots, 1½ in. apart. Cut dowel rod to 6 in.; insert in center of 8 in. cake top. Cut an 8 in. cake circle with a center hole cut out to fit over dowel rod; position on cake top. Fill inside dowel rod with fondant to hold wired flower. Position awning sections between garland points, resting tops against dowel rod; attach sections with royal icing. Pipe tip 3 beads in royal icing at base and seams of awning. Insert flower on wire at top of awning. Assemble cakes. Position flowers around pillars. Attach horses to pillars with melted candy. Serves 60.

*Combine Lemon Yellow with Golden Yellow for yellow shown. Combine Leaf Green with Lemon Yellow for green shown. Combine Violet with Rose for lavender shown.

†Brand confectionery coating.

▶ Crowned Heads

Pans: Round Cookie Treat, Cookie Sheet, p. 161

Colors: Brown, Copper (skin tone), p. 135

Candy: Candy Melts®† in White, Light Cocoa (1 pk. each) , p. 162; Girl Power Candy Mold, p. 164; Primary, Garden Candy Color Sets, Decorator Brush Set, p. 163

Recipe: Roll-Out Cookie, p. 114

Also: 8 in. Cookie Treat Sticks, p. 161, Parchment Triangles, p. 138; vegetable oil pan spray

Tint dough copper or brown. Prepare pan and press in dough and cookie sticks following pan instructions. Roll a ¼ in. diameter ball of dough for each nose and place on cookie sheet. Bake and cool.

Tint portions of melted white candy yellow, pink, violet and green using candy colors; tint portion of melted cocoa candy black. Mold crown candies using painting method (p. 123); refrigerate until firm. Using melted candy in cut parchment bags, pipe black string mouth, eyes and lashes. Add pink dot cheeks and bead heart lips. Attach noses. Add a few drops of water to light cocoa and black candy to thicken; pipe swirl hair. Immediately position crown candies on hair. Refrigerate until firm. Each serves 1.

▶ Her Majesty's Palace

Pan: Oval Pan Set (16½ x 12⅜ x 2 in. used), p. 148; Enchanted Castle, p. 153

Tips: 2, 2D, 3, 6, 10, 32, 129, 225, 349, p. 140-141

Colors: Rose, Kelly Green, p. 135

Recipes: Buttercream, Royal Icings, p. 114

Also: 2007 Pattern Book (Castle Flags), p. 126; White Candy Melts®† (2 pks.), p. 162; 4 in. Lollipop Sticks, p. 165; White Cake Sparkles™, p. 136; Cake Boards, Fanci-Foil Wrap, p. 225; Disposable Decorating Bags, p. 138; Meringue Powder, p. 134; Plastic Dowel Rods, p. 225; 18½ in. oval foamcore board (½ in. thick), pink construction paper, scissors, small ruler, cornstarch, waxed paper, cellophane tape

In advance: Make candy plaque castle (p. 124). Fill castle pan with melted white candy, leaving background areas between turrets open. Refrigerate until firm; unmold. Reserve ¾ cup of candy. **Also:** Make flowers and bushes using royal icing. Make 95 tip 225 drop flowers each in light and dark rose; add tip 2 dot centers in white. Make 25 tip 2D drop flowers in dark rose and 40 tip 129 drop flowers in light rose, each with tip 3 white dot centers. Make extra to allow for breakage and let dry. Make 2 tip 10 zigzag bushes on waxed paper-covered board. Attach tip 225 drop flowers; let dry. **And:** Using royal icing, ice tops of turrets smooth; sprinkle with Cake Sparkles. Outline and pipe in windows with tip 3 (pat smooth with finger dipped in cornstarch). Attach tip 225 drop flowers to turrets, window sills and around door with dots of royal icing. Add tip 349 leaves. Let dry. Trim 2 dowel rods to 9 in. Attach one full-length and two 9 in. dowel rods to back of candy plaque castle with melted candy, leaving 3 in. extended at bottom to insert into cake. Let set. Trace flag pattern on construction paper; cut 5 flags and attach to lollipop sticks with tape. Attach sticks to back of turrets with melted candy; let set.

Ice 2-layer cake smooth in buttercream (bake two 1½ in. high layers to make a 3 in. high cake). Position on foil-wrapped base board. Pipe tip 6 bead top border and tip 32 shell bottom border. Attach tip 2D and tip 129 drop flowers at bottom border; add tip 349 leaves in buttercream. Print tip 3 message.

Insert castle in cake. Attach bushes with dots of icing. Position tip 225 drop flowers around cake top, arranging in semi-circles of 5 flowers. Serves 44.

◀ Pink for a Princess

Pan: Crown, p. 151

Tips: 3, 4, 9, 16, p. 140-141

Color: Rose, p. 135

Fondant: White Ready-To-Use Rolled Fondant (24 oz.), p. 128; Garden Shapes, Heart Cut-Outs™, p. 130; Rolling Pin, Roll & Cut Mat, p. 131

Recipe: Buttercream Icing, p. 114

Also: Cake Boards, Fanci-Foil Wrap, p. 225; Piping Gel, p. 134; Gum-Tex™, p. 131, Parchment Triangles, p. 138; cornstarch

In advance: Combine 6 oz. fondant with ½ teaspoon Gum-Tex; tint rose. Roll out ⅛ in. thick. Cut out 8 flowers using medium Cut-Out. Cut 5 hearts using largest Cut-Out. Imprint center of hearts using medium heart Cut-Out. Outline hearts on outside and imprinted edges with tip 3; outline flowers. Let dry overnight on cornstarch-dusted board.

Ice cake sides and background areas smooth. Outline crown using tip 3; fill in with tip 16 stars. Using piping gel tinted rose in a cut parchment bag, pipe in centers of fondant hearts. Position hearts on cake top, securing with dots of icing if necessary. Pipe tip 4 dots at base of crown points; add tip 9 swags to connect dots. Pipe tip 3 dot centers on fondant flowers; position on cake. Print tip 3 message. Pipe tip 16 shell bottom border. Serves 12.

▼ Key to the City!

Pans: 8, 14 x 2 in. Round, p. 148
Tips: 1, 3, p. 140
Colors: Red-Red, Kelly Green, Royal Blue, Orange, Golden Yellow, Black, Violet, p. 135
Fondant: White Ready-To-Use Rolled Fondant (24 oz.), p. 128; Rolling Pin, Roll & Cut Mat, p. 131; Cutter/Embosser, p. 129; Brush Set, p. 128
Cookie: 101 Cookie Cutters Set, p. 160; Cookie Sheet, Cooling Grid, p. 161
Recipes: Buttercream, Color Flow Icings, Roll-Out Cookie, p. 114
Also: 2007 Pattern Book (Cloud, Train Smoke Cloud, Buildings in 4 Sizes), p. 126; 11¾ in. Lollipop Sticks, p. 165; Piping Gel, Color Flow Mix, p. 134; Dowel Rods, p. 224; Cake Circles, Fanci-Foil Wrap, p. 225; Parchment Triangles, p. 138; 18 in. round foamcore board (½ in. thick), white card stock paper, scissors, paring knife, marker, ruler, cornstarch

Two days in advance: Make cookies. Roll out dough ⅛ in. thick. Using patterns, cut 10 buildings in each size. Using cutters, cut train engine, 2 cars, airplane (trim off wings and bottom of tail; bake wings separately) and 3 trucks (cut front end off 2 trucks to make passenger cars for train). Bake and cool cookies. Prepare 2 recipes of color flow icing. Outline and flow in cookies with color flow (p. 124). Let dry overnight. When dry, pipe details with full-strength color flow. Add tip 3 dot lights on vehicles and tip 1 outline spokes on train wheels. Overpipe roof of train cars with tip 3. Pipe tip 3 outline windows on buildings (pat smooth with finger dipped in cornstarch).

Ice smooth 2-layer 14 in. cake (bake two 1½ in. layers to make a 3 in. high cake) and 3-layer 8 in. cake (bake one 2 in. and two 1½ in. layers to make a 5 in. high cake). Prepare cakes for stacked construction (p. 112). Make fondant train track. Tint 12 oz. fondant black; reserve remaining white. Roll out black fondant ⅛ in. thick; cut ¼ in. strips for outer rail. Pipe a thin line of piping gel along edge of foil-wrapped foamcore board; attach outer rail strips. Cut and attach inner rail the same way, positioning 1 in. from outer rail. For cross rails, cut ¼ x 1 in. black strips; attach with piping gel.

Using patterns, cut cloud and train smoke from card stock; print messages with marker. Cut lollipop sticks to 3 in. long; attach to back of train smoke cloud with full-strength color flow; let dry. Attach wings to plane cookie with full-strength color flow; let dry. Attach lollipop sticks to 3 building cookies for cake top with full-strength color flow, leaving 5 in. extending to insert in cake; let dry. Attach stick and cloud to plane with full-strength color flow; let dry. Cut two lollipop sticks to 4 in. and attach to cars and truck, leaving 3 in. extended; let dry. Cut ¼ x ½ in. strips of black fondant for lane dividers; position on 14 in. cake top, attach with damp brush 2 in. apart. Roll balls of white fondant; with color flow, attach to backs of train cars for additional support. Attach buildings and train cars to cake sides with dots of icing. Insert cars and truck in 14 in. cake. Insert buildings and plane on sticks in cake top. Cake serves 83; each cookie serves 1.

▶ Junior Firefighter

Pan: Firetruck, p. 155
Cookie: Dog Plastic Cookie Cutter, p. 160; Cookie Sheet, Cooling Grid, p. 161
Tips: 3, 12, 16, 21, p. 140-141
Colors:* Red-Red, No-Taste Red, Black, Lemon Yellow, Golden Yellow, Brown, Copper (skin tone), p. 135
Recipes: Buttercream Icing, Roll-Out Cookie, p. 114
Also: 2007 Pattern Book (Firefighter), p. 126; Cake Board, Fanci-Foil Wrap, p. 225; Rolling Pin, p. 131; craft knife, large marshmallows, toothpick, cornstarch

Roll out cookie dough. Trace firefighter pattern with toothpick and cut out with craft knife. Cut dog with cutter. Bake and cool cookies. On dog, using tip 3, pipe in spots, features and fur (smooth with finger dipped in cornstarch), outline mouth and toes. Trace details on firefighter with toothpick; outline with tip 3. Pipe in mouth, tongue, emblem and inside helmet (smooth with finger dipped in cornstarch). Cover helmet, face, body, shoes and hands with tip 16 stars. Pipe tip 3 string eyes and ears; pipe dot nose and cheeks; print letters on emblem. Pipe tip 16 pull-out star hair. Outline and pipe in steering wheel with tip 3.

Ice cake sides and background areas smooth. Outline doors, windows and body of truck with tip 3. Pipe tip 3 dot gas cap, valves and headlight and string door handles (smooth with finger dipped in cornstarch). Using tip 12, outline ladder, pipe in fenders and hubcaps. Cover truck with tip 16 stars. Pipe tip 3 dot wheel centers. Add tip 21 swirl wheels. Pipe tip 21 shell bottom border. Print tip 3 message. With dots of icing, attach a marshmallow under each cookie for support. Position cookies on cake. Cake serves 12; each cookie serves 1.

*Combine Lemon Yellow with Golden Yellow for yellow shown. Combine Red-Red with No-Taste Red for red shown.

◀ Big Shot Birthday Boy!

Pan: Little Hero, p. 154
Tips: 3, 5, 16, 233, p. 140-141
Colors:* Black, Buttercup Yellow, Royal Blue, Brown, Red-Red, Rose, Copper (skin tone), Leaf Green, Lemon Yellow, p. 135
Recipe: Buttercream Icing, p. 114
Also: 2007 Pattern Book (Gun Blast), p. 126; Cake Board, Fanci-Foil Wrap, p. 225; 11¾ in. Lollipop Sticks, p. 165; black twist licorice (2 needed), card stock, felt tip markers, cellophane tape, cornstarch, scissors

Trim hose area off bottom of cake. Ice sides and background areas smooth. Outline body, clothes and helmet with tip 3 (follow edges of cake for helmet, building up on sides as needed). Use tip 5 to outline and pipe in gun handle and shoes (build up for dimension and smooth with finger dipped in cornstarch). Pipe in mouth, tongue, whites of eyes and pupils with tip 3 (smooth with finger dipped in cornstarch). Cover face, body and clothes with tip 16 stars. Cut 2 licorice twists to 5 in. and 5½ in. long; position in left hand area. Outline hand with tip 3; cover with tip 16 stars. Overpipe hands, nose and cheeks with tip 16 stars for dimension. Add tip 16 pull-out star hair and tip 3 outline eyebrows. Pipe tip 233 pull-out grass bottom border. Trace gun blast pattern on card stock; cut out. Using markers, print message and draw confetti and streamers. Tape lollipop stick to back of gun blast and insert in cake. Serves 12.

*Combine Buttercup Yellow with Lemon Yellow for yellow shown. Combine Brown with Red-Red for brown shown.

◀ Safari Stampede

Pan: Standard Muffin, p. 149
Tip: 233, p. 140
Colors:* Leaf Green, Lemon Yellow, p., 135
Recipe: Buttercream Icing, p. 114
Also: Jungle Pals Baking Cups, Jungle Pals Candles, p. 178; Rainbow Jimmies Sprinkle Decorations, p. 136; Disposable Decorating Bags, p. 138

Lightly ice cupcakes smooth. Cover with tip 233 pull-out grass; sprinkle with jimmies. Insert candles. Each serves 1.

*Combine Leaf Green with Lemon Yellow for green shown.

◀ Surprise Packages

Pan: 9 x 13 Sheet, p. 148

Colors: Rose, Lemon Yellow, Royal Blue, p. 135

Fondant: White Ready-To-Use Rolled Fondant (96 oz.) p. 128; Square Cut-Outs™, p. 130; Rolling Pin, Roll & Cut Mat, p. 131

Candy: White Candy Melts®†, p. 162; Party Time Lollipop Mold, p. 164; Primary, Garden Candy Color Sets, Decorator Brush Set, p. 163

Recipe: Buttercream Icing, p. 114

Also: Cake Boards, Fanci-Foil Wrap, p. 225; Parchment Triangles, p. 138; 6 in. Cookie Treat Sticks, p. 161; Gum-Tex™, p. 131; blue and violet curling ribbon (1 yard each), ruler, pizza cutter, cornstarch

In advance: Make fondant bows. Tint 15 oz. fondant each yellow and rose; combine each with 2 teaspoons Gum-Tex. Roll out ⅛ in. thick; cut ¼ x 3 in. strips, 5 for each bow. Fold strips in half, brush ends with water and pinch together to form loops. Let dry on sides on cornstarch-dusted board. **Also:** Make lids. Tint 30 oz. fondant each blue and yellow. Roll out ⅛ in. thick; cut 20 lids using largest square Cut-Out; let dry. Reserve remaining fondant. **And:** Tint portions of melted white candy blue, violet, green and pink using candy colors. Mold balloon candies without sticks using painting method (p. 123); refrigerate until firm.

Cut 1-layer cake into 2 x 2 in. squares (cake makes approximately 20 squares). Prepare cakes for rolled fondant (p. 113); cover cakes with reserved fondant. Roll out remaining fondant ⅛ in. thick. Cut ¼ in. wide ribbon strips; attach to cakes and lids with damp brush. Cut cookie sticks to 3 in.; attach to bottom center of lids with melted candy. Refrigerate until firm. Attach bow loops to lids with melted candy; let set. Insert lids in cakes. Attach balloon candy to cookie stick with melted candy. Cut curled ribbon into 3 in. lengths; attach with melted candy. Each serves 1.

▶ Smiles to Go!

Candy: Smiley Face Pretzel Mold, p. 165; Candy Melts®† in White, Yellow, Orange (1 pk. each), p. 162; Primary, Garden Candy Color Sets, p. 163

Also: Party Hats Icing Decorations, p. 179; Parchment Triangles, p. 138; pretzel rods

Mold candy using layering method (p. 123). Position pretzel rods in mold; refrigerate until firm. Unmold and pipe facial features using melted candy in cut parchment bag. Attach icing decoration with melted candy. Each serves 1.

▲ Bitty Kitty

Pan: Mini Egg, p. 201

Candy: Candy Melts®† in White, Light Cocoa, p. 162; Garden Candy Color Set, Decorator Brush Set, p. 163; Pets Mold, p. 164

Also: 2007 Pattern Book (Cat Tail), p. 126; Cake Circles, p. 225; Parchment Triangles, p. 135; Cooling Grid, p. 161; waxed paper

In advance: Make cat face and tail candies. Tint portion of melted white candy pink using candy color. Mold face using painting method (p. 123); refrigerate until firm. For tail, cover pattern with waxed paper. Using melted candy in cut parchment bag, pipe in 1 tail for each treat; refrigerate until firm. Turn over tail and overpipe on back side.

Cover mini egg cake with melted candy (p. 124); let set. Position cake on waxed paper-covered cake circle. Pipe paws and claws using melted candy; let set. Attach tail and face using melted candy. Each serves 1.

†Brand confectionery coating.

▲ Face the Competition

Candy: Candy Melts®† in Orange, Red, White, Light Cocoa, p. 162; Garden Candy Color Set, Decorator Brush Set, p. 163; 4 in. Lollipop Sticks, p. 165; Sports Mold, p. 164

Also: Parchment Triangles, p. 138

Mold lollipops using painting method (p. 123); refrigerate until firm. Tint a portion of melted white candy black using candy color; tint a portion pink by adding a small amount of red candy to white. Using melted candy in cut parchment bag, pipe eyes, pupils, mouth and tongue; refrigerate until firm. Each serves 1.

▶ Babies in a Bundle

Pan: Mini Heart, p. 198

Tip: 2, p. 140

Colors: Black, Rose, Sky Blue, Creamy Peach, p. 135

Fondant: White Ready-To-Use Rolled Fondant (24 oz.), Brush Set, p. 128; Rolling Pin, Roll & Cut Mat, p. 131

Recipes: Buttercream, Royal Icings, p. 114

Also: Meringue Powder, p. 134; ⅛ in. wide white satin ribbon (12 in. needed for each cake)

Fill in the indented center of heart cakes with buttercream icing. Turn cakes pointed end up; prepare for rolled fondant (p. 113). Tint portions of fondant rose and blue. Cover cakes with fondant. For gathered top of bow, cut a 1½ x 5 in. wide strip, cutting 1 edge straight and the other wavy; gather strip at straight edge. Attach top to bundle with damp brush.

Tint portion of fondant light peach. For head, roll a 1½ in. diameter ball. For feet, roll a 1¼ x ¾ in. oval; flatten. For nose, cheeks and toes, roll small balls in peach and rose. Attach all pieces with damp brush. Add tip 2 dot eyes and string mouth in royal icing. Tie a ribbon bow to each cake. Each serves 1.

▼ Crispy Rice Slice

Pan: 6 x 2 in. Round, p. 148

Color: Brown, p. 135

Candy: Candy Melts®† in White, Light Cocoa, p. 162; Garden Candy Color Set, p. 163

Recipe: Favorite crisped rice cereal treats (2 recipes)

Also: Rainbow Jimmies Sprinkle Decorations, p. 136; Parchment Triangles, 8 in. Angled Spatula, p. 138; Smiley Flames Chunky Candles, p. 180; candy-coated chocolates, waxed paper, serrated knife

Prepare 2 recipes of cereal treats; tint approximately 2 cups of mixture brown. Press brown mixture into pan, ¼ in. deep; unmold. Press plain mixture into pan, 2 in. deep, for 1 layer; immediately unmold. Repeat for second layer. On waxed paper, press together 2 plain layers with brown layer in between; let set. With serrated knife, cut into 6 wedges. Tint melted white candy pink using candy color. Using melted candy in cut parchment bag, pipe "icing" on 3 wedges working from side to top; smooth with spatula. Immediately sprinkle wedges with jimmies. Position candy-coated chocolates for top border. Insert candle. Repeat on other 3 wedges using cocoa candy for icing. Makes 6 treats, each serves 1.

◀ Memorable Mini Mousse

Pan: Mini Tiered Cakes, p. 150

Tips: 2, 3, p. 140

Color: Rose, p. 135

Recipe: White Chocolate Mousse, Cream Cheese Mints, p. 114

Also: Wedding Shower Lollipop Mold, p. 164; Vanilla Whipped Icing Mix, p. 134; vegetable oil pan spray

In advance: Mold mousse in pan. Prepare pan cavities by spraying with a light coating of non-stick pan spray. Fill cavities with mousse; refrigerate overnight and unmold. **Also:** Make mint bells. Prepare mints recipe; press into bell molds. Unmold and let set overnight.

Prepare whipped icing; tint a portion rose. Pipe tip 3 drop strings; add tip 2 rosette flower at each string point. Position mint bells. Each serves 1.

La Quinceañera Bonita

Pans: 6, 8, 10, 12, 14 x 3 in. Round, p. 148; Mini Ball, p. 154

Tips: 2, 3, 6, 8, p. 140

Color: Rose, p. 135

Fondant: White Ready-To-Use Rolled Fondant (264 oz.), p. 128; Oval Cut-Outs™, p. 130; Cutter/Embosser, Flower Former Set, Fondant Shaping Foam, Easy-Glide Fondant Smoother, p. 129; Rolling Pin, Roll & Cut Mat, Gum-Tex™, p. 131; Brush Set, p. 128

Topper: Good Fairy, p. 218

Recipes: Buttercream, Royal Icings, p. 114; Thinned Fondant Adhesive, p. 115

Also: 2007 Pattern Book (Alphabet, Scrolls, Curls), p. 126; Heart Comfort Grip™ Cutter, p. 158; Floral Collection Flower Making Set, p. 130; Meringue Powder, p. 134; Cake Dividing Set, p. 133; Confectionery Tool Set, p. 129; 12 in. Floral Cake Decorations (3 sets), p. 219; Plastic Dowel Rods (4 sets), p. 224; 16 in. Round Silver Cake Base, Cake Circles, p. 225; Gum-Tex™, p. 131; ruler, waxed paper, cornstarch, sharp embroidery scissors, non-toxic chalk in rose and green, tea strainer, cardboard, cellophane tape, toothpicks, drinking straws

Several days in advance: Make 6 royal icing curls (p. 120). **Also:** Tint 4 oz. of fondant rose; roll out rose and 8 oz. of white fondant ⅛ in. thick. Make fondant flowers (p. 120). Make 8 fondant ovals for cake sides (p. 120). Make extras of all flowers and ovals to allow for breakage. **And:** Make 8 tassels (p. 120) using 8 oz. white fondant combined with ¾ teaspoon of Gum-Tex.

Bake and cool 2-layer 6 and 8 in. cakes (bake two 2½ in. layers for 5 in. high cakes), 2-layer 10 and 12 in. cakes (bake two 3 in. layers for 6 in. high cakes) and 1-layer 14 in. cake (2 in. high). Prepare for stacked construction (p. 112). Prepare for rolled fondant (p. 113). Tint 228 oz. of fondant rose. Cover cakes; smooth with Fondant Smoother.

Divide 6 in. cake into 6ths. At division points, in buttercream, pipe tip 3 triple drop strings 1, 1½ and 2¼ in. from top edge of cake. Pipe a curve of tip 2 dots ½ in. from top of cake. Pipe a tip 3 ball at drop string peaks; attach a rose apple blossom to each ball. Position 6 in. cake on top of 8 in. cake. Attach white pansies, apple blossoms and forget-me-nots on 8 in. cake top and down sides with royal icing.

Divide 10 in. cake into 8ths. Roll out rose fondant ⅛ in. thick; cut into eight 6 in. squares. Using straight-edge wheel of Cutter/Embosser, score quilting lines on each square, ½ in. apart. Cut out a heart from each square with cutter. Trim off 1 in. from top of heart; attach to cake top with damp brush, extending over side with point 1¾ in. from top of cake. Trim sides of hearts to fit. Position 8 in. cake on 10 in. cake. Pipe tip 2 white dots on hearts. Edge hearts with tip 3 rose dots. Add tip 3 curving lines from heart point to where hearts meet. Attach tassels at heart points with royal icing. Add 3 tip 2 white dots below curved lines. Roll ½ in. balls of white fondant and attach to bottom border of 8 in. cake with damp brush.

Stack all cakes for decorating (you will disassemble cakes for transporting and re-stack at reception). On backs of fondant ovals, pipe a tip 8 line of royal icing and attach to 12 in. cake, 1 in. from top edge and directly below tassels on 10 in. cake. Pipe tip 6 balls around ovals in rose. Trace scroll pattern around ovals with toothpick; outline with tip 3. Pipe tip 3 triple drop strings between ovals, ½, 1¼ and 2 in. from top edge of cake. Attach rose pansies with royal icing at drop string points. On 14 in. cake, pipe tip 3 bead bottom border. Remove 6, 8 and 10 in. cakes from stack for transporting. From white fondant, roll fifty ⅝ in. and forty-five ⅞ in. balls for bottom borders; let dry. Grate non-toxic chalk with a small amount of cornstarch through tea strainer; brush chalk on Floral Cake Decoration roses and leaves.

At reception: Assemble cakes. With icing and tip 3, attach ⅝ in. balls to bottom border of 10 in. cake and ⅞ in. balls to bottom border of 12 in. cake. Pipe tip 3 swirl on ⅞ in. balls in rose buttercream. Cut drinking straws to 3 in.; insert ends of curls in straws, then insert in 10 in. cake. Attach Floral Cake Decorations to silver cake base with pins. Position topper. Serves 132.

A Family's Pride

Pans: 9 x 2 in. Square Non-Stick, p. 146; 18 x 3 in. Half Round, p. 147; 6, 10, 14 x 2 in. Round, P. 148

Tips: 1, 2, 6, p. 140

Candy: Hanukkah Lollipop Mold (3), p. 197; Light Cocoa Candy Melts®† (3 pks.), p. 162

Recipe: Chocolate Buttercream Icing, p. 114

Also: Tailored Tiers™ Cake Display Set, p. 220; Monogram Picks, p. 219; Plastic Dowel Rods (2 pks.), p. 224; Cooling Grid, p. 161; 6-Point Star Cookie Cutter, p. 160; Cake Circles, Fanci-Foil Wrap, p. 225; Cake Dividing Set, p. 133; 20 in. round foamcore board (½ in.thick), ½ in. white ribbon (63 in.), double-stick tape, family photos

In advance: Mold 55 small Star-of-David candies without sticks in lollipop mold. Also mold 10-12 large Star-of-David candies using cookie cutter. Position cutter in non-stick pan; fill with melted candy to ⅜ in. high. Refrigerate until firm. **Also:** For cake top letters, place monogram picks on cooling grid over a drip pan. Cover with melted candy; tap grid lightly to remove excess. Stand letters upright until firm. **And:** Attach a small star candy at center of each large star with melted candy; let set.

Ice 2-layer cakes smooth (bake four 2 in. high 18 in. half round cakes to make 4 in. high base cake) and prepare for Tailored Tiers construction (p. 113). Stack 14 and 18 in. cakes. Divide 6 in. cake in 6ths, 10 in. cake in 10ths, 14 in. cake in 14ths and 18 in. cake in 10ths using Cake Dividing Set. Pipe tip 6 bead top borders on all cakes and bead bottom borders on 14 and 18 in. cakes. Attach small star candies with dots of icing to 6, 10 and 14 in. cakes at division marks. Pipe tip 2 curved vines between stars. Add tip 2 dots around vines. On large star candies, pipe tip 2 curving vines in chocolate buttercream. Add tip 2 C-motion randomly along vines. Pipe tip 1 dots. Attach large stars to 18 in. cake at division marks using dots of icing. Attach a small star between each large star.

At reception: Insert photos in acetate wraps from Tailored Tiers set, trimming as needed. Assemble cakes. Place 6 in. cake on 8 in. plate and 10 in. cake on 12 in. plate from Tailored Tiers set. Pipe tip 6 bead bottom border on 6 and 10 in. cakes. On 6 in. cake, pipe tip 6 rosette where letters will be positioned. Insert letters in cake top. Serves 213.

†Brand confectionery coating.

◀ It's No Wallflower!

Pan: Dancing Daisy Flower, p. 178
Tip: 16, p. 141
Colors: Orange, Leaf Green, Rose, Golden Yellow, p. 135
Recipe: Buttercream Icing, p. 114
Also: 2007 Pattern Book (Petal), p. 126; Cake Board, Fanci-Foil Wrap, p. 225; toothpicks

Lightly ice cake top smooth. Trace petal patterns with toothpick. Cover cake top and sides with tip 16 stars. Cover center of flower with tip 16 rosettes. Serves 12.

▼ Personal Posies

Pan: 8 x 2 in. Square, p. 148
Candy: White Candy Melts®†, p. 162; Dancing Daisy Flower Lollipop Mold, p. 178; 6 in. Lollipop Sticks, p. 165; Primary, Garden Candy Color Sets, p. 163; Decorator Brush Set, p. 163
Also: 2007 Pattern Book (Fence Post), p. 126; Cooling Grid, p. 161; Parchment Triangles, p. 138; green florist tape, paring knife, jelly spearmint leaves, waxed paper

In advance: Make candy flowers and fence posts. Tint portions of melted candy yellow, pink and orange using candy colors. Mold flower lollipops using painting method (p. 123); refrigerate until firm. Wrap sticks with florist tape, leaving 2 in. unwrapped at bottom for inserting in cake. Cover fence post pattern with waxed paper; using melted white candy in cut parchment bag, outline and pipe in 12 fence posts for each cake. Make extras to allow for breakage; refrigerate until firm.

Cut 1-layer square cake into 2 in. squares (8 in. cake makes about 16 treats). Tint portion of melted candy green with a little yellow. Cover cakes with melted candy (p. 124); refrigerate until firm and repeat with a second coat. (One pk. of Candy Melts will cover 4-5 mini cakes.) Attach fence posts to cake with dots of melted candy. Slice spearmint leaf in half, cut a slit in bottom edge and fit over flower stick, pinch leaf to secure. Insert flower in cake. Each serves 1.

▼ Flower Refreshers

Pans: Silicone Mini Flower Mold, p. 144; 8 x 2 in. Square, p. 148
Tips: 7, 17, p. 140-141
Colors: Lemon Yellow, Orange, Rose, p. 135
Also: Vanilla Whipped Icing Mix, p. 134; Leaf Cut-Outs™, p. 130; lemon, strawberry, orange, lime (3 oz. pk. each), unflavored gelatin (4 envelopes), vegetable oil pan spray

To make gelatin, add 1 cup boiling water and 1 envelope unflavored gelatin to each 3 oz. gelatin package; stir until dissolved then add 1 cup cold water.

Pour gelatin mixtures into mold sprayed with vegetable pan spray; refrigerate to set. For leaves, pour prepared gelatin ½ in. thick into square pan sprayed with vegetable pan spray; refrigerate to set. Prepare whipped icing mix and tint yellow, rose and orange to coordinate with gelatin. Use medium leaf Cut-Out to cut 1 leaf for each flower. Unmold gelatin flowers and pipe tip 7 petal outlines; add tip 17 rosette centers. Position leaves. Each serves 1.

▼ Tasty Daisies

Pan: Standard Muffin, p. 149

Color: Kelly Green, p. 135

Candy: White Candy Melts®†, p. 162; 4 in. Lollipop Sticks, p. 165; Decorator Brush Set, p. 163

Recipe: Favorite crisped rice cereal treats

Also: Dancing Daisy Flower Icing Decorations, Dancing Daisy Flower Baking Cups, p. 178; jelly spearmint leaves, candy-coated fruit-flavored dots, waxed paper, scissors

For stems, brush lollipop sticks with green icing color thinned with a little water. Let dry. Place baking cups into muffin pan; press cereal treats mixture into cups, filling ¾ full. Cut spearmint leaves in half. Attach leaves and icing decorations to stems using melted candy; let set. Insert stems into cereal treats; secure with melted candy. Fill cups with candy-coated dots. Each serves 1.

†Brand confectionery coating.

▲ Ring Around the Rosey

Pan: 8 x 2 in. Round, p. 148

Tips: 3, 6, 47, 233, 352, p. 140-141

Colors:* Kelly Green, Violet, Rose, Leaf Green, Lemon Yellow, Royal Blue, Orange, p. 135

Recipe: Buttercream Icing, p. 114

Also: 2007 Pattern Book (Flower Pot, Alphabet), p. 126; Flower Candle Set (2), p. 178; Cake Divider Set, p. 133; Cake Board, Fanci-Foil Wrap, p. 225; toothpick

Ice 2-layer cake smooth (bake two 1½ in. high layers for a 3 in. high cake). Divide cake into 10ths. At each division, trace Flower Pot pattern using toothpick. Pipe tip 6 lines to fill in flower pot base; add tip 47 (smooth side up) band for rim. Pipe tip 3 string stems; add tip 352 leaves. Pipe tip 233 pull-out grass bottom border. Trace message pattern on cake top using toothpick. Pipe tip 3 message. Position candles. Serves 20.

*Combine Violet with Rose for violet shown. Combine Leaf Green with Lemon Yellow for green shown.

▶ Dynamic Daisy

Pan: Dancing Daisy Flower, p. 151

Tips: 4, 8, p. 140

Colors: Lemon Yellow, Rose, p. 135

Fondant: White Ready-To-Use Rolled Fondant (24 oz.), Brush Set, p. 128; Rolling Pin, Roll & Cut Mat, p. 131

Recipe: Buttercream Icing, p. 114

Also: 2007 Pattern Book (Petal), p. 126; Gum-Tex™, p. 131; Cake Board, Fanci-Foil Wrap, p. 225; cornstarch, cotton balls, craft knife

At least 48 hours in advance: Make fondant flower petals. Mix 18 oz. fondant with 2 teaspoons Gum-Tex; tint light rose. Roll out ⅛ in. thick. Using pattern, cut 6 petals. Dust underside of each petal with cornstarch; brush ½ in. from each end with water and fold together to form a loop. Position cotton balls inside loop to hold shape and let dry on cornstarch-dusted board at least 48 hours. **Also:** Tint 2 oz. fondant dark rose; roll out ⅛ in. thick. Using narrow end of tip 8, cut approximately 90 dots; attach to petals with damp brush.

Ice cake smooth. Pipe tip 4 lines on cake sides, 1 in. apart. Pipe tip 4 ball bottom border. Tint 4 oz. fondant yellow; roll out ⅛ in. thick. Using pan as a pattern, cut flower center; position on cake. Remove cotton balls from petals and position on cake. Trim petal ends in a curve to fit flush against flower center. Roll a ⅜ in. diameter yellow fondant rope; form a spiral shape and attach to flower center with damp brush. Serves 12.

◀ Clunk A Monkey

Pan: Palm Tree, p. 151

Tips: 1, 3, 6, 8, 10, 16, p. 140-141

Colors:* Brown, Red-Red, Leaf Green, Lemon Yellow, Orange, Golden Yellow, Black, p. 135

Recipes: Buttercream, Royal Icings, p. 114

Also: 2007 Pattern Book (Smiling Monkey, Dazed Monkey), p. 126; Cake Boards, Fanci-Foil Wrap, p. 225; Parchment Triangles, p. 138; cornstarch, waxed paper, cellophane tape

At least 2 days in advance: Make monkeys using royal icing. Make 2 copies of each monkey pattern; place 1 copy on board, cover with waxed paper and secure with tape, (use 2nd copy for reference while piping). Build up body with tip 10; smooth with spatula. Pipe in tip 8 stomach (pat smooth with finger dipped in cornstarch). Pipe tip 8 ball head; pipe in face and ears with tip 3 (pat smooth with finger dipped in cornstarch). Pipe tip 6 outline legs, arms and tail. Pipe tip 3 eyes and mouth, tip 1 dot nose and outline teeth on top monkey. Pipe tip 10 dot coconut and tip 3 motion lines, ¾ in. long. Let dry.

On cake, outline trunk and leaf sections with tip 3. Fill in cake with tip 16 stars. Carefully peel off monkeys, coconut and motion lines from waxed paper; position on cake. Serves 12.

*Combine Brown with Red-Red for brown shown. Combine Brown and Orange with Golden Yellow for orange shown. Combine Leaf Green with Lemon Yellow for green shown.

▼ Pineapple Pleasure

Pan: Pineapple, p. 151

Tip: 366, p. 141

Color: Kelly Green, p. 135

Recipe: Favorite creamed gelatin (use four 3 oz. pks. of lemon gelatin for a 10 cup recipe)

Also: Vanilla Whipped Icing Mix, p. 134; Cake Board, Fanci-Foil Wrap, p. 225; Disposable Decorating Bags, p. 138; vegetable oil pan spray, pineapple tidbits (drained)

Prepare creamed gelatin recipe, adding pineapple to mixture; pour into pan prepared with non-stick spray. Refrigerate and unmold onto foil-wrapped board following recipe directions. Tint whipped icing green and pipe tip 366 leaves at top. Serves 12-16.

▼ Shady Characters Cupcakes

Pan: Standard Muffin, p. 149

Tips: 3, 5, 16, p. 140-141

Colors:* Black, Copper (skin tone), Brown, Red-Red, Lemon Yellow, Golden Yellow, p. 135

Candy: White Candy Melts®†, p. 162; Garden, Primary Candy Color Sets, Decorator Brush Set, Candy Melting Plate, p. 163; Summer Fun Candy Mold, p. 164

Recipe: Buttercream Icing, p. 114

Also: Assorted Pastel Standard Baking Cups, p. 184; 4 in. Lollipop Sticks, p. 165; Parchment Triangles, p. 138; Cake Boards, p. 225; waxed paper

In Advance: Tint portions of melted candy orange, yellow, black, rose, green and violet using candy colors. On waxed paper, using melted yellow candy in cut parchment bag, pipe pigtail shapes. Refrigerate until firm. Cut lollipop sticks to 3 in.; attach stick to back of pigtail shapes with melted candy. Mold candy sunglasses using painting method (p. 123); refrigerate until firm.

Ice cupcakes smooth. For girl cupcakes, insert pigtails in sides. Using buttercream, pipe girl's hair and overpipe pigtails with tip 16 strings. For boy cupcakes, pipe tip 16 pull-out hair. Attach sunglasses with dots of icing. Pipe tip 5 dot noses and tip 3 string smiles. Each serves 1.

*Combine Brown with Red-Red for brown shown. Combine Lemon Yellow with Golden Yellow for yellow shown. For candy, combine purple and pink candy colors for purple shown, combine green and yellow candy colors for green shown.

†Brand confectionery coating.

▼ Rainbow Fish

Pan: Tropical Fish, p. 151

Tip: 18, p. 141

Colors:* Violet, Rose, Lemon Yellow, Golden Yellow, Royal Blue, Leaf Green, p. 135

Fondant: White Ready-To-Use Rolled Fondant (72 oz.), Rolling Pin, Roll & Cut Mat, p. 131; Brush Set, p. 128

Recipe: Buttercream Icing, p. 114

Also: Seashells Candy Mold, p. 164; Fanci-Foil Wrap, p. 225; Piping Gel, p. 134; 16 x 21 in. foamcore board (½ in. thick), cornstarch, craft knife

In advance: Tint a portion of fondant rose. Marbleize fondant, blending a small amount of rose into white. Press into candy mold to make 2 shells and 2 starfish. Remove and let dry on cornstarch-dusted surface.

Prepare base board. Using craft knife, cut wave shapes on sides of foamcore board; wrap with foil.

Tint 48 oz. of fondant blue. Tint portions of remaining fondant green, pink, yellow and violet. Roll out a blue fondant rectangle, ⅛ in. thick, larger than base board. Brush board lightly with piping gel. Position fondant on board and trim ½ in. smaller than board on each side. Roll out violet and white fondant ⅛ in. thick; cut a 1½ in. white circle for eye and a ¾ in. violet circle for pupil. Position eye on cake top; attach pupil with damp brush. Cover cake with tip 18 stars.

Roll out all fondant colors ⅛ in. thick. Cut 20 tapered strips, ½ in. wide, in each color in various lengths from 2 to 3 in. Brush strips with water and attach for fins and tail. For bubbles, shape white balls in various sizes from ½ to 1¼ in.; flatten and position on board. For coral, roll ⅜ in. diameter violet logs; form a 10 in. long center branch and cut various lengths for other branches. Attach with damp brush and position on base board. For sea plants, cut ⅛ in. wide pink strips in various lengths. Attach bottom ends to base board with damp brush. Position shells and stars. Serves 12.

*Combine Violet with Rose for violet shown. Combine Lemon Yellow with Golden Yellow for yellow shown. Combine Leaf Green with Lemon Yellow for green shown. (Tint fondant colors slightly darker than buttercream colors.)

▲ Looking Very Hot!

Pan: Soccer Ball, p. 155

Tips: 1A, 4, 6, 12, 18, p. 140-141

Colors:* Lemon Yellow, Orange, Leaf Green, Black, p. 135

Recipes: Buttercream Icing, Roll-Out Cookie, p. 114

Also: 2007 Pattern Book (Large and Small Sunrays, Sunglasses, Mouth), p. 126; Cookie Sheet, Cooling Grid, p. 161; Fanci-Foil Wrap, p. 225; Orange Colored Sugar, p. 136; 18 in. round cardboard, cornstarch, paring knife, toothpick

Tint cookie dough yellow. Roll out dough and trace sunray and sunglasses patterns. Use knife to cut 11 each large and small sunray cookies and 1 sunglasses cookie using knife. Bake and cool. Position soccer ball cake in center of foil-covered board. Trace mouth pattern with toothpick. Outline and pipe in with tip 4 (smooth with finger dipped in cornstarch). Build up nose and cheeks with tip 1A ball; cover cake with tip 18 stars. Decorate sunglasses cookie. Outline and pipe in lenses with tip 4 (smooth with finger dipped in cornstarch). Outline sunglasses frames with tip 12. Position on cake. Outline sunrays with tip 6; sprinkle outlines with orange sugar. Position sunray cookies around cake. Cake serves 12; each cookie serves 1.

*Combine Leaf Green with Lemon Yellow for green shade shown.

CELEBRATE WITH CELEBRITIES!

Having the right names at the party adds to the fun. Let the stars of NASCAR® drive your theme home—a thrilling racecar cake on a fondant victory flag board sets the pace, while fun cookies and cupcakes rev up the excitement. There's plenty of fast company for kids too! The powerful new look of *Superman*™ rules the world on our planet earth candy favors…while *Strawberry Shortcake*™ reigns supreme for girls on a princess birthday cake with a ruffled fondant gown. Sometimes impressing your guests is all about who you know.

Instructions for projects shown on these two pages are on page 28.

NASCAR
HAPPY BIRTHDAY
MIKE
82
NASCAR

Party at the Winner's Circle

Product officially licensed by NASCAR®: Pan, Icing Color Set (black, blue, red, gold), p. 166

Tips: 1, 3, 16, 21, p. 140-141

Colors: Violet, Orange, Brown, Rose, p. 135

Fondant: White Ready-To-Use Rolled Fondant (66 oz.), Brush Set, p. 128; Rolling Pin, Roll & Cut Mat, p. 131; Square Cut-Outs™, p. 130

Recipe: Buttercream Icing, p. 114

Also: Cake Boards, Fanci-Foil Wrap, p. 225; Parchment Triangles, p. 138; 101 Cookie Cutters Set, p. 160; Piping Gel, p. 134; ½ in. thick foamcore board (24 x 20 in.), cornstarch

At least 1 day in advance: Prepare base board. Cut foamcore into a 21 x 17 in. oval; wrap with foil. Tint 28 oz. fondant black, 6 oz. red, 4 oz. blue; reserve 28 oz. white. Roll out all fondant 1/8 in. thick. Cut out message using alphabet cutters. Cut background squares using medium Cut-Out. Lightly brush board with Piping Gel and attach squares in checkerboard pattern. Attach message with damp brush; let dry.

Ice cake sides and background areas smooth. Pipe in window areas and headlights with tip 3 zigzags (smooth with finger dipped in cornstarch). Outline car, windows, headlights, hood, detailing, number and tires with tip 3. Pipe in bumper and side of car with tip 3 zigzags (smooth with finger dipped in cornstarch). Pipe in wheel wells, rims, hood racing stripes and window trim with tip 3 (smooth with finger dipped in cornstarch). Pipe in NASCAR logo background with tip 1; pipe NASCAR letters with tip 1 (smooth with finger dipped in cornstarch). Outline and pipe in tip 1 and 3 details on front bumper, tires and side panel. Add tip 3 stripe for spoiler. Cover car with tip 16 stars. Position cake on base board. Pipe tip 21 shell bottom border. Serves 12.

Driven By The Fans!

Pan: 8 x 2 in. Round, p. 148

Tips: 1, 1D, 2, p. 140

Colors: Royal Blue, Lemon Yellow, Black, Brown, Orange, Copper (skin tone), p. 135

Product officially licensed by NASCAR®: Icing Decorations (2 pks.), Candle, p. 166

Recipes: Buttercream, Royal Icings, p. 114

Also: 12 in. Cake Circle, Fanci-Foil Wrap, p. 225; Parchment Triangles, p. 138; Fine Tip Primary Colors FoodWriter™ Edible Color Markers, p. 128, Meringue Powder, p. 134; waxed paper

In advance: Make 116 faces on waxed paper using royal icing thinned with water. Pipe dot faces ranging from ½ in. to 7/16 in. diameter; let dry overnight. Pipe tip 1 and 2 pull-out or swirl hair using full-strength royal icing; let dry. Draw facial features using black FoodWriter.

Ice 2-layer cake smooth and position on foil-wrapped cake board. Ice top of board smooth in gray buttercream. Pipe tip 1D band bottom border. Attach faces to cake sides with tip 1 dots of icing. Position candle on cake top; position icing decoration flags next to candle. Attach car icing decorations around base of cake with icing. Serves 20.

Pit Stop for Treats

Product officially licensed by NASCAR®: Baking Cups, Icing Decorations, p. 166

Pan: Standard Muffin, p. 149

Recipe: Buttercream Icing, p. 114

Also: Spatula, p. 138

Ice cupcakes smooth with spatula. Position icing decorations. Each serves 1.

Suited for Speed

Cookie: 101 Cookie Cutters Set, p. 160; Cookie Sheet, Cooling Grid, p. 161

Tips: 1, 3, p. 140

Colors:* Black, Royal Blue, Red-Red, Christmas Red, p. 135

Recipes: Color Flow Icing, Roll-Out Cookie, p. 114

Also: Color Flow Mix, p. 134; Parchment Triangles, p. 138; Rolling Pin, p. 131

Roll out dough. Cut cookies using large boy cutter from set; bake and cool. Outline and flow in suit and helmet areas using tip 3 and color flow (p. 124); let dry. Add trims using full-strength color flow. Pipe tip 3 stripes on helmet, waist and patch; print tip 1 number and name. Each serves 1.

*Combine Red-Red and Christmas Red for red shown.

Speedway Cookies

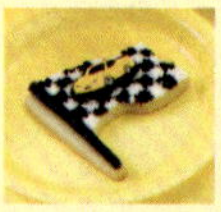

Cookie: 101 Cookie Cutters Set, p. 160; Cookie Sheet, Cooling Grid, p.161

Tips: 8, 14, p. 140-141

Color: Black, p. 135

Product officially licensed by NASCAR®: Icing Decorations, Party Bags, p. 166

Recipes: Royal Icing, Roll-Out Cookie, p. 114

Also: Rolling Pin, p. 131; Meringue Powder, p. 134

Roll out dough. Cut cookies using flag cutter from set; bake and cool. Pipe tip 8 outline pole. Using tip 14, pipe stars in groups of 4 to create checkered pattern. Attach icing decoration. Let dry. Place cookies in party bags. Each serves 1.

THE AMAZING SPIDER-MAN

Hang Around for Fun!

Pan: 8 x 2 in. Round, p. 148

Tips: 2, 3, 12, p. 140

Colors:* Leaf Green, Lemon Yellow, Black, p. 135

Recipe: Buttercream Icing, p. 114

Also: Cake Board, Fanci-Foil Wrap, p. 225; *Spider-Man™* Candle, Icing Decorations, p. 171; Cake Dividing Set, p. 133

Ice 2-layer cake smooth. Divide into 8ths, marking at top edge. Mark center of each division 1¾ in. from top edge. Pipe tip 3 triple drop strings at division points, ¾, 1¼ and 1¾ in. deep; add tip 3 diagonal lines from center point. Edge top of cake with tip 3 outline. Pipe tip 12 ball bottom border; pipe spiders on alternating balls with tip 2 ball body, head and string legs. Print tip 3 message. Position candle and icing decorations. Serves 20.

*Combine Leaf Green and Lemon Yellow for green shade shown.

◀ Web Visitors

Pan: Mini Loaf, p. 149

Candy: Candy Melts®† in White and Yellow (1 pk. each), p. 162; Garden Candy Colors Set, p. 163

Also: *Spider-Man*™ Icing Decorations, p. 171; Parchment Triangles, p. 138

Tint melted yellow candy with a small amount of green candy color to make lime green shade. Tint portions of melted white candy black and green using candy colors.

Make ¼ in. thick candy plaques (p. 124) in mini loaf cavities; unmold. Pipe webs using melted green candy in cut parchment bag; let set. Print name with melted black candy in cut parchment bag. Attach icing decoration with melted candy. Each serves 1.

†Brand confectionery coating.

▶ The Mighty Spidey!

Pans: *Spider-Man™*, p. 171; Mini Loaf, p. 149

Tips: 3, 8, 16, p. 140-141

Colors:* *Spider-Man* Icing Color Set (light blue, dark blue, red, black), p. 171; Leaf Green, Lemon Yellow, p. 135

Recipe: Buttercream Icing, p. 114

Also: 2007 Pattern Book (Web), p. 126; Cake Boards, Fanci-Foil Wrap, p. 225; ⅛ in. wide black ribbon (22 in.), cornstarch, toothpick

On a double-thick foil-wrapped board cut to fit, position 3 mini loaf cakes end-to-end to form base of cake. Position *Spider-Man* cake at top. Ice sides and background areas of Spider-Man and tops and sides of mini loaves smooth. Trace 4 web patterns across tops of mini loaf cakes with toothpick; outline webs with tip 3. Print tip 3 message. Outline tip 3 body and suit web design. Outline and pipe in black and white eye areas with tip 3 (smooth with finger dipped in cornstarch). Cover body, head, arms and hands with tip 16 stars. Pipe tip 8 ball bottom border. Serves 15.

*Combine Leaf Green and Lemon Yellow for green shown.

▲ Fast-Track Snack

Pan: Standard Muffin, p. 149
Recipe: Buttercream Icing, p. 114
Also: *Cars* Standard Baking Cups, Fun Pix®, p. 168

Ice cupcakes; insert Fun Pix. Each serves 1.

▶ Park Yourself Here!

Pan: Mini Loaf, p. 149
Also: Candy Melts®† in White, Blue, Red, Light Cocoa, Green (1 pk. each), p. 162; *Cars* Icing Decorations, p. 168; Parchment Triangles, Tapered Spatula, p. 138; toothpick

Lighten all candy colors (except white and red). For blue, mix equal amounts of blue and white. For brown ground, mix 32 light cocoa discs, 64 white discs and 3 red discs. For brown fissures, mix 10 each light cocoa and white discs.

To make candy plaques (p. 124), fill each pan cavity ¼ in. high; refrigerate until firm. Unmold and let come to room temperature. Lightly score ground outline with toothpick. Using melted candy in cut parchment bag, pipe in ground; smooth with spatula. Pipe fissures in ground, grass, clouds and name. Attach icing decorations with melted candy. Each serves 1.

†Brand confectionery coating.

▶ Jump Start the Party!

Pan: 8 x 2 in. Round, p. 149
Tips: 1, 2, 9, p. 140
Colors:* Royal Blue, Brown, Red-Red, Black, Kelly Green, p. 135
Recipe: Buttercream Icing, p. 114
Also: 2007 Pattern Book (Landscape), p. 126; *Cars* Candle, Icing Decorations, p. 168; Alphabet/Numerals Icing Decorations, p. 184; Cake Board, Fanci-Foil Wrap, p. 225; Tapered Spatula, p. 138; waxed paper, toothpick, scissors

Ice 2-layer cake smooth. Trace and cut out pattern on waxed paper, long enough to wrap around cake. Position pattern on cake side. Trace top of landscape with toothpick and remove waxed paper. Ice landscape area smooth with tapered spatula. Pipe tip 9 ball bottom border; pipe balls sized for boulders. Attach icing decorations above boulders with dots of icing. Pipe tip 1 fissures on cake sides. Pipe tip 2 pull-out grass and tip 9 zigzag clouds. Position candle and alphabet icing decoration message on cake top. Serves 20.

*Combine Brown with Red-Red and a little Black for brown shown.

©Disney/Pixar

▼ Lightning Fast!

Pan: *Cars Lightning McQueen*, p. 168
Tips: 3, 16, 21, p. 140-141
Colors: *Cars* Icing Color Set (yellow, blue, red, black), p. 168; Brown, Kelly Green, p. 135
Fondant: White Ready-To-Use Rolled Fondant (48 oz.), Brush Set, p. 128; Rolling Pin, Roll & Cut Mat, p. 131; Square, Alphabet/Number, Oval Cut-Outs™, p. 130
Recipe: Buttercream Icing, p. 114
Also: 2007 Pattern Book (Landscape), p. 126; 13 x 19 in. Cake Board, Fanci-Foil Wrap, p. 225; Piping Gel, p. 134; 22½ x 16½ in. foamcore board (½ in. thick); cornstarch, scissors, fine artist brush, cellophane tape, knife, toothpick

One day in advance: Prepare fondant board. Wrap foamcore board with foil. Tint 9 oz. fondant black, 3 oz. red, 8 oz. blue, 8 oz. brown, 2 oz. green; reserve 9 oz. white. Roll out black and white fondant ⅛ in. thick. Using medium Cut-Out, cut black and white squares. Brush back with piping gel and attach around board. **Also:** For ground and sky, roll out brown and blue fondant ⅛ in. thick. Tape landscape patterns together and trace on brown fondant with toothpick; cut ground area using knife. For sky, reverse pattern and trace on blue fondant; cut out. Position ground and sky pieces on board; trim to fit and smooth edges together. Let dry overnight.

Ice cake sides, background areas, front windshield, side windows, and blue lightning bolt smooth. Using tip 3, outline car details and number; add dot rivets on hood. Pipe in eyes with tip 3 (smooth with finger dipped in cornstarch); add tip 3 dot pupils. Cover tires with tip 16 lines. Cover car, lightning bolt and number with tip 16 stars. Add tip 3 muffler. Pipe tip 21 shell bottom border.

Position cake on fondant-covered board. Using fine artist brush and brown icing color, paint fissures in ground. Make shrubs. Roll out green fondant ⅛ in. thick. Cut two large ovals for each shrub. On each oval, using scissors or a small sharp knife, cut tapered triangles from the top horizontal edge; reserve the cut out pieces to use as additional shrub spikes. Fan out spikes. Stack the two shrubs, inserting reserved cut out spikes in between to add dimension. Attach with damp brush.

Roll out white fondant ⅛ in. thick. Cut free form clouds; attach with damp brush. Roll out red fondant ⅛ in. thick; cut message using Cut-Outs and attach with damp brush. Serves 12.

◀ *SpongeBob* Above Sea Level

Pans: *SpongeBob SquarePants*™ Mini Treats, p. 176; 6, 10 x 2 in. Round, p. 148; Standard Muffin, p. 149

Tips: 6, 12, 21, 115, p. 140-141

Colors:* Leaf Green, Lemon Yellow, Rose, Violet, Royal Blue, p. 135

Candy: Candy Melts®† in Yellow and White (1 pk. each), p. 162; Primary, Garden Candy Color Sets, Decorator Brush Set, p. 163; 6 in. Lollipop Sticks, p. 165

Recipe: Buttercream Icing, p. 114

Also: 2007 Pattern Book (Right & Left Hands), p. 126; *SpongeBob SquarePants* Party Toppers (3 pks.), Standard Baking Cups, p. 176; Flowerful Medley Sprinkle Decorations, p. 136; Decorating Comb, p. 133; Assorted Celebration Candles, p. 187; Wooden Dowel Rods, p. 224; Parchment Triangles, p. 138; Ceramic Pedestal Cake Stand, p. 222; 12 in. Round Silver Cake Base, p. 225; mini marshmallows, waxed paper, paring knife

In advance: Tint small portions of melted white candy black and blue. Make cake top candy plaque (p. 124) in Mini Treats Pan. Refrigerate until firm. For arms, cut a lollipop stick in half; dip in melted yellow candy. Let dry on waxed paper; dip and dry again. Cover hand patterns with waxed paper. Outline and pipe in with melted candy in cut parchment bag; refrigerate until firm. Attach hands to arms with melted candy; let set. With melted candy, attach arms to back of plaque, leaving 1½ in. extending. For arm supports, cut 2 marshmallows to ½ in. thick; cut a slit in side and wrap around arms. Attach 6 in. lollipop stick to back, leaving 4 in. extending at bottom to insert in cake. Let set.

Prepare 2-layer cakes for stacked construction (p. 112) and stack cakes. Ice cake smooth, sides ½ in. thick. Comb sides with wide-tooth edge of decorating comb. Pipe tip 12 icing drips on cake tops and down sides; add confetti sprinkles. On 10 in. cake, pipe tip 21 rosette bottom border. Insert candy plaque; pipe tip 115 leaf "icing bursts" around plaque. Pipe tip 12 icing drips on plaque top; insert candle. Print tip 6 message. Ice smooth 18 cupcakes; add confetti sprinkles. Position toppers. Position cake and cupcakes. Cake serves 40; each cupcake serves 1.

*Combine Leaf Green and Lemon Yellow for green shown. Combine Violet and Rose for violet shown.

▶ Spinning 360° with *SpongeBob*

Pan: *SpongeBob SquarePants*™, p. 176

Tips: 3, 16, p. 140-141

Colors:* *SpongeBob SquarePants* Icing Color Set (yellow, red, blue, brown), p. 176; Black, Kelly Green, Moss Green, p. 135

Recipes: Buttercream, Royal Icings, Roll-Out Cookie, p. 114

Also: 2007 Pattern Book (Skateboard, Right & Left Hands), p. 126; Cookie Sheet, Cooling Grid, p. 149; Cake Board, Fanci-Foil Wrap, p. 225; Yellow Candy Melts®† (1 pk.), p. 162; Decorator Brush Set, p. 163; 6 in. Cookie Treat Sticks, p. 161; Meringue Powder, p. 134; Parchment Triangles, Angled Spatula, p. 138; Rolling Pin, p. 131; paring knife, cornstarch, toothpick, waxed paper

In advance: Make skateboard cookie. Roll out dough, trace pattern with toothpick and cut out cookie with paring knife. Bake and cool. Ice smooth with royal icing. Pipe in tip 3 stripe, wheels and axles; let dry. **Also:** Make arms. Brush a 4 in. area of 2 cookie treat sticks with melted yellow candy; let set. Pipe tip 3 elbow pads (pat smooth with finger dipped in cornstarch). Make hands. Cover patterns with waxed paper; outline and fill in with melted candy in cut parchment bags; let set. Attach hands to arms with melted candy; let set.

On cake, trim off arms, hands, knees and left sleeve; trim portion of mouth in tongue area. Ice cake sides and background areas smooth in buttercream. Pipe in sleeves, building up for dimension; build up knees with a bent shape. Pipe in spots with tip 3 (pat smooth with finger dipped in cornstarch). Outline body, facial features, helmet, clothing with tip 3. Pipe in whites of eyes, mouth, tongue, teeth and tie with tip 3 (build up tongue, pat smooth). Add tip 3 dot irises and pupils (pat smooth). Cover *SpongeBob* with tip 16 stars. Pipe tip 3 outline eyelashes and belt. Pipe tip 16 shell bottom border. Attach skateboard to cake with buttercream. Insert arms, leaving 4 in. extended. Pipe in tip 3 gloves and knee pads (pat smooth). Pipe in tip 3 strap. Cake serves 12; cookie serves 1.

*Combine Kelly Green with *SpongeBob SquarePants* Yellow for green spot areas. Combine Kelly Green and Moss Green for green outline areas.

▼ Funshine Bear™ Rides the Waves

Pans: *Care Bears*™, p. 172; 16 x 2 in. Round, p. 148

Tips: 3, 12, 21, p. 140-141

Colors:* Royal Blue, Leaf Green, Lemon Yellow, Brown, Orange, Rose, p. 135

Candy: Candy Melts®† in Yellow (2 pks.), White and Dark Cocoa (1 pk. each), p. 162; Primary, Garden Candy Color Sets, p. 163

Fondant: White Ready-To-Use Rolled Fondant (48 oz.), Brush Set, p. 128; Leaf, Flower, Round Cut-Outs™, p. 130; Rolling Pin, Roll & Cut Mat, p. 131; Cutter/Embosser, p. 129

Recipe: Buttercream Icing, p. 114

Also: 2007 Pattern Book (Sunglasses, Wave, Surfboard), p. 126; Fine Tip Primary FoodWriter™ Edible Color Markers, p. 128; Gum-Tex™, p. 131; Parchment Triangles, Disposable Decorating Bags, p. 138; Cake Boards, Fanci-Foil Wrap, p. 225; 2 in. high craft block, waxed paper, cornstarch, warming tray

In advance: Make fondant surfboard, wave, sunglass frames, lenses, flowers and leaves. Add 2 teaspoons of Gum-Tex to 24 oz. fondant. Tint 8 oz. of fondant mixture green, 18 oz. blue, 2 in. balls orange and brown, 1 in. balls rose and yellow; reserve remainder white. Roll out fondant ⅛ in. thick. Using patterns and straight-edge wheel of Cutter/Embosser, cut surfboard, wave, sunglass frames and lenses. Attach lenses to frames with damp brush. Cut 1 orange and 1 rose flower using large Cut-Out; cut 1 orange and 1 yellow flower using medium Cut-Out. Cut white large flower centers using wide end of tip 12; cut white medium flower centers using narrow end of tip 12. Attach centers to flowers with damp brush. Cut 5 leaves using large Cut-Out. Let all fondant pieces dry on waxed paper-covered boards dusted with cornstarch. **Also:** Make Funshine Bear candy plaque (p. 124).

Bake and cool 1-layer round cake. Cut in half to form semi-circle; reserve remaining half for later use. Ice cake smooth. Pipe tip 21 shell bottom border. Draw motion lines on wave and detail line on surfboard with FoodWriter. Position wave on cake. Attach surfboard, flowers and leaves to cake with buttercream. Attach sunglasses to candy plaque with melted candy; position plaque on cake, supporting with foil-wrapped craft block. Print tip 3 message. Serves 20.

*Combine Leaf Green with a small amount of Lemon Yellow for green fondant color shown.

†Brand confectionery coating.

▲ Nap Snacks!

Pan: Standard Muffin, p. 149

Tips: 2, 3, 8, 12, p. 140-141

Colors:* Care Bears™ Icing Color Set (Teal, Blue, Yellow), p. 172; Red-Red, Rose, Violet, p. 135

Recipe: Buttercream, Royal Icings, p. 114

Also: White Ready-To-Use Rolled Fondant (24 oz.), p. 128; Care Bears Icing Decorations, Baking Cups, p. 172; Tapered Spatula, p. 138; Meringue Powder, p. 134; ruler, paring knife, waxed paper

One day in advance: Figure pipe bears (p. 119) on waxed paper using royal icing and tips 12, 8, 3, and 2. Let dry overnight.

Ice cupcakes smooth in buttercream. For blanket, tint fondant yellow. Roll out ⅛ in. thick; cut into 2¼ in. x 1¾ in. rectangle. Position blanket on cupcake. Attach bears with dots of royal icing. Each serves 1.

*Combine Teal and Blue for teal shown. Combine Rose with a little Yellow for rose shown. Combine Violet and Rose for violet shown.

Strawberry Reigns Supreme

Pans: *Strawberry Shortcake*™, p. 173; 10 x 2 in. Heart, p. 148

Tips: 1, 2, 3, 8, 16, 233, 349, p. 140-141

Colors:* *Strawberry Shortcake* Color Set (red, brown, skin tone), p. 173; Rose, Violet, Royal Blue, Red-Red, p. 135

Fondant: White Ready-To-Use Rolled Fondant (48 oz.), Brush Set, p. 128; Rolling Pin, Roll & Cut Mat, p. 131; Cutter/Embosser, p. 129

Recipe: Buttercream Icing, p. 114; Thinned Fondant Adhesive, p. 115

Also: 2007 Pattern Book (Right Hand, Left Hand, Wand Top/Bow Clip, Diamond, Dress Bow Flower, Side and Top Dress Overlay Sections, Dress Flower Embroidery), p. 126; White Cake Sparkles™, p. 136; Plastic Dowel Rods, p. 224; 8 in. Lollipop Sticks, p. 165; Cake Boards, Fanci-Foil Wrap, p. 225; tea strainer, large marshmallows, cornstarch, ruler, paring knife, toothpick.

In advance: Make fondant wand top, bow clip, diamonds, dress bow flower and hands. Tint a 2½ in. ball of fondant skin tone, a 2 in. ball blue and 18 oz. rose. Roll out blue fondant ⅛ in. thick, rose fondant 1/16 in. thick. Using patterns and knife, cut two each blue wand top/bow clip and rose diamond pieces. Attach diamonds to wand top and bow clip with damp brush. Thin portions of rose and blue fondant to piping consistency with a little water. Using tip 2, outline facets on diamond, outline and pipe in sparkle lines above diamonds. Lightly brush wand top and bow clip with water; sprinkle with Cake Sparkles grated through tea strainer. For wand, wrap blue fondant around lollipop stick, attaching with damp brush. Attach wand top with adhesive; let dry. Roll a small ball of blue fondant and insert on bottom of wand. Cut blue dress bow flower using pattern. For hands, roll out skin tone fondant ¼ in. thick; cut out right and left hand using patterns and knife. Wrap right hand around wand handle, attaching with damp brush. Slightly bend left hand in center. Let all pieces dry on cornstarch-dusted board.

Trim arms and hands off *Strawberry Shortcake*. Turn 1-layer heart cake point up; trim 2 in. off point and 1 in. at curves of heart. Position heart cake against bottom of *Strawberry Shortcake*. Ice cake sides, hat band, hat bow and dress areas smooth in buttercream. Tint 12 oz. fondant violet; roll out ⅛ in. thick. Using inside of *Strawberry Shortcake* pan as a pattern, cut fondant strip for hatband; cut wavy top edge. Reserve remaining violet fondant. Position hat band. Outline hat, hat band and hat bow with tip 3. Outline eyes, nose and mouth with tip 3; pipe in with tip 2 (smooth with finger dipped in cornstarch). Pipe tip 2 outline irises and dot pupils; add tip 1 dot eye highlights. Add tip 2 outline teeth, eyelashes and dot tongue. Cover hat and face with tip 16 stars. Pipe tip 16 pull-out star hair. For dress overlay, roll out reserved violet fondant ¼ in. thick; cut side and top overlay sections using patterns (reverse side pattern to make right and left side of overlay). Position on cake. For skirt ruffles, cut 1 in. wide fondant strips, twice as long as the area to be covered. You will need 11 strips to cover heart cake from bottom to top; measure width in 1 in. sections toward top. Pinch sections of strip together to form loose ruffles. Position on heart cake, overlapping strips. Trace dress flower embroidery patterns with toothpick; pipe flowers, outline stars and circles with tip 1. For each arm, cover a 3½ in. area at end of dowel rod with violet fondant; mark and pipe embroidery as above. Insert in cake sides at area where 2 cakes meet. For fur collar, shape 2 logs of white fondant, 1½ in. x 6 in. long. Taper 1 end of each strip to ¾ in. diameter; attach over shoulders with damp brush so that tapered ends meet. Cover collar with tip 233 pull-out fur. For cuffs, roll out white fondant ⅛ in. thick; cut 2 strips, 1 x 2 in. Wrap around end of arms, attaching with damp brush. Cover with tip 233 pull-out fur.

For dress bow, roll out rose fondant ⅛ in. thick. Cut a ½ x 6 in. long strip for waist; attach with damp brush. For bow loops, cut 1 x 2½ in. long strips; fold ends together to form loops and attach with damp brush. For streamers, cut two ½ x 5 in. long strips; attach with damp brush. Attach dress bow flower. In buttercream, pipe tip 8 strawberry shapes on hat (pat smooth with finger dipped in cornstarch). Add tip 1 dot seeds and tip 349 pull-out leaves. Attach clip to hat bow with icing. Place a ball of fondant in arm openings; insert hands into arms. Position large marshmallow under wand top for support. Serves 24.

*Combine *Strawberry Shortcake* Red with Red-Red for red shown. Combine Brown with Red-Red for brown shown in irises. Combine Violet with Rose for violet shown.

▶ Mighty World Hero

Pan: Mini Ball, p. 154

Color: Royal Blue, p. 135

Candy: White Candy Melts®†, p. 162; Primary, Garden Candy Color Sets, p. 163

Fondant: White Ready-To-Use Rolled Fondant (24 oz.), p. 128; Rolling Pin, Roll & Cut Mat, p. 131

Also: *Superman*™ Party Topper, *Superman* Icing Decorations, p. 167; Fine Tip Primary Colors FoodWriter™ Edible Color Markers, p. 128; Parchment Triangles, p. 138; toothpicks, wooden skewers, craft knife, map of continents for reference, candy-coated fruit dots

Tint ¾ of candy blue, tint remainder green using candy colors. For each globe, make 2 blue candy shells in mini ball pan (p. 123); unmold. Fill globe with candy and icing decoration; close halves, attaching with melted candy. Using map for reference, mark continents on globe with toothpick. Outline and pipe in continents using melted candy in cut parchment bag; let set.

Make fondant motion lines strip (p. 120). Attach tapered end at top of globe with melted candy; wind around toward back of globe and attach other end. Mark blue color between folds with FoodWriter. Attach *Superman* topper with melted candy; let set. Each treat serves 1.

†Brand confectionery coating.

▼ Skywriting *Superman*

Pans: *Superman*™, p. 167; 18 x 3 in. Half Round, p. 147

Tips: 1, 3, 6, 16, 21, p. 140-141

Colors:* *Superman* Icing Color Set (blue, yellow, red, skin tone), p. 167; Royal Blue, Lemon Yellow, Golden Yellow, Black, p. 135

Fondant: White Ready-To-Use Rolled Fondant (24 oz.), p. 128; Rolling Pin, Roll & Cut Mat, p. 131

Recipe: Buttercream Icing, p. 114

Also: 2007 Pattern Book (Large Cloud, Small Cloud), p. 126; Fanci-Foil Wrap, p. 225; Wooden Dowel Rods, p. 224; 20 in. foamcore or plywood board, paring knife, toothpicks, cornstarch

Bake and cool *Superman* and 1-layer 18 in. cakes (bake 2 half-round cakes, 2 in. high). Prepare for stacked construction (p. 112). Ice 18 in. cake smooth and position on 20 in. foil-wrapped board. Roll out fondant ⅛ in. thick. Trace cloud patterns with toothpick; cut with paring knife. Position fondant clouds on cake top. For *Superman* cake, ice sides smooth. Outline and pipe-in eyebrows with tip 1 (smooth with finger dipped in cornstarch). Outline nose and under eyes with tip 1. Outline mouth, chin, ear, neck, cape, suit and insignia with tip 3. Pipe in around eyes and under eyebrows with tip 1 (smooth with finger dipped in cornstarch). Cover face, ears, neck, cape, suit and insignia with tip 16 stars. Pipe tip 16 pull-out star hair. Pipe tip 21 shell bottom border. Position *Superman* cake on round cake. Print tip 6 message. Serves 122.

*Combine Lemon Yellow and Golden Yellow for yellow used on message. Use Yellow from *Superman* Icing Color Set for shield.

▲ Power Surge!

Pan: 10 x 2 in. Round, p. 148
Tips: 3, 4, 21, p. 140-141
Colors: Royal Blue, Red-Red,Orange, Lemon Yellow, Leaf Green, p. 135
Recipes: Buttercream Icing, Color Flow Icing (4 recipes), p. 114
Also: 2007 Pattern Book (Starburst), p. 126; Color Flow Mix, p. 134; *Superman*™ Candle, p. 167; Parchment Triangles, p. 138; Cake Boards, Fanci Foil Wrap, p. 225; fine water mister, ½ in. wide artist soft paintbrush (new), craft knife, waxed paper, sugar cubes

Four to five days in advance: Make color flow starburst (p. 124); make extra to allow for breakage. Let dry for 72 hours.

Ice 2-layer cake smooth in buttercream (bake two 1½ in. layers to create 3 in. high cake). Pipe tip 21 star bottom border. Carefully position plaque on cake, propping with sugar cubes if necessary. Position candle. Serves 28.

▼ Cupcake Bursts

Pan: Standard Muffin, p. 149
Tip: 12, p. 140
Colors:* Golden Yellow, Lemon Yellow, Royal Blue, p. 135
Candy: White Candy Melts®†, p. 162; Primary Candy Colors Set, p. 163
Recipe: Buttercream Icing, p. 114
Also: *Superman*™ Baking Cups, Icing Decorations, p. 167; Parchment Triangles, p. 138; Cake Board, p. 225; waxed paper

In advance: Make candy burst lines for cupcakes. Tint portions of melted candy blue and yellow using candy colors. Using melted candy in cut parchment bag, pipe nine 2 in. lines for each cupcake on waxed paper-covered board. Refrigerate until firm.

Cover cupcakes with tip 12 balls in buttercream. Insert candy lines in top edge of cupcakes; position icing decoration. Each serves 1.

*Combine Golden Yellow and Lemon Yellow for yellow shown.

▲ Cookie Calling Cards

Cookie: Cookie Sheet, Cooling Grid, p. 161; Circle Metal Cutter, p. 158; Cookie Spatula, p. 161
Color: Royal Blue, p. 135
Recipes: Buttercream Icing, Roll-Out Cookie, p. 114
Also: *Superman*™ Icing Decorations, Treat Bags, p. 167; Rolling Pin, p. 131; Spatula, p. 138

Roll out dough. Cut cookies; bake and cool. Ice smooth; position icing decorations on top. Place in treat bags. Each serves 1.

◀ *Dora* Kicks Into High Gear!

Pans: *Dora the Explorer*™, p. 177; Mini Ball, p. 154
Tips: 3, 5, 16, 21, p. 140-141
Colors:* *Dora the Explorer* Icing Color Set (pink, brown, skin tone), p. 177; Orange, Royal Blue, Sky Blue, Red-Red, Black, Lemon Yellow, p. 135
Recipe: Buttercream Icing, p. 114
Also: 2007 Pattern Book (Small and Large Soccer Ball Hexagons), p. 126; Cake Boards, Fanci-Foil Wrap, p. 225; toothpicks, cornstarch

Trim off backpack area on *Dora* cake. Ice cake sides and background areas smooth. Outline hair, body, facial features, clothes and shoes with tip 3. Pipe in whites of eyes, irises, pupils and highlights with tip 3 (smooth with finger dipped in cornstarch). Pipe in mouth and tongue with tip 5 (smooth with finger dipped in cornstarch). Pipe in bracelet, number, shoe ties and soles with tip 3 (smooth with finger dipped in cornstarch). Cover face, hair, clothes, body and shoes with tip 16 stars. Pipe tip 21 shell bottom border.

Lightly ice mini ball cake. Trace large and small hexagon patterns with toothpick. Cover ball with tip 16 stars. Position ball next to *Dora* cake. Serves 13.

*Combine Royal Blue with Sky Blue for blue shown. Combine *Dora* Brown with Black and a little Red-Red for hair. Combine *Dora* Brown with Lemon Yellow for shirt outline. Combine Orange with Red-Red for tongue.

▶ *Elmo*'s Been Wrapping

Pans: *Elmo* Face, p. 177; 16 x 2 in. Round, p. 149
Tips: 5, 16, p. 140-141
Colors: Black, No-Taste Red, Orange, Violet, Rose, Royal Blue, Leaf Green, Lemon Yellow, Golden Yellow, p. 135
Fondant: White Ready-To-Use Rolled Fondant (24 oz.), Brush Set, p. 128; Round Cut-Outs™, p. 130; Rolling Pin, Roll & Cut Mat, p. 131
Recipe: Buttercream Icing, p. 114
Also: 2007 Pattern Book (Party Hat), p. 126; Wooden Dowel Rods, p. 224; Flowerful Medley Sprinkle Decorations, p. 136; Gum-Tex™, p. 131; Cake Board, Fanci-Foil Wrap, p. 225; 18 in. triple-thick cardboard circle or ½ in. thick foamcore board, cornstarch, paring knife, waxed paper, toothpick, ruler

In advance: Make fondant party hat. Tint 4 oz. of fondant yellow; combine with ¼ teaspoon Gum-Tex. Roll out ⅛ in. thick. Trace pattern with toothpick; cut hat with knife. Let dry on cornstarch-dusted board. Reserve remaining fondant for gift packages.

Ice 1-layer round cake smooth and prepare for stacked construction (p. 112). Position on cardboard base wrapped with foil. Tint portions of fondant in all colors except black; roll out ⅛ in. thick. Using craft knife, cut various size gifts from 1½ in. squares to 2½ x 1¼ in. rectangles. Position gifts on cake sides. Cut ⅛ to ¼ in. wide strips for ribbons and star-shaped bows; roll ⅜ in. balls, flatten and shape into teardrops for round bows. Attach bows and ribbons to gifts with damp brush. For party hat, cut ½ in. wide violet strips for stripes; cut various color circles using smallest Cut-Out. Attach stripes and circles with damp brush. Position *Elmo* cake on foil-covered board cut to fit. Ice smooth eyes, mouth and nose (smooth with finger dipped in cornstarch). Cover face with tip 16 stars. Position *Elmo* on round cake. Insert dowel rod in top side of round cake to support party hat. Position party hat. Print tip 5 message. Add confetti sprinkles on round cake top. Serves 50.

SCOOBY-DOO!

◀ Scoop-Happy *Scooby*

Pan: Standard Muffin, p. 149

Candy: White Candy Melts®† (3 pks.), p. 162; Primary, Garden Candy Color Sets, Decorator Brush Set, p. 163

Also: White Standard Baking Cups, p. 184; Rainbow Nonpareils Sprinkle Decorations, p. 136; *Scooby-Doo!* Party Toppers, p. 175; Parchment Triangles, p. 138; ice cream, ice cream scoop

Tint 1 pk. each of white candy pink, blue and yellow using candy colors (3 pks. will make approximately 15 treats). Make candy shells in baking cups (p. 123). For solid bases, fill baking cups ½ in. deep with melted candy; refrigerate until firm. Carefully peel baking cups from candy shells and bases; attach bases to shells with melted candy; let set. Using melted candy in cut parchment bag, pipe beads along seam; refrigerate until firm. Fill cups with ice cream; sprinkle with nonpareils. Position topper. Each serves 1.

†Brand confectionery coating.

▶ *Scooby's* Road Food

Pans: *Scooby-Doo!*™, p. 175; Hexagon Set (12 x 2 in. used), p. 148

Tips: 3, 4, 6, 8, 16, 21, p. 140-141

Colors:* *Scooby-Doo!* Icing Color Set (brown, yellow, black, teal), p. 175; Christmas Red, Creamy Peach, Orange, Violet, Rose, Kelly Green, Leaf Green, Lemon Yellow, p. 135

Recipe: Buttercream Icing, p. 114

Also: 2007 Pattern Book (Mystery Van Bumper, Ice Cream, Tires), p. 126; Cake Boards, Fanci-Foil Wrap, p. 225; 4 in. Lollipop Sticks, p. 165; Tapered Spatula, p. 138; Rainbow Nonpareils Sprinkle Decorations, p. 136; candy cherry, cornstarch, toothpick, cellophane tape, 20 x 24 in. foamcore board (½ in. thick)

Bake and cool *Scooby-Doo!* and 1-layer hexagon cakes. Trim 1 in. off bottom edge of *Scooby-Doo!* cake. Cut foamcore board to fit cakes and wrap with foil; position cakes. Ice cake sides, top of hexagon, and hamburger area of *Scooby-Doo!* cake smooth. Trace bumper pattern on hexagon with toothpick. Mark window frame, measuring ½ in. wide at top and ⅜ in. wide at sides and bottom. Outline hexagon with tip 3; fill in with tip 16 stars. Print tip 4 message. Pipe tip 21 shell bottom border.

On *Scooby-Doo!* cake, trace ice cream pattern on cake top. Outline face, ears, tongue, body, paws, collar and tag with tip 3. Pipe in eyes, inside ears, nose, mouth, tongue and tag with tip 3 (smooth with finger dipped in cornstarch). Add tip 3 dot pupils and outline eyebrows. Cover *Scooby-Doo!* and collar with tip 16 stars. Overpipe tag and link with tip 3; print tip 3 initials. Pipe in ice cream bowl with tip 3 (pat smooth with finger dipped in cornstarch). Add tip 3 lines. Starting with bottom scoop, pipe in ice cream with tip 8; shape with spatula. Overpipe bottom edge of each scoop with tip 6, smooth. Pipe tip 6 swirls for whipped cream. Sprinkle with nonpareils; position candy cherry. Trace tire patterns on cake board; cut 2 tires and wrap with foil. Attach lollipop sticks with tape and ice smooth. Insert in bottom side of cake. Serves 29.

*Combine Leaf Green with Lemon Yellow for green shown.

◀ *Pooh* is Prepared to Party!

Pan: *Pooh*, p. 170

Tips: 3, 8, 16, 21, p.140-141

Colors: *Pooh* Icing Color Set (*Pooh* gold, red, black), p. 170

Fondant: Fondant Multi Packs in Primary and Neon Colors (1 pk. each), Brush Set, p. 128; Cutter/ Embosser, p. 129; Rolling Pin, Roll & Cut Mat, p. 131

Recipe: Buttercream Icing, p. 114

Also: 101 Cookie Cutters Set, p. 160; 4 in. Lollipop Sticks, p. 165; Gum-Tex™, p. 131; Cake Boards, Fanci-Foil Wrap, p. 225; curling ribbon in red, blue, green (8 in. each); cornstarch, scissors, waxed paper

In advance: Make fondant balloons, hat and gifts; let dry on cornstarch-dusted surface. Add ¼ teaspoon Gum-Tex to each 4 oz. package of fondant except pink. Roll out each color ⅛ in. thick. Cut 3 balloons using medium round cutter from set. Pipe tip 3 outline highlight. For hat, using straight-edge wheel of Cutter/Embosser, cut triangle 3½ x 1½ in. wide at base. Cut polka dots using narrow end of tip 8; attach to hat with damp brush. For pompom, cut a 5 x ½ in. fondant strip; cut fringed edge with scissors. Roll strip, pinching together at bottom to form pompom; attach to top of hat with damp brush. For base of hat, cut 3 strips 2 x ½ in.; cut fringed edge with scissors. Roll strips into separate pompoms; attach to hat with damp brush. For gifts, cut two 2½ in. squares and three 2½ x 3½ in. rectangles. For gift ribbons, cut ¼ in. wide fondant strips to fit; attach with damp brush. For bow loops, cut fondant strips ¼ x 2¾ in. long; fold in half and attach open ends with damp brush. Attach 2 loops and a ¼ in. ball for knot to each gift with damp brush.

Ice cake sides and background areas smooth. Outline *Pooh* and pipe in eyes and nose with tip 3 (smooth with finger dipped in cornstarch). Add tip 3 outline eyebrows, mouth and ridge above nose. Cover *Pooh* and shirt with tip 16 stars. Pipe tip 21 shell bottom border. Partially insert lollipop stick into top of cake to support hat; attach hat to stick with tip 3 dots. Position 3 balloons on cake; position curling ribbon, using smaller lengths for area above paw. Position gifts on cake. Serves 12.

DISNEY Winnie the Pooh

▶ *Mickey*, Front and Center!

Pans: *Mickey* Face, p. 170; 18 x 3 in. Half Round, p. 147

Tips: 2, 3, 5, 16, p. 140-141

Colors: *Mickey* Icing Color Set {black, copper (skin tone), *Mickey* peach}, p. 170

Fondant: White Ready-To-Use Rolled Fondant (24 oz.), Fondant Multi Packs in Primary and Neon Colors (2 pks. each), Brush Set, p. 128; Rolling Pin, Roll & Cut Mat, p. 131

Recipe: Buttercream Icing, p. 114

Also: Cake Board, Fanci-Foil Wrap, p. 225; 101 Cookie Cutters Set, p. 160; Cake Dividing Set, p. 133; Wooden Dowel Rods, p. 224; 21 in. round x ½ in. thick foamcore board, paring knife, granulated sugar, cornstarch

In advance: Make fondant candies. For 48 spice drops, shape various neon and primary colors of fondant into ¾ to ⅝ in. rounded cones. Brush with water, roll in granulated sugar. Make 27 assorted wrapped candies (p. 120). Make extras to allow for breakage and let all pieces dry on cornstarch-dusted surface.

Prepare *Mickey* and 18 in. round cake (bake four 1-layer half rounds to make one 4 in. high round cake) for stacked construction (p. 112). For *Mickey*, outline eyes, nose and mouth with tip 3. Pipe in whites of eyes, nose, pupils, mouth and tongue with tip 3 (smooth with finger dipped in cornstarch). Cover remaining areas with tip 16 stars. Ice round cake smooth; divide into 16ths. Make 16 fondant rope garlands. For each colored garland, roll 2 fondant logs 1 x 3 in. long, using 1 white and 1 neon or primary color. Twist logs together and roll into a ⅜ in. diameter rope. Cut into 5 in. lengths; brush with water and roll in granulated sugar. Using tip 2 dots of buttercream, attach ropes to sides and spice drops (in clusters of 3) to top at division points. Pipe tip 5 bead bottom border. Position wrapped candies around base of cake. Position *Mickey* cake. Make message. Roll out assorted fondant colors ⅛ in. thick; cut letters using alphabet cutters from set. Brush letters with water, coat with granulated sugar and position on cake. Serves 122.

DISNEY MICKEY MOUSE

Celebrate Around the Clock!

Pan: *Disney Princess*, p. 169; 12 x 2 in. Round, p. 149

Tips: 1, 2, 3, 8, 12, 16, 97 or 97L, 352, p. 140-141

Colors: *Disney Princess* Icing Color Set (blue, yellow, pink, skin tone), p. 169 Violet, Leaf Green, Royal Blue, Black, p. 135

Fondant: White Ready-To-Use Fondant (72 oz), p. 128; Cutter/Embosser, Easy-Glide Fondant Smoother, p.129; Rolling Pin, Roll & Cut Mat, p. 131;

Candy: White Candy Melts®† (2 pks.), p. 162; Primary Candy Color Set, Decorator Brush Set, p. 163

Recipes: Buttercream, Royal Icings, p. 114

Also: 2007 Pattern Book (Staircase, Clock Patterns), p. 126; 16 in. Cake Circles (4), Cake Boards, Fanci-Foil Wrap, p. 225; Gum-Tex™, p. 131; White Cake Sparkles™, p. 136; Meringue Powder, p. 134; Disposable Decorating Bags, p. 138; Plastic Dowel Rods, p. 224; Flower Nail No. 7, p. 138; 5½ x 2½ in. craft block, sharp craft knife, waxed paper, cornstarch

Two days in advance: Make clock. Combine ½ teaspoon Gum-Tex with 12 oz. fondant; tint light gray. Roll out ¼ in. thick; trace clock pattern (except face) and cut using knife. Roll out a 1½ in. ball of white fondant ⅛ in. thick; trace clock face pattern and cut out. Attach face to clock with damp brush. Let dry for 24 hours on cornstarch-dusted board. **Also:** Brush clock with damp brush and sprinkle with Cake Sparkles. Using royal icing, pipe tip 3 outline stripes, curliques, numbers and hands. For spire tops, roll three ½ in. diameter gray balls, flatten slightly and attach with royal icing. Let dry an additional 24 hours.

One day in advance: Make candy plaque princess (p. 224). Fill banner area of pan with melted white candy; refrigerate until firm. Tint remainder of candy light orange and pour into pan to form face and upper body; refrigerate until firm. Cut cardboard to fit exactly inside pan. Place cardboard directly on plaque and gently turn pan over to unmold, resting plaque on cardboard. Decorate plaque with royal icing. Use tip 3 to outline gloves, dress, sleeves, headband and earring. Cover dress, sleeves, headband and glove with tip 16 stars. Pipe in tip 12 hair, overpipe for dimension. Outline neckband and pipe in with tip 4 (smooth with finger dipped in cornstarch). Pipe in tip 3 earring (smooth with finger dipped in cornstarch). Outline eyes, eyebrows and mouth with tip 2. Pipe in tip 2 eyes, irises, teeth and lips. Add tip 1 dot eye highlights and string eyelashes. Using tip 3, outline banner and add message; set aside. **Also:** Make roses. Using royal icing, make 12 tip 97 or 97L (for left-handers) roses with tip 8 bases. Make extras to allow for breakage and let dry.

Prepare 1-layer round cake for rolled fondant (p. 113). Cover with white fondant; smooth with Fondant Smoother. Dowel rod area where candy plaque will be positioned. Tint 12 oz. fondant violet; tint 8 oz. fondant blue. Roll out violet fondant ¼ in. thick; cut top railing using pattern. Reroll remaining violet fondant ⅛ in. thick; using pattern, cut bottom railing, posts and half of the stairs. Roll out blue fondant ⅛ in thick and cut remaining stairs. Attach staircase pieces with damp brush. Using royal icing, outline with tip 3. Using buttercream icing, pipe tip 8 bead bottom border on left side of cake. Position roses; pipe tip 352 leaves. Position candy plaque on cake. Position clock, tucking tower behind candy plaque; trim bottom edge of clock to fit if necessary. Position foil-wrapped craft block under top of clock for support. Serves 20.

*Combine Violet with Royal Blue for blue fondant stairs.

Disney Princess

High-Spirited Holidays!

Some people take a little longer to get into the mood of the season. We'll help you win them over! You'll find color and excitement for every time of year, starting with the haunting Halloween graveyard display here. For Christmas, go tropical! Our sheet cake sends Santa and his crew to the beach, soaking in the sun and surf. For Valentine's Day, click on Love.com, a "message board" of mini cakes showing fun people and their profiles. We're also celebrating Mardi Gras, with a dazzling creole cupcake parade, decorated with festive beads and masks.

Instructions for projects shown on these two pages are on page 42.

END OF THE ROAD
BACK SOON
DIG ME!
GOOD MOURNING
R.I.P

Halloween Homebodies!

Grab a ghost, a ghoul or a grave! This haunted house display is surrounded by spooky cookie pops—a great way to greet and treat your guests.

Cookie: Pre-Baked and Pre-Assembled Halloween Cookie House Kit, p. 190; Halloween Metal Cutter Set, Nesting Ghosts Cutter Set, Halloween Mini Cutter Set, p. 191; Round Comfort Grip™ Cutter, p. 158; Cookie Sheet, Cooling Grid, p. 161; Rolling Pin, p. 131

Tips: 1, 1D, 2, 3, 4, 5, 6, 7, p. 140

Colors:* Lemon Yellow, Golden Yellow, Leaf Green, Black, Brown, Red-Red, p. 135

Recipes: Royal Icing, Roll-Out Cookie, p. 114

Also: 2007 Pattern Book (Cat Cookie Support, Large Cookie Support; Small, Medium, Large Fences), p. 126; Smiling Pumpkins Icing Decorations, p. 189; 11¾ in. and 4 in. Lollipop Sticks, p. 165; Meringue Powder, p. 134; Cake Board, p. 225; Fine Tip Neon Colors FoodWriter™ Edible Color Markers, p. 128; waxed paper, cellophane tape, shredded coconut, zip-close plastic bag, plastic tablecloth, craft foam sheets (one 12 x 36 x 1 in. deep, three 12 x 36 x 2 in. deep)

In advance: Decorate cookie house following kit instructions; set aside. **Also:** Make cookies. Tint ⅓ of dough light gray and a small portion dark gray. Roll out light gray dough; using Halloween metal cutters cut 8-10 tombstone cookies. Thin dark gray dough with water to piping consistency; outline tombstones with tip 6. Roll out plain dough. Using patterns, cut 1 cat cookie support and 30 to 36 large cookie supports. Using Halloween metal cutters, cut 4 ghosts. Using Halloween mini cutters, cut 4 bats, 2 skulls and 1 cat. Using 2 smallest nesting ghost cutters, cut 5 ghosts in each size, reversing some. Also cut 1 large round cookie for moon. Bake and cool all cookies. Cover all cookies except tombstones with thinned royal icing (p. 124); let dry. Make 4 small, 7 medium and 10 large fence sections using full-strength royal icing. Tape patterns to board and cover with waxed paper; secure with tape. Pipe tip 7 horizontal posts, tip 5 vertical posts and tip 3 points on top of posts. Make extras to allow for breakage; let dry.

Decorate cookies with royal icing. For ghosts, pipe tip 2 dot eyes and mouth, tip 1 dot pupils and tongues, tip 4 dot cheeks. For bats and cats, pipe tip 1 dot and string eyes, mouths and whiskers. Position skulls on waxed paper. Pipe tip 1 dot and string facial features. Separately pipe tip 5 outline arms, 1½ in. long; add tip 2 hands and pull-out fingers. Color lollipop sticks with violet FoodWriter. Attach ghosts, 3 bats and moon cookie to lollipop sticks with royal icing (use 11¾ in. sticks for moon, bats and 3 ghosts raised above display). Attach remaining bat cookie to moon. For tombstones, print tip 1 message; let dry. Attach supports to cookie backs with royal icing (use 2 supports for large cookies); let dry. For fence bases, cut cardboard in 1 x 1½, 1 x 2½ and 1 x 4 in. sizes. Cut 2 extra 1 x 2½ in. bases for skulls and arms. For fence sections, pipe tip 1D band (smooth side up) on each base; insert fence sections and let set. For skulls and arms, attach to base with dots of royal icing.

Assemble display using craft foam sheets. Tint coconut green (p. 119); position around house and cookies. Each cookie serves 1.

*Combine Leaf Green with Lemon Yellow for green used for skull head, hands and bat facial features. Combine Brown with Red-Red for skull arms.

◀ Is That You Coffin?

Pan: 10 in. Square, p. 148

Recipe: Ready-In-Minutes Cocoa Fudge, p. 115

Also: Halloween Cutter Set, p. 191; Dark Cocoa Candy Melts®† (3 pks.), p. 162; Parchment Triangles, p. 138; waxed paper

Reserve 2 oz. candy (approximately 20 wafers) for decorating. Prepare 2 recipes of fudge and pour into buttered pan lined with waxed paper. Refrigerate until firm and unmold. Cut shapes using coffin cutter from set. Outline trims and pipe message with melted candy in cut parchment bag. Each serves 1.

†Brand confectionery coating.

▶ A Man of Many Parts

Pan: 8 x 2 in. Square, p. 148

Tip: 5, p. 140

Colors:* Brown, Red-Red, Leaf Green, Black, p. 135

Also: Monster Head Comfort Grip™ Cutter, p. 191; Vanilla Whipped Icing Mix, p. 134; lemon gelatin (6 oz. pk.), unflavored gelatin (two ¼ oz. envelopes), orange and green spice drops, black shoestring licorice, non-stick vegetable pan spray

Add unflavored gelatin to dry lemon gelatin mix. Prepare following package directions; tint green. Lightly spray pan with non-stick vegetable spray and fill with gelatin. Refrigerate until firm. Cut gelatin heads with cutter; remove from pan. Tint portions of whipped icing brown and black. Pipe tip 5 pull-out hair; pipe in tip 5 whites of eyes and pupils. Cut green spice drop horizontally in half; position top half for nose. Cut orange spice drop in 4ths; position 2 pieces for bolts. Position licorice mouth. Each serves 1.

*Combine Brown with a small amount of Red-Red for brown shown.

▲ Getting a Face Lift

Cookie: Gingerbread Boy Metal Cutter, p. 158; Cookie Sheet, Cooling Grid, p. 161; Rolling Pin, p. 131

Candy: Halloween 2-Pack Candy Mold Set, p. 189; White Candy Melts®†, p. 162; Decorator Brush Set, Primary, Garden Candy Color Sets, p. 163

Tip: 3, p. 140

Colors:* Lemon Yellow, Leaf Green, Violet, Rose, Black, p. 135

Recipes: Buttercream Icing, Roll-Out Cookie, p. 114

Tint dough green; roll out. Cut boy cookies; trim off heads. Bake and cool. Pipe in tip 3 shirt, pants and dot toenails. Tint portions of melted candy green, yellow and black using candy colors. Mold head candies using painting method (p. 123); refrigerate until firm. Attach to cookies with melted candy; let set. Each serves 1.

*Combine Lemon Yellow with Leaf Green for green shown. Combine Violet with Rose for violet shown.

◀ Out for a Test Drive

Pans: Little Hero, p. 154; Cookie Sheet, Cooling Grid, p. 161
Tips: 3, 4, 12, 14, 16, 21, p. 140-141
Colors:* Orange, Violet, Black, Lemon Yellow, Leaf Green, Rose, p. 135
Recipes: Buttercream Icing, Roll-Out Cookie, p. 114
Also: 2007 Pattern Book (Witch Hat, Broom Bristles), p. 126; Cake Board, Fanci-Foil Wrap, p. 225; pretzel rods, cornstarch, large marshmallows, toothpick

Roll out dough. Trace hat and broom patterns on dough with toothpick; cut, bake and cool cookies. Outline hat with tip 4 and buckle on hatband with tip 3. Cover hat with tip 16 stars, hatband and buckle with tip 14 stars. Cover broom cookie with tip 16 pull-out stripes.

Trim off hose area from cake. Ice sides and background areas smooth. Extend and build up sleeves with tip 12 (pat inner sleeves smooth with finger dipped in cornstarch). Outline head, body and shoes with tip 4. Pipe in eyes, pupils and mouth with tip 4 (smooth with finger dipped in cornstarch). Build up nose with a tip 12 mound. Cover face with tip 14 stars. Pipe tip 3 dot teeth and zigzag eyebrows; pipe tip 4 dot warts on nose and chin. Add tip 16 pull-out star hair. Cover dress and shoes with tip 16 stars. Position two 6 in. pretzel rods for broomstick. Build up hands with tip 14 stars; overpipe for dimension. Pipe tip 21 star bottom border. Position hat, supporting with large marshmallows; attach broom cookie with buttercream. Cake serves 12; each cookie serves 1.

*Combine Leaf Green and Lemon Yellow for green shown. Combine Violet and Rose for violet shown.

▲ A Chummy Mummy

Cookie: Ready-To-Use Cookie Icing, p. 159; 101 Cookie Cutters Set, p. 160; Cookie Sheet, Cooling Grid, p. 161; Rolling Pin, p. 131
Tip: 3, p. 140
Recipe: Chocolate Roll-Out Cookie, p. 114
Also: Black Tube Decorating Icing, Coupler Ring Set, p. 135; candy-coated chocolates

Roll out dough. Cut cookies using largest gingerbread boy cutter from set; bake and cool.

Drizzle cookie icing over cookie. Position candy-coated chocolate eyes. Pipe tip 3 dot pupils using tube icing. Each serves 1.

▶ The Green Meanie

Pan: Spooky Ghost, p. 188
Tips: 3, 5, 16, p. 140-141
Colors:* Orange, Black, Lemon Yellow, Leaf Green, Rose, Violet, p. 135
Recipe: Buttercream Icing, p. 114
Also: Cake Board, Fanci-Foil Wrap, p. 225; cornstarch

Ice face area smooth, making sure to fill in all indentations. Use tip 5 to build up left arm area. Pipe in mouth and "whites" of eyes with tip 5 (smooth with finger dipped in cornstarch). Pipe tip 5 dot eyes with tip 3 dot pupils (smooth with finger dipped in cornstarch). Cover remainder of cake with tip 16 stars. Overpipe an additional row of tip 16 stars around face to build up hood. Serves 12.

*Combine Lemon Yellow and Leaf Green for green shown. Combine Violet and small amount of Rose for violet shown.

◀ Halloween Double-Header!

Pans: 8 x 2 in. Round, p. 148; Cookie Sheets, p. 161
Tips: 1D, 2, 16, 233, p. 140-141
Colors:* Black, Leaf Green, Red-Red, Orange, Golden Yellow, Lemon Yellow, Violet, Rose, p. 135
Recipes: Buttercream Icing, Color Flow Icing, p. 114
Also: 2007 Pattern Book (Pumpkin Heads), p. 126; Color Flow Mix, p. 134; Smiling Pumpkins Icing Decorations, p. 189; 11¾ in. Lollipop Sticks, p. 165; Parchment Triangles, p. 138; 10 in. Cake Circle, Fanci-Foil Wrap, p. 225; waxed paper

At least 48 hours in advance: Make color flow pumpkin heads (p. 124) using waxed-paper covered patterns on cookie sheets. Pipe black and dark orange outlines with tip 2 and full-strength color flow; pipe in facial features and heads using thinned color flow in cut parchment bag. Let dry. Cut lollipop stick to 10 in. Using full-strength color flow, attach pumpkin heads to lollipop stick; let set.

Ice 2-layer cake smooth. On cake sides, pipe tip 1D bands, leaving a space the width of tip 1D between each band. Pipe tip 16 rosette top border and tip 233 pull-out grass bottom border. Insert pumpkin heads in cake. Position icing decorations. Serves 20.

*Combine Orange and Red-Red for darker orange shown. Combine Lemon Yellow and Golden Yellow for yellow shown. Combine Leaf Green with a little Black for dark green shown. Combine Violet with Rose for violet shown.

▼ Pumpkin Patch Bash!

Pan: Standard Muffin, p. 148
Tip: 233, p. 140
Color: Leaf Green, p. 135
Recipe: Buttercream Icing, p. 114
Also: Smiling Pumpkins Fun Pix®, Smiling Pumpkins Baking Cups, p. 189; Halloween 6-Mix Sprinkles Assortment, p. 190

Bake and cool cupcakes. Pipe tip 233 pull-out grass. Top with confetti sprinkles; insert pick. Each serves 1.

▲ An Ominous Sign

Pan: Stand-Up Cuddly Bear Set, p. 153
Tips: 2, 3, 6, 16, 21, p. 140-141
Colors:* Kelly Green, Orange, Black, Golden Yellow, Lemon Yellow, p. 135
Recipes: Buttercream, Royal Icings, p. 114
Also: 2007 Pattern Book (Sign), p. 126; Plastic Dowel Rods, p. 224; Cake Board, Fanci-Foil Wrap, p. 225; Flower Nail No. 7, Spatula, p. 138; 6 in. Cookie Treat Sticks, p. 161; 4 in. Lollipop Sticks, p. 165; Meringue Powder, p. 134; cellophane tape, cornstarch, scissors

In advance: Make candelabra. For candles, cut cookie sticks: one 2½ in. long and four 1¾ in. long. Using tip 2, cover flower nail and candles with royal icing. Pipe tip 2 drip marks on candles and tip 3 pull-out flames with thinned royal icing; let dry. Attach candles to nail with royal icing; let dry.

Bake and cool cake using firm-textured batter such as pound cake. Trim ears, feet and muzzle from cake; round off head. Trim two dowel rods to 5½ in. for arms. Use end of flower nail to make holes in each dowel rod where sign and candelabra will be positioned. Insert dowel rods for arms, leaving 3 in. exposed on each side of body. Spatula ice body and arms, using edge of spatula to create folds of gown. Pipe in eyes, nose and mouth with tip 3 (pat smooth with finger dipped in cornstarch); pipe in tip 3 pupils. With tip 3, outline facial features; pipe section lines on face. Cover face with tip 16 stars. Pipe tip 21 swirl stem. Cut out sign pattern. Tape stick to sign; insert in arm. Insert flower nail candelabra into arm. Pipe tip 6 ball hands with pull-out thumbs. Serves 12.

*Combine Golden Yellow and Lemon Yellow for yellow shown.

◀ Jack the Joker

Pan: Iridescents! Jack-O-Lantern, p. 188
Tips: 1A, 4, 8, 12, 14, p. 140-141
Colors:* Orange, Leaf Green, Lemon Yellow, Golden Yellow, Black, Rose, p. 135
Recipe: Buttercream Icing, p. 114
Also: Cake Board, Fanci-Foil Wrap, p. 225; Spatula, p. 138; cornstarch

Place cake on foil-wrapped board. Ice cake sides smooth. Pipe in tip 4 eyes, pupils, mouth and teeth (pat smooth with finger dipped in cornstarch). Add tip 4 dot eye highlights. Pipe tip 12 outline eye sockets, eyebrows and lips. Pipe tip 1A mound for nose. With tip 4, outline stem and pipe section lines on pumpkin. Cover pumpkin and stem with tip 14 stars. Pipe tip 8 tongue (smooth with finger dipped in cornstarch). Imprint groove in tongue with edge of spatula. Serves 12.

*Combine Lemon Yellow with Golden Yellow for yellow shown. Combine Leaf Green with Lemon Yellow for green shown.

▼ Pumpkins Popping Up!

Cookie: Nesting Pumpkins Metal Cutter Set, p. 191; Cookie Sheet, Cooling Grid, p. 161; Rolling Pin, p. 131
Candy: White Candy Melts®†, p. 162; Primary, Garden Candy Color Sets, p. 163; 8 in. Lollipop Sticks, p. 165
Color: Orange, p. 135
Recipe: Roll-Out Cookie, p. 114
Also: Parchment Triangles, p. 138; Smiling Pumpkins Party Bags, p. 189

Tint dough orange; roll out. Cut pumpkins using two smallest cutters. On cookie sheet, cut stem off larger pumpkin and position smaller pumpkin on top edge. Bake and cool. Tint portions of white candy black, yellow, orange and green using candy colors. Using melted candy in cut parchment bag, outline facial features; let set. Using melted candy, pipe in open eyes, noses, mouths; let set. Pipe section lines and closed eyes; let set. Pipe in stem; let set. Add pupils; let set. Attach lollipop stick with melted candy. Each serves 1.

†Brand confectionery coating.

▲ Bewitchingly-Dressed Cookies!

Cookie: Jack-O-Lantern Cookie Treat Pan, p. 188; Cookie Sheet, Cooling Grid, 8 in. Cookie Treat Sticks, p. 161
Candy: Halloween Lollipop Kit, p. 189; White Candy Melts®†, p. 162; Primary, Garden Candy Color Sets, Decorator Brush Set, p. 163
Recipe: Roll-Out Cookie, p. 114
Also: 2007 Pattern Book (Bow Tie, Dress, Hands, Feet), p. 126; Parchment Triangles, p. 138; orange spice drops, waxed paper, card stock in violet, orange, black; orange bumpy chenille pipe cleaners (2 needed), cellophane tape

In advance: Mold hat without stick using mold from kit and painting method (p. 123). Tint portions of melted white candy green and blue using candy colors; refrigerate until firm.

Prepare jack-o-lantern cookie on cookie stick following pan directions; bake and cool. Tint portions of melted candy orange, black and yellow using candy colors. Cover cookie with melted candy (p. 124); let set. Using melted candy in cut parchment bags, pipe in eyes, pupils and mouth, add section outlines and dot cheeks. Cut spice drop into nose shape; attach with melted candy. Attach hat with melted candy. Twist pipe cleaners around stick for arms and legs. Cut bow tie, dress, hands and feet from card stock using patterns; attach with tape. Each serves 1.

▶ Tops in His Field

Pan: 8 in. Round, p. 147
Tip: 6, p. 140
Colors: Moss Green, Red-Red, Christmas Red, Royal Blue, Brown, Ivory, Golden Yellow, p. 135
Fondant: White Ready-To-Use Rolled Fondant (24 oz.), Fine Tip Primary Colors FoodWriter™ Edible Color Markers, Brush Set, p. 128; Cutter/Embosser, Fondant Shaping Foam, p. 129; Rolling Pin, Roll & Cut Mat, p. 131
Cookie: Gingerbread Boys Nesting Cutter Set, p. 195; 8 in. Cookie Treat Sticks, p. 161
Candy: Pumpkins Mold, p. 207; Candy Melts®† in Orange and Green (1 pk. each), p. 162
Recipes: Buttercream Icing, p. 114; Thinned Fondant Adhesive, p. 115
Also: 2007 Pattern Book (Hat, Hatband), p. 126; Gum-Tex™, p. 131; Confectionery Tool Set, p. 129; Petite Autumn Leaves Icing Decorations (3 pks.), p. 207; Cake Dividing Set, p. 133; paring knife, cornstarch, toothpick

At least 48 hours in advance: Make fondant scarecrow (p. 121).

Mold 27 pumpkins using painting method (p. 123). Ice 2-layer cake smooth; divide into 10ths. For fence, roll out white fondant 3/16 in. thick. Cut 10 fence posts 5/8 in. x 4 in. long, and 10 rails, 5/8 in. x 2½ to 3 in. long. Score woodgrain effects using straight-edge wheel of Cutter/Embosser. Trim pieces to fit and attach to cake sides at division points with dots of icing. Pipe tip 6 bead bottom border in buttercream. Insert scarecrow. Attach pumpkin candies and leaves icing decorations with dots of icing. Serves 20.

†Brand confectionery coating.

◀ Fall's Fave Face

Pan: Pumpkin Pie, p. 207
Colors: White-White, Orange, Rose, Black, Lemon Yellow, p. 135
Recipe: Favorite pie crust (2 recipes)
Also: 2007 Pattern Book (Hat, Eyes, Nose), p. 126; Blue Colored Sugar, Chocolate Jimmies Sprinkle Decorations, p. 136; Rolling Pin, Roll & Cut Mat, p. 131; Decorator Brush Set, p. 163; 4 in. Lollipop Sticks, p. 165; apple pie filling (3 cans), uncooked thin spaghetti, checkered fabric (¼ yd.), paring knife, toothpick

Prepare 2 crust recipes and roll out top and bottom crust for 1 recipe. Place bottom crust in pan and fill with apple filling. Position top crust and crimp edges with fork. Cut small slits in eye areas. Bake and cool pie. Roll out 2nd crust recipe. Trace patterns (hat, eyes, nose) with toothpick; cut. Brush shapes with water; sprinkle hat with blue sugar and hat band area with jimmies. Bake pieces at 400°F until light brown; let cool. For hair, combine white-white and yellow icing colors and brush onto 12 lengths of spaghetti, 4 in. long; let dry.

Paint eyes with white-white and pupils with black icing color. For nose, combine orange color with white-white and brush on. Paint cheeks with rose and mouth with black icing color. Insert lollipop sticks at top edge of pie to support hat. Position eyes, nose and hat. Insert hair below hat. Shape fabric into a scarf and position. Serves 8.

◀ A Little Autumn Spice

Pan: Dimensions® Cascade, p. 145

Colors: Orange, Golden Yellow, Red-Red, p. 135

Fondant: White Ready-To-Use Rolled Fondant (24 oz.), Brush Set, p. 128; Confectionery Tool Set, Fondant Shaping Foam, p. 129; Rolling Pin, Roll & Cut Mat, p. 131

Recipe: Pumpkin Apple Spice Cake, p. 114

Also: Harvest Mini Metal Cutter Set, p. 207; Gum-Tex™, p. 131; Flower Former Set, p. 129; non-toxic pastel chalk, tea strainer, cornstarch

One day in advance: Make fondant leaves (p. 121). Combine 24 oz. of fondant with 2 teaspoons of Gum-Tex™. Divide fondant into 6 portions; tint light orange, dark orange, light yellow, dark yellow, light red, dark red.

Bake and cool cake; position on plate. Position leaves around cake. Serves 12.

▶ Pops to Crow About

Candy: Smiley Face Lollipop Mold, p. 164; Candy Melts®† in White, Yellow, Orange, Green, Peanut Butter, p. 162; Garden Candy Color Set, p. 163; 6 in. Lollipop Sticks, p. 165; Silver Foil Bon-Bon Cups, p. 184; Decorator Brush Set, p. 163

Also: Parchment Triangles, p. 138; Rolling Pin, p. 131; large gumdrops, jelly fruit disks, craft knife

Melt 1 part peanut butter Candy Melts with 2 parts white Candy Melts and fill candy molds. Add sticks and refrigerate until set; unmold. Use black-tinted candy in cut parchment bag to pipe mouth and stitch marks. Use white melted candy in cut parchment bag to pipe whites of eyes; let dry and pipe black pupils. Pipe triangle nose with orange candy. Make collars (p. 124).

Cut large gumdrops in half, horizontally; roll out fruit disks to slightly elongate shape. Attach top of gumdrop to fruit disks and fruit disks to lollipop with melted candy. Use melted candy to pipe hat band and pull-out hair under hat. Insert stick through hole in collar; attach collar with melted candy. Each serves 1.

◀ Meal Markers

Pan: Mini Loaf, p. 149

Colors: Royal Blue, Lemon Yellow, Black, Golden Yellow, p. 135

Candy: Orange, White Candy Melts®†, p. 162; Primary, Garden Candy Color Sets, Candy Melting Plate, Decorator Brush Set, p. 163

Fondant: White Ready-To-Use Rolled Fondant (24 oz.), p. 128

Also: 6-Mix Autumn Sprinkle Assortment, p. 207; Parchment Triangles, p. 121, plastic ruler, embroidery scissors

Reserve 1 Candy Melts disk for each plaque to make easel. Mold candy plaques (p. 124) ¼ in. thick in pan cavities. Refrigerate until firm; unmold. Brush melted candy on edges and dip in sprinkles. Refrigerate until firm. Make pilgrims (p. 121). Attach to plaque with melted candy.

For name, tint orange candy with red candy color. Pipe names and facial features using melted candy in cut parchment bag. Make easels using reserved Candy Melts wafers. Cut wafers in half; cut one side flat to create a right angle. Attach 2 easels to back of each plaque with melted candy; let set. Each serves 1.

▼ The Most Pop-ular Guy!

Cookie: Round Cookie Treat Pan, 8 in. Cookie Treat Sticks, Cookie Sheet, Cooling Grid, p. 161; Comfort Grip™ Santa Hat Cutter, p. 195

Tips: 3, 13, p. 140-141

Colors: Christmas Red, Black, p. 135

Recipes: Royal Icing, Roll-Out Cookie, p. 114

Also: Meringue Powder, p. 134; Red Colored Sugar, p. 136; light corn syrup, cornstarch

Roll out a portion of dough; cut hat cookies. Press remaining dough into treat pan cavities, inserting sticks. Bake and cool all cookies. Cover cookies with thinned royal icing (p. 124), red for hats and white with a little red added for round faces. Immediately sprinkle hats with red sugar. Attach hats to heads with full-strength royal icing. Pipe tip 3 dot eyes and nose (smooth with finger dipped in cornstarch); pipe in mouth. Add tip 13 large rosette pompom and rosette fur trim on hat. Pipe tip 13 pull-out star hair, moustache, beard and eyebrows. Each serves 1.

▼ Tropical Yule Tree

Pan: Palm Tree, p. 151

Tips: 2, 3, 8, 16, p. 140-141

Colors:* Leaf Green, Kelly Green, Christmas Red, Red-Red, Sky Blue, Violet, Orange, Brown, Golden Yellow, Lemon Yellow, p. 135

Candy: Candy Melts®† in White, Yellow, Red, Green, Blue, p. 162; Gift Truffles Candy Mold, p. 165; Decorator Brush Set, p. 163

Recipes: Buttercream, Royal Icings, p. 114

Also: Meringue Powder, p. 134; Cake Board, Fanci-Foil Wrap, p. 225; waxed paper

In advance: Make 40 lights in various colors using royal icing. On waxed paper, pipe tip 8 bead; add tip 2 outline hanger at top. Make extras to allow for breakage and let dry. Mold 7 candy gifts using painting method (p. 123). Refrigerate until firm; unmold.

Place cake on foil-wrapped board, cut to fit. Pipe tip 3 trunk and leaf lines in buttercream; cover trunk and leaves with tip 16 stars. Position lights and candy gifts. Cake serves 12; each candy serves 1.

*Combine Christmas Red with Red-Red for red shown. Combine Golden Yellow with a little Lemon Yellow for yellow shown. Combine Leaf Green and Kelly Green for dark and light green shown. Combine Orange, Golden Yellow, Brown and Red-Red for dark brown shown on trunk lines. Combine Orange, Golden Yellow and Brown for light brown shown on trunk.

▲ A Hearty Ho-Ho-Ho!

Pans: Party Hat, p. 153; Oval Set (10¾ x 7⅞ in. used), p. 148

Tips: 12, 21, p. 140-141

Colors: Red-Red, Kelly Green, Black, Copper (skin tone), p. 135

Fondant: White Ready-To-Use Rolled Fondant (24 oz.), Brush Set, p. 128; Rolling Pin, Roll & Cut Mat, p. 131; Easy-Glide Fondant Smoother, p. 129

Recipe: Buttercream Icing, p. 114

Also: 101 Cookie Cutters Set, p. 160; Fanci-Foil Wrap, p. 225; Tapered Spatula, p. 138; paring knife, 24 x 14 x ½ in. thick foamcore board or triple-thick cardboard

On 1-layer oval cake, cut 2 in. from one long edge. On hat cake, trim bottom flat. Position cakes, cut sides together, on foil-wrapped cardboard, cut to fit. Fill in gaps and cover seam between cakes with icing. Prepare hat cake for rolled fondant (p. 138); ice oval cake smooth. Tint 8 oz. fondant red, 1 oz. green, 1 oz. black. Cover hat cake with red fondant; smooth with Fondant Smoother. Roll out black, green and remaining red fondant ⅛ in. thick. Using knife, cut a 3 in. black circle for mouth and a 1½ in. red heart shape for tongue; position on cake top. Using cutters, cut green "H" and "O" letters; attach with damp brush. For beard, starting where cakes meet, pipe tip 21 lines, overpiping for dimension and extending to a point below chin. Pipe tip 12 elongated reverse shell moustache. For eyes, roll 1½ x ¼ in. diameter ropes in black fondant; position. Pipe tip 21 elongated shell eyebrows and tip 12 ball nose. Using tip 12, cover hat brim and pompom areas with buttercream; fluff with spatula. Serves 22.

▶ Sun, Sand and Santa

Pan: 12 x 18 x 2 in. Sheet, p. 148
Tips: 2, 3, 4, 6, 8, 12, 13, 101s, p. 140-141
Colors:* Copper (skin tone), Red-Red, Christmas Red, Kelly Green, Black, Brown, Lemon Yellow, Golden Yellow, Orange, Royal Blue, p. 135
Cookie: Holiday Cutter Set, p. 195; Cookie Sheet, Cooling Grid, p. 161
Fondant: White Ready-To-Use Rolled Fondant (24 oz.), Brush Set, p. 128; Leaf, Round Cut-Outs™, p. 130; Rolling Pin, Roll & Cut Mat, p. 131
Recipes: Buttercream, Royal Icings, p. 114
Also: 2007 Pattern Book (Surfboard), p. 126; Seashells Candy Mold, p. 164; 4 in. Lollipop Sticks, p. 165; Piping Gel, p. 134; Plastic Dowel Rods, p. 224; Flower Former Set, p. 129; Gum-Tex™, p. 131; Cake Boards, Fanci-Foil Wrap, p. 225; pretzel rods, granulated brown sugar, mini candy-coated chocolates, waxed paper, aluminum foil, cardboard, cornstarch, vegetable pan spray, craft knife, tissue paper, plastic ruler, ⅛ in. green ribbon (6 in.)

In advance: Make 4 fondant palm trees (p. 120), beach chair (p. 120), surfboard, table, snowman and 8 seashells. For surfboard, tint 2 oz. of fondant Lemon Yellow with a little Golden Yellow. Roll out ⅛ in. thick; cut shape using pattern. Cut a hole for Santa's support stick using tip 8. Let dry on cornstarch-dusted board. For table, tint 2 oz. fondant green. Roll out ⅛ in. thick and cut table top with medium round Cut-Out. For table base, roll a 1¼ x ½ in. diameter log; thread onto a lollipop stick cut to 3¼ in., leaving 2 in. of stick extended. Attach base to top with damp brush; let dry. Make fondant snowman (p. 120). For seashells, tint a 1½ in. ball of fondant copper, knead together with white fondant to marbleize. Press fondant into cornstarch-dusted molds; unmold and let dry. Make Santa, Mrs. Santa, reindeer and 2 elf cookies (p. 120).

Ice 1-layer sheet cake smooth in buttercream. For water, tint piping gel blue; using spatula, spread on cake top. Sprinkle beach area with brown sugar sand. Divide cake sides in 3 in. sections; pipe tip 3 drop strings from division points. Attach mini chocolates. Pipe tip 8 ball bottom border. Insert Santa in surfboard and insert in cake. Cut plastic dowel rod in four 2 in. sections; insert in cake then insert palm trees. Insert reindeer cookie in cake top; attach ribbon reins with royal icing. Position snowman and standing elf. Sprinkle additional brown sugar sand where other elf will lay; spread with spatula to create "sand angel." Position elf, Mrs. Claus in chair and seashells. For drinking glass, roll a ⅝ in. diameter white fondant log. Tint a small ball of fondant yellow; roll out ⅛ in. thick and cut a ¼ x 2¼ in. long strip for lemonade. Wrap around glass, attaching with damp brush. Roll log to blend in strip; trim log to ⅝ in. Position on table. Cake serves 36; each cookie serves 1.

*Combine Red-Red and Christmas Red for red shown. Combine Lemon Yellow and Golden Yellow for yellow shown. Combine Brown with Red-Red for brown shown.

▶ Chilling in the Sunshine

Cookie: Cookie Sheet, Cooling Grid, p. 161; Comfort Grip™ Gingerbread Boy Cutter, p. 195
Candy: Ice Cream Candy Mold, p. 164; Candy Melts®† in Yellow and Peanut Butter, p. 162; Decorator Brush Set, p. 163
Tips: 1, 1s, 2, 3, 12, 124, p. 140
Colors:* Black, Leaf Green, Lemon Yellow, Rose, Violet, p. 135
Recipes: Royal Icing, Grandma's Gingerbread, p. 114
Also: Meringue Powder, p. 134; Rolling Pin, p. 131; large gum drops, candy corn, cornstarch, granulated sugar, waxed paper

In advance: Mold candy ice cream cones using painting method (p. 123). Refrigerate until firm; unmold.

Cut, bake and cool gingerbread boys; ice smooth with royal icing. Pipe tip 2 sunglass lenses; outline frames with tip 3. Outline and pipe in bathing suits and sandals with tip 3 (smooth with finger dipped in cornstarch). For man's suit, add tip 3 dots. Add tip 3 outline straps on sandals and lady's swimsuit. Pipe tip 124 ruffle hat brim; pipe in top of hat with tip 12. Add tip 2 hat band. Pipe tip 1 outline mouth for lady, tip 3 outline mouth for man. Add tip 3 dot cheeks and tip 2 pipe in lips. For noses, cut tip off candy corn; attach with icing. For Sun Block bottle, roll out gum drops on waxed paper sprinkled with sugar. Cut a 1 in. rectangle bottle and a ¼ in. square for top. Pipe tip 1s message. Attach candy cones and bottle to cookies with melted candy. Each serves 1.

*Combine Violet and a little Rose for violet shown. Combine Leaf Green with a little Lemon Yellow for light green shown.

†Brand confectionery coating.

▼ Ski Bum Bear

Pan: Stand-Up Cuddly Bear Set, p. 153
Tips: 1A, 5, 233, p. 140
Colors: Black, Christmas Red, p. 135
Fondant: White Ready-To-Use Rolled Fondant (24 oz.), Primary Colors Fondant Multi Pack, p. 128; Rolling Pin, Roll & Cut Mat, p. 131
Recipes: Buttercream Icing, p. 114; Thinned Fondant Adhesive, p. 115
Also: 2007 Pattern Book (Skis), p. 126; Plastic Dowel Rods, p. 224; Cake Boards, Fanci-Foil Wrap, p. 225; 8 in. Lollipop Sticks, p. 165; Flower Former Set, p. 129; Gum-Tex™, p. 131; sugar ice cream cone, paring knife, drinking straw, cornstarch

At least one week in advance: Make skis (p. 121) using pattern and green fondant mixed with 1 teaspoon Gum-Tex. Make braces for inserting skis into cake (p. 121).

Also in advance: Make ski pole baskets. Roll out red fondant ⅛ in. thick; cut 2 circles using wide end of tip 1A. Make a hole in the center of circles using a lollipop stick. Let dry. Make hat: Trim off 1 in. from open end of sugar cone. Cover cone in red fondant. Set aside.

Bake and cool bear cake using firm-textured batter such as pound cake. Trim off arms. For new arms, cut 2 plastic dowel rods to 6 in. long; insert with 3 in. extending from cake. Ice pads of feet and inside ears smooth. Outline facial features using tip 5; pipe in nose with tip 5 (smooth with finger dipped in cornstarch). For front paws, shape 1½ x ½ in. thick ovals of white fondant. Shape a finger area on each paw and wrap around a 1½ in. piece of drinking straw. Insert a lollipop stick at end of each paw and insert stick into dowel rod arms.

Cover bear with tip 233 pull-out fur. For scarf, roll out red fondant ⅛ in. thick; cut a strip ½ x 14 in. long. For fringe, cut slits in ends with knife. Wrap around cake. For tongue, shape a small log of fondant; indent at center and attach with damp brush. Use fondant to shape a 1 in. ball pompom and a 6 x ½ in. log for hat brim; flatten brim. Attach to hat with damp brush and position on cake. For ski poles, insert 8 in. lollipop sticks through baskets. Roll a thin log of fondant; wrap around stick, attaching to bottom of basket with damp brush. Immediately before serving, insert ski poles through straws in paws; secure with icing if needed. Insert skis on braces in pads of feet. Serves 12.

▲ Leading the Christmas Cheer!

Pan: Party Hat, p. 153
Tips: 3, 8, 18, p. 140-141
Colors: Red-Red, Black, Kelly Green, Copper (skin tone), p. 135
Fondant: White Ready-To-Use Rolled Fondant (24 oz.), Brush Set, p. 128; Rolling Pin, Roll & Cut Mat, p. 131
Recipe: Buttercream Icing, p. 114
Also: 2007 Pattern Book (Santa Face), p. 126; Cooling Grid, p. 161; 4 in. Lollipop Sticks, p. 165; Cake Board, Fanci-Foil Wrap, p. 225; ruler, craft knife, toothpicks

Trim top of hat cake to a point; trim pompom portion even with rest of cake. Mark face pattern starting 4 in. from top point of cake. Ice smooth a 3 in. area below marking for face. Ice rest of cake smooth in red. Mark pattern areas with toothpick. Pipe tip 3 dot eyes and nose. Pipe tip 18 swirl beard and moustache. Add tip 3 string mouth. Pipe tip 8 swirl fur on hat brim, pompom and bottom of coat.

Tint three 2¼ in. balls of fondant black, three 1½ in. balls of fondant green and four 2 in. balls of fondant red. For arms and legs, shape each red fondant ball into a 2½ in. log; insert lollipop stick at one end and insert in cake. For shoes, shape two of the black fondant balls into 2½ x 1½ x 1 in. thick ovals. Attach to legs with dots of icing. For belt, roll out remaining black fondant ball ⅛ in. thick; cut a 1 x 10 in. strip and position on cake, trimming as needed. For buckle, flatten a 1½ in. green ball into a square shape; cut out center and attach with damp brush. For gloves, flatten and shape remaining green balls; cut a small notch for thumb. Attach gloves to arms with dots of icing. Pipe tip 8 swirl fur cuffs on legs and sleeves. Serves 12.

▼ Holly Hearth

Pans: 9 x 13 x 2 in. Sheet, p. 148; 10½ x 15 x 1 in. Jelly Roll, p. 149

Fondant: Primary, Natural Colors Fondant Multi Pack (1 pk. each), Brush Set, p. 128; Leaf Cut-Outs™, p. 130; Rolling Pin, Roll & Cut Mat, p. 131

Recipe: Favorite crisped rice cereal treats (3 batches)

Also: 2007 Pattern Book (Fireplace Garland), p. 126; Candy Melts®† in White, Green (1 pk. each) and Light Cocoa (3 pks.), p. 162; Floral Collection Flower Making Set, p. 130; Flower Former Set, p. 129; Wooden Dowel Rods, p. 224; Gum-Tex™, p. 131; Disposable Decorating Bags, p. 138; Cake Board, Fanci-Foil Wrap, p. 225; Cinnamon Drops Sprinkle Decorations, p. 194; peppermint stick candy, paring knife, ruler, waxed paper, cornstarch

One day in advance: Make 6 candy garlands. Melt 7 oz. of green candy; thicken with 1 or 2 drops of water. Place pattern on board; cover with waxed paper. Using melted candy in cut disposable bag, pipe in pattern with tiny zigzags. Refrigerate for a few minutes, then overpipe. Position cinnamon drop berries and refrigerate until firm.

Also in advance: Make candy plaque (p. 124) base and mantel. Pour 3 pks. of melted cocoa Candy Melts, ½ in. thick in sheet pan; refrigerate until firm, unmold. Bring to room temperature before trimming. Using ruler and knife, cut into 13 x 5 in. base and 13 x 4 in. mantel.

Combine each package of red, green and yellow fondant with ¼ teaspoon of Gum-Tex. For bows, roll out fondant 1⁄16 in. thick. Cut 6 strips 3 x ¼ in.; fold ends into center of strip to form loops; attach with damp brush. For streamers, cut two ¾ x ¼ in. strips for each bow. For knot, roll a 1⁄16 in. ball. Attach streamers and ball with damp brush. Let dry on cornstarch-dusted board. For holly leaves, roll out fondant 1⁄16 in. thick. Cut 30 leaves using holly cutter from Floral Collection Set. Place on thick foam and score veins using veining tool from set. Let dry on medium flower formers dusted with cornstarch. Cut peppermint sticks for candles: one 4 in., two 3 in. and two 2¼ in. For candle flames, roll out fondant ⅛ in. thick; cut 5 flames using smallest leaf Cut-Out. Let dry on cornstarch-dusted board. Attach to candles with melted candy. For fireplace flames, combine a small piece of red fondant with a ½ in. ball of yellow fondant to make orange; marbleize by kneading in a 1 in. yellow fondant ball. Roll out ⅛ in. thick; cut 8 flames using smallest leaf Cut-Out. Let dry on cornstarch-dusted board.

Make fireplace (p. 119) using 3 recipes of cereal treats. Position mantel. For logs, combine light and dark brown fondant. Shape ½ in. diameter logs, three 3½ in. long, three 2 in. long and two ½ in. long. Score wood lines with knife; attach in fireplace, along with flames, using melted cocoa candy. Shape 1¼ x ¾ in. fondant stones; attach around opening with melted candy. Attach candles, holly leaves, cinnamon drop berries, garlands and bows with melted candy. Serves 24.

†Brand confectionery coating.

▲ The Giftmobile

Pan: 11 x 7 x 1½ in. Non-Stick Biscuit/Brownie, p. 146

Candy: White Candy Melts®† (2 pks.), p. 162; Garden Candy Color Set, Candy Flavorings Set, p. 163

Recipe: Ready-In-Minutes Cocoa Fudge, p. 115

Also: 18 pc. Holiday Metal Cutter Set, p. 195; Santa Fun Pix®, p. 193; Twinkling Trees Sprinkle Decorations, p. 194; Cake Board, p. 225; Parchment Triangles, p. 138; waxed paper

Prepare fudge recipe, substituting white for dark cocoa Candy Melts and adding green color and ⅛ teaspoon mint flavor. Pour mixture into waxed paper-lined pan. Immediately top with sprinkles. Refrigerate until firm. Cut fudge with sleigh cutter from set; position on waxed paper-covered board. Using melted candy in cut parchment bag, pipe trim on sleigh top. Tint portions of melted white candy green using candy color. Pipe runner on sleigh bottom. Insert Santa pick. Each serves 1.

▼ Santa Drops In

Pan: Standard Muffin, p. 148

Tip: 3, p. 140

Colors: Red-Red, Kelly Green, Black, Golden Yellow, p. 135

Recipes: Buttercream, Royal Icings, p. 114

Also: 6-Mix Christmas Sprinkles Assortment, p. 194; Smiling Santa Standard Baking Cups, Icing Decorations, p. 193; 4 in. Lollipop Sticks, p. 165; Parchment Triangles, p. 138; Meringue Powder, p. 134; scissors, waxed paper, craft block, spice drops (red and black), large red spice drops

In advance: Make Santa. For torso, insert lollipop stick through large red spice drop, leaving ¾ in. extending at top to support head. Insert bottom of stick into waxed paper-covered craft block. For legs, attach two red spice drops to torso with icing, narrow end up. For shoes, cut two black spice drops horizontally in half. Attach top halves down using royal icing. For arms, slice red spice drop vertically in half. Attach arms to body with royal icing. Pipe tip 3 zigzags in royal icing for fur trim on suit. Add tip 3 zigzag belt, cuffs, outline buckle and dot gloves. Attach icing decoration head with royal icing; let dry.

Ice cupcakes smooth; sprinkle with Christmas jimmies. Insert Santa in cupcake, trimming lollipop stick as needed. Each serves 1.

◀ Shoveling Snowcones!

Pans: Step-By-Step Snowman, p. 192; Cookie Sheet, Cooling Grid, p. 149
Colors: Red-Red, Kelly Green, Black, p. 135
Fondant: White Ready-To-Use Rolled Fondant (96 oz.), p. 128; Rolling Pin, Roll & Cut Mat, p. 131
Candy: White Candy Melts®†, p. 162; Decorator Brush Set, p. 163
Recipes: Buttercream Icing, p. 114; favorite crisped rice cereal treats
Also: Yellow, Pink, Blue, Lavender, Orange, Dark Green Colored Sugars, p. 136; Confectionery Tool Set, p. 129; Cake Boards, Fanci-Foil Wrap, p. 225; sugar ice cream cones

For snowcones, prepare cereal treats and shape into 7 ball halves, 3 in. diameter. Cover treats with melted candy (p. 124); sprinkle with colored sugars. Let set. Dip top edge of sugar cones in melted candy; attach cereal treats and let set.

Prepare snowman cake for rolled fondant (p. 113). Place cake on triple-thick foil-wrapped board cut to fit cake plus 8 in. at bottom for arm area. Tint 12 oz. of fondant red, 4 oz. green and 1 oz. black; reserve remainder white. Cover face area with white and hat area with red fondant. Roll out green fondant ⅛ in. thick; cut a ⅝ in. wide strip for hatband and attach with damp brush. Roll 1¾ x ⅛ in. diameter logs for eyes and 4 x ⅛ in. diameter log for mouth. Roll two 1½ in. balls for cheeks and one 1¼ in. ball for nose; flatten slightly. For tongue, tint a ¾ in. ball of white fondant with a little red color; roll out ⅛ in. thick and cut a 1¼ in. half oval. Score line in tongue with veining tool. Attach all pieces with damp brush. For neck, shape 8 oz. of fondant into a 5 x 2 x 1¼ in. thick log; position at bottom of cake. Roll out white fondant ⅛ in. thick; cut an 8 x 6 in. piece to support cones and position below neck. For each arm, shape 24 oz. of fondant into an 11½ x 1½ in. diameter log; flatten slightly. Attach to head with damp brush and curve around cake board. Shape ends into mitts with thumbs. Position cones, slightly lifting hands to fit. Cake serves 12; each cone serves 1.

†Brand confectionery coating.

▶ Gifts Around the Globe

Pan: Sports Ball, p. 155; Mini Ball, p. 154; 10 x 2 in. Round, p. 148
Tips: 3, 12, p. 140
Colors: Black, Orange, Royal Blue, Red-Red, Violet, Rose, p. 135
Fondant: White Ready-To-Use Rolled Fondant (24 oz.), Brush Set, p. 128; Rolling Pin, Roll & Cut Mat, p. 131
Recipes: Sugar Mold, p. 115; Buttercream, Royal Icings, p. 114
Also: Decorator Preferred™ 6 in. Smooth-Edge Decorator Plate, p. 223; Santa Bobbling Toppers, Petite Twinkling Trees Icing Decorations (3 pks.), p. 193; Piping Gel, Meringue Powder, p. 134; "Hidden" Pillars, p. 221; 6 and 12 in. Cake Circles, Fanci-Foil Wrap, p. 225; paring knife, scissors, cornstarch, spoon, ruler, granulated sugar, 4 in. lightweight bowl or cup

Several days in advance: Make sugar mold head and hollowed snowglobe body (p. 115). Using thinned royal icing, paint inside of both body halves to help fondant stick; let dry. Tint 5 oz. of fondant red, 4½ oz. blue, 2 oz. violet, 1 oz. black, ½ oz. each orange and pink (use a little Red-Red color for pink); reserve remainder white. Roll out blue fondant ⅛ in. thick. Cut a circle about 7½ in. diameter. Brush inside of back body half with piping gel; attach blue circle for sky background. Smooth and trim as needed. Roll out white fondant ⅛ in. thick. Cut a 7½ x 4 in. strip for hills; trim to shape, attach with damp brush and smooth. Cover inside of front body half around window with white fondant.

Attach body and head halves together with royal icing; let dry. Attach head to body with royal icing; trim seams and window with tip 3 bead border and let dry. Using fondant, shape 1 x ½ in. carrot nose, ¼ in. ball eyes, ½ in. flattened ball cheeks, 1¾ x ⅛ in. rope mouth. Attach with royal icing. For hat, shape a 3 x 4 in. long fondant cone; attach with royal icing. For brim, roll a 20 x ¼ in. diameter fondant rope; shape into zigzag and attach over hat with damp brush. For pompom, roll a 1 in. ball; attach. For scarf, roll out violet fondant ⅛ in. thick; cut a 11 x ½ in. strip. Wrap and attach around neck with royal icing. Using scissors, cut slits at ends for fringe. Ice top of separator plate fluffy with royal icing. Position snowman. Attach icing decorations and topper inside body with royal icing.

Ice 1-layer cake smooth with buttercream. Pipe tip 12 zigzag puff bottom border. Position icing decorations on border. Prepare cake for push-in pillar construction (p. 112) using hidden pillars trimmed to height of cake. Position snowman on cake. Serves 14.

▶ Dapper Dude

Pan: Stand-Up Cuddly Bear Set, p. 153
Tips: 3, 8, 12, 17, p. 140-141
Color: Black, p. 135
Fondant: White Ready-To-Use Rolled Fondant (24 oz.), p. 128; Primary Colors Fondant Multi Pack, Brush Set, p. 128; Rolling Pin, Roll & Cut Mat, p. 131
Recipes: Buttercream Icing, p. 114; Thinned Fondant Adhesive, p. 115
Also: 4 in. Lollipop Sticks, p. 165; Gum-Tex™, p. 131; Clear Vanilla Extract, p. 134; Cake Board, Fanci-Foil Wrap, p. 225; toasted coconut marshmallows, pretzel rods, cornstarch, freezer paper, scissors

At least 48 hours in advance: Make fondant hat and broom (p. 121). Let dry overnight on cornstarch-dusted board.

Bake cake using firm-textured batter such as pound cake; let cool. Trim off ears and arm area near face. Pipe tip 8 ball eyes and cheeks (flatten and smooth with finger dipped in cornstarch). Pipe tip 3 dot pupils and outline mouth. For nose, combine a small amount of red fondant with yellow; shape into a 1 in. cone. Cut a lollipop stick to 3 in. and insert in bottom of nose; insert in cake. Build up arms with tip 12. Cover cake and overpipe arms and cheeks with tip 17 stars. Position broom in hand area; overpipe hand with tip 12 and cover with tip 17 stars. For pipe, trim lollipop stick to 3 in; insert stick into marshmallow. Tint a small amount of vanilla black and brush on stick; let dry. Insert into cake. Position hat. Serves 12.

◀ Warm in Any Storm

Pan: Mini Ball, p. 154
Tip: 17, p. 141
Color: Royal Blue, p. 135
Fondant: White Ready-To-Use Rolled Fondant (24 oz.), Brush Set, p. 128; Rolling Pin, Roll & Cut Mat, p. 131
Recipe: Buttercream Icing, p. 114
Also: Scissors, paring knife, chocolate chips, candy corn

Ice mini ball cakes smooth. Tint fondant blue and roll out ¼ in. thick. Cut a 4 in. square for hat; shape into a cone and attach to cake with icing. Pipe tip 17 zigzag brim and rosette pompom. For scarf, cut an 8 x 1½ in. strip; wrap around cake. Using scissors, cut slits at ends for fringe. Shape a small ball of fondant into a knot; attach with damp brush. Position chocolate chip eyes and mouth, candy corn nose. Each serves 1.

▲ Frosty's Festive Face

Pan: Snowman Cookie Treat, p. 192
Tips: 2, 4, 7, 47, 126, 352, p. 140-141
Colors: Violet, Kelly Green, Royal Blue, Red-Red, Black, p. 135
Recipes: Royal Icing, Roll-Out Cookie, p. 114
Also: 8 in. Cookie Treat Sticks, p. 161; Meringue Powder, p. 134; ¾ in. wide green satin ribbon (16 in. per bow), candy corn, cornstarch

Bake cookies on sticks following pan directions; cool. Pipe in face and hat with tip 7 (smooth with finger dipped in cornstarch). Add tip 126 band brim. Pipe tip 47 (smooth side up) hat band. Add tip 352 leaves and tip 2 dot berries. Pipe tip 4 dot eyes. Add tip 2 dot pupils and pipe in mouth. Pipe tip 4 dot cheeks (flatten with finger dipped in cornstarch). Attach candy corn nose with icing. Tie ribbon bow around cookie stick. Each serves 1.

▶ Playing Winter Ball

Cookie: Cookie Sheet, Cooling Grid, p. 149; Holiday Metal Cutter Set, p. 195
Tips: 2, 7, p. 140
Colors: Orange, Red-Red, Royal Blue, Brown, Black, p. 135
Fondant: White Ready-To-Use Rolled Fondant (24 oz.), Brush Set, p. 128; Rolling Pin, Roll & Cut Mat, p. 131
Recipes: Royal Icing, Roll-Out Cookie, p. 114
Also: Meringue Powder, p. 134; paring knife, mini chocolate chips, cornstarch

Cut cookies using snowman cutter; bake and cool. Pipe in body and head with tip 7 (smooth with finger dipped in cornstarch). Tint portions of fondant blue and brown. Roll out blue fondant ⅛ in. thick. Cut cap shape using paring knife. Score seam lines with end of brush; attach cap to cookie with damp brush. Attach mini chip eyes and mouth with icing. Pipe tip 2 pull-out nose. Add tip 2 seams and stitching lines on baseball body. Shape brown fondant into teardrops for shoes; add tip 2 outline laces; let dry. Attach shoes with icing. Each serves 1.

◀ A Winter Delight

Pans: 6, 10 x 2 in. Round, p. 148

Tips: 1, 7, p. 140

Colors:* Kelly Green, Leaf Green, Lemon Yellow, Royal Blue, Violet, Black, Rose, Orange, p. 135

Fondant: White Ready-To-Use Rolled Fondant (24 oz.), Brush Set, p. 128; Rolling Pin, Roll & Cut Mat, p. 131; Cutter/Embosser, p. 129

Recipes: Buttercream, Royal Icings, p. 114

Also: 2 in. and 2½ in. Globe Pillar Sets, p. 220; Decorator Preferred™ 8 in. Smooth Edge Separator Plate, p. 223; Nesting Snowflakes Cutter Set, Holiday Mini Cutter Set, p. 195; Cake Boards, Fanci-Foil Wrap, 12 in. Round Silver Cake Base, p. 225; Cake Dividing Set, p. 133; Flower Spike, p. 224; Meringue Powder, p. 134; ⅛ in. wide white satin ribbon, waxed paper, wire cutters, 18-gauge white wire, craft block, serrated knife, ruler, cornstarch, scissors

In advance: Make cake top snowflake and holder (p. 121). Reserve remaining blue fondant.

Ice 2-layer cakes smooth; prepare for push-in pillar construction (p. 112). Using cake dividing set, divide 6 in. cake into 6ths and 10 in. cake into 10ths. Tint fondant: 6 oz. violet, 5 oz. each light green and dark green, 1 oz. each black and orange. Roll out reserved blue and violet fondant ⅛ in. thick; using knife cut eight 1¼ in. squares in each color. Roll out light green and dark green fondant ⅛ in. thick; using tree cutter from mini set, cut 8 trees in each color. Position alternating color squares on cake sides at division points in diamond formation. Attach alternating color trees to squares with damp brush. Pipe tip 1 outline snowflakes on cake sides between diamonds. Pipe tip 7 ball top and bottom border.

Make 4 snowmen (p. 121). Fill flower spike with fondant. Insert snowflake holder in spike; insert into center of top cake. Tie ribbon through blue fondant snowflake and hang on hook. Serves 40.

*Combine Kelly Green and Lemon Yellow for light green shown. Combine Violet and Rose for violet shade shown.

▶ Snow Dancing

Pan: Mini Snowman, p. 192

Tips: 4, 10, p. 140

Colors:* Black, Lemon Yellow, Leaf Green, Royal Blue, Rose, Christmas Red, Kelly Green, Orange, Violet, Copper (skin tone), Brown, p. 135

Fondant: White Ready-To-Use Rolled Fondant (24 oz.), Brush Set, p. 128; Rolling Pin, Roll & Cut Mat, p. 131; Cutter/Embosser, p. 129

Recipe: Buttercream Icing, p. 114

Also: 2007 Pattern Book (Mouth, Teeth), p. 126; Confectionery Tool Set, p. 129; ruler, sharp knife, miniature candy cane

On mini cakes, trim off hat brim and ¼ in. across top of hat. Turn cakes. Ice bottom half of cake smooth; build up sides with icing to create a triangle shape. Ice face smooth; build up with icing to create a round shape. Pipe tip 4 dot nose. Tint fondant: 1 in. ball rose, 1¾ in. ball violet, 2 in. ball black, 2½ in. ball red, 1½ in. ball each blue, brown, yellow and orange; reserve remaining white. Make and position fondant arms, legs, clothes and facial features (p. 121). Position candy cane on mitten. Each serves 1.

*Combine Leaf Green with Lemon Yellow for light green shown.

◀ Branches & Berries

Pans: Iridescents! Tree, p. 192, Mini Loaf, p. 149

Color: Kelly Green, p. 135

Also: White Candy Melts®†, p. 162; Garden Candy Color Set, p. 163; Vanilla Whipped Icing Mix, p. 134; Cake Board, Fanci-Foil Wrap, p. 225; potato peeler, cheese plane, paring knife, solid vegetable shortening, red spice drops

In advance: Make candy curls (p. 124); set aside.

Tint whipped icing light green. Ice tree cake fluffy with spatula. Position candy curls, completely covering cake. Cut spice drops in half; position on cake. Serves 12.

† Brand confectionery coating.

▼ Tree-mendously Generous

Pan: 12 x 18 x 2 in. Sheet, p. 148

Fondant: Primary Colors Fondant Multi Pack, Brush Set, p. 128; Rolling Pin, Roll & Cut Mat, p. 131

Candy: White Candy Melts®† (6 pks.), p. 162; Garden Candy Color Set, p. 163; 6 in. Lollipop Sticks, p. 165

Also: Star Plastic Cookie Cutter, p. 160; Cooling Grid, p. 149, paring knife, ruler, cornstarch

In advance: Make fondant loops and star (p. 121).

Bake 1-layer cake using firm-textured batter such as pound cake. Cut into 48 2-inch squares with paring knife. Cover squares with candy (p. 124); let dry. For cake ribbons, roll out various colors of fondant ⅛ in. thick. Cut ¼ in. wide strips to fit across top and sides of cakes; attach with damp brush. Stack cakes in tree shape on serving plate, placing 21 for bottom layer, 14 for second layer, 7 for third layer, 4 for fourth layer, 1 for top layer. Attach loops to packages and lollipop stick to back of star with melted candy. Insert star on top. Serves 47.

▶ Forest Festivity

Pans: Standard Muffin, p. 148; Cookie Sheet, Cooling Grid, p. 149

Colors: Kelly Green, Leaf Green, p. 135

Candy: White Candy Melts®† (1 pk. makes approximately 6-8 bases), p. 162; Primary, Garden Candy Color Sets, p. 163; 4 in. Lollipop Sticks, p. 165

Recipes: Roll-Out Cookie, p. 114; favorite crisped rice cereal treats

Also: White Standard Baking Cups, p. 184; 18 pc. Metal Holiday Cutter Set, p. 195; Parchment Triangles, p. 138; Cake Board, Fanci-Foil Wrap, p. 225; Rolling Pin, p. 131; ¼ in. wide white satin ribbon, white cardstock, waxed paper, black marker, non-stick vegetable oil pan spray, single hole punch

Tint ½ cookie dough Kelly Green and ½ Leaf Green; roll out. Cut cookies using tree cutter from set; bake and cool. Tint portions of melted candy pink, yellow, violet and blue using candy colors. For tree bases, make candy shells in baking cups (p. 124). Prepare cereal treat recipe. Fill shells with treat mixture; cover top evenly with additional melted candy to seal. Refrigerate until firm.

On waxed paper-covered board, pipe treetop stars and starbursts using melted candy in cut parchment bags; refrigerate until firm. On tree cookies, using melted candy, pipe dot lights and attach lollipop sticks to back; refrigerate until firm. Attach stars and starbursts with melted candy. Carefully peel baking cups from bases; insert tree cookies. Punch hole in cardstock; print names. Attach cards with ribbon. Each serves 1.

◀ Soldier of Love

Pans: Fanci-Fill Pan Set, p. 144; Cookie Sheet, Cooling Grid, p. 149
Tips: 2, 3, 4, 21, p. 140-141
Colors: Rose, Copper (skin tone), Brown, Black, Red-Red, p. 135
Recipes: Buttercream, Royal Icings, Roll-Out Cookie, p. 114
Also: 101 Cookie Cutters Set, p. 160; 11¾ in. Lollipop Sticks, p. 165; Cake Board, Fanci-Foil Wrap, p. 225; Parchment Triangles, p. 138; Spatula, p. 138; Meringue Powder, Vanilla Whipped Icing Mix, p. 134; Colored Sugars in Pink and Red, p. 136; waxed paper, white curling ribbon, cherry pie filling (21 oz.), paper, marker, cornstarch

In advance: Make heart arrowheads, bow and message with royal icing. For arrowheads, on waxed paper-covered board, pipe 5 to 7 tip 3 bead hearts; let dry. For bow, trace upper half of medium heart cutter from set for pattern. For bow string, draw a line connecting one side of heart to the other, 1¼ in. from top curve of heart. Cover pattern with waxed paper; outline bow with tip 3, leaving bow string area open. Let dry, then turn over. Cut and position a lollipop stick to fit opening for bow string and overpipe; let dry. Pipe tip 4 message on waxed paper-covered board; let dry.

Prepare dough; tint ⅓ copper (skin tone) and ⅔ rose; roll out. Cut Cupid cookie using largest gingerbread boy cutter from set and copper dough. Roll a small ball of copper dough for nose and attach. Cut 12 heart cookies using smallest heart cutter from set. Sprinkle 6 hearts with pink sugar and 6 with red sugar. Bake and cool all cookies.

Decorate Cupid with royal icing. Pipe tip 2 string facial features; outline and pipe in glasses with tip 2. Pipe in tip 4 pants and strap (smooth with finger dipped in cornstarch). Pipe tip 3 swirl hair; let dry. Trim lollipop sticks to various lengths from 7 to 11¾ in.; attach to backs of heart and Cupid cookies with royal icing and let dry. Tie curling ribbon to sticks. For arrows, trim 4 lollipop sticks to 3 in.; attach arrowheads with royal icing. Pipe tip 2 pull-out feathers on ends of arrows; let dry. Attach bow and arrows to Cupid with royal icing; let dry.

Bake cake following instructions included with pan. For cake filling, prepare 1 package of whipped icing mix following directions. Fold in cherry pie filling. Fill cake. Spatula ice cake with buttercream. Pipe tip 21 shell bottom border. Position message. Insert Cupid and heart cookies in cake top. Cake serves 12; each cookie serves 1.

▼ Fondest Flowers

Candy: White Candy Melts®†, p. 162; Hearts Candy Mold, p. 199, Primary Candy Colors Set, p. 163
Cookie: Cookie Sheet, Cooling Grid, 8 in. Cookie Treat Sticks, p. 161; Rolling Pin, p. 131
Tip: 3, p. 140
Color: Rose, p. 135
Recipes: Color Flow Icing, Roll-Out Cookie, p. 114
Also: Heart, Round Cut-Outs™, p. 130; Color Flow Mix, p. 134; jelly spearmint leaves, scissors

Tint portion of melted white candy red using candy color. Mold 1 heart candy for each treat; refrigerate until firm. Roll out dough; for each treat, cut 1 round cookie using large Cut-Out and 4 heart cookies using medium Cut-Out. Bake and cool. Outline heart cookies with tip 3 and full-strength color flow; flow in with thinned color flow. Let set. Attach cookie stick to back of round cookies, heart cookies to front of round cookies and heart candy to center of treats with white melted candy; let set. Cut spearmint leaf lengthwise in half. Attach to stick with melted candy; let set. Each serves 1.

†Brand confectionery coating.

▶ Give Your Heart Away

Pans: 10½ x 15½ x 1 in. Jelly Roll, Cookie Sheet, Cooling Grid, p. 149
Tip: 3, p. 140
Colors: Red-Red, Rose, p. 135
Fondant: White Ready-To-Use Rolled Fondant (24 oz.), p. 128; Rolling Pin, Roll & Cut Mat, p. 131; Brush Set, p. 128
Recipes: Buttercream Icing, p. 114; Quick-Pour Fondant Icing, p. 115
Also: From the Heart Nesting Cutter Set, p. 200; ruler, paring knife

Bake and cool cake in jelly roll pan. Cut mini cakes using largest heart cutter. Cover cakes with quick-pour fondant icing (p. 115); let set. Tint portions of rolled fondant rose and red. For stripes, roll out rose fondant ⅛ in. thick; cut into ¼ in. wide strips. Position strips ¼ in. apart on cake top; trim ends to fit and attach with damp brush. For cake top heart, roll out red fondant ⅛ in. thick. Cut heart using smallest cutter; attach with damp brush. In buttercream, pipe tip 3 bead hearts on cake sides, approximately ¾ in. apart. Each serves 1.

▶ Hug-Lovin' Cupcakes

Pan: Standard Muffin, p. 149

Colors:* Rose, Red-Red, Christmas Red, Black, p. 135

Fondant: White Ready-To-Use Rolled Fondant (24 oz.), Brush Set, p. 128; Rolling Pin, Roll & Cut Mat, p. 131

Recipe: Buttercream Icing, p. 114

Also: White Candy Melts®†, p. 162; 4 in. Lollipop Sticks, p. 165; Hearts Plastic Nesting Cutter Set, Hearts Standard Baking Cups, p. 199; Fine Tip Primary Colors FoodWriter™ Edible Color Markers, p. 128; Gum-Tex™, p. 131; Cake Board, p. 225; cornstarch, waxed paper

In advance: Make fondant hearts, bows, hands and shoes. Add 1 teaspoon Gum-Tex to 8 oz. of fondant; tint half rose and half red. For hearts, roll out fondant ⅛ in. thick; cut using 2nd smallest cutter. For bows, shape ½ in. triangle loops and ¼ in. diameter ball knot. Attach to heart with damp brush. For legs, cut lollipop sticks to 3 in.; attach to back of hearts with melted candy. For arms, on a 3 in. stick, shape white fondant hands ½ in. long; attach to back of hearts with melted candy. For boy's shoes, tint a portion of fondant black. Shape ⅝ in. oval shoes; insert leg sticks through shoes, leaving 1¼ in. exposed at bottom for inserting in cupcake. Let all fondant pieces dry on waxed paper-covered board dusted with cornstarch.Ice cupcakes smooth in buttercream. Draw faces with FoodWriter. Insert hearts in cupcakes. Each serves 1.

*Combine Red-Red and Christmas Red for red shade shown.

◀ Snuggle Bugs

Pans: Mini Ball, p. 154; Cookie Sheet, Cooling Grid, p. 149

Candy: Candy Melts®† in White and Red, p. 162; Deep Heart Truffles Mold, p. 165; Garden Candy Color Set, Decorator Brush Set, p. 163

Also: Parchment Triangles, p. 138; Cake Board, p. 225; waxed paper, craft block, uncooked spaghetti, candy-coated chocolates, toothpick

In advance: Make antennae. Cut uncooked spaghetti 3 in. long, paint with melted red candy; let dry on waxed paper-covered board. Tint portion of melted white candy dark pink using candy color. Mold deep heart truffle; refrigerate until firm and unmold.

Tint portions of melted white candy light pink and black using candy colors. Cover mini ball cake with light pink candy (p. 124); let set. Using melted candy in cut parchment bag, pipe facial features, hearts on body. Attach head to body and candy-coated chocolates to antennae ends with melted candy. With toothpick, make small holes in top of head with toothpick and insert antennae. Each serves 1.

▶ For The Hearty Appetite

Pans: SweetHeart, p. 198; Mini Muffin, p. 149

Tip: 32, p. 141

Colors: Red-Red, Rose, p. 135

Fondant: White Ready-To-Use Rolled Fondant (72 oz.), Brush Set, p. 128; Cutter/Embosser, Easy-Glide Fondant Smoother, p. 129; Rolling Pin, Roll & Cut Mat, p. 131

Recipe: Buttercream Icing, p. 114

Also: Nesting Hearts Plastic Cutter Set, Hearts Remembered Icing Decorations (3 pks.), p. 199; White Mini Baking Cups, p. 184; Cake Board, Fanci-Foil Wrap, p. 225, plastic ruler

Bake and cool 2-layer SweetHeart cake (bake two 1½ in. high layers for a 3 in. high cake) and 16 mini cupcakes. Prepare SweetHeart cake for rolled fondant (p. 113). Tint 36 oz. of fondant rose and a 3 in. ball red; reserve remaining white. Cover cake with rose fondant; smooth with Fondant Smoother. Roll out white fondant ⅛ in. thick. Using Cutter/Embosser, cut a 3½ x 32 in. long strip; attach to bottom border with damp brush curving over top edge with fingers. Smooth with Fondant Smoother. Roll out rose fondant ⅛ in. thick. Using Cutter/Embosser, cut 20 strips, ¼ x 3½ in. high. Attach to cake sides with damp brush, 1½ in. apart. Roll out red fondant ⅛ in. thick; cut 20 hearts using 1¼ in. cutter from set. Attach hearts to cake sides with damp brush. On cupcake tops, pipe tip 32 swirl in buttercream. Position large heart icing decorations. Position cupcakes on SweetHeart cake. Cake serves 12; each cupcake serves 1.

▲ Making An Electrical Connection

Pans: Mini Loaf, Cookie Sheet, Cooling Grid, p. 149

Tip: 2, p. 140

Colors:* Moss Green, Lemon Yellow, Rose, Royal Blue, Violet, Brown, Orange, Red-Red, Christmas Red, p. 135

Fondant: White Ready-To-Use Rolled Fondant (48 oz.), Neon, Natural Colors Fondant Multi Packs, Brush Set, p. 128; Rolling Pin, Roll & Cut Mat, p. 131; People Cut-Outs™, p. 130

Recipes: Buttercream Icing, Color Flow Icing, Roll-Out Cookie, p. 114

Also: Color Flow Mix, p. 134; 101 Cookie Cutters Set, p. 160; Parchment Triangles, p. 138; Fine Tip Primary Colors FoodWriter™ Edible Color Markers, p. 128; Cake Board, Fanci-Foil Wrap, p. 225; ruler, paring knife

Prepare mini cakes for rolled fondant (p. 113); cover with white fondant. For photo backgrounds, tint 1½ in. balls of white fondant green, yellow and violet; tint 1 in. balls rose and light blue. Roll out ⅛ in. thick; cut 1½ x 2 in. rectangles. Attach to cakes with damp brush.

Roll out natural and neon fondant ⅛ in. thick. Cut natural heads and neon clothes using people Cut-Outs. Shape arms to fit. Roll small balls for noses. Attach with damp brush. Using full-strength color flow, pipe tip 2 pull-out or swirl hair. Draw features and messages using FoodWriter.

Roll out dough; cut cookies using medium and small heart cutters and alphabet cutters. For dot cookie, roll a ½ in. ball of dough; flatten slightly. Bake and cool all cookies. Tint color flow red and rose. Outline cookies with tip 2 (p. 124). Flow in with thinned color flow in parchment bag with opening cut to size of tip 2; let set. Position cakes and cookies. Each serves 1.

*Combine Red-Red and Christmas Red for red shown. Combine Violet with Rose for violet shown. Combine Brown with a little Red-Red for brown shown.

▼ Flirtation Cakes

Pan: 9 x 13 x 2 in. Sheet, p. 148

Tip: 3, p. 140

Colors:* Rose, Violet, Lemon Yellow, Sky Blue, Creamy Peach, p. 135

Fondant: White Ready-To-Use Rolled Fondant (24 oz.), p. 128; Rolling Pin, Roll & Cut Mat, p. 131

Recipes: Buttercream Icing, p. 114; Quick-Pour Fondant Icing, p. 115

Also: Nesting Hearts Plastic Cutter Set, p. 199; Cooling Grid, p. 149; paring knife, ruler

Bake and cool 1-layer sheet cake, 1¼ in. high. Cut into 2 in. squares using knife. Prepare cakes for poured fondant by icing lightly with buttercream. Divide poured fondant into 5 portions; tint rose, blue, peach, violet and yellow. Cover cakes with poured fondant (p. 124); let set.

Tint 5 portions of fondant slightly darker than poured fondant shades. Roll out ⅛ in. thick. Cut a heart to match each cake color using smallest cutter from set. Position on cakes. Pipe tip 3 dots in buttercream. Each serves 1.

*Combine Violet with a little Rose for violet shown.

▶ Val Gals

Cookie: Cookie Sheet, Cooling Grid, p. 149; Nesting Hearts Plastic Cutter Set, 8 in. Cookie Treat Sticks, p. 199

Tips: 2, 4, 21, p. 140-141

Colors: Copper (skin tone), Violet, Rose, Lemon Yellow, Black, Red-Red, p. 135

Recipes: Royal Icing, Roll-Out Cookie, p. 114

Also: Cake Board, p. 225; Disposable Decorating Bags, p. 138; Meringue Powder, p. 134; waxed paper, cornstarch, ruler

In advance: Make bows. Using royal icing, on waxed paper, outline and pipe in 2 in. wide x 1 in. high bow shape with tip 4 (smooth with finger dipped in cornstarch); let set. Add tip 4 ball knot; let set.

Roll out dough. Cut heart cookies using 2nd largest cutter; bake and cool. Outline and pipe in tip 2 sunglasses and mouth. Position cookies on waxed paper-covered board. Pipe tip 21 pull-out star hair, curving into a flip at end; let set. Attach cookies to sticks and bows to cookies with royal icing; let set. Each serves 1.

▲ An Arrow For Your Beau

Pans: Standard Muffin, Cooling Grid, p. 149

Colors:* Red-Red, Rose, p. 135

Candy: Candy Melts®† in White and Red (1 pk. each), p. 162; 4 in. Lollipop Sticks, p. 165

Recipe: Buttercream Icing, p. 114

Also: Hearts Remembered Baking Cups, p. 199; Hearts Mix Sprinkle Decorations, p. 200; Heart Cut-Outs™, p. 130; Spatula, Parchment Triangles, p. 138; Cake Circle, p. 225; waxed paper, scissors, ruler

In advance: Make candy hearts for arrow. Place medium and small heart Cut-Outs on waxed paper-covered cake circle. Pipe in hearts using melted red candy in cut parchment bag; tap gently to spread evenly into corners. Refrigerate until firm; unmold. Trim lollipop stick to 3½ in.; position on waxed paper-covered cake circle. Pipe pull-out feathers on ends of stick using melted white candy in cut parchment bag; let set. On edge of medium heart, pipe scallops with melted red candy; let set. Attach hearts to stick with melted candy; let set.

Ice cupcakes smooth with spatula; add sprinkles. Position arrow; using a cut parchment bag, pipe a small mound of icing behind medium heart for support. Each serves 1.

*Combine Red-Red and Rose for pink shade shown on cupcakes.

▼ Using The Right Line

Pans: Oval Pan Set (13½ x 9⅞ x 2 in. used), p. 148; Stand-Up Cuddly Bear Set, p. 153; Standard Muffin, p. 149

Tips: 3, 4, 12, 16, p. 140-141

Colors:* Violet, Royal Blue, Rose, Lemon Yellow, Golden Yellow, Kelly Green, Brown, Black, p. 135

Recipes: Buttercream Icing, p. 114; Thinned Fondant Adhesive, p. 115

Fondant: White Ready-To-Use Rolled Fondant (72 oz.), p. 128; Heart Cut-Outs™, p. 130; Rolling Pin, Roll & Cut Mat, p. 131; Easy-Glide Fondant Smoother, p. 129

Also: 8 in. Lollipop Sticks, p. 165; Cake Boards, Fanci-Foil Wrap, p. 225; Fine Tip Primary FoodWriter™ Edible Color Markers, p. 128; Decorator Brush Set, p. 163; Gum-Tex™, p. 131; Dowel Rods, p. 224; 2 ft. pink ribbon, cornstarch, paring knife, plastic ruler

In advance: Make fondant hearts and bait bucket (p. 121). Tint 30 oz. violet, 18 oz. blue, 1 oz. each yellow, rose and green. Add 1 teaspoon Gum-Tex to blue; add ⅛ teaspoon Gum-Tex each to 1½ in. balls of violet and white fondant.

Bake and cool 2-layer oval and stand-up bear cakes (use firm-textured batter such as pound cake for bear) and prepare for stacked construction (p. 112). Ice oval cake smooth in rose buttercream. For dock, roll out violet fondant ⅛ in. thick; using oval pan as a pattern, cut an oval approximately 1 in. larger overall. Position on cake; smooth with Fondant Smoother. For dock posts, cut ⅞ in. wide x 3 in. long strips; attach to cake sides, 2½ in. apart, with damp brush. For water, roll out blue fondant ⅛ in. thick; cut 1¼ in. wide strip to fit around cake bottom border. Using a paring knife, cut waves along top edge. Attach with damp brush. On bear cake, trim off arm that touches mouth. For hands, roll out two 1½ in. diameter balls of white fondant. Cut 2 lollipop sticks to 3 in. Insert 1 in. deep into hands then insert in arm areas on front of cake. Build up arms with tip 12. Using tip 4 and buttercream, pipe in nose, ears, and pads of feet (smooth with finger dipped in cornstarch). Outline eyes and mouth with tip 3. Cover bear with tip 16 stars. For fishing pole, cut 12 in. of ribbon; tie into a bow at end of a lollipop stick. For fishing line, attach a heart to end of remaining ribbon with fondant adhesive; let dry. Tie onto stick leaving approximately 9 in. hanging.

Position bear cake on oval cake. Insert fishing pole. Position bait bucket and hearts. Serves 32.

*Combine Lemon Yellow with Golden Yellow for yellow shown. Combine Violet with Rose for violet shown.

▲ Cupcake Parade

Pan: Standard Muffin, p. 149

Tip: 1M (2110), p. 141

Colors: Violet, Kelly Green, Lemon Yellow, Rose, p. 135

Fondant: White Ready-To-Use Rolled Fondant (24 oz.), p. 128; Leaf Cut-Outs™, p. 130; Rolling Pin, Roll & Cut Mat, p. 131

Candy: Smiley Face Lollipop Mold, p. 164; White Candy Melts®†, p. 162; Primary, Garden Candy Color Sets, Decorator Brush Set, p. 163

Recipe: Buttercream Icing, p. 114

Also: Standard Cupcakes 'N More™ Dessert Stand, p. 137; Color Mist™ Food Color Spray in Green, Yellow, Pink, Violet, p. 135; Colored Sugars in Dark Green, Yellow, Pink, Lavender, p. 136; Gum-Tex™, p. 131; Gold Foil Standard Baking Cups, p. 184; Parchment Triangles, p. 138; 6 in. Cookie Treat Sticks, p. 161; ruler, embroidery scissors, glue gun, paring knife, assorted Mardi Gras masks, beads, bows, craft block, 1½ in. wide ribbon (8 in.)

In advance: Make candy faces. Tint portions of melted candy skin tone using orange color from Primary Set and black using black from Garden Set. Mold faces without sticks filling cavities ½ full. Refrigerate until firm. **Also:** Make fondant hats and masks. Tint 6 oz. fondant each in violet, green, rose and yellow. Add 1 teaspoon Gum-Tex to each fondant color. For hats, roll 3 cone shapes, 1¾ x ½ in. wide, tapering to a point. Flatten slightly. Attach to heads with melted candy. Using toothpick, score lines across hats to resemble fabric; bend down points. Roll ⅜ in. fondant balls and attach to points with melted candy. For headband, cut a 2 x ⅜ in. strip; attach with candy. Using melted black candy in cut parchment bag, pipe eyes and mouth; let set. For masks, cut 1¼ in. diameter fondant circles; cut each in half. Using paring knife, cut curve on straight bottom and 2 small eyeholes. Attach to faces with melted candy. Cut feathers using smallest leaf Cut-Out; trim off bottoms for side feathers. Score vein lines using toothpick. Bend feathers; attach to faces with melted candy. For fringe, cut strips 1¼ x ⅜ in. wide; cut slits using scissors. Attach to faces with melted candy.

Decorate dessert stand by attaching bead garlands to bottom row with hot glue. Pipe tip 1M swirl on cupcake tops. Spray tops with Color Mist; sprinkle with matching sugars. Position faces on cupcakes. Position cupcakes. For topper, cut craft block to a 2 in. diameter x 1½ in. high circle. Wrap sides with ribbon. Attach masks and beads to cookie treat sticks with hot glue; insert in container. Attach beads to base and top of craft block with hot glue. Attach bows to masks with hot glue. Position topper on stand; secure with hot glue. Each serves 1.

†Brand confectionery coating.

◀ The King's Cake

Pan: Crown, p. 151
Tips: 3, 5, 14, 16, p. 140-141
Colors:* Lemon Yellow, Golden Yellow, Rose, Kelly Green, Violet, p. 135
Recipe: Buttercream Icing, p. 114
Also: 2007 Pattern Book (Large, Medium and Small Diamonds, Large and Small Circles and Ovals), p. 126; Piping Gel, p. 134; Cake Board, Fanci-Foil Wrap, p. 225; Spatula, Parchment Triangles, p. 138; toothpick, cornstarch

Ice cake sides and background areas smooth. Mark patterns with toothpick. Using buttercream and tip 3, outline pattern areas in yellow and fill in with white. Outline crown with tip 3; fill in with tip 16 stars. On base of crown, pipe 7 circles with tip 5, building up for dimension (pat smooth with finger dipped in cornstarch). Pipe tip 14 pull-out stars around circles. Tint piping gel rose, green and violet. Pipe in pattern areas using tinted piping gel in cut parchment bag. Pipe tip 3 ball bottom border. Serves 12.

*Combine Lemon Yellow with Golden Yellow for yellow shown. Combine Violet with Rose for violet shown.

▶ Mask Munchies

Cookie: Heart Nesting Plastic Cutter Set, p. 160; Cookie Sheet, Cooling Grid, p. 149; 6 in. Cookie Treat Sticks, p. 161
Tips: 2A, 3, 5, 12, 67, p. 140-141
Colors: Rose, Kelly Green, Lemon Yellow, Violet, p. 135
Recipes: Royal Icing, Roll-Out Cookie, p. 114
Also: 2007 Pattern Book (Masks), p. 126; Meringue Powder, p. 134; cornstarch, toothpicks

Cut cookies using 3½ in. (2nd largest) cutter; bake and cool. Lightly trace mask patterns on cookies with toothpick. Outline and fill in mask with tip 5 (pat smooth with finger dipped in cornstarch). On yellow mask, pipe tip 67 pull-out feathers; add tip 3 dots. On rose mask, pipe pull-out crown points using tip 2A for 3 center points and tip 12 for points on each side. Add tip 5 ball to each point. Pipe tip 5 zigzag fur on top edge of mask; add tip 5 dots. Attach cookies to sticks with royal icing; let dry. Each serves 1.

◀ The Ultimate Party Hat!

Pan: Fanci-Fill 2-Piece Non-Stick Set (8¾ x 2 in. pans) , p. 144
Colors:* Lemon Yellow, Golden Yellow, Rose, Kelly Green, Violet, p. 135
Fondant: White Ready-To-Use Rolled Fondant (48 oz.), p. 128; Round, Alphabet/Number Cut-Outs™, p. 130; Rolling Pin, Roll & Cut Mat, p. 131; Cutter/Embosser, p. 129; Brush Set, p. 128
Recipe: Buttercream Icing, p. 114
Also: 2007 Pattern Book (Crown Arches, Cross), p. 126; Cake Board, p. 225; Flowerful Medley Sprinkle Decorations, Cake Sparkles™ in Purple, Green and Pink, p. 136; Gum-Tex™, p. 131; Vanilla Whipped Icing Mix, p. 134; paring knife, toothpicks, cornstarch, waxed paper, ruler, cake plate

Several days in advance: Make fondant cake top pieces. Mix 24 oz. fondant with 2 teaspoons Gum-Tex; tint yellow. Roll out 3⁄16 in. thick. Cut 8 arch strips, 8½ x 1 in. wide. Cover arch patterns with waxed paper; dust with cornstarch. Position strips on patterns, resting on sides; let dry. **Also:** Using pattern, cut out cross. Insert toothpick in bottom and let dry on cake board dusted with cornstarch. Roll and stack 1¼ and 2 in. diameter fondant balls for cross base; stack together and make center hole using toothpick. Remove toothpick; position on cornstarch-dusted board. Reserve remaining yellow fondant. For jewel pieces, tint 4 oz. portions of fondant purple, rose and green. Roll out ⅛ in. thick. Using smallest round Cut-Out, cut 50 circles in each color. Brush tops with water and sprinkle with matching color Cake Sparkles.

Prepare 2-layer cake mix; bake and cool cake following pan directions. Prepare whipped icing mix, and add confetti sprinkles. Fill and assemble cake following package directions. Ice smooth. Roll out reserved yellow fondant ⅛ in. thick. Cut a ¾ in. wide strip for top and bottom borders, long enough to wrap around cake; position on cake. Using damp brush, attach fondant circles ¼ in. apart on arches and border strips. Roll out violet fondant ⅛ in. thick; cut letters and "!" using Cut-Outs. Attach message with icing. Insert cross in base; position on cake top. Position arch pieces. Serves 24.

*Combine Lemon Yellow with Golden Yellow for yellow shown.

◀ Shamrock Snack

Pan: Shamrock, p. 200

Cookie: Metal Shamrock Cutter, p. 200; Cookie Sheet, p. 149

Also: Cake Release, p. 132; hot roll mix (2 pks.), 3 lbs. ready-made spinach dip (or favorite recipe), sliced white bread

Prepare hot roll mix following package directions. Prepare pan with Cake Release. Press dough into pan for final rising time. Bake, remove and cool following roll mix directions. Cut shamrocks from white bread using cutter; toast on cookie sheet in 400°F oven for 7 to 8 minutes or until edges are golden brown. Hollow out shamrock bread loaf leaving a ½ in. rim of crust. Cut away void areas between petals and stem. Fill with spinach dip. Position shamrock on serving tray with toasts. Serves 24-30.

▶ Dublin Derby

Pan: Mini Ball, p. 154

Colors:* Leaf Green, Lemon Yellow, Golden Yellow, Black, p. 135

Fondant: White Ready-To-Use Rolled Fondant, Brush Set, p. 128; Rolling Pin, Roll & Cut Mat, p. 131

Recipe: Buttercream Icing, p. 114

Also: Shamrock Fun Pix®, p. 200; cornstarch, cotton balls, paring knife

Prepare cakes for rolled fondant (p. 113). For each cake, tint a 2¾ in. ball of fondant green, a 1¾ in. ball black and a 1 in. ball yellow. Cover cakes with green fondant and smooth. Roll out all fondant ⅛ in. thick. For brim, cut a 5 in. green circle; place on cornstarch-dusted board. Attach cake to brim with buttercream. Shape slight curves in brim and let dry, supporting curved areas with cotton balls. For hatband, cut a 10 x ⅜ in. black rectangle; for buckle, cut a ½ x ¾ in. yellow rectangle and cut out center. Attach with damp brush. Trim shamrock pick to 1 in.; insert in cake. Each serves 1.

*Combine Leaf Green with a little Lemon Yellow for green shown. Combine Lemon Yellow with a little Golden Yellow for yellow shown.

▼ Irish Pride

Cookie: Gingerbread Boy Metal Cutter, p. 158; Cookie Sheet, Cooling Grid, p. 149

Tips: 2, 3, 4, 7, p. 140

Colors:* Lemon Yellow, Golden Yellow, Leaf Green, Kelly Green, Orange, Black, Red-Red, Christmas Red, Copper (skin tone), p. 135

Recipe: Royal Icing, Roll-Out Cookie, p. 114

Also: Shamrock Fun Pix®, p. 200; Cake Release, p. 132; Meringue Powder, p. 134; Rolling Pin, p. 131; round toothpicks, cornstarch

Tint dough copper. Roll out and cut boy cookies; reserve some dough. Brush a toothpick with Cake Release; position at end of one hand. Thin reserved dough with water; pipe tip 3 ball nose, ears and fingers. Bake and cool cookies; remove toothpick. Using royal icing, pipe in tip 3 socks, shirt, shoes and striped overalls. Add tip 7 band suspenders, tip 4 ball buttons (flatten and smooth with finger dipped in cornstarch). Pipe tip 2 outline buckles on shoes. Pipe in tip 3 mouth; add tip 3 zigzag beard and dot eyes. Pipe tip 2 outline eyebrows and dot tongue. Pipe in tip 4 hat with tip 3 outline brim and hat band. Add tip 4 outline hat buckle. Insert Shamrock pick in hand which held toothpick. Each serves 1.

*Combine Red-Red with Christmas Red for red shown. Combine Leaf Green with a little Lemon Yellow for green shirt. Combine Lemon Yellow with a little Golden Yellow for yellow button and buckle.

†Brand confectionery coating.

See instructions on facing page.

▶ Going for the Gold

Pan: Little Pirate, p. 154
Tips: 3, 4, 6, 7, 12, 16, 21, p. 140-141
Colors:* Kelly Green, Leaf Green, Golden Yellow, Lemon Yellow, Black, Orange, Copper (skin tone), p. 135
Recipes: Buttercream Icing, Roll-Out Cookie, p. 114
Also: 2007 Pattern Book (Leprechaun Hat), p. 126; Cookie Sheet, Cooling Grid, p. 149; Cake Boards, Fanci-Foil Wrap, p. 225; Rolling Pin, p. 131; Spatula, p. 138; foil-wrapped candy coins, large marshmallows, toothpick, knife, cornstarch, paring knife

Roll out dough; trace hat pattern using toothpick. Cut out cookie; bake and cool. Outline hat with tip 3; fill in hat and brim with tip 16 stars. Pipe in tip 12 hat band and buckle (smooth with finger dipped in cornstarch).

Trim facial features from cake. Ice sides and background areas smooth. Pipe in mouth with tip 7 and tongue with tip 4 (smooth with finger dipped in cornstarch). Add tip 3 string eyes. Cover face with tip 16 stars; overpipe nose. Outline pot with tip 3; pipe in with tip 12. Smooth with spatula. Add tip 12 band rim. Outline rest of body with tip 3; build up arm areas with tip 12. Cover arms, legs and shoes with tip 16 stars. For socks, pipe tip 16 vertical stripes in alternating light and dark green. Pipe tip 16 star hands. Pipe tip 6 outline shoe buckles. Add tip 16 swirl hair, beard and pull-out star eyebrows. Pipe tip 21 star bottom border.

Position hat cookie on cake; position large marshmallow to support cookie overhang. Position candy coins. Cake serves 12; cookie serves 1-6.

*Combine Leaf Green with a little Lemon Yellow for light green used on cuffs and socks.

See instructions on facing page.

▶ Leprechaun Lids!

Candy: Cordial Cups Mold, p. 165; Green Candy Melts®†, p. 162
Fondant: White Ready-To-Use Rolled Fondant, p. 128; Rolling Pin, Roll & Cut Mat, p. 131; Brush Set, p. 128
Colors:* Black, Lemon Yellow, Golden Yellow, p. 135
Recipe: Peanut Butter Filling, p. 115
Also: Cake Board, p. 225; waxed paper, paring knife

Mold cordial cups following mold package directions; refrigerate until firm. Fill cups with Peanut Butter Filling; seal top with melted candy. Refrigerate until firm; unmold. For hat brims, trace 2 in. circles on waxed paper-covered board. Pipe in circles with melted candy; refrigerate until firm. Remove waxed paper from circles and attach to cups with melted candy. Tint a 1½ in. ball of fondant black and a ½ in. ball yellow; roll out ⅛ in. thick. for hat band, cut 5 x 3/16 in. strips in black; attach with damp brush. For buckle, cut out ¼ in. squares in yellow. Cut out a small square from center with knife; attach with damp brush. Each serves 1.

*Combine Lemon Yellow with a little Golden Yellow for yellow shown.

▶ Wearing His Spring Coat

Pans: Stand-Up Lamb, p. 201; Mini Loaf, p. 149
Tip: 2, p. 140
Colors:* Rose, Brown, Red-Red, p. 135
Also: Vanilla Whipped Icing Mix, p. 134; Straight Spatula, p. 138; Cake Board, Fanci-Foil Wrap, p. 225; White Candy Melts®†, p. 162; Assorted Jordan Almonds, p. 227; shredded coconut, vegetable shortening, zip-close plastic bag, potato peeler or cheese plane, cornstarch

In advance: Make candy curls (p. 124). Bake and cool lamb cake using firm-textured batter such as pound cake. Ice face and ears smooth; pipe tip 2 dot eyes, nose and inside ears (pat smooth with finger dipped in cornstarch). Add tip 2 string mouth. Ice remainder of cake and cover with candy curls. Tint coconut green (p. 119) and sprinkle around cake. Position Jordan Almonds. Serves 12.

*Combine Brown with Red-Red for brown shown.

†Brand confectionery coating.

▶ Tiptoe Through Tulips

Pan: 3-D Bunny, p. 201
Tips: 1, 2, 3, 18, p. 140-141
Colors: Rose, Royal Blue, Black, Leaf Green, p. 135
Fondant: White Ready-To-Use Rolled Fondant (24 oz.), p. 128; Flower Former Set, p. 129; Rolling Pin, Roll & Cut Mat, p. 131
Candy: White Candy Melts® † (2 pks.), p. 162; Garden Goodies 2-Pack Mold Set, p. 164; Primary, Garden Candy Color Sets, Decorator Brush Set, p. 163
Recipes: Buttercream, Royal Icings, p. 114; Gum Paste, p. 115
Also: 2007 Pattern Book (Ears, Eyes), p. 126; Gum Paste Mix, p. 131; Meringue Powder, p. 134; Cookie Sheet, 6 in. Cookie Treat Sticks, p. 161; 8 in. Cake Circle, Fanci-Foil Wrap, p. 225; Flower Former Set, p. 129; Parchment Triangles, p. 138; shredded coconut, zip-close plastic bag, waxed paper, 1 in. wide satin ribbon (12 in.), cornstarch, paring knife, toothpicks,

In advance: Make candy tulips. Melt 2 pks. of white candy; tint ⅓ cup each in violet, rose, yellow using candy colors. Tint 1 cup lime green (mix equal amounts of green and yellow tinted candy); reserve remainder white. Mold candies using painting and layering methods (p. 123); refrigerate until firm, unmold. Flatten bottom of each candy by placing on a warm cookie sheet or warming tray. Stand candies on waxed paper-covered board; pipe puddle bases around tulips using melted candy in cut parchment bag. Refrigerate until firm. Make ears. Prepare gum paste. Roll out ⅛ in. thick; using pattern and knife, cut ears. Position in medium flower former heavily dusted with cornstarch. Tint a 2 in. ball of gum paste rose; roll out ⅛ in. thick and cut 2 ear centers using pattern. Attach centers to ears with damp brush. Bend one ear to curl and let dry overnight.

Bake and cool bunny cake using firm-textured batter such as pound cake. Trim off ears. Generously ice around nose and ear area to form oval head. Lightly ice face. Tint a 1 in. ball of fondant rose; roll out ⅛ in. thick. Cut a 1¼ x ⅝ in. oval and attach for mouth. For lower lip, roll a log of white fondant 1¼ in. x ¼ in. diameter; attach with buttercream. For muzzle, roll two ovals, 1 x ½ in. high; flatten slightly and attach. For nose, shape and attach a rose oval ½ x ⅜ in. high. Lightly ice eye area with buttercream; trace eye pattern with toothpick. Outline eyes with tip 2; pipe in whites of eyes and pupils with tip 3 (smooth with finger dipped in cornstarch). Add tip 1 dot highlights. Cover cake with tip 18 stars. Attach cookie treat sticks to backs of ears with melted candy; let set. Insert ears in cake. With royal icing, cover sides and back of ears with tip 18 stars. Tie ribbon into bow; attach with buttercream. Tint coconut green (p. 119) and sprinkle around cake. Position candy tulips. Cake serves 12; each candy serves 1.

◀ All Eggs in One Basket

Pan: Huggable Teddy Bear, p. 153

Tips: 2, 2A, 4, 8, 16, 233, p. 140-141

Colors:* Royal Blue, Brown, Red-Red, Rose, Black, Leaf Green, Lemon Yellow, p. 135

Recipes: Buttercream Icing, Roll-Out Cookie, p. 114

Also: 2007 Pattern Book (Ear, Front Paw, Back Paw), p. 126; Petite Eggs Icing Decorations, p. 202; Bunny/Ducks Mix Sprinkle Decorations, p. 203; Cookie Sheet, Cooling Grid, p. 161; Cake Boards, Fanci-Foil Wrap, p. 225; paring knife, large marshmallows, cornstarch, toothpick

Roll out cookie dough; trace patterns with toothpick. With knife, cut one each ear, front and back paw. Reverse patterns and repeat. Bake and cool cookies and cake. Ice cake sides smooth. Using tip 4, pipe in inside ears and back paw pads on cookies, tongue on cake. Using tip 4, outline and pipe in mouth; build up nose (pat smooth with finger dipped in cornstarch). Build up cheeks with tip 2A. Pipe in whites of eyes using tip 4 (pat smooth); pipe in pupils (pat smooth). Build up basket area on tummy; cover with tip 8 basketweave. Edge top of basket with tip 8 rope border. Cover bunny and cookies with tip 16 stars. Pipe tip 8 rope basket handle. Position ears, supporting with marshmallows; position paws. Position icing decoration eggs in basket. Pipe tip 2 pull-out grass around eggs. Pipe tip 233 pull-out grass bottom border. Add sprinkles on grass. Cake serves 12; each cookie serves 1.

*Combine Leaf Green and Lemon Yellow for green shown. Combine Brown with Red-Red for brown shown.

▶ Rabbit's Haul

Pan: Step-By-Step Bunny, p. 201

Colors: Rose, Brown, p. 135

Fondant: White Ready-To-Use Rolled Fondant (72 oz.), p. 128; Rolling Pin, Roll & Cut Mat, p. 131

Candy: Orange Candy Melts®† (1 pk.), p. 162; Primary Candy Color Set, p. 163

Recipes: Buttercream Icing, p. 114; favorite crisped rice cereal treats

Also: Cookie Sheet, Cooling Grid, p. 149; Piping Gel, p. 134; Disposable Decorating Bags, p. 138; Cake Boards, Fanci-Foil Wrap, p. 225; sugar cones, shredded coconut, vegetable shortening, granulated sugar, jelly spearmint leaves, waxed paper

In advance: Make carrots. Prepare crisped rice cereal treats; fill sugar cones with mixture, mounding slightly at top. Melt candy; add orange candy color to brighten and thin with a small amount of vegetable shortening. Cover cones with melted candy (p. 124). Let set on waxed paper-covered board. For stems, cut spearmint leaves lengthwise in half; roll out lightly on surface sprinkled with granulated sugar. Attach leaves to cones with melted candy; set aside.

Position bunny cake on triple-thick foil-wrapped board cut to fit cake plus 8 in. at bottom for arm area. For neck, roll an 8 oz. piece of fondant into a 5 in. long x 1¼ in. diameter log; position at bottom of bunny cake. Roll out fondant ⅛ in. thick; cut an 8 x 5 in. rectangle base to support cones and position at bottom of cake. For each arm, shape 24 oz. of fondant into an 12 x 1½ in. diameter log; flatten slightly. Attach tapered ends to neck with icing and curve around cake board. Shape hands for paw and thumb areas. Trim rectangle base to fit arms if needed. Ice cake and arms with spatula, building up nose and muzzle area. Tint a 2 in. ball of fondant rose and a 1½ in. ball brown. Press coconut on cake and arms, leaving inside of ears open. Roll out rose fondant ⅛ in. thick; cut ovals to fit inside ears and position. Shape thin logs for eyes and whiskers and a ¾ in. flattened ball for nose; position on cake. Slightly lift arms and position carrots. Cake serves 12; each carrot serves 1.

Cottontail Carousel

Pan: 9 x 13 x 2 in. Sheet, p. 148
Tips: 1, 3, p. 140
Colors:* Violet, Rose, Kelly Green, Brown, p. 135
Cookie: Easter Cutter Collection, p. 203; Circle Metal Cutter, p. 158; Cookie Sheet, Cooling Grid, p. 149; Rolling Pin, p. 131
Candy: White Candy Melts®†, p. 162; Primary, Garden Candy Color Sets, p. 163; 6 in. Lollipop Sticks, p. 165
Recipes: Color Flow Icing, Roll-Out Cookie, p. 114; favorite crisped rice cereal treats
Also: Color Flow Mix, p. 134; Parchment Triangles, p. 138; pastel candy-coated chocolates, pink gumballs, pink curling ribbon (12 in. for each treat), white card stock, marking pen, cellophane tape, scissors, knife

Prepare cereal treats and press into pan, 1 in. thick. Cut 1 base for each treat using circle cutter. Tint portions of melted white candy pink, green and yellow using candy colors. Cover bases with melted candy (p. 124). Attach candy-coated chocolates to side with melted candy; let set.

Roll out dough and cut 1 bunny for each treat; bake and cool. Using full-strength color flow, outline bunny, ear and saddle with tip 3; let set. Flow in using thinned color flow in cut parchment bag. Pipe tip 1 dot eye, string mouth and feet with full-strength color flow; let set.

Wrap lollipop sticks with curling ribbon; secure with tape. Cut a small hole in gumball; insert on end of stick. Attach bunny with melted candy. Insert stick into base. Cut flags from card stock; write names and tape to stick. Each serves 1.

*Combine Violet with Rose for violet shown.

▲ Easter Parade Pops

Pan: Non-Stick Cookie Sheet, p. 146
Colors:* Rose, Violet, Golden Yellow, Kelly Green, p. 135
Fondant: White Ready-To-Use Rolled Fondant (24 oz.), Brush Set, p. 128; Quick Ease Roller, p. 129; Roll & Cut Mat, p. 131
Candy: Candy Melts®† in Yellow, Blue, Light Cocoa, White (1 pk. each), p. 162; Primary and Garden Candy Color Sets, p. 163; Cordial Cups Candy Mold, p. 165; Garden Goodies 2-Pack Mold Set, p. 164; 6 in. Lollipop Sticks, p. 165
Also: Circle Metal Cookie Cutter, p. 158; Floral Collection Flower Making Set, p. 130; Parchment Triangles, p. 138; paring knife, 6 in. ruler, waxed paper, craft block, cornstarch

In advance: Make candy pieces. For faces, tint melted white candy flesh tone using pink, yellow and orange candy colors. Position circle cookie cutter on non-stick cookie sheet; fill ⅛ in. deep. Refrigerate until firm; unmold. For man, using blue candy, mold 1 solid cordial cup hat and one 2¼ in. diameter circle for brim on waxed paper. Mold woman's hat using yellow candy and garden set mold. Refrigerate all until firm; unmold.

Trim off ⅛ in. at top of man's head to fit hat. Place faces on waxed paper-covered board; pipe hair, facial features, moustache and cheeks on faces using melted candy in cut parchment bag. Attach hat pieces with melted candy; let set.

Tint portions of fondant rose, violet, yellow and green. Roll out ⅛ in. thick. Cut rose, violet and yellow flowers using apple blossom cutter from flower making set. Cut green leaves using smallest rose leaf cutter from set; trim around leaf edges. For flower centers, roll small balls of white fondant; attach with damp brush. For feather, cut a 2 x ½ in. wide leaf shape with knife; cut slits to feather edges. For hatbands, cut 3 x ⅜ in. high strips. For bow ties, cut 5 x ⅝ in. high strips. Brush ends with water; fold ends to meet at center; pinch center together. Cut a 1 x ¼ in. high strip for knot and attach around center with damp brush. For woman's hat bow, cut a 5 x 1 in. high strip; repeat same procedure as other bows, without center knot. Attach sticks to heads and bow ties to sticks with melted candy. Attach remaining fondant pieces with melted candy. Insert in craft block to set. Each serves 1.

*Combine Violet and Rose for violet shown.

▶ Bunches for Bunny!

Cookie: Bunny Cookie Treat Pan, 6 in. Cookie Treat Sticks, p. 201; Cookie Sheet, Cooling Grid, p. 149; Rolling Pin, p. 131
Tip: 3, p. 140
Colors: Rose, Black, Kelly Green, p. 135
Recipes: Royal Icing, Roll-Out Cookie, p. 114
Also: 2007 Pattern Book (Paw), p. 126; Oval Cut-Outs™, p. 130; Meringue Powder, p. 134; candy corn, white chenille bumpy pipe cleaners, white heavyweight card stock, pencil, scissors, cornstarch, paring knife

Roll out a portion of dough; cut an oval cookie for each treat using largest Cut-Out. Using knife, cut one long side of cookie straight. Bake and cool oval cookies and bunny treat cookies on sticks. Cover oval and bunny cookies with thinned royal icing (p. 124); let set. Twist a pipe cleaner around each stick for arms (p. 119). Attach oval cookie to stick with royal icing, positioning straight edge against bunny neck. Using tip 3, pipe dot and string facial features, pipe in inside ears (smooth with finger dipped in cornstarch). Attach candy corn carrots to oval cookie with dots of icing; let set. Pipe tip 3 pull-out stems on carrots. Using pattern and card stock, cut 2 paws for each bunny. Bend arms together in front of oval cookie. Attach paws with royal icing; let set. Each serves 1.

▲ Ballerinas Are Tutu Cute!

Tips: 2, 3, 8, 104, p. 140
Colors:* Black, Rose, Violet, Lemon Yellow, Golden Yellow, Royal Blue, p. 135
Cookie: Easter Cutter Collection, Nesting Bunnies Plastic Cutter Set, p. 203; Cookie Sheet, Cooling Grid, p. 149; Rolling Pin, p. 131
Recipes: Royal Icing, Roll-Out Cookie, p. 114
Also: Meringue Powder, p. 134; cornstarch

Roll out dough; cut bunny head and carrot cookies using cutters from sets. Bake and cool. Attach head to top of carrot with royal icing. Ice cookies (pat smooth with finger dipped in cornstarch). Pipe tip 8 outline legs using heavy pressure. With tip 3, pipe dot shoes with string straps; outline and pipe in leotard, ears and bow. Pipe tip 2 outline eyes and mouth; add tip 3 dot nose and cheeks. Pipe tip 104 ruffle. Each serves 1.

*Combine Violet with Rose for violet shown. Combine Lemon Yellow with Golden Yellow for yellow shown.

▶ On the Wing this Spring!

Pan: Mini Ball, p. 154

Cookie: Easter Mini Cutter Set, p. 203; Cookie Sheet, Cooling Grid, p. 149

Tips: 3, 16, p. 140-141

Colors: Orange, Black, Lemon Yellow, p. 135

Recipes: Buttercream Icing, Roll-Out Cookie, p. 114

Also: Straight Spatula, p. 138; Cake Board, Fanci-Foil Wrap, p. 225; large marshmallows, scissors, cornstarch

For each chick, cut, bake and cool 4 tulip cookies for wings and feet, bake and cool ½ mini ball cake for head. For body, slightly trim marshmallow vertically to lay flat on board. Position head and body, cut side down, on a foil-wrapped cake board, cut to fit. Ice head and body fluffy. Pipe tip 16 pull-out feathers on wing cookies and top of head. Ice feet smooth. Pipe tip 3 ball whites of eyes, pupils and cheeks (flatten and smooth with finger dipped in cornstarch). Ice mouth area smooth; add tip 3 outline beak, tapering lines to corners of beak. Attach wings and feet to body with dots of icing. Each serves 1.

Egg Expedition

Pan: Long Loaf, p. 149

Colors: Kelly Green, Leaf Green, Rose, Lemon Yellow, Violet, Brown, p. 135

Fondant: White Ready-To-Use Rolled Fondant (24 oz.), Brush Set, p. 128; Rolling Pin, Roll & Cut Mat, p. 131

Cookie: Easter Mini Cutter Set, Hoppy Easter Colored Metal Cutter Set, Easter Cutter Collection, p. 203; Cooling Grid, p. 149

Recipe: Buttercream Icing, p. 114

Also: 2007 Pattern Book (Large and Small Treetops and Trunks, Grass), p. 126; Primary and Neon Fine Tip FoodWriter Edible Color Markers, p. 128; 8 in. Lollipop Sticks, p. 165; Cake Boards, Fanci-Foil Wrap, p. 225; Parchment Triangles, p. 138; White Candy Melts®†, (1 pk.), p. 162; Flowerful Medley Sprinkle Decorations, p. 136; Clear Vanilla Extract, p. 134; Disposable Decorating Bags, p. 138; scissors, craft knife, waxed paper, cornstarch, craft foam block, toothpick

In advance: Make fondant bunnies, tulips, leaves, treetops and trunks. For bunnies, roll out white fondant ⅛ in. thick; cut 3 bunny shapes using cutters from each set. Let dry on waxed paper-covered board, dusted with cornstarch. Reserve a 2½ in. ball of white; tint remaining fondant: 12 oz. leaf green, a 2½ in. ball of brown and 1½ in. balls of rose, yellow and violet. Roll out rose, yellow and violet ⅛ in. thick; cut 4-5 tulips in each color using mini cutter. Let dry. Roll out green and brown fondant ⅛ in. thick; trace treetop and trunk patterns with toothpick and cut 3 large and 2 small of each. Cut leaves for tulips using ears from mini bunny cutter. Let all dry. Reserve remaining green fondant. For flower stems, cut 14 lollipop sticks in half; tint vanilla green and brush on sticks. Let stems dry in craft block. Draw features and decorated egg on bunnies with FoodWriters. Using reserved white fondant, roll small balls for bunny tails and logs for standing bunny's arms; attach with damp brush. Attach confetti sprinkles with dots of melted candy. Attach treetops to trunks with melted candy; let set. With melted candy, attach trees and bunnies to lollipop sticks, attach tulips and leaves to stems. Let set.

Ice 2-layer cake smooth (bake two 1½ in. high layers for a 3 in. high cake). Roll out reserved green fondant ⅛ in. thick. Trace grass pattern with toothpick, making a separate section for each cake side. Cut grass with knife; attach to cake sides. Draw grass blades with FoodWriter. Attach tulips to grass with dots of icing, trimming sticks as needed. Insert trees and bunnies. Serves 12.

†Brand confectionery coating.

▲ Lady Liberty

Pans: Star, p. 154; 9 x 5 in. Loaf, p. 149

Tips: 1s, 2, 2A, 3, 14, 21, p. 140-141

Colors:* Black, Royal Blue, Teal, Kelly Green, Lemon Yellow, Red-Red, p. 135

Candy: Summer Fun Lollipop Mold 2-Pk. Set, p. 164; White Candy Melts®†, p. 162; Primary, Garden Candy Color Sets, Decorator Brush Set, p. 163; 11¾ in. Lollipop Sticks, p. 165;

Recipes: Buttercream, Royal Icings, Color Flow Icing, p. 114

Also: 2007 Pattern Book (Lady Liberty), p. 126; Piping Gel, Color Flow Mix, Meringue Powder, p. 134; Plastic Dowel Rods, p. 224; 16 in. Cake Circles (2), Cake Boards, Fanci-Foil Wrap, p. 225; Patriotic Candles, p. 204; Parchment Triangles, p. 138; waxed paper, white florist tape, 22-gauge florist wire (20 pieces, 13 in. long)

At least 72 hours in advance: Make color flow statue (p. 124) using pattern. Make starburst (p. 119). Make candy. Tint portion of melted candy blue, red, yellow and green using candy colors. Mold candy boats using painting method (p. 123). On waxed paper, pipe a 1 in. diameter circle stand for each boat, using white candy in cut parchment bag; refrigerate until firm. Attach ships to stands with melted candy; let set.

Prepare base board. Wrap double-thick cake board with foil. Cut loaf cake vertically in half and stack for pedestal. Prepare star cake and pedestal cake for Stacked Construction (p. 112). Ice cakes smooth in gray. On pedestal, pipe a tip 2A band at top border and a double-high tip 2A band at bottom border; overpipe lowest band for dimension. Divide sides into 5ths, marking divisions between top and bottom border. Pipe tip 3 vertical lines at division marks and horizontal lines at edges of top and bottom bands. Pipe tip 2 outline windows and tip 3 outline door. Add tip 3 brick lines on upper tip 2A band at bottom border. Pipe tip 3 vertical lines at edge of top border. Pipe in tip 3 heavy line bricks at corners of pedestal. Pipe tip 3 bead top and bottom borders on star cake. Pipe tip 21 rosette candleholders; insert candles. Position cakes on base board. Cut two 4 in. lengths of plastic dowel rod; insert in star cake behind pedestal. Insert starburst wires in dowel rods. Insert statue in pedestal. Tint piping gel blue and cover base board. Position boats. Cake serves 20; each candy serves 1.

*Combine Teal with a little Kelly Green for green used on statue.

†Brand confectionery coating.

▲ Uncle Sam Wants Cupcakes!

Pan: Standard Muffin, p. 149

Recipe: Buttercream Icing, p. 114

Also: Uncle Sam Bobblehead Toppers, Patriotic Stars Baking Cups, p. 204; Patriotic Mix Sprinkles Decorations, p. 205

Ice cupcakes smooth; top with sprinkles. Position Uncle Sam topper. Each serves 1.

▲ Country Coolers

Cookie: Stars Nesting Metal Cutter Set, p. 158; 6 in. Cookie Treat Sticks, p. 161; Patriotic Cupcake and Cookie Stencils, p. 205; Rolling Pin, p. 131; Cookie Sheet, Cooling Grid, p. 149

Recipe: Roll-Out Cookie, p. 114

Also: Red, Blue Colored Sugars, p. 136; White Candy Melts®†, p. 162; Cake Boards, p. 225; Parchment Triangles, p. 138; Patriotic Stars Party Bags, p. 204; ½ gallon brick vanilla ice cream (makes about 8 treats), curling ribbon, waxed paper, serrated knife

At least 1 day in advance: Make cookie and ice cream stars. Roll out dough just under ⅛ in. thick. Cut cookies using 2nd largest star cutter; bake and cool. Using serrated knife, cut ice cream into ½ in. thick horizontal slices. Cut stars using 2nd largest cutter. Sandwich ice cream stars between two cookies. Insert cookie stick and freeze a few hours until very solid. Remove from freezer and coat bottom cookie with melted candy; let set. Turn sandwich over and place on cooling grid; cover with melted candy (p. 124). Freeze until firm. Position stencils on sandwich tops. Lightly spread melted candy over open areas; immediately sprinkle with colored sugar. On edges of stars, pipe melted candy in cut parchment bag; immediately sprinkle with blue sugar. Tie curling ribbon onto sticks. Place sandwiches in treat bag; wrap and freeze until serving. Each serves 1.

▲ Ribbon of Remembrance

Pan: Ribbon, p. 151

Tips: 16, 18, p. 140-141

Colors: Red-Red, Royal Blue, p. 135

Recipe: Buttercream Icing, p. 114

Also: Cake Board, Fanci-Foil Wrap, p. 225; toothpick, ruler

Ice cake sides smooth. Mark ⅝ in. wide stripe areas on cake top with toothpick. Cover cake top with tip 16 stars. Add tip 18 star bottom border. Serves 12.

▶ Bursting in Air!

Pan: Star, p. 154

Tips: 2, 21, p. 140-141

Colors: Royal Blue, Red-Red, p. 135

Recipes: Buttercream Icing, Color Flow Icing, p. 114

Also: 2007 Pattern Book (1¼, 2, 5, 7 in. Patriotic Stars), p. 126; Color Flow Mix, p. 134; 8 in. Lollipop Sticks, p. 165; Parchment Triangles, p. 138; Red, Blue Colored Sugars, p. 136; Cake Boards, Fanci-Foil Wrap, p. 225; waxed paper

At least 2 days in advance: Make color flow stars (p. 124): 1 each 7 in. blue and 5 in. red stars; 5 each 2 in. blue and red stars; and 5 each 1¼ in. blue and red stars. Outline and flow in following instructions; while still wet, sprinkle with colored sugars. Let dry on waxed paper-covered cake boards.

Ice cake smooth. Pipe tip 21 star bottom border. Attach 1¼ in. stars to end of lollipop sticks with full-strength color flow. Pipe a tip 21 mound of buttercream in center of cake top. Insert 5 of the sticks into mound, aligning ends with star points; insert remaining sticks between star points, aligning with opposite sticks. Pipe tip 21 mound on both sides of sticks at edge of cake; position 2 in. stars on mounds. Position 7 in. star in center of cake; attach 5 in. star on top with full-strength color flow. Serves 12.

Days to Treasure

In years to come, you'll think of the big milestone moments. Where you were. Who was there. And if the cake was as amazing as these, it will be part of your memories too. Look inside, as gum paste bridesmaids try to catch the bridal bouquet on the perfect shower centerpiece. When baby's on the way, we have the adorable nursery shown here, filled with fondant furnishings and toys. For Christening, it's a lovely tower of cupcakes, each topped with a cookie bassinet. Our latest dessert ideas capture the excitement and fun of all life's big events like never before.

Instructions for projects shown on these two pages are on page 72.

B
A
B
Y

Room To Grow

Everyone will want to peek into the nursery! From the drawers to the floor, it's filled with baby's favorite things. A perfect shower centerpiece and dessert: the loaf cake dresser is accented with great fondant details.

Pans: 9 x 5 in. Loaf, p. 149; Mini Stand-Up Bear Set, p. 153
Tips: 1, 2, 3, 8, 13, p. 140-141
Colors: Copper (skin tone), Rose, Royal Blue, Lemon Yellow, Violet, Kelly Green, Orange, Black, Brown, p. 135
Fondant: White Ready-To-Use Rolled Fondant (72 oz.), Brush Set, p. 128; Cutter/ Embosser, p. 129; Rolling Pin, Roll & Cut Mat, p. 131
Recipes: Buttercream, Royal Icings, p. 114; Thinned Fondant Adhesive, p. 115
Also: 2007 Pattern Book (Lampshade), p. 126; Baby Candy Mold 2-Pk. Set, p. 164; 11¾ in. Lollipop Sticks, p. 165; Baby Blocks Containers, p. 227; Rocking Horses, Shower Rattles, p. 226; 13 x 19 in. Cake Boards, Fanci-Foil Wrap, p. 225; Gum-Tex™, p. 131; Meringue Powder, p. 134; ruler, sharp embroidery scissors, sharp knife, freezer paper, cornstarch, cellophane tape

In advance: Make fondant duck, bear, train, lamp, decorative drawer panels, dresser tops and open drawer (p. 122).

Bake and cool 3 loaf cakes and bear cake using firm-textured batter such as pound cake. Assemble dresser. Stack 2 full loaves; cut third loaf in half. Position half loaf to make tall dresser section. Trim all sides evenly; ice smooth with buttercream. On front, pipe tip 3 vertical line at center point of 2 full loaves and horizontal lines at loaf seams. Attach decorative drawer panels with buttercream. Position dresser tops. On bear cake, trim off back, stomach, muzzle, neck, arms, legs and ears to resemble baby. For legs, roll 2 fondant logs, 2 x 1 in. diameter; push into cake. For feet, roll two ¾ in. balls; flatten and attach with buttercream. For arms, roll 2 fondant logs, 2¼ x ½ in. diameter; attach to cake with buttercream. For hands, roll ⅞ in. fondant balls; attach with damp brush. Outline neck and wrists with tip 3, pipe in eyes and mouth with tip 2. Cover body and face with tip 13 stars; overpipe ears and nose. Pipe tip 3 pull-out lines on fingers; overpipe with tip 13 stars.

Make fondant blanket (p. 122). Immediately position in open drawer. Roll a ¾ in. ball of fondant for rocking horse base and position inside drawer; position rocking horse. Position lamp base; insert lamp on stick. Attach shade to top of lamp with icing. Position cakes, blocks, rattles, rocking horse and train on foil-covered double-thick board; position duck, bear and lamp on dresser tops. Serves 21.

Rattle & Roar!

Cookie: Cookie Sheet, Cooling Grid, p. 149
Tips: 2, 9, p. 140
Colors: Rose, Sky Blue, p. 135
Candy: Baby Shower Mold, p. 229; Candy Melts®† in Blue, Pink, White, p. 162; Decorator Brush Set, p. 163
Recipes: Royal Icing, Roll-Out Cookie, p. 114
Also: Teddy Bear Plastic Cookie Cutter, p. 160; Parchment Triangles, p. 138; Meringue Powder, p. 134; Rolling Pin, p. 131; light corn syrup, cornstarch

One day in advance: Mold candy rattles using painting method (p. 123). Refrigerate until firm; unmold. Bake and cool cookies. Outline cookies with tip 2 and full-strength royal icing; flow in with thinned royal icing using cut parchment bag. Let set overnight.

Decorate bears with full-strength royal icing. Pipe tip 9 dot muzzle; add tip 2 dot eyes and nose, string mouth. Outline and pipe-in diaper with tip 2 (smooth with finger dipped in cornstarch). Attach rattles with melted candy. Each serves 1.

Cradle Cuties

Fondant: White Ready-To-Use Rolled Fondant, Brush Set, p. 128; Fine Tip Neon Color FoodWriter™ Edible Color Markers, p. 128
Color: Copper (skin tone), p. 135
Also: Baby Cradles, p. 227; Mini Hearts Candies, p. 229; ¾ in. wide satin ribbon in pink or blue (10 in. per favor); glue gun

In advance: Make heads. Tint portion of fondant copper. For head, roll a ⅞ in. ball of fondant. Roll a small fondant ball for nose; attach with damp brush. Let dry overnight.

Draw eyes and mouth with black FoodWriter. Fill cradles with candies. For pillows, shape rectangles using 1 in. ball of white fondant; position in cradle. Position head on pillow and add candies around head. Make bow using 10 in. of ribbon; trim as needed and attach to cradle with hot glue. Each serves 1.

†Brand confectionery coating.

▲ Peek-A-Boo Bags

Candy: Pillow Mints, p. 227
Also: Drawstring Sachets, p. 227; 1¼ in. wooden craft balls, fleshtone craft paint, paint brush, hot glue gun, pink and blue tissue paper, fine-tip black permanent marker, ⅛ in. wide satin ribbon in blue and pink

Paint wooden balls with craft paint; let dry. Draw eyes and mouths on balls with permanent marker. Line sachets with tissue paper. Fill sachets with mints; attach heads with hot glue. Tie bow on sachets using 10 in. of ribbon; make hair bows using 3 in. ribbon; trim as needed and glue to girl heads. Each serves 1.

▶ Best Gift Ever!

Pans: 10 x 2 in. Heart Pan, p. 147; Mini Loaf, p. 149
Tips: 4, 5, p. 140
Colors: Royal Blue, Rose, Black, Copper (skin tone), p. 135
Fondant: White Ready-To-Use Rolled Fondant (48 oz.), Brush Set, p. 128; Round Cut-Outs™, p. 130; Rolling Pin, Roll & Cut Mat, p. 131; Easy-Glide Fondant Smoother, p. 129
Recipes: Buttercream, Royal Icings, p. 114
Also: 101 Cookie Cutters Set, p. 160; 8 in. Lollipop Sticks, p. 165; Cake Board, Fanci-Foil Wrap, p. 225; Gum-Tex™, p. 131; Meringue Powder, p. 134; black shoestring licorice, ⅞ in. wide pink ribbon, cornstarch, large marshmallows, florist wire

At least 48 hours in advance: Tint 8 oz. fondant copper; mix with ½ tsp. of Gum-Tex. Make fondant head, ears and foot (p. 121).

Bake and cool 1-layer (2 in. high) 10 in. heart cake (use firm-textured batter such as pound cake) and one mini loaf cake, 1 in. high. Position heart cake, pointed end up, on foil-wrapped board, cut large enough to fit gathered top piece. Fill in indented center of heart with buttercream. Cut sides of loaf cake at an angle to taper toward bottom; bottom should measure 3½ in. wide. Loaf cake will support gathered top piece. Prepare cakes for rolled fondant (p. 113); cover separately with fondant and smooth with Fondant Smoother. For gathered top, roll out fondant 1 in. thick; cut a 5 x 12 in. rectangle. Gather rectangle at its base into a triangular shape, curving the top two points outward and forming folds with your fingers. Position loaf cake so that tapered side is 1 in. above point of heart cake; position gathered fondant top over loaf cake, attaching to heart cake with damp brush.

For head support, insert 2 marshmallows on sticks into cake sides, extending about 4 in. Position head. Insert 2 sticks in top of foot and insert end in cake. Write tip 5 message in buttercream. Make ribbon bow and position at neck of bundle. Serves 13.

▶ A Buggy of Bargains!

Pan: Baby Buggy, p. 152
Tips: 3, 8, 12, 18, p. 140-141
Colors:* Rose, Leaf Green, Lemon Yellow, Golden Yellow, Royal Blue, Violet, Copper (skin tone), p. 135
Fondant: White Ready-To-Use Rolled Fondant (24 oz.), Brush Set, p. 128; Heart Cut-Outs™, p. 130; Rolling Pin, Roll & Cut Mat, p. 131
Recipes: Buttercream, Royal Icings, p. 114
Also: 2007 Pattern Book (Shopping Bags), p. 126; Fine Tip Neon Colors FoodWriter™ Edible Color Markers, p. 128; Circle Metal Cookie Cutter, p. 158; Cake Board, Fanci-Foil Wrap, p. 225; Gum-Tex™, p. 131; Meringue Powder, p. 134; paring knife, pink curling ribbon, waxed paper, cornstarch

Two days in advance: Combine 12 oz. of fondant with 1 teaspoon of Gum-Tex; reserve remaining fondant. Make fondant baby, shopping bags, hearts and cell phone (p. 122).

Ice background areas of buggy cake smooth in buttercream. Using light rose and white buttercream, pipe checkerboard design with tip 18 stars in alternating color squares. Pipe tip 3 outline ribs on hood in dark rose. Fill in hood with tip 18 stars in light rose. Add tip 18 zigzag buggy brim in light rose. Add tip 8 outline wheel spokes and dot wheel center (flatten and smooth with finger dipped in cornstarch). Pipe tip 12 outline wheel rims and buggy handle in light rose. Position hearts, shopping bags, face and cell phone. Serves 12.

*Combine Leaf Green with Lemon Yellow for green shown. Combine Lemon Yellow with Golden Yellow for yellow shown.

▼ The Toddler Track

Pans: Mini Loaf, p. 149; Choo-Choo Train Set, p. 155
Tips: 2, 3, 14, 16, 21, 101, p. 140-141
Colors: Sky Blue, Copper (skin tone), p. 135
Recipes: Buttercream, Royal Icings, Roll-Out Cookie, p. 114
Also: 2007 Pattern Book (Smoke Cloud), p. 126; Shower Rattles, Baby Bears, Rocking Horses, p. 226; Cake Board, Fanci-Foil Wrap, p. 225; Gingerbread Boy Metal Cutter, p. 158; Round Cut-Outs™, p. 130; 4 in. Lollipop Sticks, p. 165; Meringue Powder, p. 134; Rolling Pin, p. 131; 8½ x 11 in. white card stock, 4 in. blue/white candy sticks (2), fine-tip marker, scissors, cornstarch, cellophane tape

Bake and cool train and 2 mini loaves using firm-textured batter such as pound cake.

Tint a small portion of cookie dough copper. Roll out copper dough; cut 1 gingerbread boy for baby. Roll out untinted dough and use large round Cut-Out to cut 4 wheels and medium Cut-Out to cut 10 wheels. Bake and cool. Ice wheels smooth with royal icing; let dry. Outline wheels, spokes and pipe rosette centers with tip 16 on large wheels and tip 14 on medium wheels. For baby cookie, use royal icing and tip 2 to pipe dot eyes, string mouth and tie on bonnet. With royal icing, pipe tip 101 ruffle for bonnet and pipe in tip 3 diaper (smooth with finger dipped in cornstarch). Attach lollipop stick to back of cookie with royal icing, leaving 1½ in. extended at bottom. Set aside.

Ice mini loaves smooth. Pipe tip 16 star top and bottom borders. Cut 12 lollipop sticks to 3½ in. and push into mini loaf top for playpen railings. With royal icing, attach 2 lollipop sticks, cut to 4 in., for front and back top railing and 2 sticks, cut to 2 in., for side top railings. Join top railings in corners with tip 3 royal icing balls.

On train engine, ice bottom sections, windows and top of smokestack smooth. Outline train and cover top of smokestack and cab with tip 21 pull-out lines. Pipe tip 21 swirl on front of cab and tip 21 pull-out lines for cowcatcher. Cover remainder of train with tip 16 stars. Attach wheels on all cakes with icing; attach candy sticks to large wheels with royal icing. Insert candy sticks in cakes to connect cars. Cut out smoke cloud pattern from card stock, write message and tape to lollipop stick; insert stick into cake. Position baby in playpen and toys on last car. Cake serves 14; each cookie serves 1.

◀ A Court of Many Colors

Pans: Mini Wonder Mold, Classic Wonder Mold, p. 150
Tips: 1, 2, 3, 4, 5, p. 140
Colors:* Rose, Violet, Lemon Yellow, Golden Yellow, Kelly Green, Royal Blue, Creamy Peach, Black, p. 135
Fondant: White Ready-To-Use Rolled Fondant (72 oz.), Brush Set, p. 128; Rolling Pin, Roll & Cut Mat, p. 131
Recipes: Buttercream, Royal Icings, p. 114
Also: 2007 Pattern Book (Bride and Bridesmaids Hangers, Bodices, Streamers and Bows), p. 126; 6 in. Lollipop Sticks, p. 165; Fine Tip Neon Colors FoodWriter™ Edible Color Markers, p. 128; Gum-Tex™, p. 131; Meringue Powder, p. 134; Cake Board, Fanci-Foil Wrap, p. 225; waxed paper, cellophane tape; cornstarch

At least 2 days in advance: Make 1 bride and 6 bridesmaid hangers. Tape waxed paper over patterns. Using royal icing, pipe tip 4 bridesmaid and tip 5 bride hangers; make extras to allow for breakage and let dry. **Also:** Use patterns to make bride and bridesmaid bodices, streamers and bows. For bridesmaids, tint 7 oz. fondant each rose, violet, green, yellow, blue and peach. Add ¼ teaspoon Gum-Tex to 3 oz. of each color; reserve remaining 4 oz. for skirts. For bride, add ¼ teaspoon Gum-Tex to 3 oz. white fondant. Roll out all fondant ⅛ in. thick. Cut bodices, streamers and bows. Let dry on board dusted with cornstarch. Attach lollipop sticks to bodice backs with royal icing; let set.

Prepare 1 Classic and 6 Mini Wonder Mold cakes for rolled fondant (p. 113). Cover Classic cake with 15 oz. white fondant; cover mini cakes with reserved tinted fondant. Decorate bridal gown. With buttercream, pipe tip 2 bead flowers with dot center on skirt; cover bodice with tip 1 cornelli lace. Insert bodice in skirt. Cut a 3 x ¼ in. wide fondant sash; attach to waist with damp brush, wrapping around in back. Write name on streamer with FoodWriter. Attach bow, streamer and hanger to cake with royal icing. Decorate bridesmaid dresses in buttercream. Pipe tip 3 lines, tip 2 dots and tip 1 swirls on skirts. In matching color fondant, cut 1½ x ⅛ in. wide sashes; attach to waist with damp brush. Write names on streamers with FoodWriter. Attach bows, streamers and hangers with royal icing. Bride cake serves 12; each bridesmaid cake serves 1.

*Combine Lemon Yellow with Golden Yellow for yellow shown. Combine Violet with Rose for violet shown.

▶ Pair of Hearts

Pan: SweetHeart, p. 148
Tips: 2, 4, 6, 101, p. 140-141
Color: Rose, p. 135
Recipes: Buttercream, Royal Icings, p. 114
Also: 2007 Pattern Book (Center Heart, Script), p. 126; Flower Nail No. 7, p. 138; Cake Boards, Fanci-Foil Wrap, p. 225; Meringue Powder, p. 134; waxed paper, toothpick

In advance: Make tip 101 roses using royal icing. Make 72 white roses and 34 rose-colored roses, all with tip 4 bases. Make extras to allow for breakage and let dry.

Bake and cool two heart cakes. Trace center heart pattern on cake tops with toothpick. Ice cakes smooth in buttercream with white center hearts. Using script pattern, trace name on center heart; pipe name with tip 4. Create scroll shapes around center heart using tip 2 dots. Attach roses around center heart with buttercream. Pipe tip 6 bead bottom borders; attach roses over border with icing. Each cake serves 12.

◀ Catch The Excitement

Pans: 8, 12 x 2 in. Round, p. 148

Tips: 2A, 3, 6, 12, 104, 366, p. 140-141

Colors: Violet, Kelly Green, Rose, Copper (skin tone), Brown, Christmas Red, Moss Green, Kelly Green, Golden Yellow, Lemon Yellow, Orange, p. 135

Fondant: White Ready-To-Use Rolled Fondant (24 oz.), Brush Set, p. 128; Rolling Pin, Roll & Cut Mat, p. 131

Recipes: Buttercream, Royal Icings, p. 114

Also: 2007 Pattern Book (Hand/Arm), p. 126; 14 in. Plate, 7¾ and 6½ in. Columns (1 each), Glue-On Plate Legs (6), Bottom Column Bolt from Tall Tier Cake Stand, p. 222; Flower Nail No. 7, p. 138; Gum Paste Mix (3 cans), p. 131; Meringue Powder, p. 134; Wooden Dowel Rods, p. 224; Cake Boards, p. 225; cornstarch, sharp knife, 3½ in. craft foam ball, waxed paper, 24-gauge green cloth-covered florist wires (7½ in. long, 15 pieces), green florist tape, 1 x 18 in. long wire-edge ribbon, super-strong glue for plastics, scissors

In advance: Make gum paste hands/arms (p. 121). **Also:** Using royal icing, make 45 tip 104 roses with tip 12 bases. Pipe first 3 petals in Golden Yellow and next two rows in white. Make extras to allow for breakage and let dry. Glue legs to bottom of 14 in. plate; let dry.

Ice 2-layer 8 in. and 1-layer 12 in. cakes smooth and prepare for Center Column and Stacked Construction (p. 112). Assemble column using one 6½ and one 7¾ in. column and position cakes on plate. Pipe tip 6 bead bottom border on 12 in. cake. Print tip 3 message. Wrap each wire with florist tape to add dimension, then tape wires together. Cut a hole in side of craft foam ball to accommodate wires; cut a second hole in bottom of ball to fit column. Position ball over column, attaching with royal icing. Ice ball with royal icing and attach roses; add tip 366 moss green leaves in royal icing and let dry. Insert wires in craft foam ball. Tie ribbon bow around wires.

At reception: Pipe a tip 2A line of buttercream icing behind lower part of arms where they will rest against 8 in. cake; attach to cake. Serves 60.

▶ Romantic Setting

Pan: 8 x 2 in. Square, p. 148

Tips: 2, 3, p. 140

Colors: Rose, Golden Yellow, Black, p. 135

Fondant: White Ready-To-Use Rolled Fondant (48 oz.), Brush Set, p. 128; Spiral Pattern Fondant Roller, Rolling Pin, Roll & Cut Mat, p. 131; Cutter/Embosser, p. 129

Recipes: Buttercream Icing, Color Flow Icing, p. 114

Also: 2007 Pattern Book (Ring, Bow, Flower), p. 126; Color Flow Mix, p. 134; Cake Board, Fanci-Foil Wrap, p. 225; Parchment Triangles, p. 138; 4 in. Lollipop Sticks, p. 165; waxed paper, non-stick pan spray, ruler

At least 2 days in advance: Make color flow ring, 4 bows and 4 flowers (p. 124) using patterns. Prepare 2 recipes of color flow. Outline bow, flower and ring band with tip 2, outline diamond with tip 3; flow in using cut parchment bag. Make extras to allow for breakage and let dry for 2 days. When dry, using full-strength color flow, attach two lollipop sticks to outer bottom edges of ring; add one at center of diamond and background, extending to top of ring to reinforce. Let dry.

Ice 2-layer cake smooth. Roll out fondant ¼ in. thick. Using straight-edge wheel of Cutter/Embosser, cut an 8 x 4 in. rectangle for each cake side. Imprint spiral design with Pattern Roller. Attach to cake sides; smooth at corners and trim to fit if needed. Roll ⅛ in. diameter logs of fondant to fit each top and corner edge of cake; attach with damp brush. Roll ½ in. diameter fondant balls for bottom border; attach with buttercream. On flowers, pipe a tip 2 swirl in full-strength color flow. Attach flowers to bows and bows to cake with full-strength color flow. Insert ring in cake top. Serves 20.

▶ Virtual Vases

Pans: 9 x 13 x 2 in. Sheet, p. 148; Non-Stick Cookie Pan, p. 146; Cooling Grid, p. 149
Tip: 12, p. 140
Fondant: White Ready-To-Use Rolled Fondant, Brush Set, p. 128; Square, Round Cut-Outs™, p. 130; Rolling Pin, Roll & Cut Mat, p. 131
Candy: White Candy Melts®†, p. 162; Garden, Primary Candy Color Sets, p. 163
Also: Flower Picks, p. 219; paring knife

In advance: Make candy platforms. Using candy colors, tint portions of melted candy yellow, pink and blue. Place large Cut-Outs on non-stick pan and fill ⅛ in. high with melted candy; refrigerate until firm and unmold. Reserve excess candy.

Bake and cool 1-layer cake using firm-textured batter such as pound cake. Using medium Cut-Outs, imprint top of cake with squares and circles. Cut out at imprints using paring knife.

Cover cakes with reserved melted candy (p. 124). Immediately insert toothpick in center of cake top to make a hole for flower pick. Attach cakes to candy platforms with melted candy. Remove toothpick; refrigerate cakes until firm. Roll out fondant ⅛ in. thick. For square cakes, cut 2 x ¼ in. strips for sides and an 8 x ¼ in. strip for top border; attach with damp brush. For circle cakes, cut dots with narrow end of tip 12 and an 8 x ¼ in. strip for top border; attach fondant with damp brush. Insert picks. Each serves 1.

†Brand confectionery coating.

▲ Perched in Paradise

Cookie: Heart Plastic Nesting Cutter Set, p. 160; Cookie Sheet, Cooling Grid, p. 149
Tips: 3, 7, 224, 349, p. 140-141
Colors:* Kelly Green, Rose, Golden Yellow, Lemon Yellow, p. 135
Candy: White Candy Melts®†, p. 162; Wedding Shower Lollipop Mold, p. 164
Recipes: Royal Icing, Roll-Out Cookie, p. 114
Also: Cake Board, p. 225; Rolling Pin, p. 131; Meringue Powder, p. 134; ½ in. wide ribbon (4 in. per cookie), waxed paper

In advance: Make flowers. Using royal icing, pipe 10 each tip 224 drop flowers in rose and yellow; add tip 3 dot centers. Make extras to allow for breakage; let dry. Also mold 2 bird candies without heart portion using melted white candy. Refrigerate until firm; unmold.

Roll out dough. Cut cookie using second largest heart cutter. Trim ½ in. off bottom point. Bake and cool. Pipe tip 7 outline cage using royal icing; position bird candies. Pipe tip 7 outline perch and bottom border. Attach flowers to border; add tip 349 leaves. Form a loop with 4 in. of ribbon; attach ends with icing. Attach loop and flowers at top with icing. Add tip 349 leaves. Each serves 1.

*Combine Golden Yellow and Lemon Yellow for yellow shown.

▼ Rock Solid Romance

Cookie: 101 Cookie Cutters Set, p. 160; Cookie Sheet, Cooling Grid, p. 149
Tip: 2, p. 140
Colors: Golden Yellow, Black, p. 135
Recipes: Color Flow Icing, Roll-Out Cookie, p. 114
Also: Color Flow Mix, p. 134; paring knife

Roll out dough; cut ring using large circle cutter, cut out center using medium circle cutter. Use small heart cutter to cut diamond; trim edges to create diamond shape and position on cookie sheet touching ring. Bake and cool. Outline ring and diamond using tip 2 and full-strength color flow; let set. Pipe in ring and diamond with thinned color flow; let set. Each serves 1.

▲ Limo of Love

Cookie: 101 Cookie Cutters Set, p. 160; Cookie Sheet, Cooling Grid, p. 149
Tips: 2, 3, 7, 24, p. 140-141
Colors:* Royal Blue, Brown, Red-Red, Lemon Yellow, Black, p. 135
Fondant: White Ready-To-Use Rolled Fondant, p. 128; Rolling Pin, Roll & Cut Mat, p. 131
Recipes: Royal, Color Flow Icings, Roll-Out Cookie, p. 114
Also: Color Flow Mix, Meringue Powder, p. 134; Cake Board, p. 225; small fruit-flavored disc candies, cardboard, cornstarch, paring knife, waxed paper

In advance: On waxed paper-covered board using royal icing, make 4 tip 24 swirl drop flowers for each cookie. Pipe tip 2 dot centers. Make extras to allow for breakage; let dry.

Cut cookies using car cutter; bake and cool. Outline car and window areas using tip 3 and full-strength color flow; let dry. Flow in car using thinned color flow; let dry. Using royal icing, pipe in wheels with tip 7 (smooth with finger dipped in cornstarch). Pipe tip 7 outline running board and wheel wells. Add tip 3 dot hubcaps and headlights. Pipe tip 3 curving outline streamer; attach flowers. For disc candy faces, pipe tip 2 dot eyes, outline mouth and pull-out hair.

For veil, roll out white fondant ⅛ in. thick. Cut a 3 x 1 in. wide piece, narrowing to ½ in. wide. Attach veil with dots of icing; attach heads in window. Pipe tip 3 zigzag crown. Each serves 1.

*Combine Brown and Red-Red for brown shown.

▶ A Case of True Love

Pan: 6-Cavity Heart Silicone Mold, p. 144

Recipe: Truffles, p. 115

Also: White Ready-To-Use Rolled Fondant, p. 128; Red, Light Cocoa Candy Melts®†, p. 162; Engagement Rings, p. 215; Spatula, p. 138; Cookie Sheet, p. 149

For each ring case, make two ¼ in. thick candy shells (p. 123) in heart mold. Refrigerate until firm; unmold by turning mold cavities inside out and gently peeling away from shell. Prepare truffle mixture with cocoa Candy Melts. Fill bottom shell halfway with mixture; seal at halfway point with melted candy. Refrigerate until firm. For ring holder, shape a 1½ in. ball of fondant into a pillow and position in bottom shell. Make a slit in pillow with edge of spatula; insert ring. Attach top shell with melted candy; refrigerate until firm. Each serves 1; each package of Red Candy Melts makes three ring cases.

▼ Single No More

Pan: 12 x 18 x 2 in. Sheet (2), p. 148

Tips: 2, 4, p. 140

Colors:* Rose, Kelly Green, Lemon Yellow, Golden Yellow, p. 135

Fondant: White Ready-To-Use Rolled Fondant (24 oz.), p. 128; Rolling Pin, Roll & Cut Mat, p. 131

Ornament: Double Heart Pick, p. 219

Recipe: Royal Icing, p. 114

Also: Floral Collection Flower Making Set, Confectionery Tool Set, p. 130; Flower Former Set, p. 129; Gum-Tex™, p. 131; Circle Metal Cutter, p. 158; 14 in. Round Silver Cake Base, Cake Boards, p. 225; White Candy Melts®† (9 pks.), p. 162; Cooling Grid, p. 149; Meringue Powder, p. 134, cornstarch, waxed paper

In advance: Make fondant flowers and leaves. Mix 12 oz. of fondant with 1 teaspoon Gum-Tex; divide into thirds and tint rose, green and yellow. Using Floral Collection cutters, cut 20 each rose and yellow pansies and 20 each rose and yellow apple blossoms. Place flowers on thick foam and cup centers using medium ball tool. Let dry on cornstarch-dusted flower formers. Also cut 20 each large and small leaves using rose leaf cutter from set. Place leaves on thin foam and score vein lines with veining tool. Let dry on cornstarch-dusted flower formers.

Bake and cool two 2 in. high sheet cakes using firm-textured batter such as pound cake. Using circle cutter, cut 40 cakes. Cover cakes with melted candy (p. 124). One pack of Candy Melts will double-coat 4 to 5 cakes. Refrigerate until firm. Seal bottom of cakes with melted candy; let set on waxed paper-covered boards. Divide each cake into 6 sections; pipe tip 2 triple drop strings, ½ to 1 in. deep, at division points. Pipe tip 2 ball at division points. Pipe tip 2 ball centers on flowers. Add tip 4 bead bottom borders.

At reception: Stack cakes on base, in ascending layers of 18, 11, 7, 3 and 1. Attach fondant flowers and leaves with icing. Insert pick. Each serves 1;

*Combine Lemon Yellow with Golden Yellow for yellow shown.

▲ Bridal Bouquets

Cookie: 101 Cookie Cutters Set, p. 160; Cookie Sheet, Cooling Grid, p. 161

Tips: 3, 131, 224, 352, p. 140-141

Colors: Kelly Green, Rose, Lemon Yellow, Violet, p. 135

Recipes: Royal Icing, Roll-Out Cookie, p. 114

Also: Meringue Powder, p. 134; Rolling Pin, p. 131; cardboard, ⅛ in. wide white ribbon (12 in. per cookie), waxed paper, scissors

In advance: Make tip 131 and tip 224 drop flowers on waxed paper using royal icing specified for each cookie. For 2-tone rose-colored cookies, use light and dark rose. For assorted color cookies, use violet, rose and yellow. Add tip 3 dot centers in white for all flowers. Make extras to allow for breakage and let dry.

Roll out dough. Cut cookies using starburst cutter from set; bake and cool. Pipe tip 3 outline stems; add tip 352 leaves at starburst points. Attach flowers with dots of icing; add tip 352 leaves between flowers. Tie ribbon into bow; attach with icing. Each serves 1.

◀ Uncork the Memories!

Pan: 8 x 2 in. Round, p. 148

Tips: 2, 3, 5, 8, 789, p. 140

Colors:* Royal Blue, Leaf Green, Lemon Yellow, Violet, Rose, Black, p. 135

Recipes: Buttercream, Color Flow Icings, p. 114

Also: 2007 Pattern Book (Champagne Bottle, Glass), p. 126; 25th Anniversary Pick, p. 219; White Candy Melts®†, p. 162; 8 in. Lollipop Sticks, p. 165; Parchment Triangles, p. 138; Color Flow Mix, p. 134; 18- and 22-gauge cloth-covered florist wire, florist tape, hot glue, waxed paper

At least 3 days in advance: Outline and flow in champagne bottle and glasses using patterns, color flow and tips 2 and 3 (p. 124). For glasses, flow in champagne area without outlining. **Also:** Make bubbles on waxed paper using thinned color flow in cut parchment bag. Make 30 single ½ in. diameter bubbles and 25 single ⅜ in. diameter bubbles; also make bubble groupings for rims of glasses using various sizes (largest at ⅞ in. diameter). Let dry at least 48 hours.

At least 1 day in advance: Assemble bubble spray. Cut six 22-gauge florist wires from 11 to 14 in. long. Tape wires together 3½ in. from bottom. Cut spikes on Anniversary Pick to ½ in. long. Cut two 18-gauge florist wires to 6 in. long; attach to pick with hot glue. Position the pick at center of 22-gauge wire grouping; bend wires to create spray look. Attach bubbles to spray with melted candy; let set. Attach spray at top of bottle; attach a lollipop stick cut to 7 in. at bottom of bottle with melted candy, positioning bottle at an angle on the stick; let set. On glass for cake top, attach an 8 in. stick at an angle, extending stick 4 in. at bottom; let set. Using full-strength color flow, attach bubbles to glasses. On glass for cake side, pipe tip 8 pull-out spikes, 1 in. long.

Ice sides of 2-layer cake smooth in buttercream. Make scallop pattern. Cut a 3 in. wide strip of waxed paper, long enough to wrap around cake. Mark scallops on top edge of strip using wide end of tip 789; position tip so that its curve is ½ in. deep from top edge of strip. Mark scallops approximately 2¼ in. apart on strip. Cut out marked area. When icing has crusted, position pattern around cake. Ice top and pattern area on sides smooth with blue buttercream; remove pattern. Pipe tip 5 double drop strings on scallops and loops above scallop points. Pipe tip 8 ball bottom border varying ball sizes. Insert glass on cake side; insert bottle and glass on cake top. Serves 20.

*Combine Leaf Green with Lemon Yellow for green shade shown. Combine Violet with Rose for violet shade shown.

†Brand confectionery coating.

▶ Their Golden Moment

Pans: 6, 8, 10 x 2 in. Round, p. 148

Tips: 3, 4, p. 140

Color: Golden Yellow, p. 135

Fondant: White Ready-To-Use Rolled Fondant (48 oz.), p. 128; Rolling Pin, Roll & Cut Mat, Spiral Pattern Roller, p. 131

Recipes: Buttercream, Royal Icings, p. 114

Also: 50th Anniversary Pick, p. 219; 7½ in. Twist Legs (2 pks.), 8, 10 in. Plates from Crystal-Clear Cake Divider Set, p. 220; 12 in. Round Silver Cake Base, Cake Boards, p. 225; Nesting Hearts Plastic Cutter Set, p. 160; 101 Cookie Cutters Set, p. 160; Gum-Tex™, p. 131; 4 in. Lollipop Sticks (2 pks.), p. 165; Meringue Powder, p. 134; ½ in. white ribbon (40 in.), double-stick tape, cornstarch

At least 2-3 days in advance: Make fondant hearts. Knead 2 teaspoons of Gum-Tex into 24 oz. of fondant. Roll out fondant ⅛ in. thick. Using 2½ in. nesting cutter, cut 40 to 50 large hearts; using 1¾ in. nesting cutter, cut 50 to 60 small hearts. Make extras to allow for breakage and let dry on cornstarch-dusted board for 2 days. Using royal icing, pipe tip 3 outlines with curls on hearts; let dry. Attach lollipop stick to back of each heart and to Anniversary Pick with royal icing; set aside.

Ice tops of 2-layer cakes in white and sides in yellow; prepare for Separator Plate and Pillar Construction (p. 112). To make swags, roll out fondant ⅛ in. thick. Imprint spiral design using Pattern Roller. Cut out circle using largest round cutter; cut swag 1 in. above bottom of circle using largest round cutter. Repeat to make 19 swags. Attach 8 swags to 10 in. cake, 6 swags to 8 in. cake and 5 swags to 6 in. cake with buttercream. Cut a fondant circle for each swag point using large end of tip 4; attach with royal icing. Pipe tip 4 bead bottom borders on all cakes. **At reception**: Assemble cakes. Insert fondant hearts and Anniversary Pick. Attach ribbon around base with double-stick tape. Serves 60.

▼ Monogrammed Memories

Pan: Oval Pan Set (16½ x 12⅜ in. used), p. 148

Tips: 2, 5, p. 140

Colors:* Royal Blue, Violet, p. 135

Fondant: White Ready-To-Use Rolled Fondant (96 oz. needed), Brush Set, p. 128; Rolling Pin, Roll & Cut Mat, p. 131; Easy-Glide Fondant Smoother, p. 129

Recipes: Buttercream, Color Flow Icings, p. 114

Also: 2007 Pattern Book (Monogram Alphabet), p. 126; Color Flow Mix, Piping Gel, p. 134; Parchment Triangles, p. 138; 12 in. Floral Cake Decorations, p. 219; Cake Boards, Fanci-Foil Wrap, p. 225; ½ in. thick oval foamcore or plywood board 2 in. larger than pan diameter, waxed paper, cellophane tape, non-stick vegetable pan spray, paper towels

At least 2 days in advance: Make color flow monogram (p. 124). Enlarge letter patterns to desired size using copy machine. Outline with tip 2 and flow in using cut parchment bag. Make extras to allow for breakage and let dry for 2 days. Make 90 color flow dots on waxed paper using tip 2 and thinned color flow; let dry.

Tint fondant blue. Wrap foamcore board with foil and brush with piping gel. Cover with fondant; smooth with Fondant Smoother. Prepare 1-layer cake for rolled fondant (p. 113). Cover with fondant and smooth with Fondant Smoother. Position cake; pipe tip 5 bead bottom border with buttercream. Carefully remove monogram and dots from waxed paper; attach with tip 2 and thinned color flow. Position floral decorations. Serves 22.

*Combine Royal Blue with Violet for blue shown.

◀ Ivy League Dreams

Pans: 6, 10, 14 x 2 in. Round, p. 148

Tips: 2, 18, p. 140-141

Color: Moss Green, p. 135

Fondant: White Ready-To-Use Rolled Fondant (24 oz.), p. 128; Rolling Pin, Roll & Cut Mat, p. 131

Recipes: Buttercream Icing, p. 114; Thinned Fondant Adhesive, p. 115

Also: 2007 Pattern Book (Script Alphabet), p. 126; Glowing Graduate Topper, p. 206; Tailored Tiers Cake Display Set, p. 220; Floral Collection Flower Making Set, p. 130; Confectionery Tool Set, Flower Former Set, p. 129; Gum-Tex™, p. 131; Meringue Powder, p. 134; 16 in. Round Silver Cake Base, Cake Circles, p. 225; Plastic Dowel Rods, Flower Spikes, p. 224; 22-gauge florist wire (one 14 in. length, three 18 in. lengths, fifty-seven 6 in. lengths), green florist tape, cornstarch, favorite family or school photos

In advance: Make ivy leaves. Mix 8 oz. fondant with 1 teaspoon Gum-Tex; tint green. Roll out 1/16 in. thick; cut approximately 150 ivy leaves using cutter in Floral Collection Set. On thin foam, vein leaves with veining tool. Let leaves dry on either side of flower formers dusted with cornstarch; vary positions to create assorted shapes.

Make ivy stems: Wrap 6 in. wires with florist tape. Attach 2 ivy leaves to each using thinned fondant adhesive. Using florist tape, attach 12 ivy stems to the 14 in. wire for small spray, 15 stems to one 18 in. wire for medium spray. Tape together two 18 in. wires and attach 30 stems with florist tape for longest spray. Attach additional leaves to main stem of each spray using thinned fondant adhesive. Set aside.

Ice 2-layer 6, 10 and 14 in. cakes smooth; prepare for Tailored Tiers Construction (p. 113). Using pattern, trace message with toothpick. Pipe tip 2 message on sides. Pipe tip 18 shell top and bottom borders on all cakes. Insert photos in acetate wraps; attach to Tailored Tiers Separators.

At reception: Assemble cakes. Insert a flower spike at the back of each tier. Position ends of ivy sprays in spikes and wrap around cake. Trim off excess if necessary. Position topper. Serves 103.

▶ Success Mini Cakes

Pan: 12 x 18 x 1 in. Jelly Roll, p. 149

Cookie: 101 Cookie Cutters Set, p. 160; Cookie Sheet, Cooling Grid, p. 149

Tip: 2, p. 140

Colors:* Red-Red, Christmas Red, Brown, Black, Royal Blue, Copper (skin tone), Lemon Yellow, Golden Yellow, p. 135

Recipe: Buttercream Icing, p. 114

Also: White Candy Melts®†, p. 162; Graduation Icing Decorations, p. 206; paring knife

Imprint 1 in. high cake with graduate shapes using small girl cutter from set (1 cake makes approximately 18 graduates). Cut out with paring knife. Cover cakes with melted candy (p. 124); refrigerate until firm. Pipe tip 2 dot and string facial features, zigzag hair. Outline and pipe in tip 2 gown, collar, shirt and tie; add tip 2 dot feet, pull-out fingers. Attach icing decorations with melted candy. Each serves 1.

*Combine Red-Red with Christmas Red for red shown. Combine Lemon Yellow with Golden Yellow for yellow shown. Combine Brown with Christmas Red for brown shown.

†Brand confectionery coating.

▶ Capping Off the Year

Pans: Oval Set (16½ x 12⅜ x 2 in. used), p. 148; Topping Off Success, p. 206
Tip: 21, p. 141
Color: Royal Blue, p. 135
Fondant: Primary Colors Fondant Multi Pack, Brush Set, p. 128; Cutter/Embosser, p. 129; Rolling Pin, Roll & Cut Mat, p. 131
Recipe: Buttercream Icing, p. 114
Also: Blue Candy Melts®† (2 pks.), p. 162; Primary Candy Color Set, p. 163; 101 Cookie Cutters Set, p. 160; Cake Board; Fanci-Foil Wrap, p. 225; Confectionery Tool Set, p. 129; Plastic Dowel Rods, p. 224; ruler, cornstarch, ½ in. thick foamcore board

In advance: Make graduation cap candy plaque (p. 124) in pan using 2 pks. Candy Melts tinted a deeper shade by adding blue from candy color set. Refrigerate until firm; unmold.

Ice 1-layer cake smooth. Pipe tip 21 shell bottom border. For cord, roll two ¼ in. diameter fondant ropes, twist together and position on candy plaque hat; flatten slightly. For tassel, shape a 1 x 2 in. yellow teardrop. Position at end of cord; trim to fit. Add a ½ in. fondant ball for knot. Score fringe lines using veining tool from Confectionery Tool Set. For button, shape a ¾ in. ball of blue fondant; flatten and attach with damp brush. Make fondant message and confetti. Roll out various colors of fondant ⅛ in. thick; cut letters using alphabet cutters from set. For confetti, cut 6 x 1 in. wide fondant strips in each color. Cut strips into ⅛ in. squares. Position message and confetti on cake.

Cut two dowel rods to 3½ in. long; insert in cake where top of candy plaque cap will rest. Cut one dowel rod to 2 in.; position where bottom point of cap will rest. Position cap; secure with icing. Serves 22.

See instructions on facing page.

◀ Double-Major Celebration!

Pans: Smiley Grad, p. 206; Party Hat, p. 153
Tips: 5, 16, 18, p. 140-141
Colors:* For both cakes–Christmas Red, Rose, Black, Lemon Yellow, Golden Yellow; For male–Royal Blue, Brown; For female–Copper (skin tone), Red-Red, p. 135
Fondant: White Ready-To-Use Rolled Fondant (24 oz. per cake), p. 128; Rolling Pin, Roll & Cut Mat, p. 131
Recipe: Buttercream Icing, p. 114
Also: Plastic Dowel Rods, p. 224; Cake Board, Fanci-Foil Wrap, p. 225; Hand Plastic Cookie Cutter, p. 160; ½ in. thick foamcore board, serrated knife, cornstarch

In advance: Make fondant hands. Tint portions of fondant copper or brown. Roll out ¼ in. thick; using cookie cutter, cut 2 hands, reversing one to make left hand. Trim wrist area off hands. On cornstarch-dusted board, let right hand dry flat; wrap left hand around dowel rod trimmed to 5 in. for diploma.

Trim off void area under mortarboard on Smiley Grad cake and pompom on Party Hat cake. Position cakes on foil-wrapped foamcore board cut to fit, placing Party Hat cake narrow end up. Ice smooth eyes, mouth and pupils (smooth with finger dipped in cornstarch). Build up nose with tip 5; cover face with tip 16 stars. Pipe tip 16 swirl hair. Pipe tip 5 string eyebrows on male and eyelashes on female. Pipe tongue with tip 5. Cover mortarboard with tip 18 stars; add tip 5 dot button. Pipe tip 5 balls for cord; add tip 5 string tassel. For arms, cut dowel rod into two 6 in. lengths. Insert into sides of Party Hat cake, extending 4 in. from body. Roll out white fondant ⅛ in. thick; cover 4 in. of dowel rod arms. Using tip 5, outline and pipe in V-neck area on female; pipe in shirt, tie and collar on male. Ice gown smooth with spatula; insert hands into arms, trimming to fit if needed. Shape 2 in. fondant balls in black or white for feet and attach. Each cake serves 24.

*Combine Lemon Yellow and Golden Yellow for yellow shown. Combine Brown with Christmas Red for brown shown.

Blue Mist

Pans: 10, 16 x 2 in. Square, 8, 12 x 2 in. Round, p. 148
Tips: 16, 17, p. 141
Colors:* Royal Blue, Black, p. 135
Fondant: White Ready-To-Use Rolled Fondant (408 oz. needed), Brush Set, p. 128; Fondant Shaping Foam, Cutter/Embosser, Easy-Glide Fondant Smoother, p. 129; Rolling Pin, Roll & Cut Mat, p. 131
Recipe: Buttercream Icing, p. 114
Also: Fluted Bowl Separator Set (2), p. 220; Cake Circles, Fanci-Foil Wrap, p. 225; Cake Dividing Set, p. 133; Decorator Favorites Pattern Press Set, p. 137; White Candy Melts®†, p. 162; Plastic Dowel Rods (3 pks.), p. 224; Gum-Tex™, p. 131; Confectionery Tool Set, p. 129; 23 in. square x ½ in. high plywood board, 3 in. diameter x 2½ in. high craft block, 18-gauge florist wire (8 in. long, 45 pieces needed), ½ in. wide white ribbon (92 in.), double-stick tape, cornstarch, hot glue gun, waxed paper, craft knife

In advance: Make large and small fondant ribbon roses (p. 123). Combine 6 teaspoons of Gum-Tex with 72 oz. of white fondant. To make 45 large ribbon roses, roll out fondant ⅛ in. thick; cut three 1 x 6 in. long strips for each rose. Follow general rolling instructions, but add strips and open petals as you roll. Let dry on cornstarch-dusted board. On 38 of the large roses, make a small hole in bottom center with craft knife; attach 18-gauge wire with melted candy. To make 105 small ribbon roses without wires, cut a 1 x 6 in. long fondant strip for each rose; roll and let dry following directions. Assemble topper using 1 fluted bowl (p. 122).

Bake 2-layer 8 in. cake (4 in. high), 3-layer 12 in. round cake (bake three 2 in. high cakes to create a 6 in. high cake); 2-layer 16 in. square cake (bake two 1½ in. high layers to create a 3 in. high cake) and four 2-layer 10 in. square cakes (bake eight 1½ in. high cakes to create four 3 in. high cakes). Stack the four 10 in. cakes edge-to-edge on foil-wrapped plywood board to create a 20 in. square cake. Prepare cakes for stacked (p. 112) and Fluted Bowl Separator Set construction (p. 113). Prepare cakes for rolled fondant (p. 113). Tint remaining fondant blue. Cover cakes with fondant and smooth with Fondant Smoother. Stack 16 and 12 in. cakes on 20 in. cake.

For 12 in. round, divide cake into 16ths; mark 1¼ in. and 4¾ in. from bottom of cake. Using large scroll from Pattern Press Set, imprint designs at division marks. Outline imprints with tip 17. Attach a small ribbon rose in center of upper and lower scrolls with melted candy. Add tip 16 shell bottom border. Sponge above and below scrolls and on cake top with thinned buttercream icing, dabbing areas with crumpled paper towels.

For 16 and 20 in. squares, pipe tip 16 pull-out lines 1 in. apart on cake tops. Add tip 16 shell bottom borders. Attach small ribbon roses at bottom border of base cake with buttercream.

For 8 in. round, mark cake 2 in. from bottom; sponge top half of cake with thinned buttercream as on 12 in. cake. Attach small roses just below sponged area with melted candy. Add tip 16 shell bottom border.

At reception: Position the second fluted bowl on 12 in. cake; position 7 large ribbon roses without wires in center of bowl. Attach ribbon to cake base with double-stick tape. Position 8 in. cake and topper. Serves 384**.

Little Loves

Pan: Silicone Mini Heart, p. 144
Tip: 3, p. 140
Colors: Royal Blue, Black, p. 135
Fondant: White Ready-To-Use Rolled Fondant (24 oz. will cover 12-14 cakes; 12 oz. will make approximately 40 to 45 ribbon roses), Brush Set, p. 128; Rolling Pin, Roll & Cut Mat, p. 131; Easy-Glide Fondant Smoother, p. 129
Recipe: Buttercream Icing, p. 114
Also: Italic Make-Any-Message Press Set, p. 137; Gum-Tex™, p. 131; plastic ruler, scissors, cornstarch, paper towels, sharp knife

In advance: Make fondant ribbon roses (p. 123).

Trim cakes to 1 in. high. Prepare cakes for rolled fondant (p. 113). Cover cakes with fondant; smooth with Fondant Smoother. For cakes with roses, sponge tops with thinned buttercream, dabbing areas with crumpled paper towels. Attach ribbon roses with buttercream. For monogrammed cakes, imprint cake tops with letter press. Outline letters with tip 3. Each serves 1.

*Combine Royal Blue with a small amount of Black for blue shown.

†Brand confectionery coating.

Glittering Garden

Pans: 6, 10 x 2 in. Round, p. 148
Tip: 3, p. 140
Fondant: White Ready-To-Use Rolled Fondant (24 oz.), p. 128; Rolling Pin, Roll & Cut Mat, p. 131
Recipe: Buttercream Icing, p. 114
Also: Flower Picks (3 pks.), p. 219; Ceramic Pedestal Cake Stand, p. 222; Floral Collection Flower Making Set, p. 130; Confectionery Tool Set, Candy Melting Plate p. 129; Spatula, p. 138; Cake Circles, p. 225; Plastic Dowel Rods, p. 224; cornstarch

At least 48 hours in advance: Make fondant flowers. Roll out white fondant ⅛ in. thick. Using pansy cutter from Floral Collection Set, cut 70 flowers. Place on thin foam from Floral Collection Set; soften petal edges with ball tool from Confectionery Set. Move to thick foam; cup center using dog bone tool. Let flowers dry in melting plate cavities dusted with cornstarch. For flower centers, roll ⅛ in. fondant balls; attach with damp brush.

Spatula ice 2-layer cakes; prepare for stacked construction (p. 112). Position cakes on stand. Attach fondant flowers to bottom borders with tip 3 dots of icing. Insert food-safe flower picks in cake top; do not remove PVC sleeves. Serves 38.**

**The top tier is often saved for the first anniversary. The number of servings given does not include the top tier.

A Diamond's Promise

Pans: 6, 10, 14 x 2 in. Round, p. 148

Tip: 2, p. 140

Colors:* Lemon Yellow, Golden Yellow, p. 135

Fondant: White Ready-To-Use Rolled Fondant (24 oz.), p. 128; Rolling Pin, Roll & Cut Mat, p. 131

Recipes: Buttercream, Royal Icing, p. 114

Also: Monogram Picks, p. 219; Tailored Tiers™ Cake Display Set, p. 220; 16 in. Round Silver Cake Base, p. 225; Plastic Dowel Rods, p. 224; Gum-Tex™, p. 131; Meringue Powder, p. 134; Confectionery Tool Set, Flower Former Set, p. 129; Floral Collection Flower Making Set, p. 130; Cake Dividing Set, p. 133; ½ in. wide white ribbon (51 in.), double-stick tape, cornstarch, toothpick

Several days in advance: Make 750 forget-me-nots. Combine 2 teaspoons of Gum-Tex with 24 oz. of fondant. Roll out fondant ⅛ in. thick. Using Forget-Me-Not cutter from Floral Collection Set, cut 750 flowers. Place flowers on thick foam and cup centers with dogbone tool; let dry on small flower formers dusted with cornstarch. Add tip 2 dot centers in royal icing.

Ice 2-layer cakes smooth and prepare for Tailored Tiers construction (p. 113). Divide 6 in. cake into 6ths, 10 in. cake into 10ths and 14 in. cake into 14ths. Using toothpick, mark diagonal lines between adjacent top and bottom division points, creating a diamond design. Mark a smaller diamond shape ½ in. inside each large diamond shape; pipe tip 2 beads on small diamond markings. Attach 24 flowers on each large diamond and a flower in center with tip 2 dots of buttercream.

At reception: Assemble cakes on separators. Attach ribbon to cake base using double-stick tape. Insert food-safe monogram picks in cake top; do not remove PVC sleeves. Serves 116.**

*Combine Lemon Yellow and Golden Yellow for yellow shown.

**The top tier is often saved for the first anniversary. The number of servings given does not include the top tier.

Pinstriped Panache

Pans: 6, 10, 14 x 2 in. Round, p. 148
Colors: Kelly Green, Brown, Royal Blue, p. 135
Fondant: White Ready-To-Use Rolled Fondant (72 oz.), Neon Colors Fondant Multi Pack, p. 128
Ornament: 6½ in. Cake Bow, p. 219
Recipe: Buttercream Icing, p. 114
Also: Cake Boards, p. 225; Dowel Rods, p. 224; 2 and 2½ in. Globe Pillar Sets, 3 in. Globe Base Set, p. 220; 8, 12, 16 in. Smooth Edge Separator Plates, p. 223; Decorator Brush Set, p. 163; White Cake Sparkles™ (4 pks.), p. 136; craft knife, ruler, plastic wrap, waxed paper

Ice 2-layer cake tops smooth, lightly ice sides, Prepare for Globe Pillar Set construction.

Reserve 24 oz. white fondant. Tint remaining fondant: 24 oz. ivory, using a small amount of brown icing color; 1 oz. dark green using icing color. For light green, combine 9 oz. white with a 1 in. diameter ball of dark green. For medium green, combine 6 oz. white with remaining dark green fondant. Add a small amount of royal blue icing color to light and medium green. For dark violet, combine 4 oz. white with 2½ oz. violet from Multi Pack. For medium violet, combine 9 oz. white with 1 oz. violet. For light violet, combine 10 oz. white fondant and a 1 in. ball of violet fondant. Cover fondant with plastic wrap and place a damp towel over wrap to prevent drying. Roll fondant into logs approximately pencil-diameter in various colors to cover cake sides. Trim logs to approximately 4¼ in. long, just slightly longer than height of cakes (measure cake before cutting to be certain). Brush logs with water and sprinkle with Cake Sparkles. Position logs side-by-side on cake sides, alternating colors, securing with buttercream icing, if necessary. Trim top edges even with cake tops.

At reception: Assemble cakes. Position cake bow.** Serves 116.*

Hugs and Kisses All Around

Pans: 6, 10, 14 x 2 in. Square, p. 148; 12 x 18 x 2 in. Decorator Preferred® Sheet, p. 147

Tip: 18, p. 141

Color: Rose, p. 135

Fondant: White Ready-To-Use Rolled Fondant (24 oz.), p. 128; Rolling Pin, Roll & Cut Mat, p. 131

Cookie: 101 Cookie Cutters Set, Nesting Hearts Plastic Cutter Set, p. 160; 8 in. Cookie Treat Sticks, p. 161

Ornament: Classic Couple, p. 218

Recipe: Buttercream Icing, p. 114

Also: 2007 Pattern Book (Cake Top Heart), p. 126; White Candy Melts®†, p. 162; Fanci-Foil Wrap, p. 225; Gum-Tex™, p. 131; Plastic Dowel Rods, p. 224; 20 in. square x ½ in. thick foamcore board, ½ in. wide pink ribbon (80 in.), double-stick tape, cornstarch, waxed paper, small paring knife

In advance: Make cake top heart, cake side hearts, X's and O's. Add 2 tsp. of Gum-Tex to 24 oz. of fondant. Tint 12 oz. fondant light rose and 12 oz. dark rose. Roll out fondant ⅛ in. thick. In light rose, cut 20 each X's and O's using cutters from set. In dark rose, cut 36 cake side hearts using 2½ in. heart from nesting set. Using cake top heart pattern cut heart from dark rose fondant. Make extras of all fondant pieces to allow for breakage; let dry on cornstarch-dusted board.

Attach cookie stick to back of cake top heart with melted candy; let dry.

Bake three 12 x 18 in. cakes. Also bake 2-layer 6, 10 and 14 in. cakes (bake two 1½ in. high layers to create 3 in. high cakes). For bottom 18 in. square cake, position one 18 x 12 in. layer on foil-wrapped foamcore board. Cut a second 18 x 12 in. layer into two 18 x 6 in. halves. Position one half cake against 18 x 12 in. layer on board for an 18 in. square; repeat for top 18 in. layer, so that seams are perpendicular to each other. Ice all cakes smooth and prepare for stacked construction (p. 112). Pipe tip 18 shell bottom borders. Attach X's and O's to sides of 6 and 14 in. cakes and hearts to sides of 10 and 18 in. cakes with buttercream.

At reception: Insert cake top heart. Position ornament.** Attach ribbon to cake base using double-stick tape. Serves 294.*

*The top tier is often saved for the first anniversary. The number of servings given does not include top tier.

**Always place a separator plate, or cake board cut to fit, on the cake where you position any figurine or ornament. This protects both the cake and your keepsake. For extra stability, secure your figurine to the plate with double-stick craft tape.

†Brand confectionery coating.

Freefalling Flowers

Pans: 6, 10, 14 x 2 in. Round, p. 148; 18 x 3 in. Half Round, p. 147

Tips: 3, 5, p. 140

Color: Ivory, p. 135

Fondant: White Ready-To-Use Rolled Fondant (288 oz.), p. 128; Rolling Pin, Roll & Cut Mat, Spiral Pattern Fondant Roller, p. 131; Easy-Glide Fondant Smoother, Cutter/Embosser, p. 129

Recipes: Buttercream, Royal Icings, p. 114

Also: Flower Former Set, Confectionery Tool Set, p. 129; Floral Collection Flower Making Set, p. 130; Gum-Tex™, p. 131; Meringue Powder, p. 134; 7½ in. Crystal-Clear Twist Legs (3 pks.), p. 220; 8, 12, 16 in. Plates from Crystal-Clear Cake Divider Set, p. 220; Fanci-Foil Wrap, p. 225; 20 in. diameter x ½ in. thick plywood board, ½ in. wide white ribbon (63 in.), double-stick tape, cornstarch, paring knife, ruler

In advance: Make fondant flowers, curved bands and bow. Combine 2 tablespoons Gum-Tex with 72 oz. of fondant. For flowers, roll out fondant ⅛ in. thick; using cutters from flower making set, cut 400 apple blossoms and 400 pansies. Position flowers on thick foam; using small ball tool, cup centers. Let flowers dry on cornstarch-dusted board. Using royal icing, pipe tip 3 dot centers on apple blossoms and tip 5 dot centers on pansies. For curved bands, roll out fondant ⅛ in. thick; imprint spiral design with pattern roller. Using straight-edge wheel of Cutter/Embosser, cut 90 strips 1½ x 2 in. long; let dry on back of small flower formers dusted with cornstarch. Make extras to allow for breakage. To make bow (p. 123), roll out fondant ⅛ in. thick; imprint spiral design. Cut 15 strips 1 x 7 in. long to make loops; let dry. Using royal icing, pipe tip 3 beads on one edge of each loop; let dry on side on a cornstarch-dusted board. Pipe tip 3 beads on other edge; let dry. Assemble bow with royal icing on waxed paper-covered cake circle, using 7 loops for bottom layer, 4 for middle, 1 for top; let dry.

Wrap plywood base with foil. Prepare 2-layer cakes (for 18 in. cake, bake four 2 in. high half rounds to make a 4 in. high cake) for push-in pillar construction (p. 112). Prepare cakes for rolled fondant (p. 113). Tint 216 oz. fondant ivory; cover cakes and smooth with Fondant Smoother. Attach curved bands to cake sides with royal icing; let set. Between each strip, pipe a row of tip 5 beads with royal icing; attach an apple blossom at top of each row. Randomly attach remaining flowers to top and sides of cakes with royal icing. Attach bow at top with royal icing. Attach ribbon to cake base with double-stick tape. Serves 262.*

◀ Linked in Love

Pans: 6, 10, 14 x 2 in. Square, p. 148

Tip: 5, p. 140

Color: Ivory, p. 135

Candy: Roses Classic, Roses in Bloom Molds, p. 165; White Candy Melts®† (6 pks.), p. 162

Ornament: Bianca, p. 217

Recipe: Buttercream Icing, p. 114

Also: Circle Metal Cookie Cutter (6), p. 158; Flower Former Set, p. 129; Plastic Dowel Rods, p. 224; 3 in. Grecian Pillars (2 pks.), p. 221; Cookie Sheet, p. 149; 7, 11 in. Square Separator Plates (2), p. 223; Cake Boards, Fanci-Foil Wrap, p. 225; 16 in. square x ½ in. thick foamcore board, ½ in. wide ivory ribbon, double-stick tape, freezer paper

In advance: Make candy roses, medallions and bands. Mold 36 large roses using Roses in Bloom mold; mold 288 small roses using rose portion only from Roses Classic mold. For candy medallions, mold 36 candy circles; place circle cutter on cookie sheet and fill ⅛ in. high with melted candy. Refrigerate all candies until firm; unmold. Make 20 large and 16 small candy bands. Cut 20 strips of freezer paper 3½ x ¾ in. wide and 16 strips 2¾ x ¾ in. wide. Spread an even layer of melted candy over each strip; let set until slightly firm. Position on outside of flower formers, using large formers for large strips and medium formers for small strips. Make extra to allow for breakage and refrigerate until firm.

Assemble candy medallions. Using melted candy, attach 1 large rose at center of candy circle and 8 small roses around center. Refrigerate until firm.

Bake and cool 2-layer cakes (bake two 1½ in. layers to make 3 in. high cakes). Ice cakes smooth and prepare for Pillar Construction (p. 112). Pipe tip 5 bead top and bottom borders. Position candy medallions at equal distance on cake sides, 2 on each 6 in. cake side, 3 on each 10 in. side, 4 on each 14 in. side. Using melted candy, attach large strips to medallions on 14 in. cake, small strips on other cakes.

At reception: Assemble cakes. Attach ribbon to cake base with double-stick tape. Position ornament.** Serves 148.*

**Always place a separator plate, or cake board cut to fit, on the cake where you position any figurine or ornament. This protects both the cake and your keepsake. For extra stability, secure your figurine to the plate with double-stick craft tape.

†Brand confectionery coating.

▶ Songbird Sonata

Pans: 6 x 2 in. Round, Petal Pan Set (12 x 2 in.), p. 148

Tips: 2, 18, p. 140-141

Colors: Violet, Moss Green, Creamy Peach, Buttercup Yellow, Rose, p. 135

Ornament: Song of Love Cake Topper, p. 218

Recipes: Buttercream Icing, p. 114; Gum Paste, p. 115

Also: Floral Collection Flower Making Set, p. 130; Flower Former Set, Confectionery Tool Set, p. 129; Gum Paste Mix, Rolling Pin, Roll & Cut Mat, p. 131; Decorator Brush Set, p. 128; Plastic Dowel Rods, p. 224; Cake Boards, Fanci-Foil Wrap, p. 225; ½ in. wide white ribbon (44 in.), double-stick tape, tea strainer, non-toxic pastel chalks, cornstarch

In advance: Make gum paste flowers and leaves. Divide prepared gum paste recipe into 4ths; tint violet/rose combination, yellow, peach and green. Make 130 violet/rose forget-me-nots, 10 yellow pansies, 85 yellow apple blossoms and 50 small peach daisies. Roll out gum paste ¹⁄₁₆ in. thick. Cut flowers using corresponding cutter from flower making set; use smallest daisy cutter for daisies. Position forget-me-nots, pansies and apple blossoms on thick foam; cup centers using ball tool. Position daisies on thin foam; thin and lengthen petals with ball tool. Let dry on small flower formers dusted with cornstarch. Grate non-toxic chalk through tea strainer and brush on flowers. For 10 fantasy flowers, attach an apple blossom to center of 10 pansies with damp brush. Let dry in small flower formers dusted with cornstarch. pipe tip 2 dot center in all flowers. Make 65 green leaves. Roll out green gum paste ¹⁄₁₆ in. thick; cut leaves using leaf cutter from set. Position leaves on thin foam. Imprint vein lines with veining tool. Let dry on small flower formers dusted with cornstarch.

Ice 2-layer round and petal cakes smooth (for petal cake, bake two 1½ in. layers to create a 3 in. high cake). Prepare cakes for stacked construction (p. 112). Pipe tip 18 shell bottom borders. Position ornament.** On round cake, attach flowers and leaves around ornament and cascading down sides with buttercream. On petal cake, attach flowers and leaves in garland formation, 1¼ in. deep. Attach ribbon to cake base with double-stick tape. Serves 40.*

*The top tier is often saved for the first anniversary. The number of servings given does not include the top tier.

◀ Uplifting Lilies

Pans: 8, 12, 16 x 2 in. Round, p. 148

Tips: 2, 3, 5, 14, 67, 363, p. 140-141

Ornaments: Bianca, p. 217; Lighted Revolving Base, p. 219

Recipes: Royal, Buttercream Icings, p. 114

Also: 10, 14 in. Spiral Separator Sets, p. 220; Lily Nail Set, p. 138; Stamen Assortment (3 pks.), p. 129; Plastic Dowel Rods, p. 224; Cake Circles, Fanci-Foil Wrap, p. 225; 18 in. round x ½ in. thick foamcore or plywood board; 2 in. foil squares, ½ in. wide white ribbon (57 in.), double-stick tape, ruler, toothpicks

Several days in advance: Make 100 lilies using royal icing, 1⅝ in. lily nail and tips 67 and 14 (p. 118). Insert stamens, using all varieties, and let dry 1 to 2 days.

Ice 2-layer cakes smooth in buttercream and prepare for alternate 2-plate set-up with Spiral Separator Set (p. 113). Use toothpicks to make guide marks ⅜ in. apart along top edge of each cake. Pipe tip 3 lines at guide marks down cake sides; start with a ¾ in. line, then pipe 1⅛ in., 1½ in., 1⅞ in. and 2¼ in. lines. Reverse order of lines from the 2¼ line, ascending to the next ¾ in. line. Repeat for all cake sides. Pipe tip 3 balls at end of lines and tip 2 balls on lines.

Position lilies along top borders. Pipe tip 5 fleur de lis on back base of each lily to support on cake. Pipe tip 363 shell bottom borders.

At reception: Assemble cakes on stands. Attach ribbon to cake base with double-stick tape. Position ornament on base and base on cake.** Serves 156.*

▶ Black & White Classic

Pans: 6, 10, 14 x 2 in. Round Pan, p. 148

Tip: 6, p. 140

Fondant: White Ready-To-Use Rolled Fondant (126 oz.), p. 128; Rolling Pin, Roll & Cut Mat, p. 131; Easy-Glide Fondant Smoother, p. 129

Recipe: Buttercream Icing, p. 114

Also: 12 in. Floral Cake Decorations (2 pks.), p. 219; 2½, 5 in. Curved Pillars, p. 221; 8, 12 in. Smooth-Edge Separator Plates (2 each), p. 223; Plastic Dowel Rods, p. 224; Cake Circles, 16 in. Round Silver Cake Base, p. 225; ⅝ in. wide black ribbon (3 yds.), ½ in. wide white ribbon (51 in.), cellophane tape

Prepare 2-layer cakes for rolled fondant (p. 113). Cover cakes with fondant; smooth with Fondant Smoother. Prepare cakes for 2-plate and pillar construction (p. 112). Cut a strip of black ribbon to fit around each cake; overlap ends and secure with tape. Pipe tip 6 bead bottom borders. Attach white ribbon to cake base with tape. Position rose sprays. Serves 116.*

*The top tier is often saved for the first anniversary. The number of servings given does not include the top tier.

Unveiling a Masterpiece

Pans: 6, 8, 10 x 2 in. Round, Hexagon Set (15 in. used), p. 148

Tips: 1, 2, 4, p. 140

Fondant: White Ready-To-Use Rolled Fondant (552 oz.), Brush Set, p. 128; Rolling Pin, Roll & Cut Mat, p. 131; Easy-Glide Fondant Smoother, p. 129

Ornament: Good Fairy Cake Topper, p. 218

Recipe: Buttercream Icing, p. 114

Also: Gum-Tex™, p. 131; White Candy Melts†, p. 162; Confectionery Tool Set, p. 129; 8 in. Smooth-Edge Separator Plates (2), p. 223; Embroidered Wrapped Pillars, p. 221; Cake Dividing Set, p. 133; Plastic, Wooden Dowel Rods, p. 224; Cake Boards, Fanci-Foil Wrap, p. 225; 28 in. diameter x ½ in. thick plywood board, 8 in. diameter x 4¼ in. high wood or craft block, ½ in. wide ribbon (100 in.), double-stick tape, cornstarch

Several days in advance: Make 6 large and 24 medium ribbon roses (p. 123). Combine 48 oz. of fondant with 4 teaspoons of Gum-Tex. Roll out fondant ⅛ in. thick. For large roses, cut 6 in. long x 1 in. strips; for medium roses, cut 6 in. long x ½ in. wide strips. Using remaining mixture, make 12 bow loops (p. 123) using 5 in. long x 1½ in. wide strips. Let all dry on cornstarch-dusted surface. Reserve any leftover fondant for veils.

Prepare six 2-layer 8 in. round cakes, one each 2-layer 6 in. and 10 in. round cake, and one 2-layer 15 in. hexagon cake for Stacked and Pillar Construction (p. 112). Prepare cakes for rolled fondant (p. 113); cover cakes with fondant and smooth with Fondant Smoother. Divide 8 in. cakes into 4ths; decorate only the 2 sections of each cake which will face outward after assembly. Mark scallops from division points, 2½ in. from base at lowest point. Pipe tip 1 sotas below scallops. Position cakes on foil-wrapped plywood board. Cover 8 in. diameter craft block with foil; position in center of cakes on board. Pipe tip 4 bead bottom borders. Roll out fondant ⅛ in. thick; cut twelve 6 x 3½ in. high strips. Make 12 swags (p. 123). Attach to cake with damp brush.

Position hexagon cake on triple-thick cake boards cut to fit. On each side, mark lowest scallop point in center, 1¾ in. from base of cake. At hexagon corners, mark 3¾ in. from base. Connect corners to lowest scallop point to form curves. Divide 10 in. cake into 12ths; mark 1 division at base, next division 2 in. up, next 3 in. up, then top edge of cake; reverse with descending markings at 3 in., 2 in. and base. Repeat process for other half of cake. Connect marks to form scallops. Position 10 in. round on hexagon cake; pipe tip 1 sotas on tops and scallop areas of both cakes. Edge hexagon scallop with tip 2 beads; pipe tip 4 bead bottom border on 10 in. cake. Make 12 fondant swags for 10 in. cake using 4 in. x 3 in. high strips; attach with damp brush. Divide 6 in. cake into 6ths. Mark 1 division at base, next division 1½ in. up, next 2½ in. up, then top edge of cake; reverse with descending markings at 2½ in. and 1¼ in., meeting back at base marking. Connect marks to form scallops. Pipe tip 1 sotas below scallops. Make 6 fondant swags using 4 x 3 in. high strips; attach to cake with damp brush. Mark 8 in. round cakes where hexagon cake will rest. Combine 96 oz. of fondant with 8 teaspoons of Gum-Tex; add reserved fondant. Make 6 fondant veils (p. 123). Attach between 8 in. cakes with damp brush, ½ in. from markings for hexagon cake. Attach medium ribbon roses at swag points of 8, 10 and 6 in. cakes with melted candy.

At reception: Position hexagon cake on 8 in. cakes with 8 in. round foil-wrapped craft block in center; position 6 in. cake on plates and pillars. Pipe tip 4 bead bottom border on hexagon cake. Attach bow loops with damp brush at end of veils. Attach large ribbon roses with damp brush where loops meet. Attach ribbon to cake base using double-stick tape. Position ornament.** Serves 212.*

**Always place a separator plate, or cake board cut to fit, on the cake where you position any figurine or ornament. This protects both the cake and your keepsake. For extra stability, secure your figurine to the plate with double-stick craft tape.

†Brand confectionery coating.

Beaucoup Beauty

Pans: 6, 8, 10 x 3 in. Round, p. 148
Tips: 2, p. 140
Color: Rose, p. 135
Ornaments: 6½ in. Cake Bows (3), p. 219
Fondant: White Ready-To-Use Rolled Fondant (80 oz.), p. 128; Rolling Pin, Roll & Cut Mat, p. 131; Easy-Glide Fondant Smoother, p. 129
Recipe: Buttercream Icing, Royal Icing, p. 114
Also: Cakes 'N More 3-Tier Party Stand, p. 222; Floral Collection Flower Making Set, p. 130; Confectionery Tool Set, Flower Former Set, p. 129; Gum-Tex™, p. 131; Meringue Powder, p. 134; Cake Circles, p. 225; ⅞ in. wide brown satin ribbon (76 In. long), double-stick tape, cornstarch

In advance: Add 1 teaspoon Gum-Tex to 12 oz. of white fondant; tint rose. Make 200 forget-me-not flowers. Roll out fondant ⅛ in. thick; cut flowers using forget-me-not cutter from flower-making set. Cup flowers on thick foam using ball tool. Add tip 2 white dot centers in royal icing. Let dry on small flower formers dusted with cornstarch. **Also:** Tint cake bows rose following package instructions.

Place 1-layer cakes (3 in. high) on same-size cake circles and prepare for rolled fondant (p. 113). Cover cakes with fondant; smooth with Fondant Smoother. Wrap ribbon around base of each cake; secure with tape. Attach flowers with dots of icing.

At reception: Position cakes on stand. Position bows on cake tops. Serves 48.*

*The smallest tier is often saved for the first anniversary. The number of servings given does not include the smallest tier.

When Hearts Beat as One

Pan: Silicone Mini Heart Mold, p. 144

Tips: 5, 7, 102, p. 140-141

Colors: Royal Blue, Kelly Green, Rose, Orange, Brown, p. 135

Fondant: White Ready-To-Use Rolled Fondant (64 oz. will decorate 25 cakes), Brush Set, p. 128; Rolling Pin, Roll & Cut Mat, p. 131; Cutter/Embosser, p. 129

Recipes: Buttercream Icing, Chocolate Fondant, p. 114

Also: Cakes 'N More 3-Tier Party Stand, p. 222; Hearts Plastic Nesting Cutter Set, p. 160; Flower Nail No. 7, p. 138; Dark Cocoa Candy Melts®†, p. 162; paring knife, waxed paper

Bake and cool cakes; unmold. Prepare one chocolate fondant recipe. Prepare cakes for rolled fondant (p. 113). Roll out white fondant ⅛ in. thick. Cut fondant heart using 3rd smallest cutter and position on cake tops, trimming to fit heart shape. Roll out chocolate fondant ⅛ in. thick. Cut 8 x 1½ in. wide strips; wrap around cake sides, trimming to fit. Tint 4 oz. portions of fondant each in rose, blue, green and orange; roll out ⅛ in. thick. Cut 8 x ½ in. strips; attach on cake sides with damp brush. Pipe tip 5 dots on color strips. For each cake, make a tip 102 rose with tip 7 base (p. 118). Attach rose to cake top with dots of icing.

At reception: Position cakes on stand. Each serves 1.

†Brand confectionery coating.

SPECIAL SECTION

Catchy Themes!

Take your party theme further. Don't just rely on candles and baking cups to tell folks they're at a jungle animals party. Build the whole jungle! Use a cool cake stand to carry the look—our stairstep 3-Tier Party Stand does it right, complete with a tier-to-tier network of tree vines. And wait until you see this stand as a water slide and a roller coaster! Stands and separators are no longer behind the scenes—they complete the scene. Check out our globe separators, turned into sports balls and puffy fish. If you want your theme to really hit home—take a stand!

Instructions for projects shown on these two pages are on page 98.

Star-Studded Celebration

With one simple shape, your party plan falls into place. We've given stars shining faces, added a galaxy of dazzling colors and given cereal treats and pizzas a new star power!

Sizzling Stars Cake: In advance: Make fondant message stars, cake side stars and swags (p. 122). Bake and cool 8, 10 and 12 in. round cakes (2 in. high) and 18 cupcakes in Silicone Baking Cups. Cover cakes with rolled fondant (p. 113). Pipe tip 1M (2110) swirl in buttercream on cupcakes; immediately top with Confetti Sprinkles from Flowerful Medley Assortment. In royal icing, pipe tip 2 dots and messages on message stars. Tie curling ribbon bows on sticks. Divide 12 in. cake in 15ths, 10 in. cake in 12ths, 8 in. cake in 10ths; attach swags and stars at division points with damp brush. Position cakes on Cakes 'N More Party Stand; position cupcakes and insert message stars and Chunky Star Candles. Cakes serve 44; each cupcake serves 1.

Star-Studded Centerpiece: Tint Roll-Out Cookie Dough (p. 114) in various colors. Cut cookies using Nesting Stars Metal Set; sprinkle with matching Colored Sugars. Bake and cool. Attach to 11¾ in. Lollipop Sticks with melted Candy Melts. Pipe tip 2 dot eyes, pupils and string smiles in buttercream. For base, cut Dazzling Dots Treat Bags in 2½ in. wide strips; wrap around a 6 x 2½ in. craft circle, secure with tape. Tie a curling ribbon bow on each cookie stick; insert cookies in block. Each serves 1.

Cereal Treat Sparklers: For stars, add ¼ teaspoon Gum-Tex™ to yellow from Primary and Neon Fondant Multi Pack. Roll out ⅛ in. thick and cut using 2¼ in. cutter from Nesting Stars Metal Set. Brush lightly with water; sprinkle with Yellow Colored Sugar. Let dry on cornstarch-dusted board. Attach lollipop stick cut to 3 in. with melted Candy Melts. Prepare favorite crisped rice cereal treats, adding Rainbow Nonpareils to mixture; press 1 in. thick into a prepared 9 x 13 in. Sheet Pan. Unmold and cut in 4½ x 1½ in. pieces. Roll out other Multi Pack colors ⅛ in. thick and cut 6 x ½ in. wide strips; wrap around treats, attaching with damp brush. Insert stars. Each serves 1.

Pizza Pie in the Sky: Prepare your favorite pizza dough. Roll out and cut stars using Star Copper Cutter. Add pizza sauce, cheese and your favorite toppings. Bake at 350°F for 8-10 minutes, until edges are golden brown and cheese is bubbly. Each serves 1.

Big Name Stars: Use 2 pks. of White Candy Melts to make and decorate 5-6 plaques; reserve 2 wafers per plaque for easels. Tint portions of 1 pk. pink, orange, yellow, green, blue and violet using Primary and Garden Candy Color Sets. Mold ¼ in. thick plaques (p. 124) in Mini Loaf Pan and 2 stars for each in Stars Mold. Pipe names and trim using melted candy. For easel backs, cut wafers straight on bottom and angled on side; attach easels to back and stars to front of plaque with melted candy. Each serves 1.

A. Set Off Skyrockets!

In advance: Using royal icing, make wired stars (p. 119). **Also:** Make candies. For numbers, place cutters from ABC & 123 set on Non-Stick Cookie Pan; fill ⅜ in. deep with melted Yellow Candy Melts®†. Refrigerate until firm; unmold and attach to 11¾ in. lollipop sticks with melted candy. For letters, tint portions of melted white candy using Garden Candy Colors Set. Mold in Alphabet Mold using layering method (p. 123). Cut a ring from a 12 in. cake circle, removing 9 in. from center; place under a craft foam circle with a 9 in. opening at center. Secure cake circle with straight pins. Wrap with foil. In chocolate buttercream, ice smooth 2-layer 6, 8 and 10 in. cakes (3 in. high); prepare for stacked construction (p. 112). Position on Ceramic Pedestal Cake Stand. Pipe tip 21 shell bottom border on 10 in. cake, pipe tip 18 shells for remaining borders; twist 12 in. wired stars together and insert in flower spike. Insert spike in cake top. Insert numbers. Position stand in center of craft foam circle. Insert 6 in. wired stars in craft block base, in a circle arrangement. Serves 60.

B. 40 Reasons for Chocolate!

In advance: Tint portions of melted white candy using Garden Candy Colors Set. Mold candies in Numbers Mold ¼ in. thick; refrigerate until firm. Pipe 1½ in. circle bases on waxed paper, using melted cocoa candy in cut parchment bag; let set. Attach numbers to bases with melted candy. Bake and cool 1½ in. high cake in 9 x 13 Sheet Pan. Cut cakes using Circle Metal Cutter. Cover with melted Light Cocoa Candy Melts (p. 124); let set. Place cakes on waxed paper; divide in 8ths. Using melted candy, pipe zigzag garlands; add dots at division points and pipe bead bottom border. Position numbers. Each serves 1.

C. Cookie Gift

Cut tinted Roll-Out Cookie Dough using 2nd and 3rd largest Nesting Stars cutters and number cutters from 101 Cookie Cutters Set; sprinkle with Colored Sugars. Bake and cool; attach to 11¾ in. lollipop sticks with White Candy Melts. Wrap 2 in. wide white ribbon and 1½ in. wide brown ribbon around a 6 x 2 in. craft block; secure with pins. Curl 18 in. lengths of curling ribbon; gather at center and secure with 22-gauge florist wire. Tie 10 in. lengths of curling ribbon to cookie sticks. Insert cookies and ribbon in craft block. Each serves 1.

†Brand confectionery coating.

Marking Milestones

It's a party for the ages, with big, bright cookie and candy toppers noting the banner year. Chocolate makes the milestone easier to swallow.

Family Pride

Your roots are strong–celebrate them with a dessert everyone can relate to. There's a heartwarming family tree cake to share, plus nametag cookies that honor each individual.

D. Our Family's Branching Out

In advance: Cut Roll-Out Cookie Dough using Circle Metal Cutter; cut a hole at top using narrow end of tip 4; bake and cool. Using royal icing, pipe 20 tip 2D swirl drop flowers with tip 3 dot centers on waxed paper. Using thinned royal icing in cut parchment bag, pipe 1 and 1½ in. circle faces on waxed paper; let dry. Attach faces to cookies with royal icing. Using thinned royal icing in cut bag, pipe dot nose. Using full-strength royal icing, pipe hair with tips 3 and 13. Draw eyes and mouth with FoodWriter™ markers. **Also:** Make 12 branches using 18-gauge wrapped florist wire, using one 14 in. and one 10 in. length for each branch. Twist the 2 lengths together leaving 4 in. length of single wire at bottom. Wrap with florist tape, adding 3 Green Leaves and leaving 4 in. at bottom untaped. Tape on an 8 in. wire for side branch; add 2 leaves. Ice smooth 2-layer 12 in. round cake (3 in. high) in buttercream and prepare for tall-tier stand construction (p. 112) using one 6½ and one 7¾ in. column for tree trunk. Pipe tip 21 shell bottom border and tip 18 shell top border. Print tip 4 message. Attach flowers with icing and add tip 352 leaves. Insert branches in center column; if all wires won't fit, attach to outside of column with melted candy, then wrap with floral tape. Lightly ice trunk; overpipe with tip 21 stripes. Thread a 12 in. curling ribbon through hole in cookie; tie onto branches. Cake serves 40; each cookie serves 1.

E. Do Your Name Proud!

For 3-letter names, cut 1¾ in. high rectangles of Roll-Out Cookie Dough, 3 in. wide; add ¾ in. more to width for each additional letter. For easel backs, cut 1¼ in. square cookies; cut diagonally in half to make 2 for each cookie. Cut large initial cookies using letter cutters from 101 Cutters Set. Bake and cool all cookies. Tint melted White Candy Melts using Primary and Garden Candy Color Sets. Mold smaller letters ½ in. deep in Alphabet Mold. Cover initial cookies with melted candy (p. 124). Attach letters and easel backs to cookie plaques with melted candy. Each serves 1.

Please see our Product Shops (p. 125-230) for specific decorating items used in this section; find recipes on pages 114-115.

Wild Water Park!

Fondant kids ride the tide on a multi-level water slide! Our 3-Tier Party Stand makes this new-wave design possible, with its flowing presentation of small, medium and large cakes.

A. Big Splash Birthday Bash

In advance: Tint 24 oz. fondant Royal Blue, 16 oz. each Black and Copper (skin tone), 8 oz. Brown/Red-Red combination and 2 oz. each Lemon Yellow/Golden Yellow combination, Orange, Rose, Violet/Rose combination and Leaf Green; reserve 10 oz. White. Make fondant kids (p. 122). Make water slides (p. 122). Ice 2-layer 6, 8 and 10 in. round cakes (3 in. high) smooth in buttercream; cover cake tops with blue-tinted piping gel. Roll out blue fondant ⅛ in. thick; using pattern from Pattern Book, cut wave strips 2 in. and 1 in. high, long enough to wrap around each cake. Attach 2 in. wave to cake with icing; attach 1 in. wave to 2 in. wave with damp brush. Position cakes on Cakes 'N More 3-Tier Party Stand. Cut sign from paper; draw message and border with markers. Tape to 11¾ in. lollipop sticks; trim as needed and insert in cake. Position slides and kids. Serves 60.

B. Sunshine Centerpiece

Tint melted white Candy Melts®† using Primary and Garden Candy Color Sets. Mold lollipops using painting method (p. 123), Summer Fun Candy Mold and 6 in. Sticks. Also mold sunglasses candy. Mold sun ¼ in. deep in Round Comfort Grip™ Cutter on Non-Stick Cookie Sheet. Trace Sun Features and Sun Rays patterns from 2007 Pattern Book on waxed paper; pipe in using melted candy; let set. Attach rays, face pieces and 11¾ in. stick with melted candy. Cut 18 in. lengths of curling ribbon; gather together in 3 groups of 5 and secure with florist wire; tie single ribbons to each lollipop. Pour dried beans in plastic bucket; add a craft foam circle, cut to fit. Insert lollipops and ribbon groups. Each candy serves 1.

C. Sun Gelatin

Mix two 3 oz. pks. of orange gelatin and three 1 oz. pks. of unflavored gelatin; prepare following orange gelatin directions. Pour in prepared 9 x 13 x 2 in. Sheet Pan. Refrigerate overnight. Spray Daisy Comfort Grip™ cutter with pan spray; cut sun shapes. Using tinted Whipped Icing Mix, pipe in tip 12 face, tip 3 facial features. Each serves 1.

D. Candies in Paradise

Tint white Candy Melts using Candy Color Sets. Mold blue base ⅜ in. deep in Round Comfort Grip Cutter on Non-Stick Cookie Sheet. Mold trees in Summer Fun Mold using painting method (p. 123); attach to base with candy. For each chair, cut striped gum in 1¼ and ¾ in. pieces; attach with candy. Attach sour candy disk face to chair with candy; pipe facial features, hair, body and bathing suits with melted candy. Ice top of base with candy; sprinkle with brown sugar. Position chairs. Each serves 1.

Safari Scene

This amazing Amazon adventure is easy to swing. Let our lively Jungle Pals products be your guide—colorful toppers, cutters, bags and baking cups give easy cakes and treats a coordinated look.

E. Jungle Fun Cake

Two days in advance: Make 7 palm trees (p. 120). **Also:** Make 4 monkeys using pattern from 2007 Pattern Book and royal icing with tips 1, 2 and 6. Make a fondant hook for each monkey using green-tinted fondant. Roll a 1½ x ⅛ in. diameter log; shape a ¼ in. hook at one end. Let dry on cornstarch-dusted board. Attach hook to back of monkey's raised arm with royal icing; let dry. Ice smooth 1-layer 6, 8 and 10 in. cakes in buttercream. Position on plates from Cakes 'N More 3-Tier Party Stand. Pipe tip 16 pull-out grass. Attach Jungle Pals Icing Decorations 1 in. apart on cake sides. Pipe in water area on cake top using tinted Piping Gel in cut parchment bag. Sprinkle brown sugar for sand. Insert palm trees, trimming as needed. Pipe tip 16 pull-out grass. For vines between trees, twist three 18 in. lengths of 22-gauge florist wire together; make 2 groups and twist around trees from highest to lowest tiers. Position monkeys on vines. Pipe tip 16 leaves on vines. Position Jungle Pals Cake Toppers. Serves 30.

F. Congo Cupcakes

Bake and cool cupcakes in Standard Muffin Pan using Jungle Pals Baking Cups. Ice smooth in buttercream. Position Jungle Pals Cake Toppers. Add tip 352 pull-out leaves. Each serves 1.

G. Cookies in the Wild

In advance: Make 3 palm trees. Cover back of Mini Ball Pan with aluminum foil and spray with vegetable pan spray. Using green royal icing, pipe tip 366 leaves; let dry. Attach leaves to pretzel rods with royal icing; let dry. Cut Roll-Out Cookie Dough using horse, giraffe, lion and elephant cutters from Animal Pals 50-Pc. Cutter Set; bake and cool. Outline and flow in cookies with color flow (p. 124); let dry. Add tip 2 details with full-strength color flow; let dry. Attach 4 in. Lollipop Sticks to backs with full-strength color flow. Wrap 8 x 2 in. craft circle with foil; cut Jungle Pals Party Bags into 2 in. strips and attach to craft block sides with cellophane tape. Cut green curling ribbon into 24 in. lengths; curl. Gather ribbon in 4-strand clusters, secure with 22-gauge cloth-covered florist wire and insert in craft block. Insert animals and trees. Each serves 1.

Please see our Product Shops (p.125-230) for specific decorating items used in this section. Find recipes on pages 114-115.

A. Coast to Coast Cakes

In advance: Tint 62 oz. of Ready-To-Use Gum Paste: 24 oz. Royal Blue, 2 oz. each dark Royal Blue, Lemon Yellow/Golden Yellow combination, Kelly Green, Red-Red/Christmas Red combination, Orange and Violet, 1 oz. each Copper (skin tone) and Brown. Reserve 24 oz. White. Make roller coaster tracks, cars and people (p. 123). In buttercream, ice smooth 2-layer 6 in. cake (4 in. high) and 8 in. cake (3 in. high), 1-layer 10 in. cake (2 in. high). Position cakes on Cakes 'N More 3-Tier Party Stand. On cake sides, pipe tip 9 outline roller coaster track; pipe a tip 4 vertical line every 1½ in. under track; add criss-cross lines to connect vertical lines. Pipe a tip 4 flag at each dip of track (smooth with finger dipped in cornstarch). Add tip 233 pull-out grass bottom borders. Position hill sections and cake top curves; support hills with 11¾ in. lollipop sticks. Roll out white gum paste ⅛ in. thick. Cut ¼ in. wide strips for bottom of side rail; attach on each side of track with damp brush. Cut ½ x 1½ in. long slats and attach across track with damp brush. Attach vertical side rails to track with royal icing; let dry several hours. Cut ¼ in. wide strips for top of side rail; attach with damp brush. With FoodWriter markers, draw facial features. Attach heads and hands to shirts with royal icing. Position people in cars; pipe tip 2 hair. Attach cars to track with royal icing. Cut flags and sign from construction paper using patterns; print message and draw borders with markers. Tape to lollipop sticks and insert in cake. Serves 46.

B. Crispy Carousel

In advance: Cut 4 horses from Roll-Out Cookie Dough using cutter from 50-Piece Animal Set. Bake and cool. Decorate using Color Flow: Outline and fill in horses with tip 3; let dry. Pipe tip 3 outline reins, legs and mouth, dot eyes; pipe in saddle, hooves, tail. Add tip 3 pull-out mane. Make canopy poles. Cut four 11¾ in. lollipop sticks to 8½ in. for outer poles and one to 10 in. for center pole. Attach curling ribbon to outer poles with color flow in a spiral formation; let dry. Prepare 2 recipes of your favorite crisped rice cereal treats. Press in prepared 10 x 2 in. Round Pan; unmold on foil-wrapped board. Divide top of treat in 4ths; measure 2 in. from edge. Make a hole at each division for outer poles using 11¾ in. lollipop stick. Make a hole for center pole at midpoint of outer poles. Divide sides of treat in 12ths using Cake Divider Set. Using full-strength color flow, pipe tip 13 zigzag garland, 1 in. deep. Attach mini candy-coated chocolates and spice drop halves. Pipe tip 16 star bottom border; attach regular size candy-coated chocolates. For canopy, cut a 12 in. circle from white paper. Divide in 12ths. Using markers, outline and fill in sections. With scissors, cut a slit from edge of one section to center. Fold circle to create cone; secure with double-stick tape. For flag, cut a 3 x ½ in. triangle from paper; color with marker. Insert poles in treat; press treat mixture around sticks to secure. Attach cookies and candy-coated chocolates to poles with color flow; let dry. Position canopy. Attach flag with tape. Serves 14. Each cookie serves 1.

C. Ferris Wheel Fun

In advance: Make kids on waxed paper using royal icing. Pipe tip 2 ball heads, pipe in tip 3 square seats and outline arms. Add tip 2 dot hands. Pipe tip 1 facial features and hair; let dry. Using Round Comfort Grip™ Cutter, cut Ferris Wheel cookie from Roll-Out Dough; bake and cool. For yellow base top, prepare favorite crisped rice cereal treat recipe; press in prepared 9 x 13 x 2 in. Sheet Pan. Unmold and cut, using Circle Metal Cutter; using stick candy, make a hole in center. Cover wheel cookies with thinned royal icing and cereal treats with melted Yellow Candy Melts®† (p. 124). For white base bottom, place round Comfort Grip cutter on non-stick cookie sheet; fill ¼ in. deep with melted white candy. Refrigerate until firm. On Ferris wheel cookies, pipe tip 8 spokes in royal icing; add tip 3 dot axle (smooth with finger dipped in cornstarch). Attach kids with royal icing; add tip 3 dots on spokes. Cut stick candy to 6 in.; attach to cookie back with melted candy, leaving 3¼ in. extending. Attach base top to base bottom with melted candy; attach candy-coated chocolates to side with melted candy. Pipe a small amount of melted candy in center hole of treat; insert candy stick. For banner, cut a 2½ x ¾ in. piece of card stock; write name with marker. Tape banner to candy stick. Each serves 1.

†Brand confectionery coating.

Thrill Rides!

Big fun at every turn! A rockin' roller coaster in gum paste connects the cakes on our 3-Tier Party Stand. The side attractions are cool too—a munchable merry-go-round and Ferris wheel combine cookies and cereal treats.

Please see our Product Shops (p.125-230) for specific decorating items used in this section; find recipes on pages 114-115.

HAPPY BIRTHDAY
ROBERT
A
C
VICKI
JOSHUA

Fish Story

Big, bold fish are the hook for a snappy new party look. Watch them swim all over the tiered cake—we've covered our new Globe Separators with fondant to create a great 3-D presentation.

A. Cool School Cake

In advance: Make 7 fish bodies using two 2½ in. Globe Pillar Sets. Tint 72 oz. White Ready-To-Use Rolled Fondant Royal Blue, 8 oz. each Orange, Rose, Lemon Yellow/Golden Yellow combination, Leaf Green/Lemon Yellow combination, 4 oz. Violet/Rose combination, 1 oz. Black; reserve 2 oz. White. Roll out fondant ⅛ in. thick; cut 2½ x 8 in. long strips. Brush globes with Piping Gel and cover with fondant; smooth with fingers. Prepare 2-layer 8 and 12 in. Round cakes for rolled fondant (p. 113) and globe pillar construction (p. 113). Position 12 in. cake on 14 in. Round Silver Cake Base and 8 in. cake on 10 in. Smooth-Edge Separator Plate. Insert 4 pillars and position fish; cut pillars to ¾ in. above fish. Cover extended pillar area with blue fondant. Position 8 in. cake. Cut 2 pillars from Globe Set to 5½ in.; insert in cake top. Insert a 9 in. pillar at back of cake; cover 3 in. of extended pillar area with blue fondant. Position 3 fish over pillars. Roll out fondant ⅛ in. thick; cut cake side fish bodies using medium Round Cut-Outs™. Attach with damp brush. Cut all fins, lips and eyes from fondant and attach with damp brush. Cut white fondant bubbles using narrow end of tip 8; attach with damp brush. In buttercream, pipe tip 14 C-motion bottom borders. Add ribbon to cake base. Serves 60.

B. Fish Out Of Water

Prepare crisped rice cereal treats recipe and press into prepared Mini Ball Pan cavities. Unmold onto waxed paper. Attach ball halves with melted White Candy Melts®† to form bodies. Tint portions of melted white candy using Primary and Garden Candy Color Sets. Dip bodies in melted candy, smooth until entire treat is covered; let dry on waxed paper. For eyes, pipe black candy pupils on white gumballs. For fins, cut fruit slices lengthwise in half; attach to body with melted candy. For mouth, cut fruit slice in a v-shape; attach mouth and eyes with melted candy. Each serves 1.

C. Fish Sticks

Wrap a 4 x 8 x 1 in. thick craft foam block with foil. Wrap 1 in. wide ribbon around side, secure with straight pins. Cut circles from cheddar cheese slices using medium Round Cut-Out. Attach 8 in. Lollipop Stick to each circle with tip 3 dots of cream cheese. Cut fins from red or yellow pepper; attach with cream cheese. Cut v-shaped mouth from pimiento; attach. Pipe tip 3 dot eye with cream cheese. Using narrow end of tip 7, cut a circle from black olive for pupil; attach. Insert sticks in craft block; position parsley on block. Each serves 1.

†Brand confectionery coating.

Good Sports

A unique cake construction can be the most valuable player in your decorating lineup. Team up our Globe Pillar Sets with rolled fondant to create sports balls for every season.

D. A Fan For All Seasons!

In advance: Make sports balls (p. 122) using 2½ and 3 in. Globe Pillar Sets. Tint a portion of white fondant Brown/Red-Red combination. Add ½ teaspoon Gum-Tex to 6 oz. white fondant and Brown/Red-Red fondant; roll out ⅛ in. thick. Cut football using cutter from 101 Cookie Cutters Set; cut goal post using pattern from 2007 Pattern Book (p. 126). For football, cut ¼ in. wide stripes and ⅛ in. wide laces; attach with damp brush. Ice smooth 2-layer 6 and 10 in. cakes in buttercream and prepare for globe pillar construction (p. 113). Position cakes on 8 and 12 in. Smooth Separator Plates. Attach football to front and 8 in. Lollipop Sticks to back of goal post with Thinned Fondant Adhesive; let dry. Insert goal post in cake. Pipe tip 17 pull-out grass at goal post base and bottom borders. Print tip 5 message. Stack cakes on globes. Serves 40.

E. Cookie Competitors

Tint ½ of Roll-Out Cookie Dough in Copper (skin tone) and ½ Light Brown/Red-Red. Cut cookies using Gingerbread Boy Metal Cutter. Roll small balls for noses; position on cookies; bake and cool. Decorate on waxed paper, using royal icing. Pipe in tip 3 clothes and tip 4 shoes; pat smooth. Add tip 2 dot eyes, outline smiles, clothing stripes, hair, hair bands and face mask. Let dry. Attach Baseball Mitts, Soccer Balls and Footballs Icing Decorations with dots of icing. Each serves 1.

F. Catch These Candies!

Tint portions of melted White Candy Melts®† using Garden and Primary Candy Colors; reserve some white and also use Candy Melts in Orange and Light Cocoa. Mold lollipops on 8 in. sticks using Sports Lollipop Mold and painting method (p. 123). Also mold candies in Stars Mold; refrigerate until firm. Using melted candy in cut parchment bags, overpipe lines and stitching on balls. Wrap 6 x 2 in. round craft foam block with foil. Cut 25 strands of white curling ribbon 24 in. long; curl. Insert lollipops in craft block at staggered heights. Gather 5 groups of ribbons (5 in each) and secure with 3 in. lengths of 22-gauge white cloth-covered wires. Insert wires in craft block. Attach candy stars to sides of block with melted candy.

G. Trading Cards

Make copies of Name Card Patterns from 2007 Pattern Book. Cut out; color in design and print name using color markers. Position toppers from Sports Topper Sets by name cards.

Please see our Product Shops (p. 125-230) for specific decorating items used in this section; find recipes on pages 114-115.

In Full Flower

The 3-Tier Party Stand is the ideal place to plant this garden of goodies. Its terraced levels give the loop petal petit fours room to breathe—and also allow space for fun accents like the fondant bees and butterflies.

A. Abuzz About the Cakes!

In advance: Add 1 teaspoon Gum-Tex to 8 oz. White Ready-To-Use Rolled Fondant. Tint ¼ each in dark shades of Violet, Rose, Lemon Yellow and Orange. Make 6 fondant flower bow loops (p. 123) for each mini cake. Let dry overnight on cornstarch-dusted large flower formers. **Also:** Tint 2 oz. fondant each in Black, Lemon Yellow, Orange, Leaf Green and 1 oz. each in Light Rose and Medium Violet; reserve a ½ in. ball of white. Add ¼ teaspoon Gum-Tex to each. Make bees and butterflies (p. 122). Bake and cool 1-layer 6, 8 and 10 in. round cakes and 14 cakes in Silicone Mini Flower Mold. Prepare cakes for rolled fondant (p. 113). For mini cakes, tint 12 oz. each of white fondant in light shades of Violet, Rose, Lemon Yellow and Orange. For round cakes, tint 36 oz. fondant light Kelly Green. Cover cakes with fondant; smooth with fondant smoother. Roll out remaining tinted fondant from mini cakes ⅛ in. thick; cut 25 flowers in each color using pansy cutter from Floral Collection Flower Making Set. Roll out leaf green ⅛ in. thick; cut 12 leaves using large rose leaf cutter from set. Let flowers and leaves dry on small flower formers dusted with cornstarch. Roll and attach ⅛ in. ball flower centers. Pipe a tip 8 ball of royal icing at center of mini cakes; attach bow loops. Roll ½ in. diameter fondant ball flower centers; flatten and attach with royal icing. Position round cakes on plates from Cakes 'N More 3-Tier Party Stand. For fence, roll out white fondant ⅛ in. thick; cut fence posts using pattern from 2007 Pattern Book. Attach ½ in. apart with damp brush. Attach pansies at bottom borders with royal icing. Insert flower spikes in cake. Insert bees and butterflies. Position mini cakes and leaves. Round cakes serve 30; each mini cake serves 1.

B. You'll Bee There!

Mold candy plaques (p. 124), filling Mini Loaf Pan ⅜ in. deep with White Candy Melts®†. Tint portions of candy green/yellow combination, yellow and black using Primary and Garden Candy Color Sets. Mold bees in Garden Goodies Mold using painting method (p. 123). On candy plaques, pipe outline border and name using melted candy in cut parchment bags. Attach bee candy and Dancing Daisy Flower Icing Decoration with melted candy. For easel back, cut a Candy Melts wafer in half; attach flat side to back of plaque with melted candy. Each serves 1.

C. Fresh-As-A-Daisy Sandwich!

Cut bread slices using Flower Plastic Cutter. Spread with ham or chicken salad. Cut a circle of cheese for flower center using wide end of tip 1A; position on sandwich. Cut thin strips of chives; position on petals. Position lettuce leaf. Each serves 1.

†Brand confectionery coating.

A Magical Marriage

Set off on a new path for your wedding cake design. The 3-Tier Party Stand is perfect for a sweeping romantic statement, as a winding lovers' lane links diamond-embossed fondant cakes accented by fairy tale toppers.

D. Cinderella Wedding

In advance: Make fondant Flowers using pansy and apple blossom cutters (p. 122). **Also:** Trace Pathway patterns from 2007 Pattern Book onto ¼ in. foamcore boards; cut pathways, brush boards with piping gel and cover with reserved white fondant from flowers. Bake and cool 1-layer 6 in. round cake, two 2-layer 8 in. round cakes (3 in. high) and 10 in. round cake (3 in. high). Cover one cake with white fondant; immediately mark 1½ in. divisions on top and bottom. Score sides using straight-edge wheel of Cutter/Embosser to imprint diagonal lines from adjacent top and bottom markings. Brush imprints with non-toxic pink chalk grated through tea strainer. Repeat for all cakes. Roll and attach ¼ in. fondant balls to cake top points and where lines meet. Prepare one 8 in. cake and 6 in. cake for stacked construction; dowel rod 6 in. cake for ornament.

At reception: Position cakes and pathways on Cakes 'N More 3-Tier Party Stand. Pipe tip 5 bead bottom borders. Attach flowers and leaves to bottom borders and to edges of pathways with buttercream. Position Castle and Horse & Carriage ornaments.†† Serves 86.**

**The top tier is often saved for the first anniversary. The number of servings given does not include top tier.

††Always place a separator plate or cake board cut to fit, on the cake before you position any figure or ornament. This protects both the cake and your keepsake. For extra stability, secure your figurine to the plate with double-stick craft tape.

E. Serenity Centerpiece

Roll out Ready-To-Use Gum Paste ⅛ in. thick and cut 13 stars using largest Cut-Out. Brush with water and sprinkle with White Cake Sparkles™; let dry on cornstarch-dusted board. Hot glue stars to end of white florist wires, 7 in. long. Glue 13¾ in. Roman Column to top of 8 x 1 in. high craft foam circle; glue Love's Duet ornament to column. Attach 1 in. wide ribbon around craft block; secure with straight pins. Glue 1 pk. of Lily Sprays, silk roses, small silk flowers and stars to craft block; add flowers around column and ornament.

F. Magic Wand Cookies

From Roll-Out Dough, cut cookies using smallest cutter from Nesting Stars Set; bake and cool. Cover cookies with thinned color flow (p. 124); sprinkle with White Cake Sparkles; let dry. Cut 3 x ¾ in. cardstock nametags. Write names using black marker. Attach 8 in. Lollipop Sticks to stars with full-strength color flow; let dry. Cut 15 in. lengths of curling ribbon; tie around stick. Tape name tag to stick. Position "Glass" Slipper. Each serves 1.

Please see our Product Shops (p.125-230) for specific decorating items used in this section. Find recipes on pages 114-115.

Step-By-Step

Decorating Guide

Decorating help starts here! Whatever cake you want to make from this Yearbook, you'll find out how to make it happen on the following pages. Whether you're creating a cake for the first time or need a quick brush-up on a technique, it's easy when you use this handy guide as you decorate.

Cake Preparation

Think of your cake as the canvas on which you will create beautiful icing decorations. To achieve the masterpiece you want, it is essential that your canvas be smooth and free of crumbs. These steps for preparing and icing your cake will result in the perfect decorating surface essential for your work of art.

BAKING THE CAKE

Follow recipe directions for specific baking instructions and recommended batter amounts for the pan size you choose. Prepare the pan by generously greasing the inside using a pastry brush or paper towel and solid vegetable shortening. For best results, do not use butter, margarine or liquid vegetable oil. Spread the shortening so that all indentations are covered. Sprinkle about 2 Tablespoons of flour inside the pan and shake so that the flour covers all greased surfaces. Turn pan upside down and tap lightly to remove excess flour. If any uncovered spots remain, touch up with shortening and flour. Or use Bake Easy™ Non-Stick Spray or Cake Release (p. 132) to coat the pan—no grease or flour needed. Pour batter into pan and place in pre-heated oven.

After cake has baked the specified time, remove it from the oven and let it cool in the pan on a cake rack for 10 minutes. Run a thin knife between the cake and side of the pan. Unmold from pan by placing cooling rack against cake and turning both cooling rack and pan over. Lift pan off carefully. Cool at least one hour and brush off loose crumbs prior to icing.

CUTTING AND WRAPPING A CAKE BOARD

For round, square and sheet cakes, you don't need to cut a cake board. Simply buy a ready-made board that is 2 in. larger than your cake. (For example, if the cake is 8 in. diameter, buy a 10 in. round board.) For shaped cakes, cut a board to fit. Turn pan upside down and trace outline onto your cake board. Cut board with a craft knife, leaving 1 in. extra around outline.

To wrap, trace your cut board onto Fanci-Foil, making the outline 3-4 in. larger than the board. Cut Fanci-Foil along the outline. Place your board, white side down, on top of your cut foil. Cut deep slits at several points along foil edge, creating tabs of foil to wrap neatly around the board. Secure foil tabs to the board with tape.

LEVELING THE CAKE

After the cake has cooled at least one hour, you'll need to level the top of the cake. This can be done using a serrated knife or the Cake Leveler (p. 132).

Using a Serrated Knife

Place the cake on a cake board, then place the board on a Trim 'N Turn Cake Stand (p. 133). While slowly rotating the stand, move the knife back and forth across the top of cake in a sawing motion to remove the crown. Try to keep knife level as you cut.

Using the Wilton Cake Leveler

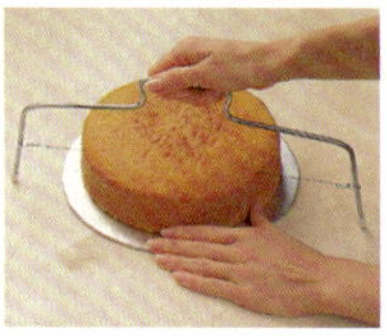

Position the ends of the cutting wire (or feet on large leveler) into the notches at the desired height. With legs standing on the work surface, cut into the crusted edge using an easy sawing motion, then proceed by gently gliding wire through the cake.

TORTING THE CAKE

Torting adds extra height, drama and taste to the cake when the layers are filled with icing, pudding or fruit filling. A serrated knife or the Cake Leveler may be used to cut a cake into multiple layers.

Using a Serrated Knife

Divide cake sides and mark equal horizontal points with dots of icing or toothpicks all around. Place one hand on top of the cake to hold it steady and rotate the stand. While slowly turning the cake, move the knife back and forth to cut the cake along the measured marks. Repeat for each additional layer.

Using the Cake Leveler

Torting is easily accomplished with the Cake Leveler. Simply follow the same directions as for leveling.

Separating the Layers

Carefully slide the top torted layer onto a cake board to keep it rigid and safe from breakage. Repeat for each additional layer.

FILLING THE LAYERS

Fill a decorating bag with medium consistency icing and use a large round tip, like tip 12. Or simply use the coupler without mounting a tip.

Starting with the bottom layer, leveled side up, create a dam of icing just inside the edge of the cake (about ¾ in. high and ¼ in. from the outside edge). Fill with icing, preserves or pudding. Place next layer on top, level; repeat. Finish with top layer leveled side down.

ICING THE CAKE

For better results, use a revolving turntable like professional decorators do...see our Revolving Cake Stand and Trim 'N Turn Cake Stand on p. 133.

Using a Spatula

The trick to keeping crumbs out of your icing is gliding your spatula on the icing—*never allow it to touch the surface of the cake.* Place a large amount of thin consistency icing on the center of the cake.

Spread icing across the top, pushing toward edges. Smooth the top using the edge of the spatula.

Sweep the edge of the spatula from the rim of the cake to its center then lift it off and remove excess icing.

Cover the sides with icing. Smooth sides by holding the spatula upright with the edge against the icing and slowly spinning the turntable without lifting the spatula from the icing surface. Return excess icing to the bowl and repeat until sides are smooth.

Rotate the cake slightly and repeat the procedure, starting from a new point on the rim until you have covered the entire top surface. Smooth the center of the cake by leveling the icing with the edge of your spatula. For easier smoothing, it may help to dip the spatula into hot water, wipe dry and glide it across the entire surface. Set the cake aside and allow the icing to crust over for at least 15 minutes before decorating. At that point you may also lay Non-Stick Parchment Paper (p. 132) on the iced cake top and gently smooth with the palm of your hand.

Using a Decorating Tip

Trim a 16 in. Featherweight bag to fit tip 789. Fill bag half full with icing. Hold bag at 45° angle and lightly press tip against cake. Squeeze a ribbon of icing in a continuous spiral motion to cover cake top, with last ribbon forcing icing over edge of cake top.

To ice the sides, squeeze icing as you turn the cake slowly. Repeat the process until the entire cake side is covered.

Smooth sides and top with spatula, same as above.

Icing Basics

In this section, we've listed general descriptions of icings, their uses, qualities and consistencies. Use this information to determine the right icing for your cake. Refer to our recipes for homemade icings (p. 114) along with color instructions below, to create the look and taste you want.

ICING USAGE GUIDE

Icing Type	Flavor/Description	Consistency	Best Used For...	Coloring	Storage/Freshness	Special Information
Buttercream (Wilton Mix or homemade)	Sweet, buttery flavor. Tastes/looks great for most decorating.	Thin-to-stiff depending on amount of corn syrup or sugar added (sugar stiffens).	Icing cakes smooth. Borders, writing, flowers, decorations.	Yields all colors. Most deepen upon setting. Let set 2-3 hours for deep color. Some may fade in bright light.	Can be refrigerated in airtight container for 2 weeks. Iced cake stores at room temperature for 2-3 days.	Flowers remain soft enough to be cut with a knife.
Snow-White Buttercream (homemade)	Sweet, almond flavor. Ideal for wedding cakes.	Thin-to-stiff depending on amount of corn syrup or sugar added (sugar stiffens).	Icing cakes smooth. Borders, writing, flowers, decorations.	Yields truer colors due to pure white base color. Creates deep colors. Most colors deepen upon setting.	Can be refrigerated in airtight container for 2 weeks. Iced cake stores at room temperature for 2-3 days.	Air-dried flowers have translucent look. Flowers remain soft enough to be cut with knife.
Wilton Ready-To-Use Decorator White (4.5 lb. tub)	Sweet, vanilla flavor. Convenient, ready-to-spread icing. Pure white color ideal for tinting.	Thin-to-medium. No need to thin for spreading.	Spreading on cakes right from the can. Piping stars, shells, messages and more.	Yields truer colors due to pure white base color. Creates deep colors. Most colors deepen upon setting.	Leftover icing can be refrigerated for 2 weeks. Iced cake stores at room temperature for 2-3 days.	Available for purchase through Wilton Yearbook, at www.wilton.com or any authorized Wilton retailer.
Wilton Ready-To-Use Decorator White (1 lb. size)	Sweet, vanilla flavor. Convenient, ready-to-spread icing. Pure white color ideal for tinting.	Stiff. Make roses right from the can.	Shells, stars, flowers—use from container. Icing cakes, writing, leaves—thin with milk, water or corn syrup.	Yields truer colors due to pure white base color. Creates deep colors. Most colors deepen upon setting.	Leftover icing can be refrigerated for 2 weeks. Iced cake stores at room temperature for 2-3 days.	Available for purchase through Wilton Yearbook, at www.wilton.com or any authorized Wilton retailer.
Wilton Ready-To-Use Decorator Chocolate	Sweet chocolate flavor. Convenient ready-to-spread icing.	Stiff. Make roses right from the can.	Shells, stars, flowers—use from container. Icing cakes, writing, leaves—thin with milk, water or corn syrup.	Recommended when black or brown icing is needed. Add a little black icing color to chocolate for a better tasting black icing.	Leftover icing can be refrigerated for 2 weeks. Iced cake stores at room temperature for 2-3 days.	Available for purchase through Wilton Yearbook, at www.wilton.com or any authorized Wilton retailer.
Royal (made with Wilton Meringue Powder)	Very sweet flavor. Dries candy-hard for lasting decorations.	Thin-to-stiff, depending on the amount of water added.	Flower making, figure piping, making flowers on wires. Decorating cookies and gingerbread houses.	Yields deep colors. Some colors may fade in bright light. Requires more icing color than buttercream to achieve the same intensity.	Icing can be stored in airtight, grease-free container at room temperature for 2 weeks. Air-dried decorations last for months.	Bowls and utensils must be grease-free. Cover icing with damp cloth to prevent crusting.
Rolled Fondant (homemade or Wilton Ready-To-Use Rolled Fondant)	Covers cakes with a perfectly smooth, satiny surface. Easy and fast to use. Knead in flavor of your choice.	Dough-like. Fondant Is rolled out before being applied to cake. Stays semi-soft on cake.	Any firm-textured cake, pound cake or fruit cake. Cutting, molding and modeling decorations.	White yields pastels to deep colors. Wilton pre-colored fondant is also available in pastel shades and in Multi Packs for fondant decorations in a variety of colors.	Excess can be stored 2 months in an airtight container. Do not refrigerate or freeze. Iced cake stores at room temperature for 3-4 days.	Prior to applying fondant, cake should be lightly covered with a glaze or buttercream icing to seal in freshness and moisture.
Whipped Icing Mix (Wilton Mix)	Light, delicate vanilla flavor. Holds shape like no other mix. **For chocolate icing,** add ½ cup of sifted cocoa powder.	Velvety, perfect for stars, roses, borders, garlands and writing.	Icing cakes. Most decorations. Toppings on pies, puddings, tarts and more.	Yields any color.	Can be refrigerated in airtight container. Iced cake stores at room temperature for 2-3 days.	Exclusive Wilton formula. Available for purchase through Wilton Yearbook, at www.wilton.com or any authorized Wilton retailer.
Fluffy Boiled Icing (homemade)	Marshmallow-like flavor. 100% fat-free.	Very fluffy. Sets quickly.	Icing cakes smooth and fluffy. Borders, figure piping, writing, stringwork.	Yields pastels to deep colors.	Use immediately. Iced cake can be stored at room temperature.	Serve within 24 hours.
Stabilized Whipped Cream (homemade)	Creamy, delicate sweetness.	Light, thin-to-medium.	All cakes but especially those decorated with fruits. Borders, large tip work, writing.	Yields pastels only.	Use immediately. Iced cake must be refrigerated.	Texture remains soft on decorated cake.

COLORING ICING

Using Color

When planning your cake, think about color. Choosing appropriate colors for your cake will help you capture the mood you want for the occasion. Gather inspiration from the theme of your celebration. The icing colors you choose should carry that theme and personalize your decorating. Look around, notice everyday objects—from a garden in bloom, to the clothes people wear. Which colors appeal to you? Use your favorite colors in your decorating. Don't be afraid to try something different. Have fun using rich, bright colors and different color combinations. Begin by making a monochromatic cake, decorated all in white or in a single, pale color. Try using decorations in contrasting colors on an all-white background. Decorate using all pastels or all primary colors. Experimenting with color will help you decide which colors work to make your cake designs spectacular!

Mixing Colors

Begin with white icing and use concentrated Icing Colors (p. 135) which will not affect your icing consistency. (Using ordinary liquid food colors can thin your icing and affect your ability to pipe certain decorations.) If you are tinting icing dark brown or black, begin with chocolate icing—your icing will not have the aftertaste that large amounts of icing color can produce. If you are tinting a large area red, use No-Taste Red.

Dip a fresh toothpick into the color, then swirl it into the icing. Add color a little at a time until you achieve the shade you desire. Always use a new toothpick each time you add color; you want to avoid getting icing in your jar of color. Blend the icing well with a spatula.

Consider the type of icing you are using when mixing color. Icing colors intensify or darken in buttercream icing about 1-2 hours after mixing. Royal icing requires more color than buttercream icing to achieve the same color intensity.

Always mix enough of each icing color to complete your entire cake. For example, if you are going to decorate a cake with pink flowers and borders, color enough icing for both. It is difficult to duplicate an exact shade of any color, and you will want to keep your colors consistent on your cake.

Bag Striping Effects

You can easily pipe two-tone decorations just by adding a different color inside the bag before you put in your tinted icing. This is how you pipe flowers with natural light and dark tones or make a rainbow-colored clown suit to brighten up the party.

Brush Striping

Produces more intense multiple colors because it is done with straight icing color brushed into the bag. Apply one or more stripes of icing color with a decorating brush, then fill the bag with white or pastel-colored icing. As the icing is squeezed past the color, your decorations will come out striped.

Spatula Striping

Produces two-tone and realistic pastel tones for flowers and figure piping. It is done with pastel-colored icing, striped inside the decorating bag with a spatula. After striping, fill the bag with white icing or another shade of the same color as the striping. Squeeze out decorations with soft contrasts.

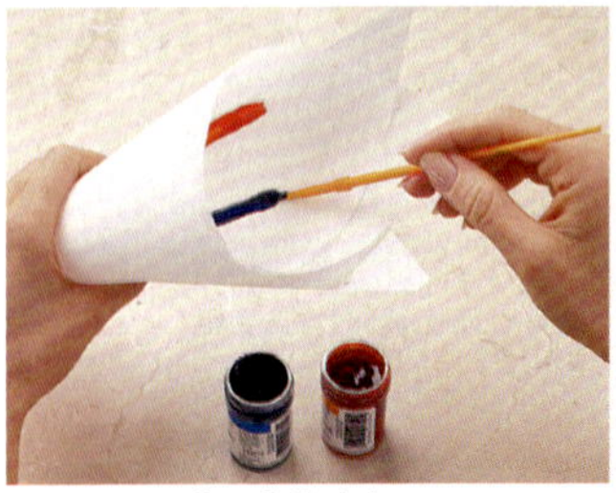

Brush Striping

Spatula Striping

Three Essentials of Cake Decorating

Every decoration you make is the result of three things working together: the consistency of your icing, the position of the bag (that is, the way you are holding it) and the amount and type of pressure you apply to the bag. You'll know when you have everything right because you'll get perfect results time after time. This will take practice. The more you concentrate on perfecting these three essentials, the sooner you will achieve perfect results.

ICING CONSISTENCY

If the consistency of your icing is not right, your decorations will not be right either. Just a few drops of liquid can make a great deal of difference in your decorating results. Many factors can affect icing consistency, such as humidity, temperature, ingredients and equipment. You may try using different icing consistencies when decorating to determine what works best for you. As a general guideline, if you are having trouble creating the decorations you want and you feel your icing is too thin, add a little more confectioner's sugar; if you feel your icing is too thick, add a little more liquid. In royal icing recipes, if adding more than ½ cup confectioner's sugar to thicken icing, also add 1-2 additional teaspoons of Meringue Powder (p. 134).

Stiff icing is used for figure piping and stringwork and for decorations like roses, carnations and sweet peas with upright petals. If icing is not stiff enough, flower petals will droop. If icing cracks when piped out, icing is probably too stiff. Add light corn syrup to icing used for stringwork to give strings greater elasticity so they will not break.

Medium icing is used for decorations such as stars, shell borders and flowers with flat petals. If the icing is too stiff or too thin, you will not get the uniformity that characterizes these decorations.

Thin icing is used for decorations such as printing and writing, vines and leaves. Leaves will be pointier, vines will not break and writing will flow easily if you add 1-2 teaspoons light corn syrup to each cup of icing. Thin icing is used to ice cakes smooth. Begin with your prepared icing recipe, then add small amounts of the same liquid used in the recipe (usually milk or water) until the proper spreading consistency is reached.

CORRECT BAG POSITION

The way your decorations curl, point and lie depends not only on icing consistency but also on the way you hold the bag and the way you move it. Bag positions are described in terms of both angle and direction.

Angle

Angle refers to the position of the bag relative to the work surface. There are two basic angle positions, 90° (straight up) and 45° (halfway between vertical and horizontal).

90° angle
or straight up, perpendicular to the surface.

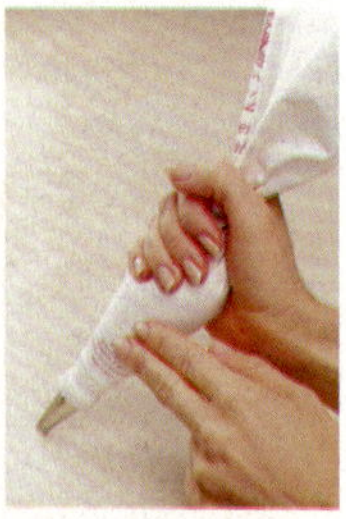

45° angle
or halfway between vertical and horizontal.

Direction

The angle in relation to the work surface is only half the story on bag position. The other half is the direction in which the back of the bag is pointed.

Correct bag direction is easiest to learn when you think of the back of the bag as the hour hand of a clock. When you hold the bag at a 45° angle to the surface, you can sweep out a circle with the back end of the bag by rolling your wrist and holding the end of the tip in the same spot. Pretend the circle you formed in the air is a clock face. The hours on the clock face correspond to the direction you point the back end of the bag.

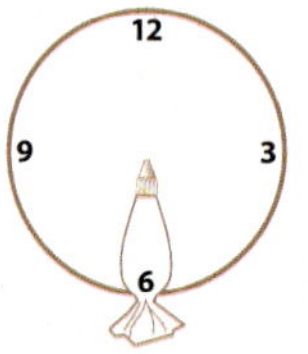

Back of bag at 6:00

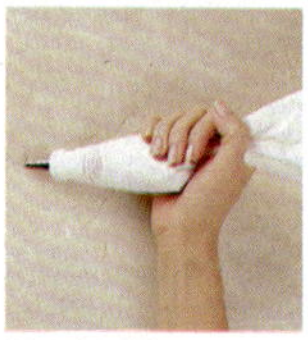

Back of bag at 3:00

The technique instructions in this Decorating Guide will list the correct direction for holding the bag. When the bag direction differs for left-handed decorators, that direction will be listed in parentheses. For example, when a bag is to be held at 3:00 for a right-handed decorator, it should be held at 9:00 for a left-handed decorator.

One more thing…since most decorating tip openings are the same shape all the way around, there's no right side and wrong side up when you're squeezing icing out of them. However, some tips, such as petal, ruffle, basketweave and leaf have irregularly shaped openings. For those you must watch your tip position as well as your bag position. If the tip opening must be in a special position, the instructions will tell you.

PRESSURE CONTROL

In addition to having the proper icing consistency and the correct bag position, you'll need to master three types of pressure control: heavy, medium and light. The size and uniformity of your icing designs are affected by the amount of pressure you apply to the bag and the steadiness of that pressure. (In other words, how you squeeze and relax your grip on the decorating bag.) Your goal is to learn to apply pressure so consistently that you can move the bag in a free and easy glide while just the right amount of icing flows through the tip. Practice will help you achieve this control.

Heavy Pressure **Medium Pressure** **Light Pressure**

Storing Cakes

Take some final precautions and store your cake the best way possible. After all, your time, effort and creativity have made it very special! Beware of the following factors, which can affect the look of your decorated cake.

Sunlight and fluorescent lighting will alter icing colors. Keep your cake stored in a covered box and out of direct sunlight and fluorescent lighting.

Humidity can soften royal icing and gum paste decorations. If you live in a climate with high humidity, prepare your royal icing using only pure cane confectioner's sugar (not beet sugar or dextrose), add less liquid and add 1 more teaspoon Meringue Powder (p. 134) to the recipe.

Heat can melt icing and cause decorations to droop. Keep your decorated cake as cool as possible and stabilize buttercream icing by adding 2 teaspoons Meringue Powder per recipe. Protect your cake by placing it in a clean, covered cake box. Avoid using foil or plastic wrap to cover a decorated cake—these materials can stick to icing and crush delicate decorations. The icing that covers your cake determines how it should be stored—in the refrigerator, at cool room temperature, or frozen, if storing for longer than 3 days. If you want to store your iced cake in a different way than noted, make a small test cake.

Icing type determines care. See chart on p. 109 for storage information.

NOTE: Cakes with thoroughly-dried royal icing decorations should be stored according to the type of icing that covers the cake. However, if royal icing decorations are to be put on a cake that will be frozen, it is recommended that these decorations be placed on the cake after thawing so that they don't bleed from condensation or become soft.

Transporting Tiered Cakes

Moving a tiered cake from one location to another does not have to be difficult. It can be quite easy! Following some simple guidelines ensures that your cake will arrive safely—whether you are traveling hundreds of miles or just a few.

Before Moving Cakes

Be certain the cake is constructed on a sturdy base made of three or more thicknesses of corrugated cardboard. Base tiers of very heavy cakes should be placed on a foam core or plywood base, ½ in. thick. Cakes on pillars must be transported unassembled. Toppers, candles and ornaments should be removed from cakes when they are being moved. For stacked cakes, move the entire assembled cake. Or, for a larger quantity of tiers, transport unassembled and assemble at the reception. Be sure to have with you the equipment and icings you will need to finish any decorating needed after assembly at the reception.

For a cake which combines stacked and 2-plate construction, take tiers apart, keeping stacked tiers as units. Boxing the cake makes transportation easier. Not only does it protect the tiers from damage, but it keeps the tiers clean—free from dirt, dust and bugs. Place the boxes on carpet foam or a non-skid mat on a level surface in the vehicle to prevent shifting. Keep the boxes flat; never place on a car seat. Boxed cakes can also be transported in the trunk of the car, except in hot weather, because air conditioning will not reach the trunk area. It's also important to find out about the reception location before the event. Knowing what to expect when you arrive can make your delivery and setup so much easier. Call the reception hall a few days before the event to get an idea of the conditions you will encounter there. Ask whether the room is located upstairs or downstairs. Find out what is the best location for bringing the cake into the building. That way you can park in the right place the first time and minimize the distance your cake has to travel from your car. Also ask how far in advance the cake can be set up so that you can plan your day and reduce the stress.

In Pan

Take tiers apart if constructed in Center Column or Push-In Leg method. Leave columns or legs in place. Position the plates on crumpled foil or in shallow pans if they do not sit level. Remove pillars from tier plates; plates stay in position.

In Box

Place the cakes in clean, covered, sturdy boxes that are sized to the base board of each cake. This prevents shifting within the box and possibly crushing the sides of the cake. If the box is too big, roll pieces of masking tape sticky side out and attach to the inside bottom of the box. Position the cake base on top of the tape, securing the base in the box. For taller decorations, prop up box top and sides, secure with masking tape.

On Non-Skid Foam

If tiers cannot be boxed, they can be transported on large pieces of non-skid foam. Place the foam on the floor of the vehicle, then carefully place the tiers centered on each piece of foam. Remove any ornament or fragile decorations before transporting.

At Your Destination

Before you bring in the cake from your car, walk the path you will have to travel to the set-up site. Be alert for any bumps along the way and note any tight spaces you will have to maneuver around. Make sure the cake table is level—it's a good idea to bring a level to check this on setup day. Request a cart on wheels to move the cake into the reception area. This is easier and safer than carrying by hand. Remove the cakes from the boxes on the reception table by cutting the sides of the boxes and sliding the cakes out. Bring along a repair kit, including extra icing, prepared decorating bags and tips, flowers and spatulas, just in case it is necessary to make any repairs. Once the cake is assembled, take a picture to establish that the cake was in perfect condition when you left it.

Cake Baking and Serving Guides

The charts below are based on baking recommendations from the Wilton Test Kitchen; your results may vary depending on oven performance or altitude in your area. For large cakes, always check for doneness after they have baked for 1 hour.

Serving amounts are based on party-sized portions of 1½ x 2 in. or smaller wedding-sized portions of approximately 1 x 2 in. Cakes from 3 to 6 in. high, baked in the same size pan, would yield the same number of servings because they follow the same pattern of cutting. Cakes shorter than 3 in. would yield half the number of servings indicated for that pan. Number of servings are intended as a guide only.

Icing amounts are very general and will vary with consistency, thickness applied and tips used. Icing amounts allow for top and bottom borders.

4 IN. HIGH CAKES (using 2 in. high pans)

The figures for 2 in. pans are based on a 2-layer, 4 in. high cake. Fill pans ½ to ⅔ full.

PAN SHAPE	SIZE	NUMBER SERVINGS PARTY	NUMBER SERVINGS WEDDING	CUPS BATTER 1 LAYER, 2 IN.	BAKING TEMP.	BAKING TIME MINUTES	APPROX. CUPS ICING TO ICE AND DECORATE
Round	6 in.	12	12	2	350°	25-30	3
	8 in.	20	24	3½	350°	30-35	4
	9 in.	24	32	5½	350°	30-35	4½
	10 in.	28	38	6	350°	35-40	5
	12 in.	40	56	7½	350°	35-40	6
	14 in.	63	78	10	325°	50-55	7½
	16 in.	77	100	15	325°	55-60	9
Square	6 in.	12	18	2	350°	25-30	3½
	8 in.	20	32	4	350°	35-40	4½
	10 in.	30	50	6	350°	35-40	6
	12 in.	48	72	10	350°	40-45	7½
	14 in.	63	98	13½	325°	45-50	9½
	16 in.	80	128	15½	325°	50-55	11
Heart	6 in.	8	14	1½	350°	25-30	3½
	8 in.	18	22	3½	350°	30-35	4½
	9 in.	20	28	4	350°	30-35	6
	10 in.	24	38	5	350°	30-35	8½
	12 in.	34	56	8	325°	45-50	9
	14 in.	48	72	10	325°	45-50	10
	15 in.	50	74	11	325°	40-45	11
	16 in.	64	94	12½	325°	40-45	12
Petal	6 in.	6	8	1½	350°	25-30	4
	9 in.	14	18	3½	350°	35-40	6
	12 in.	38	40	7	350°	35-40	9
	15 in.	48	64	12	325°	50-55	11
Hexagon	6 in.	10	12	1¾	350°	30-35	3
	9 in.	20	26	3½	350°	35-40	5
	12 in.	34	40	6	350°	40-45	6
	15 in.	48	70	11	325°	40-45	9
Oval	7¾ x 5⅝ in.	9	13	2½	350°	25-30	3
	10¾ x 7⅞ in.	20	26	5	350°	25-30	4
	13½ x 9⅞ in.	30	45	8	350°	35-40	5½
	16½ x 12⅜ in.	44	70	11	325°	40-45	7½
Sheet	7 x 11 in.	28	32	5½	350°	30-35	5
	9 x 13 in.	45	50	7	350°	35-40	6
	11 x 15 in.	60	74	11	325°	35-40	8
	12 x 18 in.	72	98	14	325°	45-50	10

3 IN. HIGH CAKES (using 3 in. high pans)

The figures for 3 in. pans are based on a 1-layer cake which is torted and filled to reach 3 in. high; fill pans ½ full.

PAN SHAPE	SIZE	NUMBER SERVINGS PARTY	NUMBER SERVINGS WEDDING	CUPS BATTER 1 LAYER, 2 IN.	BAKING TEMP.	BAKING TIME MINUTES	APPROX. CUPS ICING TO ICE AND DECORATE
Round	6 in.	12	12	3	350°	35-40	3
	8 in.	20	24	5	350°	55-60	4
	10 in.	28	38	8	325°	65-75	5
	12 in.	40	56	10½	325°	60-65	6
	14 in.	63	78	15	325°	75-85	8
	16 in.	77	100	18	325°	75-85	9
	18 in. Half, 2 in. layer	110*	146*	9**	325°	60-65	10½
	18 in. Half, 3 in. layer	110*	146*	12**	325°	60-65	10½
Sheet	9 x 13 in.	45	65	11½	325°	70-75	5
	11 x 15 in.	60	90	16	325°	80-85	6½
	12 x 18 in.	72	108	20	325°	85-90	8
Square	8 in.	20	32	6½	350°	60-65	4½
	10 in.	30	50	9	325°	65-75	6
	12 in.	48	72	14	325°	65-75	7½
	14 in.	63	98	19	325°	65-75	9½
Contour	7 in.	6	11	3½	350°	45-50	2
	9 in.	11	17	5½	350°	45-50	2½
	11 in.	16	24	8	325°	80-85	3
	13 in.	22	39	13	325°	75-80	4
	15 in.	32	48	16	325°	75-80	5

For pans 10 in. and larger, we recommend using a heating core (p. 147) to insure even baking. Use 2 cores for 18-in. pans.

*Two half rounds. **For each half round pan.

For additional pan information, check out ***www.wilton.com***

General Cake Cutting Guides

The diagrams below will give you a general plan for cutting the most popular cake shapes. They will help you serve more attractive, uniform pieces while reaching your targeted number of servings. Diagrams show only one size in each shape; you will use the same general technique to cut each size cake in that shape.

WEDDING CAKES—1 x 2 in. slices

The diagrams show how to cut popular shaped wedding tiers into slices approximately 1 x 2 in. and 2 layers high (about 4 in.) For cakes shorter than 3 in. you will need to cut wider slices to serve a proper portion; even if a larger serving size is desired, the order of cutting is still the same. Before cutting the cake, remove the top tier, which is usually saved for the first anniversary and is not included in our serving amounts for wedding cakes in this book. Begin by cutting the 2nd tier, followed by the 3rd, 4th and so on.

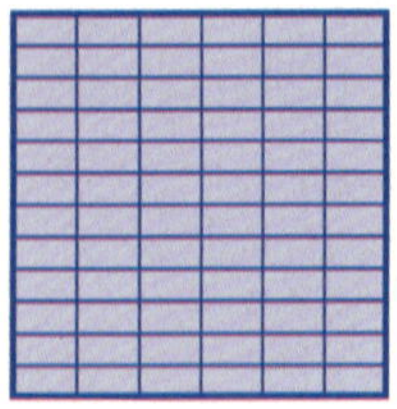

12 in.

Square Tiers:

Move in 2 in. from the outer edge and cut vertically, top to bottom. Slice and serve 1 in. pieces of cake. Now move in another 2 in. and repeat process until the entire tier is cut.

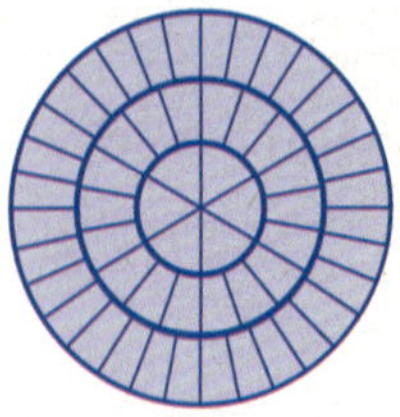

12 in.

Round Tiers:

Move in 2 in. from the tier's outer edge and cut a circle. Slice and serve 1 in. pieces from around the circle. Now move in another 2 in. and cut another circle. Repeat process until the tier is completely cut. The center core of each tier and the small top tier can be cut into 4ths, 6ths, or more, depending on size.

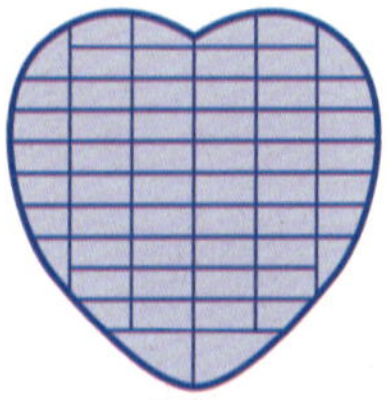

12 in.

Heart Tiers:

Divide the tiers vertically into 2 in. wide rows. Within rows, slice and serve 1 in. pieces of cake.

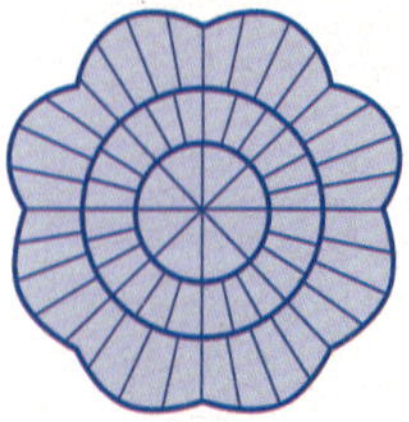

15 in.

Petal Tiers:

Cut similar to round tiers as diagram shows.

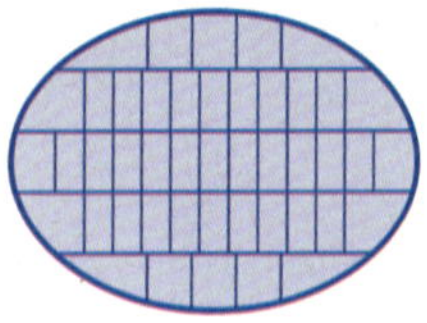

13½ x 9¾ in.

Oval Tiers:

Move in 2 in. from the outer edge and cut across. Slice and serve 1 in. pieces of cake. Now move in another 2 in., repeat process until the entire tier is cut.

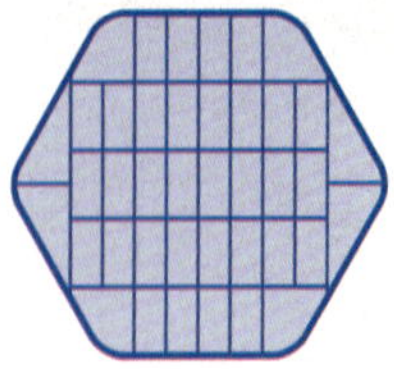

12 in.

Hexagon Tiers:

Move in 2 in. from the outer edge and cut across. Slice and serve 1 in. pieces of cake. Now move in another 2 in., repeat process until the entire tier is cut.

PARTY CAKES—1½ x 2 in. slices

Follow the diagrams above to cut party cakes (from 3 to 6 in. high), but adjust for the larger party-size slices. For cakes shorter than 3 in. you will need to cut wider slices to serve a proper portion; even if a larger serving size is desired the order of cutting is still the same.

Rounds:

To cut round cakes, move in 2 in. from the cake's outer edge; cut a circle and then slice approximately 1½ in. pieces within the circle. Now move in another 2 in. and cut another circle; slice approximately 1½ in. pieces. Continue until the cake is completely cut. Note: 6 in. diameter cakes should be cut in wedges, without a center circle. Cut petal and hexagon cakes similar to round cakes.

Squares:

To cut square cakes, move in 2 in. from the outer edge and cut top to bottom, then slice approximately 1½ in. pieces. Now move in another 2 in. and continue until the entire cake is cut.

Sheets:

Cut sheet cakes similar to square cakes.

Tiered Cake Construction

There are many methods of constructing tiered cakes. Here are some used in this book. Visit www.wedding.wilton.com for more construction methods.

TO PREPARE CAKE FOR ASSEMBLY

Place base tier on a sturdy base plate of 3 or more thicknesses of corrugated cardboard. For heavy cakes, use foam core or plywood. Base can be covered with Fanci-Foil Wrap and trimmed with Tuk-'N-Ruffle or use Ruffle Boards® (p. 225). Each tier of your cake must be on a cake circle or board cut to fit. Place a few strokes of icing on boards to secure cake. Fill and ice layers before assembly.

Adding Dowel Rods to Tiered Cakes

Use the upper tier for size reference when determining dowel rod placement. All the dowel rods must be placed within the area you will mark (see steps below) to provide adequate support.

1. Center a cake board the same size as the tier above it on base tier and press it gently into icing to imprint an outline. Remove. Use this outline to guide the insertion of the dowel rods.

2. Insert one dowel rod into cake straight down to the cake board. Make a knife scratch on the rod to mark the exact height. Pull dowel rod out.

3. Cut the suggested number of rods (see note below) the exact same length, using the mark on the first one as a guide.

4. Insert rods into tier, spacing evenly 1 ½ inches in from the imprinted outline. Push straight down until each touches the cake board. Repeat this procedure for every stacked or pillared tier on the cake.

NOTE: The larger and more numerous the tiers, the more dowels needed. If the tier above is 10 in. or less, use six ¼ in. wooden dowels. Use 8 dowel rods for 16 in. and 18 in. cakes; on these larger tiers, use ½ in. plastic dowel rods in the base tier. When using white plastic dowel rods that are wider and provide more support, the number needed may be less.

Stacked Construction

Stacking is the most architectural method of tiered cake construction. Tiers are placed directly on top of one another and pillars are not used. Cakes are supported and stabilized by dowel rods and cake boards.

1. Dowel rod all tiers except top tier.

2. Position the middle tier on the base tier, centering exactly.*

3. Repeat with the top tier.

4. To stabilize tiers further, sharpen one end of a long dowel rod and push it through all tiers and cake boards to the base of the bottom tier. To decorate, start at the top and work down.

*Finely shredded coconut or confectioner's sugar, placed in area where cake circles or plastic plates will rest, helps prevent frosting on the cake from sticking.

Separator Plate (2-Plate) and Pillar Construction

This most dramatic method features 2, 3 or more single cakes towered together. Use separator plates and pillars (p. 221, 223).

1. Set cake tiers on separator plates 2 in. larger in diameter than cakes.

2. Dowel rod cakes and position separator plates on tiers with feet up. (Note: Connect only same size separator plates with pillars.)

3. Position pillars over feet on separator plates.

4. Carefully set cake plate on pillars. Continue adding tiers this way.**

**Assemble cakes when you arrive at the reception or party.

Push-In Pillar Construction

Simple assembly—no dowel rods needed! Use any type of Wilton Push-In Pillars (p. 221) and Plates (p. 223).

1. Mark tier for push-in pillar placement. Use the separator plate for the next tier above, gently pressing it onto the tier, feet down, making sure it is centered. Lift plate away. The feet will leave marks on the icing to guide the position of pillars when you assemble the tier. Repeat this process for each tier, working from largest to smallest tier. The top tier is left unmarked.

2. Place each tier on its separator plate, securing with icing.

3. Position push-in pillars at marks, and insert into tiers. Push straight down until pillars touch the cake plate.

4. To assemble, start with the tier above the base tier. Place the feet of the separator plate on the pillar openings. Continue adding tiers in the same way until the cake is completely assembled.**

Center Column Construction (Tall Tier Stand)

1. Use boards the same size as tiers, or if tiers are shaped, cut boards to fit. Make a waxed paper pattern for each tier except the top tier in order to find the exact center for the columns. Fold the pattern in quarters. Snip the point to make a center hole. Test the hole for size by slipping it over a column, adjust size if necessary. Trace hole pattern on prepared cake board and cut out. Also cut a hole in the top tier board to allow for the column cap nut. Save patterns for marking cake tops later.

2. The base tier of the cake will rest on a 14, 16 or 18 in. plate. (18 in. plate is footed. Do not use a bottom plate smaller than 14 in.) To add legs to bottom plate, turn it upside down; using extra strength glue designed for plastic, attach the six legs, positioning the legs over each of the ribs on the plate.

3. Prepare and ice tiers and position on prepared cake boards. Make the center holes for the columns in all tiers except the top tier. Mark the top of the cakes with corresponding waxed paper pattern. Cut the hole by pressing the Cake Corer Tube (p. 222) through the tier right down to the bottom. Hold the corer upright, remove cake corer and push the upper part down to eject the cake center.

4. Screw in a column to the prepared base plate and bottom column bolt from underneath the plate. Slip the next size tier on its plate over the column.

5. Add a second column and position the next size tier on its plate, slipping it over the column. Finally, add on the top plate only, securing the top column nut. Place the top tier on the plate and decorate bottom border.**

Globe Pillar Set Construction

These elegant pearl-look globes are available in separate sets of four 2 in., 2½ in. or 3 in. globes. The 3 in. globes are to be used to support the base cake only. They have a reinforced center channel which eliminates the need for pillars. The 2 and 2½ in. sets should be used with 9 in. "Hidden" Pillars (included in set); do not use these sets to support the base cake. Your cake design may use a base board instead of the 3 in. globes to support the base cake as shown below.

1. Position separator plate holding base cake on 3 in. Globe Base Set or a thick base board. Using the separator plate which will hold the cake above, mark base cake for pillar placement (see Push-In Pillar construction, p. 112). Lift plate away.

2. Insert pillars through cake centered over marked area to rest on its separator plate or base board. Place the correct size globe (2½ in. for cake shown here) over the pillars. Mark pillars where they extend above globes. The cut pillars should be equal to the height of the base cake plus the height of each globe.

3. Trim pillars at markings with craft knife or serrated edge knife.

4. Insert pillars in base cake. Position globes over pillars.

5. Position the tier above on globes.

6. Add additional sets for more tiers.

Tailored Tiers Construction

Our Tailored Tiers Cake Display Set (p. 220) features fabric-wrapped separators which add great texture to your tiered design. The top 2 tiers are decorated on same-size boards, then transported to the reception on larger boards, so that cakes can be easily transferred to the separator plates during assembly. Bottom borders are then added to these tiers. The recommended display for Tailored Tiers separators includes a 14 in. base cake, a 10 in. center cake and a 6 in. top cake.

1. Ice cakes; place 14 in. base cake on 16 in. base board wrapped in foil or 16 in. Silver Cake Base (p. 225). Place 10 in. center and 6 in. top cakes on same size boards. Mark 14 in. and 10 in. cakes for placement of dowel rods. Center the 8 in. plate from the Tailored Tiers set on top of the 14 in. cake and press it gently into icing to imprint an outline. Remove. Use this outline to guide the insertion of dowel rods.

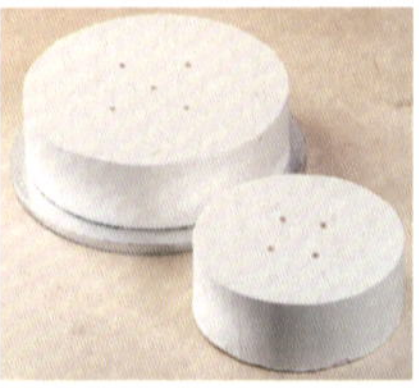

2. Dowel rod 14 in. cake (see page 112). Place the 6 in. plate from set on top of the 10 in. cake and repeat process for marking and inserting dowel rods. Complete decorating on cakes, except bottom borders of 10 in. center and 6 in. top cakes, which will be done at reception. Attach 10 in. and 6 in. cakes to larger boards before transferring to reception.

3. Place the 12 in. plate (spikes up) on table. Center the large (7¼ in.) separator over the plate and press down over the spikes. Position one 8 in. plate (spikes down) on top of the large separator. Place the second 8 in. plate (spikes up) on table. Center the small (4¼ in.) separator over the plate and press down over the spikes. Position the 6 in. plate (spikes down) on top of the small separator.

4. At reception: Position the large separator, with 8 in. plate on bottom and 12 in. plate on top, on the base cake. Remove 10 in. and 6 in. cakes from their larger boards. Position 10 in. cake on large separator.

5. Add bottom border to 10 in. cake. Position the small separator, with 6 in. plate on bottom and 8 in. plate on top, on the 10 in. cake. Position 6 in. cake on small separator. Add bottom border.

To Use Acetate Wrap for Tailored Tiers

1. Insert photos, patterned paper or fabric in pockets of acetate wrap. Trim inserted items as needed to fit.
2. Wrap acetate around separator and fasten Velcro® ends.

Alternate 2-Plate Set-Ups

The Fluted Bowl and Spiral Separator Sets shown below are assembled similar to 2-Plate and Pillar Construction (p. 112)—the separators provide support instead of pillars; each set includes 2 separator plates. Cakes must still use dowel rods to support cakes and secure the separators.

Fluted Bowl Separator Set (p. 220)

Spiral Separator Set (p. 220)

Dowel rod base cake as for 2-Plate & Pillar Construction. Position smaller plate from set on base cake (spikes up). Position Fluted Bowl or Spiral Separator over spikes. Position next tier on larger plate from set. Position plate (spikes down) on separator.

Using Rolled Fondant

The dough-like consistency of fondant makes it the perfect medium for creating ruffles and braids, stately molded accents, distinctive borders, fun trims and beautiful flowers. Decorators agree that fondant is an icing that is truly easy to work with. It's even easier with Wilton Ready-To-Use Rolled Fondant (p. 128)—no mixing, no mess!

COVERING THE CAKE

How do you cover a cake with fondant that's perfectly smooth, without wrinkles or air bubbles? The flexibility of fondant is your secret weapon. Just follow our instructions for the right ways to knead, roll out and lift the fondant, and you'll find that covering a cake is easy. For instructions on covering Square, Petal and other cake shapes, see the *Celebrate® With Fondant* book, p. 127.

1. Prepare cake by lightly covering with buttercream icing.
2. Before rolling out fondant, knead it until it is a workable consistency. If fondant is sticky, knead in a little confectioner's sugar. Lightly dust your smooth work surface or the Roll & Cut Mat and your rolling pin with confectioner's sugar to prevent sticking. Roll out fondant sized to your cake (see "Fondant Amounts," at right). To keep fondant from sticking, lift and move as you roll. Add more confectioner's sugar if needed.

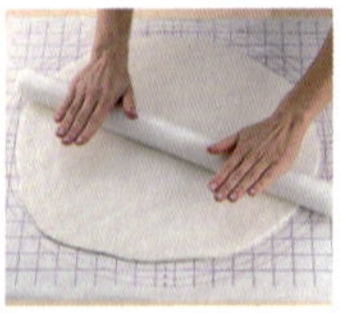

3. Gently lift fondant over rolling pin and position on cake.

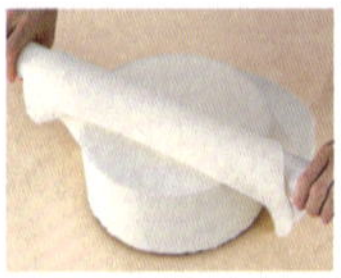

4. Shape fondant to sides of cake with Easy-Glide Smoother. We recommend using the Smoother because the pressure of your hands may leave impressions on the fondant. Use the straight edge of the Smoother to mark fondant at the base of cake. Trim off excess fondant using a spatula or sharp knife.

5. Smooth and shape fondant on cake using Easy-Glide Smoother. Beginning in the middle of the cake top, move the Smoother outward and down the sides to smooth and shape fondant to the cake and remove air bubbles. If an air bubble appears, insert a pin on an angle, release air and smooth the area again.

COVERING LARGE CAKES

In most cases, the smaller your cake, the easier it will be to cover with rolled fondant. However, there is an easy way to position and smooth fondant on cakes that are 12 in. diameter or larger. Follow the steps below to lift fondant onto the cake without tearing.

1. Cover cake lightly with buttercream icing. Roll out fondant sized to fit your cake.

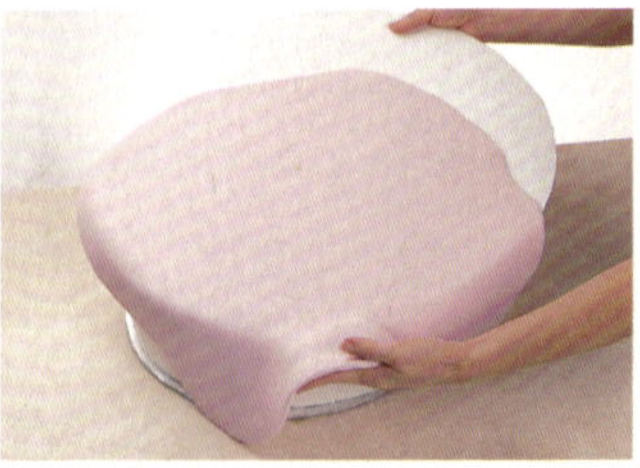

2. Slide a large cake circle that has been dusted with confectioner's sugar under the rolled fondant. Lift the circle and the fondant and position over cake. Gently shake the circle to slide the fondant off and into position on the cake. Smooth and trim as described at left.

FONDANT AMOUNTS

Use this chart to determine how much Ready-To-Use Rolled Fondant to buy. Wilton Fondant is available in 24 oz. (1 lb., 8 oz.) or 80 oz. (5 lb.) packages. Amounts listed do not include decorations.

Cake Shape	Cake Size	Fondant
Rounds 4 in. high	6 in.	18 oz.
	8 in.	24 oz.
	10 in.	36 oz.
	12 in.	48 oz.
	14 in.	72 oz.
	16 in.	108 oz.
	18 in.	140 oz.
Rounds 3 in. high	6 in.	14 oz.
	8 in.	18 oz.
	10 in.	24 oz.
	12 in.	36 oz.
	14 in.	48 oz.
	16 in.	72 oz.
	18 in.	108 oz.
Ovals 4 in. high	7¾ x 5⅝ in.	24 oz.
	10¾ x 7⅞ in.	36 oz.
	13 x 9⅞ in.	48 oz.
	16½ x 12⅜ in.	72 oz.
Hearts 4 in. high	6 in.	18 oz.
	8 in.	26 oz.
	9 in.	32 oz.
	10 in.	36 oz.
	12 in.	48 oz.
	14 in.	72 oz.
	16 in.	96 oz.
Petals 4 in. high	6 in.	18 oz.
	9 in.	30 oz.
	12 in.	48 oz.
	15 in.	72 oz.
Squares 4 in. high	6 in.	24 oz.
	8 in.	36 oz.
	10 in.	48 oz.
	12 in.	72 oz.
	14 in.	96 oz.
	16 in.	120 oz.
Hexagons 4 in. high	6 in.	18 oz.
	9 in.	36 oz.
	12 in.	48 oz.
	15 in.	84 oz.

HOW TO COLOR AND FLAVOR FONDANT

You can easily tint our White fondant or the Rolled Fondant recipe (p. 115) using Wilton Icing Colors (p. 135). Using a toothpick, add icing color, a little at a time, and knead into fondant until color is evenly blended. Wilton Ready-To-Use Rolled Fondant has a mellow flavor which can be enhanced using Wilton Butter Flavor, Clear Vanilla Extract or Almond Extract (p. 134). Knead flavor into fondant until well blended.

Recipes

The cakes, cookies and other desserts in this Yearbook were made using our favorite kitchen-tested recipes. Follow these instructions for decorated desserts that look and taste their best!

ICING RECIPES

Buttercream Icing

½ cup solid vegetable shortening
½ cup butter or margarine [1]
1 teaspoon Clear Vanilla Extract (p. 134)
4 cups sifted confectioner's sugar (about 1 lb.)
2 tablespoons milk [2]

Cream butter and shortening with electric mixer. Add vanilla. Gradually add sugar, one cup at a time, beating well on medium speed. Scrape sides and bottom of bowl often. When all sugar has been mixed in, icing will appear dry. Add milk and beat at medium speed until light and fluffy. Keep bowl covered with a damp cloth until ready to use. For best results, keep icing bowl in refrigerator when not in use. Refrigerated in an airtight container, this icing can be stored 2 weeks. Rewhip before using. Makes 3 cups.

[1] Substitute all-vegetable shortening and ½ teaspoon Wilton No-Color Butter Flavor (p. 134) for pure white icing and stiffer consistency.

[2] Add 2 tablespoons light corn syrup, water or milk per recipe to thin for icing cake.

Chocolate Buttercream Icing

Add ¾ cup cocoa (or three 1 oz. unsweetened chocolate squares, melted) and an additional 1 to 2 tablespoons milk to Buttercream Icing recipe. Mix until well blended. For a unique change of pace, use ⅛ to ¼ teaspoon Wilton Candy Flavors (p. 163) in place of vanilla extract.

Chocolate Mocha Icing: Substitute freshly brewed strong coffee for milk in recipe.

Darker Chocolate Icing: Add 4 more unsweetened chocolate squares (or ¼ cup sifted cocoa powder) and 1 more tablespoon of milk to Chocolate Buttercream Icing.

Snow-White Buttercream Icing

⅔ cup water
4 tablespoons Meringue Powder (p. 134)
12 cups sifted confectioner's sugar (about 3 lbs.)
1¼ cups solid vegetable shortening
¾ teaspoon salt
¾ teaspoon No-Color Almond Extract (p. 134)
¾ teaspoon Clear Vanilla Extract (p. 134)
½ teaspoon No-Color Butter Flavor (p. 134)

Combine water and meringue powder; whip at high speed until peaks form. Add 4 cups sugar, one cup at a time, beating at low speed after each addition. Alternately add shortening and remainder of sugar. Add salt and flavorings; beat at low speed until smooth. Makes 7 cups.

NOTE: Recipe may be doubled or halved. If halved, yield is 3 ½ cups.

Royal Icing

3 tablespoons Meringue Powder (p. 134)
4 cups sifted confectioner's sugar (about 1 lb.)
6 tablespoons water [3]

Beat all ingredients at low speed for 7-10 minutes (10-12 minutes at high speed for portable mixer) until icing forms peaks. Makes 3 cups.

[3] When using large countertop mixer or for stiffer icing, use 1 tablespoon less water.

Stabilized Whipped Cream Icing

½ pint (1 cup) heavy whipping cream
2 tablespoons confectioner's sugar
2 tablespoons Piping Gel (p. 134)
½ teaspoon Clear Vanilla Extract (p. 134)

Combine whipping cream and sugar in mixing bowl. Whip to soft peak stage. Add Piping Gel and vanilla, then continue to whip until stiff peaks form. Do not overbeat. Makes 1 ½ to 2 cups.

As an alternative, you can use frozen non-dairy whipped topping or packaged topping mix. Thaw frozen whipped topping in refrigerator before coloring or using for decorating. Use packaged topping mix immediately after preparing. Do not allow either to stay at room temperature, as it becomes too soft for decorating. Store decorated cake in refrigerator until ready to serve.

Heated Wilton Ready-To-Use Decorator Icing (p. 134)

Open icing container, remove foil. Microwave at 30% (Defrost) Power for 20-30 seconds, stirring at least once, until ready to pour. If a microwave is unavailable, icing container can be heated on a warming tray or in a pan of hot water on a stove.

Color Flow Icing Recipe (full-strength for outlining)

¼ cup + 1 teaspoon water
4 cups sifted confectioner's sugar (about 1 lb.)
2 tablespoons Color Flow Mix (p. 134)

With electric mixer, using grease-free utensils, blend all ingredients on low speed for 5 minutes. If using hand mixer, use high speed. Color flow icing "crusts" quickly, so keep bowl covered with a damp cloth while using. Stir in desired icing color. Makes approx. 2 cups color flow icing.

Thinned Color Flow: In order to fill an outlined area, the recipe above must be thinned with ½ teaspoon of water per ¼ cup of icing (just a few drops at a time as you near proper consistency). Use grease-free spoon or spatula to stir slowly. Color flow is ready for filling in outlines when a small amount dropped into the mixture takes a count of ten to disappear.

NOTE: Color flow designs take a long time to dry, so plan to do your color flow piece up to 1 week in advance.

Poured Cookie Icing

This icing dries to a shiny, hard finish. Great to use as icing or to outline and fill in with tip 2 or 3.

1 cup sifted confectioner's sugar
2 teaspoons milk
2 teaspoons light corn syrup

Place sugar and milk in bowl. Stir until thoroughly mixed. Add corn syrup; mix well. For filling in areas, use thinned icing (add small amounts of light corn syrup until desired consistency is reached).

COOKIE RECIPES

Roll-Out Cookies

1 cup unsalted butter, softened
1 ½ cups granulated sugar
1 egg
1 ½ teaspoons Clear Vanilla Extract (p. 134)
½ teaspoon No-Color Almond Extract (p. 134)
2 ¾ cups all-purpose flour
2 teaspoons baking powder
1 teaspoon salt

Preheat oven to 400°F. In mixing bowl, cream butter with sugar until light and fluffy. Beat in egg and extracts. Mix flour, baking powder and salt; add to butter mixture 1 cup at a time, mixing after each addition. Do not chill dough. Divide dough into 2 balls. On a floured surface, roll each ball into a circle approximately 12 in. wide and ⅛ in. thick. Dip cookie cutter in flour before each use. Bake cookies on ungreased cookie sheet 6-7 minutes or until cookies are lightly browned. Makes about 3 dozen cookies. Recipe may be doubled.

Chocolate Roll-Out Cookies

¾ cup butter or margarine, softened
1 cup granulated sugar
2 eggs
1 teaspoon vanilla
3 squares (3 oz.) unsweetened chocolate, melted and cooled
3 cups all-purpose flour
1 teaspoon baking powder

Preheat oven to 375°F. In large mixing bowl, beat together butter and sugar with mixer until light and fluffy. Add eggs and vanilla; mix well. Blend in chocolate. Combine flour and baking powder; gradually add to butter mixture, beating until smooth. Cover and chill until firm, about 1 hour. Roll out dough approximately ⅛ in. thick. Dip cookie cutter in flour before each use. Bake cookies on ungreased cookie sheet 8-10 minutes or until cookies are lightly browned. Remove to rack and cool thoroughly. Makes 2-2 ½ dozen cookies.

Grandma's Gingerbread

5 to 5 ½ cups all-purpose flour
1 teaspoon baking soda
1 teaspoon salt
2 teaspoons powdered ginger
2 teaspoons ground cinnamon
1 teaspoon ground nutmeg
1 teaspoon ground cloves
1 cup solid vegetable shortening
1 cup granulated sugar
1 ¼ cups unsulphured molasses [4]
2 eggs, beaten

Preheat oven to 375°F. Thoroughly mix flour, soda, salt and spices. Melt shortening in large saucepan. Cool slightly. Add sugar, molasses and eggs to saucepan; mix well. Add 4 cups dry ingredients and mix well.

Turn mixture onto lightly floured surface. Knead in remaining dry ingredients by hand. Add a little more flour, if necessary, to make firm dough.

On a floured surface, roll ¼ in. thick for cut-out cookies. Bake on ungreased cookie sheet. Small and medium-sized cookies for 6-10 minutes, large cookies for 10-15 minutes. Makes 40 medium-sized cookies.

NOTE: If you're not going to use your gingerbread dough right away, wrap in plastic and refrigerate. Refrigerated dough will keep for a week. Remove 3 hours before using so it softens and is workable.

[4] Substitute 1 ¼ cups light corn syrup for molasses to make Blonde Gingerbread.

SPECIALTY RECIPES

Pumpkin Apple Spice Cake

3 eggs
2 cups granulated sugar
¾ cup vegetable oil
1 can (15 oz.) pumpkin (not pumpkin pie filling)
⅓ cup milk or apple juice
1 teaspoon vanilla extract
3 cups all-purpose flour
2 teaspoons ground cinnamon
¼ teaspoon ground cloves (optional)
1 teaspoon salt
1 teaspoon baking soda
1½ cups finely chopped, peeled apples (about 2 medium)
½ cup chopped walnuts (optional)

Preheat oven 350°F. Spray pan with vegetable pan spray. In large bowl, beat eggs with electric mixer until they turn a light yellow color. Gradually add sugar, oil, pumpkin, milk and vanilla; beat thoroughly. Combine flour, cinnamon, cloves, if desired, salt and baking soda; add to egg mixture and mix well. Stir in apples and, if desired, nuts. Spoon into prepared pan. Bake 55-60 minutes or until toothpick inserted in center comes out clean. Let cool in pan 15 minutes. Remove from pan and cool completely on wire rack.
Makes 10-12 servings

White Chocolate Mousse

(see Memorable Mini Mousse, p. 19)

1 ½ cups heavy whipping cream
2 envelopes unflavored gelatin
6 tablespoons cold water
6 oz. cream cheese, softened
1 cup granulated sugar
½ teaspoon Clear Vanilla Extract (p. 134)
2 ½ cups milk
½ teaspoon lemon juice
2 packages (3.3 oz. ea.) white chocolate flavor instant pudding and pie filling

Whip cream until soft peaks form, set aside. Soften gelatin in cold water; heat in microwave on high, 20-30 seconds until dissolved. Cool. Beat cream cheese and sugar until light and fluffy. Add vanilla, milk and lemon juice; mix well. Add gelatin mixture, stir to combine. Add 2 packages of pudding mix. Fold in whipped cream. Refrigerate until firm, at least 3 hours or overnight. Recipe may be halved.

Wilton Gelatin Treats

This recipe yields a firmer gelatin, recommended for molding and cutting shapes.

2 packages (3 oz. ea.) flavored gelatin
1 ¼ cups boiling water

Completely dissolve gelatin in boiling water. Lightly spray pan or baking cups with vegetable pan spray. Slowly pour gelatin into pans or cups. Refrigerate until set, at least 3 hours. Unmold.

ROLLED FONDANT AND GUM PASTE RECIPES

Fondant is rolled out and used as a covering for any firm-textured cake, pound cake or fruit cake, which is traditionally first covered with a layer of marzipan to seal in flavor and moistness of the cake. A light layer of buttercream icing or apricot glaze may also be used. Cakes covered with rolled fondant can be decorated with royal or buttercream icing. Wilton also offers convenient Ready-To-Use Rolled Fondant (p. 128) in assorted colors for easy-to-handle fondant with no mixing.

Rolled Fondant

1 tablespoon plus 2 teaspoons unflavored gelatin
¼ cup cold water
½ cup Wilton Glucose (p. 131)
2 tablespoons solid vegetable shortening
1 tablespoon Wilton Glycerin (p. 131)
Icing color and flavoring, as desired
8 cups sifted confectioner's sugar (about 2 lbs.)

Combine gelatin and cold water; let stand until thick. Place gelatin mixture in top of double boiler and heat until dissolved. Add glucose, mix well. Stir in shortening and just before completely melted, remove from heat. Add glycerin, flavoring and color. Cool until lukewarm. Next, place 4 cups confectioner's sugar in a bowl and make a well. Pour the lukewarm gelatin mixture into the well and stir with a wooden spoon, mixing in sugar and adding more, a little at a time, until stickiness disappears. Knead in remaining sugar. Knead until the fondant is smooth, pliable and does not stick to your hands. If fondant is too soft, add more sugar; if too stiff, add water (a drop at a time). Use fondant immediately or store in airtight container in a cool, dry place. Do not refrigerate or freeze. When ready to use, knead again until soft. This recipe makes approx. 36 oz., enough to cover a 10 x 4 in. round cake.

Extra-Firm Rolled Fondant

Use this recipe for a fondant with the extra body and pliability ideal for making drapes, swags and elaborate decorations.

1 to 2 teaspoons Gum-Tex™ (p. 131)
24 oz. Ready-To-Use Rolled Fondant (p. 128)

Knead Gum-Tex™ into fondant until smooth. Store in an airtight container or tightly wrapped in plastic.

Apricot Glaze

Ideal for preparing a cake for fondant or for crumb-coating cakes before icing.

1 cup apricot preserves

Heat preserves to boiling, strain. Brush on cake while glaze is still hot. Let dry. Glaze will dry to a hard finish in 15 minutes or less. Makes enough to cover a 10 x 4 in. cake.

Gum Paste

Clay-like gum paste can be rolled thinner than fondant for finer detail. Gum paste dries hard and is meant for decoration only; remove from cake before serving.

1 tablespoon Gum-Tex™ (p. 131)
3 cups sifted confectioner's sugar (about ¾ lb.)
1 heaping tablespoon Glucose (p. 131)
4 tablespoons warm water
1 cup sifted confectioner's sugar (about ¼ lb.; save until ready to use)

In a large bowl, mix Gum-Tex™ into 3 cups confectioner's sugar. Make a well in the center and set aside. Mix water and glucose in a glass measuring cup and blend; heat in microwave on high for about 30 seconds until mixture is clear. Pour into well of 3 cups confectioner's sugar and mix until well blended (mixture will be very soft). Place mixture in a plastic bag and seal tightly; let mixture rest at room temperature for 8 hours or overnight. Knead remaining confectioner's sugar into gum paste when you are ready to use it. As you work it in, gum paste will whiten and soften.

Thinned Fondant Adhesive

Use this mixture when attaching dried fondant to other fondant decorations or for attaching freshly-cut fondant pieces to lollipop sticks or florist wire.

1 oz. Wilton Ready-To-Use Rolled Fondant (p. 128) (1½ in. ball)
¼ teaspoon water

Knead water into fondant until it becomes softened and sticky. To attach a fondant decoration, place mixture in decorating bag fitted with a small round tip, or brush on back of decoration. Recipe may be doubled.

Gum Paste Adhesive

1 tablespoon Wilton Meringue Powder (p. 134)
1 tablespoon water

This easy-to-make "glue" will hold your gum paste flowers and other decorations together. Mix Meringue Powder and water together; add more water if mixture is too thick. Brush on decorations.

Chocolate Fondant

1 pk. (14 oz.) Dark Cocoa Candy Melts®* (p. 162)
½ cup light corn syrup
24 oz. White Ready-To-Use Rolled Fondant (p. 128)
Brown or Black Icing Color (optional)

Melt Candy Melts® following package directions. Add corn syrup; stir to blend. Turn out mixture onto waxed paper; let stand at room temperature to dry and harden several hours. Wrap well and store at room temperature until ready to continue with recipe.

Knead small portions of candy mixture until soft and pliable. Knead softened mixture into fondant until smooth and evenly colored. If darker color is desired, knead in icing color.

Quick-Pour Fondant Icing

6 cups sifted confectioner's sugar (about 1½ lbs.)
½ cup water
2 tablespoons light corn syrup
1 teaspoon Almond Extract (p. 134)
Wilton Icing Colors (p. 135)

Cakes should be covered with apricot glaze (see recipe above) or a thin coating of buttercream icing. Let set 15 minutes before covering with fondant.

Place sugar in saucepan. Combine water and corn syrup. Add to sugar and stir until well mixed. Place over low heat. Don't allow temperature of fondant to exceed 100°F. Remove from heat, stir in flavor and icing color. To cover, place cake or cookies on cooling grid over a drip pan. Pour fondant into center and work towards edges. Touch up bare spots with spatula. Let set. Excess fondant can be reheated. Makes 2½ cups.

*Brand confectionery coating.

SUGAR MOLDING TECHNIQUE

Sugar Mold Recipe

2 cups granulated sugar
4 teaspoons water

Place sugar in a large mixing bowl. Mix sugar, making sure there are no lumps. Make a well in sugar and add water (if you are tinting sugar, blend icing color into water at this point). Rub mixture in hands and knead for about 1 minute or until well-blended and mixture packs like wet sand. Be sure there are no lumps in mixture.

NOTE: Keep sugar mixture covered with a damp cloth when not in use.

Hollowed Sugar Mold

Mix a triple batch of the sugar mold recipe. Dust half Sports Ball Pan (p. 155) with cornstarch to prevent sticking. Fill pan to ½ in. from top. Press firmly with heel of hand; scrape a small angled spatula at a 45° angle to remove excess sugar. Cut a board to 5½ in. to fit over bottom side of mold; place board on top of sugar and unmold. With knife remove ¼ in. from bottom and ⅛ in. from top of sugar molds. For Mini Ball molds, fill cavities. Follow instructions above.

For window, immediately after unmolding, cut 2 circles of plastic wrap to the size of a large round cookie cutter. Place circles on sugar mold in window area. Position cutter on wrap. Window area will remain wet. Let mold dry 3 to 4 hours. Remove cutter and gently scoop out wet sugar, leaving a ¼ in. thick shell. Smooth inside and edge with your fingers. Place molded sugar, round side down, on cardboard circle to finish drying for about 24 hours, or place on cookie sheet in 200°F oven for 20 minutes. Let cool to room temperature before touching.

CANDY RECIPES

Basic Ganache and Truffles

14 oz. Candy Melts®* (p. 162)
½ cup heavy whipping cream

Chop Candy Melts®* (you can use a food processor). Heat whipping cream in saucepan just to boiling point. Do not boil. Remove from heat and add chopped Candy Melts, stir until smooth and glossy.

Ganache Glaze: If mixture is too thick, add 1 to 2 tablespoons whipping cream. Position cake on wire rack over drip pan. Pour glaze onto center and work out toward edges.

NOTE: Cake may be iced first in buttercream. Let icing set, then pour on ganache glaze. If cake has a perfect surface, no other icing is needed.

Whipped Ganache: Follow recipe above, using 1 cup whipping cream. Allow mixture to set and cool to room temperature (mixture will have the consistency of pudding, this may take 1-2 hours). Whip on high speed with an electric mixer until light and soft peaks form.

Truffles: Add 1 tablespoon liqueur for flavor, if desired. Stir until smooth and creamy. Refrigerate until firm. Roll into 1 in. diameter balls. Can be used as center for dipped candies, served plain or rolled in nuts, coconut or cocoa powder. Store truffles in refrigerator up to 3 weeks. Makes about 2 dozen (1 in.) balls.

Candy "Clay"

14 oz. package of Candy Melts®† (p. 162)
⅓ cup light corn syrup

Melt Candy Melts® following package directions. Add corn syrup and stir to blend. Turn out mixture onto waxed paper and let set at room temperature to dry. Wrap well and store at room temperature until needed. Candy clay handles best if hardened overnight.

To Use

Candy clay will be very hard at the start; knead a small portion at a time until workable. If candy clay gets too soft, set aside at room temperature or refrigerate briefly. When rolling out candy clay, sprinkle work surface with cornstarch or cocoa (for cocoa clay) to prevent sticking; roll to approximately ⅛ in. thick.

To Tint

White candy clay may be tinted using Candy Color or Icing Color. Knead in color until well blended.

To Store

Prepared candy clay will last for several weeks at room temperature in an airtight container.

Peanut Butter Filling

1½ tablespoons butter, softened
½ cup chunky style peanut butter, room temperature
¾ cup sifted confectioner's sugar

Cream butter with peanut butter. Stir in confectioner's sugar, blending well. Add more confectioner's sugar as necessary to make thick enough to form into a ball. Use filling as a candy center for dipping, or as a center between 2 layers of coating. Makes approximately 30 candy centers.

Ready-In-Minutes Cocoa Fudge

20 oz. (approximately 4½ cups) Dark Cocoa Candy Melts®* (p. 162)
1 can (14 oz.) sweetened condensed milk (not evaporated)

Melt Candy Melts® in microwave-safe container using microwave on low power. Add milk; stir until blended. Microwave an additional 2 to 3 minutes on medium power; stir until fudge develops a sheen. Pour mixture into buttered 7 x 11 in. non-stick Biscuit/Brownie pan and refrigerate until firm.

Cream Cheese Mints

2 oz. cream cheese, softened
¼ teaspoon peppermint candy flavor
Desired icing color
2 cups confectioners' sugar
Granulated sugar

Blend cheese with flavoring and color; mix in sugar. Knead until mixture is firm, adding more sugar if needed. Roll mixture into balls. Dip one side in a small amount of granulated sugar. Press, sugar side down, in candy mold. Unmold immediately onto waxed paper. Makes approximately 12-15 mint bells.

Tip Techniques

Your icing turned out great—now you're ready to learn how to pipe beautiful shapes on your cake. Stars, shells, dots, lines and other techniques are the foundation of your decorating knowledge. We'll tell you step-by-step how to pipe each one, including the angle, pressure and movement to use for a uniform look. With practice, you can build on these basics to create many other impressive designs.

ROUND TIPS

Dot

Pipe dots for flower centers, faces, figure piping and border effects. When making large dots, lift the tip as you squeeze to allow icing to fill out completely.

Practice With: Tip 3
Icing Consistency: Medium
Bag Position: 90°
Hold Tip: Slightly above surface

1. Hold the bag straight up with the tip slightly above the surface. Squeeze the bag and keep point of the tip in icing until the dot is the size you want.
2. Stop squeezing the bag completely before you lift the tip from the dot.
3. Lift tip up and pull away from piped dot.

Ball

An important technique to master, the ball shape makes bold borders and is the first step to learn for figure piping. Vary the basic look by adding stars, dots or spirals on the ball shapes.

Practice With: Tip 9
Icing Consistency: Medium
Bag Position: 90°
Hold Tip: Slightly above surface

1. Squeeze the bag, applying steady even pressure. As the icing begins to build up, raise the tip with it, but keep the tip end buried in the icing.
2. Stop squeezing as you bring the end of the tip to the surface.
3. Lift the tip up and pull away from your piped ball. Use the edge of the tip to shave off any point so that your ball is nicely rounded.

Bead

If you can pipe a shell, you can pipe a bead—the movements are similar. To pipe a bead heart, simply pipe one bead, then a second, joining the tails. Smooth together using a decorator's brush.

Practice With: Tip 5
Icing Consistency: Medium
Bag Position†: 45° at 3:00 (9:00)
Hold Tip: Slightly above surface

1. Squeeze as you lift tip slightly so that icing fans out.
2. Relax pressure as you draw the tip down and bring the bead to a point.
3. To make a bead border, start the end of your next bead so that the fanned end covers the tail of the preceding bead to form an even chain.

Cornelli Lace

The lacy design of this freehand technique depends on continuous curving strings that do not overlap or touch.

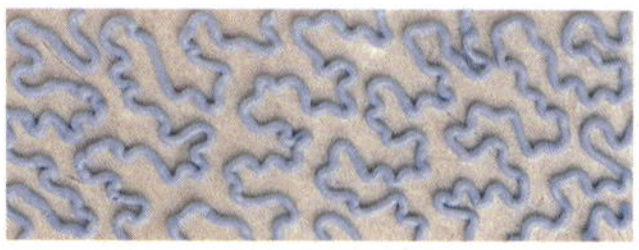

Practice With: Tip 1 or 2
Icing Consistency: Thin
Bag Position: 90°
Hold Tip: Close to cake so icing attaches without scraping cake with tip and without flattening icing strings

Beginning and ending at edges, pipe a continuous string of icing, curve it up, down and around until area is covered. Make certain strings never touch or cross. Don't leave any loose ends! Stop pressure; pull tip away.

Printing

Practice With: Tip 3 with message press
Icing Consistency: Thin
Bag Position†: 45° at 3:00 (9:00)
Hold Tip: Lightly touching surface

You may pipe letters freehand, pipe over a pattern traced with a toothpick, or pipe after imprinting letters with a pattern press. If you are using a pattern press, let icing crust slightly, then imprint the message. With a steady, even pressure, squeeze out a straight line, lifting the tip off the surface to let icing string drop. To prevent tails from forming, be careful to stop squeezing before you touch tip to surface and pull away. Be sure the end of the tip is clean before you go on to another line.

Writing

Practice With: Tip 5
Icing Consistency: Thin
Bag Position†: 45° at 3:00 (9:00)
Hold Tip: Lightly touching surface

You may pipe letters freehand, pipe over a pattern traced with a toothpick, or pipe after imprinting letters with a pattern press. If you are using a pattern press, let icing crust slightly, then imprint the message. Steadily squeeze, gliding along the surface in a smooth, continuous motion. Use your arm, not your fingers, to form each line, letter or word. Keep your wrist straight, moving your entire forearm as a single unit. After you begin to master the curves and swings of the letters, lift the tip up slightly as you write. You'll find you have more control if you let the icing draw out slightly over the surface as you write.

Outline

Characters or designs are often outlined first, then piped in with stars or zigzags. Outlines are used for facial features, too. Color Flow plaques are also outlined before icing is flowed into the shape.

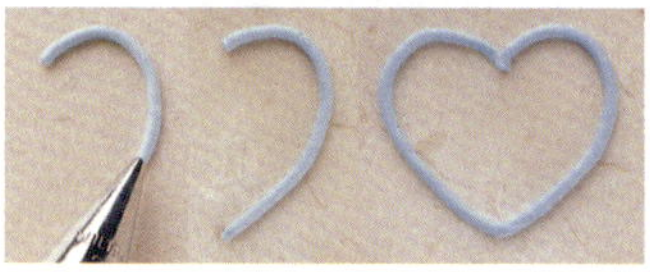

Practice With: Tip 3
Icing Consistency: Thin
Bag Position†: 45° at 3:00 (9:00)
Hold Tip: Slightly above surface

1. Touch tip to surface. Raise the tip slightly and continue to squeeze.
2. The icing will flow out of the tip while you direct it along the surface.
3. To end, stop squeezing, touch tip to surface and pull away.

Drop Strings

These flowing strings are a beautiful way to adorn the sides of a cake. The trick to making drop strings is to pull the bag toward you as the string drapes down. If you "draw" the string with the tip, you won't achieve a pretty curve and your strings will tend to break. Pipe at eye level to your cake so that strings line up evenly. The Cake Dividing Set (p. 133) is a great help in accurately dividing and marking your cake for even drop strings.

Single Drop Strings

Practice With: Tip 3
Icing Consistency: Stiff
Bag Position†: Shoulder level at 4:30 (7:30)
Hold Tip: Lightly touching surface to attach

1. With a toothpick, mark horizontal divisions on cake in the width you desire. Touch tip to first mark and squeeze, pausing momentarily so that icing sticks to surface.
2. While squeezing, pull the bag toward you. Continue squeezing to allow the icing to drape naturally into an arc. Icing will drop by itself—do not move the tip down with the string. The end of the tip should be the same distance from the surface as the width from point to point on your cake.
3. Stop pressure before you touch tip to second mark to end string. Repeat, keeping drop strings uniform in length and width.

Multiple Drop Strings

Try a different color for each row of multiple drop strings—put holiday colors together to really dress up your cake.

To add multiple rows of strings, mark the cake for the deepest row and pipe that row. Return to the first drop string point, squeeze the bag, and drop a string with a slightly shorter arc than in the first row. Join the end of this string to the end of the corresponding string in the first row. Repeat the process for a third row of drop strings above the second.

STAR TIPS

Star

Practice With: Tip 16
Icing Consistency: Medium
Bag Position: 90°
Hold Tip: Between $\frac{1}{8}$ and $\frac{1}{4}$ in. above surface

1. Hold the decorating bag straight up, with the tip between $\frac{1}{8}$ and $\frac{1}{4}$ in. above the surface, while using your other hand to hold the tip steady. Squeeze the bag to form a star. Increasing or decreasing the pressure changes the size of the star.
2. Stop squeezing the bag completely before you lift the tip from the star.
3. Lift the tip up and pull away from piped star.

Pull-out stars add even more dimension to your cake. To make them, hold bag at a 45° angle to surface. As you squeeze out icing, pull tip up and away from cake. When your mound is high enough, stop pressure and pull tip away. Work from bottom to top of area to be covered with pull-out stars.

Star Fill In

Because these close-together stars require so much piping from the same bag, it's a good idea to keep replenishing the icing. Replenish icing when it gets soft or stars will be poorly defined.

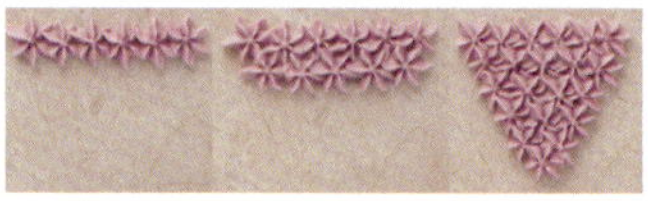

Practice With: Tip 16
Icing Consistency: Medium
Bag Position: 90°
Hold Tip: $\frac{1}{4}$ in. above surface

1. Pipe a row of stars evenly and close together, adjusting the tip position slightly each time so that the points of the stars interlock and cover the area without gaps.
2. Pipe a row of stars beneath the first, again adjusting tip position to close any gaps.
3. Continue to fill in entire area.

Zigzag

A quick and popular way to fill in outlined areas, perfect for ribbed sweater and cuff effects. You can use tight zigzags to cover the entire side of your cake—they look great!

Practice With: Tip 16
Icing Consistency: Medium
Bag Position†: 45° at 3:00 (9:00)
Hold Tip: Lightly touching surface

1. Steadily squeeze and move your hand in a tight up and down motion.
2. Continue piping up and down with steady pressure. To end, stop pressure and pull tip away. For more elongated zigzags, move your hand to the desired height while maintaining a steady pressure. For a more relaxed look, just increase the width as you move the bag along.
3. Repeat as you move in a straight line with consistent up/down motion.

†The technique instructions in this Decorating Guide will list the correct direction for holding the bag. When the bag direction differs for left-handed decorators, that direction will be listed in parentheses. For example, when a bag is to be held at 3:00 for a right-handed decorator, it should be held at 9:00 for a left-handed decorator.

Zigzag Puff
This is the fluffy look you want for making clouds or smoke and to add dimension as a side border.

Practice With: Tip 17
Icing Consistency: Medium
Bag Position†: 45° at 3:00 (9:00)
Hold Tip: Lightly touching surface

1. Begin to pipe with a light pressure, then use heavier pressure toward the center of the puff, then return gradually to a light pressure to form the tapered end.
2. To end each puff, stop pressure and pull tip away.
3. Repeat as you move in a straight line to form a row of puffs.

Shell
Most popular icing technique of all, the shell is the basis for many borders. Lift tip slightly when piping shells to avoid a bumpy look.

Practice With: Tip 21
Icing Consistency: Medium
Bag Position: 45° at 6:00
Hold Tip: Slightly above surface

1. Hold the bag in the 6:00 position so that you can pull the bag toward you. The tip should be slightly above the surface.
2. Squeeze hard, letting the icing fan out generously as it lifts the tip—do not lift the bag. Gradually relax your pressure as you lower the tip until it touches the surface.
3. Stop pressure and pull the tip away, without lifting it off the surface, to draw the shell to a point.
4. To make a shell border, start the end of your next shell so that the fanned end covers the tail of the preceding shell to form an even chain.

Reverse Shell
Opposite-facing shells look spectacular as top and bottom borders and as framed areas on your cake—they add a wonderful motion effect. The look is even fancier finished with a dot or a star at the center of each shell curve.

Practice With: Tip 21
Icing Consistency: Medium
Bag Position: 45° at 6:00
Hold Tip: Slightly above surface

1. As you begin to form a shell, squeeze hard, letting the icing fan out.
2. Form a curve, moving the tip from 9:00 (3:00) to 12:00 to 6:00. Relax pressure and lower the tip, pulling straight toward you at 6:00 to form a tail.
3. Repeat with another shell, curving from 3:00 (9:00) to 12:00 to 6:00.
4. To make a reverse shell border, pipe a chain of swirling reverse shells, with the fan end of each new shell covering the tail of the previous shell. If you are making the border on a round cake, turn the cake as you go so that the back of the bag is at 6:00 and you are working toward yourself.

Rope
Finish your piped baskets with pretty edging and handles. Excellent for western or nautical themed cakes. You can make a great-looking rope with star or round tips (or basketweave tips, ridged or smooth side up).

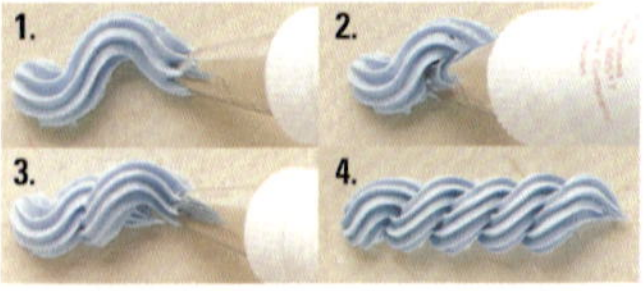

Practice With: Tip 21
Icing Consistency: Medium
Bag Position†: 45° at 4:30 (7:30)
Hold Tip: Lightly touching surface

1. Using a steady, even pressure, move the tip in a gentle sideways "S" curve. Stop pressure and pull tip away.
2. Insert tip under the bottom curve of the "S" shape.
3. Squeeze the bag with steady pressure as you pull down, then lift the tip. Move up and over the tail of the "S" as you continue to squeeze and form a hook.
4. Keep spacing as even as possible and "S" curves uniform in thickness, length and overall size. Be sure to tuck the tip into the bottom curve of the previous "S" before you begin squeezing to insure the clean, continuous look of a rope.

e-Motion
These continuous e-shaped loops work best on a bottom border, or as a western lariat. If you have to stop on your border to change positions, push in your tip at the end of the "e" and continue piping to keep a smooth look.

Practice With: Tip 16
Icing Consistency: Medium
Bag Position†: 45° at 3:00 (9:00)
Hold Tip: Slightly above surface

1. Starting with bag at a 45° angle, and at bottom edge, squeeze out icing with even pressure, moving tip up to the right…
2. …and around as if writing the letter "e."
3. Repeat to complete the border, using a steady, even pressure. To end, stop pressure, pull tip away. You can vary the look of the e-motion border by making tight e's or stretched e's.

Rosette
Practice With: Tip 16
Icing Consistency: Medium
Bag Position: 90°
Hold Tip: Lightly touching surface

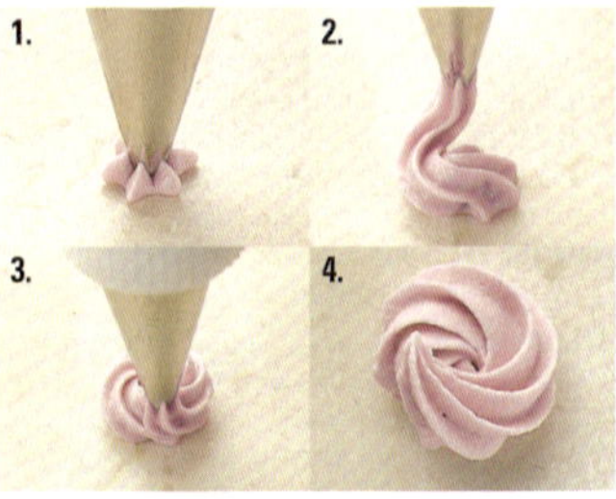

1. Keeping the tip slightly above the surface, squeeze out icing to form a star and, without releasing pressure, move the tip in a tight, complete rotation, starting at 9:00 (3:00), moving to 12:00. . .
2. then to 3:00 (9:00) and 6:00. . .
3. and ending back at 9:00 (3:00).
4. Stop pressure and lift tip away.

MULTIPLE TIPS

Swirl Drop Flower
The swirled look adds a nice motion effect to the cake. You must squeeze and turn at the same time.

Practice With: Tips 2D, 3; use Large Coupler
Icing Consistency: Use royal icing: medium for flower, thin for center
Bag Position: 90°
Hold Tip: Slightly above surface

1. Turn your wrist in toward you before piping. Hold bag straight up, just touching the surface. You will turn wrist a full twist. Starting with the flat of your knuckles at 9:00 (3:00). As you squeeze out the icing, slowly turn your hand, with knuckles ending at 12:00.
2. Stop squeezing and lift the tip away.
3. Make a tip 3 dot flower center, holding your bag straight up and keeping the tip buried as you squeeze. Stop squeezing, then pull your tip up and away.

BASKETWEAVE TIPS
Try using different tips to vary the woven effects.

Practice With: Tip 47
Icing Consistency: Medium
Bag Position†: 45° at 6:00 for vertical stripes; at 3:00 (9:00) for horizontal bars
Hold Tip: Lightly touching surface, serrated side up

1. Squeeze out a vertical stripe of icing from top to bottom (shown ridged side up).
2. Squeeze out short horizontal stripes of icing across the vertical stripe starting at the top. Spacing between stripes should be the same as the width of the tip opening. Squeeze next vertical stripe over ends of horizontal stripes. Start next set of horizontal stripes by burying the tip under the first vertical stripe.
3. Repeat vertical lines then horizontal lines until you achieve basketweave effect. Each new set should fit between the previous set.

PETAL TIPS

Ruffle
Everyone loves a ruffle's graceful motion—ruffles always add interest to your cake. Use them as a top border, to frame a plaque or to trim doll dresses and baby bonnets.

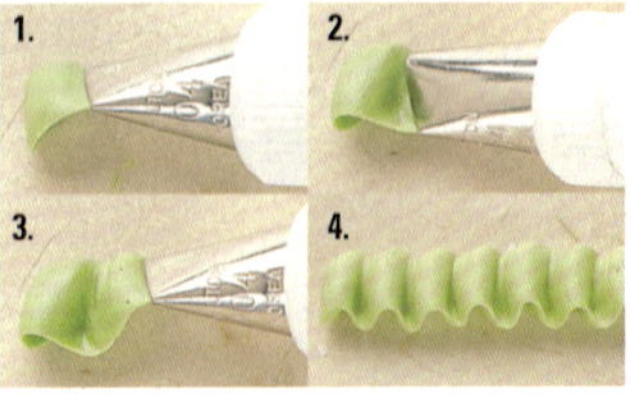

Practice With: Tip 104
Icing Consistency: Medium
Bag Position†: 45° at 3:00 (9:00)
Hold Tip: Wide end lightly touching surface with narrow end facing down and away from surface

1. Keep the wide end of your tip touching the cake with the narrow end down. Move wrist up to pull up icing.
2. Move wrist down to complete one curl of the ruffle.
3. Repeat up and down motion.
4. Raise and lower the narrow end as you move around the cake. Repeat this motion for the entire ruffle.

Bow
The bow has many uses. Create a different look by using a different tip: round, star and petal will work.

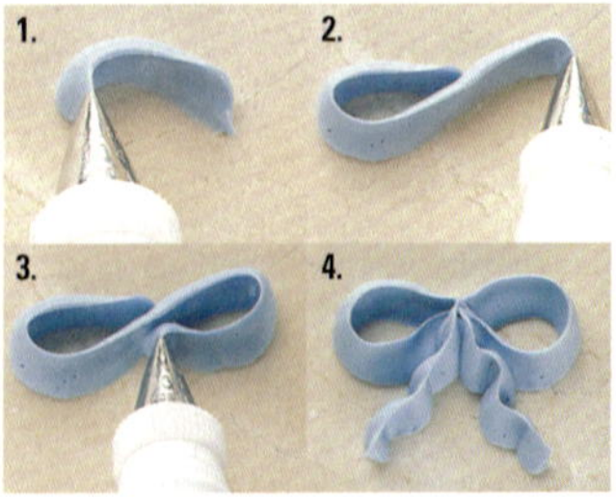

Practice With: Tip 104
Icing Consistency: Medium
Bag Position: 45° at 6:00
Hold Tip: Wide end touching surface, narrow end straight up

1. With narrow end of tip pointing straight up, squeeze, moving the tip up and around to the left and back to the starting point.
2. Continue around, making a second loop on the right.
3. The two loops will form a figure 8.
4. While holding bag in the same position, return to the center and squeeze out two streamers.

DECORATING WILTON SHAPED CAKES STEP-BY-STEP

When decorating a cake that's simply covered with stars, here are the easy steps involved.

1. Ice sides and other areas smooth per instructions.

2. Outline details.

3. Pipe in facial features, small details.

4. Cover areas with stars, stripes, zigzags or dots.

5. Add message. Edge top and base with borders. Attach flowers or trims.

Flower-Making Techniques

Explore beautiful flowers like the sweet pea or carnation, which add lovely color to your cake design. Create the magnificent rose—the most popular icing flower of all. With practice, your flowers will have the just-picked look of real garden flowers.

FLOWER NAIL FLOWERS

Using a Flower Nail

The nail is a revolving platform you hold in your hand to conveniently build roses and other flowers. It allows you to work close up, to turn for easy piping and to remove your completed flowers without damage, to dry.

The key to making the flower on the nail is to coordinate the turning of the nail with the formation of each petal.

Attach a square of waxed paper on the flat surface of the flower nail using a dot of icing. Pipe your flower directly on the waxed paper. Hold the flower nail between the thumb and forefinger of your left (right) hand (use other fingers to support nail) and roll it slowly counterclockwise (clockwise for lefties) as you press out icing with the decorating bag held in the right (left) hand. Your right (left) hand moves in and out, or up and down, as it holds the decorating bag and tip at just the right angle (in most cases 45°) and keeps the icing flowing at an even speed. After piping, slide the waxed paper with flower off the nail to dry.

The Wilton Rose

NOTE: If you are going to be placing your roses on your cake immediately, waxed paper squares are not needed. To remove finished roses, use the Flower Lifter (p. 138). Slide flower from lifter onto cake, using a spatula.

Practice With: Tips 104, 12
Icing Consistency: Royal or stiff buttercream
Bag Position†: Base 90° (straight up); petals 45° at 4:30 (7:30)
Hold Tip: For base, slightly above nail; for petals, wide end touching base
Flower Nail: #7

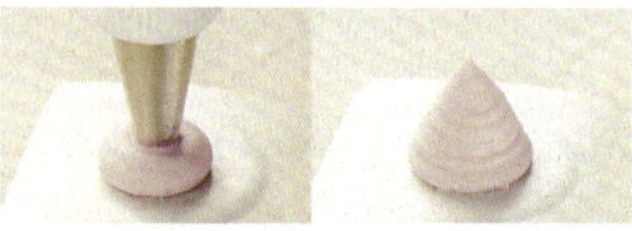

1. Make the rose base, using tip 12 and flower nail #7. Hold the bag straight up, the end of tip 12 slightly above the center of your waxed paper-covered flower nail, which is held in your other hand. Using heavy pressure, build up a base, remembering to keep your tip buried as you squeeze. Start to lift the tip higher, gradually raise the tip, and decrease the pressure.
2. Stop pressure, pull up and lift away. The rose base should be 1½ times as high as the rose tip opening.

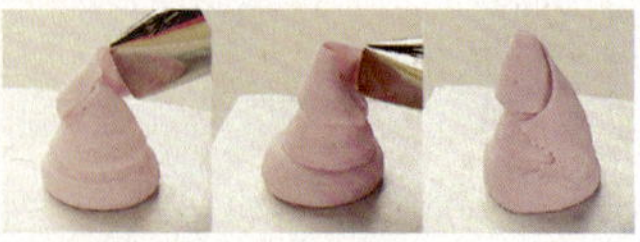

3. Make the center bud, using tip 104. Hold nail containing base in your left (right) hand and bag with rose tip 104 in right (left) hand. Bag should be at a 45° angle to the flat surface of the nail and in the 4:30 (7:30) position. The wide end of the tip should touch the cone of the icing base at or slightly below the midpoint, and the narrow end of the tip should point up and angled in over top of base.
4. Now you must do 3 things at the same time: squeeze the bag, move the tip and rotate the nail. As you squeeze the bag, move the tip up from the base, forming a ribbon of icing. Slowly turn the nail counterclockwise (clockwise for lefties) to bring the ribbon of icing around to overlap at the top of the mound, then back down to starting point. Move your tip straight up and down only; do not loop it around the base.
5. Now you have a finished center bud.

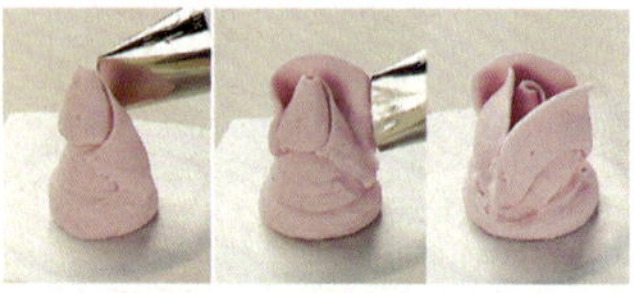

6. Make the top row of 3 petals. Touch the wide end of tip to the midpoint of bud base, narrow end straight up.
7. Turn nail, keeping wide end of tip on base so that petal will attach. Move tip up and back down to the midpoint of mound, forming the first petal.
8. Start again, slightly behind end of first petal, and squeeze out second petal. Repeat for the third petal, ending by overlapping the starting point of the first petal. Rotate the nail ⅓ turn for each petal.

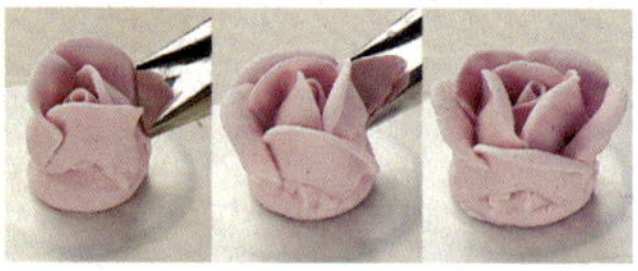

9. Make the middle row of 5 petals. Touch the wide end of tip slightly below center of a petal in the top row. Angle the narrow end of tip out slightly more than you did for the top row of petals. Squeeze bag and turn nail moving tip up, then down, to form first petal.
10. Repeat for a total of 5 petals, rotating the nail ⅕ turn for each petal.
11. The last petal end should overlap the first's starting point.

12. Make the bottom row of 7 petals. Touch the wide end of tip below the center of a middle row petal, again angling the narrow end of tip out a little more. Squeeze bag and turn nail to end of fingers, moving tip up, then down to form first petal.
13. Repeat for a total of 7 petals, rotating the nail ⅐ turn for each petal.

14. The last petal end should overlap the first's starting point.
15. Slip waxed paper and completed rose from nail. This is the completed Wilton Rose.

†The technique instructions in this Decorating Guide will list the correct direction for holding the bag. When the bag direction differs for left-handed decorators, that direction will be listed in parentheses. For example, when a bag is to be held at 3:00 for a right-handed decorator, it should be held at 9:00 for a left-handed decorator.

Rosebud

Finish your petit fours or cupcakes with one pretty rosebud. Made in buttercream, this flat flower can be piped directly on the cake.

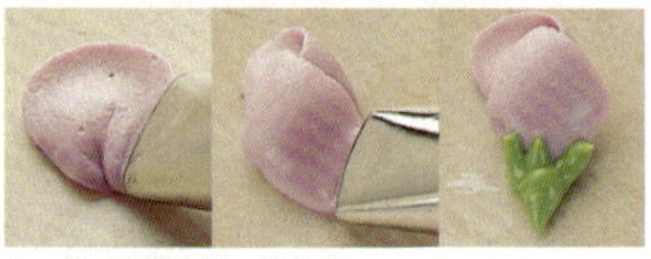

Practice With: Tips 104, 3
Icing Consistency: Stiff consistency buttercream for petals, thin consistency for sepals and calyx
Bag Position†: 45° at 4:30 (7:30) for petals; 45° at 6:00 for sepals and calyx

1. Using tip 104, make the base petal. Keep the narrow end of the tip raised up and slightly to the right (left for lefties). While squeezing, move the tip along the surface away from you in a straight line about ¼ in. long. Pause, then continue squeezing as the icing fans out. Returning the tip to the original position and halfway back, start to release pressure, move tip to starting point, stop pressure and pull tip away.
2. Using tip 104, make the overlapping petal. Touch the wide end of the tip to the outside edge of completed petal. The bag is positioned as for the base petal, at 4:30 (7:30); hold it steady in this position until the second petal is completed. As you continue squeezing, the icing will catch the edge of the base petal and roll over it naturally. When the second petal looks complete, stop pressure completely, touch the tip back down to the surface and pull tip away.
3. Using tip 3, make the sepals and calyx. Form the middle sepal first by squeezing and letting icing build up. Lift the bag up and away from the flower. Stop pressure as you pull away to form the point of the sepal. Repeat, making a sepal on the left and right sides. For the calyx, insert tip into the base of the center sepal. Squeeze, letting the icing build up. Slowly draw the tip toward you, relaxing pressure as you move away from the flower. Stop pressure, pull away. You may want to blend the calyx into the stem using a damp brush.

Sweet Pea

One of the fastest, easiest-to-make flowers; works beautifully as part of a floral cascade. Try piping them in variegated shades.

Practice With: Tips 104, 3
Icing Consistency: Buttercream—stiff for petals, thin for calyx
Bag Position†: For center petal and calyx 45° at 6:00; for left petal 45° at 4:30 (7:30); for right petal, 45° at 7:30 (4:30).
Hold Tip: Wide end touching surface; narrow end straight up

1. Make the center petal. Squeeze the bag and lift the tip slightly off the surface (about ¼ in.) as the icing moves forward and curls. Continue to squeeze without changing position. Relax pressure and return the tip to the surface. Stop squeezing, pull tip away.
2. Make the side petals. Position your bag slightly to the left of the center petal. Follow the same procedure as you did for the center petal—squeeze, and while the petal curls, lift the tip, relaxing your pressure and lowering the tip back to the surface. Stop squeezing and pull away. Repeat for the right side petal, holding the tip to the right of the center petal.
3. Make the calyx as above with tip 3.

Apple Blossom

Pipe apple blossoms about the size of a penny and dry them on Flower Formers (p. 138).

Practice With: Tips 101, 1
Icing Consistency: Stiff royal icing
Bag Position: 45° for petals; 90° for dots
Hold Tip: Wide end touching surface, with narrow end pointed out.
Flower Nail: #7

1. Use tip 101 and hold bag at a 45° angle to flower nail with wide end of tip touching nail center, narrow end pointed out ⅛ in. away from nail surface.
2. Squeeze bag and turn nail as you move tip ⅛ in. out from nail center and back, relaxing pressure as you return to starting point.
3. Repeat procedure to make 4 more petals. Add 5 tip 1 dots for center.

LILY NAIL FLOWERS

Using a Lily Nail

The lily nail helps you achieve deeply cupped flowers. You use different size nails for small and large flowers—nails range from ½ to 2½ in. in diameter. To produce flowers in your lily nail, it must first be lined with aluminum foil. This makes removal of the flower from the nail possible. To prevent the foil in your lily nail from moving when piping flowers, squeeze a dab of icing in the nail before adding the foil. Place a 2 in. square of aluminum foil in bottom half of the lily nail. Gently press the top half down into the foil, lift off.

Some flowers require a shallower foil cup. For those flowers, push foil halfway into the nail. Hold the lily nail between the thumb and forefinger on your left (right) hand and roll it slowly counterclockwise (clockwise) as you press out icing with the decorating bag held in your right (left) hand. Remove the foil cup with flower and set aside to dry.

Lily

If petals split while piping, widen tip slightly by inserting a thin spatula into the opening.

Practice With: Tips 68, 14
Icing Consistency: Stiff royal icing
Bag Position†: For petals 45° at 3:00 (9:00); for center 90°
Hold Tip: For petals, lightly touching surface of nail, wide opening parallel to surface; for center, slightly above flower line.

1. Line 1⅝ in. lily nail with foil. Use tip 68. Touch center well of nail with tip and squeeze, pulling petal up and over edge of foil cup. Decrease pressure as you reach end of petal and hesitate before you stop pressure and pull tip away, drawing petal to point.
2. Pipe two more petals.
3. Pipe three more petals between open spaces.
4. Add tip 14 star center and push in stamens.

NOTE: Stamens are not to be eaten.

FLORAL GREENERY

Leaves

Practice With: Tips 352, 67, 366
Icing Consistency: Buttercream thinned with corn syrup
Bag Position: 45° at 6:00
Hold Tip: Lightly touching surface; wide opening parallel to surface

Basic Leaf	**Veined Leaf**	**Large Leaf**
Tip 352	**Tip 67**	**Tip 366** Use large coupler

1. Squeeze hard to build up the base and, at the same time, lift the tip slightly.
2. Relax pressure as you pull the tip toward you, drawing the leaf to a point.
3. Stop squeezing and lift away.

Vines

Practice With: Tip 3
Icing Consistency: Thin
Bag Position: 45° at 3:00 (9:00)
Hold Tip: Lightly touching surface

1. Touch your tip lightly to the surface as you start to squeeze, then lift slightly above the surface as you draw out the stem.
2. Move tip gently up and down to form "hills and valleys." To end the line, stop squeezing and pull the tip along the surface.
3. Add secondary curved stems, starting at main stem, stopping pressure as you pull to a point.

Other Decorating Techniques

Combing

Practice With: Icing Sculptor™, Decorating Comb or Triangle, Trim 'N Turn Cake Stand (p. 133)
Icing Consistency: Medium-to-thin buttercream

Cover the cake with a slightly thicker coating of icing so the comb's ridges will not touch the cake. Comb immediately after icing cake, while icing is soft. Using a turntable helps to keep the movement smooth. Use the Icing Sculptor™, Decorating Comb or Decorating Triangle to add different contoured effects to your iced cake. Choose the type of effect you want—wide or narrow—then run that edge around your cake to form ridges. Ridges will be deep or shallow depending on the Icing Sculptor™ blade or the side of Decorating Comb or Triangle you use.

Icing Sculptor™

Select the sculpting blades you want and slide into holder. Press sculptor into iced cake as you rotate cake on turntable. The 64 blades included can create hundreds of different effects! Mix and match between the 14 edge designs to achieve the perfect look for your cake.

Pattern Press

The trick to uniform designs and steady writing and printing is using a pattern press (p. 137). Simply imprint the press onto all types of icing, including fondant. Use the vine pattern press on cake sides for a beautiful botanical effect.

Practice With: Tips 3, 16
Icing Consistency: Medium
Bag Position: 45° at 3:00
Hold Tip: Slightly above surface

1. Lightly press pattern onto your iced cake to imprint the design.
2. Outline the imprinted design with icing, using the tip of your choice. Change the tip to change the look of each pattern.

Tinting Shredded Coconut

Place desired amount of coconut in plastic bag, add a few drops of color and knead until color is evenly blended. Dry on waxed paper.

Attaching Bunny Arms

(see Bunches for Bunny!, p. 67)

Twist thin center section of pipe cleaner around cookie treat stick to form arms. For an even, thick look, fold and bend back pipe cleaner at each thin section. When bent, each arm should measure approximately 4¼ in. long.

Starburst

(see Lady Liberty, p. 68)

Using royal icing on waxed paper-covered board, pipe approximately 200 tip 14 stars each in red and blue; let dry. Using royal icing, attach stars to florist wire, about 1 in. apart. Cut 2 lollipop sticks to 4 in; tape a group of 10 wires to each stick to make starburst sprays.

Fireplace

(see Holly Hearth, p. 51)

Press double recipe of cereal treats into jelly roll pan, 1 in. high. Unmold and cut into three 11 x 3¾ in. wide pieces. Prepare another recipe of cereal treats and press 1 in. high, into half of jelly roll pan, lengthwise. Unmold and cut two 11 x 3¾ in. wide pieces. Stack 3 layers together on candy plaque base, attaching with melted white candy. Cut fireplace opening 5 in. wide x 1 in. deep with paring knife. Cut dowel rods to 3 in. high; insert on each side of opening. Cut a cake board to 10 x 3 in.; position on top of stack. Stack and attach 2 remaining cereal treat layers; insert 2 dowel rods cut to 2 in. high. Roll out black fondant ⅛ in. thick. Cut a 5 x 3 in rectangle and attach inside opening with melted white candy. Using melted white candy in cut bag, pipe lines on cereal treat layers to form 1½ in. wide bricks.

Swing

(see A Swinging Party, p. 10)

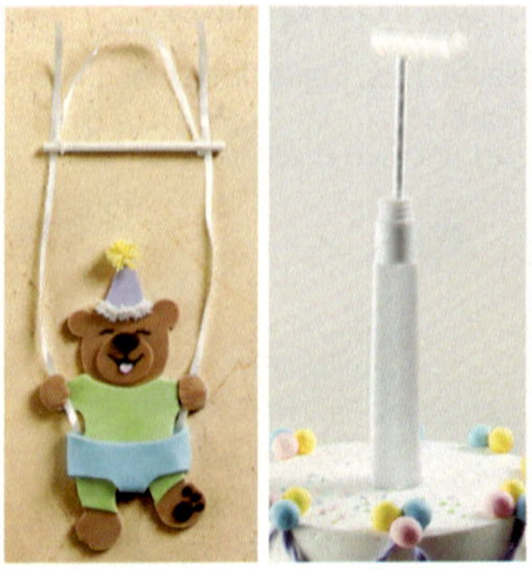

1. Cut a cookie treat stick to 4 in. long. To suspend bear from stick, tie the 8 in. ribbons which are attached to bear's paws to ends of stick, so that 4 in. of ribbon separates stick and paws.
2. Make center pole. Tape 2 wooden dowel rods together; cut at one end to make a 22 in. long pole. Wrap with white satin ribbon 12 in. from top; secure ends with hot glue. For top bar, cut a plastic dowel rod to 3 in. long. Using knife, poke a hole the diameter of center pole, ¾ in. from end. Insert center pole; secure with hot glue.
3. For hanging swing on pole, cut a 7 in. length of white curling ribbon. Tie each end on stick, next to the ribbon held by bear. At party, insert center pole in columns of assembled cake; hang swing from pole.

Wired Stars

(see Set off Skyrockets, p. 98)

Using royal icing, make 250 tip 17 stars in various colors; let dry on waxed paper-covered boards. Cut 24-gauge florist wire into 25 12 in. lengths and 150 6 in. lengths. Attach 6 pairs of stars to 12 in. and 5 pairs of stars to 6 in. wires with royal icing; let dry.

Figure Piping Techniques

Figure piping is a way to really add personality to your cake. Your figures can be as lifelike or cartoonish as you want them to be. Begin with a base, then add familiar shapes such as dots, balls and strings to give the figure personality.

Monkeys

(see Clunk A Monkey, p. 24)

Make 2 copies of each monkey pattern; place 1 copy on board, cover with waxed paper and secure with tape, use 2nd copy for reference while piping. Build up body with tip 10; smooth with spatula. Pipe in tip 8 stomach (pat smooth with finger dipped in cornstarch). Pipe tip 8 ball head; pipe in face and ears with tip 3 (pat smooth with finger dipped in cornstarch). Pipe tip 6 outline legs, arms, and tail. **For bottom monkey**, pipe tip 3 dot eyes and outline mouth, tip 1 dot nose. **For top monkey**, pipe tip 3 outline eyes, tip 1 dot nose; pipe in tip 3 mouth, and tip 1 outline teeth.

Care Bears

(see Nap Snacks, p. 32)

1. Pipe bodies on waxed paper using royal icing. Pipe tip 12 log torso, the same length as the icing decoration head.
2. Insert tip 8 in torso; pipe pull out arms and legs.
3. Add tip 3 pull out dot tail and tip 2 bead heart. Position icing decoration head and let dry overnight.

Other Decorating Techniques

Santa, Mrs. Santa, Reindeer, Elf Cookies

(see Sun, Sand and Santa, p. 49)

Tint dough copper and roll out. Using cutters from set, cut 4 gingerbread boy cookies and 1 reindeer cookie. Place on cookie sheet. Using dough thinned with water, pipe tip 6 dot ears and nose on 2 elf cookies and tip 4 dot nose on Santa and Mrs. Claus cookies. Bake and cool. **For Mrs. Claus,** immediately after removing from oven, carefully bend cookie at waist and let cool on cardboard frame used to make beach chair. Decorate cookies with royal icing. **For elves,** pipe in tip 3 swimsuit; add tip 2 string eyes, hair and mouth. **For reindeer,** ice smooth. Pipe tip 2 dot hooves, nose and eye; string antlers. Add tip 3 string harness. **For Santa and Mrs. Claus,** pipe in tip 3 swimsuits (pat smooth with finger dipped in cornstarch). On Santa, add tip 4 zigzag fur trim and tip 3 string suspenders, tip 2 dot mouth and string eyes, tip 13 pull-out beard, tip 6 pull-out moustache. For Santa, standing elf and reindeer, attach lollipop sticks to back with icing. On Mrs. Claus, pipe tip 2 glasses, mouth and swirl hair; add tip 3 hat with tip 101s brim.

Royal Icing Curls

(see La Quinceañera Bonita, p. 20)

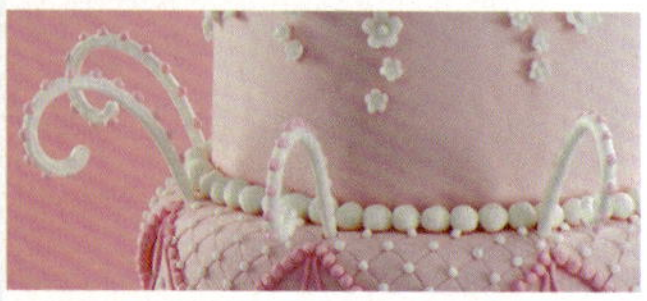

Tape curls pattern to cake boards and cover with waxed paper. Outline patterns with tip 8; let dry. Add tip 3 dots in rose to edge of curls; let dry and set aside.

Fondant/Gum Paste Techniques

Fondant Snowman

(see Sun, Sand and Santa, p. 49)

For head and body, roll 1½ in. and 2 in. balls of white fondant; attach with damp brush and let dry. Brush with piping gel and cover with brown sugar; let dry. For hat, roll a ¾ x 1 in. log of yellow fondant; attach to head with royal icing. For hat band and chin strap, tint a 1 in. fondant ball Red-Red with a little Christmas Red. Roll out ⅛ in. thick; cut ⅛ in. strips and attach with damp brush. Attach hat on snowman using royal icing. Pipe tip 3 dot eyes, buttons and mouth with royal icing. Add tip 6 pull-out nose.

Beach Chair

(see Sun, Sand and Santa, p. 49)

Cut a 2¾ x 4¾ in. cardboard frame for drying fondant chair; wrap with foil and bend to form a 45° angle. Support frame with crumpled foil and dust with cornstarch. Roll out fondant ⅛ in. thick; cut a 1¾ x 4 in. long strip. Carefully bend strip and let dry on frame. Using royal icing, pipe tip 3 stripes; let dry. Remove chair from frame. For legs, trim lollipop sticks to 1¼ in. and attach to back of chair with royal icing.

Palm Trees

(see Sun, Sand and Santa, p. 49 and Jungle Fun Cake, p. 101)

Combine 10 oz. of fondant with 1 teaspoon of Gum-Tex; tint green. Roll out fondant ⅛ in. thick. Using large leaf Cut-Out™, cut 6 or 7 leaves for each tree; cut slits in sides to form individual leaves. Make extras to allow for breakage and let dry on backs of cornstarch-dusted large flower formers. For bottom layer of leaves, pipe a tip 12 mound of royal icing on waxed paper; insert 3 or 4 leaves. Support leaves with tissue and let dry. For top layer, repeat process, piping mound in center of bottom layer, inserting 3 leaves in mound and supporting with tissue until dry. Cut end of pretzel rod level. Turn over leaf grouping and pipe a tip 12 mound; attach pretzel rod at level end; let dry. For Santa scene, attach mini candy-coated chocolates to leaves with icing.

Fondant Star Flames and Candles

(see Make Some Noise!, p. 8)

Tint 34 oz. fondant rose, 32 oz. blue, 26 oz. green, 24 oz. yellow, 6 oz. violet. Also tint 2 oz. portions in a darker shade of each color. For flames, roll out dark yellow fondant ⅛ in. thick; cut 5 stars using medium Cut-Out. Lightly brush stars with water and sprinkle with Cake Sparkles; let dry on cornstarch-dusted board. **For wicks,** attach 1¼ in. long pieces of licorice to backs of stars with adhesive; let dry. **For candles,** cut 4 dowel rods to 5 in. long and 1 to 6 in. long. Roll out all light colors except yellow ⅛ in. thick and cut strips 2½ x 5 or 6 in. long (length of dowel rod). Wrap strips around dowel rods (use green for 6 in. candle); trim off excess and smooth with fingers. **For spiral trim,** roll out dark shaded fondant ⅛ in. thick; cut ¼ x 8 in. strips. Attach strips around dowel rods with damp brush; let dry. Insert a matching-color fondant ball at top of each dowel rod. Insert wicks.

Party Hats

(see Plenty of Fun to Go Around, p. 8)

Follow project instructions for tinting fondant. For hats, roll out light colors ⅛ in. thick. Lightly brush sugar cones with piping gel and wrap fondant around cones. Trim to fit and smooth with heel of hand. Reserve remaining light colored fondant. Decorate hats using darker fondant shades; roll out ⅛ in. thick. For stripes, cut 18 x ¼ in. strip; wrap around cone, attaching with damp brush. For polka dots, cut circles using small end of tip 2A; attach with damp brush. For fringe, cut 1 in. wide strips; using scissors, cut ⅛ in. wide slits, ¾ in. deep. Cut into 2½ in. long sections, roll into small tufts, fluff with fingers. Attach to bottom edge of hat with damp brush; repeat as needed to cover entire edge. For pompom, cut fondant strips ¾ in. wide x 1½ in. long; cut ⅛ in. slits, roll into shape and attach to hat with damp brush. Let hat dry on waxed paper-covered cake circles.

Fondant Ovals

(see La Quinceañera Bonita, p. 20)

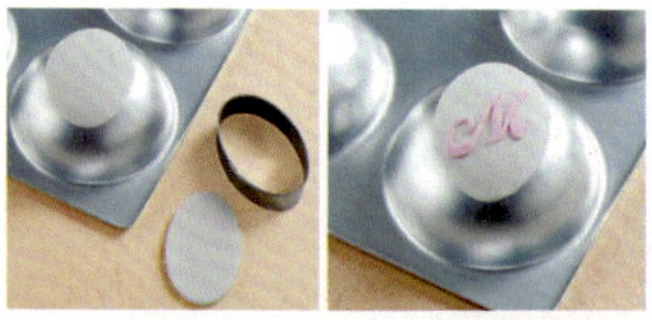

Mix 12 oz. of white fondant with 1 teaspoon of Gum-Tex. Roll out fondant ⅛ in. thick; cut ovals using largest oval Cut-Out. Let ovals dry at least 48 hours, until firm, on back of mini ball pan cavities dusted with cornstarch. Using Alphabet pattern, trace desired letter on oval with toothpick; outline letter with tip 2 and rose royal icing. Set aside.

Fondant Tassels

(see La Quinceañera Bonita, p. 20)

Form eight 1⅜ in. long teardrop shapes and ⅜ in. balls from fondant/Gum-Tex mixture; set aside. Roll out fondant 1⁄16 in. thick; cut into 1¾ in. wide x 2 in. long strips. Use embroidery scissors to cut fringe almost to the top edge of strips. Wrap strips around teardrop-shaped fondant pieces; trim off excess fondant and pinch strip together at top. Attach ball shape to top of tassel with thinned fondant adhesive; set aside.

Fondant Flowers

(see La Quinceañera Bonita, p. 20)

Tint 4 oz. of fondant rose; roll out rose and 8 oz. of white fondant ⅛ in. thick. Using cutters from Floral Collection Set, cut 16 large pansies and 6 apple blossoms in rose; cut 60 pansies, 50 apple blossoms and 30 forget-me-nots in white. Cup flowers on thick foam using ball tool from Confectionery Set and let dry on small flower formers. Using royal icing, pipe tip 3 dot centers in white; let dry.

Fondant Motion Lines

(see Mighty World Hero, p. 34)

Tint fondant blue, roll out 1⁄16 in. thick. Using knife, cut a 1½ x 11 in. strip. Gather strip and form folds in fondant by placing one skewer under bottom edge of strip and one on top, next to the first skewer. Repeat with more skewers to form three folds. Remove skewers and gather fondant at each end. Pinch one end of fondant strip and taper; trim as needed.

Fondant Wrapped Candies

(see Mickey, Front and Center!, p. 38)

Shape neon and primary colors of fondant into 1 x ½ in. x ⅝ in. rectangles or 1 in. balls with flat bottoms. Roll and cut two ¾ x 1½ in. wrapper strips for each candy. Brush one long edge with water, then form pleat. Cut slits in opposite sides of rectangles and balls and insert pleated ends to attach.

Pilgrims

(see Meal Markers, p. 47) Tint melted white candy with a little orange. Mold candy faces (p.123) in Candy Melting Plate cavities. Using fondant, make clothes and hair; roll out ⅛ in. thick. **For collars,** cut a ¼ x 1½ in. white strip; cut out a notch in center and attach to face with melted candy. **For man's hat,** tint fondant black, blue, and yellow (combine Lemon Yellow and Golden Yellow for yellow shown). Cut a black strip 1 x ⅝ in., tapering to ½ in. wide at top. Attach to face with candy. **For hatband,** cut a ⅛ in. blue strip; trim to fit and attach to hat with damp brush. **For brim,** cut a ¼ x 1¼ in. black strip. Attach to face with damp brush. **For buckle,** hand shape a yellow log into a square; attach with damp brush. **For top of woman's bonnet,** cut a 1⅜ x ⅝ in. white strip, tapering ends to 1⅛ in. wide toward bottom; attach to face with melted candy. **For woman's brim,** cut a ¼ x 1½ in. white strip; attach with melted candy. **For hair,** cut small pieces of yellow fondant; using scissors, cut slits for fringe; attach to bonnet with damp brush.

Scarecrow

(see Tops in His Field, p. 46) Add ½ teaspoon of Gum-Tex to 4 oz. fondant and tint ivory. Roll out fondant ⅛ in. thick; cut scarecrow and 1 extra head piece for 3D effect using largest Gingerbread Boy Cutter; reserve some fondant for collar. Let dry on board dusted with cornstarch. Attach additional head to body with damp brush; let dry. Tint 2 oz. fondant each in Red-Red/Christmas Red combination, Brown/Red-Red combination, blue and yellow. Roll out colors ⅛ in. thick; using largest boy cutter, cut red shoes, blue pants and white shirt. Cut a ¼ in. square in pants with paring knife; attach a small piece of brown fondant with damp brush for patch. Using paring knife, cut yellow hay and hair strips, ½ x 1½ in. for each shoe, 1 x ¾ in. for each hand and three 1 x 1 in. sections for hair. Cut slits with paring knife to fringe edges. Attach strips to hand areas, head and shoes with damp brush. Attach shoes, shirt and pants to body with damp brush. Use FoodWriters™ to draw shirt checks and cuffs and patch stitching. Trace hat pattern on brown fondant and hatband pattern on blue fondant with toothpick; cut out with paring knife. On thin foam, ruffle edge of hat with ball tool from confectionery set. Attach to head with damp brush. Cut ¼ x 1 in. blue strips for suspenders and roll ⅜ in. red dots for buttons; attach. Roll out reserved ivory fondant ⅛ in. thick; cut ¼ x 2½ in. collar; place on thin foam and ruffle with ball tool from set. Attach to shirt in a semicircle with damp brush. Shape ¼ in. oval white eyes and a ¼ in. triangle red nose; attach. Using black FoodWriter, draw freckles, pupils and mouth. Attach body to cookie stick with thinned fondant adhesive; let dry.

Fondant Leaves

(see A Little Autumn Spice, p. 47)

Tint fondant following project directions; roll out 1/16 in. thick. Using mini cutters, cut approximately 8 leaves of each color in various shapes. Position on thick shaping foam. Thin edges with large ball tool from confectionery set; move to thin shaping foam. Score vein lines using small end of veining tool from set. Let dry on small flower formers dusted with cornstarch; to vary shape, position leaves on inside and outside of flower formers. Grate chalk and a small amount of cornstarch through tea strainer; brush on leaves.

Cake Top Snowflake and Holder

(see A Winter Delight, p. 54) Tint 6 oz. fondant blue. Roll out ⅛ in. thick; cut snowflake using 3 in. cutter from set. Reserve remaining blue fondant. Cut hole for ribbon using narrow end of tip 7. Let dry on cornstarch-dusted cake board. Using royal icing, pipe tip 1 vein lines and dot. For holder, cut white wire to 16 in. long; shape into a curve with a hook on end. Using royal icing, pipe tip 7 balls. Insert hook in craft block; let dry.

Snowmen

(see A Winter Delight, p. 54)

Using serrated knife, cut 4 pillars from globe sets to 8 in. long; insert in cake. Position 2½ and 2 in. globes on pillars to form snowmen. For scarves, roll out fondant ⅛ in. thick. Cut strips 10 x ¼ in. wide; wrap around neck, overlap and attach with small amount of water. Trim scarves as needed; cut fringed edges with scissors. For eyes and buttons, roll ¼ in. balls; for mouth, roll ⅛ in. balls. For nose, roll orange fondant into a ¼ x ½ in. cone. Attach facial features and buttons with tip 1 dots of royal icing.

Skis and Braces

(see Ski Bum Bear, p. 50)

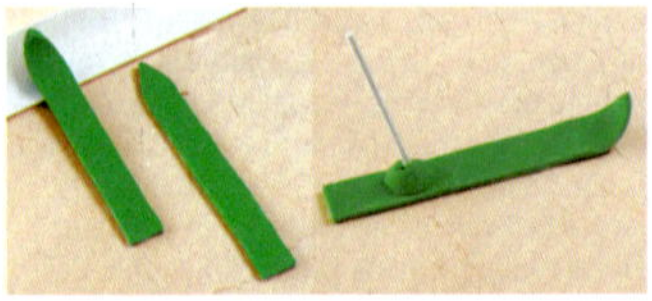

Tape one curved edge of a medium flower former to a waxed paper-covered board, so that former sits upright, with curve facing toward the board. Roll out fondant ⅛ in. thick and, using pattern, cut 2 skis. Curve end up inside flower formers and let dry. **To make braces,** cut an 8 in. lollipop stick in half. Roll a ¾ in. ball of fondant; flatten bottom and attach to top of ski, approximately 2 in. from back, with thinned fondant adhesive. Brush end of lollipop stick with water and insert into fondant at an angle, facing back of ski. Shape fondant around stick to secure. Repeat for second ski; let dry.

Fondant Broom

(see Dapper Dude, p. 53) Mix yellow fondant from Primary Colors Multi Pack with ½ teaspoon of Gum-Tex®. Roll out ⅛ in. thick. Cut an 8 x 2 in. strip; with scissors, cut 1¼ x ⅛ in. fringe. Wrap a 1½ x ½ in. log around tip of pretzel rod, extending 1 in. beyond end. Brush back of fringed fondant with damp brush and wrap around pretzel end, shaping into broom. Let dry overnight on cornstarch-dusted board.

Fondant Hat

(see Dapper Dude, p. 53) Mix green fondant from Primary Colors Multi Pack with ½ teaspoon of Gum-Tex®; roll out ⅛ in. thick. **For brim,** cut a 5 in. circle with a 2¼ in. circle cut out at center. Let dry on cornstarch-dusted board. Cut a 3 in. circle for top of hat and turn over. **For hat sides,** cut a 10 x 2 in. strip; wrap around top of hat, attach with fondant adhesive (p. 115). Support inside with double-thick strip of freezer paper, facing shiny side toward fondant. Let dry overnight. Remove freezer paper and attach hat to brim with thinned fondant adhesive. **For hatband,** roll out red fondant ⅛ in. thick; cut a 10 x ½ in. strip; attach with damp brush. Let dry overnight on cornstarch-dusted board.

Fondant Arms, Legs, Clothes, Facial Features

(see Snow Dancing, p. 54) Roll out black and white fondant ⅛ in. thick. Using patterns, cut mouth and teeth. Attach teeth to mouth with damp brush; position on cake. Roll ⅛ in. balls for eyes, ⅝ in. balls for cheeks; attach with damp brush. Roll out blue, red, green and rose fondant ⅛ in. thick. **For jacket,** cut ¼ x 3 in. strips for stripes; use narrow end of tip 10 to cut green circles for polka dots. Attach to jackets with damp brush. **For scarves,** cut ½ x 3 in. neck and two ½ x 2 in. streamers; attach with damp brush. Roll a ⅜ in. ball for knot; attach. Roll ¼ in. black fondant logs; cut a 1⅞ in. piece for each leg, a 1⅜ in. piece for each arm and a 4½ in. piece for earmuff band. Shape 1 x ⅝ in. diameter pieces for feet, ¾ in. balls for mittens and earmuffs; flatten and shape thumbs in mittens. Assemble arms, legs and earmuffs next to cakes. Shape a 1½ x 3 in. violet hat, a 1 x 3 in. red hat, two ¾ in. balls each for yellow hair and brown hair, a 3 x ½ in. crescent for orange hair. Shape hair, adding texture marks with small ball tool or layered look with veining tool; position on cakes. Shape and position 3 x 1 in. white hat bands and ½ i... ball pompom. Indent textured look on hats with small ball tool.

Fondant Loops and Star

(see Tree-mendously Generous, p. 55) Roll out various colors of fondant ⅛ in. thick. For bow loops, cut strips ¼ x 2 in.; cut 40 loops each in red, blue, green and yellow. Pinch ends together to form loops; let dry on side on cornstarch-dusted board. Cut star from yellow fondant using cutter. Cut ⅛ in. wide yellow strips for star swirl and lines. Shape swirl and attach along with lines with damp brush; let dry.

Fondant Hearts & Bait Bucket

(see Using the Right Line, p. 59) **For hearts,** roll out all colors ⅛ in. thick; cut approximately 14 hearts using medium Cut-Out. Let dry on cornstarch-dusted board. **For bucket,** dust muffin pan cavity with cornstarch. Roll out white fondant mixture ⅛ in. thick; press into cavity, smoothing with fingers. Trim off excess and let dry; unmold. Using FoodWriter™ markers, print messages on hearts and buckets.

Fondant Head, Ears, Feet

(see Best Gift Ever!, p. 72)

Roll out copper fondant mixture ¼ in. thick; cut head using largest round cutter from 101 Cookie Cutters Set. Cut ears using medium round Cut-Out, trim to shape and attach to head with damp brush. **For hair curl,** insert a 2 in. piece of licorice in head. In royal icing, pipe tip 4 outline mouth, dot eyes and cheeks. Shape a small ball of copper fondant for nose; attach with damp brush. Shape reserved copper fondant into an oval foot, 3¼ long x 1½ in. wide x ½ in. thick; for toes, roll five ⅜ in. balls; attach with damp brush. With lollipop stick, indent two ¼ in. deep holes in top of foot to mark for insertion of sticks.

Gum Paste Hands and Arms

(see Catch the Excitement, p. 75) Prepare 3 cans of gum paste; divide into 4ths. Using copper and brown colors, tint each portion in a different skin tone. Roll out ⅜ in. thick. Using pattern and knife, cut 14 pairs of hands/arms; reverse pattern for opposite hand. Trim a few sets of arms to 8 or 9 in. **For fingernails,** tint 1 oz. fondant each in violet, rose, red and coral (combine orange and rose for coral). Roll out 1/16 in. thick. Using scissors, slightly pinch small opening of tip 2A to form fingernail shape; cut out fingernails. Attach to fingers with damp brush; for thumbnails, cut fingernail in half and attach. **For sleeves,** tint 6 oz. fondant each in violet, kelly green and rose; roll out ⅛ in. thick. Using arm pattern, cut strips in various lengths for sleeves; attach to arms with damp brush. **For bracelets,** tint 1 oz. fondant lemon yellow; reserve some white. Roll out yellow ⅛ in. thick and cut 1½ x ¼ in. strip; curve to form bracelet shape and attach with damp brush. **For white bracelets,** roll ¼ in. or ⅜ in. balls and attach. Let all pieces dry on cornstarch-dusted surface.

Fondant Duck, Bear, Train, Lamp, Decorative Drawer Panels, Open Drawer, Blanket

(see Room to Grow, p. 71)

Add 4 teaspoons of Gum-Tex® to 55 oz. of white fondant; tint 2 oz. each brown and violet, 8 oz. each yellow, rose and green, 15 oz. light blue; reserve 12 oz. white for open drawer. Mold yellow duck, brown bear and blue train in candy mold heavily dusted with cornstarch; press fondant in molds, pop out and let dry on cornstarch-dusted board. Using royal icing and tip 2, pipe in top and window of train engine, add bow, dot and outline trims on duck and train; pipe in duck's beak. Pipe tip 1 dot and string facial features on bear.

For lamp, cut 2 lampshade patterns from freezer paper. Roll one pattern into a round lampshade shape, with shiny side of paper facing out; tape to hold shape and dust with cornstarch. Roll out violet fondant ⅛ in. thick; position 2nd pattern on top and cut out with knife. Wrap fondant around paper lampshade, seal ends with damp brush; let dry overnight. Remove freezer paper pattern. Roll out remaining violet fondant ⅛ in. thick. Turn lampshade upside down and trace circle on fondant; cut out with knife. Attach circle to top of lampshade with thinned fondant adhesive; let dry. Using royal icing, pipe tip 3 dot top and bottom borders. Roll out green, blue, pink and yellow fondant 1⁄16 in. thick; cut out dots using small end of tip 8. Attach dots to lampshade with damp brush. Roll a 1½ in. ball of green fondant and flatten into an oval for base; set aside. Cut lollipop stick to 10 in. and attach a 1¼ in. white fondant ball to end of stick with damp brush; flatten top of ball and let dry. Position lamp parts following cake instructions.

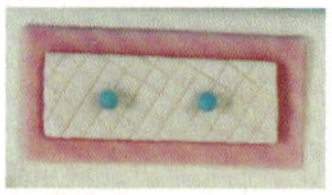

For 6 decorative drawer panels, roll out rose, yellow, green and white fondant ⅛ in. thick. Cut 3½ x 1¾ in. rectangles: 2 rose, 2 yellow and 1 green. Cut five 3 x 1⅛ in. white rectangles. Score quilting lines on white pieces with straight-edge wheel of Cutter/Embosser. Trim edges evenly. Attach white to color rectangles with damp brush; let dry. For handles, roll tiny balls of blue fondant; attach with tip 2 dots of royal icing. **Make 2 dresser tops.** Roll out blue fondant ⅛ in. thick; cut a 5½ x 5 in. piece for tall dresser section and a 5 x 4⅞ in. piece for short dresser section. Let dry on cornstarch-dusted board.

For open drawer, roll out reserved white fondant mixture ⅛ in. thick. Cut 2 sides, 2 x 2½ in. each; cut 1 front, 4¾ x 2½ in; cut 1 bottom, 4¼ x 2 in. Let all pieces dry on cornstarch-dusted surface. When dry, attach pieces with fondant adhesive. Attach decorative front panel.

For blanket, roll out reserved white fondant ⅛ in. thick; cut a 5 x 6 in. rectangle. Roll out green, rose, blue and yellow fondant ⅛ in. thick; cut out five ⅛ in. wide strips in each color. Position strips on rectangle, alternating colors and leaving a ½ in. border on each blanket edge. Lightly roll out into blanket shape. On border, cut slits with scissors for fringe effect.

Fondant Baby, Shopping Bags, Hearts, Cell Phone

(see A Buggy of Bargains!, p. 73)

Combine 12 oz. of fondant with 1 teaspoon of Gum-Tex®; reserve remaining fondant. Tint portions of fondant mixture light copper, rose, violet, blue, green and yellow. Roll out all colors ⅛ in. thick. Using circle cutter, cut out face in light copper. **For ears,** use large opening of tip 12 to cut two ¾ in. circles in copper; trim one side to fit head. Attach to side of face with damp brush. Let face dry on waxed paper-covered board dusted with cornstarch. Cut out shopping bags using pattern. Reroll rose fondant to ¼ in. thick. Using largest Cut-Out, cut 3 hearts. **For cell phone,** cut a 2¼ x ½ in. rectangle ; cut a ½ in. strip for antenna. **For hand,** roll a ⅝ in. ball of copper fondant; wrap around cell phone. Indent fingers with brush handle. Make extras of all pieces to allow for breakage and let dry on waxed paper-covered board dusted with cornstarch.

Using royal icing, decorate baby. Pipe tip 3 dot eyes and pipe in mouth. Add tip 3 dot cheeks, nose and tongue. Roll out rose fondant ⅛ in. thick. Cut a ⅜ x 2 in. strip for hair bow. Fold ends into center and pinch to form bow. Attach a small ball for center knot with damp brush. Write store names on bags and message on hearts with FoodWriters™. Attach ribbon strips to fondant hearts with royal icing.

Fondant Bassinet Back, Back Scallops, Pillow, Blanket Top Edge and Baby

(see An Angel Among Us, p. 82)

Roll out fondant ⅛ in. thick. Using patterns, cut bassinet back and pillow. **For bassinet back scallops,** cut 10 circles using smallest round Cut-Out; cut circles in half. Roll out fondant ⅜ in. thick. Using patterns, cut blanket top edge. Tint 2 oz. fondant peach; roll out ⅛ in. thick. Cut baby head using medium round Cut-Out; trim ⅛ in. off bottom edge. Reserve remaining peach fondant. Let all pieces dry on waxed-paper covered surface dusted with cornstarch.

Attach pillow and blanket top edge pieces to bassinet back with thinned fondant adhesive. Attach head to meet blanket top edge. Draw eyes and mouth with black FoodWriter. Using reserved peach fondant, roll small balls for nose, ears and cheeks; attach with damp brush. Roll 4 fondant logs, 2 x ⅜ in. diameter, tapered at top end. Attach logs to bassinet back piece with damp brush, even with bottom edge. Roll out fondant ¼ in. thick. Using pattern, cut skirt; position over logs, pressing and smoothing to create ruffled look. Trim as needed and let dry.

Attach 6 in. lollipop stick to back of bassinet back piece with royal icing; let dry. Pipe tip 2 outline and swags where blanket top edge meets skirt; attach a royal icing drop flower at each swag point. Attach bassinet scallops around top edge of bassinet with thinned fondant adhesive.

Fluted Bowl Topper

(see Blue Mist, p. 85)

Hot glue 6 in. plate from bowl set to fluted bowl. Cover 3 x 2½ x 3 in. round craft block with fondant; attach inside bowl on plate with hot glue. Insert large roses on wires in craft block.

Sports Balls

(see A Fan For All Seasons!, p. 105)

For basketballs, tint 6 oz. fondant Orange/Red-Red/Brown combination. **For remaining balls** use white . Roll out ⅛ in. thick; cut 2½ x 8 in. strips for 2½ in. globes, 3 x 10 in. strips for 3 in. globes. Brush globes with Piping Gel and cover with fondant, making 1 baseball, soccer ball, golf ball and basketball in each size. Smooth with palm of hand. **For golf ball,** imprint dimples using dogbone tool from Confectionery Tool Set. Draw stitching lines on baseball with red FoodWriter marker. Trace large and small Soccer Ball Patterns from 2007 Pattern Book; outline and fill in with black FoodWriter. Draw basketball seams with black FoodWriter.

Bees and Butterflies

(see Abuzz About the Cakes!, p. 106)

For bees, roll a 2 x ¾ in. wide teardrop body. Curve point up to form stinger. **For head,** roll a 1 in. yellow ball; attach with royal icing. Roll out yellow fondant ⅛ in. thick; cut ¼ in. stripes; attach to body with damp brush. **For antennae,** cut 1 in. pieces of dried spaghetti; dip in black icing color and let dry. Insert in head. Roll tiny balls of fondant for end of antennae and facial features; attach with damp brush. **For wings,** roll out white fondant ⅛ in. thick; cut using smallest Heart Cut-Out. Attach to 1 in. lengths of spaghetti with royal icing; let dry. Insert in body. Insert bees on 8 in. lengths of 18-gauge florist wire. **For butterflies,** roll out orange and violet fondant ⅛ in. thick. Cut wings using large and medium Heart Cut-Outs. Cut each heart in half and attach smaller to larger half with damp brush; let dry on large Flower Formers dusted with cornstarch. Roll ½ in. ball for head, three graduated-size balls for body; attach to wings with royal icing. Roll and attach balls for facial features with damp brush and insert antenna as for bees. Pipe outline mouth with royal icing. Attach to florist wires with royal icing.

Fondant Pansies and Apple Blossoms

(see Cinderella Wedding, p. 107)

Add 2 teaspoons Gum-Tex to 26 oz. of White Ready-To-Use Rolled Fondant. Tint 8 oz. Rose, 2 oz. Kelly Green; reserve remaining white. In rose, cut 95 flowers using pansy cutter and 145 flowers using apple blossom cutter from Floral Collection Flower Making Set; cup petals on thick foam using ball tool from Confectionery Tool Set. Add tip 3 dot centers in buttercream on apple blossoms; roll ⅛ in. fondant balls for pansy centers; attach with damp brush. In green, cut 70 leaves using small leaf cutter from set; mark veins using veining tool on thin foam. Let pansies and leaves dry on small Flower Formers dusted with cornstarch; dry apple blossoms on cornstarch-dusted board.

Fondant Kids

(see Big Splash Birthday Bash, p. 100)

Tint 24 oz. fondant Royal Blue, 16 oz. each Black and Copper (skin tone), 8 oz. brown/red-red combination and 2 oz. each Lemon Yellow/Golden Yellow combination, Orange, Rose, Violet/Rose combination and Leaf Green; reserve 10 oz. White. **For inner tubes,** shape a 1½ in. black ball into a log, then into a ring. Make 1 in. ball bodies and ¾ in. ball heads using copper or brown. **For arms and legs,** shape ½ in. balls into logs; cut slits for fingers with craft knife. Attach kid pieces with damp brush, positioning bodies in various ways. **For bathing suits,** roll out fondant 1⁄16 in. thick; cut strips and shape around body, attaching with damp brush. Let dry several hours. Roll and attach a small ball for nose; draw facial features with FoodWriter marker. Pipe tip 2 hair using royal icing; let dry. Attach kids to inner tubes with damp brush.

Water Slides

(see Big Splash Birthday Bash, p. 100)

Trace patterns from 2007 Pattern Book on cardboard; cut slides and bend to curve slightly. Wrap with foil and ice smooth with blue royal icing; let dry. Roll out white fondant ¼ in. thick; cut a 1 in. wide strip to fit each slide. Wrap strip around back and fold over edges of slide to make rail; trim off excess.

Fondant Message Stars, Cake Side Stars and Swags

(see Sizzling Stars Cake, p. 98)

Tint fondant: 4 oz. each royal blue, violet and orange, 18 oz. lemon yellow, 22 oz. rose and 28 oz. leaf green/lemon yellow combination. Add ¼ teaspoon Gum-Tex to 4 oz. portions in each color. Reserve 12 oz. white. Roll out colors ⅛ in. thick. Cut message stars using 3 largest cutters from Nesting Stars Metal Set; cut 8 cake side stars in each color using medium Star Cut-Out. Let dry on cornstarch-dusted board. Brush stars with water; sprinkle with White Cake Sparkles™ and let dry. Attach 8 in. lollipop sticks to backs of message stars with royal icing. Make 37 swags. Roll out white fondant ⅛ in. thick. Cut a circle using Circle Metal Cutter; cut swag ½ in. from bottom edge. Add Cake Sparkles as above.

Rollercoaster Track, Cars and People

(see Coast to Coast Cakes, p. 102)

Roll out blue gum paste ⅛ in. thick. **For hill sections,** cut three 2 in. wide strips, 10 in. long (connecting 6 in. to 8 in. cake), 11 in. long (connecting 8 in. to 10 in. cake) and 15 in. long (connecting 6 in. to 10 in. cake). Let dry on side using Hill patterns from 2007 Pattern Book to form curve. Also cut flat cake top curved tracks using pattern. Roll out white gum paste ⅛ in. thick; cut 160 vertical side rails, ¼ x ½ in. long; let dry. **Also:** Make 6 gum paste cars. Shape rectangles 1 x 2 x ¾ in. thick; for seats, cut 2 slits in top with craft knife. **And:** Make 12 people. Roll out various colors of fondant ⅛ in. thick. Using People Cut-Outs™, cut shirts (position arms up), heads. Also cut hands using foot Cut-Out; cut in half and cut slits for fingers with craft knife; let dry.

Covering Base Boards with Fondant

Cut cake boards 2 in. larger in diameter than your cake, unless otherwise directed, then roll out fondant about 1 in. larger than board size. Wrap board with foil.

1. Lightly coat board with piping gel to help the fondant stick to the foil.

2. Roll out fondant to desired size, ¼ in. thick. Position over board using a rolling pin, draping fondant over edge.

3. Trim excess fondant from edges under bottom of board. Smooth top and sides with Easy-Glide Smoother.

Fondant Veils

(see Unveiling a Masterpiece, p. 93)

For base underneath each veil, shape a 7 oz. piece of fondant into a 4½ in. long teardrop shape. Position between 8 in. cakes, with wide end at cake base. Measure 8 oz. pieces of fondant. Roll out ¼ in. thick. Cut an 8½ in. wide x 7 in. long strip for each veil. Position 5 plastic dowel rods over and under strip to form pleats. Remove dowel rods. Gather and pinch top ends of veil together to shape. Position over teardrop shape on cake.

Fondant Swags

(see Unveiling a Masterpiece, p. 93)

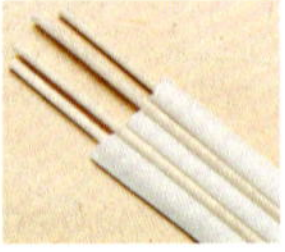

Roll out fondant ⅛ in. thick on Roll & Cut Mat lightly dusted with cornstarch. Cut strips following dimensions stated in project instructions. Form pleats in fondant by placing a wooden dowel rod under bottom edge of fondant strip and one on top, next to the first dowel rod. Repeat with more dowel rods to form 3 pleats. Remove dowel rods, gather ends together and brush with water. Position swags on cake and shape pleats with veining tool; attach with damp brush.

Bow Loops

(see Unveiling a Masterpiece, p. 93 and Abuzz About the Cakes!, p. 106)

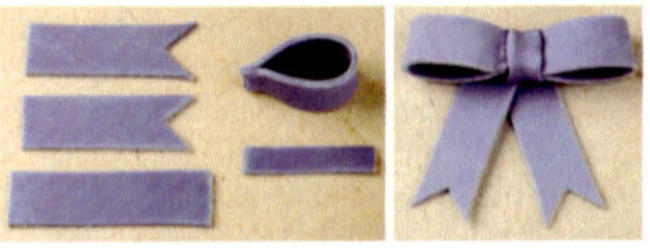

Roll out fondant ⅛ in. thick on Roll & Cut Mat lightly dusted with cornstarch. For *Unveiling a Masterpiece* cut strips 5 in. long x 1½ in. wide. For *Abuzz About the Cakes*, cut strips 3 in. long x ⅛ in. wide. Fold over and brush ends with damp brush. Dry loops on large flower formers dusted with cornstarch.

Fondant Ribbon Roses

(for Unveiling a Masterpiece, p. 93)

Roll out fondant ⅛ in. on Roll & Cut Mat lightly dusted with cornstarch. Cut strip following dimensions stated in project instructions. Begin rolling from one end of strip, gradually loosening roll as flower gets larger, attaching with damp brush. Use veining tool between spirals to open up petals; let dry on cornstarch-dusted board.

(for Blue Mist, p. 85) Combine 6 teaspoons of Gum-Tex with 72 oz. of white fondant. To make 45 large ribbon roses, roll out fondant ⅛ in. thick; cut three 1 x 6 in. long strips for each rose. Follow general rolling instructions above, but add strips and open petals as you roll. Let dry on cornstarch-dusted board. On 38 large roses, make a small hole in bottom center of rose with craft knife; attach 18-gauge wire with melted candy. Reserve 7 large roses without wires. To make 105 small ribbon roses without wires, cut a 1 x 6 in. long fondant strip for each rose; roll and let dry following directions.

For Little Loves mini cakes, make a small ribbon rose for cake tops. Trim bottom flat as needed.

Candy Making Techniques

USING CANDY MELTS®*

Fast-melting confectionery coating wafers are the key to easy candy making. Smooth texture and great taste make Candy Melts® your most convenient option for molding. Check out all the great colors on p. 162.

To Melt

Chocolate Pro™ Electric Melting Pot (p. 162): The most convenient way to melt—no microwave or double boiler needed! Melts large amounts of Candy Melts® in minutes.

Double boiler method: Fill lower pan with water to below level of top pan. Bring water to simmer, then remove from heat. Put Candy Melts® in top pan and set in position on lower pan. Stir constantly, without beating, until smooth and completely melted.

Microwave method: In microwave-safe container, microwave 1 package Candy Melts® at 30% power or defrost setting for 1 minute. Stir thoroughly. Continue to microwave and stir at 30 second intervals until smooth and completely melted. Candy Melts® may also be melted in a disposable decorating bag. Melt as described above, squeezing bag between heating intervals to blend Candy Melts® together. When completely melted, snip off end of bag and squeeze melted Candy Melts® into molds. Throw away bag when empty.

NOTE: Confectionery coating will lose its pouring and dipping consistency if overheated, or if water or other liquid is added. If coating is overheated, add 2 teaspoons hydrogenated vegetable shortening per 14 oz. Candy Melts®.

To Mold (1 color candies)

Pour melted candy into clean dry mold; tap lightly to remove air bubbles. Place mold on level surface. Refrigerate until bottom of mold appears frosty or until candy is firm. Pop out candy. For lollipops, fill molds, tap to remove air bubbles, position sticks in mold. Rotate sticks to thoroughly cover with candy so they remain securely in place. Refrigerate to set, pop out lollipops.

To Color

Add Candy Colors (p. 163) to melted Candy Melts® a little at a time. Mix thoroughly before adding more color. Colors tend to deepen as they're mixed. Pastel colored candies are most appetizing, so keep this in mind.

To Flavor

The creamy, rich taste of Candy Melts® can be enhanced by adding approx. ¼ teaspoon oil-based Candy Flavor (p. 163) to 14 oz. (one pack) of melted Candy Melts®. Never use alcohol based flavorings; they will cause candies to harden.

Multicolored Candy

Painting Method

It's easy to mold with different areas of color—just use a decorator brush to "paint" the mold with melted Candy Melts®. Refrigerate a few seconds until coating hardens, then fill mold to top with melted candy. Remember, only fill in one section of the mold at a time and let harden before adding more colors. Look for other ways to color and flavor your candy in our *Candy Making Beginner's Guide* (p. 126).

Marbleizing Method

Separately melt two different colors of Candy Melts®. Stir colors together, using a lollipop stick to draw lines in mixture. Do not overmix. Quickly spoon or place into molds while mixture is still soft. Tap. Refrigerate until firm; unmold.

Layering Method

Pour melted Candy Melts® into dry molds to desired height. Refrigerate until partially set. Pour melted contrasting color to desired height. Refrigerate until partially set. Repeat until desired number of layers are formed; refrigerate until firm and unmold.

SPECIALTY TECHNIQUES

Candy Shells

Fill pan or mold to the top edge with melted candy. Tap on counter to remove air bubbles. Let chill in refrigerator for 10-15 minutes or until a ¼ in. shell has formed. Pour out excess candy, smooth top edges with spatula and chill for 15-20 minutes longer. Carefully unmold shells (if you have difficulty removing shells, place in freezer for 2-3 minutes, then unmold). Excess candy can be reheated and reused.

For unmolding shells from silicone molds, peel mold back, pushing candy shell out from bottom of mold.

Candy Shells in Baking Cups

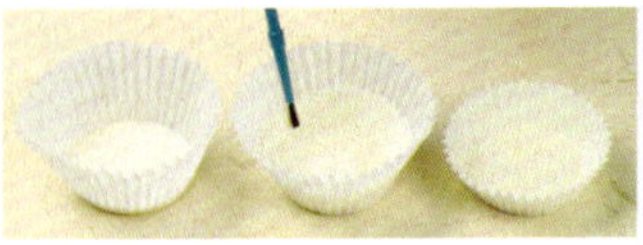

Add 1 to 2 Tablespoons of melted candy in the bottom of a standard baking cup. Brush candy slightly up sides, about halfway to top, forming an even edge. Refrigerate 5 to 8 minutes. Repeat process if desired, for a thicker shell. Refrigerate until firm. Carefully peel baking cup off candy shell.

Candy Faces

Make faces in the Candy Melting Plate (p. 163); fill cavities with melted Candy Melts® using a cut decorating bag. Refrigerate until firm and unmold.

Place faces on waxed paper-covered board and decorate facial features using melted candy in cut bag.

*Brand confectionery coating

Candy Plaques

Use pans as molds when making solid decorative plaques. If your pan has detail, it may be painted in desired colors as you would for any candy mold.

Pour melted candy into center of pan cavity. Tap pan gently on counter to eliminate bubbles. Candy should be about ⅛ to ¼ in. thick. Place pan in refrigerator for approximately 10-15 minutes until firm (check occasionally; if coating becomes too chilled, it will crack). Unmold onto hand or soft towel (tap gently, if necessary).

Funshine® Bear Candy Plaque

(see Funshine® Bear's Radical Ride, p. 32)

Tint small portions of White Candy Melts®* with red and orange candy color. Tint a small portion of Dark Cocoa Candy Melts®* black using candy color. For light brown shade, combine melted White and Dark Cocoa candy; add red candy color. In Care Bears® pan, mold detail areas in this order using melted candy in cut parchment bag: orange nose, refrigerate until set; white muzzle, mouth, tummy, and red heart on hip, refrigerate until set.

Using melted yellow candy in cut disposable bags, fill pan, except for rainbow area. Refrigerate until firm. Unmold onto waxed paper-covered board; let come to room temperature. Outline eyes and inside of mouth using melted black candy in cut parchment bag; let set. Add whites of eyes, brown irises, black pupils and white eye highlight; making sure to let each color set before adding another. Let set.

For sun on tummy, position medium round Cut-Out on waxed paper-covered board. Fill Cut-Out with melted yellow candy, tap on surface to level and refrigerate until firm. Unmold circle; attach to tummy with melted candy. Pipe sun rays, eyelids, brows and mouth using melted orange candy in cut parchment bag; let set.

Scarecrow Collars

(see Pops to Crow About, p. 47)

Flatten foil bon bon cups, trim ⅛ in. of foil around edges. Create a ruffled look by pressing edges of cup around your finger every ½ in. Paint peanut butter/white candy mixture on cups; refrigerate until firm. Peel off cup. Using craft knife, cut hole in center of collar large enough to accommodate lollipop stick.

Candy Curls

(see Branches & Berries, p. 55 and Wearing His Spring Coat, p. 64)

Melt 1 pk. Candy Melts®; add 2 tablespoons shortening. For tree, tint green using color from Garden Set. Pour candy into mini loaf cavities, 1 in. thick for 1 plaque, ½ in. thick for a second plaque. Refrigerate until firm; unmold. Let candy come to room temperature. Run potato peeler or cheese plane across narrow edge of candy plaque to make various size curls. For more open curls, use cheese plane, for tighter curls, use potato peeler. Position curls on cake.

Tree Bases

(see Forest Festivity, p. 55)

Place cereal treats mixture on waxed paper covered board sprayed with vegetable pan spray; shape into a rectangle measuring ¾ in. high. Use medium round Cut-Out to cut 1 base for each tree. Make a candy shell in a standard baking cup (p. 123). Fill shell with cereal treat base; fill gaps and seal with melted candy; refrigerate until firm.

*Brand confectionery coating

COLOR FLOW

Working With Color Flow

1. Trace your design pattern onto parchment paper, then tape paper onto a cake circle or the back of a cookie pan. Cover with waxed paper; smooth and tape. Using tip 2 and parchment bag half-filled with full strength Color Flow, squeeze, pull and drop icing string following pattern outline. Stop, touch tip to surface and pull away. If you will be using the same color to fill in, let outline dry a few minutes until it "crusts." To prevent bleeding of different colors, let outline dry 1-2 hours before filling in.
2. Thin Color Flow mixture with water. Cut opening in parchment bag to the size of tip 2. Fill in design with thinned Color Flow.
3. Let decorations air dry thoroughly, at least 48 hours. To remove, cut away waxed paper from board, then turn over and peel waxed paper off the Color Flow piece.

Hint: For curved decorations, dry pieces on flower formers.

To easily remove dried Color Flow, pull waxed paper backing over the edge of a table with one hand, while holding decoration with other hand. Waxed paper will pull off naturally. Or, with dried Color Flow resting on cookie sheet, place cardboard sheet over Color Flow, lift and turn over so that top of decoration rests on cardboard. Lift off waxed paper.

Since any moist icing will break down Color Flow, either position Color Flow decorations on cake shortly before serving or place on sugar cubes positioned on a piece of plastic wrap cut to fit.

Superman Starburst

(see Power Surge, p. 35)

Prepare 4 color flow recipes; tint 1 each red and orange, 1 ¾ yellow and ¼ green. Position pattern on waxed paper-covered board. For added support, make a base layer of the starburst. Using tip 3, outline starburst with full-strength red color flow; let set. Flow in with thinned yellow color flow; let dry 48 hours. Overpipe outline with full-strength red color flow. Flow in sections with thinned red, followed by orange and yellow. As you fill in design, lightly mist piped color flow with water to keep moist. Immediately after starburst is filled in, use a damp brush, ½ in. wide, to blend colors, brushing from each point and along sides to center of design. Continue lightly misting with water as you brush each section. Let dry for 48 to 72 hours. Pipe tip 4 message in full-strength color flow; let dry.

Color Flow Statue

(see Lady Liberty, p. 66)

Tint portions of color flow green (combine Teal with a little Kelly Green) and yellow. Using full-strength color flow and waxed paper-covered pattern, outline body, folds of gown, torch and flame with tip 2. Flow in with thinned color flow in cut parchment bag. Let dry 48 hours. Attach lollipop stick to back using full-strength color flow; let dry. Pipe tip 1s dot and string facial features using full-strength color flow; let dry.

COVERING CAKES AND COOKIES WITH CANDY MELTS®* OR POURED ICINGS

A quick and easy way to give a professional-looking finish to all your baked goods! For Candy Melts®, melt following package directions. For icings, follow recipe directions to reach pouring consistency. Place cooled cakes or cookies on cooling rack positioned over cookie sheet or pan. Pour or pipe candy or icing on center of item, spreading to edges with a spatula so that candy or icing drips down and covers sides. Let dry.

2007 PRODUCT SHOPS

FIND IT FAST... ORDER WITH EASE!

Welcome to the most complete selection of cake decorating products anywhere! Here you'll find all the great Wilton tools, ingredients, accents and more you need to create every design in this Yearbook.

Go ahead and browse! Our shops are conveniently organized to help you find what you need fast. Whether you're decorating a batch of holiday cookies or creating a 3-tiered wedding cake, it's easy to find everything on your list.

When you're ready to buy, we make it a breeze! Charge your order 4 easy ways at your convenience:

PHONE TOLL-FREE
800-794-5866
8:00 am-4:30 pm, Monday-Friday CST
(RETAIL CUSTOMERS ONLY)

FAX TOLL-FREE
888-824-9520
24 HOURS A DAY/7 DAYS A WEEK

ORDER ON-LINE
www.wilton.com
24 HOURS A DAY/7 DAYS A WEEK

MAIL YOUR ORDER
Use the convenient retail order form in this book.

Se Habla Español!
Para mas informacion, marque 800-436-5778

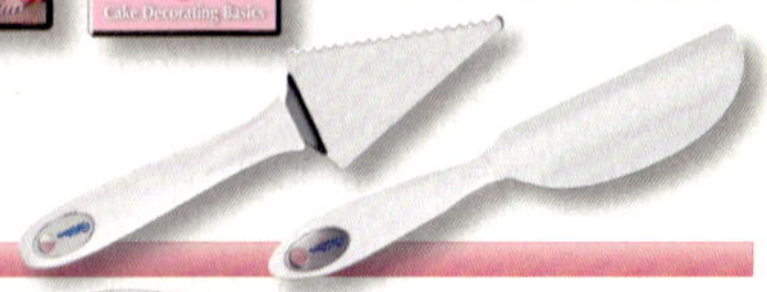

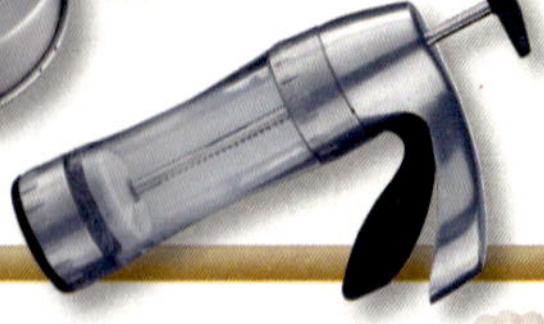

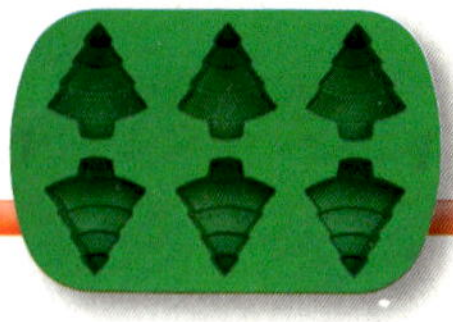

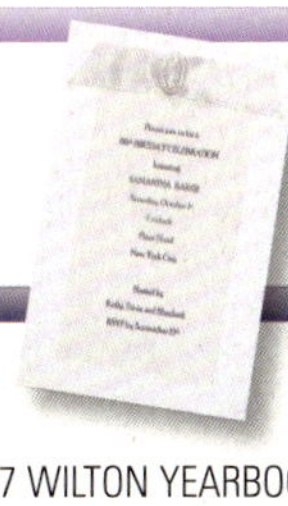

Instructional

Find inspiration with Wilton how-to books and videos. There's something perfect for your next celebration, from kids' birthday cakes to multi-tiered wedding designs.

Specialty Publications

The Wilton School—Decorating Cakes

This exciting book presents what Wilton has learned in 78 years of teaching cake decorating, in an easy-to-follow format that reflects today's lifestyles. *Decorating Cakes* is designed to appeal to anyone who wants to make great-looking cakes for families and friends.

- 30 exciting cakes with complete instructions and product listings
- 103 technique instructions, shown step-by-step, including borders, flowers, fondant and more
- Helpful recipes, tip chart, serving and cutting charts, glossary of terms
- In-depth sections on baking cakes, preparing icing, using decorating tips, cutting and transporting cakes
- Product guide, which shows and explains the equipment and ingredients required for decorating

Soft cover, 116 pages.
902-S-904

Cake Decorating Beginner's Guide

With this exciting book, anyone can decorate a fantastic-looking cake the very first time! Wilton, the #1 name in cake decorating, shows beginners everything they need to know, step-by-step. The *Beginner's Guide* makes decorating easy to learn and fun to do for everyone!

- How to bake and ice perfect cakes
- How to mix any color icing with ease
- 15 fantastic cake ideas to decorate in 6 steps or less
- Step-by-step decorating instructions for stars, rosettes, drop flowers and more

Soft cover, 40 pages.
902-S-1232

Candy Making Beginner's Guide

You'll be amazed at the fantastic candies you can make using this book. The possibilities are endless, using the great selection of Wilton Candy Melts®* and Candy Molds. The *Beginner's Guide* shows you how, step-by-step, so you will make great-looking candies your very first time. It's a great new way to add fun to parties and create impressive gifts. The *Beginner's Guide* has the information you need to start making candy like a pro.

- 20 incredible candy ideas—all made in a few easy steps!
- Easy ways to melt perfectly every time
- Painting color details in candy
- How to make classic creme-filled and dipped candies
- Great candy gift and favor ideas

Soft cover, 40 pages.
902-S-1231

*Brand confectionery coating.

Uses of Decorating Tips

Valuable quick reference and idea book for any decorator. Features five of the most popular decorating tip families and explains what each does. Shows the versatility of many tips by presenting varied cake designs. Soft cover, 48 pages.
902-S-1375

NEW!

2007 Yearbook of Cake Decorating

It's our biggest edition ever! In 2007, the Yearbook expands to 232 pages, with more than 220 extraordinary cake and dessert ideas for all occasions. It's the ultimate resource for professional bakers and anyone who wants to serve something special. You'll find magnificent wedding tiers, festive holiday cakes and cookies, favorite character desserts and more. Our Theme Parties special section is packed with exciting celebration ideas, including a spectacular rollercoaster, a safari scene kids will love and a charming Cinderella wedding with a dramatic castle and coach cake. Featuring step-by-step decorating instructions, technique resource guide, product section and website link to more great designs. Soft cover.
English 1701-S-3501
Spanish 1701-S-3503

NEW!

2007 Pattern Book

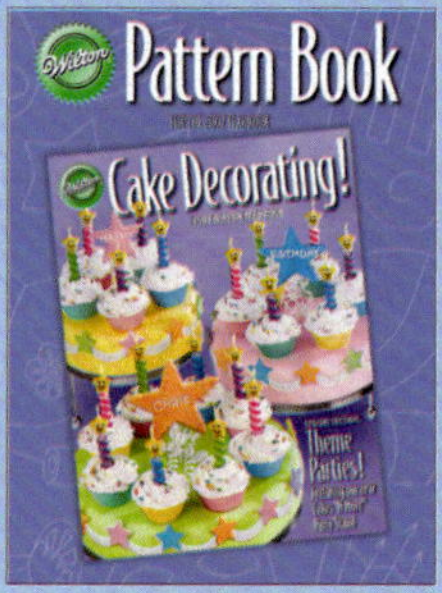

Duplicate many of the beautiful cake designs featured in the 2007 Yearbook and on the Wilton website. Includes over 100 decorating outlines to transfer to your cake. Easy-to-follow instructions. Soft cover, 60 pages of patterns.
408-S-2007

Celebrate! with Fondant

It's the first book to feature fondant done the Wilton way—using our exciting cake designs, step-by-step instructions and convenient fondant products. Celebrate! with Fondant makes fondant cakes easy and fun for everyone. See how to make more than 40 terrific cakes, along with alternate ways to decorate every design and suggestions for the perfect occasions to serve them.
Soft cover, 120 pages.
902-S-911

Wilton Party Favors

Includes all you need to know about making these favors with ease. Step-by-step instructions help you complete a party's worth of favors in just a few hours. A convenient section on favor-making tools and techniques. Plus information on buying the great Wilton products used to make each design.
Soft cover, 48 pages.
908-S-119

Instructional Videos

NOW ON DVD!

How to Make Wedding Cakes

Invaluable lessons on how to design and assemble tiered cakes for weddings, showers, anniversaries and other special occasions. Hints for transporting and serving also included in this 60-minute video. DVD material matches VHS.
DVD 901-S-256
VHS 901-S-128

BAKE DECORATE CELEBRATE!™ Complete First Season Set

NEW!

It's the ultimate introduction to cake and dessert decorating on video! Includes all 13 episodes from the first season of the popular PBS series, which makes it easy for anyone to create something great. In every episode, hosts Nancy Siler and Melanie Glasscock focus on a specific theme such as *Kids Birthdays, Garden Party Desserts* or *Chocolate Treats*, They'll decorate specialty projects based on that theme and give you related decorating ideas to make the celebration complete. A *Decorating Basics* segment will give you easy first steps for success, while a *Decorating Tips* chapter shows all kinds of beautiful designs you can create with just one featured tip. 4 discs, approx. 6 hours.
DVD 901-S-121

How to Make Icing Flowers

Learn how to make roses, Easter lilies, violets, pansies, daisies, poinsettias and more! Five cake designs incorporate all the flowers included in this 60-minute video. DVD material matches VHS.
DVD 901-S-258
VHS 901-S-119

NEW!

Cake Decorating Basics

See the essentials of creating amazing cakes and desserts, step by step! Everything from tools to icings, baking perfect cakes, decorating stars, shells, flowers and more is covered in this 60-minute program.
DVD 901-S-120

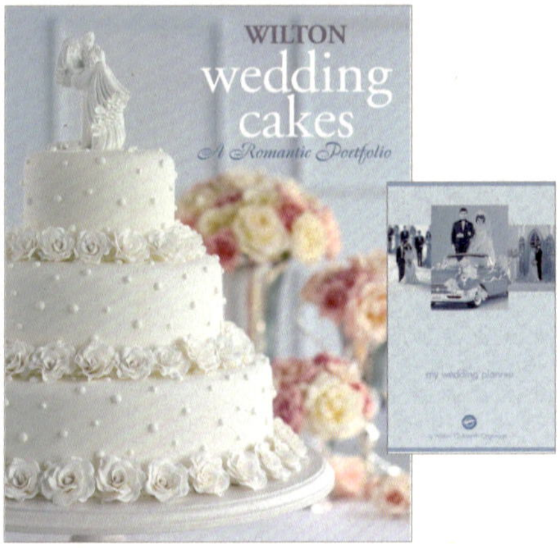

Wilton Wedding Cakes— A Romantic Portfolio

Our exciting new collection of tiered cakes makes the romantic wedding of every bride's dreams a reality. *A Romantic Portfolio* sets the bride's imagination free, with 38 exquisite cakes that express love in many ways. It's all here—beautiful seasonal designs, elegant shapes, classic and contemporary looks. There is a cake for every taste—along with coordinating ornament, favor suggestions and tiered cake accessories.

A Romantic Portfolio will inspire decorators as well as brides. Every design includes step-by-step decorating instructions, product checklists and serving amounts. Used with our comprehensive construction guide, patterns, techniques and recipes, *A Romantic Portfolio* has everything decorators need to recreate each cake to perfection. Soft cover, 144 pages.
902-S-907

NEW!

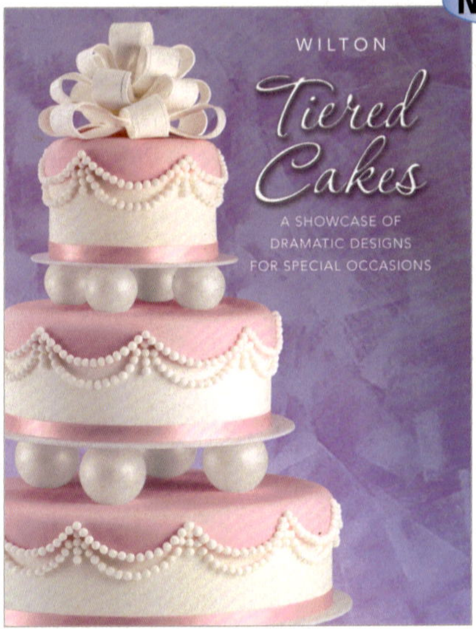

Wilton Tiered Cakes

If you are planning a wedding, a shower or any big event, Wilton Tiered Cakes will show you the perfect way to top it off. Experience today's most contemporary looks in reception cakes! See how exciting it can be to mix up colors on a wedding cake using textured fondant or floral accents. Find an anniversary cake that's as much fun as a scrapbook, with tiers surrounded by family photos. Discover creative new construction ideas like our cute teddy bear tower with fondant baby blocks as separators. It's all here—38 amazing cake designs—along with complete instructions, techniques, construction and cutting guides, and great Wilton products. Soft cover, 128 pages.
902-S-1108

Cake Decorating

Create your greatest cakes with the essentials decorators count on. Time-saving tools. Precise tips. Quality icings. Plus, the most exciting new products for fondant decorating!

fondant fun!™

Wilton presents the easy system for fondant decorating! Convenient, Ready-To-Use Rolled Fondant. Cut-Outs™ that create fun shapes. Icing Writer™ to add vivid designs. Easy-to-use tools that help you roll, cut and color to achieve exciting new decorations!

WHITE READY-TO-USE ROLLED FONDANT

Fondant has never been more convenient and easy for decorating! With Wilton Ready-To-Use Rolled Fondant, there's no mess, no guesswork. The 24 oz. (1½ lbs.) package covers an 8 in. 2-layer cake plus decorations; the 80 oz. (5 lbs.) package covers a 2-layer 6 in., 8 in. and 10 in. round tiered cake plus decorations. Pure white. Certified Kosher.

1. Roll out.

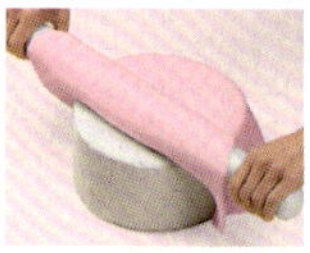

2. Layer over cake.

3. Trim and decorate.

24 oz. (1½ lbs.) Pk.
710-S-2076

80 oz. (5 lbs.) Pk.
710-S-2180

COLOR FONDANT MULTI PACKS

Convenient four-pouch assortments of primary, neon, pastel or natural colors are perfect for making multi-colored decorations. The color is already mixed in. . . no kneading, no mess, no guesswork. Great for flowers, borders and fun shapes. Each 17.6 oz. package contains four 4.4 oz. packs. Certified Kosher.

Primary Colors
Green, Red, Yellow, Blue
710-S-445

Neon Colors
Purple, Orange, Yellow, Pink
710-S-446

Pastel Colors
Blue, Yellow, Pink, Green
710-S-447

Natural Colors
Light Brown, Dark Brown, Pink, Black
710-S-448

ICING WRITER™

Squeeze on colorful accents —flowers, swirls, messages and more—with this ready-to-use icing! It's easy to control for precise decorating: Just squeeze the bottle and icing flows smoothly from the built-in round tip. Trace imprinted shapes made with Cut-Outs or draw dazzling freehand designs. Dries to a smooth, satin finish. 3 oz. bottle. Certified Kosher.

Blue
710-S-2227

Red **710-S-2225**
Yellow **710-S-2226**
White **710-S-2228**
Green **710-S-2229**
Pink **710-S-2230**
Violet **710-S-2231**

Brush Set

Add a special touch of color to your fondant-covered cake! It's easy and fun with these fine-bristle brushes and Icing Writer™. Three tip designs—round, square and bevel—help you achieve different painted effects. Also great for applying water or adhesive to attach fondant decorations.
1907-S-1207 Set/3

FOODWRITER™ EDIBLE COLOR MARKERS

Use like ink markers to add fun and dazzling color to countless foods. Kids love 'em! Decorate on fondant, color flow, royal icing, even directly on cookies. Brighten everyday foods like toaster pastries, cheese, fruit slices, bread and more. Each set includes five .35 oz. FoodWriter pens. Certified Kosher.

Primary Colors Sets

Yellow, Green, Red, Blue, Black

Fine Tip 609-S-100 Set/5
Bold Tip 609-S-115 Set/5

Neon Colors Set

Purple, Orange, Pink, Light Green, Black

Fine Tip
609-S-116
Set/5

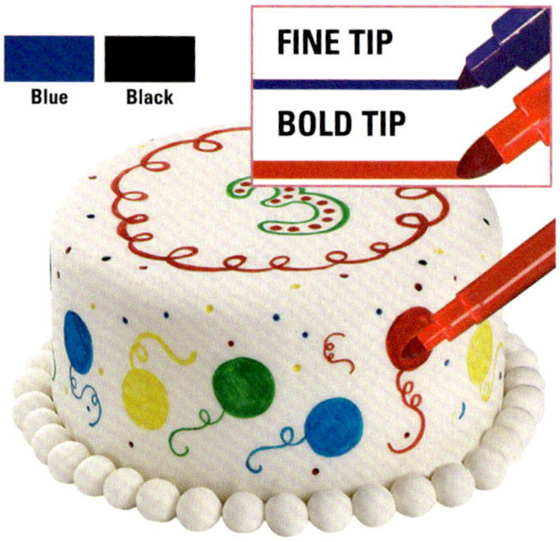

Color Tray

Become a true fondant artist with this convenient tray! Pour in Icing Writer™ and use with the Brush Set at left to add vivid designs to your fondant cakes.
1907-S-1208

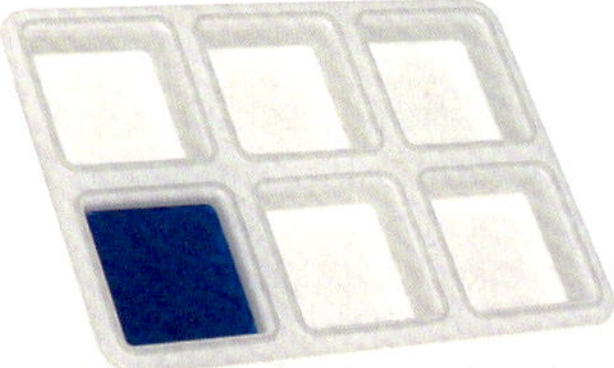

SHIMMER DUST™

Give your fondant decorating that added dash of color—sprinkle on Shimmer Dust! Just brush your fondant-covered cake top or fondant Cut-Outs with water and sprinkle lightly over the dampened area.
Total net wt. .47 oz. Certified Kosher.

Elegant
Silver, Gold, Pearl
703-S-212 Set/3

Primary
Red, Green, Blue
703-S-210 Set/3

Bright
Pink, Yellow, Orange
703-S-211 Set/3

Fondant Tools and Accessories

NEW!

Flower Stamen Assortment

Finish your royal icing or gum paste flowers with a beautiful natural look using one of these 3 lovely stamen styles. Just pipe a dot of icing for your flower center, cut stamens to desired size, insert and let dry. Includes 60 each in Pearl, Glitter and Fluffy styles. May be tinted (except Pearl) with Wilton Icing Colors added to vanilla extract. 2½ in. long with stamen on each end.
1005-S-410 Pk./180

Fondant Shaping Foam

Thick and thin squares are the ideal soft surface for shaping flowers, leaves and other fondant or gum paste cutouts. Use the thin square for thinning petal edges with a ball tool, carving vein lines on leaves and making ruffled fondant strips. Use the thick square for cupping flower centers. Thin: 4 x 4 x ⅛ in. Thick: 4 x 4 x 1 in.
1907-S-9704 Set/2

Confectionery Tool Set

Invaluable tools for shaping and imprinting, helping you achieve lifelike fondant or gum paste flowers. Ideal for marking patterns in fondant cakes, shaping marzipan fruits. Includes plastic Dogbone, Umbrella, Shell, Ball and Veining tools.
1907-S-1000 Set/5

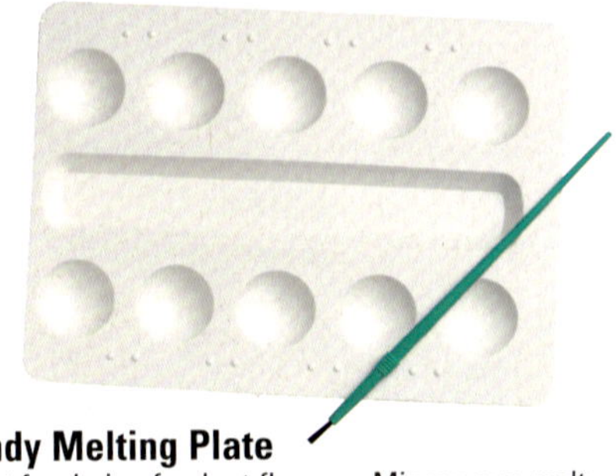

Candy Melting Plate

Great for drying fondant flowers. Microwave-melt up to 11 Candy Melts®* colors at one time for less mess. Plastic with non-slip grip edge. Includes decorating brush.
1904-S-8016 Set/2

*Brand confectionery coating.

Quick Ease Roller

Makes it easy to prepare small pieces of fondant and gum paste for cutting flowers and designs. Wooden roller fits comfortably in palm of hand.
1907-S-1202

Fondant Ribbon Cutter/Embosser Set

This easy-to-use tool is the perfect way to add beautiful textured fondant ribbons, stripes and bows to your cake. Just choose the cutting and embossing wheel designs you want, slide the washer, core, wheels and spacers on the roller handle, and roll on top of your fondant. (We suggest brushing the assembled roller with shortening for easy release.) The perfectly cut ribbon strips are ready to place right on your cake! Produces ribbon widths from ¼ in. to 3¾ in. when combining spacers. Complete set includes: 8 embossing wheels: (4 striped, 4 beaded); 9 spacers (one ⅓ in., two each ¼, ½, ¾ and 1 in. wide); 9 cutting wheels (3 straight, 3 wavy, 3 zigzag); roller handle with detachable core; assembly hardware.
1907-S-1203 Set/26

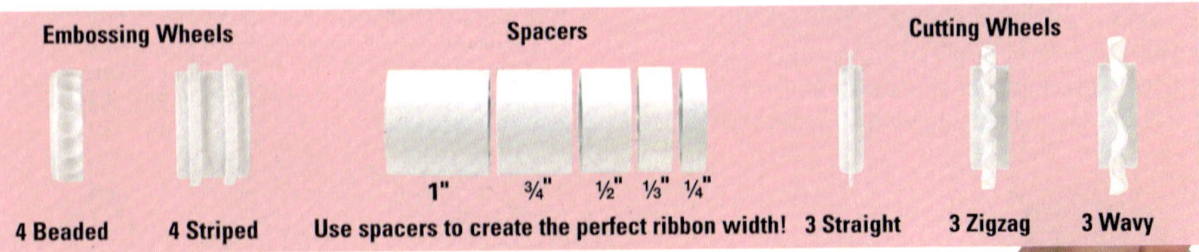

Fondant Decorative Punch Set

Add exciting 3-dimensional decorations in fondant with this easy-to-use tool. In seconds, you can punch out fondant accents with elegant openwork shapes like diamonds and flowers. As you punch, the disk imprints a detailed design that adds a pretty touch of texture to any cake. The comfortable angled handle holds your choice of 8 design disks. Also great for adding fondant detail to cupcakes and cookies. Disks turn to lock into place.
1907-S-1204 Set/9

Flower Former Set

Dry fondant or icing leaves and flowers in a convex or concave shape. Three each of 1½, 2 and 2½ in. wide holders, all 11 in. long.
417-S-9500 Set/9

Cutter/Embosser

Three detachable wheels—straight, wavy and ridged—for cutting and for embossing patterns on fondant. Light, easy-rolling design cuts at the perfect angle. Comfortable handle also stores wheels.
1907-S-1206

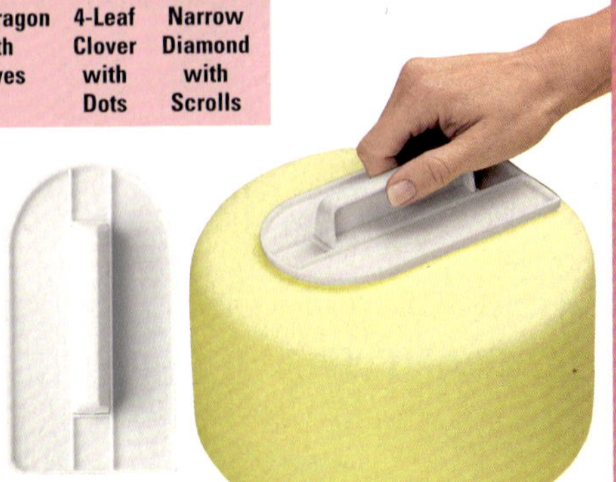

Easy-Glide Fondant Smoother

Essential tool for shaping and smoothing rolled fondant on your cake. Works great on top, edges and sides! Shapes fondant to sides of cake so that no puffed areas appear. Trim any excess with a sharp knife. 6¼ in. long x 3¼ in. wide.
1907-S-1200

Celebrate!® With Fondant

It's the first book to feature fondant done the Wilton way—using our exciting cake designs, step-by-step instructions and convenient fondant products. *Celebrate! with Fondant* makes fondant cakes easy and fun for everyone. See how to make more than 40 terrific cakes, along with alternate ways to decorate every design and suggestions for the perfect occasions to serve them. Soft cover, 120 pages.
902-S-911

Fondant Tools and Accessories

CUT-OUTS™

With Cut-Outs, it's easy to make fun 3-D shapes for your fondant cakes and cupcakes. Just roll out fondant, press down with Cut-Out and lift away. Remove shapes with a small spatula.

Stainless steel shapes range from ⅝ in. to 2½ in.

- Fast, fun way to brighten any fondant cake!
- Great assortment of shapes for any occasion.
- Perfect for highlighting with Icing Writer™.

Crinkle Shapes
Circle, Square, Triangle, Heart
417-S-444 Set/4

Fancy Shapes
Flower, Leaf, Oval, Heart
417-S-445 Set/4

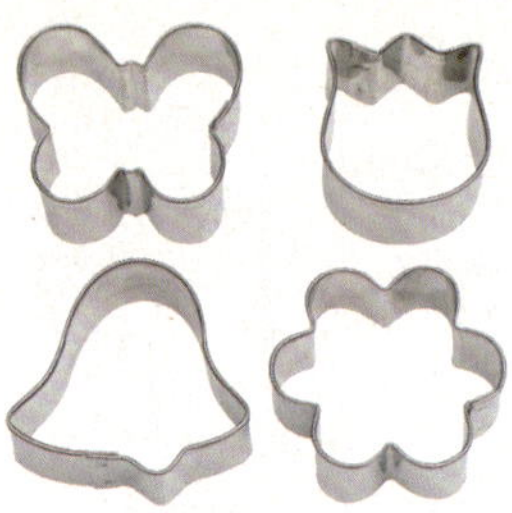

Garden Shapes
Butterfly, Tulip, Bell, Flower
417-S-443 Set/4

Daisy
Durable plastic.
417-S-439
Set/3

Oval
417-S-438
Set/3

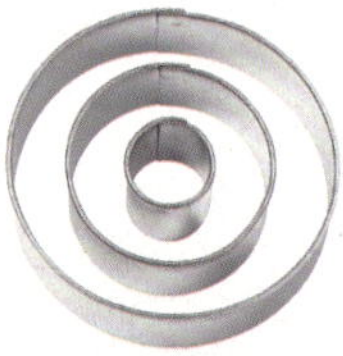

Round
417-S-432
Set/3

Square
417-S-431
Set/3

People
417-S-441
Set/6

Heart
417-S-434
Set/3

Star
417-S-433
Set/3

Flower
417-S-435
Set/3

Funny Flower
417-S-436
Set/3

Leaf
417-S-437
Set/3

Alphabet/Number
417-S-442
Set/37

FONDANT AND GUM PASTE DECORATION SETS

Floral Collection Flower Making Set
Make incredibly lifelike gum paste flowers. Full-color how-to book includes many arranging ideas and step-by-step instructions. Kit includes 24 plastic cutters, 1 leaf mold, 3 wood modeling tools, protector flap, 40-page instruction book and 2 foam squares for modeling.
1907-S-117 Set/32
Book only 907-S-117

Stepsaving Rose Bouquets Flower Cutter Set
Create gorgeous fondant and gum paste roses and forget-me-nots using book and cutters in this set. Cutters include large and small rose, rose leaf, calyx and forget-me-not.
1907-S-1003 Set/6

Floral Garland Cutter/Ejector Set
Quickly and easily cuts and positions fondant or gum paste flowers on cakes. Includes ejector, 5 cutters and instructions.
1907-S-1001 Set/7

ROLLING PINS AND MAT

NEW!

Spiral Pattern Roller

This easy-to-use roller adds an exciting swirled texture to fondant cake decorations. Its lightweight design makes it easy to imprint evenly, creating a perfect look for your cake. Sized just right for preparing small amounts of fondant to create bow loops, swags, flat flowers and more. Perfect for use with Wilton Ready-To-Use Rolled Fondant, Fondant Multi Packs and Cut-Outs. Just roll out fondant with a smooth rolling pin, then re-roll with the Spiral Pattern Roller to imprint incredible texture. Imprint width is 9¼ in.; 2 in. diameter.
1907-S-1224

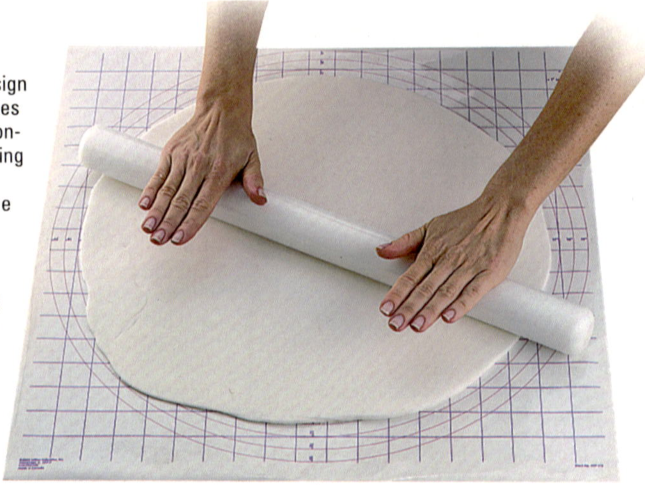

20 in. Rolling Pin

Its extra-wide, smooth design is perfect for covering cakes with rolled fondant. The non-stick surface makes handling large pieces of fondant easy—just dust the surface with confectioner's sugar and roll out fondant to the size you need, then use the Wide Glide Rolling Pin to lift the fondant from your work surface to the cake. Great for rolling out pastry dough and pie crusts, too. 20 x 1½ in. diameter.
1907-S-1210

9 in. Rolling Pin

Roll out fondant evenly, in the perfect thickness for easy cutting and shaping, with this 3-piece non-stick roller. Roll to the perfect ⅛ in. height used for cutting many fondant decorations, using the slide-on guide rings. Easy to handle—just the right size for preparing small amounts of fondant to place on your cake. Perfect for use with Fondant Multi Packs and Cut-Outs™. 9 x 1 in. diameter.
1907-S-1205

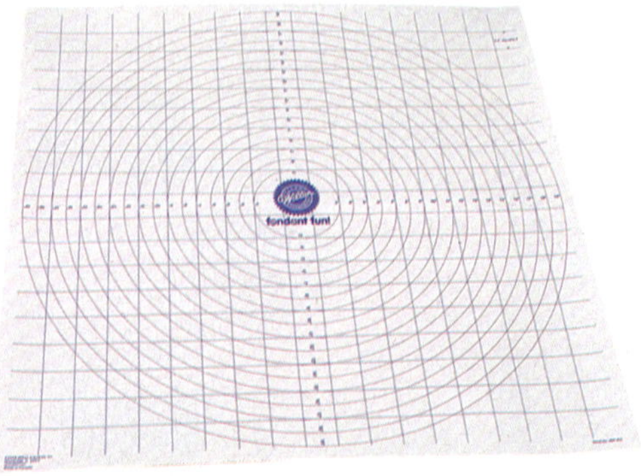

Roll & Cut Mat

For precise measuring, rolling and cutting of fondant or dough. Pre-marked circles for exact sizing. Square grid helps you cut precise strips. Non-stick surface for easy release. 20 in. square with circles from 3 in. to 19 in. diameter.
409-S-412

Use mat to roll out and cut fun shapes!

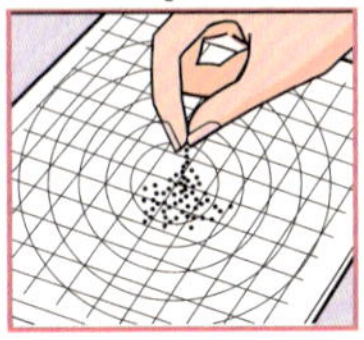

1. Sprinkle Rolling Pin and Roll & Cut Mat with confectioner's sugar.

2. Place fondant on the mat. Roll about ⅛ to ¼ in. thick.

3. Cut pieces with Decorative Punches, Cutter/Embosser (p. 129), or Cut-Outs™ (p. 130).

Gum Paste and Ingredients

NEW!

READY-TO-USE GUM PASTE

No mixing! Create beautiful handmolded flowers right from the box.

Now you can have gum paste on hand whenever you need it! With Ready-To-Use Gum Paste, there's no mixing, no mess—just tint, roll out and cut to create incredible floral bouquets for your cakes. Follow the easy instructions included and use with Wilton Gum Paste Floral Kits to make roses, daisies, apple blossoms, tulips and many more beautiful blooms. 1 lb.
707-S-130

Gum Paste Mix

Just add water and knead. Workable, pliable dough-like mixture molds into beautiful flowers and figures. 1 lb.
707-S-124

Gum-Tex™

Makes fondant and gum paste pliable, elastic, easy to shape. Plastic resealable lid. 6 oz.
707-S-117

Glucose

Essential ingredient for making fondant and gum paste from scratch. Use with Wilton Gum-Tex™. 12 oz.
707-S-107

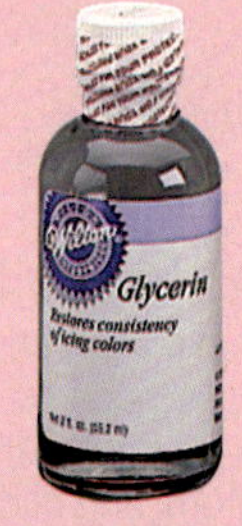

Glycerin

Stir into dried out fondant, gum paste and icing color to restore consistency. 2 oz. Certified Kosher.
708-S-14

Comfort Grip™ Kitchen Tools

NEW!

They make decorating and kitchen tasks easier! Lightweight, comfortable tools with contoured handles and quality blades of silicone or stainless steel.

Pastry Brush

Flexible silicone bristles are great for brushing on Cake Release, shortening or hot glazes. More durable than nylon bristles. Comfortable ergonomic handle; 8½ in. long.
409-S-6056

Cake and Pie Server

Slice and serve with greater control! The comfortable ergonomic handle with thumb rest and angled blade makes lifting every slice easier. Serrated stainless steel blade cuts even the first slice cleanly. 9 in. long.
409-S-6058

Cookie Spatula

Angled stainless steel blade moves cookies from pan to plate with ease. Slides easily under cookies—great for serving brownies and bar cookies, too. Comfortable ergonomic handle with thumb rest. 9 in. long.
409-S-6054

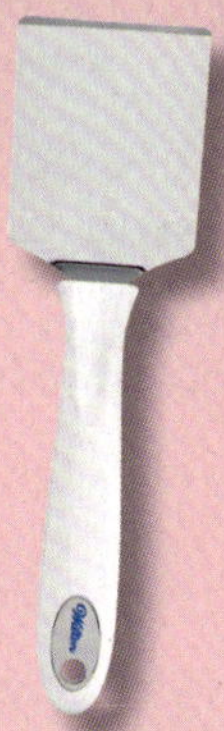

All-Purpose Spatulas

Blend and mix with greater comfort, more control and less fatigue, thanks to the contoured Comfort Grip™ handle. Flexible silicone blade is ideal for blending icing and removing from bowls or icing containers—great for all-around kitchen use. Stain and odor resistant.
9 in.
409-S-6050
12 in.
409-S-6052

Cake Knife/Spatula

This stainless steel knife is perfect for torting cakes—it cuts layers cleanly and has the width you need to transfer layers without breakage. Use the smooth edge for spreading icing or filling on cake layers. It's easy to control, with a lightweight nylon handle that is comfortable in any hand. 15 in. long
409-S-6048

Baking Accessories

Bake Easy!™ Non-Stick Spray

For cakes that turn out beautifully every time, start by spraying pans with Bake Easy. This convenient non-stick spray helps your cakes release perfectly with fewer crumbs for easier icing and a flawless look for decorating. Just a light, even coating does the job. Use Bake Easy for all mixes and recipes—cupcakes, brownies, breads and more. Versatile for all types of baking and cooking. 6 oz.
702-S-6018

Cake Release

No need to grease and flour your baking pan—Cake Release coats in one step. Simply spread Cake Release lightly on pan bottom and sides with a pastry brush and add batter. Cakes release perfectly without crumbs every time, giving you the ideal surface for decorating. In convenient dispensing bottle. 8 oz. Certified Kosher.
702-S-6016

BAKE-EVEN STRIPS

Cakes bake perfectly level and moist, without cracking, when you wrap these strips around the pan before baking. Oven-safe, instructions and clips included.

Small Set

Two 1½ in. high strips, 30 in. long. Enough for two 8 or 9 in. round pans.
415-S-260 Set/2

Large Set

Four 1½ in. high strips, 36, 43, 49 and 56 in. long. Enough for one each: 10, 12, 14, 16 in. round pans.
415-S-262 Set/4

CAKE LEVELERS

Cake Leveler

Make your cake top perfectly level for precise decorating—just place adjustable wire in notches to desired height up to 2 in. and glide through the cake. Makes torting easy, too! For cakes up to 10 in. wide.
415-S-815

Large Cake Leveler

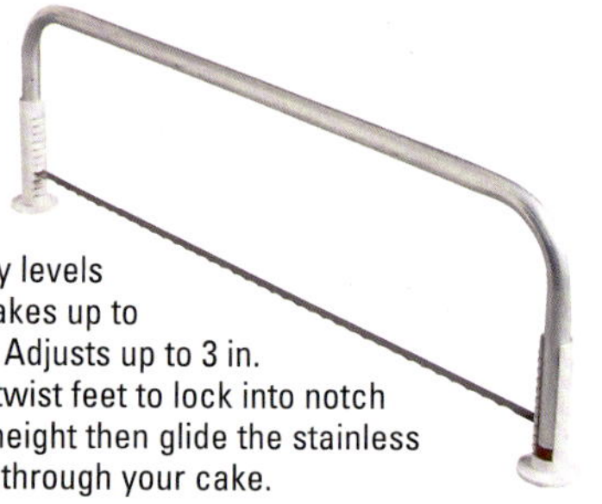

Blade easily levels and torts cakes up to 18 in. wide. Adjusts up to 3 in. high—just twist feet to lock into notch at desired height then glide the stainless steel blade through your cake.
417-S-1198

Non-Stick Parchment Paper

Use Wilton silicone-treated non-stick parchment to line baking pans and cookie sheets—a non-fat alternative that saves cleanup time. Roll out cookie dough between 2 sheets, dough won't stick and will easily transfer to your cookie sheet. You can even reuse it for the next batch. Oven-safe to 400°F, parchment is great for conventional ovens, microwaves and the freezer. Double roll is 41 square feet, 15 in. wide. Certified Kosher.
415-S-680

6-Piece Covered Mixing Bowl Set

Perfect for preparing decorating icings—clear lids snap on tight to keep icing the right texture. Includes one each 1, 2 and 3 quart nesting bowls with easy-grip handles and easy pour spouts for better control. Rubberized base keeps bowls from sliding on countertops. Measurements clearly marked for precise mixing. Dishwasher safe.
417-S-469 Set/6

CAKE STENCILS VARIETY PACK

Our collection of 4 stencil designs gives you several ways to make birthday and everyday cakes more festive. Decorating with stencils is so easy—just place on your iced cake, then sprinkle away with Wilton Cake Sparkles™, add exciting Wilton Sugars in a rainbow of colors or use Color Mist™ food color spray. Also works beautifully with Wilton Rolled Fondant—fill in designs with sugars or decorate with FoodWriter™ Markers. Includes Happy Birthday, Flower, Swirl and Heart designs.
417-S-148 Pk./4

Decorating Stands

A quality cake stand is a must for easy decorating. Stands lift your cake off the work surface so you can create borders conveniently. And they rotate as well, allowing you to decorate all the way around the cake without straining.

Tilting Cake Turntable

It tilts! Decorate any part of your cake conveniently!

The Tilting Cake Turntable moves to 3 preset angles—12°, 24°, and level—and locks in place, making every decorating technique easier! 6 in. high turntable smoothly rotates in any of the angled positions for effortless decorating of top borders, stringwork, lettering on top and sides of cake, more. Includes lock to prevent rotation. Non-slip bottom, 12 in. diameter.
307-S-894

Professional Turntable
Extra strength and effortless turning for decorating tiered wedding cakes. Heavy-duty aluminum stand is 4½ in. high with 12 in. diameter plate. Holds cakes up to 16 in. diameter.
307-S-2501

Revolving Cake Stand
Turns in either direction on easy-rotating ball bearings. 3 in. high, 11 in. diameter plate is white molded plastic. Holds cakes up to 10 in. diameter.
415-S-900

Trim 'N Turn Cake Stand
Turns smoothly on hidden ball bearings for easy decorating and serving. Flute-edged 12 in. plate is white molded plastic. Holds cakes up to 10 in. diameter.
2103-S-2518

Decorating Tools

ICING SCULPTOR™

Now your cakes can have an elegant sculpted finish that will give them a beautiful professional look. It's easy with the Icing Sculptor. Just insert any combination of the 64 design blades—mix and match between the 14 sculpting edges to create your favorite customized effects. Then glide the comb over the iced cake sides to create attractive ridges that will beautifully frame your design. Create hundreds of pattern combinations—wide or narrow ridges, dramatic swirls and vertical designs too.

Includes sculptor handle, 64 design blades and complete instructions. This versatile tool has a patent pending.
2104-S-12 Set/66

So Easy!
Select the sculpting blades you want and slide into handle. Press sculptor into iced cake as you rotate cake on turntable.

So Versatile!
Mix and match between the 14 edge designs on 64 blades to achieve the perfect look for your cake.

Includes 8 of each 2-Sided Design Blade

Decorating Comb
Run edge across your iced cake to form beautiful ridges. 12 x 1½ in.; plastic.
417-S-156

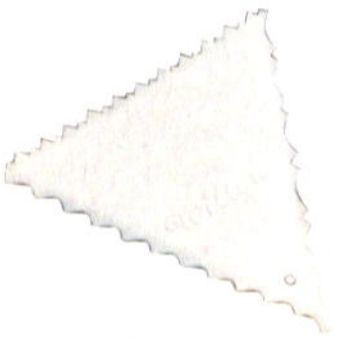

Decorating Triangle
Each side adds a different contoured effect to iced cakes. Easy to hold; 5 x 5 in.; plastic.
417-S-162

Garland Marker
Adjusts to 7 preset widths and varying depths to easily mark perfectly uniform garlands on cake sides. Instructions included.
409-S-812

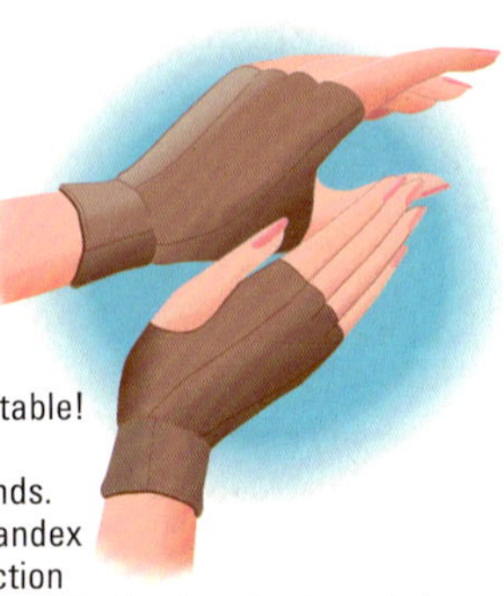

Hand & Wrist Support Gloves
Makes decorating and other creative tasks more comfortable! Use whenever you work with your hands. Their exclusive spandex and nylon construction supports vital areas of the hand and wrist to help you work more comfortably, while the breathable fabric reduces perspiration. Hand & Wrist Support Gloves promote circulation and massage muscles to reduce fatigue. Lightweight, fingerless design gives you the freedom of motion you need for all kinds of tasks including computer work, painting, sewing, knitting, quilting, crocheting and more. Machine or hand wash.
417-S-488 Pk./2

Cake Dividing Set
Measures equal sections of your cake for precise placement of garlands, stringwork and other designs. Cake Dividing Wheel marks up to 16 divisions on cakes up to 20 in. diameter. Garland Marker adjusts to 7 widths. Instructions included.
409-S-806 Set/2

Practice Board with Patterns Set
Includes stand and 20 full-size patterns. 9 x 6 in.
406-S-9464

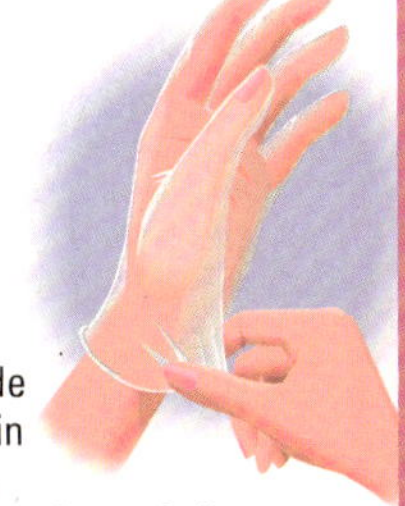

All-Purpose Decorating Gloves
Food-safe disposable gloves keep your hands clean, odor-free and protected in and out of the kitchen. Prevent color stains when tinting fondant, keep fingerprints off homemade candy, eliminate burning of skin when cutting hot, spicy foods. Great when working with craft paint and glue too. Easy to slip-on, gloves fit either hand.
417-S-1642 Pk./20

Icings

All Wilton icings are formulated for decorating as well as taste. That's because Wilton insists on providing you with the perfect consistency icing for decorating. Our quality ingredients mean better results for you.

Creamy White Buttercream Icing Mix

Our convenient mix has the delicious taste and creamy texture of homemade buttercream icing. Use just as you would your favorite buttercream recipe. Makes 1½ to 2 cups. Enough to ice a 1-layer 8 in. cake. Certified Kosher.
710-S-112

Vanilla Whipped Icing Mix

Our light, whipped icing is the ideal texture for decorating in an easy-to-make, delicious mix. Just add ice water and it whips up velvety-smooth for icing or decorating. Light and delicate flavor. Makes 4 cups. Certified Kosher Dairy.
710-S-1241

Meringue Powder

Primary ingredient for royal icing. Stabilizes buttercream, adds body to boiled icing and meringue. Replaces egg whites in many recipes. Resealable top opens for easy measuring. 4 oz. can makes 5 recipes of royal icing; 8 oz. can makes 10 recipes. 16 oz. can makes 20 recipes. Certified Kosher.
4 oz. can 702-S-6007
8 oz. can 702-S-6015
16 oz. can 702-S-6004

Color Flow Mix

Create dimensional flow-in designs for your cake. Just add water and confectioner's sugar. 4 oz. can makes ten 1½ cup batches. Certified Kosher.
701-S-47

Piping Gel

Pipe messages and designs or glaze cakes before icing. Use clear or tint with icing color. 10 oz. Certified Kosher.
704-S-105

READY-TO-USE DECORATOR ICINGS

Wilton makes the only ready-to-use icing that is the perfect consistency for decorating. The pure white color is best for creating true vivid colors using Wilton Icing Colors. Rich and creamy, with a delicious homemade taste. Certified Kosher.

Large Tub

Ideal thin-to-medium consistency for use in Wilton Method Cake Decorating Classes in a convenient easy-carry tub. Great for icing cakes, making borders, messages and more. Contains 9 cups—enough to decorate ten 8 or 9 in. round cake layers.
White 704-S-680

1 lb. Can

Ideal stiff consistency for making roses and flowers with upright petals. One 16 oz. can covers two 8 or 9 in. layers or one 9 x 13 in. cake.
White 710-S-118
Chocolate 710-S-119

READY-TO-DECORATE ICING

Anyone can decorate with Wilton Ready-to-Decorate Icing! Brilliant colors and easy-to-use tips make it a breeze to add an exciting finishing touch to treats—without mixing or mess. Just slip one of the four free tips over the nozzle and start the fun. Decorating couldn't be easier!

Colors match Wilton Icing Colors (p. 135). 6.4 oz. Certified Kosher.

Red	Green	White	Black	Pink
710-S-4400	710-S-4401	710-S-4402	710-S-4404	710-S-4406
Blue	**Violet**	**Yellow**	**Orange**	
710-S-4407	710-S-4408	710-S-4409	710-S-4410	

Four FREE decorating tips included:

Small Round Tip For dots and outlining

Leaf Tip For basic and ruffled leaves

Large Round Tip For writing and printing

Star Tip For stars, swirls and pretty borders

Flavorings

Decorators trust Wilton flavorings for great taste that won't change icing consistency. Wilton flavors are concentrated—only a drop or two adds delicious taste to icings, cakes, beverages and other recipes.

NO-COLOR FLAVORINGS

Recommended by and used in Wilton Method Classes, these delicious flavors won't change your icing color. Essential for making pure white icings for wedding cakes and maintaining vibrant colors in all your decorating. Certified Kosher.

Clear Vanilla Extract

2 oz.
604-S-2237
8 oz.
604-S-2269

No-Color Butter Flavor

2 oz.
604-S-2040
8 oz.
604-S-2067

No-Color Almond Extract

2 oz.
604-S-2126

Pure Vanilla Extract

The world's finest vanilla is from Madagascar. Unmatched flavor and aroma to enhance cakes, puddings, pie fillings, custards, salad dressings and more. 4 oz.
604-S-2270

Tube Icings, Gels

Tube Decorating Icings

The same high quality as our Ready-To-Use Decorator Icing, in a convenient tube. Create flowers, borders and more. Ideal for small areas of color on character cakes. Use with our Tip and Nail Set or Coupler Ring Set and any standard-size Wilton metal tip (not included). Colors match Wilton Icing Colors shown at right. 4.25 oz. Certified Kosher.

Violet 704-S-242
Red 704-S-218
Lemon Yellow 704-S-236
Orange 704-S-212
Pink 704-S-230
Royal Blue 704-S-248
Leaf Green 704-S-224
Kelly Green 704-S-227
Chocolate 704-S-254
White 704-S-200
Black 704-S-206

Coupler Ring Set

Attach Wilton standard size metal decorating tips onto Wilton tube icings to create any technique.
418-S-47306 Set/4

Tip and Nail Set

Tips easily twist onto Wilton tube icings to create many decorating techniques. Includes Star, Round, Leaf and Petal Tips, Flower Nail.
418-S-47300 Set/5

Tube Decorating Gels

Add shimmering accents, colorful highlights and sparkle to your decorating with these transparent gels. Create a beautiful stained-glass effect and add distinctive writing and printing. Great for cakes and cookies. Colors match Wilton Icing Colors shown at right. .75 oz. Certified Kosher.

Red 704-S-318
Pink 704-S-330
Violet 704-S-342
Lemon Yellow 704-S-336
Orange 704-S-312
Royal Blue 704-S-348
Leaf Green 704-S-324
Brown 704-S-354
White 704-S-302
Black 704-S-306

Tube Icing and Gel Color Chart

Lemon Yellow	Orange	Red	Pink
Violet	Royal Blue	Leaf Green	† Kelly Green
† Chocolate	Brown	White	Black

†Not available in gel.

Icing Colors

Wilton color is made to produce deeper, richer color by adding just a small amount. Our concentrated gel formula helps you achieve the exact shade you want without thinning your icing. You'll find a rainbow of colors, ready to blend together for creating your own custom shades.

*Note: Large amounts of these colors may affect icing taste.

Use No-Taste Red for large areas of red on a cake. When using Black, start with chocolate icing to limit the amount of color needed.

‡Daffodil Yellow is an all-natural color. It does not contain Yellow #5. The color remains very pale.

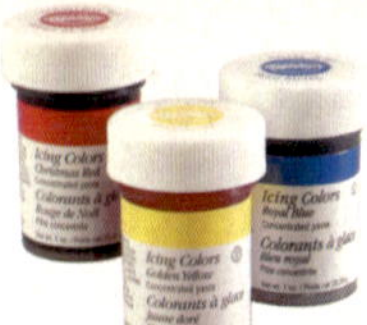

Single Bottles
1 oz. Certified Kosher.

Ivory 610-S-208	Daffodil Yellow‡ 610-S-175	Buttercup Yellow 610-S-216	Golden Yellow 610-S-159	Lemon Yellow 610-S-108	Copper (skin tone) 610-S-450	Creamy Peach 610-S-210	Rose Petal Pink 610-S-410	Terra Cotta 610-S-206	Orange 610-S-205
Red-Red* 610-S-906	Christmas Red* 610-S-302	Red (no-taste) 610-S-998	Rose 610-S-401	Burgundy 610-S-698	Pink 610-S-256	Violet 610-S-604	Delphinium Blue 610-S-228	Cornflower Blue 610-S-710	Royal Blue 610-S-655
Sky Blue 610-S-700	Teal 610-S-207	Kelly Green 610-S-752	Leaf Green 610-S-809	Moss Green 610-S-851	Juniper Green 610-S-234	Brown 610-S-507	Black* 610-S-981		

Primary 4-Icing Colors Set

Lemon Yellow, Sky Blue, Christmas Red, Brown in .5 oz. jars. Certified Kosher.
601-S-5127 Set/4

White-White Icing Color

Stir in to whiten icing made with butter or margarine. Perfect for wedding cakes. 2 oz. Certified Kosher.
603-S-1236

8-Icing Colors Set

Lemon Yellow, Sky Blue, Christmas Red, Brown, Orange, Violet, Pink and Leaf Green in .5 oz. jars. Certified Kosher.
601-S-5577 Set/8

Glycerin

Stir into dried out icing color to restore consistency. 2 oz. Certified Kosher.
708-S-14

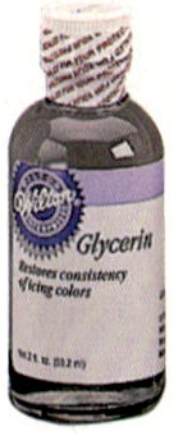

12-Icing Colors Set

Our most popular collection creates the spectrum of primary colors plus skin tones, teal and burgundy. Lemon Yellow, Teal, No-Taste Red, Brown, Copper (skin tone), Violet, Pink, Burgundy, Golden Yellow, Royal Blue, Black, Kelly Green in .5 oz. jars. Certified Kosher.
601-S-5580 Set/12

Pastel 4-Icing Colors Set

Willow Green, Cornflower Blue, Creamy Peach, Rose Petal Pink in .5 oz. jars. Certified Kosher.
601-S-25588 Set/4

Garden Tone 4-Icing Colors Set

Buttercup Yellow, Delphinium Blue, Aster Mauve, Juniper Green, in .5 oz. jars. Certified Kosher.
601-S-4240 Set/4

Color Mist™ Food Color Spray

This easy-to-use spray gives decorators the versatility and dazzling effects of an airbrush in a convenient can! Creates a rainbow of excitement on so many desserts. Use it to transform a plain iced cake with sensational color, add splashes of holiday color to iced cookies and cupcakes. Great for party desserts—highlighting whipped topping or ice cream with color. No mess, taste-free formula; add a little color or a lot.

Colors match Wilton Icing Colors above. 1.5 oz. Certified Kosher.

Red 710-S-5500	Blue 710-S-5501	Yellow 710-S-5502	Green 710-S-5503
Violet 710-S-5504	Pink 710-S-5505	Black 710-S-5506	Orange 710-S-5507

Sprinkles

SPARKLING SUGARS

Put that extra dazzle in your decorating! These easy-pour sugars have a coarse texture and a brilliant sparkle that makes cupcakes, cookies and cakes really shine. 8 oz. bottle. Certified Kosher.

White
710-S-992

Lavender/White
710-S-993

Rainbow
710-S-991

SHAPED SPRINKLES

Pour on the fun! Great shapes and colors add a dash of excitement to cakes, cupcakes, ice cream and more. Certified Kosher.

Rainbow Nonpareils
3 oz. **710-S-772**

White Nonpareils
3 oz. **710-S-773**

Cinnamon Drops
3 oz. **710-S-769**

Rainbow Jimmies
2.5 oz. **710-S-776**
6.25 oz.
710-S-994

Chocolate Jimmies
2.5 oz. **710-S-774**

COLORED SUGARS

Extra-fine sugar is excellent for filling in brightly colored designs on cakes, cupcakes and cookies. 3.25 oz. bottle. Certified Kosher.

Blue
710-S-750

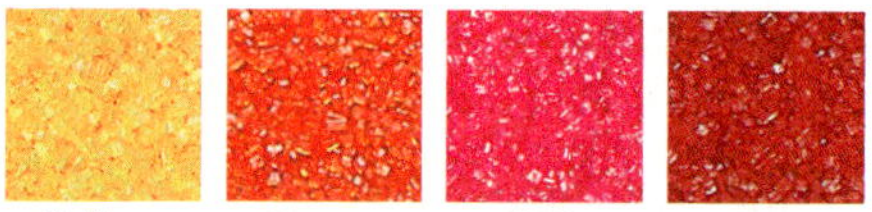

Yellow
710-S-754

Orange
710-S-759

Pink
710-S-756

Red
710-S-766

Lavender
710-S-758

Light Green
710-S-752

Dark Green
710-S-764

Black
710-S-762

4-MIX ASSORTMENTS

They're so convenient! Assorted sugars in an easy-pour flip-top bottle. Top cupcakes, ice cream and other goodies. Certified Kosher.

Brights Sugars
Includes Yellow, Light Green, Lavender, Pink.
710-S-651

Primary Sugars
Includes Red, Dark Green, Blue, Yellow.
710-S-650

6-MIX ASSORTMENTS

They're so convenient! Assorted fun shapes in an easy-pour flip-top bottle. Top cupcakes, ice cream and other goodies. Certified Kosher.

Flowerful Medley
Includes Confetti, Colorful Leaves, Daisies, Pastel Hearts, Wild Flowers, Butterflies.
710-S-4122

Animals and Stars
Includes Cows, Stars, Dinosaurs, Stars and Moons, Bears, Dolphins.
710-S-4123

Nonpareils
Includes Pink, Orange, Green, Red, Yellow, Purple.
710-S-4125

Jimmies
Includes Pink, Orange, Green, Red, Yellow, Blue.
710-S-4127

CAKE SPARKLES™

Add shimmering color to cakes, cupcakes, cookies and ice cream! Brilliant edible glitter in a great variety of colors, great for stencilling, highlighting messages, snow scenes. .25 oz. Certified Kosher.

Silver
703-S-1285

White
703-S-1290

Yellow
703-S-1272

Purple
703-S-1266

Blue
703-S-1314

Red
703-S-1284

Green
703-S-1278

Pink
703-S-1260

Orange
703-S-1308

Black
703-S-1302

Cupcakes 'N More® Dessert Stands

Individually decorated cupcakes are the perfect way to add a personal touch to celebrations. Now, with Cupcakes 'N More, you have the perfect way to serve them! The look is fresh and fun, featuring bold silver-finished wire spirals to securely hold each cupcake. The twisting, towering design is perfect for any setting—showers, kids' birthdays, weddings, holidays and more.

Easy to assemble!
Just stack each layer of cupcakes onto the locking center rod.

Keeps looking great!
Non-toxic, silver-finished metal has a durable non-chip finish.

Collapsible design
Stores easily and safely.

Angled holders
Give the best view of cupcake tops!

Large
15 in. high x 18 wide.
Holds 38 cupcakes.
307-S-651

Standard
12 in. high x 13 wide.
Holds 23 cupcakes.
307-S-826

So many exciting ways to serve!

Dessert Tables

Table Centerpieces

Wedding and Shower Party Favors

Press Sets

Block Letter Press Set
Includes Best, Happy, Wishes, Anniversary, Birthday and Congratulations. Letter holder. Word height ⅞ in.
2104-S-2077
Set/6

Make-Any-Message Letter Press Set
Imprint the perfect sentiment! Press words up to 10½ in. wide, letters ¾ in. high.
2104-S-10
Set/56

Designer Pattern Press Set
Imprints elegant designs for easy overpiping. Includes symmetrical swirl, small and large fleurs de lis, corner flourish, flower, heart bow, scroll and curlicues.
2104-S-3112 Set/8

Italic Make-Any-Message Press Set
Pretty and sophisticated letters for a custom message. Press words up to 10½ in. wide, letters ¾ in. high.
2104-S-2277
Set/58

Decorator Favorites Pattern Press Set
Includes double heart; fleur de lis; medallion; open heart; closed scroll; heart; large, medium and small C-scrolls; crest; double scroll and vine.
2104-S-3160
Set/12

Script Message Press Set
Combine the words Best, Happy, Wishes, Birthday, Anniversary, and Congratulations. Word height ⅞ in.
2104-S-2061
Set/6

Decorating Bags

Featherweight® Decorating Bags

Use these easy-handling bags over and over. Lightweight, strong and flexible polyester will never get stiff. Coated to prevent grease from seeping through. May be boiled; dishwasher safe. Instructions included. Sold singly.

8 in. 404-S-5087
10 in. 404-S-5109
12 in. 404-S-5125
14 in. 404-S-5140
16 in. 404-S-5168
18 in. 404-S-5184

Disposable Decorating Bags

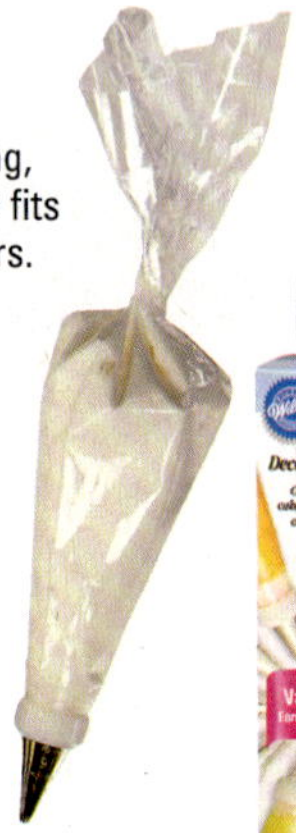

Just use, then toss. Strong, flexible plastic. 12 in. size fits standard tips and couplers. Also perfect for melting Candy Melts®* in the microwave. Instructions included.

2104-S-358 Pk./12

2104-S-1358 Pk./24

*Brand confectionery coating.

Disposable Decorating Bag Dispenser Box

50 Pack

Now in convenient Value Packs! These dispenser boxes make it easy to pull out one bag at a time, so you can keep your decorating space uncluttered. Instructions included.

2104-S-1273 Pk./50

2104-S-1249 Pk./100

Parchment Triangles

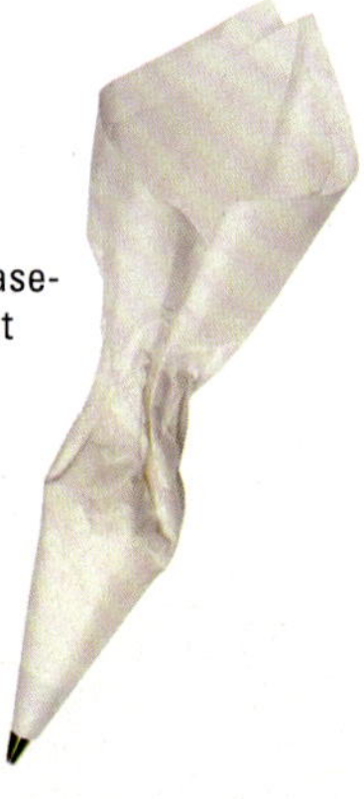

Make your own disposable decorating bags with our grease-resistant vegetable parchment triangles. The professional's choice for convenience and quick bag preparation. Instructions included.

12 in. 2104-S-1206 Pk./100

15 in. 2104-S-1508 Pk./100

Spatulas

ROSEWOOD

Quality rosewood handle spatulas have been favorites for years. They have strong, flexible stainless steel blades and sturdy handles.

Straight Blade

11 in.; 6 in. blade.
409-S-7695
8 in.; 4¼ in. blade.
409-S-6044

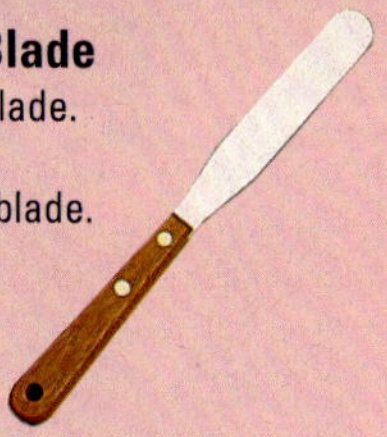

Angled Blade

12 in.; 6¼ in. blade.
409-S-135
8 in.; 4½ in. blade.
409-S-739

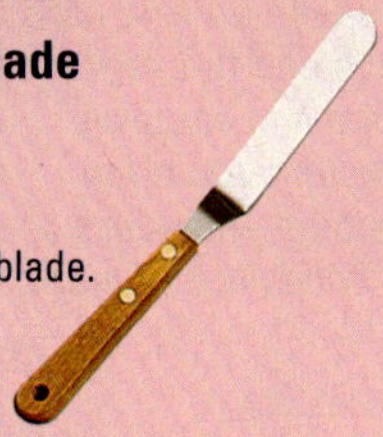

Tapered Blade

8 in.; 4 in. blade.
409-S-518

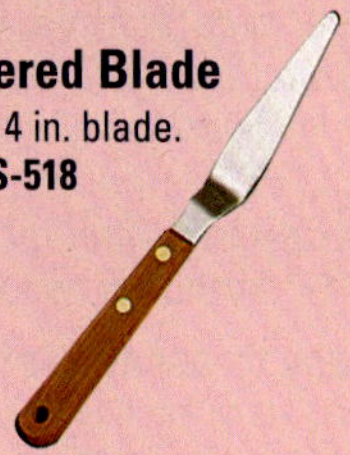

COMFORT GRIP™

Decorate with greater comfort, more control and less fatigue, thanks to contoured handle with finger pad. Flexible stainless steel blade is perfect thickness for gliding over icing.

Straight Blade

15 in.; 10⅛ in. blade.
409-S-6030
11 in.; 6 in. blade.
409-S-6018
9 in.; 4½ in. blade.
409-S-6006

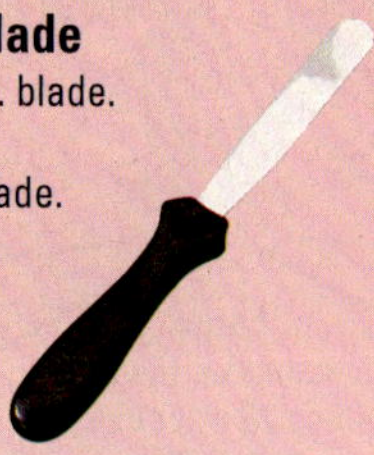

Angled Blade

15 in.; 9⅞ in. blade.
409-S-6036
13 in.; 7¾ in. blade.
409-S-6024
9 in.; 4½ in. blade.
409-S-6012

Tapered Blade

9 in.; 4 in. blade.
409-S-6003

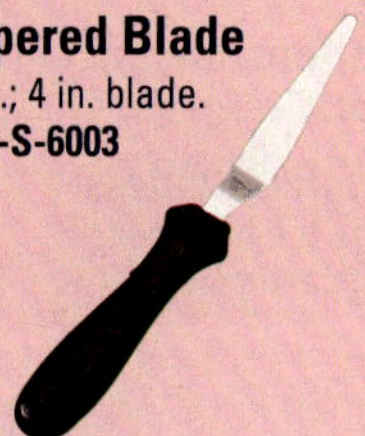

Tip Accessories

Maintain the quality of your Wilton metal decorating tips with these tools.

Tip/Coupler Dishwasher and Storage Bag

Place nylon mesh bag in dishwasher silverware rack for easy tip and coupler cleaning. Tips not included. 5¾ x 6 in.
417-S-1640 Pk./2

Tip Saver

Restores bent tips to their proper shape; opens clogged tips. Place tip over pointed or cone-shaped end, put on cover and twist back and forth to reshape. Heavy-duty plastic.
414-S-909

Tip Covers

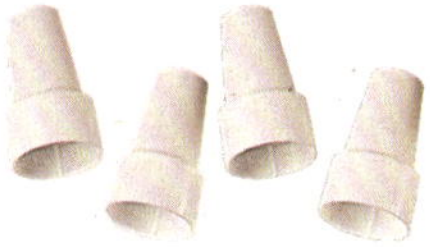

Take filled bags along for touch ups—just slip over tip and go. Plastic.
414-S-915 Pk./4

Tip Brush

Great for cleaning small tip openings. Plastic bristles. ¼ x 4 in. long.
418-S-1123

Tipsaver Cases

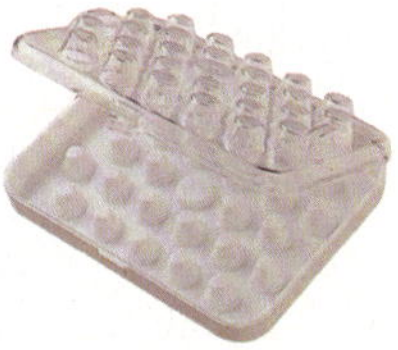

Small case holds 26 tips; large case holds 52 tips Tips not included.
Small 405-S-8773
Large 405-S-7777

DECORATING COUPLERS

Couplers make it easy to change decorating tips on the same icing bag.

Standard Coupler

Fits all decorating bags and standard tips.
411-S-1987

Large Coupler

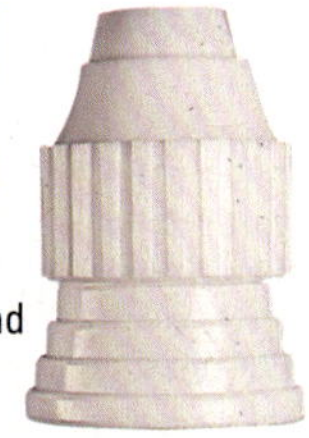

Use with large decorating tips and 14 to 18 in. Featherweight Bags.
411-S-1006

Flower-Making Accessories

Flower Lifter

Easily transfers buttercream flowers from nail to cake without damage. Angled design keeps your hands from touching the cake. Detachable blades for easy cleaning. Plastic. 5¼ in. long.
417-S-1199

Flower Nail No. 7

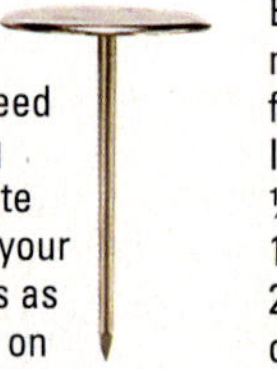

For basic flower making. Provides the control you need when piping icing flowers. Just rotate the nail between your thumb and fingers as you pipe a flower on the head. Stainless steel. 1½ in.
402-S-3007

Lily Nail Set

Essential for making cup flowers. Includes ½, 1¼, 1⅝ and 2½ in. diameter cups.
403-S-9444 Set/8

Flower Former Set

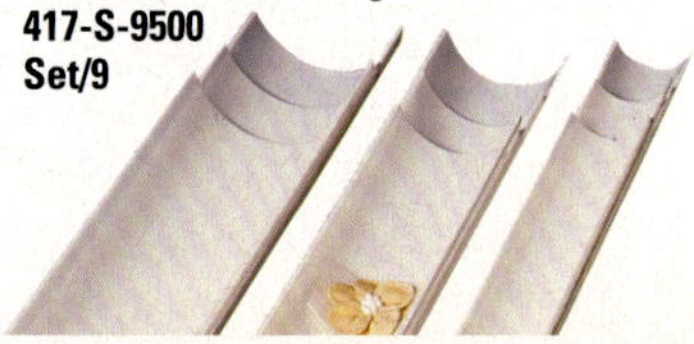

Dry icing leaves and flowers in a convex or concave shape. Three each of 1½, 2 and 2½ in. wide holders, all 11 in. long.
417-S-9500 Set/9

Decorating Sets

53 Piece Cake Decorating Set

"The Works". Decorate many advanced wedding, floral and basketweave cakes as well as basic cakes. Set includes: metal decorating tips 2, 3, 5, 7, 12, 16, 18, 21, 32, 48, 67, 101, 103, 104, 129, 225, 349 and 352; 24 disposable 12 in. decorating bags, two tip couplers, 5 icing colors (.5 oz. each): Golden Yellow, Moss Green, Rose Petal, Cornflower Blue; one 1¼ in. flower nail No. 9; 8 in. angled spatula; storage tray and a 40-page book: *Cake Decorating Beginner's Guide*.
2104-S-2546 Set/53

25 Piece Cake Decorating Set

A solid foundation set for decorating. Set includes: metal decorating tips 3, 16, 32, 104 and 352; 12 disposable 12 in. decorating bags; two tip couplers; 4 icing colors (.5 oz. each): Lemon Yellow, Pink, Sky Blue, Leaf Green; 1¼ in. flower nail No. 9; instruction booklet.
2104-S-2536 Set/25

18 Piece Cake Decorating Set

Perfect for Wilton character cakes! Set includes: metal decorating tips 4, 12, 18 and 103; 6 disposable 12 in. decorating bags; 2 tip couplers; 5 liquid color packets (.067 fl. oz. each): Yellow, Red, Green, Orange, Blue; instruction booklet.
2104-S-2530 Set/18

101 Piece Tool Caddy Collection

This convenient caddy contains our most complete collection of tools, colors and flavors for the cake decorator. It's a great way to organize, carry and store the essentials—tips, couplers, colors, spatulas and more. Lift-out tray holds tips, couplers, brushes and colors securely. Upright storage prevents spills and makes it easy to find what you need. Generous storage area keeps books, spatulas, bags and other large supplies neatly organized.
2109-S-861
Set/101

Includes These Tools:

- 8 Icing Colors: Golden Yellow, No-Taste Red, Brown, Violet, Pink, Royal Blue, Black, Kelly Green in .5 oz. jars
- 3 Couplers (2 standard, 1 large)
- 2 Tip/Coupler Dishwasher and Storage Bags
- Tip Cleaning Brush
- 24 Disposable 12 in. Decorating Bags
- 3 Professional Reusable Decorating Bags (8, 10 and 16 in.)
- 4 Tip Covers
- Tip Saver
- 1 in. Flower Nail No. 7
- 3 Spatulas (8 and 13 in. Angled, 8 in. Tapered)
- Flower Lifter
- Garland Marker
- *Decorating Cakes* Book
- 20 All-Purpose Disposable Decorating Gloves
- Practice Board with Patterns
- 2 Bake-Even Strips
- 8 oz. Clear Vanilla and No-Color Butter Flavors
- Cake Leveler
- Quick Ease Roller
- Easy-Glide Fondant Smoother
- Decorating Brush

Plus 18 Tips:

- Round: 1, 2, 2A, 3, 12
- Star: 16, 18, 21, 32
- Basketweave: 48
- Leaf: 67, 352
- Petal: 102, 103, 104, 125
- Drop Flower: 2D
- Cake Icer: 789

50 Piece Tool Caddy Decorating Set

We've put together the perfect set for both beginning and advanced decorators. The generous selection of tips, colors and tools gives you the flexibility to decorate virtually any kind of cake. There's also plenty of room to add new items and keep everything organized to save you time. Set includes all tools specified as needed in our Course I class.
2109-S-859 Set/50

Includes These 19 Tips:

- Round #2, 3, 5, 7, 12
- Open Star #16, 18, 21, 32
- Basketweave #47
- Leaf #67, 352
- Petal #101, 103, 104
- Multi-Opening #233
- Drop Flower #225
- Closed Star #133
- Large Drop Flower #2004 (2D)

Plus Tools:

- Tip Brush
- Decorating Brush
- 1½ in. Flower Nail #7
- 2 Standard Couplers
- 18 Disposable Bags
- One 10 in. Professional Bag
- 8 in. Angled Spatula
- Four .5 oz. Icing Colors: Lemon Yellow, Christmas Red, Royal Blue, Leaf Green
- Practice Board with stand
- *Cake Decorating Beginner's Guide*

Tip Sets

Deluxe Tip Set

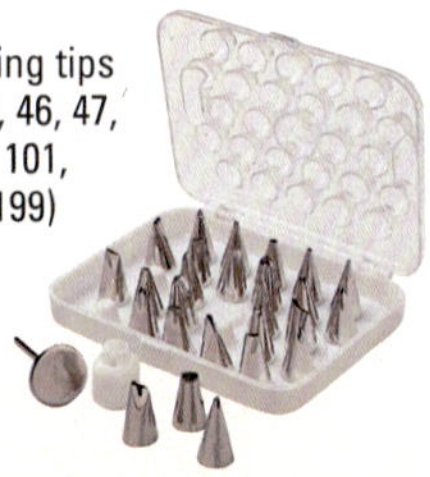

Includes: 26 metal decorating tips (2, 4, 7, 13, 16, 17, 18, 30, 42, 46, 47, 61, 65, 66, 67, 74, 78, 97, 98, 101, 102, 103, 104, 106, 107 and 199) 1¼ in. flower nail No. 9; tip coupler; plastic tipsaver case.
2104-S-6666
Set/29

Master Tip Set

Includes: 52 metal decorating tips: (1, 2, 3, 4, 6, 7, 12, 13, 16, 17, 18, 22, 24, 27, 30, 31, 32, 42, 45, 46, 47, 48, 54, 59, 61, 65, 66, 67, 68, 69, 70, 73, 74, 78, 96, 97, 98, 101, 102, 103, 104, 106, 108, 109, 123, 124, 129, 134, 136, 195, 199 and 2C); two standard tip couplers; two 1¼ in. flower nails No. 9; plastic tipsaver case.
2104-S-7778 Set/57

Tool Caddy Only

Lift out tray keeps 48 tips and 12 color jars in easy reach (tips and colors not included). Stores colors upright to prevent spilling. Plastic.
409-S-860

Decorating Tips

All tips work with standard bags and couplers, unless otherwise indicated. Nickel-plated brass. Dishwasher safe.

ROUND TIPS

Outline, lettering, dots, balls, beads, stringwork, lattice, lacework.

- #1 — 402-S-1
- #1L — 402-S-901**
- #1s — 402-S-1009
- #2 — 402-S-2
- #3 — 402-S-3
- #4 — 402-S-4
- #5 — 402-S-5
- #6 — 402-S-6
- #7 — 402-S-7
- #8 — 402-S-8
- #9 — 402-S-9
- #10 — 402-S-10
- #11 — 402-S-11
- #12 — 402-S-12
- #2A — Smaller version of 1A. 402-S-2001*
- #1A — Bold borders, figure piping. 402-S-1001*
- #230 — Fill eclairs and bismarcks. 402-S-230**
- #55 — 402-S-55
- #57 — 402-S-57
- #301 — For flat lettering. 402-S-301

DROP FLOWER TIPS

Small (106-225); medium (131-194); large (2C-1G), (great for cookie dough).

- #106 — 402-S-106
- #107 — 402-S-107
- #108 — 402-S-108**
- #109 — 402-S-109**
- #129 — 402-S-129
- #224 — 402-S-224
- #225 — 402-S-225
- #131 — 402-S-131
- #190 — 402-S-190**
- #191 — 402-S-191
- #193 — 402-S-193
- #194 — 402-S-194**
- #140 — 402-S-140
- #195 — 402-S-195**
- #2C — 402-S-2003*
- #2D — 402-S-2004*
- #2E — 402-S-2005*
- #2F — 402-S-2006*
- #1B — 402-S-1002*
- #1C — 402-S-1003*
- #1E — 402-S-1005*
- #1F — 402-S-1006*
- #1G — 402-S-1007*

PETAL TIPS

Realistic flower petals, dramatic ruffles, drapes, swags and bows.

- #59s/59° — 402-S-594
- #59 — 402-S-59
- #60 — 402-S-60
- #61 — 402-S-61
- #62 — 402-S-62
- #64 — 402-S-64
- #97 — 402-S-97
- #101s — 402-S-1019
- #101 — 402-S-101
- #102 — 402-S-102
- #103 — 402-S-103
- #104 — 402-S-104
- #150 — 402-S-150
- #116 — 402-S-116*
- #121 — 402-S-121*
- #123 — 402-S-123*
- #124 — 402-S-124*
- #125 — 402-S-125*
- #126 — 402-S-126*
- #127 — 402-S-127*
- #127D — Giant Rose** 402-S-1274

BASKETWEAVE TIPS

Tips 44, 45 make only smooth stripes; rest of basketweave tips and Cake Icer make both smooth and ribbed stripes.

- #44 — 402-S-44
- #45 — 402-S-45
- #46 — 402-S-46
- #47 — 402-S-47
- #48 — 402-S-48
- #1D — 402-S-1004**
- #2B — 402-S-2002*
- #789 — Cake Icer** 409-S-789

MULTI-OPENING TIPS

Rows and clusters of strings, beads, stars, (Use 233 for grass).

- #42 — 402-S-42
- #89 — 402-S-89
- #134 — 402-S-134**
- #233 — 402-S-233
- #234 — 402-S-234*
- #235 — 402-S-235*
- TRIPLE STAR — Triple Star* 402-S-2010

*Fits large coupler. **Tip does not work with coupler. Use with parchment or uncut bags only.

OPEN STAR TIPS

Star techniques, drop flowers; the finely cut teeth of 199 through 364 create decorations with many ridges; use 6B and 8B with pastry dough too.

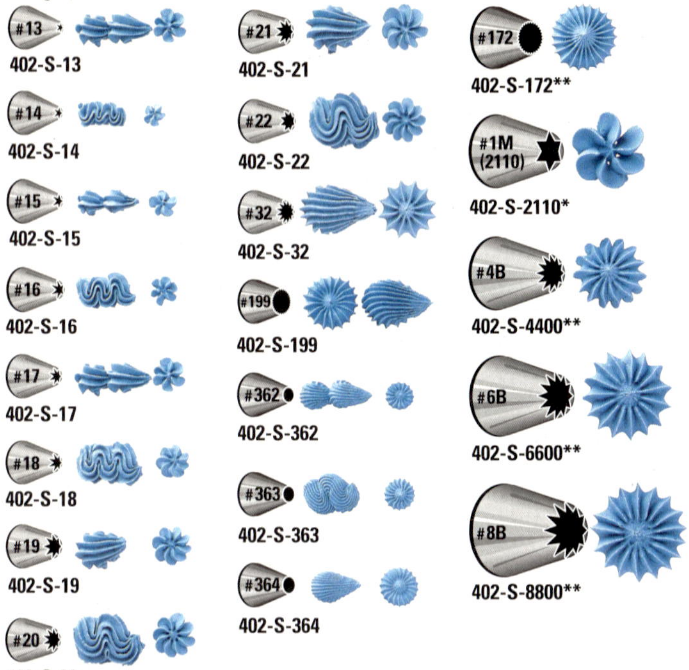

402-S-13
402-S-14
402-S-15
402-S-16
402-S-17
402-S-18
402-S-19
402-S-20
402-S-21
402-S-22
402-S-32
402-S-199
402-S-362
402-S-363
402-S-364
402-S-172**
402-S-2110*
402-S-4400**
402-S-6600**
402-S-8800**

LEFT-HANDED TIP SETS

Now left-handers can achieve the same beautiful flowers as right-handed decorators! Nickel-plated brass tips fit standard bags and couplers.

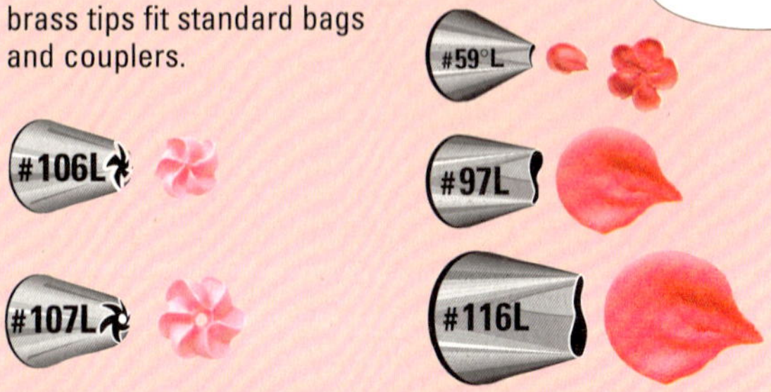

Drop Flower Set
Includes Left tips #106 and #107 for making small swirled flowers.
418-S-613† Set/2

Petal Set
Includes Left tip #59° for violets, Left tip #97 for Victorian roses and Left tip #116 for large Wilton roses.
418-S-612† Set/3

LEAF TIPS

So realistic! Ideal for shell-motion borders too.

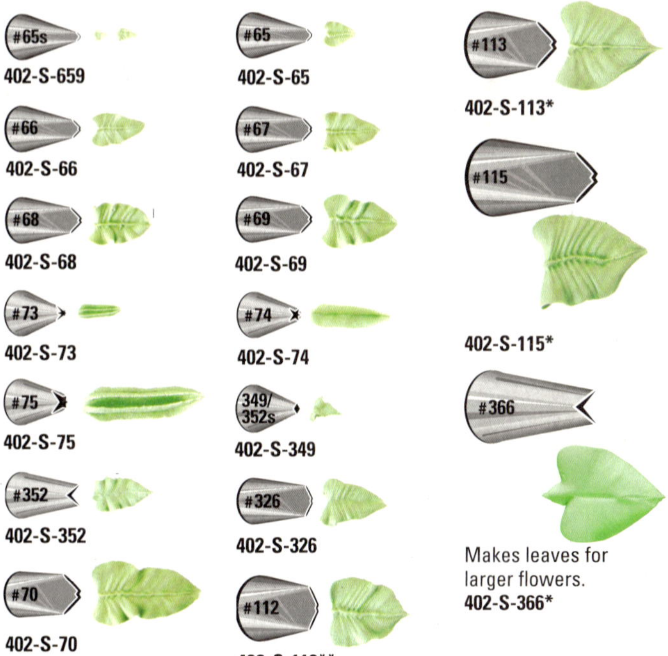

402-S-659
402-S-66
402-S-68
402-S-73
402-S-75
402-S-352
402-S-70
402-S-65
402-S-67
402-S-69
402-S-74
402-S-349
402-S-326
402-S-112**
402-S-113*
402-S-115*

Makes leaves for larger flowers.
402-S-366*

SPECIALTY TIPS

Shells, ropes, hearts, Christmas trees, ring candle holders!

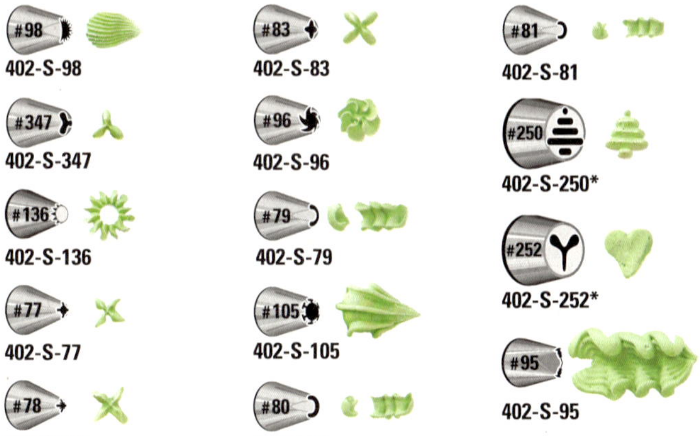

402-S-98
402-S-347
402-S-136
402-S-77
402-S-78
402-S-83
402-S-96
402-S-79
402-S-105
402-S-80
402-S-81
402-S-250*
402-S-252*
402-S-95

CLOSED STAR TIPS

Create deeply grooved shells, stars and fleurs de lis.

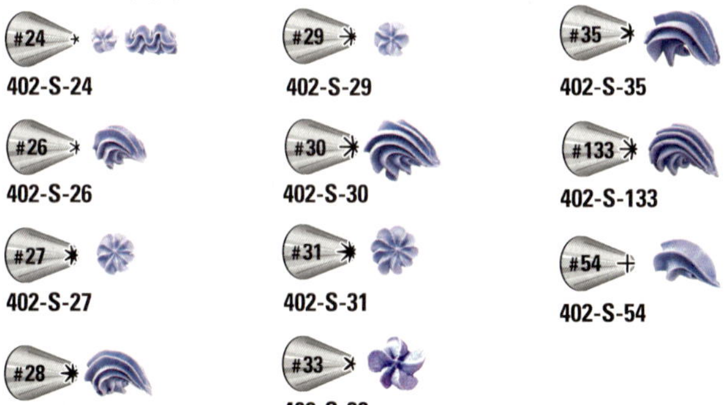

402-S-24
402-S-26
402-S-27
402-S-28
402-S-29
402-S-30
402-S-31
402-S-33
402-S-35
402-S-133
402-S-54

RUFFLE TIPS

Plain, fluted, shell-border, special effects.

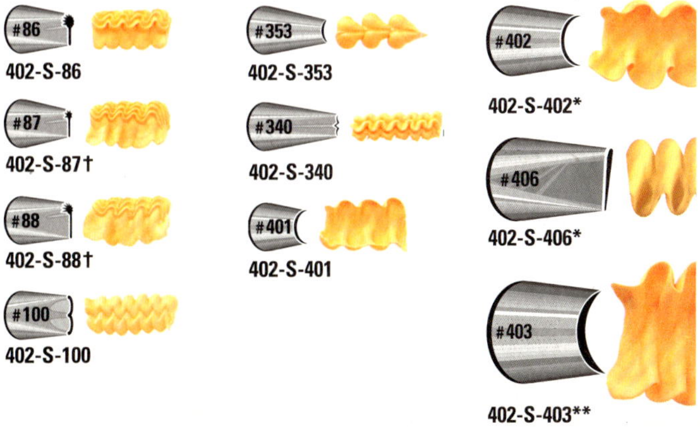

402-S-86
402-S-87†
402-S-88†
402-S-100
402-S-353
402-S-340
402-S-401
402-S-402*
402-S-406*
402-S-403**

†For left-handers.

Dessert decorator Pro™

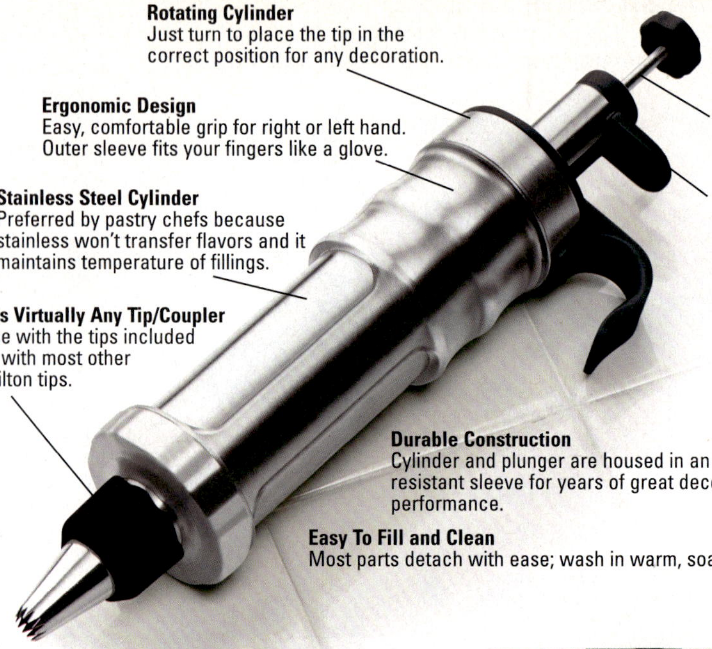

It's easy to add beautiful decorations to any dessert or appetizer in minutes! Designed for comfortable one-hand decorating and effortless tip positioning, this is the most convenient dessert tool you'll ever use.

Create beautiful decorations—shells, stars, rosettes, leaves. The great recipe book included is filled with fabulous ideas to tempt your family and friends: Decorate desserts with elegant whipped cream or icing designs. Dress up pastry shells with dramatic swirls of mousse. Add sophistication to savories with pretty piped cream cheese or seafood spread decorations. With Dessert Decorator Pro, you can do it all!
415-S-850

Dessert Decorator Pro includes all this:

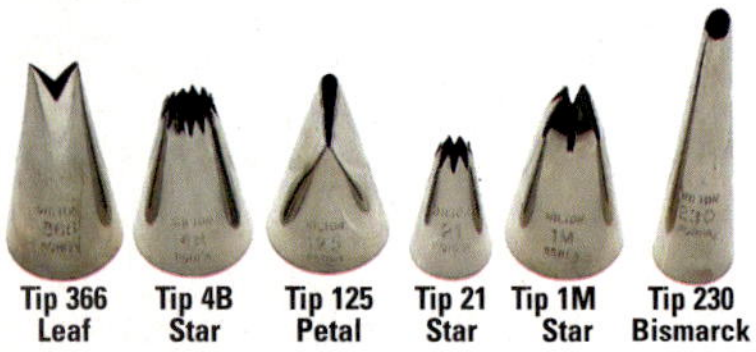

Six Durable Nickel-Plated Tips
Quality metal tips produce perfectly-shaped decorations every time.

Two Tip Couplers
Two sizes to hold standard (small) and large tips.

Tips in bag for size reference only. Tips included are shown at left.

Tip/Coupler Dishwasher and Storage Bag
Just place nylon mesh bag with tips and couplers in your dishwasher silverware rack for easy tip and coupler cleaning.

Recipes and Instructions
Includes delicious recipes and easy decorating instructions for elegant desserts and appetizers.

dessert decorator max™

Create sensational decorations for desserts and appetizers in minutes! One easy-to-use tool does it all—tops pies with fancy whipped cream lattice designs, accents deviled eggs with a pretty rosette, decorates party crackers with savory spreads, fills cupcakes with buttercream for the perfect kids' party treat. The complete set includes 6 tips and 2 couplers for making pretty designs like stars, shells, flowers, petals, lattice/basketweave, leaves and more. The Dessert Decorator Max also works with virtually any Wilton tip, giving you complete versatility. Instruction/recipe booklet is filled with easy step-by-step decorating instructions and delicious ideas for sweet and savory foods.
415-S-854

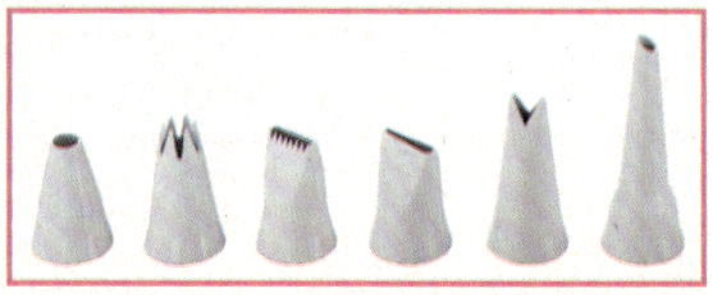

Basic Dessert Decorator

Give your cakes and pastries a beautiful finishing touch in seconds. The easy-to-control lever helps you fill and decorate all kinds of desserts. The 4 decorating nozzles included let you pipe stars, rosettes, shells and many other accents. Works great with Wilton Buttercream Icing Mix and Whipped Icing Mix, p. 134.
415-S-825

THE ULTIMATE 3-IN-1 CADDY™

The world's most versatile and safest cake carrier.

- Reversible, removable tray holds 12 standard cupcakes/ muffins or 24 minis
- Roomy base holds a 9 x 13 decorated cake when used without tray
- 4 locking latches keep baked goods secure
- Extra-thick walls provide the ultimate protection
- Wide, comfortable handle is easy to grab and go
- Textured base resists scratches when cutting cakes
- Sleek see-through design presents desserts at their best

It's the most convenient way to take along cakes, cupcakes, muffins and more! The Ultimate 3-In-1 Caddy features an exclusive reversible cupcake tray which holds 12 standard or 24 mini cupcakes. Or, remove the tray to carry up to a 9 x 13 in. decorated cake on the sturdy locking base. The see-through cover has higher sides to protect icing flowers and tall decorations. You can also use the caddy at home, to keep pies, cookies and brownies fresh for days after baking. 17.9 x 14.4 x 6.8 in. high.
2105-S-9958

Cake Caddy™

Carry decorated desserts with ease! The 6 in. high see-through plastic dome has 3 locking latches that hold the base securely in place wherever you go. Convenient handle gives you a firm grip for a safe trip from home to car to party. The elegant base is approximately 13 in. diameter and holds and stores up to 10 in. round cake or pie, cupcakes, cookies and more.
2105-S-9952

Cake Dome

An elegant way to display and protect your cake—looks great in any setting. The unbreakable polycarbonate dome gives a clear view of the cake as it rests on the graceful pedestal. The 7½ in. high crystal clear dome is the ideal height for multi-layer cakes, angel food, cupcakes and muffins. Pedestal is approximately 12½ in. diameter and can be stored inside dome. Holds up to a 10 in. round cake. Instructions and recipes included.
307-S-702

Cake Saver

The convenient way to carry decorated cakes! Its generous size accommodates borders and cake top decorations easily. Great for carrying or storing angel food, cheese cakes, pies and layer cakes. Fits a 10 in. round cake with borders or a 12 in. cake without borders. 14 in. round base and 6 in. high cover.
415-S-905

Bakeware

Wilton is the #1 bakeware brand in America. From fun novelty shapes for birthday cakes to dramatic cast aluminum styles for elegant desserts, count on Wilton for the best results.

Silicone Bakeware

Discover the convenience and easy release of flexible silicone bakeware!

- Exceptional baking performance for your favorite recipes
- Freezer, refrigerator, oven, microwave and dishwasher safe
- Resists stains and odors
- Oven safe to 500°F
- Easy and convenient storage
- Limited lifetime warranty

Pastel Silicone Baking Cups
No muffin pan needed! Bake and serve in these reusable oven-safe cups in pretty pastels.
Standard size, 2 in. diameter.
415-S-9410 Set/12

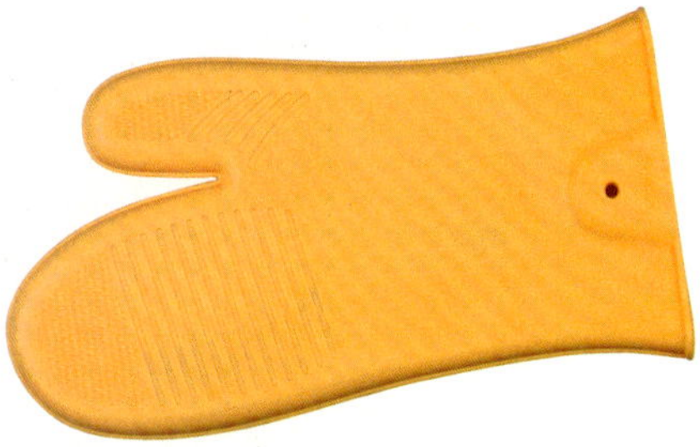

Silicone Oven Mitt
Silicone provides better protection from oven heat! Flexible design with interior and exterior textured grip for better control.
570-S-1127

NEW!

Silicone Mini Star Mold
One cake mix makes 20 to 24 mini stars. Six-cavity pan is 10⅝ x 7 in.; individual cavities are 2½ x 2½ x 1¼ in. deep.
2105-S-4819

Silicone Mini Heart Mold
One cake mix makes 20 to 24 mini hearts. Six-cavity pan is 10⅝ x 7 in.; individual cavities are 2½ x 2½ x 1¼ in. deep.
2105-S-4824

Silicone Mini Flower Mold
One cake mix makes 20 to 24 mini flowers. Six-cavity pan is 10⅝ x 7 in.; individual cavities are 2½ x 2½ x 1¼ in. deep.
2105-S-4825

Silicone Mini Rounds Mold
One cake mix makes 20 to 24 mini rounds. Six-cavity pan is 10⅝ x 7 in.; individual cavities are 2½ in. diameter x 1⅝ in. deep.
2105-S-4832

Fanci-Fill™ Cake Pan Set

NEW!

Serve delicious filling in every slice! Create filled cakes and entrees with incredible flavor combinations using these convenient non-stick pans. The patented recessed design creates a contour you can fill with ice cream, fruit, mousse and more—just bake, fill, flip and frost! The premium non-stick coating provides easy release so cakes unmold perfectly from the pan. Also great for pasta and potato entrees, molded salads and appetizers.

Set includes two 8¾ x 2 in. non-stick pans, bonus recipe booklet with 12 delicious ideas and complete instructions. Non-stick steel.
2105-S-150 Set/2

Dimensions®
DECORATIVE BAKEWARE

With our non-stick cast aluminum bakeware, anyone can create desserts with elegant shapes and spectacular detail. Heavyweight cast aluminum conducts heat extremely evenly and allows for uniquely sculpted shapes you will be proud to serve. Bake in non-stick cast aluminum as you would in any aluminum pan. Cakes and breads rise high and bake evenly. The premium non-stick surface means foods release perfectly and cleanup is a breeze. Lifetime Warranty.

Gift
11⅛ in. x 9⅝ in. x 1½ in. 10 cup capacity; takes 6½ to 7 cups of cake batter.*
2105-S-5027

Perennial
9⅝ in. diameter x 3⅛ in. 10 cup capacity; takes 6½ to 7 cups of cake batter.*
2105-S-5031

Tulip
9½ in. diameter x 4 in. 10 cup capacity; takes 6½ to 7 cups of cake batter.*
2105-S-5032

Crown of Hearts
11 in. wide x 2½ in. 10 cup capacity; takes 6½ to 7 cups of cake batter.*
2105-S-5011

6 Cavity Mini Hearts
Each cavity 4 in. x 2 in. 6 cup capacity; takes 3 to 3½ cups of cake batter.*
2105-S-5012

Queen of Hearts
9 in. diameter x 3¼ in. 10 cup capacity; takes 6½ to 7 cups of cake batter.*
2105-S-5001

Cascade
9½ in. diameter x 4¾ in. 10 cup capacity; takes 6½ to 7 cups of cake batter.*
2105-S-1199

Belle
9 in. diameter x 3¾ in. 10 cup capacity; takes 6½ to 7 cups of cake batter.*
2105-S-1186

Marquise
8¾ in. diameter x 4 in. 10 cup capacity; takes 6½ to 7 cups of cake batter.*
2105-S-1188

*For cakes, fill pans ½ to ⅔ full.

CHECKERBOARD CAKE SET

With this unique baking set, you'll create cakes with an exciting multi-colored pattern—there's style in every slice! Baking is easy with the Batter Dividing Ring included. Just place the Dividing Ring in one of the three 9 x 1½ in. pans in the set and follow instructions for adding dark and light colors of batter in the divisions. Repeat for 2 more layers, pouring the dark and light batters in opposite sections for the middle layer. Use the Dividing Ring's easy-lift handles to lift out ring before baking, then stack cakes to form the checkerboard. Enjoy two tastes in one cake—try the Golden Yellow/Chocolate recipe on the package. Great for colorful holiday cakes, too! Three pans feature oversized handles for safe lifting from the oven; each takes 5½ cups batter. Non-stick steel pans; plastic Dividing Ring.

2105-S-9961 Set/4

Non-Stick Bakeware

Our premium non-stick bakeware combines superior non-stick performance, serving convenience and elegant design, to provide the highest level of baking satisfaction.

- *Oversized handles for safe lifting of the pan*
- *Pan dimensions permanently stamped into handles*
- *Heavy-duty steel construction prevents warping*
- *Durable, reinforced non-stick coating offers superior release and easy cleanup*
- *10-Year Warranty*

CAKE AND PIE PANS

9 x 1½ in. Round Cake
2105-S-408

9 x 9 x 2 in. Square Cake
2105-S-407

11 x 7 x 1½ in. Biscuit/Brownie
2105-S-443

13 x 9 x 2 in. Oblong Cake
2105-S-411

13 x 9 x 2 in. Oblong Cake w/Plastic Cover
2105-S-423

9 x 1½ in. Pie w/Fluted Edges
2105-S-438

2105-S-408

2105-S-411

MUFFIN AND LOAF PANS

6 Cup Regular Muffin
2105-S-405

12 Cup Mini Muffin
2105-S-403

12 Cup Regular Muffin
2105-S-406

Large Loaf
9¼ x 5¼ x 2¾ in.
2105-S-402

4 Cavity Mini Loaf
5¾ x 3 x 2⅛ in.
2105-S-444

2105-S-405

2105-S-402

SPRINGFORM PANS

4 x 1¾ in. Round
2105-S-453

6 x 2¾ in. Round
2105-S-447

9 x 2¾ in. Round
2105-S-414

10 x 2¾ in. Round
2105-S-435

4 x 1¾ in. Heart
2105-S-457

9 x 2¾ in. Heart
2105-S-419

2105-S-435

2105-S-419

COOKIE PANS AND SHEETS

Small Cookie
13¼ x 9¼ x ⅝ in.
2105-S-436

Medium Cookie
15¼ x 10¼ x ¾ in.
2105-S-412

Large Cookie/Jelly Roll
17¼ x 11½ x 1 in.
2105-S-413

Jumbo Air Insulated Sheet
18 x 14 in.
2105-S-422

2105-S-412

2105-S-422

COOLING GRIDS

10 x 16 in.
2305-S-228

14½ x 20 in.
2305-S-229

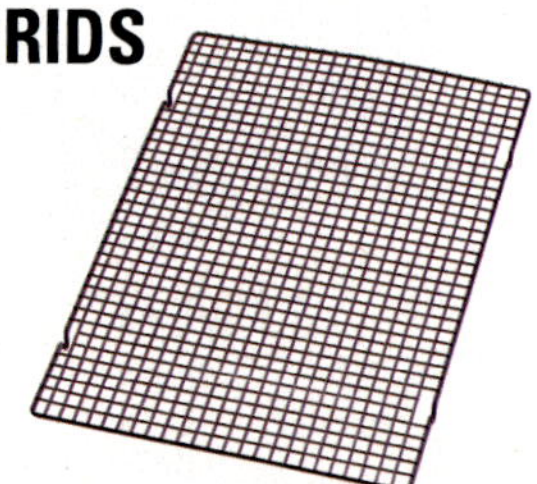

2305-S-228

13 in. Round
2305-S-230

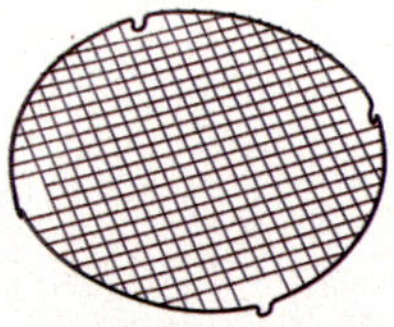

2305-S-230

3-Tier Stackable
15⅞ x 9⅞ in. stackable 3-tier grid.
2105-S-459

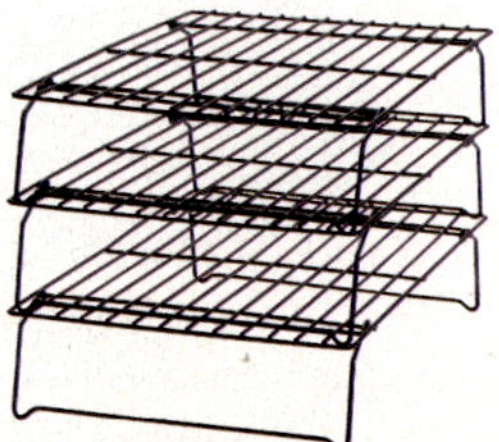

2105-S-459

SPECIALTY PANS

Fluted Tube
9¾ x 3⅜ in.
2105-S-416

6 Cavity Mini Fluted Tube
4⅛ x 2 in.
2105-S-445

Angel Food
9⅜ x 4¼ in.
2105-S-415

14 in. Pizza Crisper
14 x ⅝ in.
2105-S-420

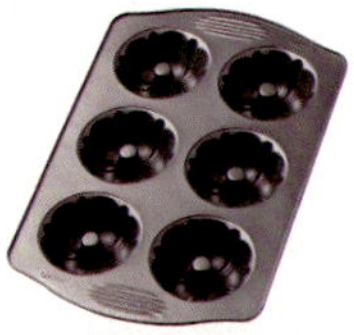

2105-S-445

2105-S-420

TART/QUICHE PANS

9 x 1⅛ in. Round
2105-S-442

11 x 1⅛ in. Round
2105-S-450

10 x 1⅛ in. Heart
2105-S-452

Round 3-Pc. Set
8 x 1⅛ in., 9 x 1⅛ in., and 10 x 1⅛ in.
2105-S-451 Set/3

Brioche 6-Pc. Set
3¼ x 1¼ in.
2105-S-6762 Set/6

Tartlet 6-Pc. Set
4¾ x 1⅞ x ½ in.
2105-S-6761 Set/6

4 in. Tart 4-Pc. Set
4 x ¾ in. with removable bottom.
2105-S-466

4 in. Tart/Quiche 6-Pc. Set
4 x ¾ in. with removable bottom.
2105-S-441

2105-S-450

2105-S-452

2105-S-6762

RATED #1 BY GOOD HOUSEKEEPING!

Decorator Preferred®

Professional Aluminum Bakeware

*Our most popular bakeware—built with the most features to help decorators bake their best. Compare these benefits to any brand and discover why Decorator Preferred was rated #1 by Good Housekeeping.**

*The May 1999 Good Housekeeping Institute Report rates this Wilton Professional Pan #1 out of 31 different 9 in. round pans.

STRAIGHT SIDES

Bake perfect 90° corners for the precise look wedding cakes require. Ordinary bakeware has rounded corners, giving cakes rounded edges.

GRIP LIP EDGES

Extra-wide rims make heavy filled pans easy to handle.

PURE ALUMINUM

The best material for baking cakes—creates a light, golden brown cake surface, beautiful for decorating.

SUPERIOR THICKNESS

Thicker than ordinary bakeware, built to distribute heat evenly for more consistent baking.

HANDCRAFTED CONSTRUCTION

Sheets and squares are handwelded for excellent detail and durability.

LIFETIME WARRANTY

Superior construction and performance designed and guaranteed to last a lifetime.

ROUNDS

What a selection of sizes—including the hard-to find 18 in. Half Round, which lets you bake and ice two halves to create one 18 in. round cake.

6 x 2 in.
2105-S-6122

8 x 2 in.
2105-S-6136

9 x 2 in.
2105-S-6137

10 x 2 in.
2105-S-6138

12 x 2 in.
2105-S-6139

14 x 2 in.
2105-S-6140

16 x 2 in.
2105-S-6141

6 x 3 in.
2105-S-6106

8 x 3 in.
2105-S-6105

10 x 3 in.
2105-S-6104

12 x 3 in.
2105-S-6103

14 x 3 in.
2105-S-6102

16 x 3 in.
2105-S-6101

18 x 3 in.
Half Round
2105-S-6100

3-Pc. Round Set
6, 10 and 14 in. diameter x 3 in. deep.
2105-S-6114
Set/3

HEARTS

Ultimate heart cake is beautiful for showers, weddings, more!

6 x 2 in.
2105-S-600

8 x 2 in.
2105-S-601

10 x 2 in.
2105-S-602

12 x 2 in.
2105-S-607

14 x 2 in.
2105-S-604

16 x 2 in.
2105-S-605

Contour

Create cakes with an elegant, rounded top edge. This is the perfect shape for positioning rolled fondant. 9 x 3 in. deep.
2105-S-6121

Heating Core

Distributes heat to bake large cakes evenly. Recommended for pans 10 in. diameter or larger. Releases easily from cake. 3½ x 3½ x 4 in. diameter.
417-S-6100

SHEETS

Extra-thick aluminum distributes heat efficiently on these large pans.

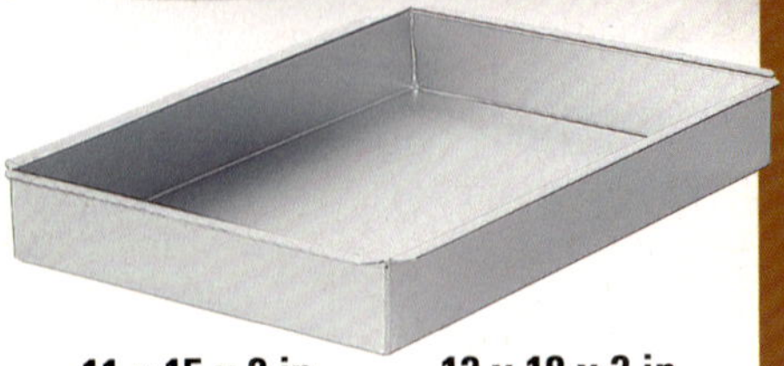

9 x 13 x 2 in.
2105-S-6146

11 x 15 x 2 in.
2105-S-6147

12 x 18 x 2 in.
2105-S-6148

SQUARES

Perfect 90° corners give you the flawless look necessary for wedding tiers.

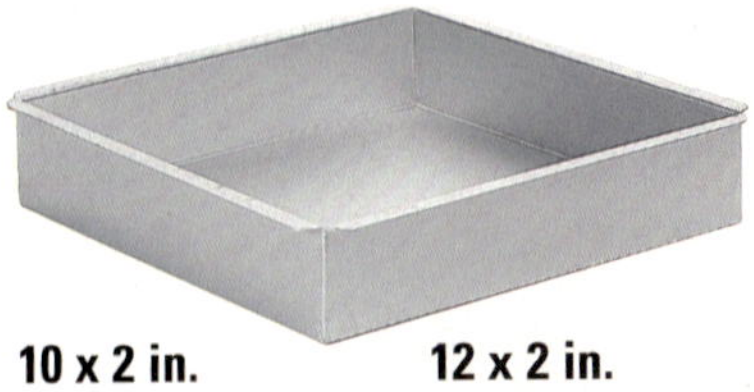

8 x 2 in.
2105-S-6142

10 x 2 in.
2105-S-6143

12 x 2 in.
2105-S-6144

Springform Pans

When shopping for a springform pan, you want strong construction and an easy-release design that will let you remove a perfect cheesecake every time. Wilton springform pans are built tough, with strong springlocks that hold up year after year. The removable waffle-textured bottom design keeps crusts from sticking while distributing heat evenly. Springlock releases sides. Aluminum.

6 x 3 in.
2105-S-4437

8 x 3 in.
2105-S-8464

9 x 3 in.
2105-S-5354

10 x 3 in.
2105-S-8465

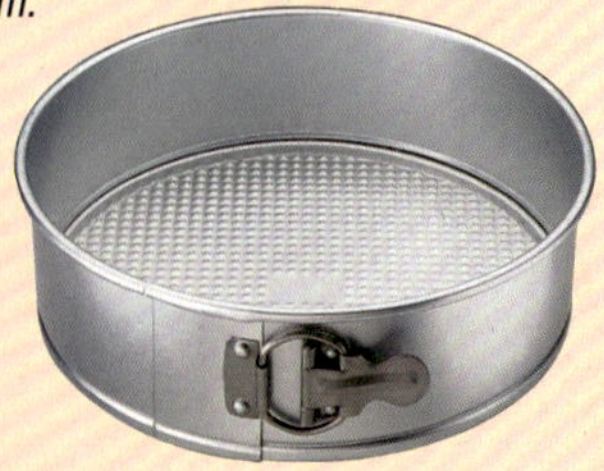

Performance Pans™

The classic aluminum pans—durable, even-heating and built to hold their shape through years of use. We named them Performance Pans because they perform beautifully. These are great all-purpose pans. You'll use them for casseroles, entrees, baked desserts and more. Wilton has sold millions of Performance Pans because decorators and bakers know they can depend on them.

SweetHeart Pan
A gently curving shape gives the classic heart a more romantic flair. Whether you accent it with pretty icing flowers or pair it with bold fondant decorations, this cake will charm guests for birthdays, Mother's Day, Valentine's Day, showers and more. Takes 1 standard mix. 10¼ x 11 x 2 in. Aluminum.
2105-S-1197

SQUARES

6 x 2 in.
507-S-2180

8 x 2 in.
2105-S-8191

10 x 2 in.
2105-S-8205

12 x 2 in.
2105-S-8213

14 x 2 in.
2105-S-8220

16 x 2 in.
2105-S-8231

ROUNDS

6 x 2 in.
2105-S-2185

8 x 2 in.
2105-S-2193

10 x 2 in.
2105-S-2207

12 x 2 in.
2105-S-2215

14 x 2 in.
2105-S-3947

16 x 2 in.
2105-S-3963

2-Pan Round Set
9 x 2 in. deep
2105-S-7908

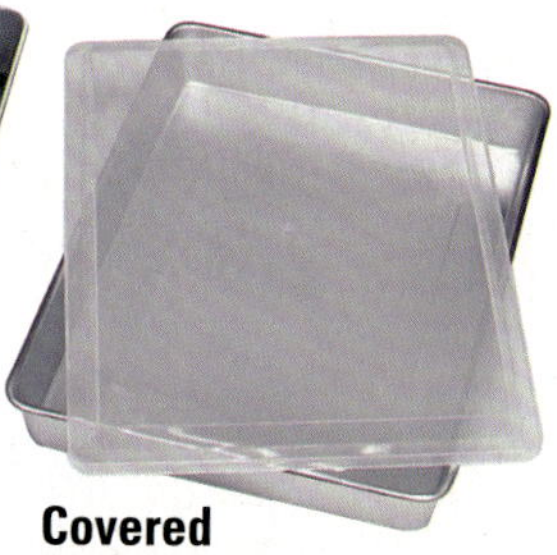

SHEETS

9 x 13 x 2 in.
2105-S-1308

11 x 15 x 2 in.
2105-S-158

12 x 18 x 2 in.
2105-S-182

Covered Baking Pan
Clear, durable cover makes it easy to transport desserts and keep them fresh at home. 11 x 15 x 2 in.
2105-S-3849

PERFORMANCE PANS™ SETS

These are the classic shapes every baker needs. Wilton has them in convenient graduated-size sets, to help you create fabulous tiered cakes or individual cakes in exactly the size you want. Quality aluminum holds its shape for years. Each pan is 2 in. deep, except where noted.

Heart Pan Set
Create the ultimate tiered heart cake—a beautiful way to celebrate showers, weddings and more. Now redesigned for a perfect fit when used with our Decorator Preferred® Heart Separator Plates shown on page 223. Includes 6, 10, 12 and 14 in. pans. Aluminum.
2105-S-606 Set/4

Round Pan Set
Includes 6, 8, 10, 12 in. pans.
2105-S-2101 Set/4

Round Pan Set, 3 in. Deep
Includes 8, 10, 12, 14 in. pans.
2105-S-2932 Set/4

Oval Pan Set
Includes 7¾ x 5⅝ in.; 10¾ x 7⅞ in.; 13½ x 9⅞ in. and 16½ x 12⅜ in. pans.
2105-S-2130 Set/4

Square Pan Set
Includes 8, 12, 16 in. pans.
2105-S-2132 Set/3

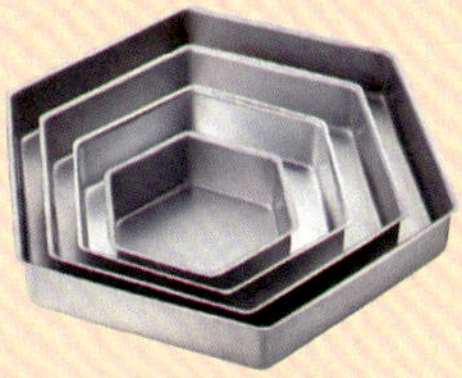

Hexagon Pan Set
Includes 6, 9, 12, 15 in. pans.
2105-S-3572 Set/4

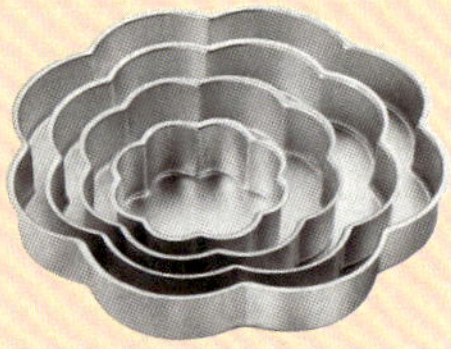

Petal Pan Set
Includes 6, 9, 12, 15 in. pans.
2105-S-2134 Set/4

Specialty Pans

CLASSIC ANGEL FOOD

If you're looking for a healthy dessert, you can't do better than angel food! It's delicious with a simple fresh fruit topping. Removable inner core sleeve, cooling legs. Aluminum.

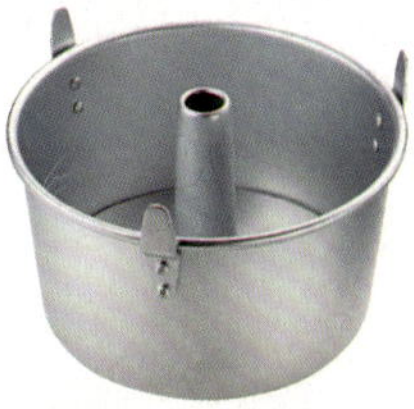

7 x 4½ in. deep
Takes ½ standard mix.
2105-S-9311

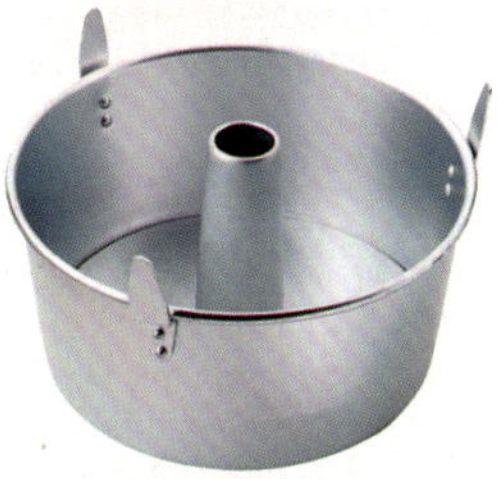

10 x 4 in. deep
Takes 1 standard mix.
2105-S-2525

Fancy Ring Mold
Beautiful sculpted pan, ideal for pound cakes, mousse and more! Takes 1 standard mix. 10 in. diameter x 3 in. Aluminum.
2105-S-5008

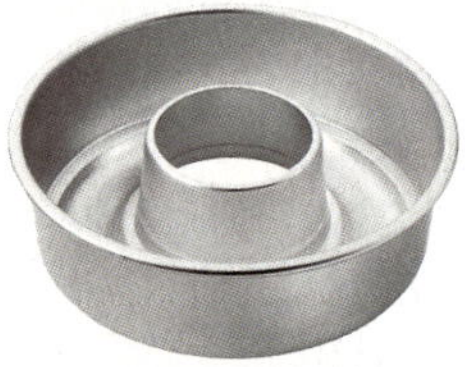

Ring Mold
Turn out spectacular cakes, gelatin molds and more. Takes approx. 1½ standard cake mixes. 10½ x 3 in. Aluminum.
2105-S-4013

Cookie Sheets and Pans

A warped sheet can ruin a batch of cookies. With Wilton Cookie Sheets, you won't worry about warping. The extra-thick aluminum heats evenly for perfectly browned bottoms. Versatile sheets are great for baking appetizers, turnovers and more.

Aluminum
Extra-thick construction heats evenly for perfectly browned bottoms.
Jumbo 14 x 20 in.
2105-S-6213
12½ x 16½ in.
2105-S-2975

Insulated Aluminum
Two quality aluminum layers sandwich an insulating layer of air for perfect browning without burning.
14 x 16 in.
2105-S-2644

Jelly Roll and Cookie Pans
Wilton pans are 1 in. deep for fuller-looking desserts.
10½ x 15½ x 1 in.
2105-S-1269
12 x 18 x 1 in.
2105-S-4854

Muffin Pans

With so many great Wilton muffin pans to choose from, you'll be making muffins —and cupcakes —more often. You'll love our mini pans for the perfect brunch muffins and the jumbo size pan for bakery-style muffins and cupcakes.

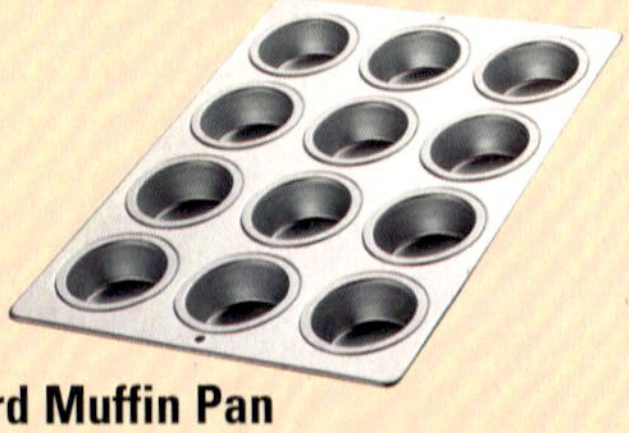

Standard Muffin Pan
Most popular size for morning muffins, after-school cupcakes and desserts. Twelve cups, each 3 in. diameter x 1 in. Aluminum.
2105-S-9310

White Standard Baking Cups **(shown on p. 184)**
Microwave-safe paper. 2 in. diameter.
415-S-2505 Pk./75

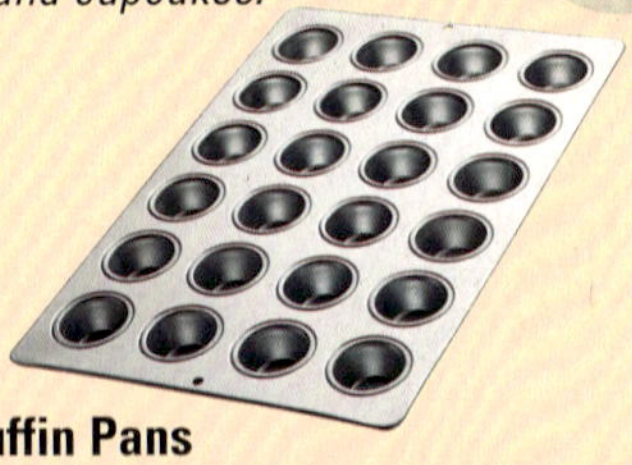

Mini Muffin Pans
Great for mini cheesecakes, brunches, large gatherings. Cups are 2 in. x ¾ in. Aluminum.
12 Cup 2105-S-2125
24 Cup 2105-S-9313

White Mini Baking Cups **(shown on p. 184)**
Microwave-safe paper. 1¼ in. diameter.
415-S-2507 Pk./100

Jumbo Muffin Pan
Make super-size cupcakes and muffins. Six cups, each 4 x 2 in. Aluminum.
2105-S-1820

White Jumbo Baking Cups **(shown on p. 184)**
Microwave-safe paper. 2¼ in. diameter.
415-S-2503 Pk./50

Loaf Pans

It's all in the crust. Wilton Loaf Pans bake bread with hearty, crisp crusts and soft, springy centers. Our superior anodized aluminum promotes better browning, resulting in the perfect texture for all your breads.

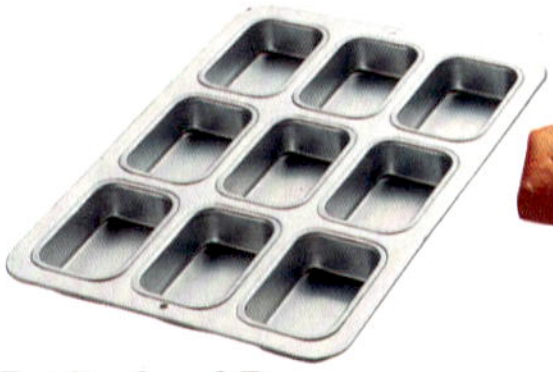

Petite Loaf Pan
Great for single-size dessert cakes, frozen bread dough. Nine cavities, each 2½ x 3⅜ x 1½ in. Aluminum.
2105-S-8466

Mini Loaf Pan
Everyone loves personal-sized nut breads or cakes. Six cavities are 4½ x 2½ x 1½ in. Aluminum.
2105-S-9791

9 x 5 in. Loaf Pan
Favorite size for homemade breads and cakes. 2¾ in. Aluminum.
2105-S-3688

Long Loaf Pan
Legs provide support for cooling angel food cakes, breads or classic cakes. 16 x 4 x 4½ in. deep. Aluminum.
2105-S-1588

Chrome-Plated Cooling Grids

Sturdy design will never rust. Great selection of popular sizes.

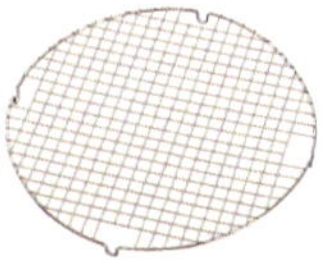

13 in. Round
2305-S-130

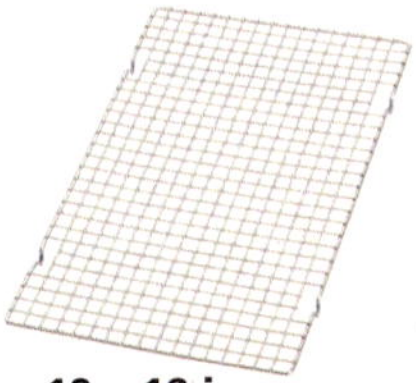

10 x 16 in.
2305-S-128

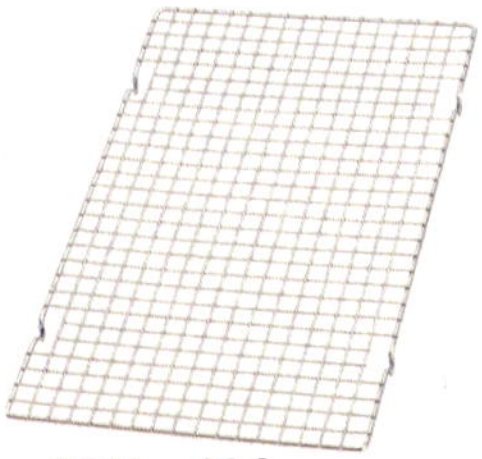

14½ x 20 in.
2305-S-129

3-Tier Stackable
Use singly or stack to save space while cooling three cake layers or batches of cookies at the same time. Individual grids are 13½ x 9¾ x 3 in. high; stacked grids are 9¾ in. high.
2305-S-151

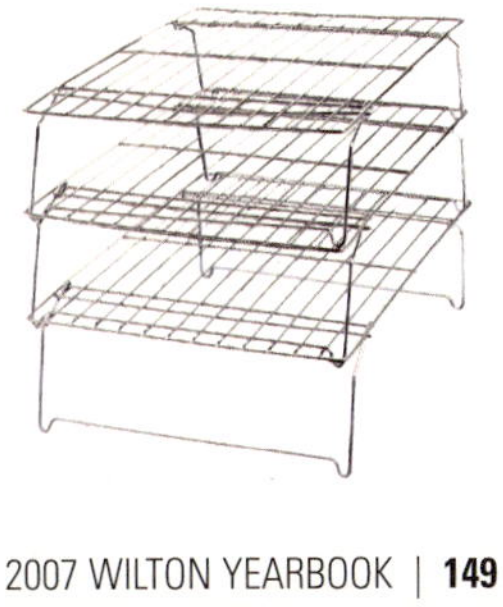

Mini Shaped Pans

Mini Tiered Cakes
One cake mix makes 10-15 mini tiered cakes, perfect for individual wedding, shower and birthday desserts. Six cavity pan is 14 x 10¾ in.; individual cavities are 4 x 4¾ x 1¼ in. deep. Aluminum.
2105-S-3209

Mini Embossed Hearts
One cake mix makes 12-18 mini hearts, beautifully scalloped for weddings, showers and brunches. Six cavity pan is 14 x 10¾ in.; individual cavities are 3½ x 3¼ x 1¼ in. deep. Aluminum.
2105-S-3210

Mini Fluted Mold Pan
One cake mix makes 12-14 mini fluted molds. Six cavity pan is 14¾ x 9¾ in.; individual cavities are 4 x 1¼ in. deep. Aluminum.
2105-S-2097

Mini Bear Pan
One cake mix makes 12-14 mini bears. Six cavity pan is 14½ x 11½ in.; individual cavities are 4⅜ x 4¾ x 1¼ in. deep. Aluminum.
2105-S-4497

Mini Train Pan
One cake mix makes 14-16 mini trains. Six cavity pan is 13¾ x 10½ x 1 in. deep; individual cavities are 4¼ x 3¾ x 1 in. deep. Aluminum.
2105-S-4499

Mini Star Pan
One cake mix makes 12-14 mini stars. Six cavity pan is 14½ x 11 in.; individual cavities are 4¾ x 1¼ in. deep. Aluminum.
2105-S-1235

Wonder Mold Pans

Mini Wonder Mold
Use with Mini Doll Picks for a quartet of party treats. Great with the Wilton Classic Wonder Mold (at right) for a color-coordinated bridal party centerpiece. One cake mix makes 4 to 6 cakes. Pan is 10 x 10 x 3 in. deep. Individual cakes are 3½ x 3 in. Aluminum.
2105-S-3020

Mini Doll Picks
4¼ in. high with pick.
1511-S-1019
Pk./4

Classic Wonder Mold
Creates an elegant 3-D shape for decorating fabulous dress designs. Use with our Teen Doll Pick to make the doll of your dreams. Pan is 8 in. diameter and 5 in. deep; takes 5–6 cups of firm-textured batter. Heat-conducting rod assures even baking. Kit contains pan, rod, stand, 7 in. brunette doll pick and instructions. Aluminum/plastic.
2105-S-565

Teen Doll Pick
Her hair and face are prettier than ever to give your Wonder Mold cakes a realism and sophistication unlike anything you've seen.
7¼ in. high with pick.

Brunette
2815-S-101
Blond
2815-S-102

Ethnic Doll Pick
Beautiful face for realistic doll cakes.
7¾ in. high with pick.
2815-S-103

Novelty Shaped Pans

NEW!

Friendly Lion Pan

He'll be the pride of all your celebrations! Kids will just love this furry, adorable creature for birthdays, school parties and special events. He's sure to please animal-lovers of all ages. One-mix pan is 12¾ x 10¾ x 2 in. deep. Aluminum.

2105-S-1012

NEW!

Tropical Fish Pan

Everyone at the party will be hooked by this fish! Catch it at kids' celebrations and school events—it's a great cake for that special fisherman's birthday. It's a keeper! One-mix pan is 12½ x 11½ x 2 in. deep. Aluminum.

2105-S-1014

NEW!

Palm Tree Pan

With this easy-to-decorate shape, you'll have your party dessert made in the shade! Whether you're celebrating a summer birthday, a retirement or a bon voyage, the Palm Tree pan is the perfect spot for colorful cakes, molded gelatin, rice cereal treats and more. One-mix pan is 14¼ x 12 x 2 in. deep. Aluminum.

2105-S-1013

NEW!

Pineapple Pan

You can almost feel the soft, tropical winds blowing and hear island music playing when you bring this festive treat to the table. Great for backyard luaus, barbeques and pool parties. Try it with gelatin salads, pineapple upside-down cake and more. One-mix pan is 14¾ x 8¼ x 2 in. deep. Aluminum.

2105-S-1018

NEW!

Dancing Daisy Flower Pan

One perfect flower makes bunches of great desserts! It's a big, bouncy blossom that's the perfect shape for cakes, molded gelatin and ice cream, brunch breads and more. Pick this daisy for Mother's Day, wedding showers and birthdays for any garden-lover. One-mix pan is 12 x 12 x 2 in. deep. Aluminum.

2105-S-1016

NEW!

Crown Pan

Treat your little princess (or prince) like royalty at their next celebration! This majestic crown cake is a fun way to honor both kids and adults alike—perfect for birthdays, school parties, Mother's and Father's Day, more! One-mix pan is 14¼ x 10½ x 2 in. deep. Aluminum.

2105-S-1015

Topsy Turvy Pan

Our topsy turvy "tiered" cake is just the right look for wacky birthdays, wild parties or special occasions. One-mix pan is 10¼ x 12 x 2 in. deep. Aluminum.

2105-S-4946

NEW!

Ribbon Pan

If there's a cause dear to your heart, bring it some attention with a bright ribbon cake or molded dessert. What a fitting way to demonstrate your support. Decorate in the colors to highlight your special cause for charity events, school activities or school fundraisers. One-mix pan is 15¼ x 9 x 2 in. deep. Aluminum.

2105-S-1017

Novelty Shaped Pans

Lady Bug Pan

These critters are so cute, you'll want them dropping in at all your celebrations. It's a pan that adapts to any environment—try it as a birthday bee, a Valentine love bug or even a friendly fly for that special gardener in your life. One-mix pan is 12 x 10 x 2 in. deep. Aluminum.
2105-S-3316

Animal Crackers Pan

Make a zoo full of fun animals with this versatile pan! Pick your favorite from the menagerie of critters on the box—pig, cat, giraffe or panda bear—or create a furry face of your own. One-mix pan is 10¾ x 9¼ x 2 in. deep. Aluminum.
2105-S-4945

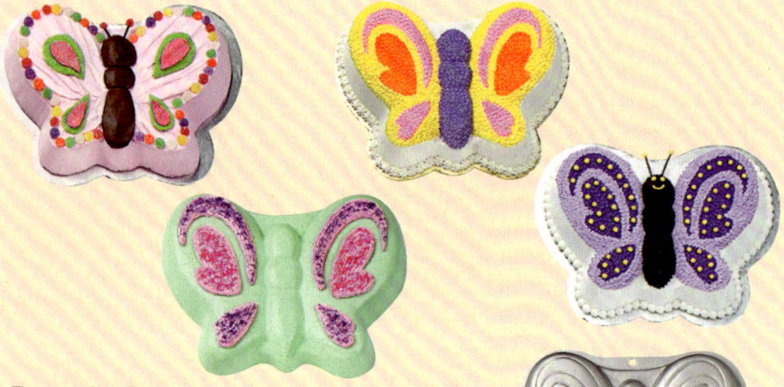

Butterfly Pan

A butterfly cake or molded salad is the perfect way to captivate! Go wild with fun colors. One-mix pan is 11 x 8½ x 2 in. deep. Aluminum.
2105-S-2079

Partysaurus Pan

Our prehistoric party animal is a must-have at all sorts of fun fests—a kid's birthday favorite. One-mix pan is 16 x 10 x 1⅞ in. deep. Aluminum.
2105-S-1280

Baby Buggy Pan

These wheels will bring squeals of delight from shower and christening guests. It's a precious carriage design fit for royalty and ready to dress up for colorful cakes or elegant salads and gelatins. One-mix pan is 11¼ x 11¼ x 2 in. deep. Aluminum.
2105-S-3319

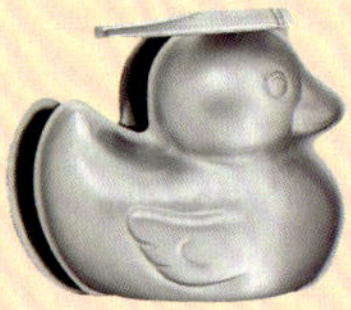

3-D Rubber Ducky Pan

This bathtime favorite will make the biggest splash for birthdays, baby showers and school celebrations. Five adorable designs included. Two-piece pan takes 5½ cups batter, 9 x 5 x 7 in. high. Aluminum.
2105-S-2094

One-Mix Book Pan

This open book details life's important chapters—birthdays, baby showers, graduations and more. Five ways to decorate included. 13 x 9½ x 2 in. deep. Aluminum.
2105-S-972

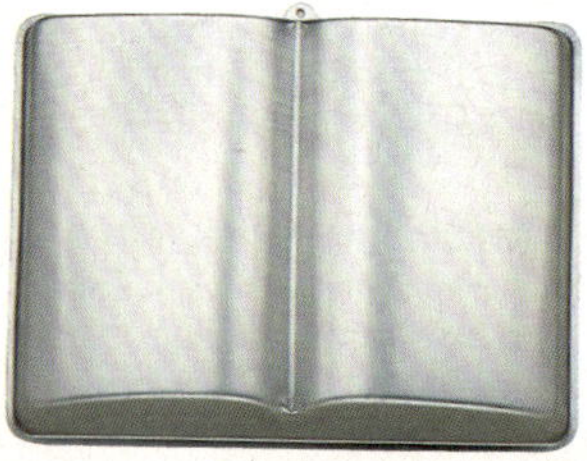

Two-Mix Book Pan

Serves up to 30. 15 x 11½ x 2¾ in. deep. Aluminum.
2105-S-2521

Novelty Shaped Pans

Party Hat Pan
When you put on this party hat, you know you're headed for fun! Customize cakes with your favorite colors and fun designs—ideal for molded desserts and salads too. What a great way to cap off any celebration, from birthdays to that New Year's Eve bash! One-mix pan is 10 x 13½ x 2 in. deep. Aluminum.
2105-S-3317

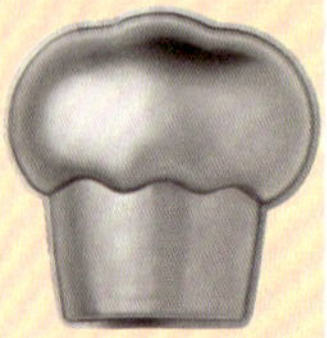

Cupcake Pan
Here's a "cupcake" cake that's big enough for the whole crowd to eat. Bake and decorate it to look like your favorite party cupcake—only bigger! Create endless color and flavor combinations, including the luscious Chocolate Supreme design on the label. One-mix pan is 9¾ x 9½ x 2 in. deep. Aluminum.
2105-S-3318

Ice Cream Cone Pan
You'll find room for this cone at any celebration, from birthdays to backyard barbecues. Like a real ice cream cone, create endless flavor and color combinations. One-mix pan is 13¾ x 9¼ x 2 in. deep. Aluminum.
2105-S-2087

Stand-Up House Pan
A delightful "welcome home". haunted houses, Easter hutches, Christmas cottages, school houses and dog houses are a few ideas for this pan. Cakes can stand up or lay flat. One-mix pan is 9 x 3 x 8¾ in. high. Aluminum.
2105-S-2070

Enchanted Castle Pan
Royal treat for little girls' birthdays or any event. Wonderful for molded sugar or ice cream. One-mix pan is 11½ x 11¾ x 2 in. deep. Aluminum.
2105-S-2031

Huggable Teddy Bear Pan
This classic never hibernates! From birthdays to baby showers to school parties, he's used all year. One-mix pan is 13½ x 12¼ x 2 in. deep. Aluminum.
2105-S-4943

Mini Stand-Up Bear Pan Set
Includes baking stand, four clips and instructions. Two-piece pan takes 1 cup of batter; standard pound cake mix makes about 4 cakes. Assembled cakes are 4 x 3¼ x 4¾ in. high. Aluminum.
2105-S-489 Set/8

Stand-Up Cuddly Bear Set
Five decorating ideas on the box! Two-piece pan takes 6⅔ cups of firm textured batter. Includes 6 clips, heat-conducting core and instructions. Pan is 9 x 6¾ x 8⅝ in. high. Aluminum.
2105-S-603 Set/10

Novelty Shaped Pans

Star Pan

Brighten birthdays, opening nights, even law enforcement occasions. One-mix pan is 12¾ x 12¾ x 1⅞ in. deep. Aluminum.
2105-S-2512

Over The Hill Tombstone Pan

Optimistically mark the passing of one more year. One-mix pan is 13 x 9¼ x 2 in. deep. Aluminum.
2105-S-1237

Horseshoe Pan

Say "good luck" at birthdays, graduations, bon voyage parties! One-mix pan is 11½ x 12 x 1¾ in. deep. Aluminum.
2105-S-3254

Guitar Pan

Whatever your musical choice, a guitar cake sets the tone for fun at your next party! Celebrate school band concerts, kid and adult birthdays! One-mix pan is 16½ x 8½ x 2 in. deep. Aluminum.
2105-S-570

Little Hero Pan

Bring their favorite figures to life! One-mix pan is 13¼ x 6½ x 2 in. deep. Aluminum.
2105-S-2077

Little Pirate Pan

Cute pirate-in-training design is easy to transform into just about any character. One-mix pan is 9 in. x 14¼ in. x 2 in. deep. Aluminum.
2105-S-2078

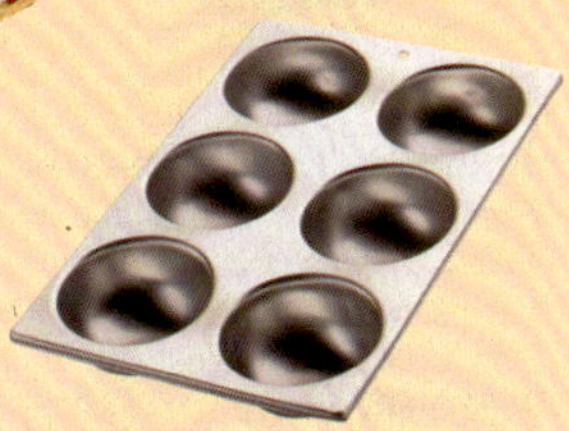

Mini Ball Pan

Ice two mini balls and push together for a 3-D effect. One cake mix makes 10–12 mini balls. Six cavities, each 3½ x 3½ x 1½ in. deep. Aluminum.
2105-S-1760

First and Ten Football Pan

Touching down at Super Bowl parties, homecomings, award dinners and much more. One-mix pan is 12 x 7¾ x 3 in. deep. Aluminum.
2105-S-6504

Novelty Shaped Pans

Train Pan
Load with delicious cargo! One-mix pan is 14 x 7¼ x 2 in. deep. Aluminum.
2105-S-2076

Choo-Choo Train Pan Set
Two-piece pan snaps together to create a cake 10 x 4 x 6 in. high. Takes 6 cups batter. Aluminum.
2105-S-2861 Set/2

3-D Cruiser Pan
Bake exciting 3-D cakes, ready to customize for all occasions. One-mix pan is 11 x 6¾ x 4 in. deep. Aluminum.
2105-S-2043

Race Car Pan
Customize it with your favorite colors and racing team identification. One-mix pan is 12½ x 9½ x 2 in. deep. Aluminum.
2105-S-1350

Tractor Pan
Down on the farm has never been so much fun. One-mix pan is 13½ x 9½ x 2 in. deep. Aluminum.
2105-S-2063

Firetruck Pan
When the occasion calls for a five-alarm celebration. One-mix pan is 15½ x 8½ x 2 in. deep. Aluminum.
2105-S-2061

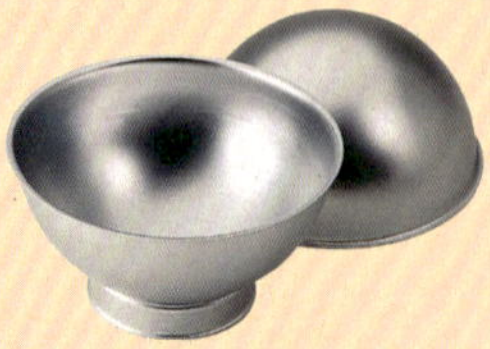

Sports Ball Pan Set
Use this four-piece set to create a perfect sports cake centerpiece. Includes two 6 in. diameter half-ball pans and two metal baking stands. Each pan half takes 2½ cups batter. Aluminum.
2105-S-6506 Set/4

Soccer Ball Pan
A great way to reward a season or a game well done! One-mix pan is 8¾ x 8¾ x 3½ in. deep. Aluminum.
2105-S-2044

Cookie Making

Wilton has just what you need to make cookies fun! Easy-to-use presses, colossal cutter sets, fun stencils, colorful icings and unique toppings sure to create unforgettable cookies!

Cookie Presses

Wilton has four great ways to press cookies—the best selection of feature-packed presses anywhere! From our Comfort Grip™ Press, designed for easy handling and filling, to our powerful cordless Cookie Master™ Plus, spritz cookie-making has never been easier!

Cookie Pro™ ULTRA II

Deluxe Cookie Press

Making traditional spritz cookies has never been so easy! Cookie Pro™ Ultra II is designed to be the easiest to fill, most comfortable press you've ever used. And, with 16 terrific shapes, including 4 fun mini cookie designs, your holiday cookie baskets will be more festive than ever! Includes complete instructions and delicious recipes.
2104-S-4018 Set/17

Twelve Disks in Festive Shapes

Plus 4 BONUS Disks For Mini Cookies!

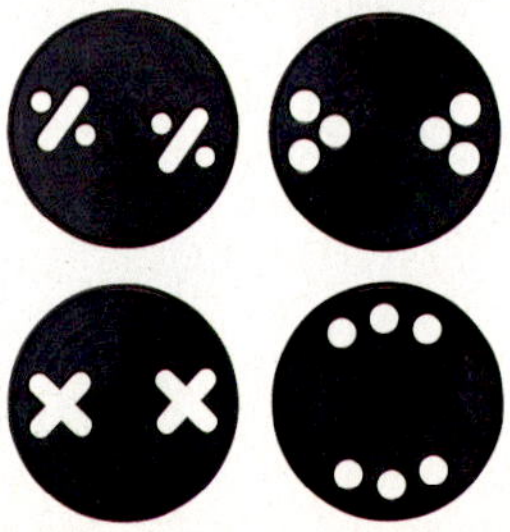

- **Arrow pointed toward the handle means press is in proper position.**
- **Soft-grip trigger for comfortable pressing, batch after batch.**
- **Ergonomic barrel designed for outstanding comfort and control.**
- **See-through barrel lets you know when to refill with dough.**
- **Non-slip bottom ring keeps press securely on cookie sheet for evenly shaped cookies.**
- **Twist-off ring with Finger Grips makes changing disks a breeze.**
- **12 full-sized shaping disks in favorite basic and holiday shapes.**
- **Plus 4 BONUS mini shaping disks for making fun bite-sized cookies.**

NEW!

COOKIE MASTER™ Plus
Cordless Cookie Press

Distinctive Cookies

Snacks & Appetizers

Desserts & More!

Our cordless cookie press is so powerful and easy to operate, you'll use it all year to create cookies, appetizers, desserts and more. Exclusive patented reverse action means there's no need to take press apart for refilling. Ergonomic design is shaped to fit in your hand for excellent comfort.

Includes 12 aluminum disks in classic and seasonal shapes, 4 accent tips for decorating and filling and 2 bonus recipe booklets—sweet and savory. Uses 4 AA batteries, not included.
2104-S-4008 Set/19

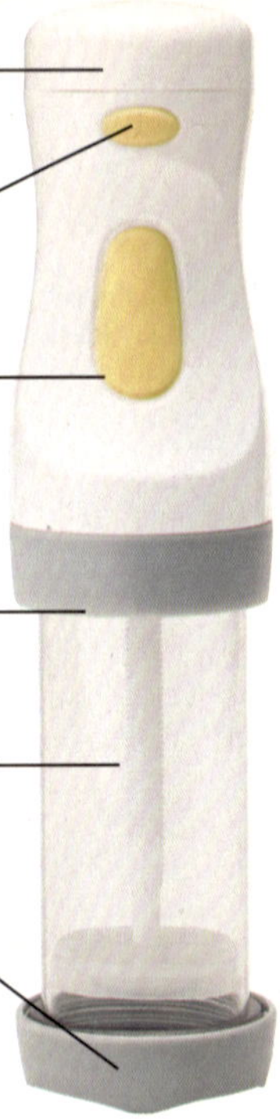

Cordless, Battery Operated
No cord means no need to be near an outlet.

Patented Reverse Action
No need to take press apart to refill—just press a button.

Ergonomic Design
Shaped to fit your hand for excellent comfort and ease of use. Sealed buttons keep food out.

Unique Dough Guard™
Keeps the dough away from the motor.

See-Through Barrel
Check progress and see how much dough is left.

Fluted Bottom
Raises press off of the cookie sheet for well-formed designs.

Twelve Disk Designs

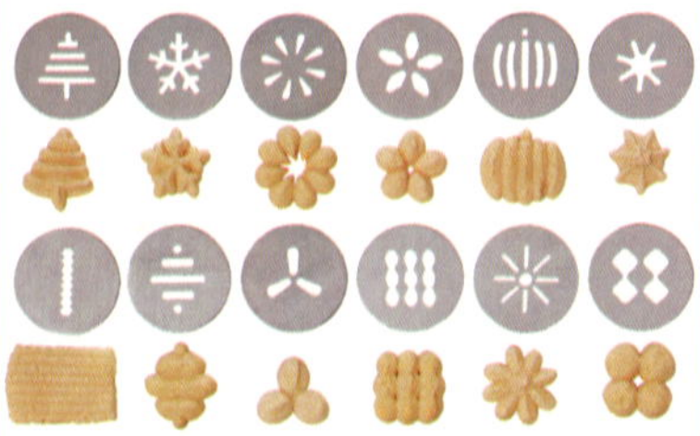

Twelve aluminum disks in classic & seasonal shapes let you create distinctive snacks, appetizers, cookies, desserts and pastries.

Four Accent Tips

Four multi-purpose accent tips make it easy to fill pastries, garnish appetizers and decorate elegant desserts.

cookie max™ cookie press

Discover the cookie press that takes convenience and comfort to the max! With the Cookie Max™, you'll see the difference from the first batch. An easy pump action gives you more control—one click of the plunger equals one perfect cookie, every time. The handle is cushioned for a sure, comfortable grip. The see-through barrel and raised bottom let you see the cookie and your remaining dough as you press. No clogging, easy cleaning.

Includes 12 plastic disks in favorite shapes, easy instructions and 3 delicious recipes.
2104-S-4003 Set/13

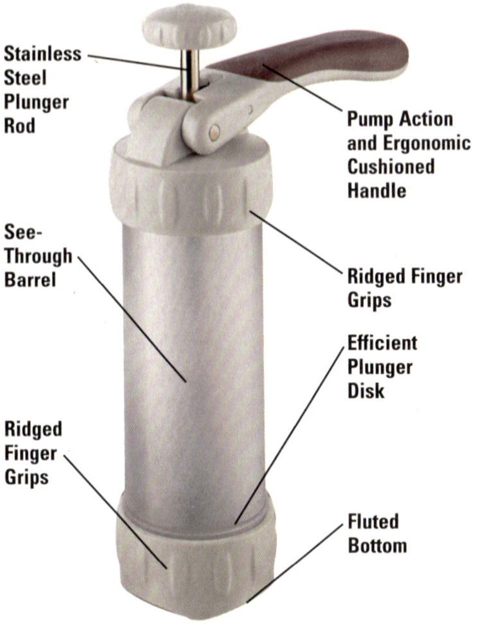

Twelve Disk Designs

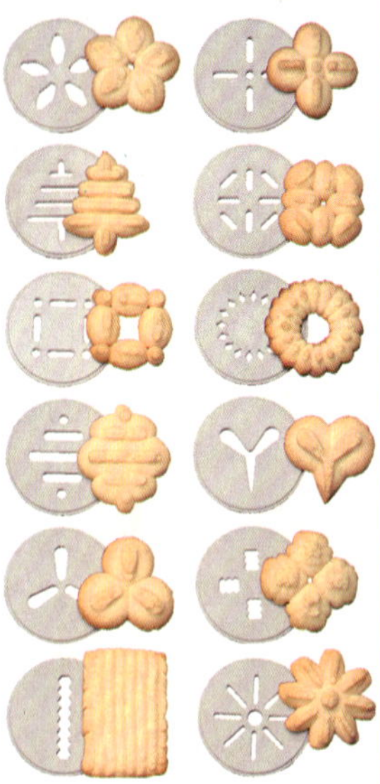

COMFORT GRIP™ Cookie Press

Experience a classic press that is truly comfortable. Its ergonomic handle feels great in any hand—the easy-squeeze action releases perfectly shaped dough. The clear barrel takes the guesswork out of refilling. Fluted bottom raises the press off the cookie sheet to help you create better shapes.

Includes 12 plastic disks in a variety of shapes plus our classic spritz recipe.
2104-S-4011 Set/13

Twelve Disk Designs

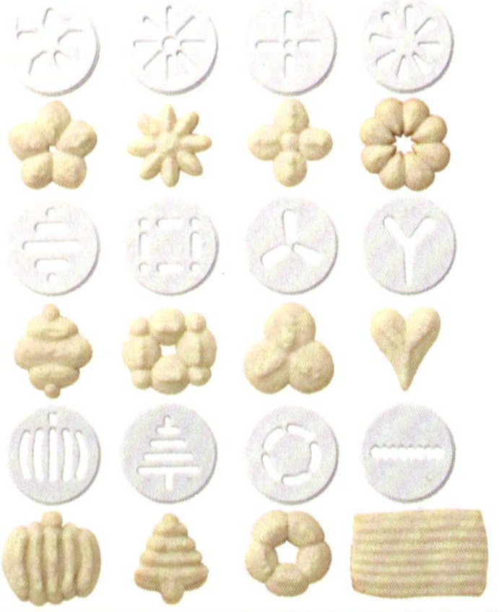

Cookie Cutters

These versatile designs are sure to spark your creativity!

COMFORT GRIP™ CUTTERS

Easy-grip stainless steel cutters with extra-deep sides are perfect for cutting so many favorite foods into spectacular shapes. Ideal for brownies, biscuits, sandwiches, sheet cakes, cheese, crispy rice treats, fudge and much more. The cushion grip gives you comfortable control even when cutting into thick desserts. Recipe included. Each approximately 4 x 4 x 1¾ in. **Each**

Round
2310-S-608

Star
2310-S-605

Teddy Bear
2310-S-609

Heart
2310-S-616

Butterfly
2310-S-614

Flower
2310-S-613

Daisy
2310-S-619

METAL CUTTER SETS

Multi-piece sets add variety. Built to last, they cut cleanly and release easily. Recipe included.

Basic

Geometric, crinkle diamond, heart, half moon, star and flower. Each approx. 3 in.
2308-S-1235
Set/6

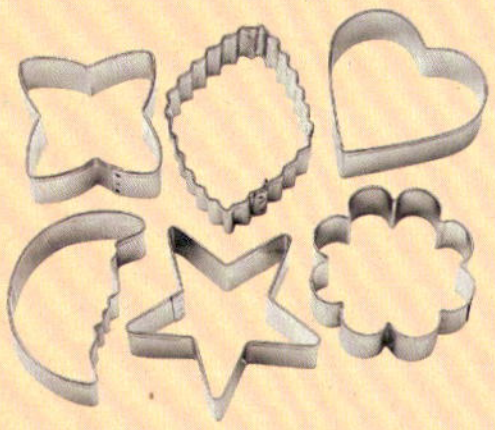

Animals

Horse, dove, lion, duck, pig and cat. Each approx. 3 in.
2308-S-1236
Set/6

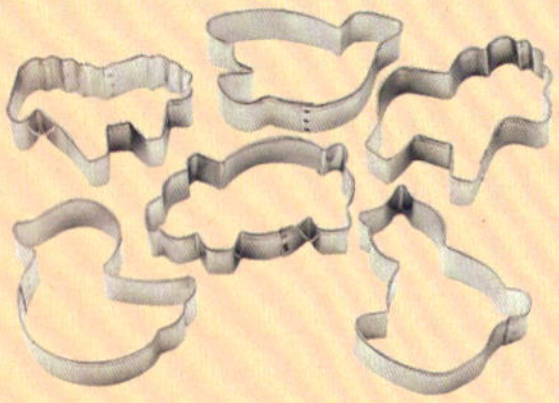

Hearts

Seven different heart cutter designs from stylized to traditional. Sizes range from 1½ to 3 in.
2308-S-1237
Set/7

Bug Buddies

Butterfly, caterpillar, bee, ladybug, dragonfly and spider. Each approx. 3 in.
2308-S-1245 Set/6

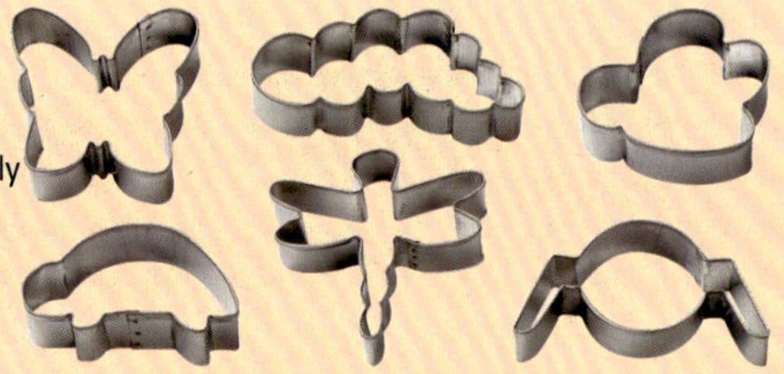

Nesting From The Heart

Two crinkled and two smooth. Largest is approx. 5 in.
2308-S-1203
Set/4

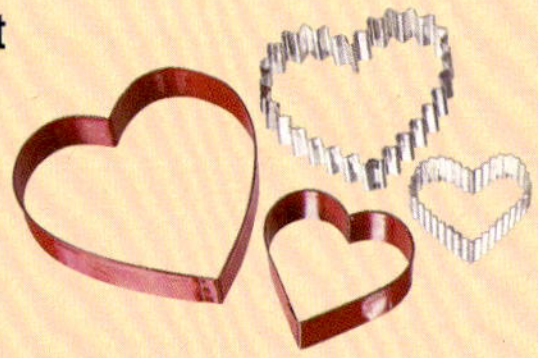

Nesting Stars

For holidays and more! Largest is approx. 5 in.
2308-S-1215
Set/4

Nesting Blossoms

Pretty flowers in four sizes. Largest is approx. 5 in.
2308-S-1204
Set/4

Mini Romantic

Butterfly, heart, bell, crinkled heart, tulip, and blossom. Each approx. 1½ in.
2308-S-1225
Set/6

Mini Noah's Ark

Horse, ark, elephant, bear, giraffe and lion. Each approx. 1½ in.
2308-S-1206
Set/6

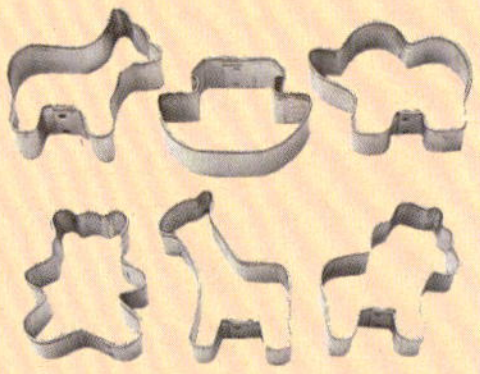

Mini Geometric Crinkle

Square, circle, heart, diamond, oval and triangle. Each approx. 1½ in.
2308-S-1205
Set/6

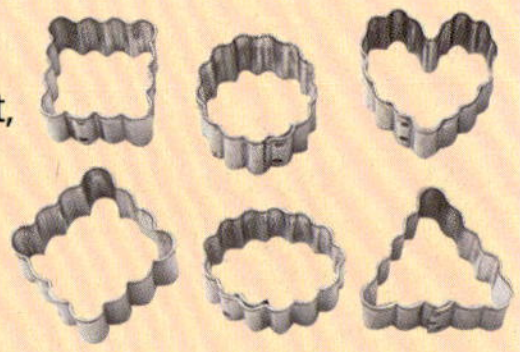

METAL CUTTERS

The classic metal cutter was Grandma's favorite but she never had all these fun shapes! Metal cutters from Wilton are built to last through years of cookie making; they cut cleanly and release with ease. Each shape is approximately 3 in.

Star
2308-S-1008

Gingerbread Boy
2308-S-1002

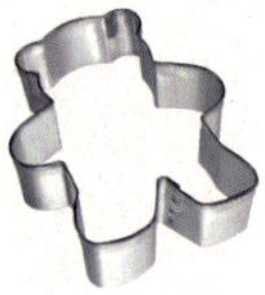

Bear
2308-S-1009

Heart
2308-S-1003

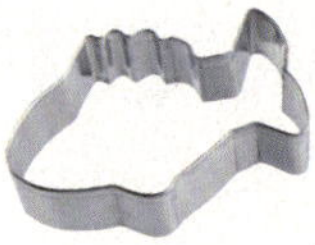

Fish
2308-S-1017

Cross
2308-S-1018

Daisy
2308-S-1007

Acorn
2308-S-1020

Maple Leaf
2308-S-1021

Oak Leaf
2308-S-1013

Butterfly
2308-S-1015

Chick
2308-S-1000

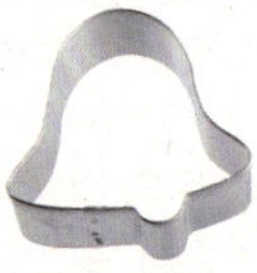

Bell
2308-S-1006

Circle
2308-S-1010

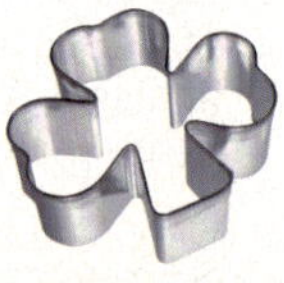

Shamrock
2308-S-1011

SOLID COPPER CUTTERS

The warmth and beauty of copper make these cutters ideal for displaying and adding that decorative touch to your kitchen after baking cookies. These beautiful, heirloom-quality copper cutters have smoothly rolled edges for that finishing touch. Each approximately 5½ in. across.

Star
2308-S-3002

Heart
2308-S-3040

WHITE COOKIE ICING

NEW!

Use this quick-setting microwavable icing to cover your cookies with a shiny finish—perfect for decorating with colorful Wilton Icing Writer™ accents! Easy to use—just heat and squeeze onto cookies using the convenient cap. Sets smooth in just 45 minutes. 10 oz. bottle covers 24 (3 in.) cookies. Certified Kosher.
704-S-481

FoodWriter™ Edible Color Markers

Use like ink markers to add fun and dazzling color to countless foods. Kids love 'em! Decorate on cookies, fondant, color flow and royal icing designs. Brighten everyday foods like toaster pastries, cheese, fruit slices, bread and more. Each set includes five .35 oz. FoodWriter pens. Certified Kosher.

PRIMARY COLORS SETS

Yellow | Green | Red | Blue | Black

Fine Tip
609-S-100
Set/5

Bold Tip
609-S-115
Set/5

NEON COLORS SET

Purple | Orange | Pink | Light Green | Black

Fine Tip
609-S-116
Set/5

STENCIL-A-COOKIE™ CUTTER & STENCIL SETS

Using the fun-shaped cutter and stencil, it's easy to serve cookies with exciting, colorful designs. Just cut cookies, then use the stencil and Wilton FoodWriter™, Cake Sparkles™, Colored Sugars or Color Mist™ Food Color Spray (each sold separately) to create dazzling shapes on top after baking. Cookies look great iced with Wilton Cookie Icing sold above. Set includes one metal cutter and two stencils (same design). Each shape approximately 4 x 4 in.
Set/3

Heart
2308-S-1401

Butterfly
2308-S-1402

Flower
2308-S-1403

Star
2308-S-1405

PLASTIC CUTTER SETS

101 Cookie Cutters!

With this set, you're covered! Make cookies featuring popular holiday and theme shapes like sports, flowers, animals and more. Or use the complete alphabet and numeral collections included to create the perfect cookie message. Great for cutting all kinds of food into fun shapes—perfect for crafting, too. Average cutter size approx. 3½ x 3½ in. Recipe included.
2304-S-1000 Set/101

A-B-C and 1-2-3 50-Pc. Cutter Set

Complete alphabet and numeral collection, great for cookies, brownies, gelatin treats, learning games, crafts and more. Average cutter size approx. 3½ x 3½ in. Recipe included.
2304-S-1054
Set/50

Animal Pals 50-Pc. Cutter Set

Everyone will go wild for cookies, foods and crafts made with this menagerie of favorite animal shapes. Shapes include fish, dog, cat, birds, butterflies, reptiles and more. Average cutter size approx. 3½ x 3½ in. Recipe included.
2304-S-1055
Set/50

PLASTIC CUTTERS

With our large variety of brightly-colored cutter shapes, the making is as much fun as the eating! Child-safe design means kids can help.

Each approx. 3 in. x 4 in.

Fish 2303-S-128 | **Dinosaur** 2303-S-112 | **Teddy Bear** 2303-S-133 | **Butterfly** 2303-S-116 | **Puppy** 2303-S-137

Star 2303-S-135 | **Hand** 2303-S-147 | **Foot** 2303-S-113 | **Girl** 2303-S-120 | **Boy** 2303-S-124 | **Dog Bone** 2303-S-123

Locomotive Engine 2303-S-139 | **6 Pt. Star** 2303-S-122 | **Heart** 2303-S-100 | **Cat** 2303-S-118 | **Duck** 2303-S-148

Cross 2303-S-141 | **Ice Cream Cone** 2303-S-111 | **Sailboat** 2303-S-129 | **Airplane** 2303-S-101 | **Flower** 2303-S-117 | **Four-Leaf Clover** 2303-S-134

PLASTIC NESTING CUTTER SETS

Your favorites in child-safe, graduated shapes. Discover all the fun ways to use our cutters—for bread shapes, stencils, sun catchers and so much more.

Teddy Bear

From cub to grizzly size! 1¾ to 6⅜ in. tall.
2304-S-1520
Set/4

Blossom

Create pretty blooms with plastic cutters in sizes from 1⅛ to 4½ in.
2304-S-116
Set/6

Heart

Great for tracing valentines! 1½ to 4⅛ in.
2304-S-115
Set/6

Star

For crafts, cookies or patterns in your iced cake. 1⅝ to 4⅝ in.
2304-S-111
Set/6

Cookie Bakeware and Accessories

COOKIE TREAT PANS

Cookie treats on a stick are so easy! Just press cookie dough into pan, insert a cookie stick, then bake, cool and decorate. Create your own cookie blossoms for that special someone; also great for rice cereal treats and candy.

Recipe included. Each pan makes 6 individual treats, 3½ in. x ¼ in. deep. Aluminum.

Star
2105-S-8102

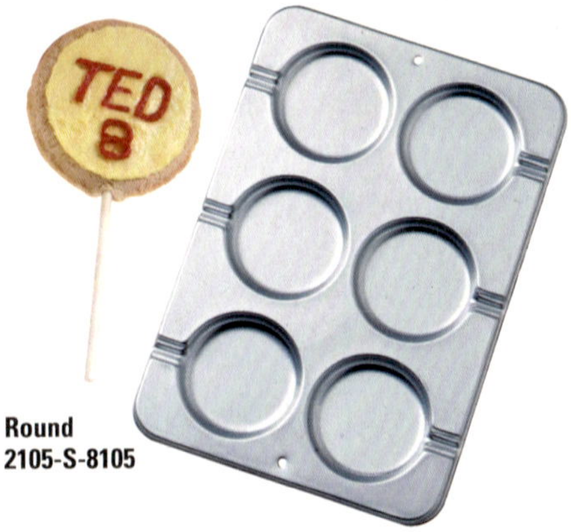

Round
2105-S-8105

Blossom
2105-S-8109

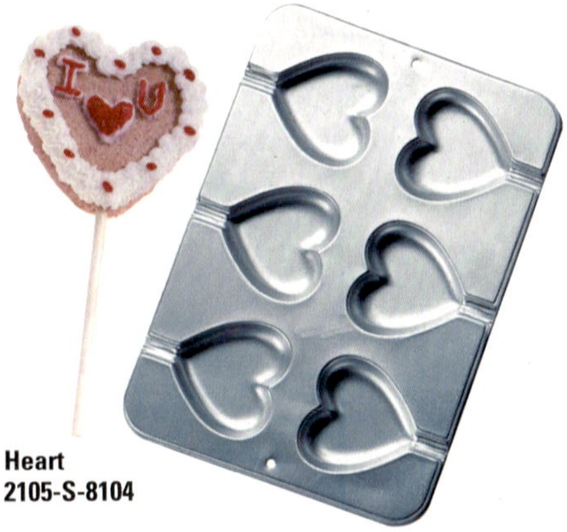

Heart
2105-S-8104

Cookie Treat Sticks

For fun cookie pops.

6 in. 1912-S-9319
Pk./20

8 in. 1912-S-9318
Pk./20

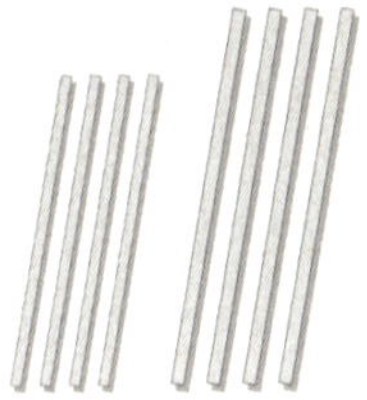

Clear Party Bags

4 x 9½ in. Each pack contains 25 bags and 25 ties.
1912-S-1240
Pk./25

GIANT COOKIE PANS

Our Giant Cookie Pans help you create a jumbo pan cookie in a shape that will be a big hit for any occasion. Specially designed for one package of refrigerated dough, they are also great for brownies and pizza!

Each shape is approximately ¾ in. deep and can be used with recipes that call for a standard 13 x 9 in. pan. Aluminum.

Round
2105-S-6201

Heart
2105-S-6203

COOKIE SHEETS

Wilton Cookie Sheets are extra thick aluminum to heat evenly for perfect, evenly-browned bottoms.

Aluminum

Extra-thick construction.

Jumbo 14 x 20 in.
2105-S-6213

12½ x 16½ in.
2105-S-2975

Insulated Aluminum

Two quality aluminum layers sandwich an insulating layer of air for perfect browning without burning.

16 x 14 in.
2105-S-2644

COOLING GRIDS

Chrome-Plated

Sturdy design will never rust.

13 in. Round
2305-S-130

10 x 16 in.
2305-S-128

14½ x 20 in.
2305-S-129

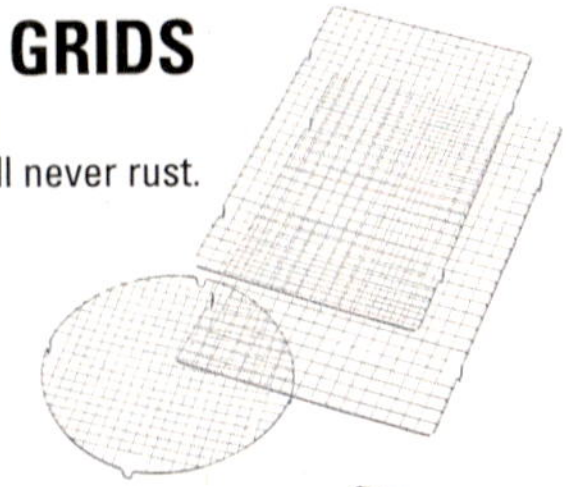

Non-Stick

Cookies and cakes won't stick with our slick non-stick coating.

13 in. Round
2305-S-230

10 x 16 in.
2305-S-228

14½ x 20 in.
2305-S-229

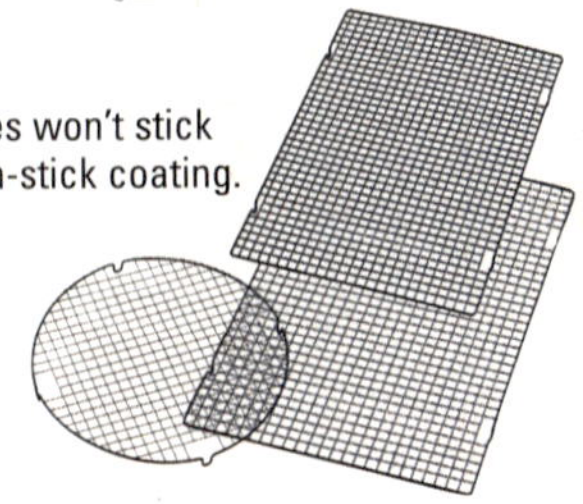

3-Pc. Stackable Chrome-Plated

Use singly or stack to save space while cooling three batches of cookies at the same time. Individual grids are 13½ x 9¾ x 3 in. high; stacked grids are 9¾ in. high.
2305-S-151

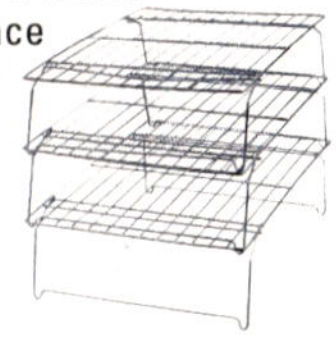

See p. 144-155 for the full line of Wilton Bakeware.

NEW!

COOKIE SPATULA

Angled stainless steel blade and smooth ergonomic handle with thumb rest—moves cookies from pan to plate with ease. Great for brownies and bar cookies, too. **409-S-6058**

SUGAR CRYSTALS

Brighten up plain cookies fast with our colorful decorating sugars. Just sprinkle these extra-fine sugars on cookies before baking. Controlling the flow is easy with our flip-top shaker bottle. Certified Kosher.

Each

Brights 4-Mix

Contains Pink, Yellow, Light Green, Lavender.
710-S-651

Primary 4-Mix

Contains Red, Dark Green, Blue, Yellow.
710-S-650

Candy Making

Let Wilton show you how great candy can be! Use our Candy Melts® and molds for beautiful candy in 3 easy steps—just melt, mold and serve.*

Candy Melting Accessories

We've made melting chocolate and Candy Melts® faster and easier than ever—so it's even more fun to make your own homemade candies! Our new collection is designed for melting candy smooth for pouring or dipping and for maintaining the texture to paint molds without constant reheating. It's just what the home candy-maker needs!*

CHOCOLATE PRO™ ELECTRIC MELTING POT

The fast and easy way to melt chocolate & Candy Melts®!*

- Melting base stays cool to the touch
- Removeable non-stick Melting Pot holds 2½ cups of melted chocolate
- Easy-pour spout
- Non-skid feet keep Chocolate Pro™ steady on counter

With the Chocolate Pro™, it's easy to melt large amounts of chocolate or Candy Melts brand confectionery coating in minutes! It's the fast and fun way to mold candies like a pro and to add the excitement of chocolate to all your desserts. With the Chocolate Pro™, you'll be able to mold lollipops and fancy dipped-center candies. Serve elegant dipped desserts like fruit, cake, cookies and fondue. Add the great taste of chocolate to potato chips and pretzels. Create flavored chocolate sauces for ice cream or silky ganache glaze to pour over cakes. The Chocolate Pro™ helps you do it all! 120 volts. UL Listed.

2104-S-9004

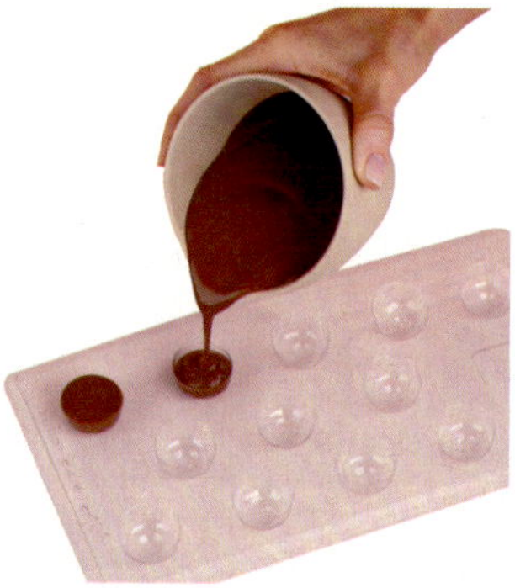

STAY-WARM CERAMIC CANDY MELTING CUPS & BOWLS

Ceramic keeps candy melted longer for easier candy-making—great for heating and pouring dessert toppings too. Microwave-safe ceramic retains heat.

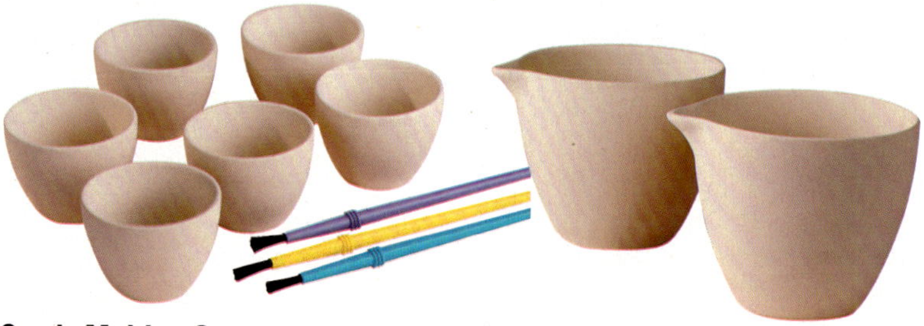

Candy Melting Cups

Cups are great for melting colors separately. Use them like an art palette for painting colors or molds—just brush candy into molds before filling. Holds heat up to ½ hour. Includes 6 cups and 6 decorating brushes. 2 x 1½ in. deep.

1904-S-1067 Set/12

Candy Melting Bowls

Bowls are ideal for filling all types of Wilton molds, when making candy plaques or lollipops. Or take them right to the table for easy dipping of pretzels, graham crackers or cookies. Holds heat up to 1 hour. 4 x 3½ in. deep.

1904-S-1076 Set/2

LOLLIPOP AND TREAT STAND

NEW!

Show off your fun lollipops and other treats for the whole party to see! This lively looping stand neatly serves up to 18 treats for the ideal celebration centerpiece. Great for marshmallows, jelly candies and caramels too—just insert on 4 in. sticks. Use the top slot to add a fun message! Assembled size 6 x 14 in. high.

1904-S-1068

Candy Melts®*

Versatile, creamy, easy-to-melt wafers are ideal for all your candy making—molding, dipping or coating. Their delicious taste can be varied by adding our Candy Flavors.

Light and Dark Cocoa are all natural, cocoa flavor; colors are artificially vanilla flavored. 14 oz. bag. Certified Kosher.

Peanut Butter
1911-S-481

Dark Cocoa
1911-S-358

Light Cocoa
1911-S-544

Chocolate Mint
1911-S-1920

Lavender
1911-S-403

Pink
1911-S-447

Yellow
1911-S-463

Orange
1911-S-1631

Blue
1911-S-448

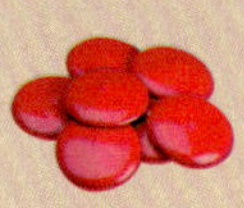

Red
1911-S-499

Green
1911-S-405

White
1911-S-498

*Brand confectionery coating.

Candy Making Tools

Squeeze Bottles

Melt candy with ease, then fill your mold without mess! Our convenient bottles are available in three sizes so you can melt the right amount of Candy Melts®* you need. Melt candy right in the bottle, then squeeze out into molds. Great way to store and reheat leftover candy.

Mini	Regular	Large
6 oz.	12 oz.	16 oz.
1904-S-1166	**1904-S-1189**	**1904-S-1167**
Pk./2		

Candy Melting Plate

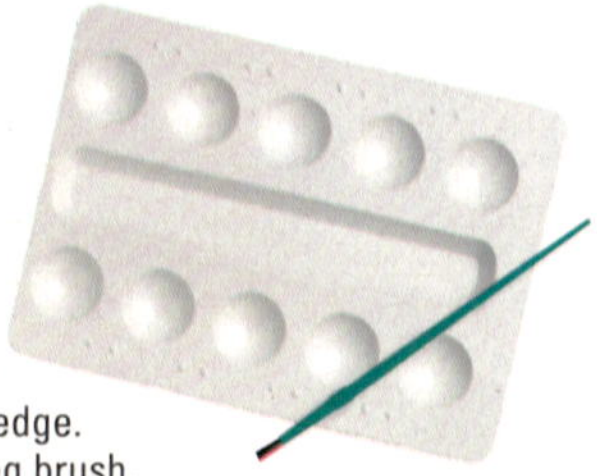

Microwave-melt up to 11 Candy Melts®* colors at one time with less mess! Plastic with non-slip grip edge. Includes decorating brush.
1904-S-8016

Metal Dipping Set

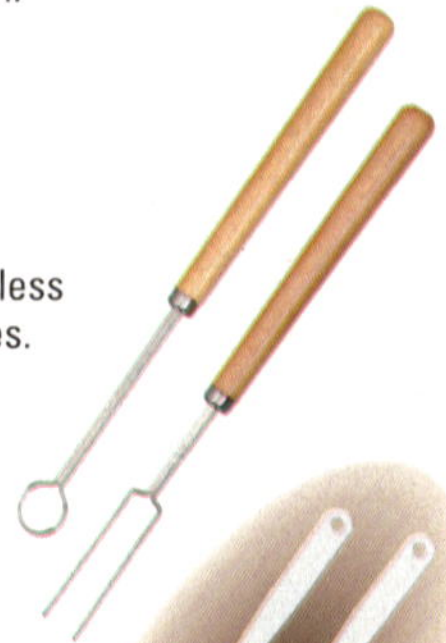

Professional-quality stainless steel with wooden handles. 8¾ in. long.
1904-S-925
Set/2

Candy Dipping Set

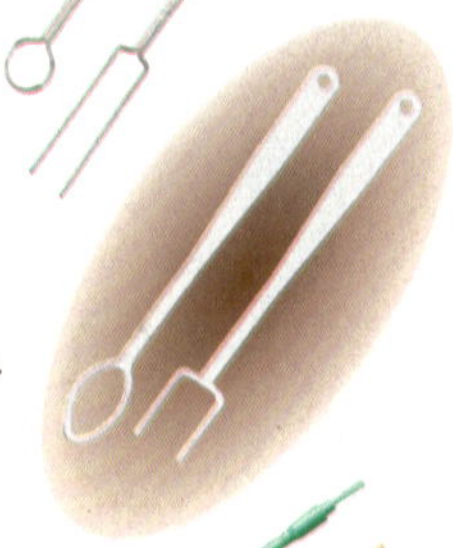

Easy-handling spoon and fork, each 7¾ in. long.
1904-S-800
Set/2

Decorator Brush Set

Plastic, durable bristles, easy-to-hold handle.
2104-S-9355
Set/3

Easy-Pour Funnel

Push-button controls flow of candy. 5 x 4 in. diameter, nylon.
1904-S-552

Candy Thermometer

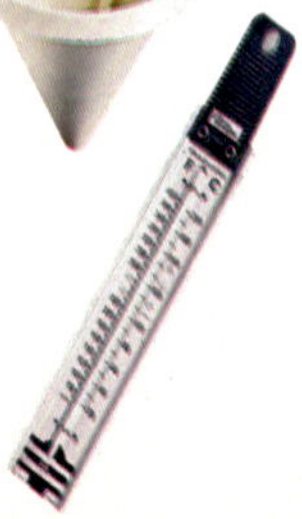

Precise measurement essential for preparing hard candy, nougat, more.
1904-S-1200

Candy Wraps and Boxes

Your homemade candy deserves a beautiful presentation. Wilton has everything you need to wrap and package your candy like a pro. Designed to keep candies fresh, protected and attractive for gift giving.

Candy Gift Boxes

For attractive gift giving and stay-fresh storage.

1 lb. White Candy Boxes Pk./3
1904-S-1172

½ lb. Candy Boxes Pk./3

White	Red
1904-S-1150	**1904-S-1152**
Gold	**Silver**
1904-S-1151	**1904-S-1153**

Gold Elastic Ties

Pre-tied with a bow. Use with Candy Gift Boxes.
1904-S-1186 Pk./5

Candy Box Liners

Padded paper liners cushion candy and prevent breakage. Use with ½ lb. Candy Gift Boxes.
1904-S-1191 Pk./4

Candy Cups

Crisply-pleated, just like professionals use. White glassine-coated paper.

1¼ in. Diameter.
1912-S-1245 Pk./75

1 in. Diameter.
1912-S-1243 Pk./100

Foil Wrappers

Bright, shiny coverings for candy and lollipops! 4 x 4 in. squares.
Pk./50

Gold
1904-S-1197

Silver
1904-S-1196

Red
1904-S-1198

Candy Bar Boxes

Designed to hold candies made in our Candy Bar Molds (p. 165), the window displays your special message.
Pk./10

White
1904-S-1157

Silver
1904-S-1159

Truffle Boxes

An elegant look, with a lock-close top that forms a perfect "bow." Holds 2-3 pieces of candy.
Pk./4

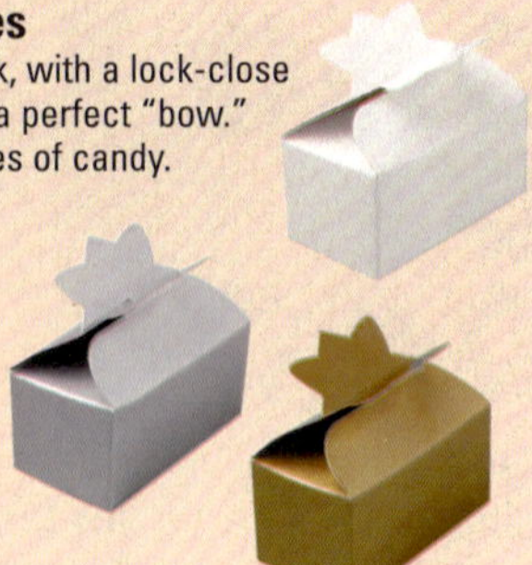

White
1904-S-1154

Silver
1904-S-1155

Gold
1904-S-1156

Candy Color and Flavoring Sets

Primary Candy Color Set

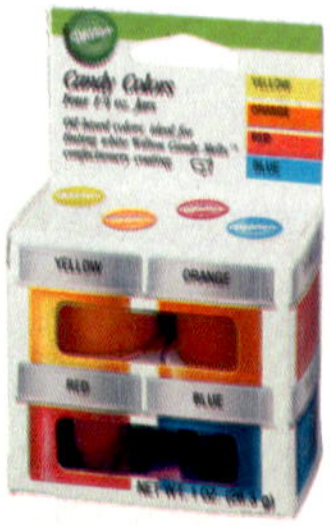

Concentrated oil-based colors blend easily with Candy Melts®. Includes Yellow, Orange, Red and Blue in .25 oz. jars. Certified Kosher.
1913-S-1299 Set/4

Garden Candy Color Set

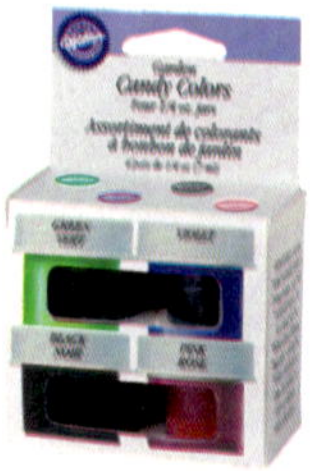

Create pretty pastel colors! Concentrated oil-based colors blend easily with Candy Melts®. Includes Pink, Green, Violet and Black in .25 oz. jars. Certified Kosher.
1913-S-1298 Set/4

Candy Flavoring Set

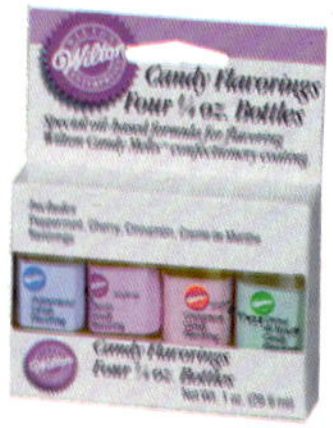

Add your favorite. Includes Peppermint, Cherry, Cinnamon and Creme de Menthe in .25 oz. bottles.
1913-S-1029 Set/4

Novelty Candy Molds

More fun shapes and greater detail make Wilton Candy Molds the world's favorite way to create candy. Look at the variety! You can do it all, from exciting kids' party treats to elegant wedding and shower favors. Molding and coloring couldn't be easier when you use Candy Melts®. Look for terrific design ideas and molding instructions on every mold package.*

LARGE CANDY MOLDS *Big and bold candies, great for favors and gifts.*

Sports Lollipop
4 designs, 4 cavities.
2115-S-4432

Party/Birthday Lollipop
4 designs, 4 cavities.
2115-S-4434

Double Heart Lollipop
2 designs, 4 cavities.
2115-S-4440

Cross/Bible Lollipop
4 designs, 6 cavities
(2 lollipop).
2115-S-4435

Candy Bar
1 design, 3 cavities.
2115-S-4431

2-PACK CANDY MOLD SETS *More shapes for more fun!*

Girl Power
10 designs, 10 cavities.
2115-S-1604 Pk./2

Baby
10 designs, 10 cavities.
2115-S-1605 Pk./2

Pets
10 designs, 11 cavities.
2115-S-1606 Pk./2

Garden Goodies Lollipop
10 designs, 10 cavities.
2115-S-1607 Pk./2

Summer Fun Lollipop
10 designs, 10 cavities.
2115-S-1608 Pk./2

Dancing Daisies Lollipop
1 design, 9 cavities.
2115-S-1430

Ice Cream
3 designs, 9 cavities.
2115-S-4367

Summer Fun
5 designs, 11 cavities.
2115-S-1741

Alphabet
26 designs, 26 cavities.
2115-S-1563

Numerals
10 designs, 10 cavities.
2115-S-1564

Stars
1 design, 12 cavities,
2115-S-1554

Rubber Ducky
1 design, 6 cavities.
2115-S-1565

Party Time Lollipop
6 designs, 8 cavities.
2115-S-1516

Seashells
5 designs, 11 cavities.
2115-S-1561

Roses and Buds Lollipop
3 designs, 9 cavities.
(4 lollipop).
2115-S-1708

Wedding Shower Lollipop
5 designs, 10 cavities.
(4 lollipop).
2115-S-1711

Roses in Bloom
1 design, 10 cavities.
2115-S-1738

Smiley Face Lollipop
1 design, 9 cavities.
2115-S-1715

*Brand confectionery coating.

Classic Candy Molds

Wilton has a great selection of traditional shapes for creating elegant gift assortments and party trays.

Cordial Cups

Mold a candy "glass" for dessert liqueurs, or fill with whipped cream and float in cocoa or coffee. 1 design, 6 cavities.
2115-S-1535

Peanut Butter Cups
1 design, 10 cavities.
2115-S-1522

Deep Heart Truffles
1 design, 7 cavities.
2117-S-100

Truffles
1 design, 12 cavities.
2115-S-1521

Roses
3 designs, 12 cavities.
2115-S-1713

Gift Truffles
1 design, 13 cavities.
2115-S-1728

Mint Discs
1 design, 16 cavities.
2115-S-1739

Dipped Spoons Mold

Use with the Dipped Spoons Kit or use your own spoons, along with Wilton Candy Melts®* and Candy Flavors, to create candy-coated spoons that stir in flavor. Contains mold (1 design, 6 cavities) and instructions.
2115-S-1722

Silicone Candy & Craft Molds

Use these versatile silicone molds to make a fun-shaped treat for your next celebration. Their flexible design is perfect for molding candy plaques, large-size cookies or creative ice sculpts. Great with Wilton Candy Melts®!*

- High-heat silicone is oven-safe to 500°F
- Stain and odor resistant
- Reusable
- Dishwasher safe

NEW!

Butterfly
Mold area is 5⅜ x 5½ x ½ in. deep.
2115-S-1038

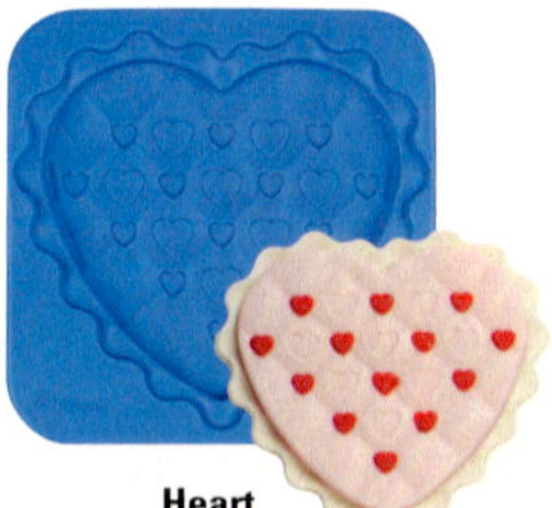

Heart
Mold area is 6¼ x 6 x ½ in. deep.
2115-S-1039

Teddy Bear
Mold area is 4¼ x 5½ x ½ in. deep.
2115-S-1040

Candy Bar Molds

Create a sweet memory for your guests . . . a candy bar featuring your special message.

Molding is easy using Candy Melts®* (p. 162). Present them beautifully in Candy Bar Boxes (p. 163). Each candy bar measures 3¼ x 1¾ x ¼ in. deep. Mold has 1 design, 4 cavities.

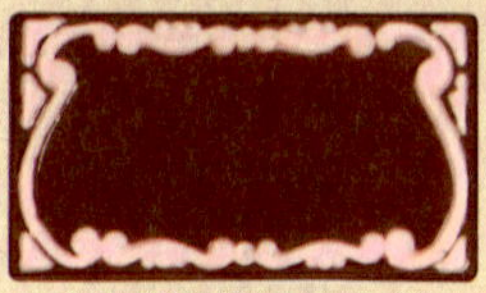

Add-A-Message
2115-S-1356

Our Wedding
2115-S-1409

Thank You
2115-S-1410

Gummy Making Kits

Kids will have a wild time making gummy shapes with Wilton for Kids kits and gummy mixes. Just mix, shake and mold to make great-tasting gummys in 10 minutes! Ages 4 and above.

Everything's included to make 16 gummys.

Each kit includes:

- Mold with 4 fun shapes, mixing bottle and funnel.
- 4 gummy mixes (.7 oz. each) in assorted artificial flavors.
- 1 packet of Sour Sugar (.7 oz.) for covering gummys.
- Easy instructions.

Glam Girl
2104-S-1616

Creepy Critters
2104-S-1617

Dinosaurs
2104-S-1620

Gummy Sour Sugar

Add a sour kick to your gummy flavors! Includes five pouches (.7 oz. each)—enough to cover 80 pieces.
1911-S-1930

Gummy Mix Refill Pack

Refill Pack includes one pouch each Green Apple, Blue Raspberry, Grape and Strawberry flavors (.7 oz. each)—enough to make 20 pieces of candy, complete instructions, and one pouch (.7 oz. each) of Sour Sugar. Artificial flavors.
1911-S-329

Pretzel Molds

NEW!

Easy to mold; position pretzel rod, spoon in your favorite melted Candy Melts®* and refrigerate to set. Ideal for lollipop sticks, too. 1 design, 6 cavities.
Smiley Face
2115-S-4437
Flowers 2115-S-4436

Accessories

Create the perfect pop with sticks in every size, cool colors too! Clear wrappers make giving easy.

Rainbow Lollipop Sticks

Add pizzazz to your pops! Food-safe plastic sticks; 5 each red, yellow, blue and green. Not for oven or microwave use. 4 in.
1912-S-9316 Pk./20

Lollipop Sticks

Sturdy paper sticks in 4 sizes. Not for oven use.

4 in.
1912-S-1006 Pk./50

6 in.
1912-S-1007 Pk./35

8 in.
1912-S-9320 Pk./25

11¾ in.
1912-S-1212 Pk./20

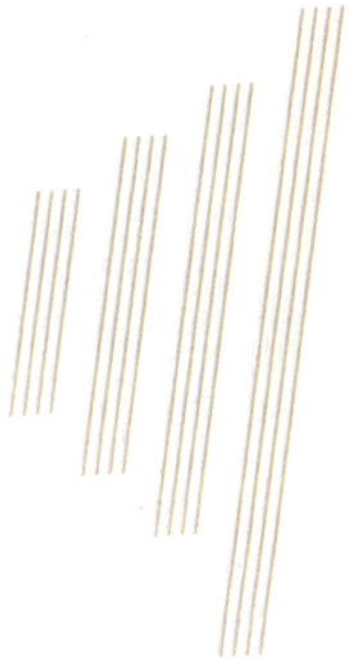

Lollipop Wrapping Kit

Cover your candy lollipops and special treats for gift-giving! Contains 18 sticks, (4 in.) 18 bags, 18 twist ties.
1904-S-1193

Clear Treat Bags

Let your fun candy and cookie treats show through! 3 x 4 in.
1912-S-2347 Pk./50

Dipped Spoons Kit

Fun to make, use or give. Use with the Dipped Spoons Mold, plus your favorite Candy Melts®* and Candy Flavors. Includes 6 plastic spoons, 6 bags, 6 twist ties and instructions.
1904-S-1192

Famous Favorites

Wilton helps you make kids feel like stars! We have a great cast of today's favorite faces and themes on fun party products for cakes, cookies and more.

NASCAR®

NEW!

Cake Pan
Start your party with a cake your pit crew will love—decorated with the excitement of *NASCAR*. It's ready to customize with your favorite driver's number and colors! Perfect for birthdays or race days. One-mix pan is 15¾ x 8¾ x 2 in. deep. Aluminum.
2105-S-2500

Icing Decorations
Mint-flavored edible sugar shapes to decorate cupcakes, cookies, ice cream and cake. Certified Kosher.
710-S-2500 Pk./9

Baking Cups
Standard size, microwave-safe paper. 2 in. diameter.
415-S-2500 Pk./50

Candle
Handpainted, clean-burning with colorful details.
3 in. high.
2811-S-2500

Icing Color Set
Includes four .5 oz. jars: Black, Red, Yellow and Blue. Certified Kosher.
601-S-2500
Set/4

Treat Bags
Fill with candy, cookies and other goodies; great for gifts and surprises, too! Includes sixteen 4 x 9½ in. bags with twist ties.
1912-S-2500
Pk./16

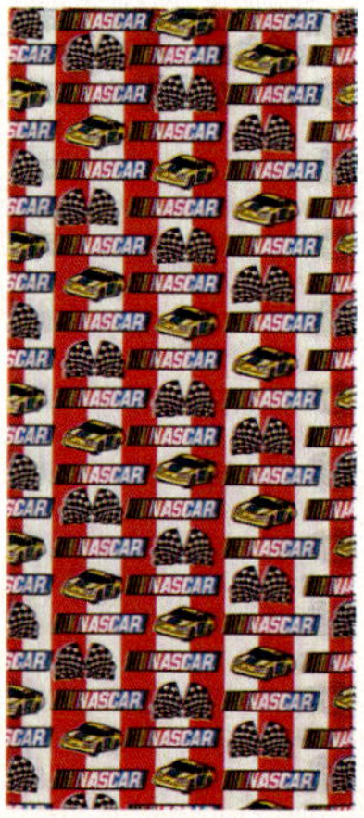

NASCAR is a registered trademark of the National Association for Stock Car Auto Racing, Inc.

SUPERMAN™

NEW!

Cake Pan
Superman™ is back to save the world and rescue your celebration! Call on this mighty World Hero for a cake that will thrill every kid—and featuring a bold new look for the *Man of Steel*™. One-mix pan is 13½ x 11½ x 2 in. deep. Aluminum.
2105-S-3350

Candle
Handpainted, clean-burning with fun details. 2½ in. high.
2811-S-3350

Icing Decorations
Mint-flavored edible sugar shapes to decorate cupcakes, cookies, ice cream and cake. Certified Kosher.
710-S-3350 Pk./9

Baking Cups
Standard size, microwave-safe paper. 2 in. diameter.
415-S-3350 Pk./50

Party Toppers
Top your treats with these exciting action figures. Handpainted, food-safe plastic is great on cupcakes, brownies, cakes and other treats. 2¼ in. high.
2113-S-3350
Set/6

Icing Color Set
Includes four .5 oz. jars: Red, Blue, Yellow, Copper (skin tone). Certified Kosher.
601-S-3350
Set/4

Treat Bags
Fill with candy, cookies and other goodies; great for gifts and surprises, too! Includes sixteen 4 x 9½ in. bags with twist ties.
1912-S-3350 Pk./16

DISNEY PRESENTS A PIXAR FILM

Cars

NEW!

Fun Pix®
Fun for cupcakes, brownies, ice cream and more. Paper, 3 in. high.
2113-S-6402 Pk./24

Cake Pan
Any party is a joy ride when you serve a cake starring *Lightning McQueen*! All the fun details you love on the big screen are here. One-mix pan is 13¾ x 6¼ x 2¾ in. deep. Aluminum.
2105-S-6400

Icing Decorations
Mint-flavored edible sugar shapes to decorate cupcakes, cookies, ice cream and cake. Certified Kosher.
710-S-6400 Pk./9

Party Toppers
Rev up the fun with treats topped with your favorites from *Disney/Pixar Cars*! Handpainted, food-safe plastic is great on cupcakes, brownies, cakes and other treats. 1¼ in. high.
2113-S-6400 Set/6

Baking Cups
Standard size, microwave-safe paper. 2 in. diameter.
415-S-6400 Pk./50

Candle
Handpainted, clean-burning with fun details. 3½ in. high.
2811-S-6400

Icing Color Set
Includes four .5 oz. jars: Red, Blue, Yellow, Black. Certified Kosher.
601-S-6400 Set/4

Treat Bags
Fill with candy, cookies and other goodies; great for gifts and surprises, too! Includes sixteen 4 x 9½ in. bags with twist ties.
1912-S-6400 Pk./16

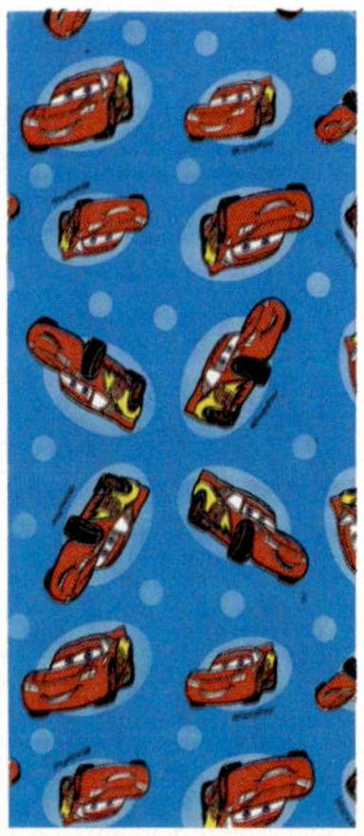

Disney Princess

Cake Pan
Fulfill every little girl's dream of becoming a princess with her very own magical *Cinderella* cake. One-mix pan is 14¼ x 9¼ x 2 in. deep. Aluminum.
2105-S-7475

Party Toppers
A royally fun way to top party treats. Handpainted, food-safe plastic is great on cupcakes, brownies, cakes and other treats. 2 in. high.
2113-S-7475
Set/6

Candle
Wish upon a *Disney* star! Handpainted, clean-burning with colorful details. 3½ in. high.
2811-S-7475

Icing Decorations
Mint-flavored edible sugar shapes to decorate cupcakes, cookies, ice cream and cake. Certified Kosher.
710-S-7475 Pk./9

Shaped Sprinkles
4-cell container for easy pouring and storing. Includes Crown, Heart, Star and Flower shapes. 2.45 oz. Certified Kosher.
710-S-7479

Icing Color Set
Includes four .5 oz. jars: Blue, Yellow, Pink and Skin Tone. Certified Kosher.
601-S-7475
Set/4

Baking Cups
Standard size, microwave-safe paper. 2 in. diameter.
415-S-7475
Pk./50

Treat Bags
Fill with candy, cookies and other goodies; great for gifts and surprises, too! Includes sixteen 4 x 9½ in. bags with twist ties.
1912-S-7475
Pk./16

Disney Winnie the Pooh

Pooh Cake Pan

He's always ready for a fun party, with his birthday balloon in hand and a happy smile on his face. One-mix pan is 13¾ x 7¾ x 2 in. deep. Aluminum.
2105-S-3100

Icing Decorations

Mint-flavored edible sugar shapes to decorate cupcakes, cookies, ice cream and cake. Certified Kosher.
710-S-3100
Pk./9

Icing Color Set

Includes four .5 oz. jars: *Pooh* (gold), Red, Green and Black. Certified Kosher.
601-S-3100 Set/4

Candles

Pooh is ready for the party. Handpainted, clean-burning with colorful details. 2-3 in. high.

***Pooh* #1 Hunny Pot**
2811-S-3102

***Pooh* and Presents**
2811-S-3100

Treat Bags

Fill with candy, cookies and other goodies; great for gifts and surprises, too! Includes sixteen 4 x 9½ in. bags with twist ties.
1912-S-3100
Pk./16

Baking Cups

Standard size, microwave-safe paper. 2 in. diameter.
415-S-3100 Pk./50

Disney Mickey Mouse

Mickey Face Pan

The world's most beloved mouse goes to the best parties! Easy-to-decorate; loved by all ages. One-mix pan is 10½ x 12 x 2 in. deep. Aluminum.
2105-S-3603

Icing Decorations

Mint-flavored edible sugar shapes to decorate cupcakes, cookies, ice cream and cake. Certified Kosher.
710-S-3600 Pk./9

Mickey with Starburst Candle

Your favorite mouse! Handpainted, clean-burning with colorful details. 3½ in. high.
2811-S-3609

Baking Cups

Standard size, microwave-safe paper. 2 in. diameter.
415-S-3610 Pk./50

Icing Color Set

Includes four .5 oz. jars: two Black plus *Mickey* Peach and Copper (lt. skin tone). Certified Kosher.
601-S-3603 Set/4

THE AMAZING SPIDER-MAN

Cake Pan
The Wizard of Webs is back in action, on a pan that will grab every guest! Kids will love the great costume detail. One-mix pan is 9 x 12 x 2 in. deep. Aluminum.
2105-S-5052

Party Toppers
He's ready to sling his next web on these exciting handpainted toppers. Food-safe plastic to use on cupcakes, brownies, cakes and other treats. 2¼ in. high.
2113-S-5052 Set/6

Candle
Handpainted, clean-burning with exciting details. 3½ in. high.
2811-S-5052

Icing Color Set
Includes four .5 oz. jars: Light Blue, Dark Blue, Red and Black. Certified Kosher.
601-S-5052
Set/4

Icing Decorations
Mint-flavored edible sugar shapes to decorate cupcakes, cookies, ice cream and cake. Certified Kosher.
710-S-5052 Pk./9

Baking Cups
Standard size, microwave-safe paper. 2 in. diameter.
415-S-5052 Pk./50

Treat Bags
Fill with candy, cookies and other goodies; great for gifts and surprises, too! Includes sixteen 4 x 9½ in. bags with twist ties.
1912-S-5052 Pk./16

MARVEL

Cake Pan
With this pan, kids can enjoy a different *Care Bear* every time! The label includes instructions and patterns for 4 of the most popular "care"acters—it's easy to give *Wish Bear™, Love-a-lot Bear™, Share Bear™* and *Good Luck Bear™* their distinctive colors and personalities. One-mix pan is 13 x 9½ x 2 in. deep. Aluminum.
2105-S-2424

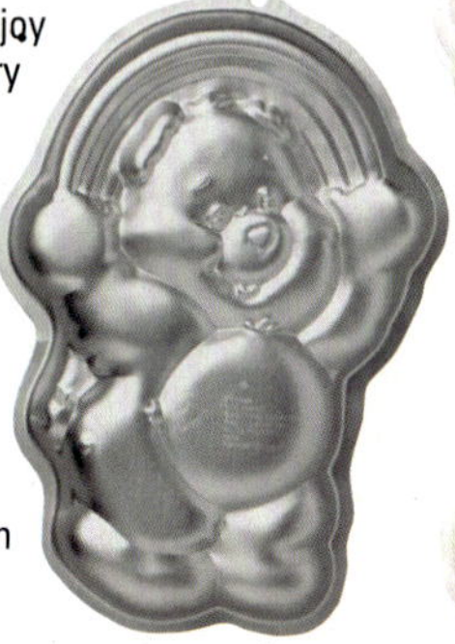

Candle
Hand-painted, clean-burning with adorable details. 3 in. high.
2811-S-2424

Icing Color Set
Includes four .5 oz. jars of Teal, Blue, Yellow and Orange. Certified Kosher.
601-S-2424
Set/4

Baking Cups
Standard size, microwave-safe paper. 2 in. diameter.
415-S-2424 Pk./50

Icing Decorations
Mint-flavored edible sugar shapes to decorate cupcakes, cookies, ice cream and cake. Certified Kosher.
710-S-2424 Pk./9

Treat Bags
Fill with candy, cookies and other goodies; great for gifts and surprises, too! Includes sixteen 4 x 9½ in. bags with twist ties.
1912-S-2424
Pk./16

Cake Pan
Everyone loves her fun and colorful look! From her bouncy hat to her sweet smile, she adds a "berry" happy touch to the party. One-mix pan is 11¼ x 10½ x 2 in. deep. Aluminum.
2105-S-7040

Icing Decorations
Mint-flavored edible sugar shapes to decorate cupcakes, cookies, ice cream and cake. Certified Kosher.
710-S-7041 Pk./9

Baking Cups
Standard size, microwave-safe paper. 2 in. diameter.
415-S-7040
Pk./50

Candle
Handpainted, clean-burning with fun details.
3¼ in. high.
2811-S-7040

Icing Color Set
Includes four .5 oz. jars: Red, Brown, Green and Skin Tone. Certified Kosher.
601-S-7040
Set/4

Treat Bags
Fill with candy, cookies and other goodies; great for gifts and surprises, too! Includes sixteen 4 x 9½ in. bags with twist ties.
1912-S-7040 Pk./16

Barbie™

Cake Pan
Celebration *Barbie* gets the party fun started for your birthday girl. This newest *Barbie* design features pretty pastels, romantic flowers and a fresh, fashionable look that's hers alone. Includes face maker (pictured below). One-mix pan is 9¾ x 13½ x 2 in. deep. Aluminum.
2105-S-8934

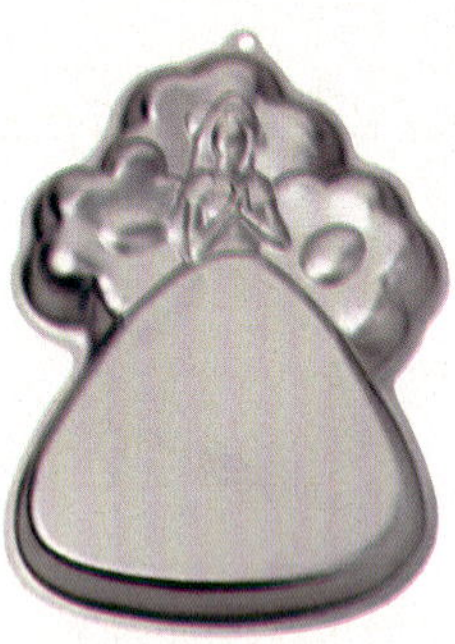

Face Maker
Place on cake top for the perfect look of Celebration *Barbie*.
504-S-8934

Candle
Barbie style makes any cake captivating! Handpainted, clean-burning with colorful details. 3½ in. high.
2811-S-8934

Shaped Sprinkles
Shake up your *Barbie* treats! 4-cell container for easy pouring and storing. Includes crown, butterfly, heart and flower shapes. 2.7 oz. Certified Kosher.
710-S-8901

Baking Cups
Standard size, microwave-safe paper. 2 in. diameter.
415-S-8934
Pk./50

Icing Color Set
Includes three .5 oz. jars (Pink, Yellow and Violet), and one .1 oz. jar of White Cake Sparkles™ edible glitter. Certified Kosher.
601-S-8934 Set/4

Icing Decorations
Mint-flavored edible sugar shapes. Certified Kosher.
710-S-8934 Pk./9

Treat Bags
Fill with candy, cookies and other goodies; great for gifts and surprises, too! Includes sixteen 4 x 9½ in. bags with twist ties.
1912-S-8934
Pk./16

Scooby-Doo!™

Cake Pan
As usual, *Scooby* gets right next to the food! This fun pan shows him about to put his canines into a big burger. One-mix pan is 10½ x 12 x 2 in. deep. Aluminum.
2105-S-3227

Mini Treats Cake Pan
Get close-up with your favorite character and create all kinds of exciting single-size desserts. Great for cakes, candy, gelatin and brownies. The pan's intense color makes baking even more fun. Four cavity pan is 11 x 9 in.; individual cavities are 3 x 5½ x ¾ in. deep. Aluminum.
2105-S-3228

Party Toppers
Scooby-Doo! is begging for attention on these fun handpainted toppers. Food-safe plastic to decorate cupcakes, brownies, cakes and other treats. 2½ in. high.
2113-S-3206 Set/6

Edible Cake Decoration Set
Surround the fun-to-eat *Scooby-Doo* wafer with the edible icing decorations and Happy Birthday message to create instant excitement on any birthday cake.
711-S-3206 Set/20

Shaped Sprinkles
Shake up your *Scooby-Doo!* treats. Convenient 4-cell container designed for easy pouring and storing. Includes *Mystery Machine, Scooby-Doo!*, bone and bat shapes. 2.55 oz. Certified Kosher.
710-S-3207

Candle
Handpainted, clean-burning with colorful details. 3¾ in. high.
2811-S-3227

Baking Cups
Standard size, microwave-safe paper. 2 in. diameter.
415-S-3227 Pk./50

Icing Decorations
Mint-flavored edible sugar shapes to decorate cupcakes, cookies, ice cream and cake. Certified Kosher.
710-S-3206 Pk./9

Icing Color Set
Includes four .5 oz. jars: Brown, Yellow, Black, Teal. Certified Kosher.
601-S-3206 Set/4

Treat Bags
Fill with candy, cookies and other goodies; great for gifts and surprises, too! Includes sixteen 4 x 9½ in. bags with twist ties.
1912-S-3227 Pk./16

Cake Pan

Everyone's favorite seafaring star will make a big splash at the party. One-mix pan is 13½ x 11¾ x 2 in. deep. Aluminum.
2105-S-5130

Mini Treats Cake Pan

Get close-up with your favorite character and create all kinds of exciting single-size desserts. Great for cakes, candy, gelatin and brownies. The pan's intense color makes baking a bubbly good time. One cake mix makes 15 mini cakes. Four-cavity pan is 11 x 9 in.; individual cavities are 3¾ x 3½ x ¾ in. deep. Aluminum.
2105-S-5131

Shaped Sprinkles

4-cell container is convenient for pouring and storing. Includes *SpongeBob* (in 2 cells), Flower and Patrick shapes. 2.8 oz. Certified Kosher.
710-S-5131

Icing Decorations

Mint-flavored edible sugar shapes to decorate cupcakes, cookies, ice cream and cake. Certified Kosher.
710-S-5130 Pk./9

Party Toppers

He's surfing your party goodies on these cool handpainted toppers. Food-safe plastic to use on cupcakes, brownies, cakes and other treats. 2 in. high.
2113-S-5130 Set/6

Edible Cake Decoration Set
Surround the neat-to-eat *SpongeBob* wafer with the edible icing decoration shapes and Happy Birthday message to create instant excitement on any birthday cake.
711-S-5130 Set/20

Baking Cups

Standard size, microwave-safe paper. 2 in. diameter.
415-S-5130 Pk./50

Candle

SpongeBob is swimming in loot—giving you a cake to treasure! Handpainted, clean-burning with colorful details. 3½ in. high.
2811-S-5130

Icing Color Set

Includes four .5 oz. jars: Yellow, Red, Blue and Brown. Certified Kosher.
601-S-5130
Set/4

Treat Bags

Fill with candy, cookies and other goodies; great for gifts and surprises, too! Includes sixteen 4 x 9½ in. bags with twist ties.
1912-S-5130
Pk./16

Dora the Explorer

Cake Pan

Wherever *Dora* goes, it's always "una fiesta"! Discover a world of party excitement with this great pan. One-mix pan is 13¾ x 10 x 2 in. deep. Aluminum.
2105-S-6300

Mini Treats Cake Pan
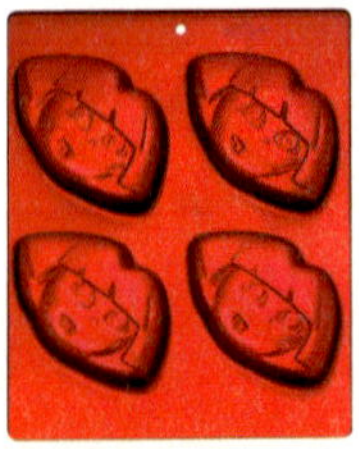

Get close-up with your favorite explorer and create all kinds of exciting single-size desserts. Great for cakes, candy, brownies and gelatin. The pan's intense color makes baking even more fun. One cake mix makes 15 mini cakes. Four-cavity pan is 11 x 9 in.; individual cavities are 3¼ x 5 x ¾ in. deep. Aluminum.
2105-S-6301

Icing Color Set

Includes four .5 oz. jars: Red, Pink, Brown and Skin Tone. Certified Kosher.
601-S-6300
Set/4

Party Toppers

Dora is ready to top your delightful party treats! Handpainted, food-safe plastic is great on cupcakes, brownies, cakes and other treats.
2¼ in. high.
2113-S-6300
Set/6

Candle

Handpainted, clean-burning with colorful details.
3¼ in. high.
2811-S-6300

Icing Decorations

Mint-flavored edible sugar shapes to decorate cupcakes, cookies, ice cream and cake. Certified Kosher.
710-S-6300 Pk./8

Baking Cups

Standard size, microwave-safe paper. 2 in. diameter.
415-S-6300
Pk./50

Treat Bags

Fill with candy, cookies and other goodies; great for gifts and surprises, too! Includes sixteen 4 x 9½ in. bags with twist ties.
1912-S-6300 Pk./16

Sesame Street

Elmo Face Cake Pan

He's sweet, lovable and popular with kids of all ages. One-mix pan is 13½ x 10½ x 2 in. deep. Aluminum.
2105-S-3461

Elmo with Crayons Candle

Elmo brings smiles to the party. Handpainted, clean-burning with colorful details.
3½ in. high.
2811-S-3463

Parade Cake Top Set

A fun birthday parade right on your cake. *Cookie Monster, Zoe, Elmo, Big Bird* in food-safe plastic.
1½ to 4 in. high.
2113-S-3460 Set/4

Icing Decorations

Mint-flavored edible sugar shapes to decorate cupcakes, cookies, ice cream and cakes. Certified Kosher.
710-S-3460 Pk./9

Baking Cups

Standard size, microwave-safe paper. 2 in. diameter.
415-S-3461
Pk./50

Treat Bags

Fill with candy, cookies and other goodies; great for gifts and surprises, too! Includes sixteen 4 x 9½ in. bags with twist ties.
1912-S-3461
Pk./16

Party

You've written the guest list—now start your decorating list here! From baking cups to candles, cake toppers to treat bags, Wilton has the great-looking designs you want.

Theme Party Products

Give your party personality! You've seen how much fun a theme party can be in our Catchy Themes special section *(p. 96)**. Now see how easy it is to pull the party together with the great selection of Wilton theme products. You'll discover favorite subjects including jungle animals, colorful flowers, over the hill tombstones and sports for every season. Find candles, party bags, baking cups, candy molds, cake pans and more—all with the Wilton touch of fun design and detail.*

JUNGLE PALS

Kids will just love these adorable creatures for birthdays, school parties and special events.

NEW!

Friendly Lion Pan
He'll be the pride of all your celebrations! One-mix pan is 12¾ x 10¾ x 2 in. deep. Aluminum.
2105-S-1012

Party Bags
20 plastic bags, 20 ties included. 4 x 9½ in.
1912-S-1012
Pk./20

Baking Cups
Standard size.
415-S-1012
Pk./50

Icing Decorations
Certified Kosher.
710-S-1012 Pk./12

Fun Pix®
Approx.
3⅛ in. high.
2113-S-1012
Set/24

Jungle Animals Topper Set
1¾ to 3 in. high.
2113-S-2095 Set/4

Candles
Approx.
2 in. high.
2811-S-1012
Set/4

DANCING DAISY FLOWER

NEW!

Pick this daisy for Mother's Day, wedding showers and birthdays for any garden-lover.

Pan
One perfect flower makes bunches of great cakes and desserts! One-mix pan is 12 x 12 x 2 in. deep. Aluminum.
2105-S-1016

Icing Decorations
Certified Kosher.
710-S-353 Pk./12

Lollipop Mold
1 design, 9 cavities.
2115-S-1430

Baking Cups
Standard size.
415-S-7812
Pk./50

Party Bags
20 plastic bags, 20 ties included. 4 x 9½ in.
1912-S-7813
Pk./20

Candles
Approx. 2 in. high.
2811-S-217
Set/6

PARTY TIME

What a great way to cap off any celebration, from birthdays to that New Year's Eve bash!

Party Hat Pan
Customize cakes with your favorite colors and fun designs—ideal for molded desserts and salads too. One-mix pan is 10 x 13½ x 2 in. deep. Aluminum.
2105-S-3317

Party Time Lollipop Mold
6 designs, 8 cavities.
2115-S-1516

Party Bags
20 plastic bags, 20 ties included.
4 x 9½ in.
1912-S-4365
Pk./20

Baking Cups
Standard size.
415-S-5365
Pk./50

Icing Decorations
Certified Kosher.
710-S-7205
Pk./12

Party Time Candles
Approx. 1½ in. high.
2811-S-860 Set/4

ICE CREAM

A refreshing look for any celebration, from birthdays to backyard barbecues.

Pan
Like a real ice cream cone, create endless flavor and color combinations. One-mix pan is 13¾ x 9¼ x 2 in. deep. Aluminum.
2105-S-2087

Candy Mold
3 designs, 9 cavities.
2115-S-4367

Party Bags
20 plastic bags, 20 ties included.
4 x 9½ in.
1912-S-3106
Pk./20

Icing Decorations
Certified Kosher.
710-S-7812
Pk./12

Baking Cups
Standard size.
415-S-121
Pk./50

Candles
Approx. 2¼ in. high.
2811-S-9349 Set/4

Theme Party Products

OVER THE HILL

The secret of aging is keeping your sense of humor! These Wilton products help anyone face those big birthdays with a smile!

Tombstone Pan
Optimistically mark the passing of one more year. One-mix pan is 13 x 9¼ x 2 in. deep. Aluminum.
2105-S-1237

Icon Candles
Candles that feature a fun hand-carved tombstone. Instant fun, great size for cupcakes too! 2½ in. high.
2811-S-8417
Pk./10

Candle
2¼ in. high.
2811-S-553

Candle Picks
3 in. high.
2811-S-786 Set/13

SMILEY FACE

Have a nice party! This friendly face has a way of making everyone happy at birthdays, housewarmings and welcome home parties.

Lollipop Mold
1 design, 6 cavities.
2115-S-1715

Party Bags
20 plastic bags, 20 ties included.
4 x 9½ in.
1912-S-2361
Pk./20

Baking Cups
Standard size.
415-S-261
Pk./50

Candles
1½ in. high.
2811-S-9351
Set/6

Pretzel Mold
Easy to mold; im sticks and lollipop sticks, too. 1 design, 6 cavities.
2115-S-4437

Candle Picks
2½ in. high.
2811-S-6327 Set/4

Chunky Candles
Thicker candles to energize any cake! They feature bold textured spirals and a fun hand-carved shape on top. 3¼ in. high.
Pk./4

Smiley Stars
2811-S-6325

Smiley Flames
2811-S-6326

RUBBER DUCKY

This bath-time favorite will make the biggest splash for birthdays, baby showers and school celebrations.

3-D Cake Pan
Five adorable designs included. Two-piece pan takes 5½ cups batter. Aluminum.
2105-S-2094

Candy Mold
1 design, 6 cavities.
2115-S-1565

Party Bags
20 plastic bags, 20 ties included. 4 x 9½ in.
1912-S-1275 Pk./20

Baking Cups
Standard size.
415-S-378 Pk./50

Icing Decorations
Certified Kosher.
710-S-293
Pk./12

Icon Candles
Feature a fun hand-carved rubber ducky. Great size for cupcakes too! 2½ in. high.
2811-S-8419 Pk./10

Candles
Handpainted details, clean-burning design. 1½ in. high.
2811-S-9337 Set/6

BASEBALL/SOFTBALL

From Little League to World Series celebrations, cover the bases with 3-D cakes, bobbling player toppers and hit candles.

Soccer Ball Pan
One-mix pan is 8¾ x 8¾ x 3½ in. deep. Aluminum.
2105-S-2044

Sports Ball Pan Set
Includes two 6 in. diameter half-ball pans and two metal baking stands. Each pan half takes 2½ cups batter. Aluminum.
2105-S-6506 Set/4

Mini Ball Pan
Ice two mini balls and push together for a 3-D effect. One cake mix makes 10–12 mini balls. Six cavities, each 3½ x 3½ x 1½ in. deep. Aluminum.
2105-S-1760

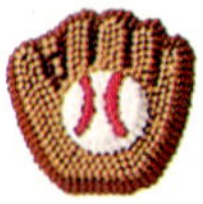

Icing Decorations
Certified Kosher.
710-S-475
Pk./9

Baking Cups
Standard size.
415-S-298
Pk./50

Take Me Out To The Ballgame Candles
Approx. 2 in. high.
2811-S-9341
Set/4

Bobbling Cake Toppers
Food-safe, with hand-painted detail. 4½ in. high.

Baseball	Softball
2113-S-5242	2113-S-5240

Sports Lollipop Mold
Makes favorite sports balls from every season. 4 designs, 4 cavities.
2115-S-4432

HOCKEY

Topper Set With Decals
Includes 1 topper, 6 candleholders, 6 candles, 1 sheet of decals.
2811-S-8422 Set/14

Baseball Topper Set*
Batter, catcher, three fielders and pitcher, 2⅛ to 2¾ in. high.
2113-S-2155 Set/6

Topper Set with Decals
Includes 1 topper, 6 candleholders, 6 candles, 1 sheet of decals.
2811-S-8425 Set/14

*CAUTION: Contains small parts. Not recommended for use by children 3 years and under.

Theme Party Products

FOOTBALL

Touching down at Super Bowl parties, homecomings, award dinners and much more.

First and Ten Football Pan
One-mix pan is 12 x 7¾ x 3 in. deep. Aluminum.
2105-S-6504

Icing Decorations
Certified Kosher.
710-S-478 Pk./9

Sports Lollipop Mold
Makes favorite sports balls from every season.
4 design, 4 cavities.
2115-S-4432

Topper Set with Decals
Includes 1 topper, 6 candleholders, 6 candles, 1 sheet of decals.
2811-S-8424 Set/14

Baking Cups
Standard size.
415-S-297
Pk./50

Football Topper Set*
Eight players and two goal posts, 1½ to 4½ in. high.
2113-S-2236 Set/10

SOCCER

A great way to reward a season or a game well done!

Soccer Ball Pan
One-mix pan is 8¾ x 8¾ x 3½ in. deep. Aluminum.
2105-S-2044

Bobbling Cake Toppers
Food-safe, with hand-painted detail.
4½ in. high.

Male Soccer	Female Soccer
2113-S-5238	2113-S-5239

Icing Decorations
Certified Kosher.
710-S-477
Pk./9

Sports Lollipop Mold
Makes favorite sports balls from every season.
4 design, 4 cavities.
2115-S-4432

Baking Cups
Standard size.
415-S-296 Pk./50

Topper Set with Decals
Includes 1 topper, 6 candleholders, 6 candles, 1 sheet of decals.
2811-S-8421 Set/14

Soccer Topper Set*
Seven players and two nets, 1¾ to 2 in. high.
2113-S-9002
Set/9

*CAUTION: Contains small parts. Not recommended for use by children 3 years and under.

BASKETBALL

Slam dunk winners! Create thrilling cakes and candies.

Sports Lollipop Mold
Makes favorite sports balls from every season.
4 design, 4 cavities.
2115-S-4432

Soccer Ball Pan
One-mix pan is 8¾ x 8¾ x 3½ in. deep. Aluminum.
2105-S-2044

Topper Set with Decals
Includes
1 topper,
6 candleholders,
6 candles,
1 sheet of decals.
2811-S-8423
Set/14

Basketball Topper Set*
Includes 1 forward, 2 centers, 3 guards and 1 hoop, 2¼ to 4 in. high.
2113-S-2237 Set/7

GOLF

Great ways to top cakes with perfect form.

Golf Topper Set*
Includes 4½ in. high golfer plus three each: 2½ in. wide greens, 4 in. high flags, 5 in. clubs and golf balls.
1306-S-7274 Set/13

Topper Set with Decals
Includes 1 topper, 6 candleholders, 6 candles, 1 sheet of decals.
2811-S-8420 Set/14

Bobbling Cake Topper
Food-safe, with hand-painted detail. 4½ in. high.
2113-S-5237

FISHING

Land the perfect cake for your angler, with bright candles and toppers.

Tropical Fish Pan
Everyone will be hooked by this fish—it's a keeper! One-mix pan is 11½ x 12½ x 2 in. deep. Aluminum.
2105-S-1014

Bobbling Cake Topper
Food-safe, with hand-painted detail. 4½ in. high.
2113-S-5236

Frustrated Fisherman Topper*
4½ in. high.
2113-S-2384

Tropical Fish Candles
Approx. 1½ in. high.
2811-S-9333
Set/4

Baking Cups

The easiest way to dress up a cupcake! Ideal for holding candy and nuts, too.

Made of microwave-safe paper unless otherwise noted. Jumbo cups are 2¼ in. diameter, standard cups are 2 in. diameter, mini cups are 1¼ in. diameter, bon bon cups are 1 in. diameter.

NEW!

Dazzling Dots
Standard
415-S-582 Pk./50
Mini
415-S-1141 Pk./75

NEW!

Snappy Stripes
Standard
415-S-581 Pk./50
Mini
415-S-1140 Pk./75

White
Jumbo 415-S-2503 Pk/50
Standard 415-S-2505 Pk./75
Mini 415-S-2507 Pk./100

Assorted Pastel
25 pink, 25 yellow, 25 blue.
Standard 415-S-394
Pk./75

Gold Foil
Wax-laminated paper on foil.
Standard 415-S-206 Pk./24
Bon Bon 415-S-306 Pk./75

Silver Foil
Standard 415-S-207
(24 pure aluminum/24 paper)
Bon Bon 415-S-307
(36 pure aluminum/36 paper)

Foil Petite Loaf Cups*
Wax-laminated paper on foil.
Gold Foil
415-S-452 Pk./24

Microwave-safe paper.
White
415-S-450 Pk./50

*Petite Loaf Cups are 3¾ x 2 in. and fit Petite Loaf Pan p. 149.

Nut and Party Cups
Mini 1¼ oz.
415-S-500
Pk./36
Standard 3¼ oz.
415-S-400
Pk./24

Party Bags

Wrap up cookies, candies, favors and more with color and fun!

Contains 20, 4 x 9½ in. bags and 20 twist ties, unless otherwise noted.
Pk./20

Clear (not shown)
1912-S-1240
Pk./25

NEW!

Dazzling Dots
1912-S-1090

NEW!

Snappy Stripes
1912-S-1089

NEW!

Wedding Cake
1912-S-1086

Wedding
1912-S-2364

Colorful Stars
1912-S-2362

Baby
1912-S-2365

Blue
1912-S-2356

Yellow
1912-S-2359

Pink
1912-S-2363

Red
1912-S-2357

PIZAZZ

A dazzling reflective pattern in 4 bright colors.

Contains 8, 4 x 9½ in. bags and 8 twist ties.
Pk./8

Silver Pizazz
1912-S-1020

Gold Pizazz
1912-S-1022

Red Pizazz
1912-S-1019

Blue Pizazz
1912-S-1021

Icing Decorations

Wilton Icing Decorations are perfect for topping cupcakes, cookies and ice cream. Mint-flavored edible shapes are Certified Kosher.

NEW!

Dazzling Dots
710-S-352
Pk./12

Alphabet/Numerals
710-S-494 Pk./70

Script Alphabet
710-S-546 Pk./62

Happy Birthday with Balloons
710-S-547 Pk./21

Cake Toppers

With Wilton toppers, a decorated cake is just minutes away! The excellent detail you expect from Wilton is evident in every design.

Circus Animals Set
Handpainted performers, 2½ to 3 in. high.
2113-S-9422 Set/4

Dinosaur Party Set
Reptile revelry! 1¾ to 2½ in. high.
2113-S-9420 Set/4

Tumbling Bears Set
Adorable acrobats, 2 to 2½ in. high.
2113-S-9421 Set/4

Small Derby Clowns Set
2 in. high with pick.
2113-S-2759
Set/6

Circus Balloons Set
12 in a bunch, 3 bunches per set, 6½ in. high.
2113-S-2366 Set/36

*CAUTION: Contains small parts. Not recommended for use by children 3 years and under.

Musical Light Show Topper

Any birthday cake will become a showstopper when this dazzling decoration is on top! The birthday message flashes brightly while the "Happy Birthday" song is played for everyone to join in. Convenient ON/OFF switch. Requires four AG13 or LR44 Alkaline Button Cell Batteries; 8 batteries included. Each set of 4 batteries lasts for 28 minutes of playing time.
2113-S-3465

Carousel Separator Set

Snaps together fast—sturdy pony pillars and separator plates provide strong support. Set includes four 9 in. high pony pillars and two 10 in. diameter separator plates.
2103-S-1139 Set/6

PARTY

DOLL PICKS

Teen Doll Pick

Her hair and face are prettier than ever—she'll give your Wonder Mold cakes a realism and sophistication unlike anything you've seen. 7¾ in. high with pick.
Brunette 2815-S-101
Blond 2815-S-102
Ethnic 2815-S-103

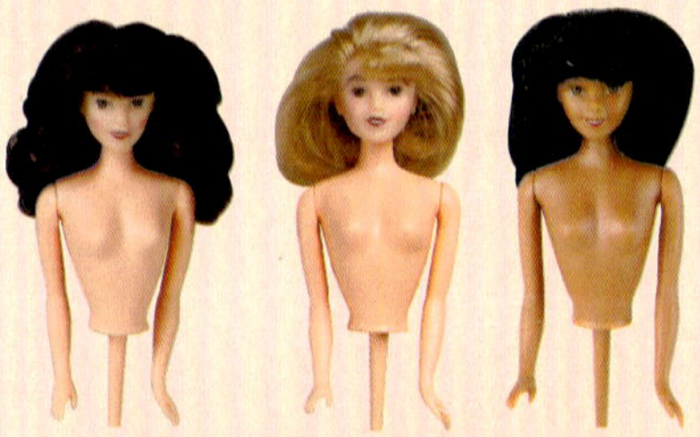

Mini Doll Pick Set

4¼ in. high with pick.
1511-S-1019 Set/4

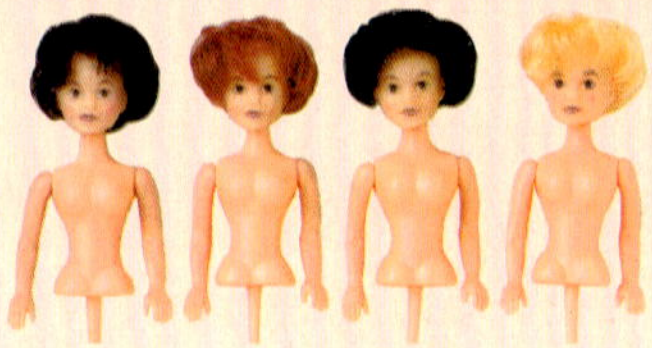

RELIGIOUS

Inspiring decorations that add a beautiful touch to spiritual events.

Inspirational Cross

Polished resin with finely sculpted scroll and bead highlighting. 5½ in. high.
202-S-398

Communion Girl†

3½ in. high.
2113-S-7878

Communion Boy†

3½ in. high.
2113-S-7886

† Designed by Ellen Williams

Candles

CANDLE SETS

Wilton gives you more choices! Top your cake with candles in the perfect colors—and check out our exciting designs on pages 186-187.

Farm

Approx. 1⅝ in. high.
2811-S-9347 Set/4

Firefighting

Approx. 1½ in. high.
2811-S-9339 Set/4

Baby Things

Approx. 2 in. high.
2811-S-855 Set/4

Fiesta

Approx. 1¾ in. high.
2811-S-9345 Set/4

Home Improvement Tools

Approx. 2¼ in. high.
2811-S-9136 Set/5

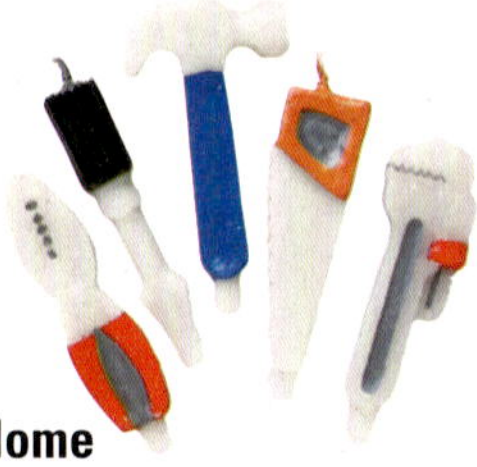

Construction Vehicles

Approx. 1¾ in. long.
2811-S-858 Set/4

Race Cars

Approx. 1¾ in. high.
2811-S-9135 Set/4

Paper Lanterns

1 in. high.
2811-S-9308 Set/6

Beach Sandals

⅜ in. high, ⅞ in. long.
2811-S-9352 Set/6

Margaritas

1¼ in. high.
2811-S-9343 Set/6

Champagne Bottles

2 in. high.
2811-S-163 Set/6

Beer Cans

1¾ in. high.
2811-S-9326 Set/6

Candles

NOVELTY

Glow-in-the-Dark

They light up the room even before you light them! These luminous candles will lend an extra touch of fun to any celebration. Assorted colors: white, yellow, green, blue. 2½ in. high.
2811-S-165
Pk./10

Glow Candle Set

Turn out the lights and get ready to serve your cake in a thrilling glow of color. Set of 4 light stick candle holders with candles gives cakes an aura of excitement that lasts up to 6 hours. No batteries needed—the glow starts when you bend the light sticks. Includes 4 each light sticks, connectors and candles. 6½ in. high.
2811-S-6215
Set/12

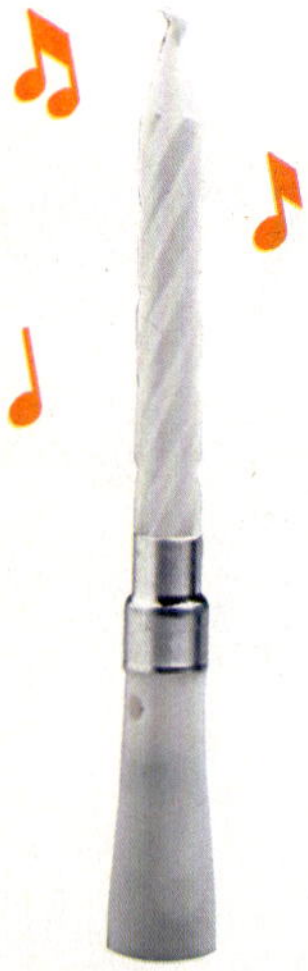

Musical Candle

Plays "Happy Birthday To You". 4¾ in. high.
2811-S-1231

Cupcakes
2811-S-8418

Stars
2811-S-8416

Icons

Highlight your party theme with candles that feature a fun hand-carved shape. Instant fun for any celebration, great size for cupcakes, too! 2½ in. high.
Pk./10

PICK SETS

Put your celebration message in lights! These bright candle picks are a unique and easy way to pick up the party theme on your cake top. Fun colors are just right for the occasion.

Happy Birthday

3 in. high.
2811-S-785 Set/15

Congratulations

3 in. high.
2811-S-787 Set/15

NUMERALS

Festive way to mark age or year. Edged in green unless specified. 3 in. high.

#2	**2811-S-9102**	**#7**	**2811-S-9107**
#3	**2811-S-9103**	**#8**	**2811-S-9108**
#4	**2811-S-9104**	**#9**	**2811-S-9109**
#5	**2811-S-9105**	**#0**	**2811-S-9100**
#6	**2811-S-9106**	**?**	**2811-S-9110**

#1
2811-S-9101

Pink #1
2811-S-240

Blue #1
2811-S-241

Longs

Sized right for larger cakes or for making a bold statement on any cake. 5⅞ in. high. **Pk./12**

White
2811-S-773

Multicolor
2811-S-777

Slenders

6½ in. high.
2811-S-1188
Pk./24

"Trick" Sparklers

Blow 'em out—they relight!
6½ in. high. **Pk./18**

Assorted
2811-S-1230

Red and Blue
2811-S-704

RAINBOW COLORS

Curly
Twisting, turning fun. 3 in. high.
2811-S-9127
Pk./12

Candle Holders
Protects cakes and keeps candles secure. Great colors, 1 in. high.
2811-S-552
Pk./24

CLASSIC

Pearlized
Watch them shimmer from the moment you light them! 2½ in. high.
Pk./10
White
2811-S-3658
Multicolor
2811-S-3665

Glitter
2½ in. high.
Pk./10
White
2811-S-248
Pink 2811-S-244
Blue 2811-S-246
Black
2811-S-247

Celebration
2½ in. high.
Pk./24
White 2811-S-207
Pink 2811-S-213
Red 2811-S-209
Blue 2811-S-210
Black 2811-S-224

Assorted Celebration
Classic spirals in attractive two-tones. 2½ in. high.
2811-S-215
Pk./24

"Trick"
Blow 'em out —they relight! 2½ in. high. Assorted: White, Yellow, Pink, Blue.
2811-S-220
Pk./10

Silver and Gold
2¼ in. high.
Pk./10
Silver
2811-S-9123
Gold
2811-S-9122

Shimmer
2½ in. high.
2811-S-3663
Pk./8

Lattice
2½ in. high.
2811-S-3656
Pk./8

Twist
2½ in. high.
2811-S-3660
Pk./8

Corkscrew
2½ in. high.
2811-S-778
Pk./8

Tricolor
2½ in. high.
2811-S-779
Pk./10

Crayons
Jumbo
3¼ in. high.
2811-S-226 Pk./8
Regular
2½ in. high.
2811-S-227 Pk./10

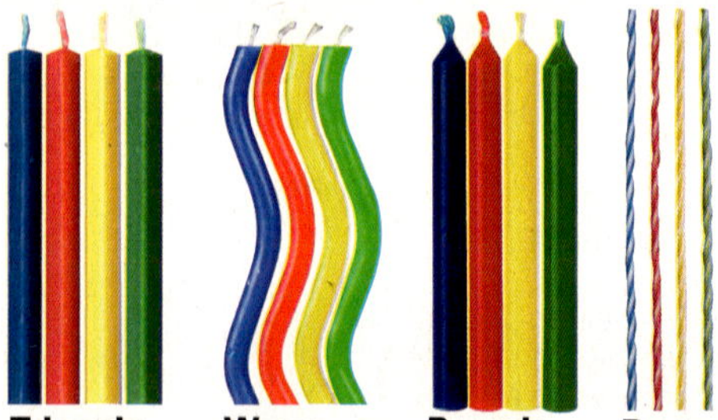

Triangle "Trick" Sparklers
2½ in. high.
2811-S-278
Pk./9

Wavy "Trick" Sparklers
2½ in. high.
2811-S-272
Pk./10

Rounds
2½ in. high.
2811-S-284
Pk./24

Party Thins
8 in. high.
2811-S-239
Pk./20

HOT COLORS

Diamond Dot
2½ in. high.
2811-S-551
Pk./20

Shimmer
2½ in. high.
2811-S-3662
Pk./8

Lattice
2½ in. high.
2811-S-3655
Pk./8

Twist
2½ in. high.
2811-S-3659
Pk./8

Corkscrew
2½ in. high.
2811-S-776
Pk./8

Tricolor
2½ in. high.
2811-S-779
Pk./10

Jumbo Crayons
3¼ in. high.
2811-S-282
Pk./8

Triangle "Trick" Sparklers
2½ in. high.
2811-S-276
Pk./9

Wavy "Trick" Sparklers
2½ in. high.
2811-S-270
Pk./10

Rounds
2½ in. in. high.
2811-S-225
Pk./24

Party Thins
8 in. high.
2811-S-237
Pk./20

SOFT COLORS

Shimmer
2½ in. high.
2811-S-3664
Pk./8

Lattice
2½ in. high.
2811-S-3657
Pk./8

Twist
2½ in. high.
2811-S-3661
Pk./8

Corkscrew
2½ in. high.
2811-S-775
Pk./8

Tricolor
2½ in. high.
2811-S-782
Pk./10

Jumbo Crayons
3¼ in. high.
2811-S-292
Pk./8

Triangle "Trick" Sparklers
2½ in. high.
2811-S-288
Pk./9

Wavy "Trick" Sparklers
2½ in. high.
2811-S-289
Pk./10

Rounds
2½ in. high.
2811-S-291
Pk./24

Party Thins
8 in. high.
2811-S-255
Pk./20

Seasonal

Wilton makes every time of year worth celebrating! With so many fun ways to serve cakes, cookies and other treats, it's easy to let everyone taste the excitement of each season.

HALLOWEEN

Bakeware

NEW!

Non-Stick Mini Pumpkin and Ghost Pan

Perfect size for trick-or-treaters! Non-stick steel releases treats easily. One mix makes 24-28 pumpkins and ghosts. 6 cavities, each 2¾ x 1¼ in. deep.
2105-S-1540

NEW!

Silicone Mini Jack-O-Lantern Mold

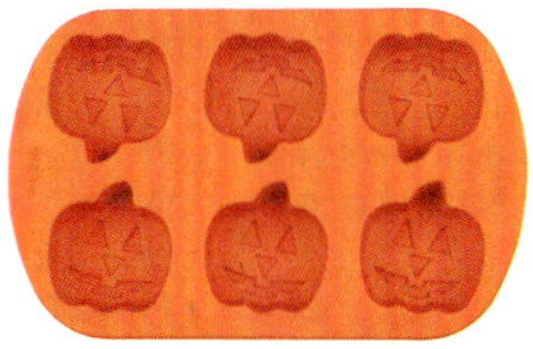

Discover the convenience and easy release of flexible silicone bakeware! Freezer, refrigerator, microwave and dishwasher safe—oven safe to 500°F. One mix makes 20-24 Jack-O-Lanterns. 6 cavities, each 2½ x 2½ x 1½ in. deep.
2105-S-4815

Petite Jack-O-Lantern Pan

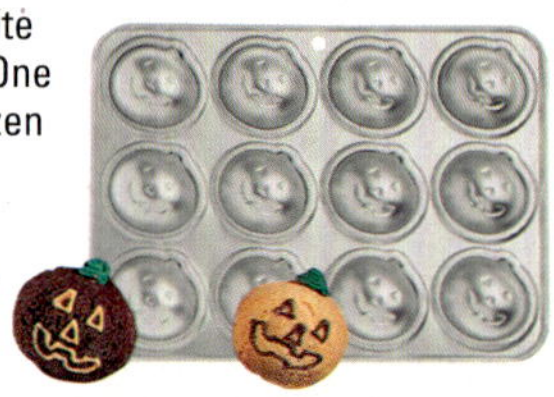

Make personal petite smiling pumpkins. One mix makes 9-13 dozen jack-o-lanterns. 12 cavities, each 2 x 2 x 1⅛ in. deep. Aluminum.
2105-S-8462

Mini Ghost Pan

Create gobs of goblins at one time! One mix makes 9-15 ghosts ready for decorating. 6 cavities, each 4 x 4⅞ x 1⅜ in. deep. Aluminum.
2105-S-3845

Spooky Ghost Pan

This appetizing apparition will be a welcome vision at all your Halloween happenings—from costume parties at home to celebrations at school. Great for easy-to-decorate cakes and gelatin desserts. One-mix pan is 11½ x 11½ x 2 in. deep. Aluminum.
2105-S-2090

Iridescents! Jack-O-Lantern Pan

The perfect holiday pan—this bright, colorful shape is as much fun for serving party treats as it is for baking a great cake! Designed for quick, easy cake decorating. Also ideal for crisped rice cereal treats, molded gelatin, bread dough and more. One-mix pan is 11¾ x 11⅛ x 2 in. deep. Aluminum.
2105-S-2059

Jack-O-Lantern Cookie Treat Pan

Create your own cookie blossoms; also great for adding fun shapes to other goodies like rice cereal treats and candy pops. Recipe included. Six-cavity pan, each cavity measures 3¼ x 3¼ x ¼ in. deep. Aluminum.
2105-S-8100

Cookie Treat Sticks

6 in. 1912-S-9319 Pk./20
8 in. 1912-S-9318 Pk./20

Colors & Icings

HALLOWEEN COLOR GUIDE

Orange	Black	Violet	White

Halloween Icing Colors Set

.5 oz. jars of Black and Orange. Certified Kosher.
601-S-3010 Set/2

FoodWriter™ Edible Color Markers

Use like ink markers to add fun, dazzling color to countless foods. Kids love 'em! Decorate on fondant, color flow, royal icing designs and cookies. Includes Black and Orange markers. .35 oz. Certified Kosher.
609-S-101 Set/2

Tube Decorating Icing

Tubes can be used with our Tip and Nail Set or Coupler Ring Set (p. 133) and any standard size Wilton metal tip. Colors match Wilton Icing Colors (p. 135). 4.25 oz. Certified Kosher.

Orange	**704-S-212**
Black	**704-S-206**
Violet	**704-S-242**
White	**704-S-200**

Color Mist™ Food Color Spray

Gives decorators the versatility and dazzling effects of an airbrush in a convenient can! Use it to transform a plain iced cake with sensational color, add splashes of holiday color to iced cookies and cupcakes. No mess, taste-free formula. 1.5 oz. Certified Kosher.

Orange	**710-S-5507**
Black	**710-S-5506**
Violet	**710-S-5504**

Ready-To-Decorate Icing

Anyone can decorate with Wilton Ready-to-Decorate Icing! Our brilliant colors and four decorating tips make it a breeze to add an exciting finishing touch to treats—without mixing or mess. 6.4 oz. Certified Kosher.

Orange	**710-S-4410**
Black	**710-S-4404**
Violet	**710-S-4408**
White	**710-S-4402**

Tube Decorating Gel

Transparent gels are great for writing messages and decorating cakes and cookies. Colors match Wilton Icing Colors (p. 135). .75 oz. Certified Kosher.

Orange	**704-S-312**
Black	**704-S-306**
Violet	**704-S-342**
White	**704-S-302**

Party

Baking Cups
Microwave-safe paper. Standard size, 2 in. diameter, Mini size, 1¼ in. diameter.
Standard Pk./50
Mini Pk./75

Smiling Pumpkin
Standard 415-S-1703
Mini 415-S-1704

Halloween Treats
Standard 415-S-1706
Mini 415-S-1707

Spooky Ghost
Standard 415-S-371

Ghost
2113-S-3464

Pumpkin
2113-S-3463

Bobbling Cupcake Toppers
Top off that special treat with these fun bobbling toppers. Food-safe design features hand-painted detail that makes even plain cupcakes more exciting. 2¼ in. high.
Pk./6

Party Bags
Colorful Halloween designs for candy and cookie treats. Unless otherwise noted, 20 plastic bags, 20 ties included. 4 x 9½ in.
Pk./20

NEW!

Shaped Smiling Pumpkin with Drawstring
Large bags are 9½ x 7 in.
1912-S-2126 Pk./15

NEW!

Smiling Pumpkin
1912-S-1224

NEW!

Halloween Treats
1912-S-2125

Spooky Ghost
1912-S-1040

NEW!

Glow-In-The-Dark Spooky Ghost
Large bags are 8¼ x 8¼ in.
1912-S-1113 Pk./10

Fun Pix®
Add a spooky touch to cakes, cupcakes, ice cream and more. Approx. 3½ in. high.

NEW!

Smiling Pumpkin
2113-S-7505
Pk./24

Foil Pumpkin
2113-S-713
Pk./12

Icing Decorations
Perfect for topping cupcakes, cookies and ice cream. Mint-flavored. Certified Kosher.

NEW!

Smiling Pumpkin
710-S-7200 Pk./12

NEW!

Halloween Treats
710-S-348 Pk./12

Petite Ghosts
710-S-3030 Pk./12

Candy

NEW!

Halloween Candy Mold 2 Pack Set
6 designs, 16 cavities.
2115-S-3057 Pk./2

NEW!

Smiling Pumpkins Lollipop Mold
1 design, 7 cavities.
2115-S-1750

NEW!

Monsters Candy Mold
4 designs, 4 cavities.
2115-S-1752

NEW!

Bats and Spiders Candy Mold
2 designs, 8 cavities.
2115-S-1754

NEW!

Halloween Lollipop Kit
More shapes, more fun—lollipop mold plus Bonus candy mold with 14 spooky designs! Everything's included! 10 oz. Wilton Candy Melts®* (5 oz. Light Cocoa, 2.5 oz. each Orange and White), Halloween Lollipop Mold (5 designs, 5 cavities), **Bonus** Halloween Candy Mold (9 designs, 9 cavities), 3 disposable decorating bags and ten 6 in. Lollipop Sticks.
2104-S-1497

Jack-O-Lantern Lollipop Mold
1 design, 8 cavities.
2115-S-1704

Spooky Ghost Candy Mold
1 design, 8 cavities.
2115-S-1407

Candy Melts®*
Ideal for all your candy making—molding, dipping or coating. Artificially vanilla flavored unless otherwise indicated. 14 oz. bag. Certified Kosher.

Orange	**1911-S-1631**	**Yellow**	**1911-S-463**
Dark Green	**1911-S-405**	**Dark Cocoa**	**1911-S-358**
Light Cocoa	**1911-S-544**	**Chocolate Mint**	**1911-S-1920**
White	**1911-S-498**	**Lavender**	**1911-S-403**

*Brand confectionery coating.

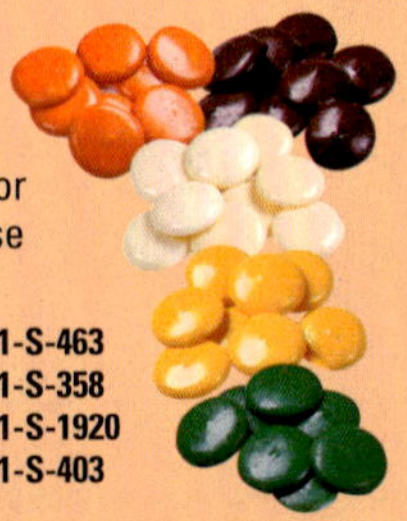

See pages 162-165 for more Wilton candy items.

HALLOWEEN

Stencil Sets

STENCIL-A-COOKIE™ CUTTER & STENCIL SETS

Using the fun-shaped stencils and cutter, it's easy to serve cookies with exciting, colorful designs for the season. Just cut cookies, then use the stencils and Cake Sparkles™ or Colored Sugars (shown at right), or Wilton FoodWriter™ Edible Color markers or Color Mist™ Food Color Spray (p. 188) to create dazzling shapes on top after baking. Set includes one metal cutter and two stencils (same design).
Set/3

Just Batty
2308-S-1413

Jack-O-Lantern
2308-S-1406

Halloween Cupcake and Cookie Stencils

Turn plain treats into ghoulish goodies with a stenciled Halloween design. Just place one of the fun designs over your baked treat, then sprinkle with Wilton Cake Sparkles™ or Colored Sugars (shown at right) or spray with Color Mist™ Food Color Spray (p. 188). 8 designs.
417-S-499

Gingerbread Kits

No baking, just fun! Everything you need is included to make one of 3 great haunted designs.

Pre-Baked Halloween Cookie House Kit

This hair-raising Halloween house is easy to build and fun to decorate! Everything's included—pre-baked cookie house pieces, orange and black decorating icing mixes, 2 bat and 2 ghost icing decorations, lots of candy for decorating, 2 decorating tips, 2 decorating bags, cardboard base and complete instructions. House measures 6¾ x 3½ x 7 in. high.
2104-S-2058

Pre-Baked and Pre-Assembled Halloween Cookie House Kit

It's already built so you can get right to the family decorating fun. Everything's included—pre-assembled cookie house, cookie chimney piece, orange and black decorating icing mixes, 2 bat and 2 ghost icing decorations, colorful candy for decorating, 2 decorating tips, 2 decorating bags, cardboard base and complete instructions. House measures 6¾ x 3½ x 7 in. high.
2104-S-2059

Sprinkles

INDIVIDUAL BOTTLES

Shake up your Halloween treats with fun colors and designs. Plastic bottles for convenient pouring and storing. Certified Kosher.

NEW!

Hallow Pumpkin Mix
2.5 oz. bottle
710-S-182

NEW!

Halloween Confetti
2.5 oz. bottle
710-S-184

NEW!

Halloween Nonpareils
3 oz. bottle
710-S-584

Ghost Mix
2.5 oz. bottle
710-S-767

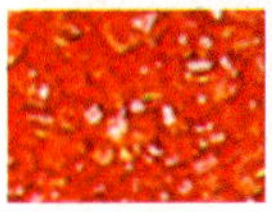

Orange Sugar
3.25 oz. bottle
710-S-759

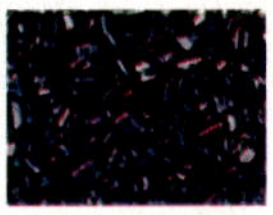

Black Sugar
3.25 oz. bottle
710-S-762

Purple Sugar
3.25 oz. bottle
710-S-758

Sparkling Sugars

A coarse texture and a brilliant sparkle. 8 oz. Certified Kosher.

Orange/White
710-S-572

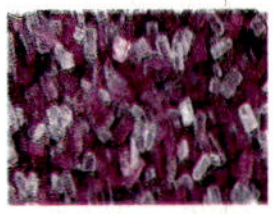

Lavender/White
710-S-571

Cake Sparkles™

Edible glitter, .25 oz. bottle. Certified Kosher.

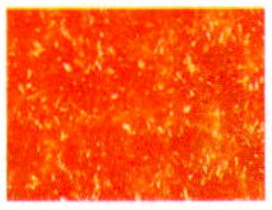

Orange
703-S-1308

Black
703-S-1302

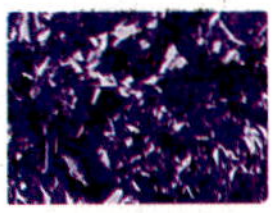

Purple
703-S-1266

ASSORTMENTS

4-Mix
Includes Halloween Mix, Halloween Nonpareils, Black and Orange Sugars. Certified Kosher.
710-S-728

6-Mix
Includes Halloween Mix, Bat Mix, Halloween Nonpareils, Black, Orange and Purple Sugars. Certified Kosher.
710-S-727

Cookie Cutters

COMFORT GRIP™ CUTTERS

These easy-grip cutters with extra-deep sides are perfect for cutting so many favorite foods into spectacular shapes. The cushion grip gives you comfortable control even when cutting thick desserts. Recipe included. Stainless steel sides, 4½ x 4½ x 1½ in. deep.

NEW!

Monster Head
2310-S-643

Pumpkin
2310-S-600

Ghost
2310-S-607

Witch's Hat
2310-S-630

GRIPPY™ CUTTERS

4 Pc. Grippy™ Set
Safe, easy cutting, with a comfortable grip and deep plastic sides. Four shapes include ghost, cat, pumpkin and bat, approx. 3½ in.
2311-S-257 Set/4

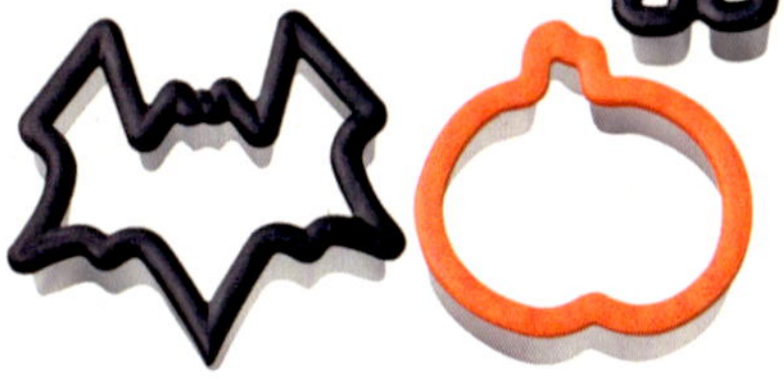

COOKIE SCOOP

Festive color and convenient design come together to make holiday baking more fun!

Scoops and releases approx. 1 Tbsp. of dough with ease. Dishwasher safe plastic.
417-S-324

NEW!

METAL CUTTERS

Put variety in your cookie-making with fun Halloween multi-shape sets. There are styles to please everyone. Recipe included.

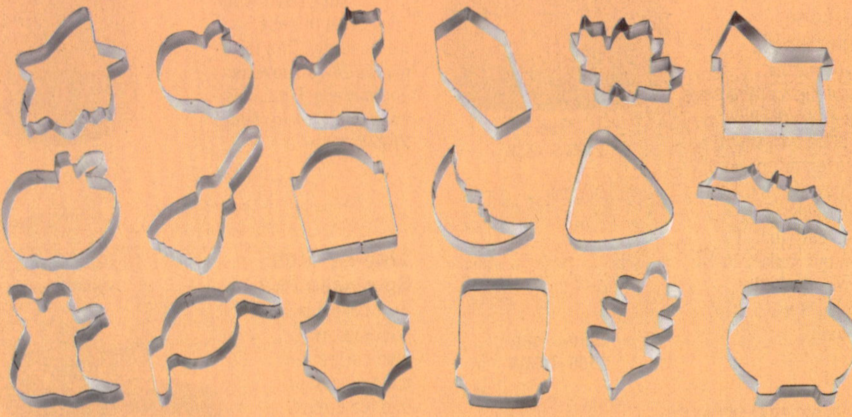

Halloween Cutter Set
Set of 18 includes witch, pumpkin, cat, coffin, maple leaf, house, apple, witch's broom, tombstone, moon, candy corn, bat, ghost, spider, spider web, Frankenstein, oak leaf and cauldron, each approx. 3 in. Metal.
2308-S-1131 Set/18

NEW!

Large Stainless Steel Pumpkin Cutter
Easy-to-use with raised handle for great control. Ideal size for gift cookies, party sandwiches, ice cream and more. Approx. 5½ in.
2308-S-1140

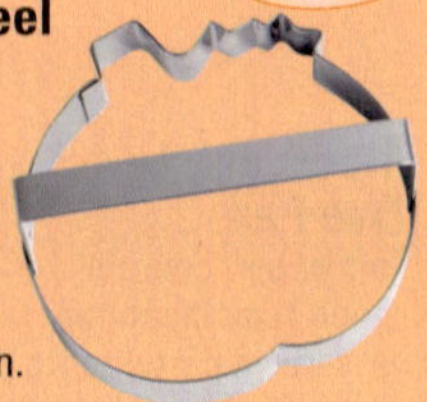

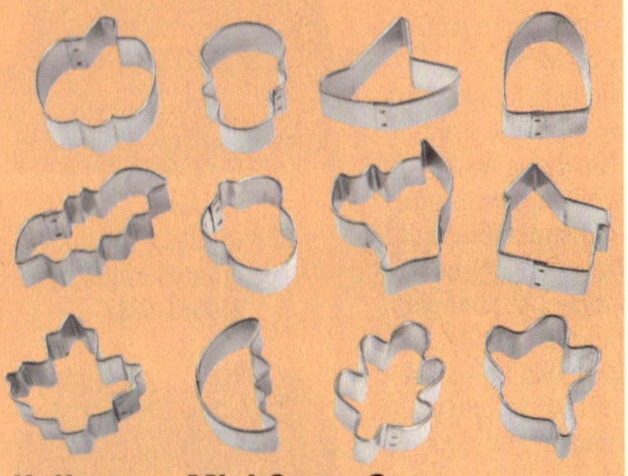

Halloween Mini Cutter Set
Set of 12 includes pumpkin, skull, witch's hat, tombstone, bat, acorn, cat, house, maple leaf, moon, oak leaf and ghost, each approx. 1½ in. Metal.
2308-S-1246 Set/12

Colorful Cutter Sets
Our metal cutters look great with their bright colors and fun shapes. Perfect for hanging until your next cookie-baking bash.

Halloween Cutter Set
Set of 9 includes bat, ghost, cat, witch, moon, witch's broom, tombstone, house and pumpkin, each approx. 3 to 3¾ in. Colored aluminum.
2308-S-2501 Set/9

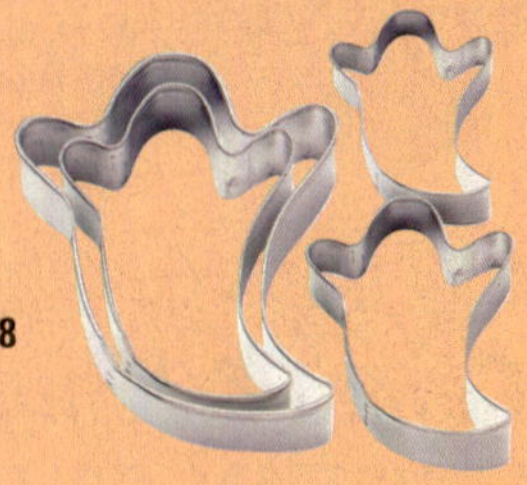

Ghosts
2308-S-1238

Nesting Cutter Sets
Create boo-tiful Halloween treats in four sizes. Each cuts neatly and is easy to handle. Sizes from 2¼ to 4 ½ in. Metal.
Set/4

Pumpkins
2308-S-1210

Spooky Shapes Cutter Set
Set of 4 includes moon, pumpkin, witch and ghost, each approx. 3 in. Coated metal.
2308-S-1200 Set/4

Halloween Mini Cutter Set
Set of 6 includes cat, bat, pumpkin, ghost, moon and skull, each approx. 1½ in. Metal.
2308-S-1211
Set/6

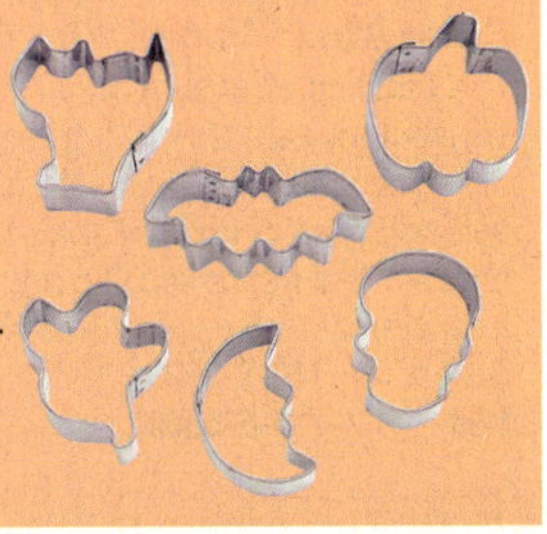

CHRISTMAS *Bakeware*

Silicone Mini Molds
Discover the convenience and easy release of flexible silicone bakeware! Freezer, refrigerator, microwave and dishwasher safe—oven safe to 500°F. One mix makes 20-24 cakes. 6 cavities, each 2½ x 2½ x 1½ in. deep.

NEW!

Tree
2105-S-4830

Snowflake
2105-S-4831

DIMENSIONS® DECORATIVE BAKEWARE
With Dimensions non-stick cast aluminum bakeware, anyone can create Christmas desserts with elegant shapes and spectacular detail. Heavyweight cast aluminum conducts heat extremely evenly. Premium non-stick surface for easy release and cleanup. Aluminum.

Gift
11⅛ x 9⅝ x 1½ in. deep. 10 cup capacity.
2105-S-5027

4 Cavity Mini Snowflakes
11 in. diameter x 2¼ in. deep. Four 1½ cup cavities; 6 cup total capacity.
2105-S-5028

Non-Stick Mini Snowman and Mitten Pan
NEW!

Perfect size for holiday gift basket treats! Non-stick steel releases treats easily. One mix makes 24-28 snowmen and mittens. 6 cavities, each 2¾ x 1¼ in. deep.
2105-S-3513

Step-By-Step Snowman Pan
Just bake, ice and decorate. He's also perfect for molding gelatin and ice cream, salads, baking bread and more. One-mix pan is 12 x 9¼ x 2 in. deep. Aluminum.
2105-S-2083

Iridescents! Tree Pan
This bright, colorful shape is as much fun for serving party treats as it is for baking! Designed for quick, easy decorating. Also ideal for crisped rice cereal treats, molded gelatin, bread dough and more. One-mix pan is 14 x 10 x 2 in. deep. Aluminum.
2105-S-2081

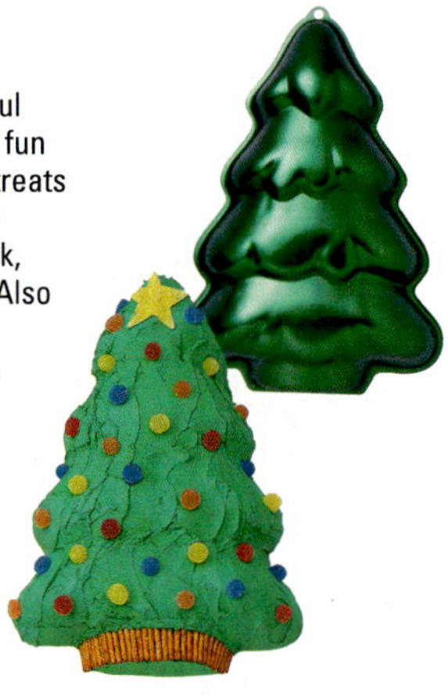

Mini Snowman Pan
Bake a blizzard of snowmen! One mix makes 12-18 snowmen. 6 cavities, each 2⅞ x 4⅝ x 1⅞ in. deep. Aluminum.
2105-S-472

Bite-Size Gingerbread Boy Pan
Bake plenty of fun little guys for everyone. One mix makes 24-36 boys. 9 cavities, each 2¾ x 3⅜ x ¾ in. deep. Aluminum.
2105-S-926

Cookie Treat Pans
Treats on a stick are so easy; just press dough or rice cereal treat mixture into the pan, insert a cookie stick, then bake, cool and decorate. Each pan makes six individual treats, approx. 4 in high x ½ in. Recipe included. Aluminum.

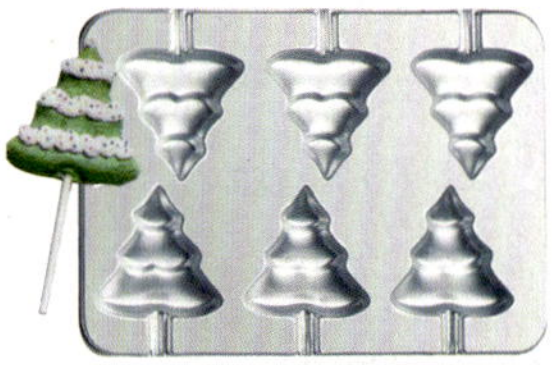

Christmas Tree
2105-S-8101

Snowman
2105-S-8107

Cookie Treat Sticks
6 in.
1912-S-9319
Pk./20

8 in.
1912-S-9318
Pk./20

Star
2105-S-8102

Colors & Icings

CHRISTMAS COLOR GUIDE
Red | **Kelly Green** | **Leaf Green** | **White**

Holiday Icing Colors Set
.5 oz. jars, Red-Red and Kelly Green. Certified Kosher.
601-S-3011 Pk./2

Color Mist™ Food Color Spray
The dazzling effects of an airbrush in a convenient can! Use it to transform a plain iced cake with sensational color, add splashes of holiday color to iced cookies and cupcakes. No mess, taste-free formula. 1.5 oz. Certified Kosher.

Green	**710-S-5503**
Red	**710-S-5500**

FoodWriter™ Edible Color Markers

Use like ink markers to add fun, dazzling color to countless foods. Kids love 'em! Decorate on fondant, color flow, royal icing designs and cookies. Includes Green and Red markers .35 oz. Certified Kosher.
609-S-102 Set/2

Ready-to-Decorate Icing
Anyone can decorate with Wilton Ready-to-Decorate Icing! Our brilliant colors and four decorating tips make it a breeze to add an exciting finishing touch to treats—without mixing or mess. 6.4 oz. Certified Kosher.

Green	**710-S-4401**
Red	**710-S-4400**
White	**710-S-4402**

Tube Decorating Icing
Can be used with our Tip and Nail Set or Coupler Ring Set (p. 135) and any standard size Wilton metal tip. Colors match Wilton Icing Colors (p. 135). 4.25 oz. Certified Kosher.

Kelly Green	**704-S-227**
Red	**704-S-218**
White	**704-S-200**

Tube Decorating Gel
Transparent gels are great for writing messages and decorating cakes and cookies. Colors match Wilton Icing Colors (p. 135). .75 oz. Certified Kosher.

Leaf Green	**704-S-324**
Red	**704-S-318**
White	**704-S-302**

Party

Baking Cups
Microwave-safe paper. Standard size, 2 in. diameter, Mini size, 1¼ in. diameter.
Standard **Pk./50**
Mini **Pk./75**

NEW!

Santa
Standard 415-S-424
Mini 415-S-406

NEW!

Snowflake
Standard 415-S-8801
Mini 415-S-8803

Bon Bon Cups
1 in.

Red Foil
415-S-314
Pk./75

Silver Foil
415-S-307
Pk./72
(36 pure aluminum 36 paper)

Gold Foil
415-S-306 **Pk./75**

Santa Bobbling Cupcake Toppers
Top off that special treat with this fun bobbling topper. Food-safe design features hand-painted detail that makes even plain cupcakes more exciting. 2 in. high.
2113-S-2005 **Pk./6**

Party Bags
Colorful Christmas designs for candy and cookie treats. Unless otherwise noted, 20 plastic bags, 20 ties included. 4 x 9½ in.
Pk./20

NEW!

Shaped Santa with Drawstring
Large bags are 9½ x 7 in.
1912-S-1328 **Pk./15**

NEW!

Santa
1912-S-1325

NEW!

Snowflake
1912-S-1395

Red/Green Mini Cups

Mixed, glassine paper. 1¼ in.
1912-S-1247
Pk./75

Petite Loaf Baking Cups

For gift breads. Fits Petite Loaf Pan (p.149). Microwave-safe paper. White.
415-S-450 **Pk./50**

NEW!
Santa Fun Pix®

Add a fun holiday touch to cakes, cupcakes, ice cream and more. 3½ in. high.
2113-S-7610
Pk./24

Icing Decorations
Perfect for topping cupcakes, cookies and ice cream. Mint-flavored. Certified Kosher.

NEW!

Santa
710-S-697 Pk./12

NEW!

Snowflake
710-S-543 Pk./12

Petite Twinkling Trees
710-S-502 Pk./12

SEASONAL

Candy

NEW!

Gift Truffle Candy Mold 2 Pack Set
10 designs, 22 cavities.
2115-S-1742 **Pk./2**

NEW!

Christmas Lights Candy Mold 2 Pack Set
3 designs, 17 cavities.
2115-S-1744 **Pk./2**

NEW!

Mini Gingerbread Candy Mold 2 Pack Set
8 designs, 22 cavities.
2115-S-1746 **Pk./2**

NEW!

Snowflake Lollipop Mold
1 design, 6 cavities.
2115-S-1705

NEW!

Christmas Character Lollipop Mold
3 designs, 6 cavities.
2115-S-1567

Santa Pretzel Mold
NEW!

Easy to mold; position pretzel rod, spoon in your favorite melted Candy Melts®* and refrigerate to set. Ideal for lollipop sticks, too. 1 design, 6 cavities.
2115-S-1501

Twinkling Trees Lollipop Mold
1 design, 10 cavities.
2115-S-1406

Candy Melts®*
Ideal for all your candy making —molding, dipping or coating. Artificially vanilla flavored unless otherwise indicated. 14 oz. bag. Certified Kosher.

Red	**1911-S-499**
White	**1911-S-498**
Dark Green	**1911-S-405**
Light Cocoa	**1911-S-544**
Dark Cocoa	**1911-S-358**
Chocolate Mint	**1911-S-1920**
Yellow	**1911-S-463**

*Brand confectionery coating.

Christmas Lollipop Kit
More shapes, more fun—lollipop mold plus Bonus candy mold with 7 jolly designs! Everything's included for making easy Christmas treats: 10 oz. Wilton Candy Melts®* (5 oz. White, 2.5 oz. each Red and Green), Christmas Characters Lollipop Mold (4 designs, 10 cavities), **Bonus** Gifts Galore Candy Mold (3 designs, 6 cavities), 3 disposable decorating bags and ten 6 in. Lollipop Sticks.
2104-S-3217

NEW!

See pages 162-165 for more Wilton candy items.

CHRISTMAS

Christmas Cookie Tree Cutter Kit

Create a beautiful Yule tree as a perfect holiday centerpiece—it's easy and fun! Just bake, stack and decorate. Kit includes 10 star cookie cutters in graduated sizes from small to large, 3 disposable decorating bags, round decorating tip, cookie and icing recipes, baking and decorating instructions for four great designs. Tree measures approx. 8 x 11 in. high.
2104-S-1555

Cookie and Stencil Sets

Holiday Cookie Set

Fun-shaped cutters and colorful sprinkles for sweet Christmas treats. Includes angel, tree, star and gingerbread boy metal cutters and 2 oz. Red and Green Sugars, 1.5 oz. Snowflake Mix, 2 oz. Christmas Nonpareils, 1.5 oz. Gingerbread Boy Mix amd 2 oz. White Nonpareils. Certified Kosher.
2109-S-5392
Set/10

Holiday Cupcake and Cookie Stencils

Turn plain treats into holiday visions. Just place one of the fun designs over your baked treat, then sprinkle with Wilton Cake Sparkles™ or Colored Sugars (shown at right) or use FoodWriter™ Edible Color Markers or Color Mist™ Food Color Spray (p. 192). 8 designs.
417-S-510

STENCIL-A-COOKIE™ CUTTER & STENCIL SETS

Using the fun-shaped stencils and cutter, it's easy to serve cookies with exciting, colorful designs for the season. Just cut cookies, then use the stencils and Cake Sparkles™ and Colored Sugars (shown right) or Wilton FoodWriter™ Edible Color Markers or Color Mist™ Food Color Spray (p. 192) to create dazzling shapes on top after baking. Sets include one metal cutter and two stencils (same design).
Set/3

Tree	Gingerbread Boy	Snowman
2308-S-1408	**2308-S-1410**	**2308-S-1409**

Sprinkles

INDIVIDUAL BOTTLES

Shake up your holiday treats with fun colors and designs. Plastic bottles for convenient pouring and storing. Certified Kosher.

Twinkling Trees Mix
2.5 oz. bottle
710-S-696

Christmas Confetti
2.5 oz. bottle
710-S-172

Christmas Nonpareils
3 oz. bottle
710-S-585

Cinnamon Drops
3 oz. bottle
710-S-769

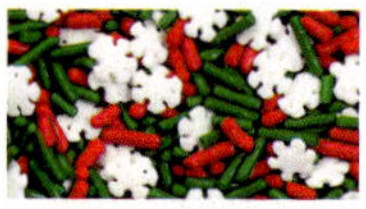

Snowflake Mix
2.5 oz. bottle
710-S-797

Chocolate Jimmies
2.5 oz. bottle
710-S-774

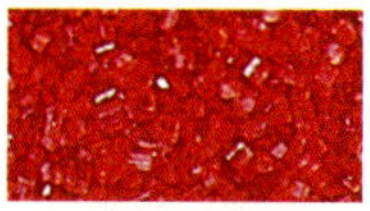

Red Sugar
3.25 oz. bottle
710-S-766

Dark Green Sugar
3.25 oz. bottle
710-S-764

Sparkling Sugars

Easy-pour sugars have a coarse texture and brilliant sparkle. 8 oz. bottle. Certified Kosher.

Holiday Mix
710-S-308

Red/ White
710-S-998

Green/ White
710-S-997

Cake Sparkles™

Edible glitter, .25 oz. bottle. Certified Kosher.

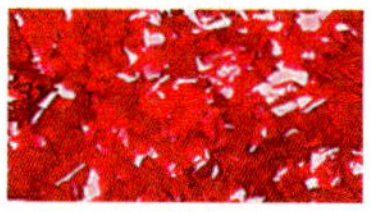

Red
703-S-1284

Green
703-S-1278

White
703-S-1290

ASSORTMENTS

4-Mix

Includes Christmas Tree Mix, Christmas Nonpareils, Dark Green and Red Sugars. Certified Kosher.
710-S-729

6-Mix

Includes Christmas Nonpareils, Confetti, Twinkling Tree Mix, Green, Red and White Sugars. Certified Kosher.
710-S-755

PLASTIC CUTTERS

Individual Cookie Cutters

Great shapes for end-of-year celebrations!
3 x 4 in. high.

Christmas Tree
2303-S-132

5-Pt. Star
2303-S-135

Cookie Cutters

COMFORT GRIP™ CUTTERS

These easy-grip cutters with extra-deep sides are perfect for cutting so many favorite foods into spectacular shapes. The cushion grip gives you comfortable control even when cutting thick desserts. Recipe included. Stainless steel sides, 4½ x 4½ x 1½ in. deep.

NEW!

Candy Cane
2310-S-644

Santa Hat
2310-S-640

Mitten
2310-S-639

Christmas Tree
2310-S-604

Gingerbread Boy
2310-S-602

Star
2310-S-631

Snowman
2310-S-634

GRIPPY™ CUTTERS

4 Pc. Grippy™ Set
Safe, easy cutting, with a comfortable grip and deep plastic sides. Four shapes include stocking, tree, star and gingerbread boy, each approx. 3½ in.
2311-S-260
Set/4

White Cookie Icing

Use this quick-setting microwavable icing to cover your cookies with a shiny finish—perfect for decorating with colorful Wilton Icing Writer™ accents! Easy to use—just heat and squeeze onto cookies using the convenient cap. Sets smooth in just 45 minutes. 10 oz. bottle covers 24 (3 in.) cookies. Certified Kosher.
704-S-481

NEW!

METAL CUTTERS & SCOOP

Put variety in your cookie-making with fun Christmas multi-shape sets. There are styles to please everyone. Recipe included.

Holiday Cutter Set
Snowflake, holly leaf, gingerbread girl, star, sleigh, tree, stocking, snowman, reindeer, ornament, candy cane, Santa hat, angel, bell, gift, wreath, gingerbread boy and mitten, each approx. 3 in. Metal.
2308-S-1132 Set/18

Holiday Mini Cutter Set
Star, angel, gingerbread girl, stocking, candy cane, ornament, teddy bear, bell, holly leaf, tree, gingerbread boy and sleigh, each approx. 1½ in. Metal.
2308-S-1250 Set/12

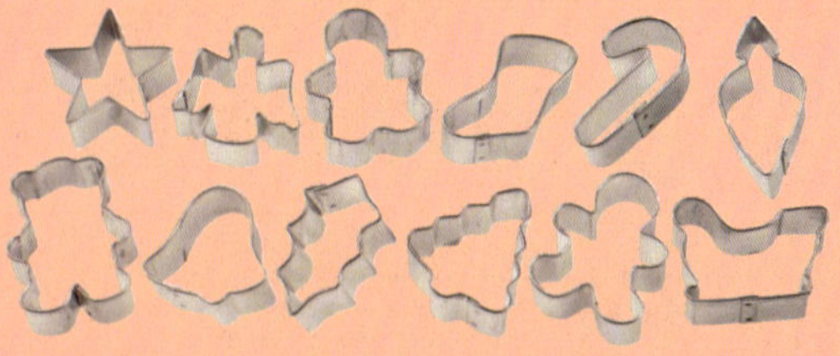

Colorful Cutter Sets
Our metal cutters look great with their bright colors and fun shapes. Perfect for hanging on the tree until your next cookie-baking bash.

Holiday Cutter Set
Candy cane, gingerbread girl, stocking, angel, star, bell, snowman, tree and gingerbread boy, each approx. 3 to 3¾ in. Colored aluminum.
2308-S-2500 Set/9

Jolly Shapes Cutter Set
Stocking, star, tree and candy cane, each approx. 3 in. Coated metal.
2308-S-1201 Set/4

Nesting Cutter Sets
Bake your favorite holiday shapes in four fun sizes! Quality metal cuts neatly and is easy to handle. Sizes from 5 to 2½ in.
Set/4

Snowflakes
2308-S-1244

Gingerbread Boys
2308-S-1239

Holiday Mini Cutter Set
Bell, gingerbread boy, holly leaf, tree, candy cane and angel, each approx. 1½ in.
2308-S-1214 Set/6

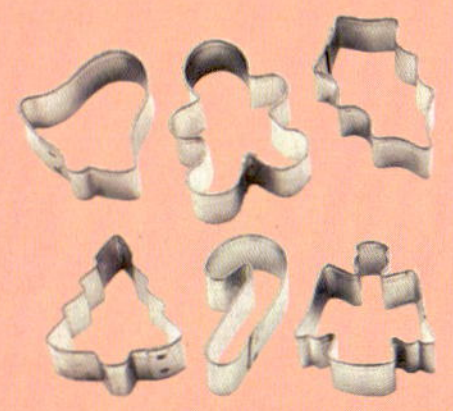

Holiday Red Cookie Scoop
Festive color and convenient design come together to make holiday baking more fun! Scoops and releases approx. 1 Tbsp. of dough with ease. Dishwasher safe plastic.
417-S-320

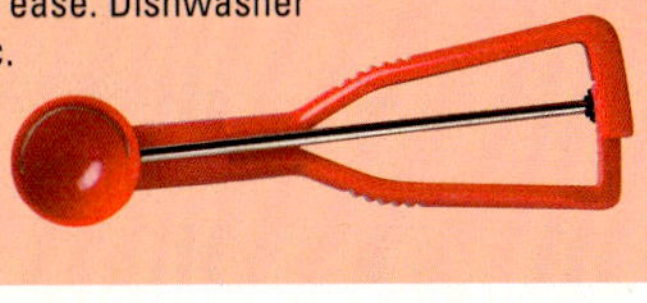

CHRISTMAS *Cookie Presses*

NEW!

Cookie Pro™ ULTRA II

Plus 4 BONUS Disks For Mini Cookies!

Making traditional spritz cookies has never been so easy! Cookie Pro Ultra II is designed to be the easiest to fill, most comfortable press you've ever used. And, with 16 terrific shapes, including 4 fun mini cookie designs, your holiday cookie baskets will be more festive than ever! Includes complete instructions and delicious recipes.
2104-S-4018 Set/17

Twelve Disks in Festive Shapes

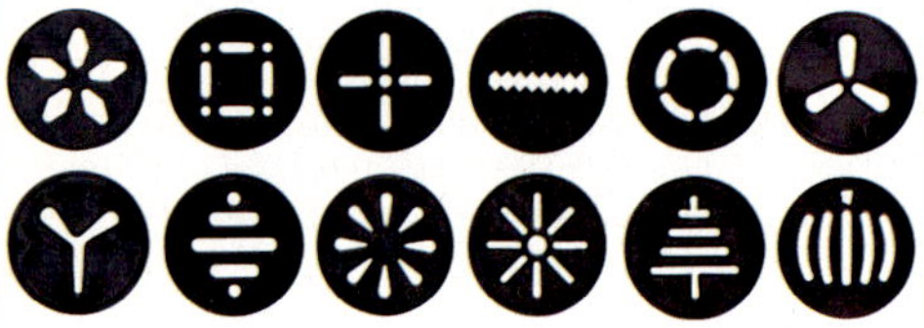

COMFORT GRIP™ Cookie Press

Experience a classic press that is truly comfortable. Its ergonomic handle feels great in your hand—the easy-squeeze action releases perfectly shaped dough. Clear barrel takes the guesswork out of refilling. Fluted bottom raises press off the cookie sheet for better-defined shapes.

Includes 12 cookie disks in a variety of shapes and our classic spritz recipe.
2104-S-4011 Set/13

12 Disk Designs

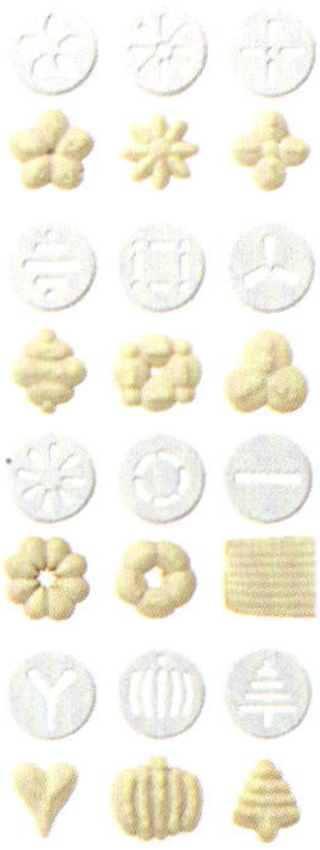

COOKIE MASTER™ Plus

Cordless Cookie Press

Our cordless cookie press is so powerful and easy to operate, you'll use it all year to create cookies, appetizers, desserts and more. Exclusive patented reverse action means there's no need to take press apart for refilling. Ergonomic design is shaped to fit in your hand for excellent comfort.

Includes 12 aluminum disks in classic and seasonal shapes, 4 accent tips for decorating and filling and 2 bonus recipe booklets—sweet and savory. Uses 4 AA batteries, not included.
2104-S-4008 Set/19

12 Disk Designs

4 Accent Tips

cookie max™ cookie press

MAXimum Control
Pump action dispenses a perfect cookie every time. 1 click of the plunger equals 1 cookie.

MAXimum Comfort
Soft cushioned pump handle reduces hand fatigue.

MAXimum Efficiency
Recessed plunger disk eliminates backflow—dough won't clog!

MAXimum Fun!
Makes 12 favorite shapes—easy instructions and 3 delicious recipes included.
2104-S-4003 Set/13

12 Disk Designs

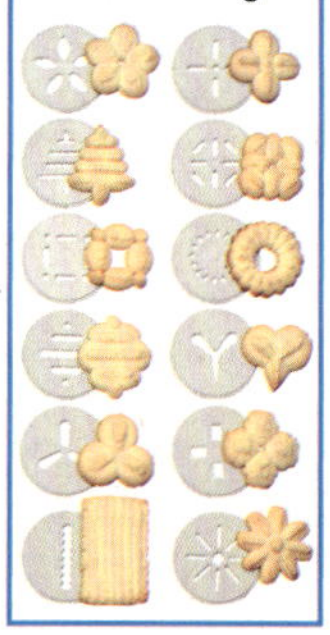

Bakeware

RECIPE RIGHT® NON-STICK

Built with all the right qualities for better baking results. Pan dimensions are embossed on handles for easy reference. Heavy-gauge construction means pans spread heat evenly and won't warp. Non-Stick coating provides exceptional quick release and easy cleanup.
5 year warranty. Aluminum.

15 in. x 10 in. Cookie Sheet
2105-S-967

12 Cup Muffin Pan
2105-S-954

24 Cup Mini Muffin Pan
2105-S-914

Bake Easy!™ Non-Stick Spray

This convenient non-stick spray helps your baked goods release perfectly. Just a light, even coating does the job. Use Bake Easy for all mixes and recipes—cookies, muffins, cupcakes, brownies, breads and more. Versatile for all types of baking and cooking. 6 oz.
702-S-6018

Gingerbread Kits

Pre-Baked Ultimate Gingerbread House Kit

Get ready for the ultimate gingerbread experience! This house is so huge, with tons of icing and colorful candy, that everyone can have a great time building and decorating to celebrate the holiday season. Everything you need is inside—pre-baked house pieces, two pre-baked trees, 3 packages of icing mix, 2 decorating bags and 2 nickel-plated tips, boy and girl icing decorations, loads of candy for decorating and complete instructions for assembling and decorating. House measures 10¾ x 9 x 11¾ in. high.
2104-S-1353

Pre-Baked Gingerbread Tree Kit

This brightly-decorated tree would look so festive on your holiday table—and it's great fun for the whole family to build and decorate. Just stack ready-made star cookies, decorate with icing and candy and add the star icing decoration tree top! Includes 14 gingerbread cookies, white and green icing mix, 3 gift and 1 star icing decorations, multi-colored candies, 2 decorating tips and 2 decorating bags and complete instructions. Tree measures 5½ x 8¼ in. high.
2104-S-2621

Pre-Baked Gingerbread House Kit

No baking—get right to the fun of assembling and decorating your festive gingerbread house. Kit includes pre-baked gingerbread house pieces, icing mix, assorted candies for decorating, decorating bag and tip, cardboard base and complete instructions with great decorating ideas. House measures 5¼ x 5½ x 4¾ in. high.
2104-S-1537

Pre-Baked and Pre-Assembled Gingerbread House Kit

The easiest-to-use gingerbread kit we've ever made! Pre-baked and pre-assembled so the family can get right to the fun of decorating. Kit includes assembled house with cardboard base, icing mix, candies, decorating bag and tip and complete instructions with great decorating ideas. House measures 5½ x 5½ x 4½ in. high.
2104-S-1516

Pre-Baked Gingerbread House Kit

Real gingerbread pieces are ready to assemble and decorate (without the mess of baking). Kit includes pre-baked gingerbread pieces, icing mix, assorted candies, decorating bag and tip, cardboard base and complete instructions with great decorating ideas. House measures 8 x 7 x 6½ in. high.
2104-S-1509

HANUKKAH

Cookie

Hanukkah Cutter Set

Includes Torah, menorah, 6-point star and dreidel, each approx. 3 in. Colored metal.
2308-S-1262
Set/4

6-Point Star Cookie Cutter

3 x 4 in. high.
2303-S-122

Sprinkles

Plastic bottles for pouring and storing. 3.25 oz. Certified Kosher.

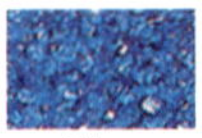

Blue Sugar
710-S-750

Yellow Sugar
710-S-754

Candy

Hanukkah Candy Kit

Everything you need to make easy, fun Hanukkah treats! Includes 10 oz. Light Cocoa Candy Melts®*, Hanukkah candy mold (6 designs, 13 cavities), 25 gold foil squares (4 x 4 in.), 2 disposable decorating bags and 5 mesh coin bags. Complete instructions. Certified Kosher.
2104-S-1328

Cake Sparkles™

Edible glitter, .25 oz. bottle. Certified Kosher.

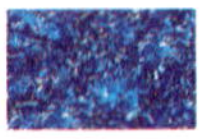

Blue
703-S-1314

Yellow
703-S-1272

White
703-S-1290

Hanukkah Lollipop Mold

5 designs, 10 cavities.
2115-S-1405

Candy Melts®*

Ideal for all your candy making—molding, dipping or coating. Artificially vanilla flavored unless otherwise indicated. 14 oz. bag. Certified Kosher.

Blue	**1911-S-448**	**Light Cocoa**	**1911-S-544**
Yellow	**1911-S-463**	**Dark Cocoa**	**1911-S-358**
White	**1911-S-498**	**Chocolate Mint**	**1911-S-1920**

*Brand confectionery coating.

See pages 162-165 for more Wilton candy items.

Colors & Icings

HANUKKAH COLOR GUIDE

Blue **Yellow** **White**

Color Mist™ Food Color Spray

The dazzling effects of an airbrush in a convenient can! Use it to transform a plain iced cake with sensational color, add splashes of holiday color to iced cookies and cupcakes. No mess, taste-free formula. 1.5 oz. Certified Kosher.

Blue **710-S-5501**
Yellow **710-S-5502**

Ready-to-Decorate Icing

Anyone can decorate with Wilton Ready-to-Decorate Icing! Our brilliant colors and four decorating tips make it a breeze to add an exciting finishing touch to treats—without mixing or mess. 6.4 oz. Certified Kosher.

Blue **710-S-4407**
Yellow **710-S-4409**
White **710-S-4402**

Tube Decorating Icing

Tubes can be used with our Tip and Nail Set or Coupler Ring Set (p. 135) and any standard size Wilton metal tip. Colors match Wilton Icing Colors (p. 135). 4.25 oz. Certified Kosher.

Blue **704-S-248**
Yellow **704-S-236**
White **704-S-200**

Tube Decorating Gel

Transparent gels are great for writing messages and decorating cakes and cookies. Colors match Wilton Icing Colors (p. 135). .75 oz. Certified Kosher.

Blue **704-S-348**
Yellow **704-S-336**
White **704-S-302**

VALENTINE

Bakeware

DIMENSIONS® DECORATIVE BAKEWARE

With Dimensions non-stick cast aluminum bakeware, anyone can create Valentine desserts with elegant shapes and spectacular detail. Heavyweight cast aluminum conducts heat extremely evenly. Premium non-stick surface for easy release and cleanup. Aluminum.

Mini Heart (shown)
Each heart is 4 x 2 in. deep. Six 1 cup cavities.
2105-S-5012

Also available, shown on p. 145.

Queen Of Hearts
9 in. x 3¼ in. 10 cup capacity.
2105-S-5001

Crown Of Hearts
11 x 2½ in. 10 cup capacity.
2105-S-5011

9 in. Non-Stick Heart Pan
Your classic heart cake will release perfectly. Cleanup is easy too. 9 x 2¼ in. deep. Non-stick steel.
2105-S-410

Heart Tart Pan
Create luscious desserts and entrees with classic fluted edges. Removable bottom. 10 x 1 in. deep. Non-stick steel.
2105-S-452

Silicone Mini Heart Mold

Discover the convenience and easy release of flexible silicone bakeware! Freezer, refrigerator, microwave and dishwasher safe—oven safe to 500°F. One mix makes 20-24 Hearts. 6 cavities, each 2⅝ x 2½ x 1½ in. deep.
2105-S-4012

Heart Springform Pans
Create elegant Valentine cheesecakes with these easy-releasing non-stick pans. Springlock sides, removable bottom for easy serving. Non-stick steel.

4 x 1¾ in. Mini
2105-S-457

9 x 2¾ in.
2105-S-419

Heart Pans
For graceful expressions of love on Valentine's Day or anytime, in just the size you need. 2 in. deep. Aluminum.

12 in.
2105-S-607

9 in.
2105-S-5176

6 in.
2105-S-600

SweetHeart Pan
Its gently curving shape gives the classic heart a more romantic flair. This cake will charm guests for birthdays, Mother's Day, Valentine's Day, showers and more. One-mix pan is 10¼ x 11 x 2 in. deep. Aluminum.
2105-S-1197

Mini Heart Pan
Great size for petit fours, individual brownies and more. One mix makes 12-18 hearts. 6 cavities, each 3⅝ x 3½ x 1 in. deep. Aluminum.
2105-S-11044

Petite Heart Pan
Bite-size muffins, brownies and cookies will win hearts. One mix makes 10-15 dozen hearts. 12 cavities, each 1¾ x 1⅝ x ½ in. deep. Aluminum.
2105-S-2432

Cookie Pans

Heart Giant Cookie Pan
Create a giant-sized pan cookie or brownie in a heart shape that will be a big hit. Ideal for refrigerated dough and brownie mix. Recipe included. Pan is 11½ x 10½ x ½ in. deep. Aluminum.
2105-S-6203

Heart Cookie Treat Pan
Just press cookie dough into pan, insert a cookie stick, then bake, cool and decorate. Also great for adding fun shapes to other goodies like rice cereal treats and candy pops. Each pan makes 6 individual treats, 3½ in. x ¼ in. deep. Aluminum.
2105-S-8104

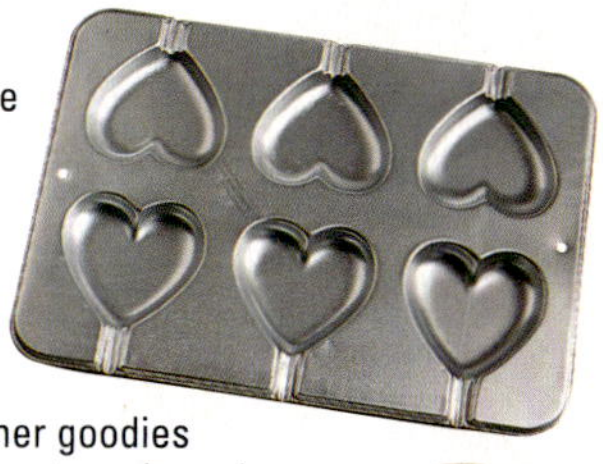

Cookie Treat Sticks
6 in. 1912-S-9319 Pk./20
8 in. 1912-S-9318 Pk./20

Colors & Icings

VALENTINE COLOR GUIDE

Red **Pink** **Violet** **White**

Color Mist™ Food Color Spray
Gives decorators the versatility and dazzling effects of an airbrush in a convenient can! Use it to transform a plain iced cake with sensational color, add splashes of holiday color to iced cookies and cupcakes. No mess, taste-free formula. 1.5 oz. Certified Kosher.

Red	**710-S-5500**
Pink	**710-S-5505**
Violet	**710-S-5504**

Valentine Icing Colors Set
Red-Red and Pink in .5 oz. jars. Certified Kosher.
601-S-5570 Set/2

Ready-to-Decorate Icing
Anyone can decorate with Wilton Ready-to-Decorate Icing! Our brilliant colors and four decorator tips make it a breeze to add an exciting finishing touch to treats—without mixing or mess. 6.4 oz. Certified Kosher.

Red	**710-S-4400**
Pink	**710-S-4406**
Violet	**710-S-4408**
White	**710-S-4402**

Tube Decorating Icing
Tubes can be used with our Tip and Nail Set or Coupler Ring Set (p. 135) and any standard size Wilton metal tip. Colors match Wilton Icing Colors (p. 135). 4.25 oz. Certified Kosher.

Red	**704-S-218**	**Violet**	**704-S-242**
Pink	**704-S-230**	**White**	**704-S-200**

Tube Decorating Gel
Transparent gels are great for writing messages and decorating cakes and cookies. Colors match Wilton Icing Colors (p. 135). .75 oz. Certified Kosher.

Red	**704-S-318**	**Violet**	**704-S-342**
Pink	**704-S-330**	**White**	**704-S-302**

Party

Baking Cups
Microwave-safe paper. Standard size, 2 in. diameter, Mini size, 1¼ in. diameter.
Standard Pk/50
Mini Pk/75

Hearts Remembered
Standard 415-S-274
Mini 415-S-268

Hearts
Standard 415-S-210
Mini 415-S-310

Party Bags
Colorful Valentine designs for candy and cookie treats. 20 plastic bags, 20 ties included. 4 x 9½ in.
Pk./20

Red Party Bags
Pk./20
1912-S-2357

Hearts Remembered
1912-S-1292

Hearts
1912-S-1269

Icing Decorations
Perfect for topping cupcakes, cookies and ice cream. Mint-flavored. Certified Kosher.

Hearts Remembered
710-S-824 Pk./18

Bon Bon Cups
Wax-laminated paper on red foil. 1¼ in. diameter
415-S-314 Pk./75

Cookie Stencils

HEART STENCIL-A-COOKIE™ CUTTER & STENCIL SET
Using the fun-shaped stencils and cutter, it's easy to serve cookies with exciting, colorful designs for the season. Just cut cookies, then use the stencils and Cake Sparkles™ and Colored Sugars (shown at right) or Wilton FoodWriter™ Edible Color Markers or Color Mist™ Food Color Spray (p. 198) to create dazzling shapes on top after baking. Sets include one metal cutter and two stencils (same design).
2308-S-1401 Set/3

Sweetheart Cupcake and Cookie Stencils
Turn plain treats into visions of love. Just place one of the fun designs over your baked treat, then sprinkle with Wilton Cake Sparkles™ or Colored Sugars (p. 200) or spray with Color Mist™ Food Color Spray (p. 198). 8 designs.
417-S-494

Candy

Roses and Buds Lollipop Mold
3 designs, 9 cavities.
2115-S-1708

Heart Lollipop Mold
2 designs, 8 cavities.
2115-S-1709

Hearts Candy Mold
1 design, 15 cavities.
2115-S-1712

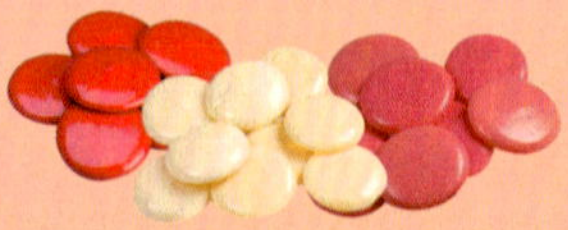

CANDY MELTS®*
Ideal for all your candy making—molding, dipping or coating. Artificially vanilla flavored unless otherwise indicated. Certified Kosher. 14 oz. bag.

Red	**1911-S-499**
Pink	**1911-S-447**
White	**1911-S-498**
Light Cocoa	**1911-S-544**
Dark Cocoa	**1911-S-358**

*Brand confectionery coating.

See pages 162-165 for more Wilton candy items.

Cookie Cutters

COMFORT GRIP™ CUTTER
This easy-grip stainless steel heart with extra-deep sides is perfect for cutting many favorite foods into heart shapes. The cushion grip gives you comfortable control even when cutting into thick desserts. Recipe included. 4½ x 4½ x 1½ in. deep.
2310-S-616

COPPER CUTTER
The warmth and beauty of solid copper make this cutter ideal for displaying and adding that decorative touch to your kitchen. This beautiful, heirloom-quality copper cutter has a smooth rolled edge with deep sides. Recipe included. 5½ in. wide.
2308-S-3040

PLASTIC CUTTERS

Nesting Hearts Cutter Set
Great for cookies, imprinting patterns in icing, cutting bread shapes and more. Sizes from 1¼ to 4⅛ in.
2304-S-115 Set/6

Heart Cutter
3 x 4 in.
2303-S-100

COMMUNION

Cross Pan
Beveled design is excellent for rolled fondant. Instructions included. One-mix pan is 14½ x 11⅛ x 2 in. deep. Aluminum.
2105-S-2509

TOPPERS

Inspirational Cross
Beautifully designed sculpted resin. 5½ in. high.
202-S-398

Communion Girl*
3½ in. high.
2113-S-7878

Communion Boy*
3½ in. high.
2113-S-7886

*Designed by Ellen Williams.

SEASONAL

VALENTINE *Sprinkles*

INDIVIDUAL BOTTLES

Shake up your Valentine treats with fun colors and designs. Certified Kosher.

NEW!

Hearts Confetti
2.5 oz. bottle
710-S-968

NEW!

Valentine Nonpareils
3 oz. bottle
710-S-625

Hearts Mix
2.5 oz. bottle
710-S-854

Kisses Mix
2.5 oz. bottle
710-S-855

Sugars

3.25 oz. bottle. Certified Kosher.

Red
710-S-766

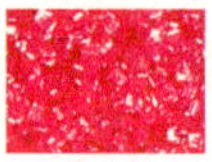

Pink
710-S-756

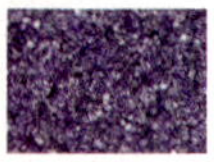

Lavender
710-S-758

Sparkling Sugars

Easy-pour sugars have a coarse texture and brilliant sparkle. 8 oz. bottle. Certified Kosher.

Red/ White
710-S-367

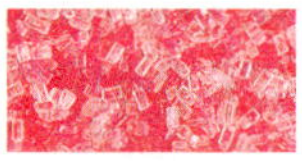

Pink/ White
710-S-366

Cake Sparkles™

Edible glitter, .25 oz. bottle. Certified Kosher.

Red
703-S-1284

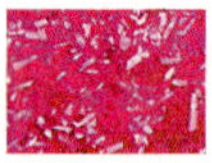

Pink
703-S-1260

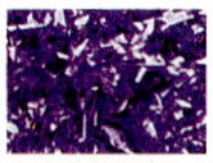

Purple
703-S-1266

ASSORTMENTS

3-Mix

NEW!

Includes Red/White, Pink/White and White Sparkling Sugars. Certified Kosher.
710-S-373

4-Mix

Includes Heart Mix, Sweetheart Nonpareils, Pink and Red Sugars. Certified Kosher.
710-S-730

6-Mix

Includes Kisses Mix, Heart Mix, Sweetheart Nonpareils, Pink, Red and Lavender Sugars. Certified Kosher.
710-S-738

Cookie Cutters

METAL CUTTERS

Put variety in your cookie-making with fun Valentine multi-shape sets. There are styles to please everyone.

Valentine Cutter Collection

Vivid Valentine colors bring a touch of romance to cookie-baking. Great variety of hearts, hugs and kisses designs. Sizes range from 1 to 5 in. Colored aluminum.
2308-S-2502 Set/9

Valentine Mini Cutter Set

Double heart, crinkle heart, O, heart with arrow, heart and X, each approx. 1½ in. Metal.
2308-S-1255 Set/6

From The Heart Nesting Cutter Set

Nesting metal cutters give you a choice of sizes, with two crinkled shapes. Largest cutter is approximately 5 in.
2308-S-1203 Set/4

Hearts Cutter Set

Love comes in all shapes and sizes. Includes seven different heart cutter designs from stylized to traditional. Sizes range from 1½ to 3 in.
2308-S-1237 Set/7

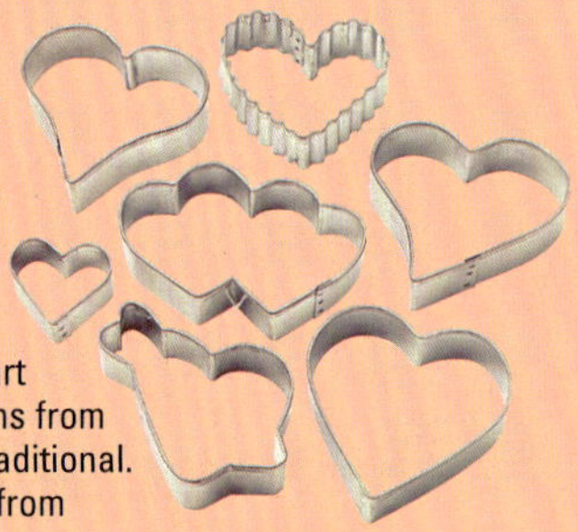

Heart Cutter

Quality metal cuts neatly and is easy to handle. 3 in. wide.
2308-S-1003

ST. PATRICK'S DAY

Shamrock Pan

Celebrate St. Patrick's Day with this fun symbol of joy and celebration. Also great for school parties, birthdays, sports celebrations and much more. One-mix pan is 11¾ x 2 in. deep. Aluminum.
2105-S-185

Shamrock Foil Fun Pix®

Add a shimmering, lucky touch to cakes, cupcakes, ice cream and more. Approx. 3½ in. high.
2113-S-1347
Pk./12

Shamrock Sprinkle Mix

NEW!

Shake up your St. Patrick's Day treats! Plastic 2.5 oz. bottle for convenient pouring and storing. Certified Kosher.
710-S-7485

Shamrock Baking Cups

Microwave-safe paper. Standard size 2 in. diameter.
415-S-357 Pk./50

Shamrock Party Bags

20 plastic bags, 20 twist ties included. 4 x 9½ in.
1912-S-2233
Pk./20

Shamrock Icing Decorations

Sugar-flavored. Certified Kosher.
710-S-286 Pk./9

Shamrock Lollipop Mold

1 design, 5 cavities.
2115-S-1545

Shamrock Green Metal Cookie Cutter

NEW!

Quality metal cuts neatly. Approx. 3 in.
2308-S-1320

Shamrock Metal Cookie Cutter

Quality metal and cuts neatly and is easy to handle. Approx. 3 in.
2308-S-1011

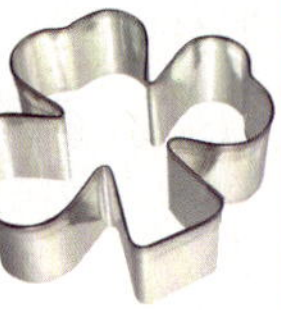

4-Leaf Clover Cookie Cutter

Cut cookies, sandwiches, use as party favors and in crafts. 3 in. wide.
2303-S-134

EASTER
Bakeware

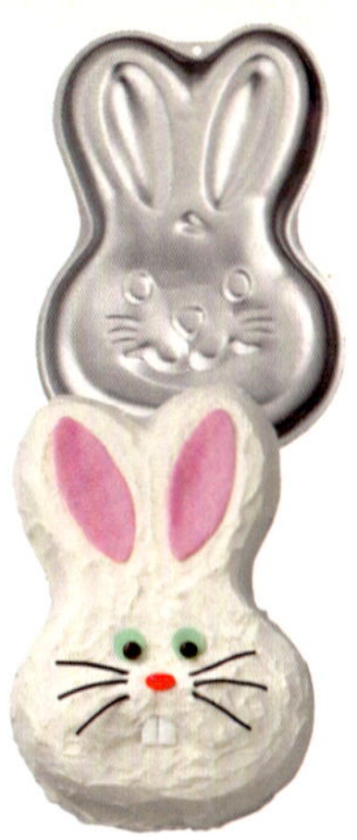

Step-By-Step Bunny Pan
Just what you need to get springtime celebrations hopping—just bake, ice and decorate! He's also perfect for molded gelatin, ice cream, salads and more. One-mix pan is 9¾ x 14 x 2 in. deep. Aluminum.
2105-S-2074

3-D Bunny Pan
Sure to get everyone's attention at your holiday brunch and beyond. Instructions for 5 different decorating ideas included. Two-piece pan is 7¼ x 7 x 4¾ in. high. Pan takes 4½ cups of pound cake batter. No heating core needed. Aluminum.
2105-S-2042
Set/2

Stand-Up Lamb Pan
A gentle symbol of springtime. This 3-D lamb will charm everyone at your Easter table. Instructions included. Two-piece pan is 10 x 4½ x 7 in. high and takes 6 cups of pound cake batter. Aluminum.
2105-S-2010
Set/2

Silicone Mini Flower Mold
Discover the convenience and easy release of flexible silicone bakeware! Freezer, refrigerator, microwave and dishwasher safe—oven safe to 500°F. One mix makes 20-24 Flowers. 6 cavities, each 2⅝ x 2¾ x 1½ in. deep.
2105-S-4034

Decorated Egg Pan
Great for molded desserts as well as cakes. Decorating instructions for five different designs included. One-mix pan is 9 x 11 x 3½ in. deep. Aluminum.
2105-S-174

3-D Egg Pan
Hatch a great Easter centerpiece! Two-piece pan takes just one cake mix. Includes 2 ring bases for level baking of each half. Each half is 9 x 6 x 2¾ in. Aluminum.
2105-S-4793
Set/4

Cross Pan
Truly inspiring for holidays, Christenings and other religious occasions. Bevel design is excellent for rolled fondant. Instructions included. One-mix pan is 14½ x 11⅛ x 2 in. deep. Aluminum.
2105-S-2509

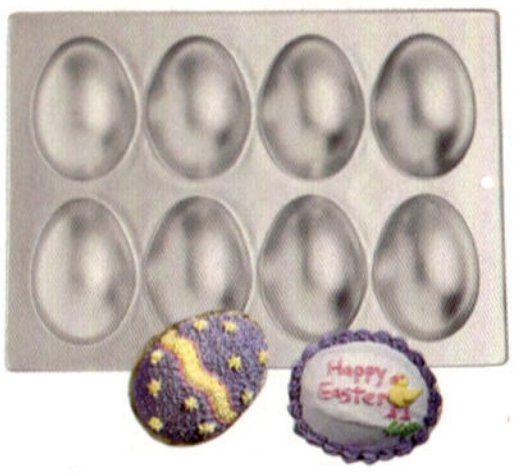

Mini Egg Pan
Make colorful place markers for the holiday table. One mix makes about 24-36 eggs. 8 cavities, each 3¼ x 2½ x 1 in. deep. Aluminum.
2105-S-2118

Mini Bunny Pan
Bake 6 treats quick as a bunny! One mix makes about 12-16 bunnies. 6 cavities, each 4⅜ x 3⅛ x ½ in. deep. Aluminum.
2105-S-4426

Cookie Pan

Bunny Cookie Treat Pan
Just press cookie dough into pan, insert a cookie stick, then bake, cool and decorate. Create your own cookie gifts for that special someone; great for adding fun shapes to other goodies like rice cereal treats and candy pops. Each pan makes 6 individual treats, 3½ x 2¾ x ¼ in. deep. Aluminum.
2105-S-8106

Cookie Treat Sticks
6 in. 1912-S-9319 Pk./20
8 in. 1912-S-9318 Pk./20

Colors & Icings

EASTER COLOR GUIDE
Pink | Violet | Yellow | Green/ Leaf Green | White

Easter Icing Colors Set
Lemon Yellow and Violet in .5 oz. jars. Certified Kosher.
601-S-5571 Set/2

Color Mist™ Food Color Spray
Gives decorators the versatility and dazzling effects of an airbrush in a convenient can! Use it to transform a plain iced cake with sensational color, add splashes of holiday color to iced cookies and cupcakes. No mess, taste-free formula. 1.5 oz. Certified Kosher.

Pink	**710-S-5505**	**Yellow**	**710-S-5502**
Violet	**710-S-5504**	**Green**	**710-S-5503**

FoodWriter™ Edible Color Markers
Use like ink markers to add fun and dazzling color to countless foods. Kids love 'em! Decorate on fondant, color flow, royal icing designs and cookies. Includes Pink and Lavender markers. .35 oz. Certified Kosher.
609-S-104 Set/2

Ready-to-Decorate Icing
Anyone can decorate with Wilton Ready-to-Decorate Icing! Our brilliant colors and four decorating tips make it a breeze to add an exciting finishing touch to treats—without mixing or mess. 6.4 oz. Certified Kosher.

Pink	**710-S-4406**	**Green**	**710-S-4401**
Violet	**710-S-4408**	**White**	**710-S-4402**
Yellow	**710-S-4409**		

Tube Decorating Icing
Tubes can be used with our Tip and Nail Set or Coupler Ring Set (p. 135) and any standard size Wilton metal tip. Colors match Wilton Icing Colors (p. 135). 4.25 oz. Certified Kosher.

Pink	**704-S-230**	**Leaf**	
Violet	**704-S-242**	**Green**	**704-S-224**
Yellow	**704-S-236**	**White**	**704-S-200**

Tube Decorating Gel
Great for writing messages and decorating cakes and cookies. Colors match Wilton Icing Colors (p. 135). .75 oz. Certified Kosher.

Pink	**704-S-330**	**Green**	**704-S-324**
Violet	**704-S-342**	**White**	**704-S-302**
Yellow	**704-S-336**		

EASTER
Party

Baking Cups
Microwave-safe paper.
Standard size, 2 in. diameter,
Mini size, 1¼ in. diameter,
Standard Pk/50
Mini Pk/75

Bunnies & Chicks
Standard 415-S-515
Mini 415-S-472

Assorted Pastel
25 pink, 25 yellow, 25 blue.
Standard 415-S-394 Pk./75

Party Bags
Colorful Easter designs for candy and cookie treats. 20 plastic bags, 20 ties included. 4 x 9½ in.
Pk./20

Bunnies & Chicks
1912-S-3104

NEW!

Bunnies & Chicks Favor Boxes
1904-S-1346 Pk./4

Icing Decorations
Perfect for topping cupcakes, cookies and ice cream. Mint-flavored. Certified Kosher.

Petite Eggs
710-S-528 Pk./12

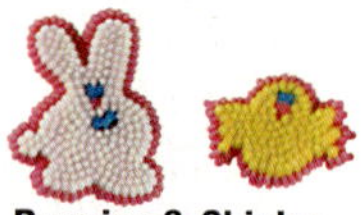

Bunnies & Chicks
710-S-368 Pk./12

Bunny Fun Pix®
Add a fun touch to cakes, cupcakes, ice cream and more. Approx. 3½ in. tall.
2113-S-2318 Pk./12

Bunny Shaped Party Bags
Colorful Easter designs for candy and cookie treats. 6⅞ x 9½ in. high.
1912-S-5150
Pk./20

NEW!

DOILIES

Serve springtime treats with sweet pastel doilies in 4 in., 8 in. and 10 in. sizes. Pretty lace-look edges. Includes 4 doilies in each size.
Pink 2104-S-5560 Pk./12
Yellow 2104-S-5559 Pk./12

Stencil Sets

STENCIL-A-COOKIE™ CUTTER & STENCIL SETS
Using the fun-shaped stencils and cutter, it's easy to serve cookies with exciting, colorful designs for the season. Just cut cookies, then use the stencils and Cake Sparkles™ and Colored Sugars (shown at right) or Wilton FoodWriter™ Edible Color Markers or Color Mist™ Food Color Spray (p. 201) to create dazzling shapes on top after baking. Sets include one metal cutter and two stencils (same design).
Set/3

Egg
2308-S-1412

Bunny
2308-S-1411

Flower
2308-S-1403

Candy

Lil' Bunnies Mini Candy Mold
4 designs, 12 cavities.
2115-S-1544

Hoppy Easter Lollipop Mold
8 designs, 9 cavities.
2115-S-1718

Candy Melts®*
Ideal for all your candy making—molding, dipping or coating. Artificially vanilla flavored unless otherwise indicated. 14 oz. bag. Certified Kosher.

Pink	**1911-S-447**
Lavender	**1911-S-403**
Yellow	**1911-S-463**
Blue	**1911-S-448**
White	**1911-S-498**
Chocolate Mint	**1911-S-1920**
Light Cocoa	**1911-S-544**
Dark Cocoa	**1911-S-358**

*Brand confectionery coating.

See pages 162-165 for more Wilton candy items.

Gingerbread

Pre-Baked and Pre-Assembled Bunny Hutch Cookie House Kit
It's the perfect springtime project and a cute centerpiece for your Easter table. So hop to it—everything is included: a pre-baked, pre-built hutch, yellow and pink decorating icing mixes, candies, pre-made icing decorations, two cookie bunny ears, two decorating bags and tips, cardboard base and complete instructions with great decorating ideas. Hutch measures 5½ x 5¼ x 6 in. high.
2104-S-1594

Easter Cupcake and Cookie Stencils
Turn plain treats into spring sensations with a stenciled Easter design. Place one of the fun designs over your baked treat, then sprinkle with Wilton Cake Sparkles™ or Colored Sugars (p. 203) or spray with Color Mist™ Food Color Spray (p. 201) 8 designs.
417-S-496 Set/8

Sprinkles

INDIVIDUAL BOTTLES

Shake up your Easter treats! Plastic bottles for convenient pouring and storing. Certified Kosher.

NEW!

Colorful Egg Mix
2.5 oz. bottle
710-S-7486

NEW!

Spring Confetti
2.5 oz. bottle
710-S-1278

Bunny/Ducks Mix
2.5 oz. bottle
710-S-870

Soft Pink Sugar
3.25 oz. bottle
710-S-896

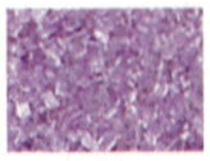
Soft Lavender Sugar
3.25 oz. bottle
710-S-897

Soft Yellow Sugar
3.25 oz. bottle
710-S-895

Soft Green Sugar
3.25 oz. bottle
710-S-898

Sparkling Sugars

Easy-pour sugars have a coarse texture and brilliant sparkle. 8 oz. Certified Kosher.

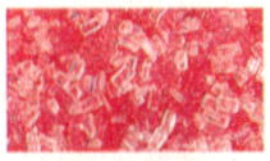
Pink/White
710-S-369

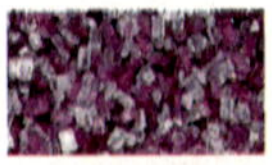
Lavender/White
710-S-371

Yellow/ White
710-S-370

ASSORTMENTS

NEW!

3-Mix

Includes Pastel Green, Yellow and Pink Sparkling Sugars. Certified Kosher.
710-S-373

4-Mix

Includes Yellow Sugar, Lt. Green Sugar, Springtime Nonpareils and Bunnies and Ducks Mix. Certified Kosher.
710-S-736

6-Mix

Includes Bunny and Ducks Sprinkle Mix, Colorful Egg, Spring Confetti, Lavender, Pink and Green Sugars. Certified Kosher.
710-S-740

Cookie Cutters

METAL CUTTERS

Put variety in your cookie-making with fun Easter multi-shape sets. There are styles to please everyone. Recipe included.

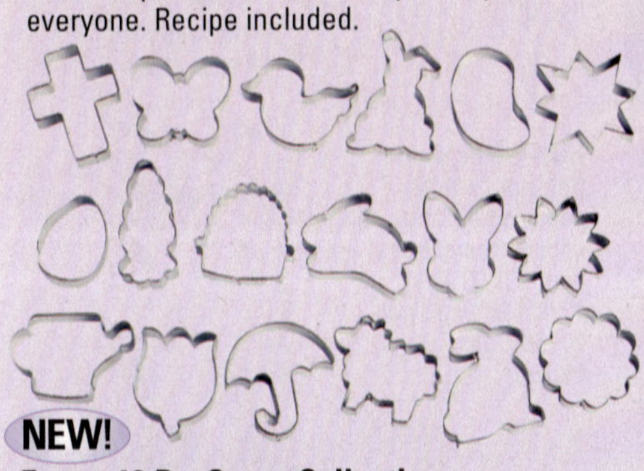

NEW!

Easter 18 Pc. Cutter Collection

Cross, butterfly, chick, bunny, jelly bean, sun, egg, carrot, basket, leaping bunny, bunny face, daisy, sprinkling can, tulip, umbrella, lamb, rabbit and flower cutters are approx. 3 in.
2308-S-1134 Set/18

Easter 9 pc. Cutter Collection

Lamb, chick, tulip, flower, bunny, egg, butterfly, bunny face, and carrot cutters are approx. 3 in. Colored aluminum.
2308-S-2503 Set/9

Hoppy Easter Colored Metal Cutter Set

Springtime favorites in pastels of the season. Tulip, egg, butterfly and bunny. Coated metal. Each approx. 3½ in.
2308-S-1207 Set/4

NEW!

Easter 12 Pc. Mini Cutter Collection

Bunny face, egg, cross, sun, carrot, chick, flower, tulip, sprinkling can, umbrella, bunny and butterfly cutters are approx. 1½ in.
2308-S-1254 Set/12

Easter Mini Cutter Set

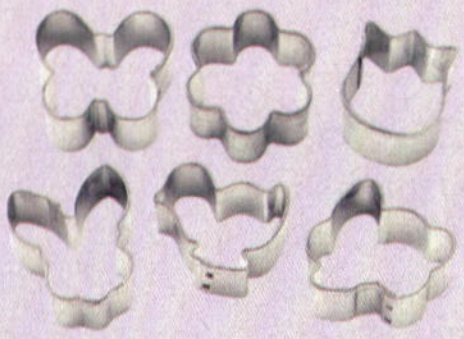

Butterfly, daisy, tulip, bunny face, chick and bunny, each approx. 1½ in. Metal.
2308-S-1209 Set/6

COMFORT GRIP™ CUTTERS

Easy-grip stainless steel cutters with extra-deep sides are perfect for cutting so many foods into seasonal shapes. The cushion grip gives you comfortable control even when cutting thick desserts. Recipe included. 4½ x 4½ x 1½ in. deep.

Bunny
2310-S-626

Chick
2310-S-625

GRIPPY™ CUTTERS

4 Pc. Grippy™ Set

Safe, easy cutting, with a comfortable grip and deep plastic sides. Four shapes include egg, butterfly, flower and bunny. Approx. 3½ in.
2311-S-258 Set/4

PLASTIC CUTTERS

Child-safe design means kids can have a great time helping. And remember all the fun ways to use our cutters—for bread shapes, stencils, sun catchers and so much more.

Easter Egg Canister Cutter Set

A fun and convenient egg canister holds a collection of Easter cutters for holiday cookies. Ten cutters, each approx. 3½ in.
2304-S-95 Set/10

Easter Bite-Size Cutter Set

Bunny, chick, tulip, egg and bunny face shapes, each approx. 1½ in.
2303-S-9319 Set/5

Nesting Bunnies Cutter Set

Sizes from 1¼ to 4⅛ in.
2303-S-9270 Set/4

Cross
2303-S-141

Duck
2303-S-148

Egg
2303-S-119

Individual Cutters

Each approx. 3 x 4 in.

SEASONAL

PATRIOTIC

Bakeware

NEW!

Silicone Mini Star Mold
Discover the convenience and easy release of flexible silicone bakeware! Freezer, refrigerator, microwave and dishwasher safe—oven safe to 500°F. One mix makes 20-24 stars. 6 cavities, each 2⅝ x 2½ x 1½ in. deep.
2105-S-4819

Stars and Stripes Pan
Decorate a grand old flag cake perfect for that July 4th cookout. Accent Old Glory with Piping Gel and fresh summer fruit. One-mix pan is 13 x 9 x 2 in. Aluminum.
2105-S-183

Star Pan
Your colorful star cake will set off sparks on the 4th and brighten parties all year long. One-mix pan is 12¾ x 1⅞ in. Aluminum.
2105-S-2512

Mini Star Pan
Personal-size desserts make everyone feel like a star. One mix makes 12-16 stars. 6 cavities, each 4¾ x 1 in. Aluminum.
2105-S-1235

Party

Baking Cups
Microwave-safe paper. Standard size, 2 in. diameter.
Pk./50

Old Glory
415-S-1262

Patriotic Stars
415-S-381

Party Bags
Colorful Patriotic designs for candy and cookie treats. Pack contains 20 plastic 4 x 9½ in. bags and 20 twist ties.
Pk./20

Old Glory
1912-S-3056

Patriotic Stars
1912-S-1254

Icing Decorations
Perfect for topping cupcakes, cookies and ice cream. Mint-flavored. Certified Kosher.

Patriotic Flags
710-S-726 Pk./9

Patriotic Stars
710-S-942 Pk./21

PARTY PICKS

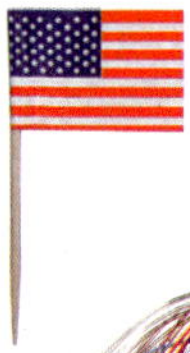

Stars and Stripes
3 in. high.
2113-S-704
Pk./40

Patriotic Foil Pix
Looks like a dazzling fireworks display on your holiday treats! Great for cakes, cupcakes. 4 in. high.
2113-S-712 Pk./12

NEW!

Bobbling Cupcake Toppers
Top off that special treat with these fun bobbling toppers. Food-safe design features hand-painted detail that makes even plain cupcakes more exciting. 2 in. high.
Pk./6

Uncle Sam
2113-S-1273

CANDLES

NEW!

Patriotic Chunkys
Feature bold textured spirals and a fun hand-carved shape on top. 3¼ in. high.
2811-S-1122 Pk./4

Beer Cans
1¾ in. high.
2811-S-9326
Set/6

Red and Blue Sparklers
6½ in. high.
2811-S-704
Pk./18

Colors & Icings

PATRIOTIC COLOR GUIDE

Red | White | Blue

Color Mist™ Food Color Spray
Dazzling effects of an airbrush in a convenient can! Transform a plain iced cake with sensational color, add splashes of color to iced cookies and cupcakes. No mess, taste-free formula. 1.5 oz. Certified Kosher.

Red	**710-S-5500**
Blue	**710-S-5501**

Tube Decorating Gel
Transparent gels are great for writing messages and decorating cakes and cookies. Colors match Wilton Icing Colors (p. 135). .75 oz. Certified Kosher.

Red	**704-S-318**
White	**704-S-302**
Royal Blue	**704-S-348**

Ready-to-Decorate Icing
Anyone can decorate with Wilton Ready-to-Decorate Icing! Our brilliant colors and four decorating tips make it a breeze to add an exciting finishing touch to treats—without mixing or mess. 6.4 oz. Certified Kosher.

Red	**710-S-4400**
White	**710-S-4402**
Blue	**710-S-4407**

Tube Decorating Icing
Tubes can be used with our Tip and Nail Set or Coupler Ring Set (p. 135) and any standard size Wilton metal tip. Colors match Wilton Icing Colors (p. 135). 4.25 oz. Certified Kosher.

Red	**704-S-218**
White	**704-S-200**
Royal Blue	**704-S-248**

Cookie Pan

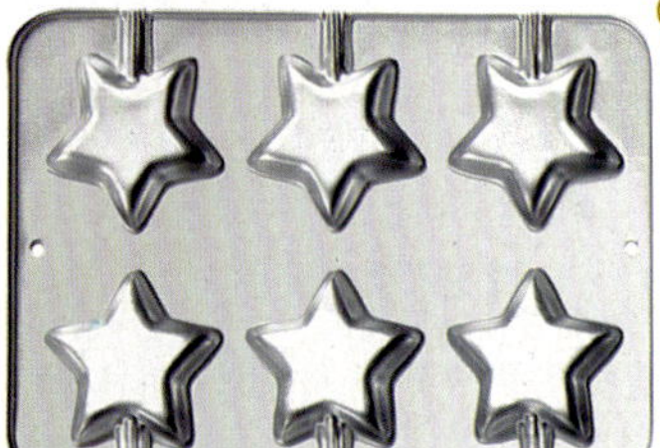

Star Cookie Treat Pan
Just press cookie dough into pan, insert a cookie stick, then bake, cool and decorate. Create cookie stars, rice cereal treats and candy pops. Pan makes 6 individual treats, 3½ in. diameter x ¼ in. Aluminum.
2105-S-8102

Cookie Treat Sticks
6 in. 1912-S-9319 Pk./20
8 in. 1912-S-9318 Pk./20

CUPCAKES 'N MORE® DESSERT STANDS

Easy to assemble!
Just stack each layer of cupcakes onto the locking center rod.

Keeps looking great!
Non-toxic, silver-finished metal has a durable non-chip finish.

Collapsible design
Stores easily and safely.

Angled holders
Give the best view of cupcake tops!

Individually decorated cupcakes are the perfect way to add a personal touch to celebrations. Now, with Cupcakes 'N More, you have the perfect way to serve them! The look is fresh and fun, featuring bold silver-finished wire spirals to securely hold each cupcake. The twisting, towering design is perfect for any setting—showers, kids' birthdays, weddings, holidays and more.
Large 15 in. high x 18 in. wide. Holds 38 cupcakes. **307-S-651**

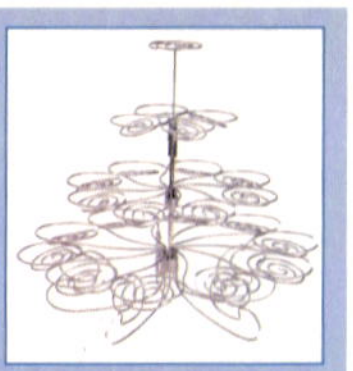

Standard
12 in. high x 13 in. wide. Holds 23 cupcakes.
307-S-826

Sprinkles

INDIVIDUAL BOTTLES

Plastic bottles for convenient pouring and storing. Certified Kosher.

NEW!

Patriotic Confetti
2.5 oz. bottle
710-S-1122

NEW!

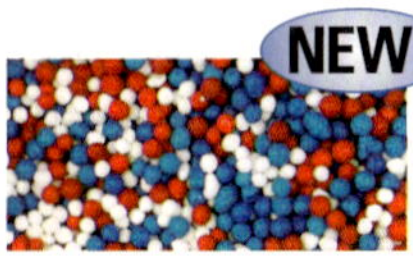

Patriotic Nonpareils
3 oz. bottle
710-S-1123

Patriotic Mix
2.5 oz. bottle
710-S-786

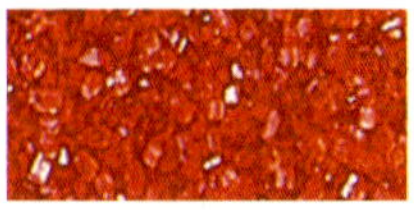

Red Sugar
3.25 oz. bottle
710-S-766

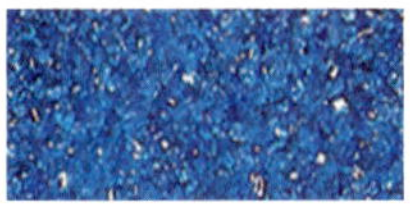

Blue Sugar
3.25 oz. bottle
710-S-750

Cake Sparkles™

Edible glitter, .25 oz. bottle. Certified Kosher.

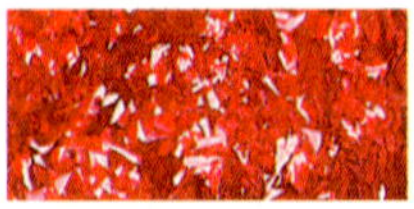

Red
703-S-1284

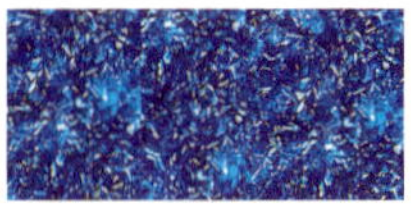

Blue
703-S-1314

ASSORTMENTS

3-Mix Sparkling Sugar
Includes Blue and White, Red and White and White Sparkling Sugars. Certified Kosher.
710-S-914

6-Mix
Includes Red and Blue Jimmies and Patriotic Mix, Red and Blue Sugar and Patriotic Sprinkle Sparks. Certified Kosher.
710-S-656

Cookie

COOKIE STENCIL SETS

Stencil-A-Cookie™ Cutter & Stencil Set
Using the fun-shaped stencils and cutter, it's easy to serve cookies with exciting, colorful designs for the season. Just cut cookies, then use the stencils and Cake Sparkles™ and Colored Sugars (shown at right) or Wilton FoodWriter™ Edible Color Markers (p. 128) or Color Mist™ Food Color Spray (p. 204) to create dazzling shapes on top after baking. Sets include one metal cutter and two stencils (same design).
2308-S-1405 Set/3

Patriotic Cupcake and Cookie Stencils
Turn plain treats into American classics with a stenciled patriotic design. Just place one of the fun designs over your baked treat, then sprinkle with Wilton Cake Sparkles™ or Colored Sugars (shown at right) or spray with Color Mist™ Food Color Spray (p. 204). 8 designs.
417-S-498

COOKIE CUTTERS

NEW!

Patriotic Colored Metal Cutter Set
Bold colors add to the fun! Favorite shapes include star, USA, flag and shooting star. Sizes from 3 to 3½ in.
2308-S-1257 Set/4

Stars Nesting Metal Cutter Set
A parade of small to large stars to create fun cookies for the 4th or all year long. Sizes from 5 to 2½ in.
2308-S-1215 Set/4

Nesting Stars Cutter Set
1⅝ to 4⅝ in.
2304-S-704
Set/6

Star Comfort Grip™ Cutter
This easy-grip stainless steel cutter with extra-deep sides is perfect for cutting so many favorite foods into star shapes. The cushion grip gives you comfortable control even when cutting into thick desserts. Recipe included.
4½ x 1½ in. deep.
2310-S-605

Star Metal Cookie Cutter
Quality metal is clean-cutting and easy to handle. 3 in.
2308-S-1008

SEASONAL

GRADUATION

Bakeware

Smiley Grad Pan
Our grinning grad is a smart choice to honor any student who's made the grade—boy or girl, kindergartner to collegian.One-mix pan is 10¼ x 12 x 2 in.deep. Aluminum.
2105-S-2073

Topping Off Success Pan
Decorate in your grad's school colors. One-mix pan is 14¾ x 11¾ x 2 in. deep. Aluminum.
2105-S-2038

Book Pans
Books detail any of life's important chapters, including graduation. Aluminum.

Two-Mix Book Pan
11½ x 15 x 2¾ in. deep. Serves up to 30.
2105-S-2521

One-Mix Book Pan
13 x 9½ x 2 in. deep.
2105-S-972

NEW!

Autograph Mat
A party memento any grad will treasure—to be filled with greetings from every guest. Includes black pen. Fits 11 x 14 in. frame, holds 5 x 7 in. photo.
1009-S-241

Party

Baking Cups
Microwave-safe paper. Standard size, 2 in. diameter.
Pk./50

NEW!

Graduation
415-S-420

Smiley Grad
415-S-294

Party Bags
Colorful grad designs for candy and cookie treats. 20 plastic bags, 20 ties included. 4 x 9½ in.
Pk./20

NEW!

Graduation
1912-S-9241

Smiley Grad
1912-S-1130

Icing Decorations
Perfect for topping cupcakes, cookies and ice cream. Mint-flavored. Certified Kosher.

NEW!

Graduation
710-S-1125 Pk./12

Petite Smiley Grad
710-S-503
Pk./12

Grad Fun Pix®
Add a fun touch to cakes, cupcakes, ice cream and more. Approx. 3½ in. tall.
2113-S-717
Pk./12

CANDLES

Candle Set
3 caps, 3 diplomas, ½ to 2 in. high.
2811-S-1800
Set/6

Champagne Bottles
2 in. high.
2811-S-163
Set/6

Toppers

BOBBLING TOPPERS
Top off that special cake with these fun bobbling toppers and watch heads turn. The food-safe design features hand-painted detail.

Bobbling Cake Toppers
Wax, approx. 4¼ in. high.

Female Grad
2113-S-462

Male Grad
2113-S-461

Bobbling Cupcake Toppers
Makes even plain cupcakes more exciting. Plastic, approx. 2 in. high.
Pk./6

NEW!

Female Grad
2113-S-1275

Male Grad
2113-S-1274

Graduation Toppers
Capture the day's excitement with our beautifully-detailed plastic toppers on a special cake.Approx. 4¼ in. high.

Female Graduate
2113-S-1821

Male Graduate
2113-S-1823

Glowing Graduate
Girl.
2113-S-1833

Successful Graduate
Boy.
2113-S-4549

Graduation Caps Set
Great party favors or cake toppers, 2 in. high.
Set/2
White 2113-S-1800
Black 2113-S-1801

AUTUMN

Pumpkin Pie Pan
Holds one 15 oz. can of pumpkin pie filling. Use for apple, peach and cherry pies, too! Ideal for ready-to-bake pie crusts.
9 x 1½ in.
Aluminum.
2105-S-3970

NEW!

Autumn Icing Colors Set
.5 oz. jars of Golden Yellow and Orange. Certified Kosher.
601-S-5583
Set/2

Sprinkles

INDIVIDUAL BOTTLES

Plastic bottles for convenient pouring and storing. Certified Kosher.

Leaves Mix
2.5 oz. bottle.
710-S-787

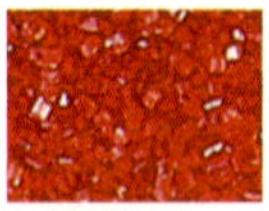
Red Sugar
3.25 oz. bottle.
710-S-766

Dark Green Sugar
3.25 oz.bottle.
710-S-764

Cake Sparkles™
Edible glitter, .25 oz. bottle. Certified Kosher.

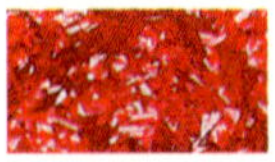
Red
703-S-1284

Dark Green
703-S-1278

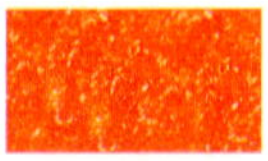
Orange
703-S-1308

Yellow
703-S-1272

ASSORTMENT

6-Mix
Includes Yellow, Red, Orange and Light Green Sugar, Leaves Mix and Chocolate Jimmies. Certified Kosher.
710-S-751

Party

NEW!

Baking Cups
Microwave-safe paper. Standard size, 2 in. diameter.
Standard Pk./50
Mini Pk./75

Autumn Leaves
Standard 415-S-430
Mini 415-S-432

Harvest
415-S-512

NEW!

Party Bags
Colorful Autumn designs for candy and cookie treats. 20 plastic bags, 20 ties included.
4 x 9½ in.
Pk./20

Autumn Leaves
1912-S-1430

Harvest
1912-S-1288

Icing Decorations
Wilton Icing Decorations are perfect for topping cupcakes, cookies and ice cream. Mint-flavored. Certified Kosher.

Petite Leaves
710-S-230 Pk./12

Leaves
710-S-3003 Pk./12

Cookie

Autumn Cupcake and Cookie Stencils
Turn plain treats into visions of the season with a stenciled Autumn design. Just place one of the fun designs over your baked treat, then sprinkle with Wilton Cake Sparkles™ or Colored Sugars (shown at left) or spray with Color Mist™ Food Color Spray (p. 135). 8 designs.
417-S-495

COMFORT GRIP™

Easy-grip stainless steel cutters with extra-deep sides. Great for cutting, cushioned plastic grip gives comfortable control. Recipe included. Approx. 4½ x 4½ x 1½ in. deep.

Oak Leaf
2310-S-633

Maple Leaf
2310-S-632

Pumpkin
2310-S-600

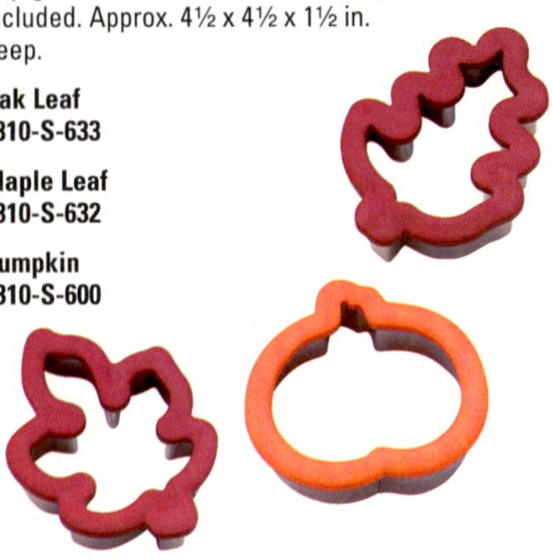

METAL CUTTERS

Leaves and Acorns Nesting Metal Cutter Set
Graduated acorns, oak and maple leaves,(3 each).
1¾ to 3¾ in.
Recipe included.
2308-S-2000
Set/9

Harvest Mini Metal Cutter Set
Six shapes: oak leaf, maple leaf, apple, pumpkin, elm leaf and acorn, each approx. 1½ in. Recipe included.
2308-S-1217 Set/6

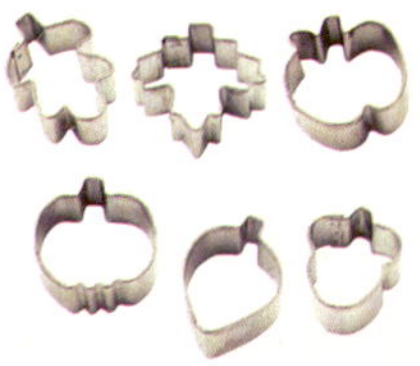

Candy

Pumpkins Candy Mold
1 design, 11 cavities.
2115-S-1558

Candy Melts®†
Ideal for all your candy making—molding, dipping or coating. Artificially vanilla flavored unless otherwise indicated. Certified Kosher. 14 oz. bags.

Red	1911-S-499	Dark Green	1911-S-405
Light Cocoa	1911-S-544	Dark Cocoa	1911-S-358
Orange	1911-S-1631	Chocolate Mint	1911-S-1920
Yellow	1911-S-463	White	1911-S-498
		Peanut Butter	1911-S-481

†Brand confectionery coating.

Peanut Butter
1911-S-481

See pages 162-165 for more Wilton candy items.

Wilton

Wedding Style

Wilton has a beautiful selection of products for today's bride. From toasting glasses to garters to favors, we'll help you design the wedding day of your dreams!

Wedding Ensembles

Fulfill your wedding day dreams with the finest coordinated wedding accessories. Nicely presented, a complete collection makes a beautiful gift. Or enjoy the flexibility of choosing individual accessories that personalize the wedding day!

Flower Basket
Held by the flower girl, as she scatters Rose Petals along the bridal path. Petals not included.

Ring Bearer's Pillow
Lovingly carried by the Ring Bearer, this beautiful pillow adds elegance to your wedding ceremony.

Guest Book
The perfect wedding keepsake—guests sign and add their good wishes on your special day.

Guest Pen and Holder
Make signing the guest book easy and elegant.

NEW!

All Occasion Guest Book
With attached pen and holder. Paper-covered. Pearlized white.
120-S-082

NEW!

Flower Basket
Crafted in satin with ribbon flowers. Ivory.
120-S-084

NEW!

Ring Bearer Pillow
Crafted in sheer, beautiful organza.
White 120-S-100
Ivory 120-S-681

NEW!

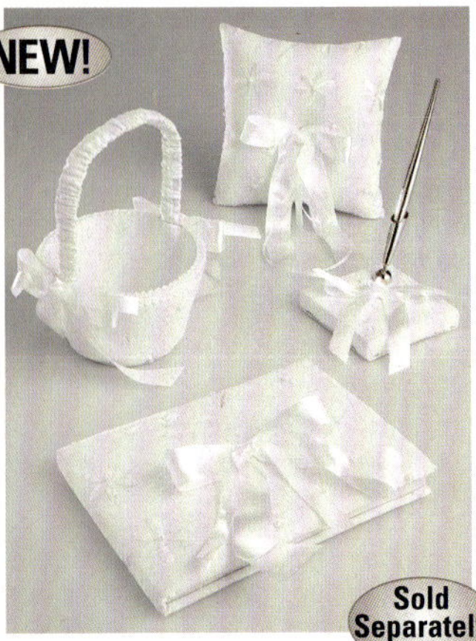

Sold Separately

Joyful
Satin bows embellish these brides' essentials. Embroidered details.

Flower Basket	**120-S-860**
Ring Bearer Pillow	**120-S-861**
Guest Book & Pen	**120-S-1027**

Sold Separately and as a Set

Timeless
Beautiful woven satin ribbon design.

Flower Basket	**120-S-604**
Ring Bearer Pillow	**120-S-101**
Guest Pen	**120-S-831**
Guest Book	**120-S-829**
Complete Set of 4	**120-S-460**

Sold Separately

Elegance
Sophistication abounds with tailored satin and ribbon trim.

Flower Basket	**120-S-331**
Ring Bearer Pillow	**120-S-334**
Guest Book & Pen	**120-S-871**

Sold Separately

Eternity
Upscale quilting with floral trim—the essence of bridal chic. Ivory.

Flower Basket	**120-S-339**
Ring Bearer Pillow	**120-S-338**
Guest Book & Pen	**120-S-328**

Sold Separately

Graceful
Sparkling rhinestone accents.

Flower Basket	**120-S-078**
Ring Bearer Pillow	**120-S-077**
Guest Pen	**120-S-076**
Guest Book	**120-S-079**
Guest Book & Pen	**120-S-072**

Sold Separately

Traditional
Gleaming white with organza and ribbon trim.

Flower Basket	**1006-S-603**
Ring Bearer Pillow	**120-S-100**
Guest Pen	**120-S-804**
Guest Book	**120-S-800**

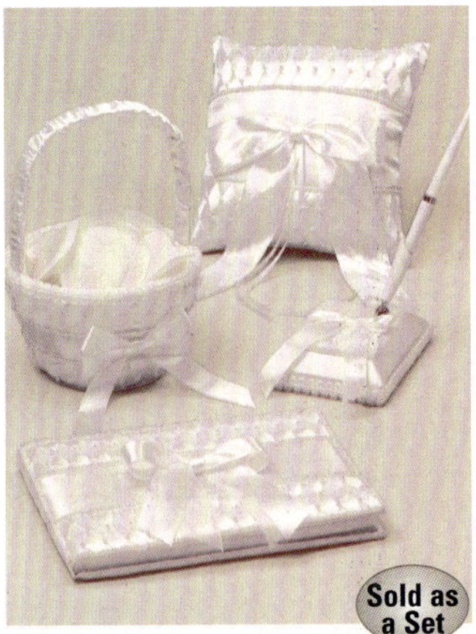

Sold as a Set

Classic
Perfect choice for the bride who appreciates elegant simplicity. Satin with satin ribbon trim. Set includes Flower Basket, Ring Bearer Pillow, Guest Pen and Guest Book.
120-S-472 Set/4

Sold as a Set

Enchanting
Inspired by the romance of a flower garden, designed in satin with fabric blooms. Set includes Flower Basket, Ring Bearer Pillow, Guest Pen and Guest Book.
120-S-083 Set/4

Wedding Day Accessories

UNITY CANDLES & TAPER SETS

NEW!

Swirl

Ornate sculpted design. Unity Candle is 9 in. high x 3 in. diameter; Taper Candles are 10 in. high.
Unity Candle 120-S-140
Taper Candles 120-S-447 Set/2

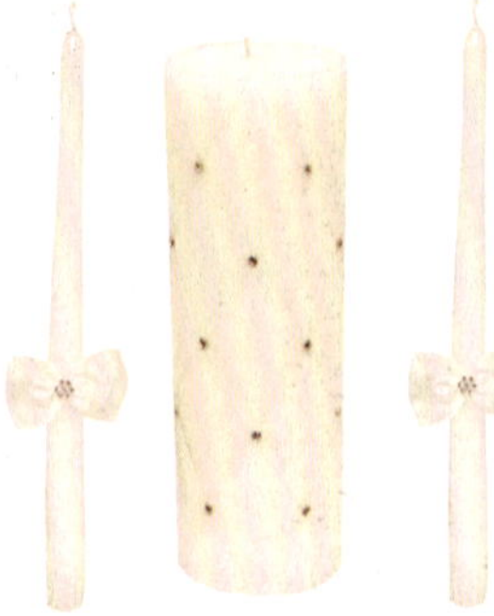

Graceful

Sparkling rhinestone accents. Unity Candle is 9 in. high x 3 in. diameter; Taper Candles are 10 in. high.
Unity Candle 120-S-461
Taper Candles 120-S-463 Set/2
Unity Candle and Taper Candles Set 120-S-065 Set/3

NEW!

Glass Candleholder Set

Bring the beauty and shimmer of crystal-look glass to your candle lighting ceremony. Elegant glass holders make a beautiful display of the unity candle and tapers. Use them after the ceremony at the reception to light the bridal table. At home, they fit perfectly with any table décor—everyday and special occasion. Ribbon trim. Unity candleholder is 5¾ in. high; holds a pillar candle up to 3¾ in. diameter. Each taper candleholder is 4¼ in. high; holds a standard size taper. Candles not included.
120-S-088 Set/3

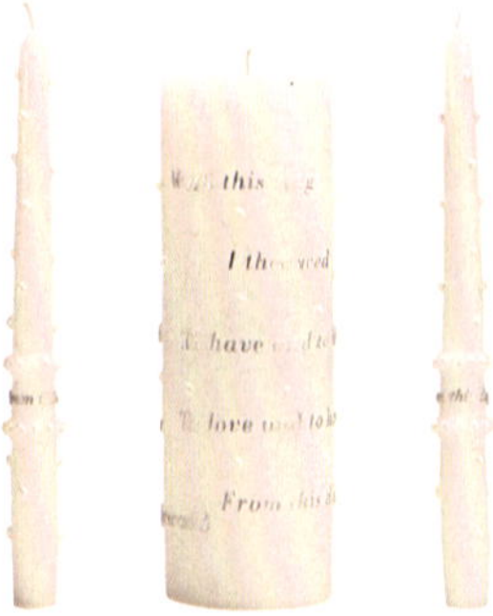

With This Ring

Words of love encircle the candle design. Unity Candle is 9 in. high x 3 in. diameter; Taper Candles are 10 in. high.
120-S-064 Set/3

Love, Honor, Cherish

Contemporary lettering. Unity Candle is 9 in. high x 3 in. diameter; Taper Candles are 10 in. high.
120-S-066 Set/3

Silver Candleholder Set

Keepsake-quality set holds the unity candle and tapers for the candle lighting ceremony, then adds the romantic glow of candlelight to your reception table. At home, you'll use the candleholders year-round for special dates, dinner parties and holidays. Silver-plated; ribbon trim. Unity candle holder is 6¼ in. high; holds a pillar candle up to 3¾ in. diameter. Each taper candle holder is 5½ in. high; holds standard size tapers. Candles not included.
120-S-448 Set/3

TOASTING GLASSES

Beautiful stemware to use at the reception, then at home!

Graceful

Height: 10½ in.
120-S-716 Set/2

Pearl

Height: 9½ in.
120-S-783 Set/2

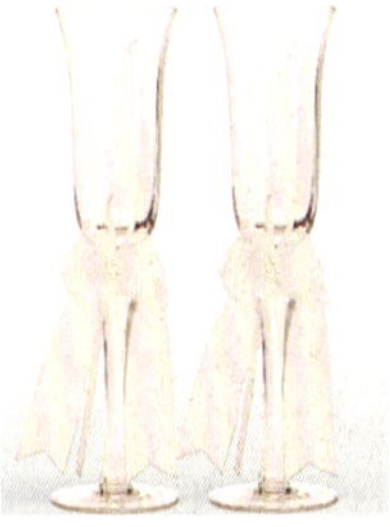

Fluted

Height: 10 in.
120-S-784 Set/2

Bride and Groom

Height: 8⅜ in.
120-S-708 Set/2

Heart Silver Toasting Glasses and Servers Ensemble

Silver-plated heart design, organza ribbon and pearl trim. Engrave for a beautiful keepsake.
120-S-232 Set/4

SERVING PIECES

Quality cake knife and servers will be used again, on special occasions at gatherings with family and friends throughout your married life. Engrave the blades to create beautiful keepsakes.

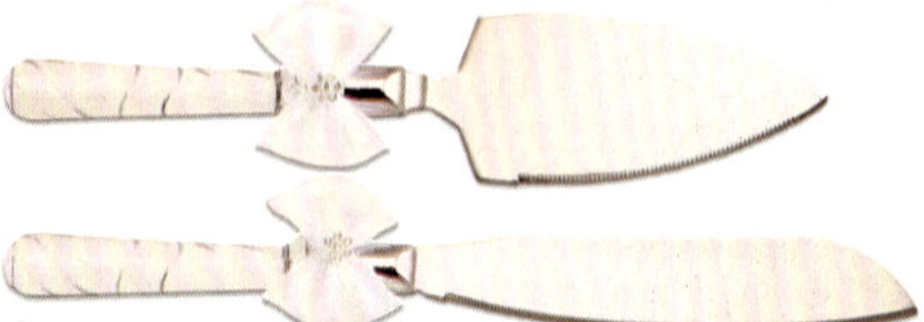

Graceful

Stainless steel blades with acrylic handles.
120-S-718 Set/2

Crystal Look

Stainless steel blades with acrylic handles.
120-S-4003 Set/2

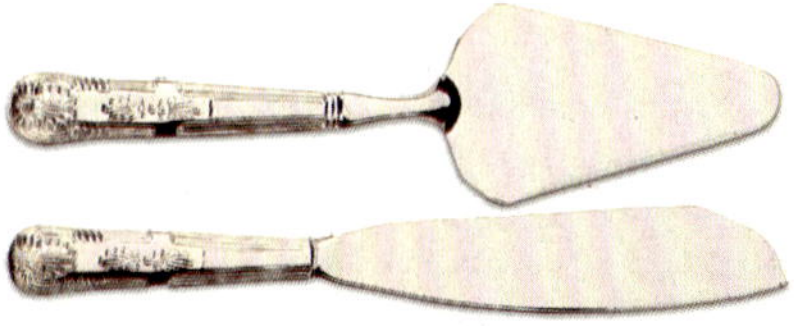

Silver

Silver-plated, with sculpting on handles.
120-S-4004 Set/2

Wedding Day Accessories

FLORAL ACCESSORIES

French Rose Wedding Bouquet
Perfect, beautiful blooms to keep or to use during the bouquet toss. Hand-crafted, fine silk flowers with wrapped stem. Bouquet measures approx. 8½ in. diameter with 4 in. stem.
120-S-1013

Fresh Look Bouquet Holder
Make bouquets for the wedding party! It's easy to do, using your favorite silk or fabric flowers.
1006-S-611

Silver Bouquet Holder
Arrange the bride's favorite flowers in this keepsake holder. Silver-plated. 7½ in. long.
120-S-651

Bouquet Collar
Slip over stems to dress up any bouquet. White Organza; 10½ in. diameter.
1006-S-992

Flower Petals
Fill the flower girl's basket, scatter on the cake table, decorate favors. Lifelike 2½ in. diameter flower petals. Approx. 300 petals in pack.

Lavender Hydrangea
1006-S-879

White Rose
1006-S-698

Blush Rose
1006-S-697

Red Rose
1006-S-695

White Rose Boutonniere
Perfect for weddings, prom, special occasions
1006-S-694

GLOVES

For all celebrations—weddings, prom, parties, Communion and costumes. In white.

Satin Long
Adult
120-S-827

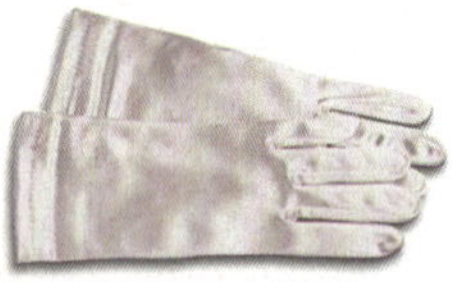

Satin Short
Adult
120-S-413

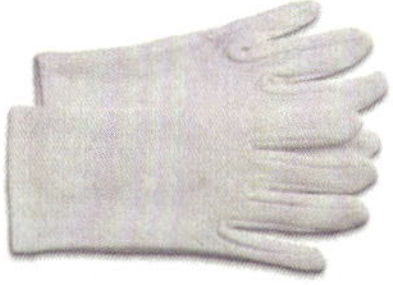

Small
Polyester.
Child
120-S-828

GARTERS

Buy one to toss, one to keep. Beautifully appointed with lace and ribbon trim.

Tossing
Ribbon, pearl and lace trim.
Blue 120-S-402
White 120-S-401

Keepsake White
Features engravable silver locket that holds two photos.
120-S-826

Car Decorating Kit
Eye-catching decorations trim the bride and groom's getaway vehicle with style! Includes: Magnetic "Just Married" sign, window clings, pre-fluffed pom-poms, streamers, balloons. Crafted of weather-resistant materials, reusable (except balloons).
1006-S-483

Autograph Mat
Let guests create wonderful wedding memories. Each size holds 5 x 7 in. photo, includes black pen.

11 x 14 in.
Fits 11 x 14 in. frame.
1009-S-508

8 x 10 in.
Fits 8 x 10 in. frame.
1009-S-1103

NEW!

Wedding Day Décor

RECEPTION GIFT CARD HOLDERS

Attractively keep the wedding gift cards together at the reception. Tulle, ribbon and flowers not included. Use the Tulle Spool (sold below) for creating puffs that decorate the Gift Card Holders.

NEW!

Gift Shape
Whimsical gift box design of sturdy metal construction with faux gem trim, extra long slot for envelopes, box opens from the top, heart-shaped lock and key. 10¾ in. high x 8 in. long x 8 in. deep
120-S-220

NEW!

Mailbox
Personalize the flag with a photo or saying at www.wiltonprint.com. Includes easy to assemble mailbox, 2 printable labels, 1 test sheet. White printed corrugated cardboard. 12 in. high x 15¼ in. wide x 10¼ in. deep.
1006-S-396

Wishing Well
A charming display for any shower, wedding, or anniversary celebration. White printed corrugated cardboard, easy to assemble. 30½ in. high x 16 in. wide x 14 in. deep.
1006-S-395

NEW!

Horizontal
White painted wire. After the reception, use as a display for flowers or photos. 12 in. high x 10 in. long x 7 in. deep.
120-S-875

Vertical
White painted wire. After the reception, use as a display for flowers or photos. 16½ in. high x 7 in. long x 7 in. deep.
120-S-330

CHAIR DÉCOR

Versatile fabrics beautifully accent party and reception chairs and more! Fabric dye changes both cover and wrap into perfect-colored accents for your wedding day!

Satin Chair Cover
Distinguish wedding party and special guest seating at your celebration —fits most standard folding and party chairs.
1006-S-131

Organza Beaded Chair Wrap
Place on a table as a lush runner, wrap a large gift, make a magnificent bow. 18 in. wide x 12 ft. long.
1006-S-382

Sparkling Ice*
Container size: 1½ in. high x 4½ in. diameter.
1006-S-342

*WARNING: CHOKING HAZARD– Small parts. Not intended for children. Not a toy–for decorative use only.

Tulle Spool
Create beautiful bows and swags, spectacular puffs, even use as ribbon for gift wrap! Simply cut to desired length. 6 in. wide x 50 yards long.
1005-S-442

Organza Pull-N-Fluff™ Bows
Create stunning bows in 3 easy steps—just pull the strings, tie and fluff! Perfect for weddings, holiday décor, gifts, more. Reusable and dyeable.

Medium	Large
8 in. diameter.	10 in. diameter.
1006-S-637	**1006-S-635**
Pk./12	**Pk./12**

BRIDAL GARLANDS

Romantic garland adds a soft glow to your wedding ambiance! You'll find so many uses for the ceremony and reception. Drape on pews and line the aisles, place along table edges and around the cake, wrap around pillars. Lighted garlands are battery operated (uses 2 D Batteries, not included).

Lighted Organza Rose
6 Ft. Length 1006-S-584

Lighted Hydrangea
6 Ft. Length 1006-S-581

Lighted White Rose
6 Ft. Length 1006-S-350

Rose Garland
Non-lighting; roses strung together by organza ribbon. 6 foot length.
1006-S-917

Centerpieces

Lighted Lantern

Straight from the pages of decorating magazines, these lighted lanterns create a party setting styled to your celebration—indoors or out! Hang or use as a centerpiece. Uses two AAA batteries, not included.
9½ in. high x 8 in. wide
1006-S-278

Paper Bells

Looking for an easy way to decorate the shower and reception without spending a lot of money? Your search ends with these favorite shapes—bells, the all-time favorite icon of the wedding day! Crafted in paper, easy to assemble.

Medium
6⅝ x 8 in.
1006-S-270 Pk./3

Small
3¼ x 4 in.
1006-S-276 Pk./7

Celebration Tree

Use it as a party decoration, displayed on the gift table, and as a centerpiece on reception tables. Easy to assemble. Metal construction. Assembled tree measures approx. 14 in. (high x 11 in. wide. (Favors and decorations shown not included.)
1006-S-571

Heart Basket

Makes a stunning table centerpiece—fill it with flowers, candy, favors, more. Includes a clear liner to securely hold smaller contents. Silvertone metal basket measures 3¾ in. high x 5 7/16 in. diameter at rim. (Decorations and candy shown not included.)
1006-S-998

Tiered Floral Centerpiece

Create an elegant display for fresh or silk flowers. Use with or without cake. Can be displayed as single tiers. Contains three 2-piece tiers. Tops remove for easy cleaning. Assembly instructions included.
120-S-822

Always festive, paper decorations are trendy, fun, and economical too! Easy to assemble. Reusable, fold to store flat.

Sweet Romance
7½ in. wide x 9⅜ in. high.
120-S-546

Happy Couple
8 in. wide x 10¼ in. high.
120-S-545

Blossoming Bride
7 in. wide x 9¼ in. high.
120-S-841

Wedding Dress
7 in. wide x 10 in. high.
120-S-547

Favor-Making Kits

Fun and festive kits personalize your favors with ease!

NEW!

Square Pail Favor Kit

Make elegant favors with personalized tags perfect for all occasions. Print the tags at www.wiltonprint.com. Food safe pails measure 2 in. high. Kit contains 18 favor pails, 18 (12 in.) satin ribbon lengths, 18 printable tags, 2 test sheets. Candy not included.
1006-S-1137 Pk./18

NEW!

Flower Pen Favor Kit

Use as a place card or a quick thank you for your guests. Personalize the cards at www.wiltonprint.com. Great for shower games, too. Black ink. Pens measure 6½ in. Kit includes 12 flower-topped pens, 12 (12 in.) satin ribbon lengths, 12 printable tags, 2 test sheets. Silk petals not included.
1006-S-928 Pk./12

NEW!

Love Potion Favor Kit

Fill to match your celebration theme and surprise your guests. Personalize the stickers at www.wiltonprint.com. Bottles measure 2¾ in. high. Kit includes 24 glass bottles with slotted corks. 24 (12 in.) satin ribbon lengths, funnel for easy filling, 24 printable stickers, 2 test sheets. Candy not included.
1006-S-1009 Pk./24

NEW!

Silver Bell Favor Kit

Set a bell at each place setting, guests will ring for the newlyweds to kiss. Personalize the place cards at www.wiltonprint.com. Bells measure 2¼ in. high. Kit contains 20 metal favor bells, 20 (12 in.) satin ribbon lengths, 20 printable place cards, 2 test sheets.
1006-S-1136 Pk./20

CD Favor Tins

Create personalized CD labels for your celebration using your computer, or hand design. Includes 12 tins, 12 adhesive labels and complete instructions. Just download template from www.wiltonprint.com.
1006-S-391
Pk./12

Favor Tins Mega Kits

Create personalized favor tins for your celebration using your computer, or hand design. Includes 25 tins, 25 adhesive labels and strips, complete instructions. Just download template from www.wiltonprint.com. Candy not included.
1006-S-8038
Pk./25

Candle Favors

Add a romantic touch to showers, receptions, every celebration. Includes 12 lightly-scented 4 in. mini candles, and 3 in. candle holders already decorated with white organza bows.
1006-S-643
Pk./12

Sweet Things™ Champagne Bottles

Make 12 favors with champagne bottle favor pedestals, ribbon, organza circles and favor tags. Candy not included.
1006-S-227 Pk./12

Heart Favor Mega Kits

Make 24 favors with heart containers, tulle circles, ribbon and favor tags. Candy not included.
1006-S-924 Pk./24

Goblet Favor Mega Kits

Make 24 favors with goblet containers, tulle circles, ribbon and favor tags. Candy not included.
1006-S-923 Pk./24

Drawstring Wrappers

Create 12 cute favors in no time at all! Kit includes pre-assembled drawstring wrapper and favor tags. Just fill and tie.
Pk./12
White 1006-S-921
Lavender 1006-S-922

Favor Containers

These beautiful containers hold favors for shower, wedding and anniversary celebrations. Perfect for mints, almonds, potpourri and small gifts.

Sweet Heart Favor Box
2¼ in. high x 2¼ in. wide. Paper.
1006-S-937 Pk./10

Flirty Fleur Favor Box
2¼ in. high x 2¼ in. wide. Paper.
1006-S-936 Pk./10

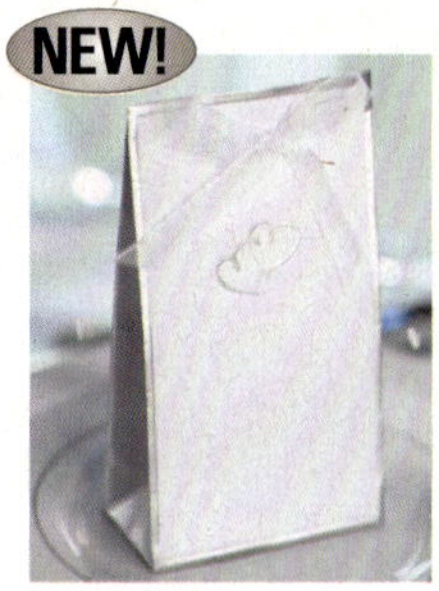

Sweet Heart Favor Bag
6 in. high x 3¼ wide x 1¾ in. deep. Includes sheer white ribbon. Paper.
1006-S-940 Pk./10

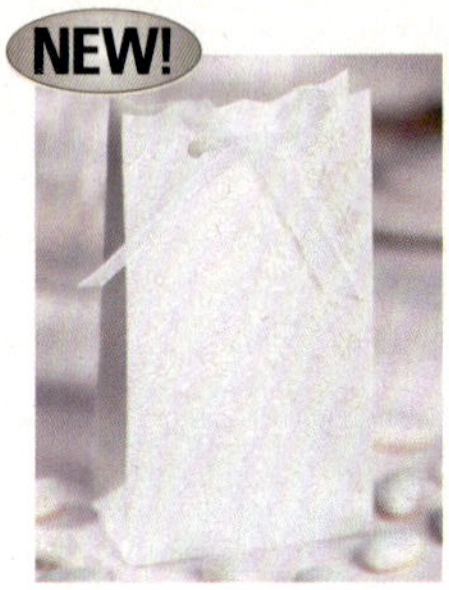

Flirty Fleur Favor Bag
6 in. high x 3¼ wide x 1¾ in. deep. Includes sheer white ribbon. Paper.
1006-S-941 Pk./10

Simple Yet Elegant Favor Bag
6 in. high x 3¼ wide x 1¾ in. deep.Includes sheer white ribbon. Paper.
1006-S-939 Pk./10

Swan
3 in. high x 1½ in. wide x 2 in. deep. Wings are moveable. Acrylic.
1006-S-369

Silver Heart Patterned Basket
3½ in. high x 3 in. wide. Metal.
1006-S-338

White Wire Rope Heart Basket
3½ in. high x 3 in. wide. Metal. Candy not included.
1006-S-687

Silver Heart Box
2 in. high x 2 in. wide. Metal.
1006-S-169

Ivory Chest
2½ in. high x 2¼ in. long x 1½ in. wide. Paper.
1006-S-515 Pk./20

Tuxedo
4 in. high. Paper.
1006-S-514 Pk./10

Heart Tab
2¼ in. high x 2¼ in. long x 2¼ in. wide. Paper.
1006-S-517 Pk./20

Silver Heart Pillow
1 in. high x 3 in. long x 2¼ in. wide. Paper.
1006-S-557 Pk./20

Champagne Glass
Clear. 2 in. high. Plastic.
1006-S-614 Pk./12

Champagne Flute
4 in. high x 1¼ in. wide. Plastic.
1006-S-193 Pk./12

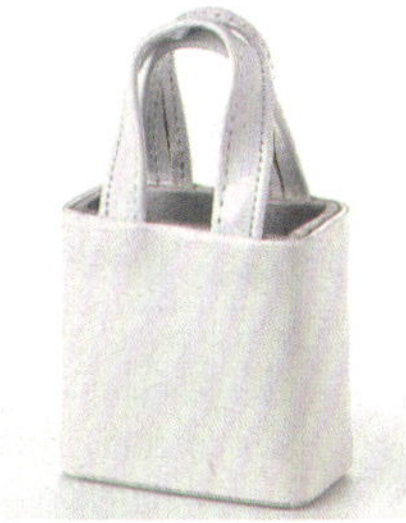

Tote
4 in. high x 2¼ in. wide x 1¼ in. deep. Vinyl.
1006-S-372

Favor Cake Box
Shaped and decorated like a slice of wedding cake. 20 boxes fit together to form a round cake tier. 4¼ in. long x 2¾ in. high.
1006-S-629 Pk./20

Cake Slice Boxes
Bakery style boxes measure 5 in. square x 3½ in. high.
415-S-955 Pk./5

Tulle Sachets; Organza and Tulle Circles

Perfect for favors, rose petals, rice, treats, gifts.

Drawstring Sachet Bags
Sheer organza fabric pouch closes with a pull of the ribbons. 3¾ x 4 in. **Pk./12**

White **1006-S-173**

Ivory **1006-S-176**

Lavender **1006-S-189**

Red **1006-S-188**

Black **1006-S-1126**

Also available:
4½ x 6¾ in. size. White.
1006-S-184 Pk./12

Organza Circles with Ribbon Trim
Shimmering organza trimmed with ribbon makes the prettiest favors, decorations, and crafts. 9 in. diameter.
Pk./25
White 1005-S-426
Ivory 1005-S-106
Pink 1005-S-107

White Tulle Circles
Makes beautiful favors and decorations! Sheer mesh fabric measures 9 in. diameter.
1005-S-7882 Pk./75

Favors

WEDDING BUBBLES

Celebrate the wedding by showering the newly married couple with shimmering bubbles. It's a fun trend and a great way to wish the bride and groom good luck!

Contains 24 .6 oz. bottles of bubbles with wands. Decorate with Favor Band (shown below) and Tulle or Organza Circles (shown on p. 214).
1007-S-8000
Pk./24

Pop Out Streamers

Great for weddings, graduations, birthdays, New Year's celebrations, surprise parties. Just aim and press lever. Each contains ten silver foil streamers that stay attached to tube for easy disposal. Streamers are over 10 feet long. Spring loaded, the streamers do not contain gunpowder or other explosives.
1006-S-932 Pkg./14

Love Knot Wands

Use after the ceremony or at the reception. 36 wands are packed in a convenient tray for reception table use. Ribbon not included. Each wand contains .16 fl. oz. bubble solution.
1007-S-8017
Pk./36

Celebration Bells

Ring for a special kiss after the ceremony and at the reception. Hand to guests exiting the church, and place one at each setting at the reception. Contains 24 bells, poem tags and ties. Bell measures 1¼ in. tall.
Silver 1007-S-8012 Pk./24
White 1007-S-8013 Pk./24

Silver-tone Pens

Perfect as shower, reception, and anniversary favors. Convenient to have on hand for games at showers and parties. Black ink. Ribbon not included.
1006-S-1008
Pk./6

Favor Accents and Leaves

Romantic accents add sparkling beauty and elegance to favors, table decorations!

Thank You Tags

Clear oval tags, imprinted in silver are threaded on 11¾ in. organza ribbon lengths. Tie onto favors, wine glass stems, napkins and more.
1006-S-927 Pk./20

Bling Rings

Use these sparkling favor accents to add beauty to favors, table decorations. Faux diamond measures 1 in. diameter.
1006-S-919 Pk./12

Engagement Rings

Sparkling favor accents to add beauty to favors, table decorations, centerpieces. Faux diamond measures ¼ in. diameter.
1006-S-115 Pk./12

Anniversary Bands

¾ in. diameter.
Pk./48
Silver 1006-S-101
Gold 1006-S-100
Pk./288
Silver 1006-S-422
Gold 1006-S-421

Lily Spray

9 in. long.
1006-S-503
Pk./12

White Pearl Spray

8 in. long.
1006-S-506
Pk./12

Glittered Doves

Coated with non-edible glitter. Do not place directly on cake.
2 x 1½ in.
1006-S-166
Pk./12

Gold

1⅞ in. long.
1005-S-6518
Pk./144
1¼ in. long.
1005-S-6712
Pk./144

Silver

1⅞ in. long.
1005-S-6526
Pk./144
1¼ in. long.
1005-S-6720
Pk./144

Green

2½ in. long leaf, 2½ in. stem.
1005-S-401
Pk./12

White Pearl Beading

Molded on one continuous 5-yard strand. Remove pearls before cutting and serving cake.
Small (4 mm) **211-S-1989**
Large (6 mm) **211-S-1990**

Satin Stripe Favor Bands

Functional and decorative, a pretty way to accent favors. Use on Drawstring Sachets, Wedding Bubbles bottles and more for an instant decoration. 2 in. wide.
1007-S-8014 Pk./12

Place Cards and Holders

An elegant way to indicate seating arrangements; and a stunning display for photos, special notes and thanks for your guests.

Sweet Heart Glass Place Card Holder
Clip on back to attach to rim of glass or napkin ring. Approx. 4¾ in. high x 2½ in. wide. Ribbon not included. (Place cards not included.)
1006-S-933
Pk./20

Clip-On Rose
It's a favor, a decorative accent, and a fashion statement. You'll find so many uses for the Clip-On Rose. Adds beauty to shower and wedding reception tables—clip on glassware, napkins, place cards, more! Fabric rose measures 3½ in. diameter. (Place cards not included.)
1006-S-467

Wedding Dress Place Card Holder
Charming place card holder can also display photos, menu, thank you notes. (Place cards not included.)
120-S-842
Pk./6

Favor Frames

Insert a favorite photo or use as a place card holder by adding your guest's name.

Silver Double Heart Place Cards
Use for every life celebration!
1006-S-752 Pk./40

Flirty Fleur
3 in. high x 4 in. wide. Easel back. Paper.
1006-S-930 Pk./10

Fleur-De-Lis
2½ in. high x 3½ in. wide. Silver-tone plastic.
1006-S-376 Pk./5

Single Heart
1 in. high x 1 in. wide. Metal.
1009-S-239

Candy

Trendy and traditional candies make great fillers for favors and candy dishes at showers, weddings, celebrations!

Wedding Bells
12 oz. bag. Sweet/tart fruit flavored.
1006-S-1140

Mint Drops
16 oz. bag. Assorted. Certified Kosher.
1006-S-788

Mini Hearts
12 oz. bag. Fruit flavored. Certified Kosher.
1006-S-797

Wedding Message Hearts
10 oz. bag; approximately 90 pieces. Mint flavored.
1006-S-371

Pillow Mints
10 oz. bag. approximately 205 pieces. Assorted. Certified Kosher.
1006-S-858

Jordan Almonds
16 oz. bag; approximately 100 pieces. Certified Kosher.
Assorted 1006-S-779
White 1006-S-778

Candy Bar Molds

Create a sweet memory for your guests, a candy bar featuring a special message.

Molding is easy using Wilton Candy Melts® (p. 162). Present them beautifully in Candy Bar Boxes. Each bar measures 3¼ in. wide x 1¾ in. tall x ¼ in. deep. 1 design, 4 cavities.

Our Wedding
2115-S-1409

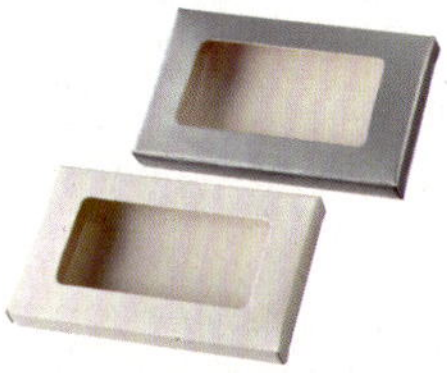

Candy Bar Boxes
The window displays your special message.
Pk./10
White 1904-S-1157
Silver 1904-S-1159

Thank You
2115-S-1410

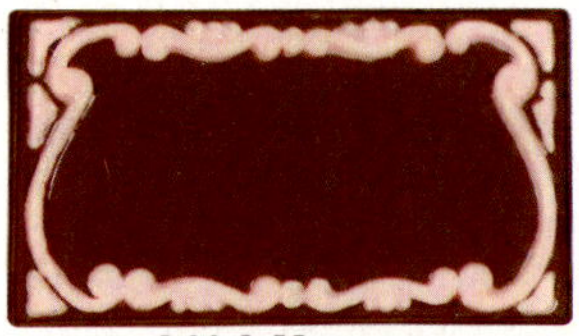

Add-A-Message
2115-S-1356

Wedding Cakes

From the keepsake figurine on top, to the impressive stand below, Wilton has something special just for your wedding cake!

Wedding Figurines

More brides choose Wilton figurines to top their wedding cakes. The rich, sculpted crafting, realistic detailing and romantic designs make these figurines perfect wedding day keepsakes.

Threshold of Happiness
Height: 5 in.
Base: 3¼ x 2 in.
Resin.
202-S-202

From This Day Forward
Height: 5 in.
Base: 3¼ x 2 in.
Resin.
202-S-319

Always and Forever Petite Embrace
Height: 3¾ in.
Base: 2½ in. diameter. Resin.
202-S-311

Bianca
Height: 5½ in.
Base: 3¾ x 3½ in.
Resin.
202-S-207

Clear Bianca
Height: 5½ in.
Base: 3¾ x 3½ in.
Acrylic. Perfect on Lighted Revolving Base (sold on p. 219).
202-S-424

Always and Forever Musical Ornament
Plays "The Wedding March". Height: 7¼ in.
Base: 4¼ in. diameter.
Resin.
215-S-310

Castle
Lights from within using 2 D batteries (not included).
Height: 7½ in.
Base: 4½ in. Resin.
111-S-2804

Just Married
Height: 5 in.
Base: 5 x 3¼ in. Resin.
110-S-864

Elegance
Height: 5½ in.
Base: 5 x 3 in. Resin.
110-S-863

Always and Forever
Height: 6½ in. Base: 7 x 5 in.
118-S-200

With This Ring
Height: 4½ in.
Base: 3½ diameter.
Resin.
202-S-313

HUMOROUS WEDDING FIGURINES

Add a lighthearted touch to the celebration. Sure to bring a smile to the face of anyone who has ever planned a wedding!

Oh No You Don't
Height: 4¼ in. Base: 6 x 3 in. Resin.
115-S-102 $19.99
Ethnic 115-S-104

Now I Have You
Height: 4¼ in. Base: 4¼ x 3¾ in. Resin.
115-S-101

The Tiff
Height: 4 in. Base: 2¼ x 2 in. Resin.
115-S-103

Forever In Your Eyes
Height: 6 in.
Base: 5 in. diameter. Resin.
110-S-903

Our Day
Height: 4¾ in.
Base: 2 x 1¾ in.
Poly resin.
Blonde/White Gown
202-S-409
Brunette/Ivory Gown (not shown)
202-S-415

Horse & Carriage
Height: 4½ in.
Base: 7 x 2½ in. Resin.
110-S-862

CAKE JEWELRY

NEW!

These toppers follow today's trends of decorating the cake with new shapes, fantasy themes, and designs that mirror other elements of your wedding day!

Good Fairy
Embellished with faux pearl blossoms and long stemmed blooms. Height: 3 in.
Base: 4 in. diameter.
120-S-490

Song Of Love
Handcrafted with sparkling rhinestones, painted hues, butterflies and flowers.
Height: 4½ in. Base: 4 in. diameter.
120-S-492

Beautiful Dreamer
Appointed with faux pearls and punched detailing.
Height: 3 in.
Base: 4 in. diameter.
120-S-493

Our First Dance
Height: 9¼ in. Base: 4⅝ in. diameter.
118-S-650
Couple Only
Height: 6 in. Poly resin.
202-S-411

Expression of Love
Height: 7¾ in.
Base: 4½ in. diameter.
101-S-931

Sweetness
Height 7¾ in.
Base: 4½ in. diameter.
101-S-153

Ethnic Expression of Love
Height: 7¾ in. Base: 4½ in. diameter.
101-S-933
Couple Only
Height: 4½ in.
Base: 2¼ x 1¾ in. Poly resin.
202-S-306

Simple Joys
Height: 8 in.
Base: 4½ in. diameter.
103-S-150

Classic Couple
Add a touch of nostalgia and retro design.
Plastic. Height: 4½ in. Base: 2 x 3 in.
Brunette 202-S-1422
Blonde (not shown) **202-S-1423**
Ethnic 202-S-1421

Love's Duet
Height: 6 in. Base: 2½ x 2¼ in.
Poly resin.
202-S-402
Ethnic 202-S-412

Lasting Love
Height: 4½ in.
Base: 2¼ x 1¾ in.
Poly resin.
202-S-302

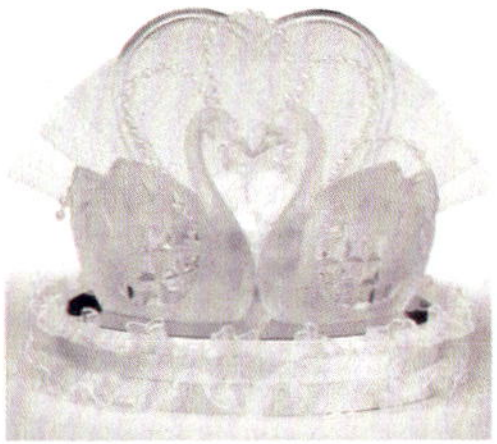

Enduring Love
Height: 5 in.
Base: 7 x 5 in. oval.
103-S-235

Reflections
Porcelain couple.
Height: 8 in.
Base: 4¾ in. diameter.
117-S-268

Spring Song
Height: 9½ in. Base: 4⅝ in. diameter.
111-S-2802
Kissing Lovebirds 5½ in. high.
1002-S-206

Petite Spring Song
Height: 7 in.
Base: 3¼ in. diameter.
106-S-159

Devotion
Height: 7 in.
Base: 4 x 2½ in. Ceramic.
111-S-2803

Inspirational Cross
Height: 5½ in. Base: 2 x 1½ in. Resin.
202-S-398

La Quinceañera
Cake top decoration or as a favor. Height: 4½ in.
Base: 2¾ in. diameter.
203-S-305

Specialty Toppers

NEW!

Cake Bow
Perfect for all celebrations—showers, weddings, birthdays! May be colored to match your celebration with Wilton Icing Colors and/or decorated with royal icing. Food-safe, non-edible, paper clay. Approx. 6½ in. high.
120-S-1103

NEW!

Floral Cake Decorations
Beautiful, realistic white roses are so versatile for decorating your tiered cake. Use them as is or color them to match any special celebration—wedding, baby shower, graduation, anniversary or holiday. Easy to tint using non-toxic pastel chalk; complete instructions on the package. Includes three 12 in. floral lengths suitable for any size or shape cake; attach with enclosed picks or with dots of icing. Food-safe, non-edible, paper clay. Each piece approx. 12 in. long.
120-S-1105 Pk./3

Floral Topper
Beautiful handmade flowers, greenery, satin ribbon. Height: 5¾ in. Base: 3¼ in. diameter, white resin.
120-S-073

CAKE PICKS

NEW!

The new look—stunning picks draw attention to your celebration—perfect for cake tops, floral arrangements, bouquets and centerpieces. Beautifully appointed with rhinestones, crafted of painted resin, except for the Flowers, which are crafted of metal. Food-safe. Approximately 5-5¼ in. high overall; the monogram letters measure 2½ in. high.

Monogram
Use individually or in groups.

Available letters:

A Monogram	1008-S-753
B Monogram	1008-S-755
C Monogram	1008-S-760
D Monogram	1008-S-732
E Monogram	1008-S-737
F Monogram	1008-S-736
G Monogram	1008-S-733
H Monogram	1008-S-754
J Monogram	1008-S-735
K Monogram	1008-S-751
L Monogram	1008-S-750
M Monogram	1008-S-759
P Monogram	1008-S-734
R Monogram	1008-S-752
S Monogram	1008-S-757
W Monogram	1008-S-761

Decorative
Perfect for wedding and anniversary celebrations.

Double Hearts
1006-S-985

Flowers
Painted hues bring these flowers to life.
120-S-528 Pk./9

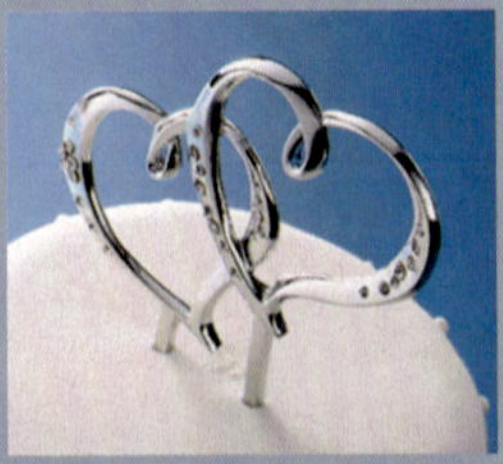

Anniversary
Silver 25th
1008-S-758
Gold 50th
1008-S-762

ANNIVERSARY ORNAMENTS

Petite 50th
Height: 5¾ in.
Base: 3¼ in. diameter.
105-S-4273

Petite 25th
Silver.
105-S-4265

50 Years of Happiness
Height: 10 in.
Base: 4⅝ in. diameter.
102-S-223

Ornament Settings and Bases

A beautiful beginning to a cake top ornament you create. Simply add the figurine of your choice, and trim with flowers, fabric tulle and accents.

Romantic Heart
2 pieces, 4⅝ in. diameter
201-S-7332

IT LIGHTS!

Lighted Revolving Base
Select just light, just rotate or both at the same time. Uses 3 AA batteries (not included). Height: 2 in. Diameter: 5 in.
201-S-453

Chapel Windows
Use with base or alone. 6½ x 5 x 1 in. deep.
205-S-3060

Gazebo Set
Easy to assemble plastic. 5 x 9 in.
205-S-3061

Floral Arch
Height: 10 in.
Base: 4⅝ in. diameter.
210-S-1987

Cake Assembly Sets

NEW!

Fluted Bowl Separator Set

The translucent bowl separator makes it easy to add designer color treatments that complement your tiered cake. Simply fill it with fresh or silk flowers, tulle or patterned fabric, or use it on its own. The curving, fluted design adds a fresh new element that works for a variety of wedding and shower cakes. Setup couldn't be simpler: the included separator plates are spiked to fit inside the top and bottom openings of the bowl for a secure presentation. Set includes 4 in. high fluted bowl and 2 smooth-edge separator plates (6 and 10 in. diameter). Holds cakes up to 9 in. diameter.

303-S-823

NEW!

Globe Pillar and Base Sets

Sophisticated pearl-look globes separate tiered cakes for a dramatic new look. The 2 and 2½ in. Pillar Sets are positioned between tiers, as globes fit over hidden pillars to provide strong support. The 3 in. Base Set features a reinforced center channel which fits over separator plate spikes to hold your base cake. Use all three sets together to create a towering 3-tier display (see inset above). The Globe Base Set is to be used under the bottom tier only; Pillar Sets will not support the base tier. Each set includes four globes and four 9 in. pillars, no pillars on Base Set.

2 in. 303-S-822 Set/8 **2½ in. 303-S-824 Set/8**

3 in. Globe Base Set 303-S-825 Set/4

9 in. Replacement Pillars Set 303-S-4005 Set/4

Spiral Separator Sets

Add an elegant touch to your special occasion cakes with these beautifully scrolled separators. The curling, openwork design in white coated metal gives cakes a light, garden style design. Setup couldn't be simpler—the smooth-edge plates are spiked to fit inside the top and bottom rings for a secure presentation. Use sets together for a high-rising construction of 3 separated tiers or use on their own to hold 2 or 3 stacked tiers.

NEW!

10 in. Set

Includes 7 x 4¼ in. high wire separator ring, 2 smooth-edge separator plates, 8 and 10 in. diameter. Holds 6, 8 or 9 in. round cakes.

303-S-8176 Set/3

14 in. Set

Includes 10½ x 4¼ in. high wire separator ring, 2 smooth-edge separator plates, 10 and 14 in. diameter. Holds round cakes 12 in. or smaller.

303-S-8175 Set/3

NEW!

Tailored Tiers Cake Display Set

Satin-look separators add beautiful texture to any tiered cake design. The elegant patterned fabric which covers the foam separators will complement most wedding, shower and anniversary designs and looks wonderful with floral arrangements. As an added bonus, use the included acetate photo wraps to customize the separators with treasured family photos, wrapping paper or an alternate fabric. It's a great way to personalize your cake for those special occasions. Set includes 2 satin brocade wrapped craft foam separators (4¼ and 7¼ in. diameter x 2 in. high), 4 smooth-edge separator plates (one 6 in., two 8 in., one 12 in. diameter) and 2 acetate photo wraps. The 4¼ in. separator holds cakes up to 6 in. diameter when used with 8 in. top plate; the 7¼ in. separator holds cakes up to 10 in. diameter when used with 12 in. top plate.

304-S-8174 Set/8

Crystal-Clear Cake Divider Set

- Sparkling clear twist legs beautifully accent your cake
- Designed for towering cakes from 6 to 14 in. diameter
- An elegant combination with Wilton Crystal-Look accessories

Clear plastic twist legs penetrate cake, rest on plate (dowel rods not needed). Includes 6, 8, 10, 12, 14 and 16 in. plastic separator plates plus 24 legs.

301-S-9450 Set/30

Additional Plates

6 in. **302-S-9730**
8 in. **302-S-9749**
10 in. **302-S-9757**
12 in. **302-S-9765**
14 in. **302-S-9773**
16 in. **302-S-9780**

7½ in. Twist Legs

303-S-9794 Pk./4

9 in. Twist Legs

Add more height to your tiers.

303-S-977 Pk./4

Grecian Pillar and Plate Set

A deluxe money-saving collection for the serious cake decorator. Decorator Preferred® scalloped-edge separator plates and 5 in. pillars. Includes 54 pieces: two each 6 in., 8 in., 10 in., 12 in. and 14 in. plates; 20 Grecian pillars and 24 pegs.
301-S-8380 Set/54

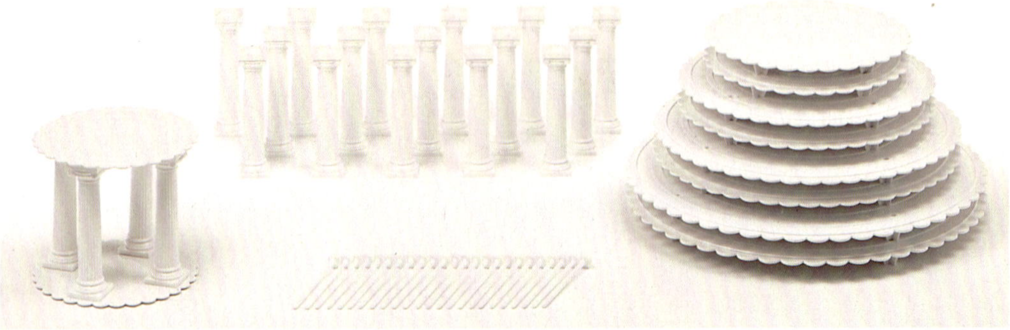

Roman Column Tier Set

Stately Roman pillars and scalloped-edge plates create beautiful settings for all tiered cakes. Includes 8 pieces: six 13¾ in. Roman columns and two super strong 18 in. round Decorator Preferred® separator plates. Lovely with the Kolor-Flo Fountain (sold on pg. 224).
301-S-1981 Set/8

Arched Tier Set

Dramatic when used with Kolor-Flo Fountain (sold on pg. 224). Includes 14 pieces: Six 13 in. arched columns, two super strong 18 in. round Decorator Preferred® separator plates and six angelic cherubs to attach to columns with royal icing or glue.
301-S-1982 Set/14

Separator Pillars

NEW! NEW! NEW!

Wrapped Pillars

Traditional 4 in. high pillars are wrapped with beautifully-textured fabric, providing an elegant new decorating option for tiered cakes.
Embroidered 303-S-980 Pk./4
Silver Lamé 303-S-981 Pk./4
Dotted 303-S-982 Pk./4

NEW!

Curved Pillars

Modern, pearlized pillars bring a contemporary look to any classic tiered cake designs.
2½ in. 303-S-658 Pk./4
5 in. 303-S-659 Pk./4

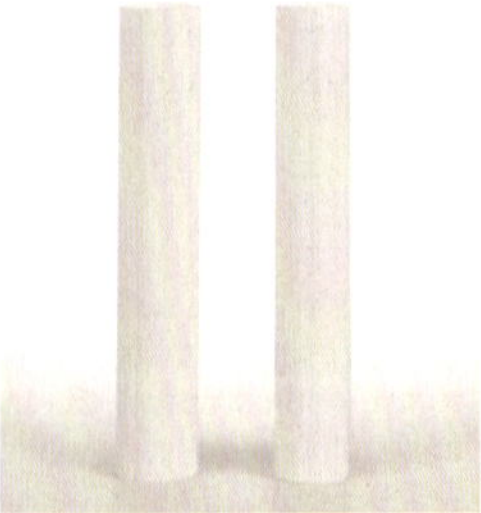

"Hidden" Pillars

Separate cake tiers slightly and create a floating illusion. Pushed into tiers as dowel rods, they fit onto all white separator plates except Tall Tier. Trimmable, hollow plastic. 6 in. high.
303-S-8 Pk./4

Grecian Pillars

Elegantly scrolled and ribbed.
3 in. 303-S-3606 Pk./4
5 in. 303-S-3703 Pk./4
7 in. 303-S-3705 Pk./4

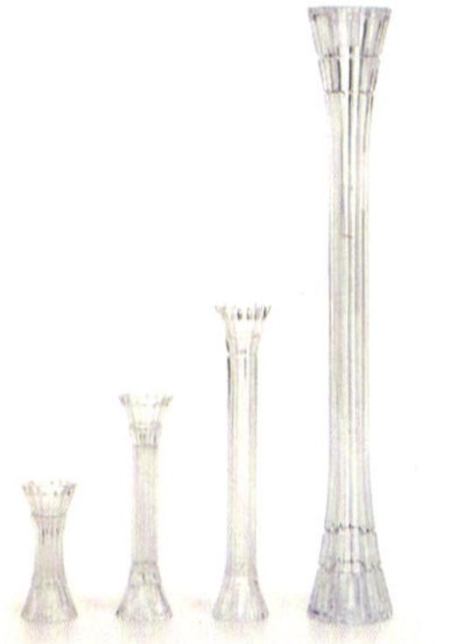

Crystal-Look Pillars

Use with Crystal-Look Plates (sold on pg. 223) and Crystal Bridge and Stairway Set (sold on pg. 224).
3 in. 303-S-2171 Pk./4
5 in. 303-S-2196 Pk./4
7 in. 303-S-2197 Pk./4
***13¾ in. 303-S-2242**
*Sold singly. Use only with 17 in. crystal plate (sold on pg. 223).

Arched Pillars

Grecian-inspired with arched support.
4½ in. 303-S-452 Pk./4
6½ in. 303-S-657 Pk./4
13 in. 303-S-9720 Pk./2

Roman Columns

Handsome pillars may be used with 16 and 18 in. plates and the Kolor-Flo Fountain (sold on pg. 224).
10¼ in. 303-S-8136 Pk./2
13¾ in. 303-S-2130 Pk./2

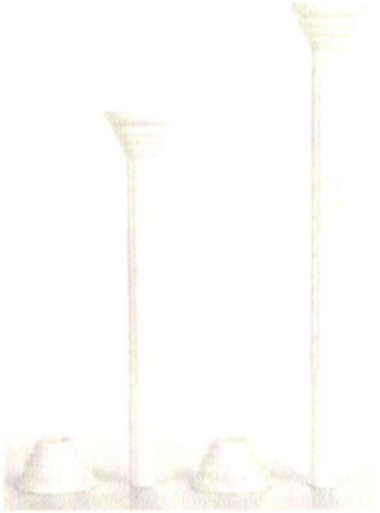

Baker's Best® Disposable Pillars with Rings

Single plate pillars.
7 in. 303-S-4000 Pk./4
9 in. 303-S-4001 Pk./4

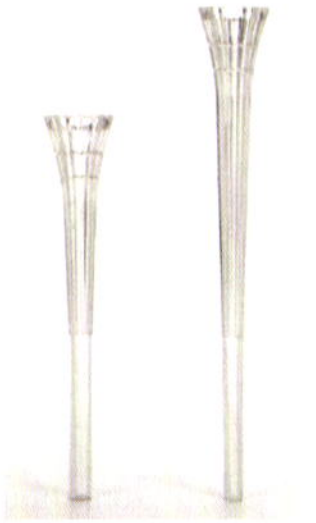

Crystal-Look Spiked Pillars

Single plate pillars. Double cake circles for extra support.
7 in. 303-S-2322 Pk./4
9 in. 303-S-2324 Pk./4

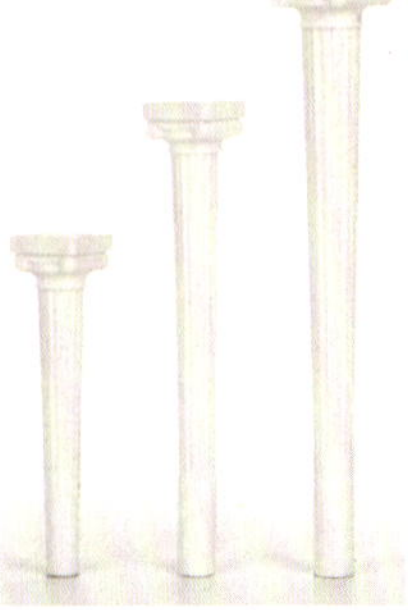

Grecian Spiked Pillars

Single plate pillars. Wide base for increased stability.
5 in. 303-S-3708 Pk./4
7 in. 303-S-3710 Pk./4
9 in. 303-S-3712 Pk./4

Cake Stands

Stunning Wilton Cake Stands are the perfect way to display your special wedding cake. Take a look—there's one perfectly suited to your wedding cake size and design.

Ceramic Pedestal Cake Stand

Present your cake with elegance on this classic ceramic stand. Its white pillar design features a gracefully sculpted base and a smooth attached 12 in. plate. Also use it to serve pies, brownies, cookies, candies and other special desserts. Holds cakes up to 10 in. diameter; stand is 4 in. high.
307-S-873

Tall Tier Cake Stand

Display your multi-tiered cakes up to 6 tiers high with this majestic stand. Lace-look plates enhance every cake design and hold tiers from 6 to 16 in. diameter. Easier to assemble than pillar construction, the twist-together center columns and strong, interchangeable plates provide stability.

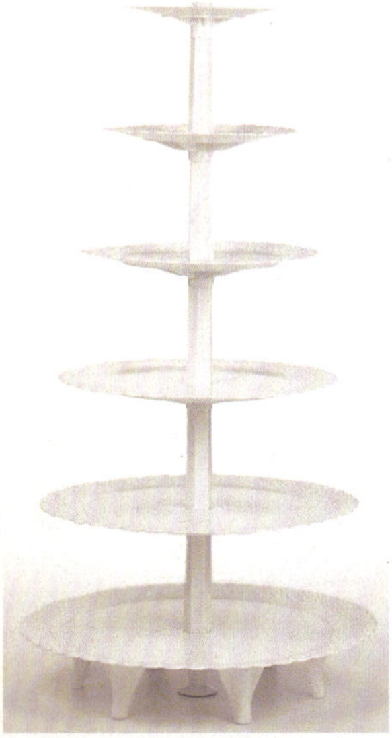

Basic Set

Includes: 5 twist-apart columns, 6½ in. high; top nut and bottom bolt; 18 in. footed base plate; 8, 10, 12, 14 and 16 in. separator plates (interchangeable, except footed base plate). Plastic.
304-S-7915 Set/13

Replacement Parts

Top Column Cap Nut **304-S-7923**
Bottom Column Bolt **304-S-7941**

Additional Plates

8 in. **302-S-7894**
10 in. **302-S-7908**
12 in. **302-S-7924**
14 in. **302-S-7940**
16 in. **302-S-7967**
18 in. **302-S-7983**

Additional Columns

6½ in. **303-S-7910**
7¾ in. **304-S-5009**
13½ in. **303-S-703**

Glue-On Plate Legs

Convert 14 or 16 in. separator plate into a footed base plate. Order 6 legs for each plate.
304-S-7930

Lady Windemere-Look 4-Arm Base

(For Use With Tall-Tier Stand)

Easily adds 4 base cakes to your tall tier cake. The 4-arm base can be used with any plate from the basic set, except the 18 in. footed base plate. Up to 3 graduated tiers can be added to the center columns. Includes 20 in. diameter 4-arm base with 4 stability pegs and base bolt. Use with 13½ in. column, bottom column bolt and four 12 in. plates, sold above.
304-S-8245

Additional Base Bolt 304-S-8253

Cakes 'N More™ 3-Tier Party Stand

Contemporary stairstep stand with crystal-clear plates puts the focus where it belongs—on your stunning cake and desserts! Constructed in metal with chrome-plated finish, stand holds 3 different size cake plates—8, 10 and 12 in. (included). Easy to set up and take apart.
307-S-859

Candlelight Cake Stand

Simple, graceful design reinforced with a crossbar for more support. Sturdy enameled metal design holds up to 40 lbs. Ideal for three stacked tiers supported by a 14 in. separator plate. Stand is 21½ in. diameter (13¼ in. center cake area) x 5 in. high and uses standard ⅞ in. candles. (Plates and candles not included.)
307-S-871

Garden Cake Stand

Our beautiful Garden Cake Stand echoes the wrought-iron look found in many formal gardens. Simply place cakes on plates and set on the stand. Painted metal stand is 23 in. high x 22 in. wide and uses 10 in., 14 in. and 18 in. scalloped separator plates (p. 223). Satellite garden stands sold individually below.
307-S-860

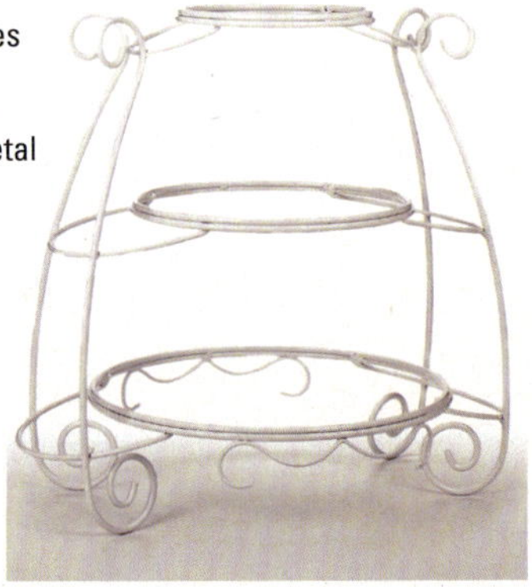

Satellite Garden Cake Stand
Painted metal; holds 12 in. separator plate.
307-S-861

Cake Corer Tube (not shown)

Essential tool easily and neatly removes center from cake tiers when tall tier stand columns are used. Ice cake before using. Serrated edge removes cake center with one push. Cleans easily.
304-S-8172

3-Tier Cake and Dessert Stand

- Beautiful cascading effect with display platforms at 6, 12 and 19 inches high
- Holds cakes up to 8, 10 and 12 inches diameter, also serves appetizers, cookies and candies

With this 3-Tier Cake and Dessert Stand, creating an elegant tiered display is easier than ever! Set up is easy—the unique design combines the ease of a lightweight foam base and 3 foam support plates with the strength and dependability of 3 grooved pillars. Also included are 3 plastic plates with rings on the bottom that insure exact orientation during set-up.

304-S-8275

CUPCAKES 'N MORE® DESSERT STANDS

Individually decorated cupcakes are the perfect way to add a personal touch to celebrations. Now, with Cupcakes 'N More, you have the perfect way to serve them! The look is fresh and fun, featuring bold silver-finished wire spirals to securely hold each cupcake. The twisting, towering design is perfect for any setting—kids' birthdays, holidays, weddings, showers, and more. Everyone will love serving themselves—and you'll love presenting your cupcakes, petits fours, candy cups, mini quiches and party favors in the center of the celebration! Easy to assemble, collapsible for easy storage.

Large Holds 38 cupcakes. **307-S-651**
Standard Holds 23 cupcakes. **307-S-826**

Standard Holds 23 cupcakes.

FLOATING TIERS CAKE STAND SETS

Round

Round plates present beautiful tiers. Set includes 17 in. high enamel coated white metal stand, 8, 12, and 16 in. smooth separator plates; instructions.

307-S-825
Set/4

Replacement Plates
(Same plates as Crystal-Clear Cake Divider Set.)

8 in. **302-S-9749**
12 in. **302-S-9765**
16 in. **302-S-9780**

Heart

Perfectly sized to heart shaped tiers. Set includes 17 in. high enamel coated white metal stand, 8, 12 and 16 in. Decorator Preferred® Heart separator plates; instructions.

307-S-872
Set/4

Replacement Plates

8 in. **302-S-60**
12 in. **302-S-62**
16 in. **302-S-64**

Separator Plates

NEW!

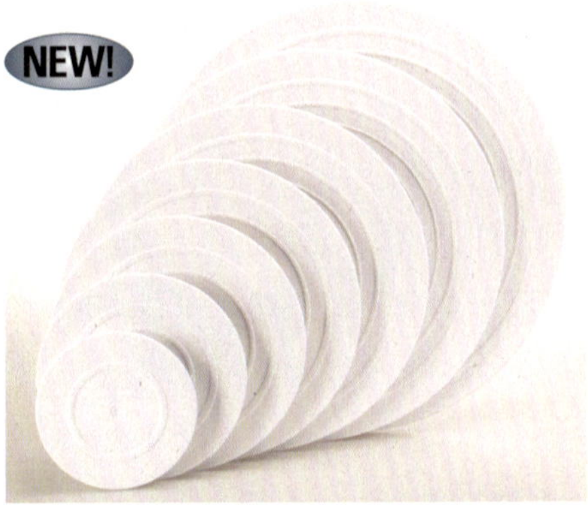

Decorator Preferred® Smooth Edge Plates

A fresh, clean shape which puts all the focus on your beautiful cake. Built for unmatched stability, with our patented Circles of Strength™ design. Plate feet fit securely on Wilton pillars, available in many styles (p. 221). Guaranteed non-breakable.

6 in. **302-S-4101**	14 in. **302-S-4105**
8 in. **302-S-4102**	16 in. **302-S-4106**
10 in. **302-S-4103**	18 in. **302-S-4107**
12 in. **302-S-4104**	

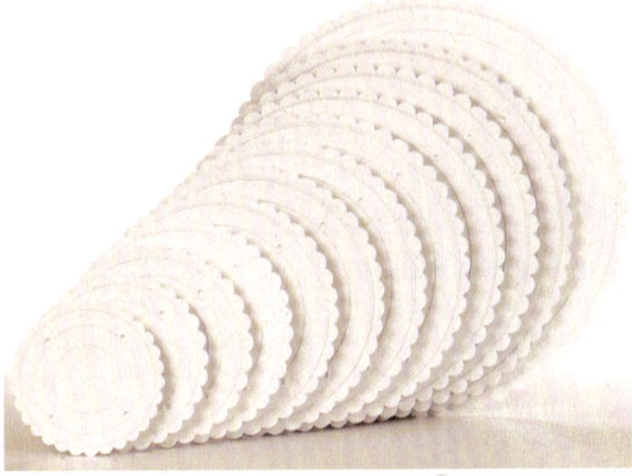

Decorator Preferred® Scalloped Plates

Our best, strongest separator plates with superior stability, beauty and scalloped edges. Guaranteed non-breakable.

6 in. **302-S-6**	12 in. **302-S-12**
7 in. **302-S-7**	13 in. **302-S-13**
8 in. **302-S-8**	14 in. **302-S-14**
9 in. **302-S-9**	15 in. **302-S-15**
10 in. **302-S-10**	16 in. **302-S-16**
11 in. **302-S-11**	18 in. **302-S-18**

Decorator Preferred® Heart Plates

Perfectly sized to fit Wilton heart pans, for a stunning tiered heart creation. Lovely scalloped edges. Guaranteed non-breakable.

8 in. **302-S-60**	14 in. **302-S-63**
10 in. **302-S-61**	16 in. **302-S-64**
12 in. **302-S-62**	18 in. **302-S-65**

Square Plates

7 in.
302-S-1004
9 in.
302-S-1020
11 in.
302-S-1047
13 in.
302-S-1063

Crystal-Look Plates

Wilton Crystal-Look plates have an elegance like no other, with ridged sides that look like cut crystal. Built with the strength and support Wilton is famous for. Use with Crystal-Look pillars (sold on p. 221).

7 in. **302-S-2013**	13 in. **302-S-2078**
9 in. **302-S-2035**	* 17 in. **302-S-1810**
11 in. **302-S-2051**	

*Use only with 13¾ in. Crystal-Look pillars (sold on p. 221).

17 in. Crystal-Look Plate and Pillar Set

Ideal style and height for use with fountains (sold on p. 224). Contains four 13¾ in. pillars and two 17 in. plates. (not shown)

301-S-1387

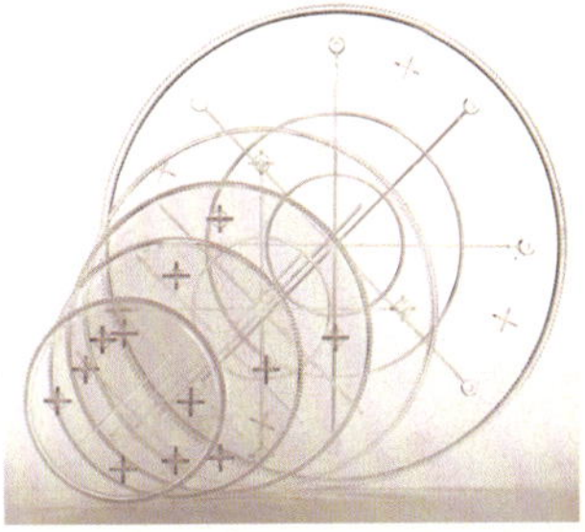

Cake Fountains and Accessories

Kolor-Flo Fountain
Professional quality fountain looks spectacular with every tiered cake design. Water cascades dramatically from three levels; simply remove top levels for smaller fountain arrangements. Intricate light system with two bulbs for added brilliance. Use with 16 or 18 in. scalloped edge plates; 18 in. smooth edge plate (p. 223). Coordinates with our 17 in. Crystal-Look Plate and Pillar Set (p. 223). Plastic fountain bowl is 9¾ in. diameter. 110-124 V, AC motor with 65 in. cord. Pumps water electrically. Directions, replacement part information included.
306-S-2599

Cascade Set for Kolor-Flo Fountain
Dome shapes redirect water over surface in non-stop streams. Set includes 4 pieces: 2½ in., 4½ in., 8 in., and 11½ in. diameter.
306-S-1172 Set/4

Fanci Fountain
Economical fountain in crystal-clear design enhances any tiered cake. Adjustable, smooth water flow. Use with 16 or 18 in. scalloped edge plates; 18 in. smooth edge plate (p. 223). Set-up instructions included. Height: 12 in. Diameter: 10 in.
306-S-2000

Replacement Parts

Bulb
306-S-1790

Cascade Set
306-S-1791

Replacement Parts for Kolor-Flo Fountain

Light Bulb
306-S-1053

Light Socket
306-S-1045

Floater Switch
306-S-1096
$14.49

Piston
306-S-1029

Cascade /Pump Connector
306-S-1088

Bottom Base
306-S-1170

Pump/Bulb Bracket
306-S-1037

Pump
306-S-1002

Upper Cascade
306-S-1118

Middle Cascade
306-S-1126

Lower Cascade
306-S-1134

Bowl
306-S-1142
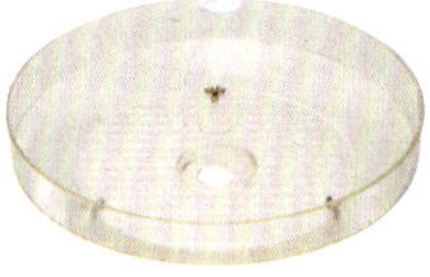

Fresh Flower Accessories

Crystal-Look Bowl
4½ in. diameter. 1½ in. deep.
205-S-1404

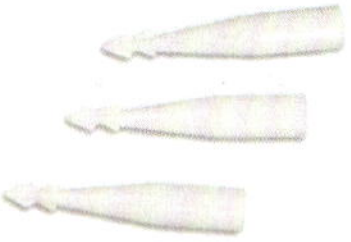

Flower Spikes
Fill with water, push into cake, add flowers. Makes cakes safe for insertion of stems or wires. 3 in. high.
1008-S-408 Pk./12

Fresh Flower Holders
Insert easily under cake tiers to hold blooms, greenery, pearl sprays, tulle puffs and more. Use with floral oasis to keep flowers fresh.
205-S-8500 Pk./2

Flower Holder Ring
Put at base of Kolor-Flo Fountain as shown at right. 12½ in. diameter x 2 in. high. 1¾ in. wide opening; inside ring diameter is 8½ in. Plastic.
305-S-435

Stairways and Bridges
Bridge the gap between lavish tiers.

Crystal Bridge and Graceful Stairway Set
Includes two stairways (16¾ in. long) and one platform (4¾ x 5 in.). Plastic.
205-S-2311
Set/3

Filigree Bridge and Stairway Set
Includes two stairways (16¼ in. long) and one platform (4¾ x 5 in.). Plastic.
205-S-2109
Set/3

Dowel Rods and Pegs

Plastic Dowel Rods
Heavy-duty hollow plastic provides strong, sanitary support for all tiered cakes. Cut with serrated knife to desired length. Length: 12¾ in. Diam.: ¾ in.
399-S-801 Pk./4

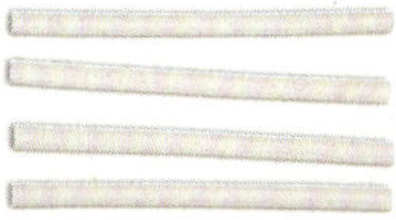

Wooden Dowel Rods
Cut and sharpen with strong shears and knife. Length: 12 in. Diam.: ¼ in.
399-S-1009 Pk./12

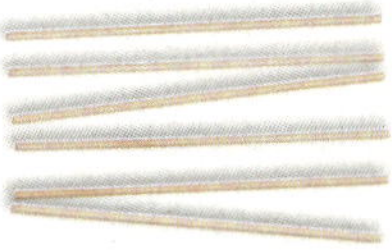

Plastic Pegs
Insure that cake layers and separator plates atop cakes stay in place. Pegs do not add support; dowel rod cake properly before using. Length: 4 in.
399-S-762 Pk./12

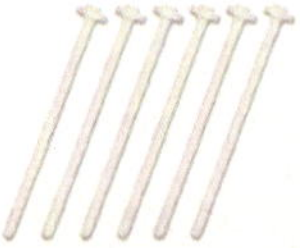

Cake Boards and Accents

Your cake will look its best when presented with quality Wilton boards, doilies and ruffled trims.

Cake Boards

Shaped cakes look best on boards cut to fit! Strong corrugated cardboard, generously-sized in rectangular shapes. Perfect for sheet and square cakes. For shaped cakes, use the pan as a pattern and cut out board to fit cake.

10 x 14 in.	**2104-S-554**	**Pk./6**
13 x 19 in.	**2104-S-552**	**Pk./6**

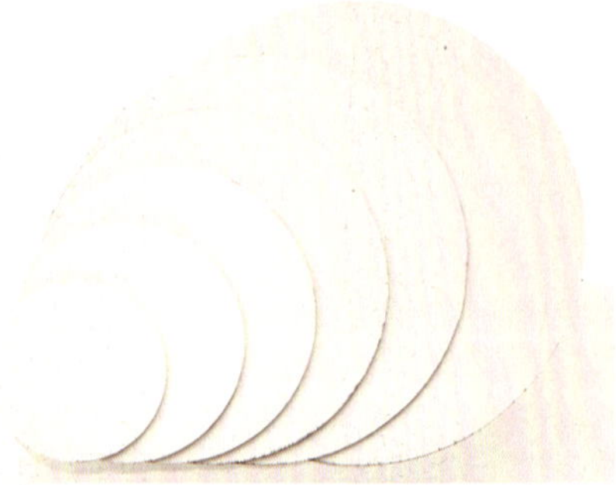

Cake Circles

Corrugated cardboard for strength and stability.

6 in. diameter	**2104-S-64**	**Pk./10**
8 in. diameter	**2104-S-80**	**Pk./12**
10 in. diameter	**2104-S-102**	**Pk./12**
12 in. diameter	**2104-S-129**	**Pk./8**
14 in. diameter	**2104-S-145**	**Pk./6**
16 in. diameter	**2104-S-160**	**Pk./6**

Silver Cake Bases

Convenient ½ in. thick silver-covered bases are grease-resistant, food-safe and reusable. Strong to hold heavy decorated cakes without an additional serving plate. Perfect for all types of cakes and craft creations.

10 in. Round	**2104-S-1187**	**Pk./2**
12 in. Round	**2104-S-1188**	**Pk./2**
14 in. Round	**2104-S-1189**	**Pk./2**
16 in. Round	**2104-S-1190**	**Pk./2**

Show 'N Serve™ Cake Boards

Scalloped edge has the look of intricate lace. Food-safe, grease-resistant coating.

10 in. diameter	**2104-S-1168**	**Pk./10**
12 in. diameter	**2104-S-1176**	**Pk./8**
14 in. diameter	**2104-S-1184**	**Pk./6**
14 x 20 in. Rectangle	**2104-S-1230**	**Pk./6**

Ruffle Boards®

Ready-to-use cake board and ruffle in one. Bleached white board and all-white ruffling complement any cake.

8 in. (for 6 in. round cake)	**415-S-950**
10 in. (for 8 in. round cake)	**415-S-960**
12 in. (for 10 in. round cake)	**415-S-970**
14 in. (for 12 in. round cake)	**415-S-980**
16 in. (for 14 in. round cake)	**415-S-990**
18 in. (for 16 in. round cake)	**415-S-1000**

Tuk-'N-Ruffle®

A pretty touch that attaches to edge of your serving tray or board with royal icing or tape.

60 ft. bolt per box.
White **802-S-1008**

6 ft. pkg. White
802-S-1991

Fanci-Foil

Serving side has a non-toxic grease-resistant surface. FDA-approved for use with food.

Continuous roll: 20 in. x 15 ft.
White **804-S-191**
Gold **804-S-183**
Silver **804-S-167**

Cake Doilies

Add instant elegance to cake plates, dessert trays, entrée and sandwich servings. Use under table centerpieces and plants, for decorations and crafts, too.

Silver Foil

4 in. Round
2104-S-90404 Pk./12
6 in. Round
2104-S-90116 Pk./18
8 in. Round
2104-S-90006 Pk./12
10 in. Round
2104-S-90007 Pk./6
12 in. Round
2104-S-90412 Pk./4

Gold Foil

4 in. Round
2104-S-90304 Pk./12
6 in. Round
2104-S-90306 Pk./18
8 in. Round
2104-S-90308 Pk./12
10 in. Round
2104-S-90310 Pk./6
12 in. Round
2104-S-90312 Pk./4

Grease-Proof White

4 in. Round	**2104-S-90204**	**Pk./30**
6 in. Round	**2104-S-90206**	**Pk./20**
8 in. Round	**2104-S-90208**	**Pk./16**
10 in. Round	**2104-S-90210**	**Pk./10**
12 in. Round	**2104-S-90212**	**Pk./6**
14 in. Round	**2104-S-90214**	**Pk./4**
10 x 14 in. Rectangle	**2104-S-90224**	**Pk./6**

Cake Accents

Romantic accents add a sparkling beauty and elegance to cakes.

White Pearl Beading

Molded on one continuous 5-yard strand. Remove before cutting and serving cake.

Small (4 mm) **211-S-1989**
Large (6 mm) **211-S-1990**

Scrolls

2¾ x 1¼ in.
1004-S-2801
Pk./24

Baby

Start planning the party—from pink to blue, and themes in between, this dazzling array of Wilton products will inspire you to make the cutest things for your baby celebration.

Baby Favor Kits

All you add is candy—adorable favor containers are packaged in larger quantities to complete your favor making in no time at all!

Baby Blocks
Featuring print-your-own tags to personalize favors—it's easy to do at **www.wiltonprint.com**. 1¾ in. squares. Multicolor pastel assortment. Includes tags with printing instructions, ribbon, blocks, 2 printing test sheets. (Candy and tulle not included.)
1006-S-284
Pk./20

Pails
Featuring print-your-own tags to personalize favors—it's easy to do at **www.wiltonprint.com**. Crafted of food-safe painted metal, pails measure 2 in. high x 2⅜ in. diameter at rim. Includes tags with printing instructions, ribbon, pails, 2 printing test sheets. (Candy, tulle, favor tie and safety pin accent not included.)
1006-S-916 (Available September 2006) **Pk./18**
Pail Only
1006-S-915

Baby Bottles
Featuring print-your-own tags to personalize favors—it's easy to do at **www.wiltonprint.com**. Bottles measure 4 in. high, ½ in. diameter opening. Multicolor pastel assortment. Includes tags with printing instructions, ribbon, bottles, 2 printing test sheets. (Candy and safety pin accents not included.)
1006-S-577 Pk./24
Bottles Only
1006-S-696 Pk./6

Drawstring Wrappers
They're pre-assembled! Just fill, tie ribbons, and add favor tag. (Candy not included.)
Pk./12
Pink
1006-S-218
Blue
1006-S-219
White
1006-S-340
Multicolor
3 each pink, blue, yellow, mint green.
1006-S-245

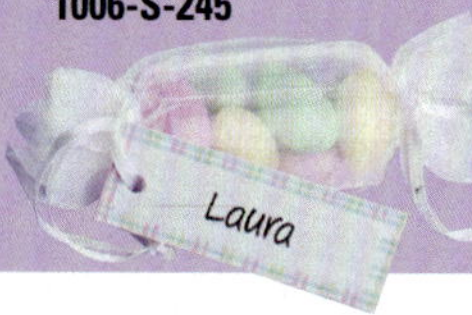

Sweet Things™ Pacifiers
Everything you need to make 6 oh-so-cute favors! Includes pacifier favor pedestals, ribbon, tulle circles, place cards, assembly instructions. (Candy not included.)
1006-S-531
Pk./6

Sweet Things™ Teddy Bears
Everything you need to make 6 adorable favors! Includes teddy bear favor pedestals, ribbon, tulle circles, place cards, assembly instructions. (Candy not included.)
1006-S-530
Pk./6

Favor Accents

Add special touches to your baby favors, gift tie-ons and table decorations.

Baby Bracelets*
Pink, blue, yellow, mint green.
1¼ in. high.
1103-S-56
Pk./6

Mini Clothes Pins*
Pink, lavender, blue, yellow, mint green.
1⅜ in. high.
1103-S-27
Pk./20

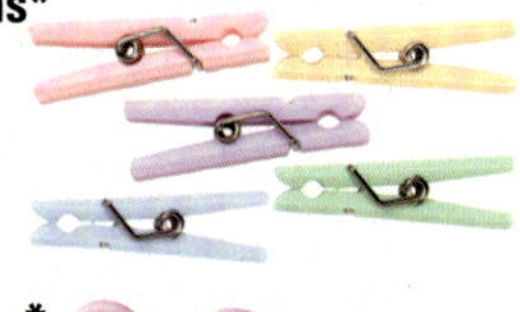

Small Safety Pins*
1½ in. long.
Pk./20
Pink 1103-S-21
Blue 1103-S-26
Multicolor
Pink, blue, yellow, mint green.
1103-S-42

Mini Baby Bottles*
Pink, lavender, blue, yellow, mint green. 1¼ in. high.
1103-S-16 Pk./20

Ethnic Newborn Baby Figurines*
1 in. high.
1103-S-30 Pk./6

Newborn Baby Figurines*
1 in. high.
1103-S-62 Pk./6

Baby Bears*
1 in. high.
Pk./6
Blue 1103-S-7
Pink 1103-S-8
Multicolor
Pink, blue, yellow, mint green. **1103-S-46**

Rocking Horses
Three blue, three pink.
2½ in. high.
1103-S-28
Pk./6

Shower Rattles*
Pink, lavender, blue, yellow, mint green.
3¾ in. high.
1103-S-29
Pk./6

Mini Rocking Horses*
1¼ in. high. Pink, lavender, blue, yellow, mint green.
1103-S-52 Pk./6

Sleeping Angels Set
A precious pose, one pink and one blue. 2 in. high x 3 in. long.
2113-S-2325
Set/2

Favor Containers

Perfect as favors, filled with candy and treats, and as gift and cake accents.

Drawstring Sachets

Ready to fill with Jordan Almonds, Rose Petals, Pillow Mints, small gifts. 3¾ in. x 4 in.
Pk./12

Pink 1006-S-179
Blue 1006-S-180
Multicolor
3 each pink, blue, yellow, mint green.
1006-S-244

Tulle Circles

NEW!

Sheer tulle circles come in an assortment of pretty pastel shades, perfect for all baby celebrations. Make cute favors, use in centerpieces, decorations and floral arrangements. Contains 5 each pink, lavender, blue, yellow, mint green. 9 in. diameter.
1006-S-288
Pk./25

Silver Plated Baby Carriage

With moveable wheels. 3 in. long x 2 in. wide x 3½ in. high.
1006-S-878

Baby Favor Bags

Delightful container for candies, small gifts and other favor treats. 3 x 5½ in. high.
1006-S-362 Pk./12

Baby Blocks Containers*

Removable lids for easy filling. Each 1¼ in. high.
2113-S-419 Set/4

Baby Cradles

Adorable as favors, cake toppers and table decorations. 2½ in. high.
Pink
1006-S-579

Blue
1006-S-578

Baby Party Bags

Colorful designs for candy and cookie treats. 20 plastic bags, 20 ties included. 4 x 9½ in.
1912-S-2365 Pk./20

Pacifier Favor Boxes*

Assembled, decorated and ready to fill with Wilton candies. Each box is 2 in. x 2 in. x 1¼ in. high.
Pk./6

Pink 1006-S-330
Blue 1006-S-331
Yellow 1006-S-332

White Flower Basket

3¾ in. wide x 2 in. high. Metal. Contents shown not included.
1006-S-990

FAVOR TIES

Instant decoration for favors, bubbles, gifts. Slip one on to close filled bags and tulle favor puffs, or use to decorate any baby favor.

Baby Bottle

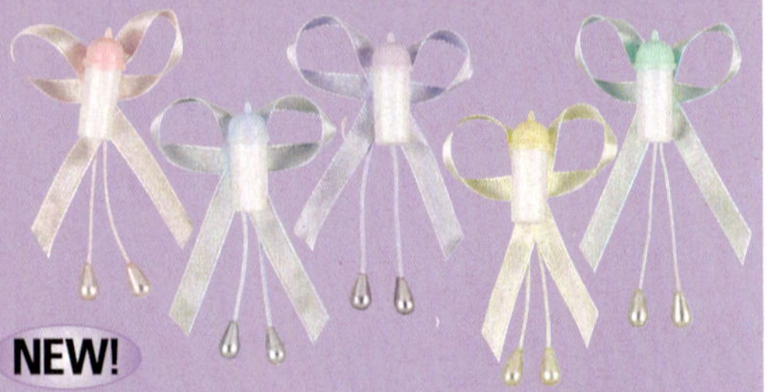

Accented with a cute baby bottle.
Pk./6

Pink 1006-S-509
Blue 1006-S-508
Multicolor
Pink, lavender, blue, yellow, mint green.
1006-S-575

NEW!

Baby Pacifier

Accented with a mini pacifier.
Pk./6

Pink 1006-S-566
Blue 1006-S-567
Multicolor
Pink, lavender, blue, yellow, mint green.
1006-S-361

NEW!

Candy

Perfect filler for favors, treat bags, candy dishes!

Baby Talk

Assorted fruit flavors. 10 oz. bag.
1006-S-1115

Mini Pacifiers

Assorted sweet/tart fruit flavors. 12 oz. bag.
1006-S-540

Mini Hearts

Assorted fruit flavors. 12 oz. bag. Certified Kosher.
1006-S-797

Mint Drops

Assorted colors. 16 oz. bag. Certified Kosher.
1006-S-788

Jordan Almonds

16 oz. bag; approx. 100 pieces. Certified Kosher.
Assorted 1006-S-779
White 1006-S-778

Pillow Mints

Assorted colors. 10 oz. bag; approx. 205 pieces. Certified Kosher.
1006-S-858

*WARNING: CHOKING HAZARD—Small parts. Not intended for children. Not a toy—for decorative use only.

Party Decorations

Add special touches to your celebration.

BABY ABC BLOCKS

NEW!

Baby Bottle Garland
Baby bottle shapes are the perfect accent for baby showers and celebrations. 8 ft. long.
1006-S-426

Centerpiece
Cute centerpiece is easy to assemble, crafted of paper with ribbon pull. Assembled centerpiece measures 8 x 5 x 14½ in. high.
1006-S-427

Lighted Lantern
Hang for a spectacular effect, or use as table decorations. Uses two AAA batteries, not included. Easy to assemble, crafted of paper, plastic, metal. 8 x 9 in. wide.
1006-S-423

Pop Up Favor Boxes
One piece construction for easy-to-assemble quick favors. Constructed of paper. Assembled size; 2¼ x 2¼ in.
1006-S-425 Pk./10

White Pail Centerpiece
Use these pails for showers and celebrations—as treat holders, centerpieces, more! Add your own creative touch by decorating with ribbon, stickers and accents, then filling with flowers. Add candy, cookies and treats, too—crafted of food-safe painted metal. Pail measures 4¾ in. high x 5⅜ in. diameter at rim. Contents shown not included.
1006-S-251

See matching favor container on p. 226!

Lighted Party Garland
Pretty fabric blooms illuminate the baby shower, christening party or the first birthday celebration! 8 ft. long garland has end-to-end connectors and includes 2 replacement bulbs and fuse. 120V, AC, UL listed. For indoor use only.
1008-S-810

Baby Memories

NEW!

Piggy Bank
Whimsical, yet practical, it's a great gift idea and fun accent for baby's room. Cute just as it is, or you can personalize with name and birthdate, pink or blue, or any design you choose. Crafted in ceramic. Has coin slot on top, removable plug on the bottom. 5¾ in. high.
1009-S-1113

Best Wishes Bear
Create a precious keepsake for the new baby. Makes a great shower gift. Includes blue and pink sheer ribbons and pen. 9¼ in. high, holds 4 x 3 in. photo. Fabric covered. (Clothespin accents not included.)
1009-S-1140

Autograph Mat
Holds a 5 x 7 in. photo, with room for autographs and good wishes from friends and family. Few gifts touch so many like this one! For use in an 11 x 14 in. frame.
1009-S-1106

Mini Favor Frames
Perfect shower favors, crafts, keepsakes. Hand out instead of cigars! 4 different designs per box, each 2⅞ x 2⅞ in. Holds 1½ x 1½ photo. Resin.
1009-S-1326 Pk./4

Rubber Ducky Theme

3-D Cake Pan
This bathtime favorite will make a big splash at baby showers. Five adorable designs included. Two-piece pan takes 5½ cups batter. 9 x 5 x 7 in. high. Aluminum.
2105-S-2094

Candles
Handpainted details, clean-burning design. 1½ in. high.
2811-S-9337 Set/6

Icon Candles
Highlight your shower theme with candles that feature a fun hand-carved rubber ducky. Instant fun, great size for cupcakes too! 2½ in. high.
2811-S-8419 Pk./10

Candy Mold
Making candy is easy to do, complete directions are included. Reusable. Use Wilton Candy Melts®† sold on p. 162. 1 design, 6 cavities.
2115-S-1565

†Brand confectionery coating.

Icing Decorations
Mint-flavored edible sugar shapes to decorate cupcakes, cookies, ice cream and cake. Certified Kosher.
710-S-293 Pk./12

Baking Cups
Microwave-safe paper. Standard size, 2 in. diameter.
415-S-378 Pk./50

Party Bags
Fill with candy, cookies and other goodies; great for gifts and surprises, too! 20 plastic bags, 20 ties included. 4 x 9½ in.
1912-S-1275 Pk./20

Baking Accessories

BAKEWARE

Mini Stand-Up Bear Pan Set
Convenient size for baking cakes and molding candy, ice cream and sugar. 4¾ in. high. Includes 2-piece pan, baking stand, four clips and instructions. Aluminum.
2105-S-489 Set/8

Stand-Up Cuddly Bear Pan Set
Five decorating ideas on one box! Two-piece pan takes 6⅔ cups of firm textured batter. Includes 6 clips, heat-conducting core and instructions. Pan is 9½ x 8⅝ in. Aluminum.
2105-S-603 Set/10

Huggable Teddy Bear Pan
From birthdays and baby showers to school parties, classic toy shape can be used all year 'round. One-mix pan is 13½ x 12¼ x 2 in. Aluminum.
2105-S-4943

Baby Buggy Pan
It's a precious carriage design for shower and christening guests and ready to dress up for colorful cakes or elegant salads and gelatins. One-mix pan is 11¼ x 11¼ x 2 in. Aluminum.
2105-S-3319

BAKING CUPS
Everyone loves the convenience of cupcakes—easy to make, to carry to the party, and simple to serve! Now, you'll make the cutest cupcakes for every baby celebration using Wilton Baking Cups! Also perfect for treats, favors, and as nut or candy cups.

Assorted Pastel
25 pink, 25 blue, 25 yellow. Standard size, 2 in. diameter. Microwave-safe paper.
415-S-394 Pk./75

†Brand confectionery coating.

CANDLES
Cute candles brighten the little one's first celebration. Handpainted details, clean-burning design.

Baby Things
Approx. 2 in. high.
2811-S-855 Set/4

Soft Colors Candles
From classic to shimmer in yellow, pink, mint and blue.

Shimmer
Shown, 2½ in. high.
2811-S-3664 Pk./8

Also available, shown on p. 187:

Rounds
2½ in. high.
2811-S-291 Pk./24

Corkscrew
2½ in. high.
2811-S-775 Pk./8

Lattice
Shown, 2½ in. high.
2811-S-3657 Pk./8

Also available, shown on p. 187:

Tricolor
2½ in. high.
2811-S-782 Pk./10

Jumbo Crayons
3¼ in. high.
2811-S-292 Pk./8

Twist
Shown, 2½ in. high.
2811-S-3661 Pk./8

Also available, shown on p. 187:

Party Thins
8 in. high.
2811-S-255 Pk./20

Candy Molds
Fun shaped reusable molds celebrate baby over and over again. Making candy is easy to do, complete directions are included! Use Wilton Candy Melts®† brand confectionery coating, sold on p. 162.

Baby Bottles Lollipop
1 design, 6 cavities.
2115-S-1560

Baby Shower
4 designs, 11 cavities.
2115-S-1710

Mini Baby Icons
5 designs, 20 cavities.
2115-S-1537

Stationery

*Printing invitations at home is so easy to do. Simply go to **www.wiltonprint.com** and see how!*

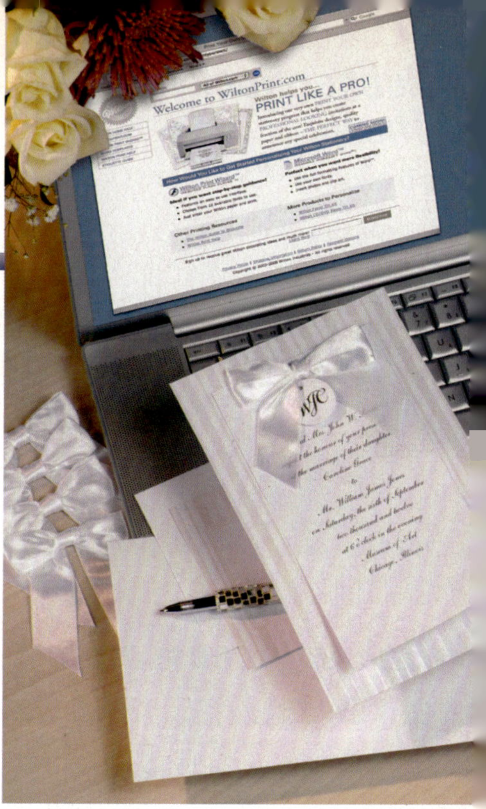

Complete Invitation Kits

Wilton Print-Your-Own Stationery is the perfect way to announce any special celebration! Complete kits are ready to personalize, print and mail! All invitation kits are crafted in 80 lb. card stock with distinctive accents and are acid- and lignin-free.

*See the complete line of Wilton stationery at **www.wiltonprint.com**.*

Simple Yet Elegant

Set of 25
Includes:
- 25 Invitations and Mailing Envelopes
- 25 Reply Cards and Envelopes,
- 25 Pre-tied Bows with Adhesives, Circle Tags and Ball Chains,
- 3 Test Sheets

1008-S-530
Set/25
Also available in Ivory.
1008-S-531
Set/25

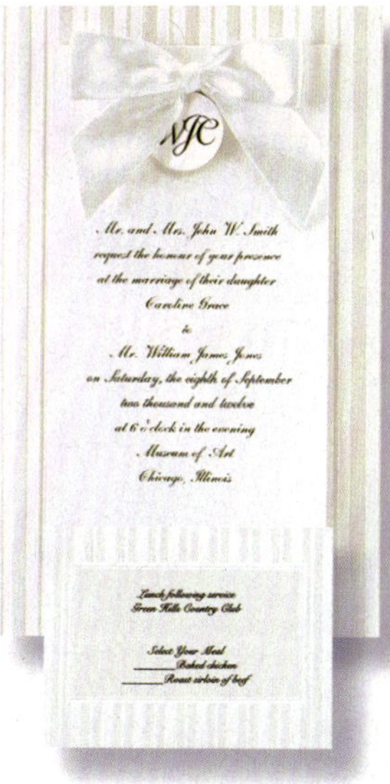

NEW! Soiree

Set of 25
Includes:
- 25 Invitations and Mailing Envelopes
- 25 Reply Cards and Envelopes
- 25 Rhinestone Buckles with Ribbons
- 3 Test Sheets

1008-S-710
Set/25

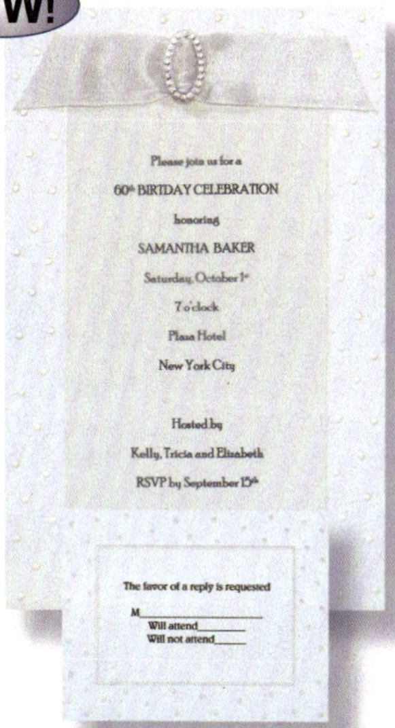

Portrait of Love

Set of 25
Includes:
- 25 Invitations and Mailing Envelopes
- 25 Reply Cards and Envelopes
- 25 Mini Frames with Adhesive Backing and Mini Frame Inserts
- 3 Test Sheets

1008-S-529
Set/25

Keeping with Tradition

Set of 50
Includes:
- 50 Invitations and Mailing Envelopes
- 50 Reply Cards and Envelopes
- 3 Test Sheets

1008-S-520
Set/50
Also available in Ivory.
1008-S-521
Set/50

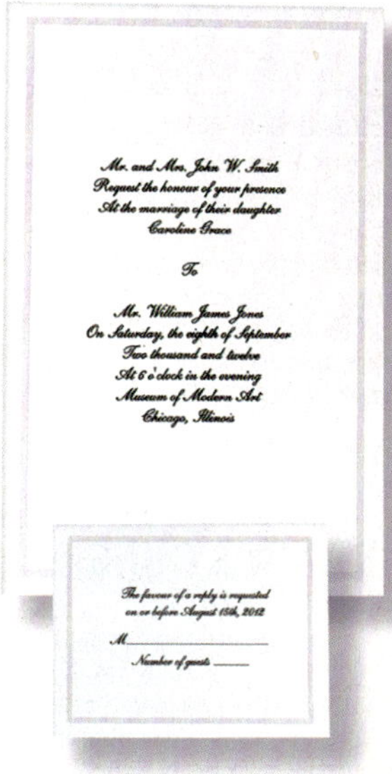

Two Hearts

Set of 50
Includes:
- 50 Invitations and Mailing Envelopes
- 50 Reply Cards and Envelopes
- 3 Test Sheets

1008-S-524
Set/50

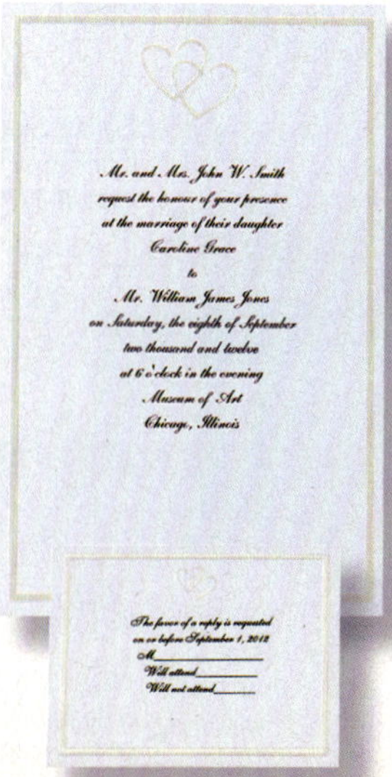

Joined Together

Set of 50
Includes:
- 50 Invitations and Mailing Envelopes
- 50 Reply Cards and Envelopes
- 3 Test Sheets

1008-S-522
Set/50

Also available in Ivory with Gold.
1008-S-523
Set/50

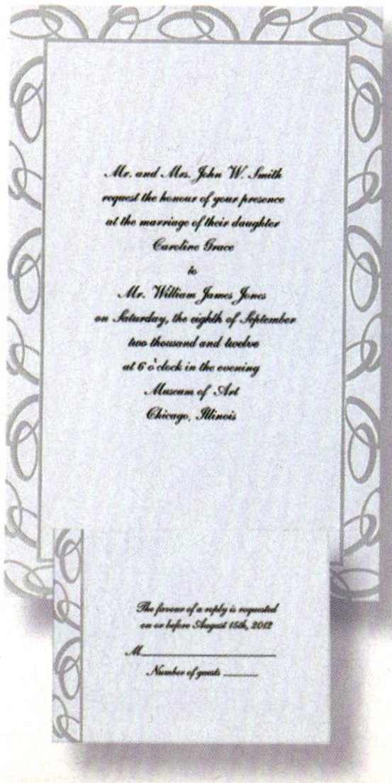

Flirty Fleur

Set of 50
Includes:
- 50 Invitations and Mailing Envelopes
- 50 Reply Cards and Envelopes
- 3 Test Sheets

1008-S-525
Set/50

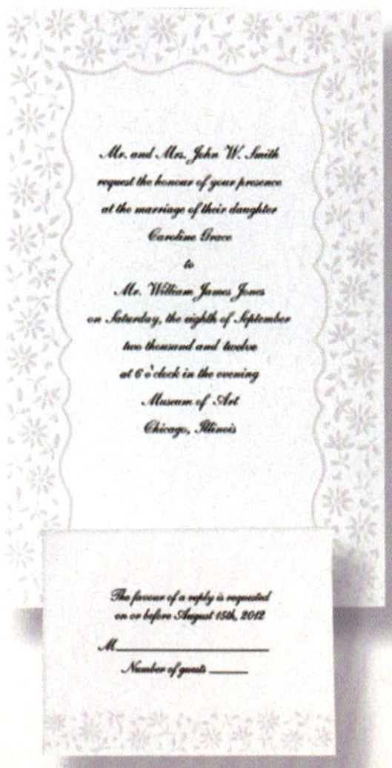

INDEX

PRODUCT SHOPS

GENERAL PRODUCT

Cake Tools & Supplies

Candy Supplies

Cookie Supplies

Fondant and Gum Paste Supplies

Icing Supplies

Instructional

Ornaments & Figurines

Party Favors & Accents

Wedding/Tiered Cake Supplies & Accessories

BAKEWARE

Numbers in parentheses indicate page numbers for designs which feature these pans.

Bakeware Essentials

Seasonal Pans

Novelty Pans

Mini Pans

Tier Pan Sets

PARTY THEME

Licensed Themes

Party Themes

*Brand confectionery coating.

Learn From The Leaders In Cake Decorating!

Celebrating 79 Years

The Wilton® School

of Cake Decorating & Confectionery Art

For almost 80 years, The Wilton School has been home to the leading authorities in cake decorating. Today, our curriculum is more extensive than ever, featuring world-class decorating specialists who give students individual guidance in their field of expertise. Whether you are a professional seeking to grow your business or a hobbyist looking to gain new skills for entertaining at home, The Wilton School is the ideal place to enjoy an unforgettable learning experience.

SIGN UP NOW FOR THESE POPULAR COURSES!

THE MASTER COURSE

The world's most comprehensive cake decorating course! In this exciting 2-week class, students learn the skills needed to become a professional cake decorator. Learn 20 borders and 15 flowers, including The Wilton Rose. Decorate with color flow, piping gel and figure piping. Create a floral birthday cake, then design, assemble and decorate a 3-tiered wedding cake with skills learned. Virtually all materials included.

SUPPLEMENTARY CLASSES *(Available during the Master Course)*

Confectionery Creations

Master candy making and decorating to expand your business or create incredible gifts using Candy Melts® brand confectionery coating (no tempering needed). Learn to make roses, leaves, ganache, boxes, baskets and more.

Introduction to Sugar Artistry

Start with basic recipes and equipment to become familiar with sugar art, then proceed to spun, pulled, molded and piped techniques. Students create flowers and leaves, a spun sugar cage, ribbons, bows and more that can be used on a cake or as accent decorative pieces.

Introduction to Rolled Fondant

Learn creative ways to work with fondant, including hand-cut and shaped flowers, ribbons and bows. Discover special icing effects on fondant—sponging, crimping and embossing.

EXPLORE OTHER GREAT CLASSES!

Cakes for Catering, Lambeth, Advanced Sugar Artistry, Chocolate Inspirations, Advanced Gum Paste and Fondant, Fondant Art.

1-DAY WORKSHOPS

Art of Sweet Tables, Holiday Icing Flowers, Holiday Candy Making, Wedding Cake Assembly, Cupcakes by Design and more!

CHECK OUT OUR WEEKEND AND BILINGUAL CLASSES!

For class schedules, details and enrollment visit **www.school.wilton.com** or call 630-810-2888 or 800-772-7111, ext. 2888.